Dr. Guernette

CLINICAL NEUROPSYCHOLOGY:
CURRENT STATUS
AND APPLICATIONS

CLINICAL NEUROPSYCHOLOGY:
CURRENT STATUS
AND APPLICATIONS

EDITED BY RALPH M. REITAN

UNIVERSITY OF WASHINGTON

and LESLIE A. DAVISON

UNIVERSITY OF CALIFORNIA, SAN FRANCISCO

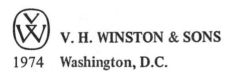 V. H. WINSTON & SONS

1974   Washington, D.C.

A HALSTED PRESS BOOK

JOHN WILEY & SONS
New York   Toronto   London   Sydney

V. H. Winston & Sons, Inc., Publishers
1511 K St. N.W., Washington, D.C. 20005

Distributed solely by Halsted Press Division, John Wiley & Sons, Inc., New York.

Library of Congress Cataloging in Publication Data:

Reitan, Ralph M
   Clinical neuropsychology: current status and applications.

   (The Series in clinical psychology)
   1. Mental deficiency. 2. Clinical psychology.
   I. Davison, Leslie A., joint author. II. Title.
   [DNLM: 1. Brain damage, Chronic—Congresses.
   2. Neurophysiology—Congresses. 3. Psychophysiology—
   Congresses. WL102 C641 1970]
   RC570.R44   616.8'588   73-22173
   ISBN 0-470-71623-1

Printed in the United States of America

CONTENTS

LIST OF CONTRIBUTORS

Numbers in parentheses indicate the pages on which the authors' contributions begin.

Arthur L. Benton, University of Iowa, Iowa City, Iowa (47)

Thomas J. Boll, University of Washington, Seattle, Washington (91)

Leslie A. Davison, University of California at San Francisco, San Francisco, California (1, 325)

Harry Klonoff, University of British Columbia, Vancouver, British Columbia (121, 179)

Hallgrim Klove, University of Bergen, Bergen, Norway (211, 237)

Morton Low, University of British Columbia, Vancouver, British Columbia (121)

Charles G. Matthews, University of Wisconsin Center for Health Sciences, Madison, Wisconsin (237, 267)

Manfred J. Meier, University of Minnesota, Minneapolis, Minnesota (289)

Robert Paris, University of British Columbia, Vancouver, British Columbia (179)

Ralph M. Reitan, University of Washington, Seattle, Washington (19, 53)

FOREWORD

Developments in clinical neuropsychology awaited interaction between psychologists and clinical neurological scientists. Such interaction has resulted in a large growth of substantive knowledge in the last 30 years. With this burgeoning of knowledge, the interest of psychologists in the brain as the organ of adaptive behavior has awakened. Norman J. Spector, Chief Psychologist of the Miami Veterans Administration Hospital, thought it particularly timely that this reawakened interest be recognized by an appropriate symposium at the convention of the American Psychological Association held in that city in September, 1970. He hoped that the symposium would address itself to what had been accomplished and what yet needed to be accomplished in this field. Largely through his efforts and persuasion, that symposium, "Clinical Neuropsychology: The Significance of Brain Damage for Human Behavior," was held.

While Spector's initiative and feeling of responsibility for the area of clinical neuropsychology was the critical input in the occurrence of the Miami APA symposium, the plan for publication of this volume was similarly developed and nurtured by one of the editors of this volume, Leslie A. Davison. The original papers in the symposium, which was chaired by Davison, were intended to provide a brief survey of the current status of clinical neuropsychology among both children (Reitan) and adults (Klove), together with a consideration of challenges and needs of each of these areas for the 1970s (Benton and Meier). Davison began organizing the plan for publication and, in consultation with Reitan, realized the need for an enlarged scope. The clinical neuropsychology of older children needed to be represented, and Boll contributed this chapter. The extensive normative data collected by Klonoff and his associates, together with data on head injuries and minimal cerebral dysfunction, was another area that needed to be covered. We also felt that an indication of the broad range of application of clinical neuropsychology would be valuable, and Klove and Matthews were asked to present material representing their extensive experience with epilepsy and mental retardation. As the volume developed, consultation between the editors became more frequent and finally we realized that we were working as coeditors rather than as editor and consultant. Thus, each editor has worked in detail on all the chapters. Davison was primarily responsible for chapters by Klonoff and his associates; Reitan had principal editorial responsibility for chapters by Boll, Klove, Matthews, and Meier.

Many different, for the most part nonoverlapping, volumes could be produced on the topic of clinical neuropsychology. As Meier concluded (this volume), review of recent developments in clinical neuropsychology which have implications for improvements of clinical assessment in this field would alone require an entire volume. In the summary chapter we also noted the need for a clinical manual of neuropsychology. Actually, two of these would be needed if each were to be sufficiently comprehensive—one covering the clinical neuropsychology of children, the other that of adults. No one volume can hope to meet all the needs for collation and summary of the data and concepts now to be found in this field. We have not here attempted the impossible task of simultaneously meeting these diverse needs, nor have we addressed ourselves to one of them alone.

Although the volume is far from inclusive of the full range of areas to which clinical neuropsychology is relevant, many relevant areas are considered. We present new data comparing the functioning of brain-damaged children and their matched controls on comprehensive measures of adaptive functioning. These data build toward the development of practically useful children's neuropsychological assessment batteries. We also present some comparative data on impaired groups of special interest—children defined as suffering minimal brain dysfunction, epileptics, and mentally retarded individuals. We summarize data on some recent developments in the field with implications for further development of neuropsychological assessment procedures, and for the solution of as-yet-unsolved clinical problems. Clinically useful descriptive information about the nature of the tests and batteries reported in the various chapters and scores for various normal and impaired groups on these variables have been included. As a special feature of this volume, we have included clinical examples at the end of many of the chapters in order to illustrate application of research results. The gulf between research findings and clinical application often is immense, and this problem needs to be addressed. Our purpose in giving case examples was to add some richness to the research findings and to help bridge the gap between research and clinical application. Above all, our main purpose throughout the book has been to explicate what we judge to be the salient issues in this field.

One sometimes hears proposals about what clinical neuropsychology should or should not be. For some it is too atheoretical and applied. For others, it is not applied enough, presently containing too little of relevance to treatment and rehabilitation for their taste. Some feel that certain clinical applications in this field rely too much on sensory-motor behavior, and not enough on more complex psychological processes, and that view is expressed in this volume by one of our contributors. We do not believe that these issues will be decided by fiat. Many motivations stimulate interest in this field. It provides an approach to the ancient and unsolved riddles of neuroanatomical-physiological bases of human behavior. It provides confrontation with the most extreme dehumanizing forces that life has to offer. It presents innumerable applied and theoretical questions. It permits, often requires, that one be both clinician and researcher. It straddles diverse disciplines. Investigators in this field will express their personal preferences, intellectual convictions, emotional propensities, and other motives in the focus and methods of their work. However, this field does require a certain attention to empirical facts, regardless of one's preferences. Where there are objective criteria for appraising the outcomes of clinical decisions, as in this field, clinicians will be forced to honor methods which contribute to valid outcomes, regardless of their unconventionality, and become skeptical of methods which do not, regardless of what prestige they may have acquired in other areas. Neuropsychological theory will be developed as quickly as it can be devised to fit the facts, and will be used insofar as it contributes to the tasks at hand. Adequate treatments for the conditions encompassed depend upon adequate understanding, based upon comprehensive and detailed description, of the nature of these conditions.

If this volume does not answer many questions, or only answers some to raise others, we hope that our efforts will spur others to join this work. It is our conviction that in this field of psychology, answers do make a difference and substantive data will quickly be put to use.

1
INTRODUCTION

Leslie A. Davison[1]

Those who read this book will probably already have some familiarity with the field of neuropsychology.[2] Yet the reader, whether clinical psychologist, neurologist, neurosurgeon, psychiatrist, or other professional perhaps less closely allied to this field, is likely to experience feelings of unfamiliarity with the subject matter of this volume, clinical neuropsychology. This subfield of neuropsychology may appear to many readers to possess more novel than recognizable features. I hope that some orientation to the terrain may make the contents of this book more useful and help open the door for its readers to other related material which could benefit their work.

CONCEPTS FREQUENTLY ENCOUNTERED IN THE STUDY OF CLINICAL BRAIN-BEHAVIOR RELATIONS

Readers not thoroughly conversant with the field of clinical neuropsychology may benefit from an attempt to distinguish among a number of different concepts frequently encountered in the field of brain-behavior relations, often

[1] I am indebted to my colleague, John C. Steinhelber, whose many careful readings of this chapter resulted in clarifications, substantive additions, and improvements in readability too numerous to cite individually.
[2] My own view of the field of clinical neuropsychology owes a great deal to Ralph M. Reitan through his writings, workshops, and private communications. I have tried to acknowledge his specific contributions as appropriate in this chapter, but he has had a much broader influence on what I have said here than could be credited by such specific references.

without adequate differentiation. *Brain damage* refers to pathological alteration of brain tissue, and is sometimes broadened to include alteration of brain physiology without structural change. *Brain lesion(s)* is a more precise concept referring to pathological alteration of brain tissue. These are physical constructs which, appropriately, are verified by physical means. *Intellectual impairment* refers to pathological reduction of those adaptive behaviors customarily grouped as intellectual. It is a psychological construct which is measured by quantifying behavior. Intellectual impairment may result from a wide variety of causes including: temporary alterations of brain physiology (e.g., alcohol intoxication); brain lesions; proximal causes described in purely psychological terms and without known physical bases such as depression, anxiety, psychoses, etc.; and interactions of the above. *Sensory motor deficit* is customarily excluded from the concept, "intellectual impairment," although sensory motor deficits have been shown to be interdependent with intellectual impairment (Luria, 1966; Reitan, 1970). Sensory-motor deficit, too, is a psychological concept which, operationally, depends upon quantification of behavior. *Personality changes* may result from brain damage. This concept refers to changes of mood and interpersonal style not easily subsumed under intellectual or sensory-motor deficit. Impairment of *adaptive functioning* is the broad concept including decrements in intellectual, sensory-motor, and personality functioning. *Organicity* is a very troublesome concept because it is widely used but carries no clear or agreed-upon definition. The term *organicity* itself has probably contributed to perpetuation of conceptual inadequacies because of its broad connotations. The liver, kidneys, spleen, colon, etc., are hardly less organic than the brain. Use of the term leads to such redundant and clumsy phrases as "organic brain damage." The concept organicity refers to a syndrome including all of the above conditions, *brain damage* (or lesions), *intellectual impairment, sensory-motor deficit*, and *personality change*. Among others, the dangers deriving from use of the concept include the fact that the entire range of included concepts may be inferred to have been established when evidence is presented bearing upon as few as one of them.

CLINICAL NEUROPSYCHOLOGY AND OTHER NEUROPSYCHOLOGICAL DISCIPLINES

The field of neuropsychology includes a number of disparate, sometimes only remotely related, disciplines of which clinical neuropsychology is only one. The principal subfields of neuropsychology are experimental neuropsychology, behavioral neurology, and clinical neuropsychology. All three subfields of neuropsychology are concerned with brain-behavior relations, but they differ in objectives and methods.[3]

[3]Dr. Manfred Meier, in a personal communication, helped to clarify my thinking about the various disciplines of neuropsychology. While I do not agree in every respect with his structuring of the field, the following discussion owes much to his views. "Behavioral neurology" is Meier's term for the traditional medical approach to brain-behavior study. See also Professor Meier's chapter in this volume.

Clinical Neuropsychology Clinical neuropsychology is concerned with developing knowledge about human brain-behavior relations, and with applying this knowledge to clinical problems (see Arthur Benton's chapter, this volume). Reitan (1966a) has described its subject matter as the psychological effects of brain lesions. Clinical neuropsychologists measure intellectual, sensory-motor, and personality deficits, and relate these deficits to brain lesions, or sometimes, to brain damage in the broader sense of including impaired physiology. The individuals whose work defines the field of clinical neuropsychology typically both conduct research on human brain-behavior relations, and perform clinical-diagnostic studies of the brain-damaged in direct application of knowledge in this field. Sometimes their work extends to therapy of the brain-damaged as well.

Clinical neuropsychology is itself a heterogeneous field occupied by individuals differing in training, methods of data gathering, and spheres of application. Although we have used the term clinical neuropsychology in the title of this book and have implied considerable breadth of coverage of that field in the subtitle, the contributors to this volume, for the most part, represent a particular approach to clinical neuropsychology. The efforts of neurologists and neurosurgeons in the behavioral field, and those of speech pathologists and some special education experts could also be termed clinical neuropsychology. Yet the activities of these specialists typically differ in important ways from the work represented on these pages. In this discussion, more for convenience than out of any sense of exclusive proprietorship, the term clinical neuropsychology will be used to refer to *comprehensive* approaches to *applied* problems concerning the *psychological* effects of brain damage in *humans*, and different terms will be used for distinguishably different approaches. Clinical neuropsychology in this tradition has roots in academic psychology, behavioral neurology, and, especially, the mental measurement or psychometric field in psychology.

Clinical neuropsychology relies on standardized behavioral observations, emphasizing psychological tests with norms and cutting scores. Behavior, in the context of this approach, is defined in operational terms and, usually, quantified on continuous distributions. Studies performed in this tradition tend to use large groups of subjects; the behavior of various patient groups is contrasted with one another and with that of controls, with the outcomes of such comparisons evaluated by means of inferential statistics. The concept of behavioral effects of brain damage is, in this approach, a very differentiated one. In his diagnostic task, the clinical neuropsychologist is not merely interested in differentiating brain damage from other diagnostic possibilities; he is also interested in making refined descriptions of clinical conditions including inferences as to location and extent of brain damage, if any, and probable medical and psychological conditions accounting for the abnormal behavior. Increasingly, he is interested in prognosis of recovery, rehabilitation potentials, and management alternatives for the patient. Measurement of adaptive function dependent upon the organic integrity of the brain is, in this approach, comprehensive, systematically including measures of all major adaptive behaviors of the human organism.

Measurement is usually standardized. The combined needs of comprehensiveness and standardization lead to the use of integrated batteries of tests which are administered in the same carefully systematized fashion to all patients assessed.

Within these broad communalities can be distinguished a number of different clinical neuropsychological approaches, two of which, at least, need to be described. These two are represented by their foremost exponents, Arthur Benton and Ralph Reitan, in this volume. Benton has conducted in-depth studies in most, if not all, of the major classical content areas in human neuropsychology. He has, thus, achieved comprehensiveness, not in the simultaneous examination of the full range of adaptive behaviors in individual subjects, but in the sequential study of these various topics. His focus has been on the empirical and theoretical elucidation of the classical problems identified by behavioral neurology. He has operationalized, differentiated, and expanded upon these concepts. In the process, he has kept a steady eye on the problems of the clinician, providing us with a wide variety of standardized tests for quantifying behavior variables related to the organic integrity of the brain. Except that he has had to rely upon nature's experiments, and has oriented his work to clinical problems, Benton could be said to have applied the approach of experimental neuropsychology to the classical problems of behavioral neurology.

Reitan's approach to clinical neuropsychology, on the other hand, has emphasized the use of standard batteries of tests that were designed to reflect, as far as possible, the full range of deficits associated with brain lesions. These batteries utilize procedures from the areas of experimental and clinical neuropsychology as well as behavioral neurology in order to maximize accurate prediction of cerebral functioning in individual subjects. His approach bears some resemblance to that of the industrial psychologist (Guion, 1965, pp. 163-169) in developing test batteries to predict job performance. This line of endeavor has resulted in establishing complementary relationships between the Halstead Neuropsychological Test Battery for adults and a number of additional tests, and in the development of neuropsychological batteries for two different age groups of children.[4] These comprehensive batteries have gained considerable acceptance based on Reitan's prodigious validation research and his provision of workshops devoted to their administration and interpretation. In the process of this validational work, Reitan has discovered and sharpened a large number of

---

[4] Although various labels have been applied to these batteries, the appropriate nomenclature, according to Reitan, is as follows: (a) The Halstead Neuropsychological Test Battery for Adults is applicable to adults and children down to 15 years. This battery is based on Halstead's original tests with some additions and deletions provided by Reitan. (b) The Halstead Neuropsychological Test Battery for Children is applicable to the age range 9-14 years, inclusive. It is basically a downward revision of the adult battery. (c) The Reitan-Indiana Test Battery for Children is used with the age group 5-8 years, inclusive. This battery has some communality in specific tests with the Halstead adult and children's batteries, and shares their basic principles of development and application. See the Appendix for a complete description of these batteries.

relationships between brain lesions and adaptive behavior. No one else has accumulated such a wealth of data characterized by variety and number of subjects, variety and comprehensiveness of behavioral measures, and replication of the same measures on all subjects. Refer to Reitan's chapter, Methodological Problems in Clinical Neuropsychology, Ch. 2 of this volume, for additional discussion of this approach pioneered by Halstead and carried forward by Reitan and by those influenced by him.

Compared with other fields involved with the development and application of psychological tests, clinical neuropsychology has shown a relative deemphasis of technical test construction problems. Since this stands in such sharp contrast to the focus in other measurement fields in psychology, which is sometimes on technical measurement problems to the exclusion of substantive psychological content, the difference probably requires some discussion. This relative deemphasis of technical test construction problems appears to have a number of distinguishable roots. (*a*) There has been some reliance by clinical neuropsychologists on already well-standardized tests, the technical construction aspects of which had previously been worked out by others. (*b*) The clinical neuropsychologist has usually been concerned with concurrent validity; thus some of the technical problems involved in predicting to criteria which mature at some later date have been obviated. (*c*) Many of the tests used by clinical neuropsychologists were originally developed not formally as tests but as standardized experiments designed to collect a particular type of data. Thus, there has been a tendency in this area to view data collection not in terms of administering psychometric tests but as performance of standardized experiments. (*d*) The criterion, brain damage, while presenting its own difficulties, is more objective than criteria for most other assessment problems in behavior pathology. (*e*) The behavioral variance with which the clinical neuropsychologist deals is, at least at its extremes, so potent, that behavioral neurology has been able to make findings which have stood the test of repeated verification despite the serious methodological weakness of nonsystematic behavioral measurement. Such extreme behavioral variance seldom occurs in other areas in psychology; when it does, one frequently encounters a lack of emphasis on technical measurement problems equal to that found in clinical neuropsychology. For example, Harlow's work on the affectional behavior of monkeys (Harlow & Harlow, 1965) illustrates this relationship. The investigator has much more motivation to concentrate on problems of validity than on other test construction problems when he is achieving success without having to place his major emphasis on item analyses, various aspects of reliability, etc. However, the relative luxury which clinical neuropsychologists have enjoyed in this regard may be approaching an end as they attempt to deal with problems characterized by increasingly subtle behavioral variance.

Experimental neuropsychology. The clinical neuropsychologist is distinguished from the experimental neuropsychologist primarily by his focus on clinical problems with human beings. The goals and professional activities of the experimental neuropsychologist are quite different. Experimental neuropsychologists do not orient their research toward the direct solution of applied problems, and seldom engage in applied work. Although the basic assumptions of comparative psychology are currently under severe challenge (Lockard, 1971), they are still reflected in the work of many experimental neuropsychologists. The primary objective of these investigators is to discover fundamental principles of brain-behavior relations, regardless of their practical applications. The basic assumption is that carefully controlled experimental situations will reveal relationships of greater generality than will direct study of naturally occurring situations. Most of the research in experimental neuropsychology is performed on animals, primarily because experimental alteration of the central nervous system of human beings is seldom possible. The experimental neuropsychologist hopes to discover, by study of nonhuman life forms, principles fundamental and sweeping enough to apply throughout the phylogenetic range and thus, ultimately, to explain human behavior. A corollary assumption embodied in this endeavor is that of continuity of neurobehavioral relationships across life forms differing greatly in morphology and behavior potentials. However, while many experimental neuropsychologists hope, ultimately, to be able to account for human behavior, others find the brain-behavior relations of animals other than man to be of intrinsic interest. Their work sometimes focuses on problems in this area even when there is no anticipation of application to human conditions.

Behavioral neurology. Behavioral neurology shares a focus on human problems of clinical significance with clinical neuropsychology, but differs in method from both experimental neuropsychology and clinical neuropsychology. The behavioral neurologist is much more likely than other neuropsychologists to emphasize conceptual rather than operational definitions of behavior, varying the operations used to elicit conceptually similar behavior as he examines different subjects. Instead of measuring behavior quantitatively on continua, as psychologists typically do, the behavioral neurologist tends to set up test situations designed to detect abnormal deviations from "normal" functioning in a dichotomous fashion. This approach places a primary emphasis on the individual case study rather than on group statistics as a source of generalizable data. For example, Luria (1966), a psychologist who has achieved a high level of training in neurology and whose work epitomizes this approach, produces methodical, highly individualized case studies employing a dazzling array of innovative test situations, apparently never repeated in exactly the same way across subjects.

Considering the interrelationships of these three neuropsychological fields—clinical neuropsychology, experimental neuropsychology, and behavioral neurology—they do not interact with as much frequency or fruitfulness as might be expected (Talland, 1969). With some few exceptions, it has not been possible to generalize from animal neuropsychology to human clinical neuropsychology because the range and complexity of human adaptive behaviors so far exceeds that of lower animals. Thus the human behaviors of greatest interest have no precise counterparts in animal analogues (Reitan, 1966a). Neuroanatomists and neurophysiologists have shown us that the human brain is organized and functions in importantly different ways from that of even our closest subhuman relatives (Geschwind, 1965). These structural and biochemical differences provide the bases for the important behavioral differences between humans and other animals (Lancaster, 1968; Luria, 1966; Reitan, 1966a). As a result of these factors, most of the voluminous and often very carefully executed experimental animal neuropsychological research contributes little to the direct solution of human clinical neuropsychological problems. Animal neuropsychological work sometimes does have heuristic value for human clinical research, focusing attention on human problems which would otherwise not have received as early investigation. However, when parallel observations are made on man and other animals, the original animal-derived generalizations frequently are revised extensively as a result of the human data. This point is illustrated in Gazzaniga's *The Bisected Brain* (1970), which summarizes human and animal work on the function of the corpus callosum.

The relationships between behavioral neurology and clinical neuropsychology have been more intimate than those between the latter and experimental neuropsychology, but communication of information has tended to flow more from the medical investigator to the psychologist than vice versa. There can be little doubt that many of our most useful insights concerning human brain-behavior relationships have derived from the clinicoanatomical studies of physician investigators (Adams, 1969). These insights and the concepts of brain function derived therefrom are rather easily assimilated by clinical neuropsychologists who attempt to give them consensually validated and comprehensive operational definitions (Benton, 1959, 1967a). There is less evidence that the knowledge and techniques produced by clinical neuropsychologists have affected medical study in this field except in an ancillary way. It seems reasonable that further significant strides in clinical neuropsychology will depend upon close collaboration between the medically trained neuroscientist and the psychologically trained clinical neuropsychologist, each of whom brings unique and essential skills to this endeavor. For some examples of fruitful collaboration of this kind see Heimburger and Reitan (1961), Penfield and Milner (1958), and in this volume, the chapters by Klonoff and Low (Ch. 6), and by Klonoff and Paris (Ch. 7).

RELATIONSHIPS BETWEEN CLINICAL NEUROPSYCHOLOGY AND ITS PRIMARY REFERRAL SOURCES: NEUROLOGY, NEUROSURGERY, AND PSYCHIATRY

The referral sources for clinical neuropsychology seem to be developing as rapidly as the area itself since clinical concern regarding the adequacy of brain functions has only been awaiting development of appropriate methodology.

Referrals come from other psychologists, cardiologists and cardiovascular surgeons, endocrinologists, internists, pediatricians, speech and hearing specialists, and many others. In current practice, however, the clinical neuropsychologist examines patients referred primarily by medical specialists in neurology, neurosurgery, and psychiatry. There appear to be particular characteristics of each of these fields which importantly affect their working relationships with clinical neuropsychology. However, the most important influence on the interactions between neuropsychologists and these referral sources is a general one; thus far, there are relatively few clinical neuropsychologists, with the consequence that the clinical neuropsychological approach is not generally well known in these referring fields. Most of these medical specialists have become accustomed to the tests and types of inferences used by clinical psychologists. They tend to expect familiar references to such information, and sometimes do not know how to receive the unfamiliar data and inferences provided by the clinical neuropsychologist.

As in any discipline, with respect to a specific content area which is not definitive of the field, great variation is present among neurologists and neurosurgeons in their familiarity with the methods and content of clinical neuropsychology. Some neurologists and neurosurgeons are frontline contributors to this field; others know very little about it. However, many neurologists and neurosurgeons will be familiar with behavioral neurology, and will possess a differentiated picture of the behavioral effects of brain damage. Thus, when the clinical neuropsychologist refers to specific functions, such as spatial praxis, being affected, and makes inferences from the pattern of such deficits to the distribution of damage in the brain, the neurologist and neurosurgeon will be in possession of similar concepts. But, despite this communality, the neurologist and neurosurgeon will sometimes encounter difficulties in utilizing the services of the clinical neuropsychologist. First, there still remain important conceptual differences about the behavioral effects of brain damage. The clinical neuropsychologists' view of brain-behavior relations is inclined to be more differentiated than that of the neurologist or the neurosurgeon. The concept of dementia is still popular in neurology, and remains an important constituent of many diagnostic syndromes. The clinical neuropsychologist's differentiated presentation of preserved and impaired adaptive functions, when the neurologist has merely questioned whether the patient is demented or not, can be confusing and frustrating to both professionals. Furthermore, neurologists and neurosurgeons are not typically acquainted with the validity data on neuropsychological tests and batteries, and may be equally unfamiliar with the meaning of various scores deriving from such procedures. Thus, they may be both unable to evaluate the raw data, and mistrustful of the conclusions derived from such data. Obviously, these are problems of education that may be corrected in time. Neurologists and neurosurgeons tend to seek and welcome objectification of adaptive function related to the physical integrity of the brain. As they become acquainted with the achievements of clinical neuropsychology, the difficulties in understanding dissipate in the face of the contributions presented.

In the current state of affairs, the neurologist, more than the neurosurgeon, is likely to encounter another difficulty in using the services of the clinical neuropsychologist. He will find the latter presenting quantified data concerning functions which he, the neurologist, has already measured in a less-quantitative manner. The conclusions from the two sets of data may not agree. The neurologist has become used to this sort of situation with respect to global measures of adaptive function like the IQ tests where he realizes that there is something to be gained from more-standardized appraisal of intellectual functions than can be derived from the mental status examination, but he may view the clinical neuropsychologist's presentation of quantified data on sensory suppression effects, finger agnosia, motor strength, and finger oscillation speed as uninvited poaching on his own territory. From the other side of it, the clinical neuropsychologist may have insufficient respect for the diagnostic power of a well-conducted neurological examination.

In practical application, the interrelations of the clinical neuropsychologist and medical neurospecialists encounter other difficulties. At the present state of development, the administration of a comprehensive neuropsychological test battery, such as the Halstead Neuropsychological Test Battery for Adults, may require most of a working day. The patient's condition may demand that this work be distributed over several days' time. Other contemporaneous diagnostic procedures, such as the pneumoencephalogram, may so limit the patient's ability to cooperate that valid psychological testing is temporarily impossible. Some of the most time-consuming tests may be among the most valuable to the neuropsychologist, and he may have a strong desire to include the entire battery in the interest of research and to obtain the most comprehensive basis from which to make clinical inferences. The lengthy neuropsychological examination is also expensive.

These are problems which must be met through close collaboration between referring specialists and clinical neuropsychologists on the one hand, and further refinement of neuropsychological test batteries on the other. In the best circumstances, the clinical neuropsychologist will be consulted during the admission planning phase so that the neuropsychological testing can be performed in proper synchrony with other procedures. Given the rushed and complicated patient care of a large teaching hospital, such synchrony is usually difficult to achieve, however, while the frequent turnover of treating personnel in such settings further complicates collaborative planning and communication of results. Further developments in clinical neuropsychology may soon lead to systematic stepwise screening procedures and more efficient comprehensive batteries; but when we attempt abbreviated procedures in our current state of knowledge, we are mindful that we may be omitting a source of information which in a particular case could be decisive.

For a number of years, clinical neuropsychology has been in possession of knowledge and techniques which could contribute substantially to the psychiatrist's diagnostic efforts when brain damage is suspected. However, psychiatrists, even more frequently than neurologists and neurosurgeons, find themselves unfamiliar with clinical neuropsychology, and perhaps somewhat uneasy with its findings which may conflict with or fall outside the focus of the conceptual lens through which they view the behavioral effects of brain damage. The popular theories of behavior in psychiatry do not facilitate articulation with neuropsychological data. The global and imprecise concepts of the organic brain syndrome and "organicity" are the most popular relevant ones in psychiatry. Psychiatrists typically have little opportunity in their training to become familiar with clinical neuropsychology. What they learn about psychological assessment usually comes from clinical psychologists, most of whom are not trained in clinical neuropsychology, or from summary reference works which frequently fail to mention clinical neuropsychology. For example, the publication, *Psychiatry*, 2nd edition, by M. T. Eaton, Jr., and Margaret H. Peterson (1969), popularly relied upon by psychiatrists preparing for their boards in psychiatry and neurology, has this to say about psychological testing in "organicity":

> Although there may be some indications of organic impairment from variations in performance on the WAIS, the most helpful test for suspected brain damage is the Bender Visual Motor Gestalt Test . . . . Other specialized tests for the assessment of intellectual performance include the Babcock-Levy test for memory deterioration, the Kohs block design, the Hanmann-Kasanin [sic.] Concept Formation test and the various tests involving sorting such as the Goldstein-Sheerer series [p. 62].

Perusal of the 10 references under "Organic Brain Syndromes" (the major heading for this topic) in the index of this same work failed to turn up a single reference to any comprehensive neuropsychological approach to the problem, nor was "neuropsychology" a heading in the index. Clinical neuropsychology also finds little coverage in comprehensive reviews of psychological testing also frequently consulted by psychiatrists in an effort to gain information about particular tests or approaches. Cronbach's recently revised (1969), widely used, and authoritative text on psychological testing, *Essentials of Psychological Testing*, contains only two index references to "Organicity," his major heading for this subject, and both of these refer to single measure relationships with dichotomous criteria of brain damage. He does not mention neuropsychology or any comprehensive approach to behavioral diagnosis of brain damage.

CLINICAL NEUROPSYCHOLOGY AND THE TRADITIONAL PSYCHODIAGNOSTIC APPROACH OF CLINICAL PSYCHOLOGY

Psychiatry, neurology, and neurosurgery have traditionally relied upon clinical psychology for psychodiagnostic assessment. Although clinical neuropsychology is gaining headway as a recognized psychodiagnostic discipline, it is, so far, represented by few practitioners. It appears unlikely that at any time in the foreseeable future the clinical need for psychological assessment of patients with known or suspected brain damage can be met by the direct services of clinical neuropsychologists or those supervised by them. The most expeditious route to dissemination of clinical neuropsychological techniques and knowledge would appear to be through providing such training to clinical psychologists. The clinical psychologist engaged in psychodiagnostic work has much to profit from the insights concerning the behavioral effects of brain damage, techniques for assessing these effects, and concepts of neural-behavioral relationships that clinical neuropsychology has to offer. If he obtains such training, new and exciting horizons will open to him and the quality of his diagnostic work will be improved to a significant extent.

Becoming an expert clinical neuropsychologist may require a degree of specialization and concentration of effort impossible to a practitioner already involved in many other activities. Nevertheless, useful training in clinical neuropsychology may be obtained by a combination of attendance at workshops such as those that have been offered by Ralph Reitan and other neuropsychologists, and selected reading and practice with the related techniques. Clinical neuropsychological training may someday be incorporated into most graduate school and internship training programs in clinical psychology. Such incorporation appears to be occurring now. Until very recently, the proportion of clinical psychologists possessing any knowledge of clinical neuropsychology appeared to be quite small. That state of affairs is now changing. Increasingly, one encounters students entering their clinical internships who have had some exposure to clinical neuropsychology and are eager to learn more about it. There must be powerful reasons for this interest, for it has to contend with the current, almost ubiquitous Zeitgeist, especially potent in many behavioristically oriented academic clinical psychology training programs, which strongly opposes psychological testing of any kind.

The current interest in clinical neuropsychology to be found among clinical psychologists probably owes something to the following facts: Recently publicized, but not always recently accomplished investigations provide considerable cross-cultural verification of certain generalizations about the psychological effects of brain damage. Investigators working in widely separated spots on the globe are beginning to communicate about this field, and frequently find that they are talking the same scientific language, at least sufficiently so as to find each other's work interesting and useful. Investigators working in such different cultures as Russia (Luria, 1966), Italy (Faglioni, Spinnler, & Vignolo, 1969), France (Hécaen & Ajuriaguerra, 1964), Norway (Klove, this volume), and the English-speaking countries (Benton, 1967a) appear to be arriving at interrelated and mutually verifying generalizations despite the obvious communication difficulties deriving from translation, varying methodological biases, varying observational methods, and varying methods of inference. This convergence fosters considerable confidence that certain brain-behavior relations are quite fundamental to the human organism regardless of cultural influence, and that the behavioral variance due to these organic factors is potent enough to filter through international barriers to communication.

In addition, although we are far from an adequate theoretical understanding of the nervous system, in working with this material one sometimes gains the impression that we are beginning to understand how the brain works—that relations between the structural conditions and physiology of the brain, on the one hand, and adaptive behavior, on the other, are rapidly becoming clearer. Luria (1966), Geschwind (1965), Pribram (1971), and others have been able to devise conceptual systems of human neuropsychology of ever-increasing breadth and precision due to the rapid accumulation of empirical data in this field.

Discoveries in neuropsychology may even help to clarify and operationalize psychodynamic concepts. For example, the concept of unconscious psychological content and processes is considered by many clinicians to be essential for adequate description and explanation of clinical phenomena such as conversion symptoms and dissociated behaviors. However, the concept has encountered serious logical difficulties, generating very complex theoretical discussions (e.g., Rubinstein, 1965). To some students, the concept appears so indefensible on logical and philosophical grounds that they are discouraged from studying the relevant clinical material and related literature. Some of the behavior of brain-bisected humans (Gazzaniga, 1970) illustrates simultaneous independence of the functioning of the two cerebral hemispheres and of the two sides of the body analogous to dissociated or unconsciously motivated behaviors. For example, the right hemisphere of these patients can be induced to perform complex adaptive behaviors about which the subject concerned is unable to make a verbal report. This is because the right hemisphere has insufficient control over the speech apparatus to make a verbal report, while the left hemisphere, which does, has insufficient information about the acts which have occurred. Gazzaniga reports that one commissurotomized patient seized his wife by the throat with his left hand, while simultaneously attempting to restrain his left hand with his right. These behaviors occur due to a known physical cause. The callossal fibers which normally interconnect and provide information exchange between the two cerebral hemispheres have, in these patients, been interrupted surgically, establishing partially independent neurobehavioral systems. Over time following the surgery, the two hemispheres learn to communicate in subtle ways so that special techniques are required to demonstrate their potential for independence of function. Some of the methods of interhemispheric communication in these cases, for example eye divergence, unverbalized cooperative strategies, and emotional cross-cuing, resemble behaviors which in noncommissurotomized patients have been conceptualized as "unconscious" or nonverbal "symbolic" communications.

These neuropsychological observations of commissurotomized patients and our knowledge of how these behaviors occur do not explain functional dissociation, conversions symptoms, and the like. However, the concept of semi-independent neurobehavioral systems within the same organism cuts through theoretical confusion concerning "unconsciously" motivated behavior and redirects our attention in such cases to careful empirical observation and delineation of interrelations among observables as distinguished from philosophizing about such behavior.

Finally, one finds in this area of endeavor an uncommon interconnection between research and clinical practice. It is quite stimulating to pick up a recent edition of a scientific journal and find that much of its contents are of potential utility in one's clinical work. Failure to find this kind of connection between current research and practice in most of the subfields of clinical psychology—psychotherapy, psychodiagnosis of functional conditions, and group behavior—constitutes, I believe, a very potent source of dissatisfaction for most clinical psychologists who were trained to be scientist-practitioners, or vice versa, but who frequently find it impossible to be scientist and practitioner in relation to the same clinical material (Ross, 1971).

DIFFERENCES BETWEEN CLINICAL PSYCHOLOGICAL AND CLINICAL NEUROPSYCHOLOGICAL APPROACHES TO THE ASSESSMENT OF BRAIN DAMAGE

The conceptual and operational differences between the approach to the assessment of brain damage which has evolved in clinical psychology and that of clinical neuropsychology should be clarified if clinical neuropsychology is to be most profitably assimilated in clinical psychology training and practice. Clinical psychology and clinical neuropsychology have developed independent approaches to some of the same clinical problems, the two approaches having few communalities despite superficial similarities which, on first examination, suggest considerable overlap. Use by clinical neuropsychologists of some tests also commonly used by clinical psychologists, such as the Wechsler series of intelligence scales, constitutes one such similarity. Another is the acceptance by clinical psychologists, as occasional additions to their test batteries, of particular tests of psychological effects of brain damage which have been developed by clinical neuropsychologists.

The major difference between the two approaches resides in their antithetical but internally consistent bodies of assumptions and techniques concerning the assessment of the behavioral effects of brain damage. The approach to this assessment problem in traditional clinical psychology involves the application of a more or less standardized battery of tests used for any and all assessment problems. The most commonly used tests are: the Wechsler series of intelligence scales, the Rorschach, the Thematic Apperception Test, the Minnesota Multiphasic Personality Inventory, the Bender Gestalt figure drawings, and the Draw-A-Person task (Lubin, Wallis, & Paine, 1971). When used to perform differential diagnoses involving questions of brain damage, some subset of these tests may be supplemented by one or more tests developed specifically for this diagnostic purpose such as the Visual Retention Test (Benton, 1963) or Stein Symbol Gestalt Test (Stein, 1970). If specific questions of future academic performance are raised, additional tests of academic skills such as the Wide Range Achievement Test (Jastak & Jastak, 1965), or reading comprehension may also be used. The tests in the nuclear battery listed above are, for the most part, what Cronbach (1969) has called "large bandwidth" devices. They each sample a wide range of behaviors which clinical neuropsychology has found to be differentially sensitive to varying types and degrees of brain damage.

"Organicity" as a unitary construct. In using this semistandardized battery, the clinical psychologist looks for evidence of reduced level of performance, qualitative indications of brain damage (such as concreteness of verbal expression), pathognomonic signs of brain damage, and diagnostic patterns on intelligence tests and on personality tests such as the MMPI. An experienced clinical psychologist will look for an "organic syndrome," or pattern of functioning, considering the profile of performance over all the tests used. The basic concept guiding this approach is that of organicity, a unitary construct. The concept includes the assumption that any and all kinds of brain damage lead to similar behavioral effects, and that behavioral differences among the brain-damaged are due primarily to severity of damage and to premorbid personality characteristics. This is a faulty assumption.

Reitan (1966a) has noted that all of the following factors have been shown to have an important bearing upon the magnitude and patterning of behavioral effects resulting from brain lesions: laterality of lesion—right or left hemisphere, site of lesion within hemisphere, causal agent(s) creating lesion(s), age of patient when lesion was incurred, and interval between damage and testing.

To this list may be added: condition of the patient at the time of assessment apart from brain damage (e.g., interaction between brain damage and drugs) (Stein, 1970), lateral motor and higher cortical function dominance (Hécaen & Ajuriaguerra, 1964), and premorbid condition of patient (Lansdell, 1971; Ruesch, Harris, & Bowman, 1945; Chapman & Wolff, 1959).

And, of course, size and severity of brain lesion(s) are important factors in determining their behavioral effects (Chapman & Wolff, 1959).

Most psychodiagnosticians trained in traditional clinical psychology would probably admit that each of these variables could influence the behavioral expression of brain damage, but it is doubtful that these factors typically are given appropriate weighting in the context of an assessment approach emphasizing the unitary concept of "organicity." This unitary conceptualization of the effects of brain damage, "organicity," so deeply entrenched in traditional clinical psychodiagnostics, appears to have resulted from the combined effects of several distinguishable influences. First, Lashley's work on the relationships between cortical ablations and the maze learning behavior of rats (Lashley, 1929) appears to have contributed to this viewpoint even though experimental neuropsychologists have since progressed far beyond the methods and conclusions of that effort. Recall that this work showed that the volume of

inADequate Ante-cedents

cortex destroyed, not its location, was the overwhelming determinant of maze learning deficit in the surgically brain-damaged rat. Lashley's concept of mass action came to be regarded by many as a verity which, in subhumans, dispensed with the potentially complex problem of differential function of cortical tissue depending upon topographical organization. As Luria (1965) noted, it appears to have been applied uncritically to humans as well.

Second, from the clinical approach to the problem, Kurt Goldstein (1952) appears to have been very influential in promulgating an overly narrow view of human brain-behavior relations. By describing the communalities exhibited in the clinical syndromes of traumatically brain-damaged humans, Goldstein was able to provide a convincing, and in many ways accurate, picture of the general effects of brain damage on human behavior. Although Goldstein did not himself ignore the variable effects of brain lesions depending upon their etiology and location, his concepts of generalized organic effects survived in much more vivid form than did his views of differential effects. His concepts of generalized organic effects, especially that of loss of the "abstract attitude," appear to have had considerable influence on clinical psychology's approach to the problem. Goldstein's contribution thus reinforced the trends derived from Lashley's work—the conceptualization of the behavioral effects of brain damage primarily as a unitary construct varying only in severity.

Third, these influences were funnelled through the methodologically oriented psychometric approach of *American Psychology* which emphasized standardized measurement, norms, and considerations of statistical reliability and validity. The net result of these several influences was the still-continuing search for a *single best* test for "organicity." If brain damage produces substantially the same qualitative effects regardless of its etiology, location, duration, etc., the task becomes that of devising the single most reliable, sensitive, and otherwise valid measure of these general effects. The development of test indices of concreteness, distortions of drawings (in the Bender Gestalt and Graham-Kendall figure drawing tests, for example), perceptual aftereffects, tasks susceptible to brain damage versus those less susceptible (e.g., Wechsler's hold versus don't hold ratio), perceptual-motor malfunction, etc., as *single measures of "organicity"* appears to owe a powerful legacy to the aforementioned influences and represents a still-prevalent acceptance of the unitary construct of organicity.

Fourth, another powerful influence in establishing the unitary concept of organicity in clinical psychology, perhaps the most powerful, was the strong impact of psychoanalysis—more broadly considered, "dynamic" psychology—on clinical psychology, and the resulting conceptualization within clinical psychology of its psychodiagnostic testing mission. With an emphasis on psychoanalysis and psychoanalytic psychotherapy as *the* methods of treatment for behavior pathology, there was considerable pessimism about the ability of brain-damaged patients to benefit from treatment. If the behavior pathology was due to structural damage, the methods of psychoanalytically oriented treatments were, theoretically, useless as therapeutic agents. With the focus on psychoanalytically oriented psychotherapy and psychoanalysis, behavior pathology due to brain damage fell outside the theoretical scope of the treatment orientation. It was important only to identify the brain-damaged as patients of poor therapeutic prognosis, not to learn anything about the effects of brain damage on behavior as a subject of intrinsic interest or to discover ways to ameliorate the effects of brain damage.

Expert application of the semistandard battery of tests already listed, can result in adequate descriptions of patients in psychoanalytic terms. This psychodiagnostic approach is classically expressed in the work of the Menninger clinical psychologists under Rappaport (Rappaport, Gill, & Schafer, 1968), especially in the work of Schafer (1948). Their approach, which involved the complete and systematic administration of their battery to all patients referred for psychodiagnostic testing, became the ideal model for the field; use of this battery (though very rarely the complete Menninger battery) was almost universally taught in clinical psychology training programs. The attainment of an acceptable level of proficiency with it requires a great deal of time and energy and the battery also requires very considerable time to administer, score, and collate in a typical case. These factors established potent conservative forces resisting extensive alterations of this battery.

With respect to the diagnosis of brain damage, the influence from this direction resulted in attempts to find indices of "organicity" in this "standard" battery of tests. Occasionally, as in the work of Baker (1956), the diagnosis of brain damage within this framework involved careful clinical observation and considerable sophistication about different kinds of organic syndromes. However, the conceptualization of the behavioral effects of brain damage appears to have become increasingly simplistic and undifferentiated under this influence. The somewhat differentiated and naturalistic pioneer work of Hermann Rorschach (1942) was, in this tradition, eventually reduced to the signs of "organicity" of Piotrowski (1937) and Hughes (1948).

UTILITY OF CLINICAL NEUROPSYCHOLOGY

This field of clinical neuropsychology is, for those of us who are engaged in it, stimulating and self-sustaining. Yet, considering the widespread disillusionment with clinical psychodiagnostic testing in the traditional model, and the recent cultural emphasis on *relevance*, the *utility* of clinical neuropsychology may require some discussion.

First, the same behavioral deficits, so far as gross adaptive consequences are concerned, may be due to widely differing causative agents and, therefore, require entirely different therapeutic measures. For example, a reading disability may be the result of an abnormal learning history in an otherwise normal individual, or the result of a structural or biochemical anomaly of the brain. Psychotic behavior, including delusions, may be the result of treatable brain damage, of essentially untreatable brain damage, or of unknown (and presently unknowable) etiology, presumed by many to be the result of the particular interpersonal learning history of the individual. Or similar behaviors may be the result of some combination of these different factors. Thus, for treatment purposes, it becomes important to detect the cause of the adaptive deficits observed, although it must be acknowledged that one is frequently unable to utilize the differential diagnostic information to design appropriate treatment because of the current paucity of treatment alternatives and poor coordinating propositions between knowledge of the condition of the nervous system and treatment techniques, and even between patterns of adaptive functioning and treatment alternatives.

While current physical diagnostic techniques in neurology such as radioisotope encephalography, angiography, pneumoencephalography, and electroencephalography frequently provide positive and unequivocal diagnostic data, some of these techniques, in certain instances, carry a limited morbidity risk. Clinical neuropsychology can make a contribution to the diagnostic process at the point where there is suspicion of brain damage, but insufficient evidence thereof to warrant such diagnostic procedures, especially when they require hospitalization of the patient. In some cases behavioral measures may reflect brain damage when measures of the physical properties of the brain short of direct inspection following craniotomy cannot document it. Further, in certain situations psychodiagnostic information may round out a syndrome picture after all reasonable physical procedures have been done.

Second, a careful specification of adaptive deficits due to brain damage may be important for disposition, management, and treatment, even when it is already known that a patient's ailment is the result of brain damage (diagnosis is in that sense not a problem). It is frequently the case that although the neurological facts are fairly well known, it is difficult if not impossible for the neurologist, neurosurgeon, or psychiatrist to extrapolate from these facts to predictions about the patient's behavior in his ambient environment so as properly to advise the patient and others involved in his life how to maximize well-being and adaptive function. It is almost as difficult for the clinical neuropsychologist to extrapolate from knowledge about brain damage to ambient behavior, but he is able to sample adaptive behavior in a controlled manner so as to make very useful and specific predictions concerning the patient's extra-test adaptive limitations, and how to minimize their impact on the patient's life and self-esteem.

A complete clinical neuropsychological examination is reasonably comprehensive with respect to adaptively significant behaviors, whereas other methods of appraising a patient's adaptive capacity are likely to omit critically important behaviors. In general, other methods of appraisal tend to rely too heavily on a patient's spontaneous verbal behavior and on nonsystematically elicited perceptual-motor and motor behavior. The spatial praxis and other simultaneous-organizational functions of the so-called "minor" hemisphere are insufficiently scrutinized in such appraisals. Even more importantly, the patient's highest cortical functions, involving the categorization of stimuli and formation of new logical relationships (analysis and synthesis) are not sufficiently appraised even by the rather wide-ranging assessment involved in the "standard" battery typically employed by clinical psychologists. Without systematic and comprehensive examination of a patient's adaptively significant behaviors and careful comparison of his pattern of functioning with the demands of the work and home environment to which he will return following hospitalization, the stage is frequently set for needless tragedies of adaptive failure. With precise knowledge of a patient's pattern of functioning, specific training and compensatory measures can be recommended. On the other side of it, a patient with obvious verbal or motor deficits may be thought of as more generally impaired than he actually is, with the consequence that he will be deprived, needlessly, of many satisfying life experiences.

Third, diagnosing brain damage can be important in establishing legal responsibility. A frequent question in liability suits involving head injury concerns the presence and adaptive significance of brain damage. The clinical neuropsychological examination can be quite valuable in such cases in objectifying the presence, quality, and extremity of adaptive deficit, if any. Such applications of clinical neuropsychology are likely to increase as medical science continues to improve its ability to preserve life in the face of brain injury.

Fourth, clinical-neuropsychological assessment is a valuable study technique with numerous applications. It can be an invaluable means of quantifying adaptive functions as dependent variables in the evaluation of experimental interventions which affect the nervous system—for example, neurosurgical treatments, chemotherapeutic or antibiotic treatments, nervous system stimulants or depressants, anesthetics, etc.

Finally, increasing our understanding of the psychological effects of brain damage and, more generally, brain-behavior relations, requires the systematic study of the behavior of human beings with brain damage of different etiologies, locations, extents, etc. Because we can seldom alter the central nervous system of humans under controlled conditions for experimental purposes alone, we shall always be dependent on nature's experiments to further our knowledge of human neuropsychology (Reitan, 1966a).

2
METHODOLOGICAL PROBLEMS IN CLINICAL NEUROPSYCHOLOGY[1]

Ralph M. Reitan

Even a casual review of most volumes or publications in the area of psychology indicates that the development of knowledge has been determined (or perhaps limited) by available methodological approaches. In most introductory psychology textbooks, for example, a great deal is presented that represents a body of knowledge. Information is given concerning concepts, methodologies, and content areas. One might find expositions in the area of verbal learning, bilateral transfer, intelligence, visual form perception, concept formation, the physiological bases of emotional behavior, or any of a number of other general or specific topics. Further, one might find comments regarding the nature of anxiety, the behavioral concomitants of depression, or the differential aspects of process versus reactive schizophrenia. The field of psychology, however, has rather neglected the systematized investigation of how such information is applied in evaluation of the individual subject. When an attempt is made to apply the available knowledge to individuals, the approach either relates almost exclusively to measurements and comparisons of level of performance or to the customary methods of clinical psychology. Level of performance may be based on data that reflect how well an individual or group of subjects learns, how well they see, what their intelligence level is, or the number of trials (or errors) needed to reach a specified criterion. The methods of clinical psychology, conversely, have emphasized the use of the case history, interview information, and psychological testing. Data derived from psychological testing has often been inadequately validated principally because of deficiencies in criterion information used to characterize the condition in question. Use of case history

[1] Preparation of this paper was supported in part by a grant (HD 02274) to the Child Development and Mental Retardation Center, University of Washington.

and interview information has never adequately overcome the problem of selectivity of data acquisition and use. The information derived customarily is a function of the special interests and "hunches" of the interviewer. Even though a standardized interview may be utilized, the information actually drawn from the interview for application to the individual subject must finally be selected and the judgments of the clinician are introduced at this time. The conclusions drawn about the individual are necessarily a function of the available information, and the use of the available information is often based upon presumptive and ill-defined subjective procedures which are sometimes referred to as clinical judgment. Decisionmaking procedures of this type have been referred to as instances of "special pleading." Thus the methods of clinical psychology, as customarily applied, often generate conclusions about individual subjects that are not documented or substantiated by empirical evidence or unbiased data-sampling procedures.

If one's interest is restricted to various content areas, abstract notions or concepts, or various types of methodologies, one need not be concerned about problems of this type. However, psychology and its various subfields supposedly are oriented toward the scientific study of human or animal behavior and, in this sense, it is important to relate the knowledge that is developed to the organism that generates the behavior. Thus, the behaving organism becomes the focal and distinct unit of relevance. While one can develop knowledge of areas such as visual form perception, emotional behavior, reading skills, or intelligence, eventually it becomes of interest to apply this information to the relevant unit. In clinical neuropsychology this unit is the individual human being. In spite of the paucity of formal inquiries, it scarcely seems necessary to offer an apology for a feeling of responsibility to develop methods for applying available knowledge to individual human subjects. For example, if research has generated information concerning the differential functions of the two cerebral hemispheres, and presumably a basis for measuring the adequacy of such functions, it would seem that such advances would be more significant if methods were also developed for application of the knowledge to individual subjects. Only in this way can the findings eventually become of practical significance.

To illustrate this point it may be well to offer a specific example. Some years ago, a resident neurological surgeon at the Indiana University Medical Center volunteered to take a battery of neuropsychological tests in order to have a better understanding of the types of examinations that might be given to his patients. After taking this extensive battery of psychological tests, that among other things yielded information concerning the differential status of the two cerebral hemispheres, he returned to obtain a brief interpretation of the results. The results indicated that this young neurosurgeon had an excellent left cerebral hemisphere, but that abilities dependent upon the right cerebral hemisphere were scarcely better than average. The left hemisphere, as is well known, subserves language functions and verbal communications whereas the right cerebral hemisphere is more intimately involved in analysis of visuospatial configurations and performance (manipulatory) activities. The differential level of this man's abilities in these two areas prompted me to offer an initial comment to the effect that the test results indicated that he probably would be much better at telling about an operation after it was over than he would be at actually doing it. The neurosurgeon looked shocked, admitted that this was correct, and confessed that he regularly was the last person to be able to identify any landmarks! The test results, in other words, had definite practical implications with respect to evaluation of the subject. He showed evidence of excellent left cerebral functioning, including a high level of verbal ability. Right cerebral functioning, conversely, was definitely poorer and he demonstrated a relatively mediocre ability in manipulatory and visuospatial problem-solving skills. While objective external criterion evidence regarding the efficiency of functioning of the two cerebral hemispheres of this subject was not available, the results did seem to be applicable to the individual human being who had taken the tests. Exactly how such applications can generally be made, however, has not been the subject of sufficient directed research and most of our knowledge, as mentioned above, is in the form of generalizations and abstractions that relate to content areas, ideas, and methodologies.

The above comments imply that some psychologists disdain an interest in individual human beings and prefer to direct their efforts to identification of abstractions and generalization that have no demonstrable application to individual subjects. However, it is equally clear that a considerable number of psychologists *are* concerned about the development of methods for applying knowledge in the field of psychology to individual human beings. Thus, for those psychologists whose professional values and activities are oriented toward the importance of the individual in his own right, the question exists as to how we can effect a transition from knowledge of content to individual application. It would seem that the appellation "clinical neuropsychology," as contrasted with "experimental neuropsychology," might require an orientation of this kind. In this area, therefore, the question becomes one of how we can draw specific differential conclusions regarding the psychological effects of brain lesions, as contrasted with the many environmental factors which may have both general and specific psychological significance for the individual person.

It would appear that the first step in attempting to answer this question would be to formulate some kind of statement of an adequate set of psychological measurements (test battery) to reflect the behavioral correlates of brain functions (Reitan, 1966a). This is not an easy task. Essentially the answer to the question requires a great deal of empirical research in order to demonstrate the kinds of abilities involved and adequate methods for their measurement. In fact, if we knew the answer to this question we would have essentially an answer to the overall problem of human brain-behavior relationships. Given these circumstances, practical necessities require that we use a "best-guess" type of approach and gradually, through acquisition of experimental data, successively improve the adequacy of the prior guesses. Many of the attempts to generate information regarding the behavioral correlates of brain lesions, judging from the literature, have not been concerned even with an attempt to make such a "best guess." Not infrequently, investigations have concerned themselves only with explorations of single tests considered individually. As described elsewhere in this volume, this approach has led to identification of a number of supposed "critical factors" in the psychology of brain-behavior relationships which in fact were nothing more than confirmation of the selective and a priori notions of individual investigators. Obviously, we will never develop a meaningful conceptualization of the extent and manner in which brain lesions alter ability structure in individual human beings if each group of subjects is studied with a different set of measurements and the measurements, in turn, are never put in a meaningful overall behavioral context. Thus, the use of single tests can scarcely contribute very significantly to an overall understanding of the behavioral correlates of brain lesions nor can a single test, considering the complexity of brain functions, be expected to serve as an adequate diagnostic instrument.

While the use of single tests in human investigations has been prompted by a desire to effect clinical diagnostic categorizations, the same type of problem (but for very different reasons) is present in animal research. Frequently the results of altered brain functions in animals are expressed behaviorally by single scores representing number of correct responses, percentages of correct responses in relation to total trials, etc. As one looks at published graphs and tables that are presented as representing the behavioral correlates of brain lesions in animals, one is confronted, just as in studies based on human subjects, with the question of whether the particular type of deficit shown really represents a meaningful concept of the behavioral correlates of brain functions for the animal in question. The point to be made is that particular and selected types of deficit shown in single variables, based either on animal or human subjects, can scarcely reflect a meaningful conceptualization of brain functions in an overall sense. This criticism is not intended to deny the value of single-variable studies but unless more extensive sets of measurements of behavior, as related to impaired brain functions, are accomplished in individual animals, the effects of brain lesions on ability structure for the individual subject will not be learned. It seems entirely conceivable that the principal correlates of brain lesions may be reflected in alterations of relationships among behavioral variables, and if this does turn out to be the case, it obviously will have been necessary to have used a sufficient number of variables to study their interrelationships and configurations. This problem may be more difficult to deal with in animal than in human studies. Sampling of a broad range of adaptive abilities in animals is complicated by communicational limitations in an attempt to give "test instructions" or in asking a meaningful question of the animal. In examining a human subject, the experimenter can give a verbal description of the nature of the task or the problem to be solved which greatly facilitates examination over a broad range of functions. In animal work, however, the task itself must be communicated through use of detailed training procedures. After this training is completed and the nature of the problem communicated, the investigator is finally in a position to study the effect of a new variable on performance of the learned task.

A more pointed critique of studies that orient themselves toward selected or individual measurements should be made and since almost all investigators in this area could be criticized in this regard, it may be most appropriate to select a personal research effort for criticism. Recently, I became interested in name-writing ability among normal and brain-damaged children. Because younger children, especially those with brain lesions, vary greatly in the ability to write their own name, the instructions used were very simple. The child was merely requested to write his name in his customary manner. Some children are able to write their names completely at the age of 6, whereas others are able only to print a few individual letters. In any case, the child's best attempt was accepted as representative of his performance. The hand that the subject used for this purpose and the amount of time required for completion of the task were recorded by the examiner. Next the child was requested to write his name again, but this time using his nonpreferred hand. He was asked to write his name in exactly the same way as on the first attempt. In this way the time for the two attempts could be compared in order to reflect facility in this performance with the preferred and nonpreferred hands. Three hypotheses were proposed for investigation. First, we postulated that normal children would require less time with the preferred hand (first trial) than would children with brain lesions. Secondly, the same directional relationship among groups of subjects was postulated for the nonpreferred hand. Thirdly, it was postulated that the relationship between time required for the two hands would differ in the two groups. Normal children should take somewhat longer with the nonpreferred hand than with the preferred hand rather regularly and consistently. Subjects with brain lesions, however, might be expected to show more variability between the two hands for several reasons. First, they presumably would have more difficulty adapting to the requirements of the task under the nonpracticed (nonpreferred hand) conditions and, therefore, generally would require more time with the nonpreferred hand, as compared with the preferred hand, than would the normal children. We also postulated that in some instances hand preference might be determined by the comparative condition of the two cerebral hemispheres. For example, an individual brain-damaged child might have principal damage to the left cerebral hemisphere, which in turn could severely impair the functional efficiency of his right upper extremity. If his right upper extremity were seriously dysfunctional as compared to his left, a factor would be present that could lead to a left-handed preference. In such cases the nonpreferred hand would also be the impaired side and the child might have special difficulties on that side with the name-writing task. Finally, we postulated that the brain-damaged subjects, in some instances, would do relatively well with the nonpreferred hand compared to their own performance with the preferred hand. These would represent instances in which the subject had left cerebral damage, but had nevertheless continued to be right-handed even though he performed relatively poorly with his right hand. In these instances brain damage would have been responsible for a poor performance with the right (preferred) hand as compared with the less-affected (nonpreferred) hand. This investigation, therefore, raised certain questions concerned with unimanual performance of a practiced and possibly overlearned type of task. Considering the current interest in comparative sensorimotor performances on the two sides of the body and their possible implications for theories of brain dysfunction (Semmes, Weinstein, Ghent, & Teuber, 1960; Semmes, 1968), the hypotheses appeared to be worth investigating.

The detailed results of these studies are given in individual publications (Reitan, 1971a, 1971b) and need only be summarized briefly here. All three hypotheses were clearly confirmed in terms of statistical analysis of the data. The brain-damaged subjects did require more time with both the preferred and nonpreferred hands and also showed a differential relationship between performances with the two hands as compared with the control subjects. In fact, the data generated from the two name-writing trials permitted classification of subjects to their correct groups with an 80%-85% accuracy rate. This was of interest in consideration of the fact that such a simple performance was involved. It appeared from the results that brain damage had a very pervasive effect that altered even highly practiced performances such as name-writing.

The second of these studies inquired as to whether the same effect occurred for older children. It seemed possible that the results obtained with younger children might have been due to the fact that the younger brain-damaged children had not yet learned very well to write their names as compared with the normal children. In older children, however, one would postulate that even the brain-damaged children had enough experience in writing their own names that learning of the task would not be a limiting consideration. Thus, if the results obtained with the younger children were confirmed with the older children, one could postulate that brain damage was responsible for some type of alteration of basic tempo in a highly practiced type of task. The comparable study for older groups of brain-damaged and control children yielded results very similar to those obtained with the younger subjects. Again, all three hypotheses were confirmed and the accuracy of classification of subjects to their groups was approximately 80%-85%.

While these studies were based on reasonable hypotheses which may have at least some general interest, they can be criticized as experimental investigations that used entirely too simplified a set of dependent (behavioral) variables. They not only used a single type of test, but also the test involved perhaps the most highly practiced type of performance that one could select. Considering the many important adaptive abilities that are probably served by the brain, one could scarcely propose that name-writing alone could be considered as a significant representation of the array of behavioral correlates of brain functions. In fact, a study of this type could easily lead to reinforcement of the tendency among many clinicians to latch onto some type of simple procedure as a basis for classifying subjects into brain-damaged and non–brain-damaged groups. This diagnostic type of effort has characterized much of the history of research on the effects of brain damage in the clinical areas and the notion seems to exist that such classification has value in its own right, even without having raised any question as to the nature of behavioral correlates of brain damage in a general, not to mention an individual, sense. Thus, if research of the type mentioned above were to lead to a simple procedure for classification of subjects in diagnostic terms, without promoting an underlying concern about more general brain-behavior relationships, the research could very possibly be a disservice. Undoubtedly the brain-damaged children included in the studies cited had many deficits other than name-writing speed and these may have been even more pronounced and consistent in identifying the brain-damaged subjects, not to mention much more meaningful in terms of characterizing the psychological changes of the brain-damaged group. Thus, while the investigation of simplified behavioral procedures and single tests may possibly contribute information of interest regarding behavioral correlates of impaired brain functions, it is important to recognize that these studies cannot supply the type of information concerned with alteration of ability structure that is necessary to understand the overall effects of brain lesions as they relate to the individual subject. Nevertheless, oversimplified studies of this kind continue to represent the major approach toward development of knowledge, not only in clinical neuropsychology but also in the area of psychology generally. It may be time, in fact, to reconsider the entire research model that is customarily taught and used in American psychology.

THE COMPARATIVE VALUE OF GENERAL VERSUS PARTICULAR INFORMATION

A consideration of the comparative values of (a) an approach that contributes to the general body of knowledge in psychology as contrasted with (b) an approach which emphasizes application of this knowledge to individual subjects might well take into consideration some of the more general principles and values that have been proposed in science. Weinberg (1970) has discussed a number of traditional values in science, weighing them with regard to present-day needs and priorities. Among the considerations he has raised is that "pure is better than applied," "general is better than particular," "search is better than codification," and "paradigm breaking is better than spectroscopy." Weinberg tends to evaluate the relative worth of pure and applied science in terms of historical considerations that render pure scientific efforts as more dignified than applied efforts. In addition, pure science may be more valued in

America because of the current social organization of the university. In this latter respect he postulates that,

> It is natural for the university professor to gravitate toward pure science, since the pursuit of pure science by and large involves little outside sanction. The pure scientist sets his own problem, and this is congenial to the university professor, who almost by definition goes where his intellectual instinct directs [p. 613].

Further, he suggests that pure science "is in a sense easier than applied science, and this may also help explain its popularity."

Of greater interest with respect to the present paper, however, is the comparative evaluation of general versus particular in science. Weinberg notes that Eugene Wigner (1964) in his Nobel lecture and Karl Popper (1959) both cited the relation between individual events and laws of nature as a basis for understanding the differential scientific value of the particular and general: "The aim of science is to subsume these individual events in laws of nature" [p. 614]. In this sense, an organized generalization would permit understanding of individual events in a broader context and, at least in categories, with relation to each other. Weinberg indicates that this ordering of values derives from the principle of scientific parsimony which recommends the more simple as compared with the more complex explanation of observed events. While Weinberg feels that this attitude is fostered in part by the desire of scientists to "cope with the information explosion," the more important consideration is that it is unnecessary to continue to be concerned with individual events if a general principle has been established which subsumes them.

Nevertheless, it is important to recognize that general principles represent abstractions and that abstractions, in turn, cannot include the wealth of information implicit in the full array of individual events. Weinberg points out,

> One can overdo this love of the general as opposed to the particular. For every general law implies particular instances only in principle. And to know in principle is not the same as knowing in fact and in detail [p. 614].

While laws of nature may be established which tend to organize individual events, "as the events become more complicated, this becomes more a matter of 'follows in principle' than 'follows in fact' " [p. 614]. He further points out that in the social sciences the relative merit of general and particular may be reversed since in these areas "one no longer makes much pretense of predicting events from general principles" [p. 614].

Probably the important point is not one of arguing for or against the value of the general or the specific but rather to consider the extent to which each may complement the other. Certain general principles of human brain-behavior relationships have been established even though no one would propose that deviations from these principles do not occur in individual instances. It becomes important to understand the limitations and qualifications of generalizations and, in fact, such understanding can be proposed as a criterion of the maturity and actual depth of understanding represented by the individual scientist. If we identify the individual human being as the unit of interest, our ultimate goal might be to develop an understanding of the way in which his brain-behavior relationships accord with general principles as well as with meaningful and unique deviations from general principles.

METHODOLOGICAL STEPS TOWARD ADVANCING KNOWLEDGE OF HUMAN BRAIN–BEHAVIOR RELATIONSHIPS

While it is easy to criticize single-variable studies and to point out the conceptual and methodological inadequacies of prior approaches to an area as complex as that represented by human brain-behavior relationships, a more challenging question relates to the recommendations for positive or progressive steps. We may conclude that the individual human subject is important in his own right and that we need to develop methods for effecting a transition from knowledge of content to application to individual subjects. Our specific aim may be to develop a method that is appropriate in drawing conclusions regarding the behavioral correlates of brain lesions in the individual person, differentiated from the many other influences on both general and specific abilities which may derive from other variables. Implementation of this aim probably requires several steps. As mentioned previously, it would appear that we must postulate some kind of answer to the question of an adequate set of behavioral measurements to reflect the correlates of brain functions. This is not an easy question to answer and we do not presently have the required information regarding the full range of psychological deficits associated with cerebral damage. Results presented in later chapters in this volume make it abundantly clear that the overall psychological deficits associated with cerebral damage may be extremely extensive in nature, both among children and adults. While this information identifies the brain as a generally significant organ with respect to behavior, it does not provide us with a basis for postulating the particular types of measurements that reflect brain functions with the least degree of overlap. It is apparent that we need a set of measurements that range over motor, sensory, psychomotor, and intellectual and cognitive functions in a number of specific content areas. The content areas, in terms of presently available knowledge, would include expressions in the area of language, spatial and temporal organization and integration, and concept formation and abstraction abilities. Further, we would postulate that tests in these areas would need to be organized so that they would reflect speed (efficiency) as well as power.

If this task were actually given separately to a number of competent investigators, it is clear that the resulting test batteries would be quite variable from one investigator to another. The question then arises as to how we can generate evidence that any particular test battery actually provides an adequate representation of brain functions. How can we be assured that the particular tests recommended are adequately extensive in their coverage and have not omitted some critical aspect of behavior related to brain functions? In other words, even though a battery of tests were recommended, we could not be sure that some kind of error in test selection had not been made which, in turn, could easily reflect prejudiced judgment and resulting misrepresentation such as that referred to above with regard to single-variable studies.

A preliminary answer to this question is provided by a method that was recommended and practiced by the late Ward C. Halstead with every patient examined in his laboratory. In brief, the plan was to collect a predetermined and standardized set of data reflecting behavioral functions in every subject. This same set of data was collected for every subject regardless of any individual differences in history, complaints, or provisional diagnoses. In fact, in the data-collection phase of the experiment with each subject a point was deliberately made to refrain from obtaining information concerning prior or present manifestations of his disorder and, in this way, avoided the problem of possible inadvertent influence of such knowledge on the data collected. The rationale behind administration of a standard and predetermined battery of tests was to permit eventual evaluation of the adequacy of this battery of tests to reflect individual variations among brain conditions. In brief, Halstead took a "best guess" regarding the types of questions that should be asked of each potential subject and then proceeded to ask these questions in a standardized and objective manner. The basic plan was to use this data, which represented the dependent variables in the research design, for predicting the independent variable, which would be represented by the full range of information independently derived from neurological evaluation which described the condition of the patient's brain. The same type of plan could be used in reverse to predict behavioral measurements from independently obtained neurological information, but this approach has not seemed as specifically relevant to development of needed information as has the alternate direction of prediction. However, an approach of this kind clearly presumes a decision regarding the relevant unit for prediction. One is hardly inclined in this context to think of an idea or concept, an area of function, or a particular point of content, as the significant endpoint in contrast to the individual human organism. In other words, the measurements that are made are based on an individual subject and the predictions to be made concern that individual subject. The method precludes the possibility of losing sight of the relevant unit.

In actual application of this method the investigator might find that he is able to make certain predictions with a satisfactory degree of reliability but that his measurements do not seem to be relevant, insofar as he can determine, to other known neurological variables which describe the brain. Conceivably, for example, the investigator might find that his results permit differential identification of subjects with and without cerebral lesions, but that he is not able to categorize subjects with cerebral lesions in accordance with the cerebral hemisphere principally damaged. Conversely, he may gradually develop clues among his dependent variables (test measures) which permit him to make such predictions regarding lateralization of damage and perhaps even to identify differential features of the test results which permit further inferences. In fact, this particular approach, if applied conscientiously by an investigator, requires him to consider in detail what additional measurements may be necessary to permit the types of predictions he wishes to make. He also is inclined by the method to consider interrelationships between the measures that may reflect critical variance with regard to various predictions. Further, the approach tends to place any set of positive conclusions that may be justified in a comparative frame of reference, differentiating those positive findings which are of real significance with respect to brain-behavior relationships from those which tend to be more incidentally associated with other effects. Finally, an approach of this type leads the investigator to consider the nature of methods of inference regarding brain-behavior relationships that are available and their possible complementary potential. This approach suffers from a lack of specificity in criteria for evaluating the adequacy of the test battery with respect to the predictions being made, since a great deal depends upon the ability of the researcher. Ideally, the approach is intended to complement the more conventional research methods.

This procedure for advancing knowledge clearly has close relationships to the usual clinical process. The differences in terms of the usual clinical process, however, are of critical significance with respect to the basic purpose of the method. The purpose, in turn, differs from the usual clinical process in that the latter is intended to reach a diagnosis of the individual subject whereas the method described above is more specifically oriented toward use of a diagnostic inference as a method for testing the adequacy of a preselected array of data. Further, the usual clinical procedure takes advantage of all available information on the individual subject at the time that it becomes available. This, in turn, makes it impossible to evaluate any predetermined set of data with respect to its adequacy for making particular predictions. Thus, Halstead's method deliberately refrains from using information other than the predetermined dependent variables (test battery) as a basis for predicting (diagnosing) the independently determined neurological findings. Curiously, a method of this type could easily be applied in many animal and human studies but rarely is used. It would seem that the method might readily reveal limitations and inadequacies of measurements, with relation to criterion information, as a study progressed, if no possible predictions of any validity seemed to be forthcoming for individual subjects. Further, application of the method would tend to limit unsystematic reporting of the great number of individual relationships among variables which may be statistically significant even though they may not be of much value in providing critical variance with respect to individual human subjects. If, for example, a study were performed in order to evaluate the relationships between impaired thyroid function in rats and maze-learning ability, it would be of interest not only to compare the maze performance of a group with thyroid deficiency and a normal group but also to take the dependent variables for the total number of rats (both normal and thyroid-deficient) and use this data as a basis for predicting the group to which each animal belonged. If these predictions, from behavioral manifestation to the underlying condition, permitted a high degree of accuracy of assignment of individual subjects, it would be apparent from the findings that adequacy of thyroid function, as defined in the particular study, was a highly significant and compelling factor with regard to maze performances. Conversely, it is entirely possible that the maze-learning data would not permit accurate classification of subjects to their groups. In this case the data would indicate that while maze-learning might be a significantly related factor, it was hardly an adequate behavioral representation, considered by itself, of normal versus impaired thyroid functioning.

Halstead applied this method in his laboratory for many years and, following his example, I have applied this method with many thousands of subjects. The next question concerns evidence of what we have learned from applications of this method.

Predicting neurological bases of behavioral deficits for individual subjects.   One of the first things that was learned using this method was that the effects of cerebral lesions manifest themselves in individual subjects in a variety of ways. It was gradually becoming clear during the 1940s, in Halstead's laboratory, that the adequacy of an individual's performance, considered by itself, was scarcely an adequate inferential model for evaluating brain functions. Halstead was very much interested in an evaluation of the comparative efficiency of performance of the preferred and nonpreferred hands on the Tactual Performance Test as another type of indicator. He felt that data of this type would yield information related to the differential integrity of the two cerebral hemispheres. However, he had not developed a very thoroughgoing procedure for application of this method at that time, as illustrated by the fact that it was not his standard practice to measure finger-tapping speed with both hands but rather only with the preferred hand.

When the Neuropsychology Laboratory at the Indiana University Medical Center was opened in 1951, a number of additional tests and procedures were employed over and beyond those that had been routinely used in Halstead's laboratory. For example, the Wechsler-Bellevue Scale (Form I) was introduced to give a more representative and adequate evaluation of general intelligence than was possible with the Henmon-Nelson Intelligence Test that had been employed by Halstead. We began routinely to measure finger-tapping speed with both hands and also, in collaborative planning with Hallgrim Klove, introduced a series of sensory-perceptual tests using the modalities of tactile, auditory, and visual functioning. The purpose of these tests was twofold: (*a*) to determine whether or not specific instances of errors in perception occurred of the type that were rarely manifested by persons with evidence of normal brain functions and (*b*) to compare the performance on the two sides of the body in order to provide additional information regarding the comparative integrity of the two cerebral hemispheres. The entire battery of tests that we were then in process of composing was based on prior experiences which were generated by use of the method recommended by Halstead. Specifically, an experiment was performed with every subject which consisted of (a) an intensive study of the test results (dependent variables) for each individual subject followed by (b) a written evaluation of these results (a set of predictions of neurological variables based on the behavioral measurements), and finally (c) an actual comparison of these predictions with the independently obtained neurological criterion information. Several guiding principles became apparent in this effort. First, the adequacy of performance of subjects with cerebral lesions customarily was somewhat reduced with relation to comparative data from appropriate control subjects, but results for individual subjects with cerebral lesions rarely deviated to such an extent that they fell outside the limits of the distribution of the normal probability curve. This finding indicated that adequacy of performance, considered by itself, could scarcely be a sole method of inference. Secondly, it was apparent that certain subjects with cerebral lesions demonstrated specific types of deficits which could be used as pathognomonic signs of cerebral damage. However, many subjects with cerebral lesions did not demonstrate deficits of this kind and, when this kind of information was not forthcoming for an individual subject, no significant information had been gained. However, when specific signs of deficit were present, especially if prior findings indicated that such findings occurred in subjects with cerebral lesions but not in subjects with normal cerebral functions, information of high validity was present to implicate the organic status of the brain. Thirdly, it became apparent that individual subjects showed varying patterns with regard to their level of performance. Some persons with brain lesions did well on particular tests and poorly on others, leading to the prospect that a number of basic patterns might be identified. These patterns appeared to relate differentially to localization of cerebral lesions and possibly also to types of cerebral lesions. Thus, it was deemed necessary to include in the overall battery of tests a sufficiently extensive range of measurements to reflect possible patterns as they might relate to neurological variables. Finally, as mentioned above, a deliberate effort was made to build into the test battery a series of comparisons of the functional efficiency of the two sides of the body since it was apparent that lesions of one cerebral hemisphere consistently tended to impair principally the performance on the opposite side of the body. A subbattery was developed which covered a range from pure motor functions (finger-tapping speed and strength of grip) through psychomotor problem-solving skills (Tactual Performance Test) to measures that were concerned solely with sensory perception. Thus, the test battery was developed, on the basis of empirical experience with individual subjects, to reflect the following methods of inference: (a) level of performance, (b) specific deficits of pathognomonic significance, (c) differential scores or patterns of ability, and (d) comparisons of the functional efficiency of the two sides of the body. These methods of inference, together with still other possible approaches, have been described in more detail elsewhere and their strengths and weaknesses specifically considered (Reitan, 1967a).

Since these several inferential methods, used in a complementary manner, appeared on the basis of experience to be helpful in making predictions for individual subjects, one could postulate that more accurate predictions might be made through their use than with conventional statistical analyses. A study concerned with this question was performed and reported (Reitan, 1964b). This study is referred to by Meier, in a somewhat different context, later in this volume. A group of 112 patients was assembled on the basis of complete and definitive neurological findings; 64 had fairly focal cerebral lesions and 48 had diffuse or generalized cerebral involvement. The patients with focal lesions were composed of four subgroups (16 subjects each) with intrinsic tumor, extrinsic tumor, cerebral vascular lesion, and focal head injury. These 64 patients also were so selected that four subjects with each type of lesion had his area of maximum involvement in one of four quadrants of the cerebral hemispheres: left anterior, left posterior, right anterior, and right posterior. Thus, it was possible to divide the total of 64 patients with focal lesions into four subgroups ($N = 16$) with involvement in each of the quadrants (in this case with each of the four types of lesions equally represented) or into four subgroups ($N = 16$) representing each of the types of lesions (with each of the four locations equally represented). The 48 patients with generalized or diffuse cerebral involvement were composed of 16 subjects with closed head injuries, 16 subjects with generalized cerebral vascular disease, and 16 subjects with multiple sclerosis.

Two studies were performed. The first of these involved the use of a rating form for prediction of various aspects of neurological involvement for each subject, based on an assessment of the array of his test scores. In order to accomplish this, the protocols (test results) for the 112 patients were placed in random order, all identifying information was concealed, and judgments were made blindly for each subject on the basis of his test results. The first judgment called for on the rating form required a decision as to whether the lesion was focal or diffuse. I did these ratings myself, with full knowledge of the overall characteristics of the group as given above with respect to the number of patients having diffuse and focal lesions, but the ratings were done consecutively from the 1st through the 112th subject without keeping any record of the number that were being classified in various categories. If a judgment was made that the lesion was diffuse, the next prediction concerned whether the underlying condition represented cerebral vascular disease, multiple sclerosis, or traumatic brain injury. If the lesion was judged to be focal, a further estimate was necessary as to the quadrant principally involved. In addition, a judgment was made as to whether the lesion represented cerebral vascular disease, intrinsic or extrinsic neoplastic disease, or traumatic brain injury.

The results of these ratings indicated that a highly significant number of correct predictions had been made on the basis of the test results. Of the 64 subjects classified neurologically as having focal lesions, 57 had been judged from psychological test results to have focal involvement and 7 to have diffuse damage. Of the 48 patients with diffuse damage, 46 were judged to have diffuse involvement and 2 to have focal lesions. In terms of identification of the quadrant of major involvement among the 64 patients with focal lesions, the overall results indicated that correct predictions had been made in 42 of the 64 instances. For 7 subjects with focal lesions a judgment had been made that the lesion was diffuse, a condition that may well have occurred principally with lesions that had been sustained some years before and, in terms of recorded neurological information, were judged as being focal, even though the acute effects of the lesion had largely disappeared. In only 4 instances among the 64 patients were errors made with respect to the hemisphere principally involved. The remaining instances of misclassification represented ones in which an error had occurred between anterior and posterior locations within a hemisphere. These results obviously were far beyond chance expectation and indicated that the test findings, when interpreted according to the several methods of inference built into the battery, had definite relevance to regional localization of damage in the cerebral hemispheres.

Even more striking results were obtained when predictions of types of lesion were made from the psychological test data. Of 112 patients, 94 were correctly classified to their appropriate groups. Among the five types of lesions represented, the following number of "hits" were obtained: intrinsic tumor, 13 of 16; extrinsic tumor, 8 of 16; cerebral vascular disease, 28 of 32; traumatic head injury, 30 of 32; and multiple sclerosis, 15 of 16. Obviously, these results could hardly represent chance influences and the only conclusion that can be reached is that the test results were closely related to the types of lesions involved. It is important to note, however, that this was a demonstrational study. The study demonstrated that the use of the test results alone was an adequate condition for reasonably accurate prediction of the corresponding neurological findings, but the study did not provide explicit information with regard to the specific nature of the psychological deficits differentially associated with the various neurological parameters.

A second study of a statistical nature was performed using the same 64 subjects with focal lesions. The purpose of this study was to compare the groups of subjects who had lesions in different locations (with types of lesions equally represented in each group) and to compare groups of subjects with varying types of lesions (with location of lesions equally represented in each group). A simple analysis of variance was performed, first with the groups composed according to locations of lesions and the analysis was then repeated with patients categorized according to types of lesions. Thirty-two mean values were present for each of the four groups, making a total of 192 possible comparisons in total. The results indicated that significant intergroup differences, according to lesion locations, were found in only 25 comparisons. Most of these differences related to comparative performances with the right and left hands rather than reflecting significant differences in various types of intellectual and cognitive performances. When the groups were composed according to types of lesion, again 192 possible mean comparisons were available. The results indicated that only 13 of these could be considered statistically significant. Ten of these 13 differences involved comparisons of the group with intrinsic cerebral tumors with the other groups. The group with intrinsic tumors tended to do somewhat more poorly than the other groups but, aside from these differences, very few significant results were obtained.

It is apparent from the results of these two studies which utilized common groups of subjects, that behavioral measurements, in a battery organized to reflect various methods of inference, are relevant to both type and location of cerebral damage. However, in a statistical analysis organized to evaluate differences in central tendency with relation to variability, relatively few significant differences were obtained. It would appear that conventional methods of statistical analysis may not be appropriate for a fully meaningful reflection of human brain-behavior relationships. In fact, many of the data characteristics that contributed significantly to individual interpretation tended to be confounded or cancelled when added into the total group. While this type of finding may be disheartening to persons who would like to see rigorous statistical documentation of the unique psychological correlates of cerebral lesions differing in type and location, it may be important to recognize that the limitation does not lie essentially with the data that can be obtained in examination of subjects but instead, at least in some instances, with statistical methods of evaluation. It would appear that we have an important problem still to solve in developing or adapting appropriate methods of data analysis to the interrelationships of behavioral data which reflect impaired brain functions.

Illustration with individual patients.   The contention of the previous section can be made much more clear by illustrating some of the observations, derived from results on individual subjects, which tend to become concealed in group comparisons. The particular subjects that will be presented have been selected for instructional purposes, but similar results could be duplicated with other patients in a great number of instances. Thus, there is nothing necessarily unique about the individual subjects selected for illustration. Our purpose will be to demonstrate first the inadequacy of level of performance as an inferential model by presenting results on a subject who performed relatively well in spite of the fact that he had a brain lesion. We shall proceed to show results on subjects who demonstrated pronounced specific deficits that occur in subjects with cerebral lesions but rarely if ever occur in persons with normal brain functions. Next, certain patterns and relationships of test results will be presented and their significance for interpretation of brain dysfunction discussed. These illustrations will then be used as models for reanalysis and further consideration of the test results for the initial patient.

Table 1 and Figure 1 present the test results for a 25-year-old postal clerk, D. J., who had experienced blackout spells over a 4-year period. These had begun just a few days after he had been kicked in the right frontal area of his

TABLE 1

Psychological Test Results for D. J., a 25-year-old Man with Right
Anterior Temporal Lobe Atrophy

PATIENT: D. J.		AGE: 25 years	EDUCATION: 12 years

Wechsler-Bellevue Scale (Form I)		Halstead's Neuropsychological Test Battery	
Verbal IQ	111	*Category Test*	22
Performance IQ	117	*Tactual Performance Test*	
Full Scale IQ	115	Right hand: 4.6 min.	
Verbal Weighted Score	56	Left hand: 4.5 min.	
Performance Weighted Score	61	Both hands: 2.5 min.	
Total Weighted Score	117	Total time:	11.6
Information	11	Memory:	6
Comprehension	13	Localization:	0
Digit Span	10	*Seashore Rhythm Test*	3
Arithmetic	10	Raw score: 27	
Similarities	12	*Speech-sounds Perception Test*	7
Vocabulary	9	*Finger Oscillation Test*	61
Picture Arrangement	9	Right hand: 61	
Picture Completion	14	Left hand: 45	
Block Design	13	*Time Sense Test* Memory:	245.5
Object Assembly	12	Visual: 15.3	
Digit Symbol	13	*Impairment Index:*	0.1

Trail Making Test	
Trails A: 24 sec., 0 errors	
Trails B: 90 sec., 3 errors	

Minnesota Multiphasic Personality Inventory	
? − 50	Pd − 60
L − 56	Mf − 44
F − 46	Pa − 53
K − 68	Pt − 60
Hs − 54	Sc − 53
D − 51	Ma − 45
Hy − 58	

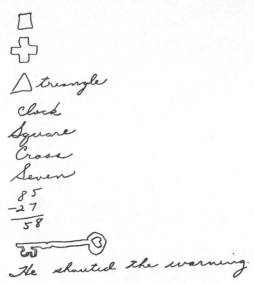

FIG. 1. Examples of writing, calculating, and drawing done by D. J.

head while playing football. During these episodes, which usually lasted about 10 to 12 min., the patient lost consciousness but had no clonic or tonic movements. While he had experienced other frequent episodes of light-headedness since this injury, he also had additional episodes with complete loss of consciousness, urinary incontinence, and amnesia. The physical neurological examination was essentially normal and laboratory findings were not contributory. The electroencephalogram demonstrated a focus in the right anterior temporal area. While skull x-rays were normal, a pneumoencephalogram demonstrated an area of mild atrophy involving the right anterior temporal lobe. Thus, neurological evidence indicated that cerebral damage appeared to be quite focal and relatively mild.

Psychological test results indicated that this man, who had completed the 12th grade in school, had a Verbal IQ of 111 and Performance IQ of 117. The subtest scores generally fell at about the average level or somewhat above and, considering the adequacy of performance, scarcely provided evidence for cerebral damage. This patient also performed very well on the Halstead Neuropsychological Test Battery. He earned an Impairment Index of 0.1, indicating that only 1 of the 10 tests in this battery (Localization component of the Tactual Performance Test) fell in the brain-damaged range. Customarily, Impairment Indexes ranging from 0.0 to 0.3 are considered to be in the normal range, 0.4 is considered borderline, and 0.5 to 1.0 represents the brain-damaged range. It is clear from these findings that this man not only had levels of general intelligence which well exceeded the average but he also performed excellently on Halstead's tests. Inspection of the entire array of test results indicates that he performed poorly on the Localization component of the Tactual Performance

Test, was a little slow in finger-tapping speed with his left hand, and took a little more time than might be expected on Part B of the Trail Making Test. However, one must expect some variability in test results for an individual subject and the overwhelming preponderance of findings were in the normal range or above. Thus, in terms of level of performance, one could scarcely conclude that this patient had any significant impairment that might support a conclusion of cerebral damage. Nevertheless, the overall set of test results contains very definite information to implicate the right anterior temporal area. Rather than being represented by level of performance, this evidence is revealed in the additional inferential methods that have been mentioned previously—specific pathognomonic signs, patterns and relationships among test results, and evaluation of the comparative efficiency of the two sides of the body. We will return to the results on this patient after having reviewed findings on additional patients.

Table 2 and Figure 2 present psychological test results for a 58-year-old man, L. B., who had completed only four grades in school and was the owner of a small restaurant. Contrast studies performed 2 days following our examination definitely indicated the presence of a space-occupying lesion in the posterior part of the right cerebral hemisphere. A craniotomy was performed and a large tumor located in the occipital-parietal area was partially removed.

The test results indicated the presence of severe impairment in terms of level of performance. While Verbal intelligence appeared to be relatively intact, the Performance intelligence of this patient was nearly at the bottom of the scale. On Halstead's tests the patient obtained normal scores only on the test of finger-tapping speed with the right hand. Thus the clear deficits shown by this patient in terms of level of performance would certainly have been a sufficient basis to reach a conclusion that the patient had sustained serious impairment of brain functions. However, cases of this kind serve an additional very useful purpose with respect to amplification of the other inferential models. Figure 2 illustrates some attempts by this subject to perform simple tasks. He had no significant language difficulties on the aphasia examination, but had great difficulties in copying simple spatial configurations. Although he worked carefully and diligently in his attempt to copy the shape of a Greek cross, he was not able to determine the proper directions in which to turn, especially on the left side of the figure. In his attempts to copy a key, the patient was trying very hard to draw the figure correctly but finally said, "I'll have to give up. Every line I put in makes it look worse." While a model was presented for the patient to copy in instances of the square, cross, triangle, and key, we also asked the patient to draw a daisy, following Sir Macdonald Critchley's procedure. In this instance, the patient is only given verbal instructions and not shown a sample to copy. This patient began with the upper petals and, after drawing the elongated petal on the lower left, felt that he had completed the entire daisy. It was apparent that this patient had great difficulty with the left side of figures, but he also demonstrated a pronounced problem in dealing with spatial configurations

TABLE 2

Psychological Test Results for L. B., a 58-year-old Man with a Right
Posterior Glioblastoma Multiforme

PATIENT: L. B.	AGE: 58 years	EDUCATION: 4 years

Wechsler-Bellevue Scale (Form I)		Halstead's Neuropsychological Test Battery	
Verbal IQ	117	*Category Test*	Unable to do
Performance IQ	63	*Tactual Performance Test*	
Full Scale IQ	92	Right hand: 15.0 min.	
Verbal Weighted Score	56	(4 blocks placed)	
Performance Weighted Score	5	Left hand: 12.0 min.	
Total Weighted Score	61	(2 blocks placed)	
Information	11	Both hands: 3.0 min.	
Comprehension	11	(discontinued)	
Digit Span	11	Total time:	30.0 min
Arithmetic	12	Memory:	3
Similarities	11	Localization:	0
Vocabulary	12	*Seashore Rhythm Test*	3
Picture Arrangement	1	Raw score: 27	
Picture Completion	0	*Speech-sounds Perception Test* 13	
Block Design	1	*Finger Oscillation Test*	
Object Assembly	0	Right hand: 54	54
Digit Symbol	3	Left hand: 40	
		Time Sense Test Memory: 323.9	
		Visual: 103.8	
		Impairment Index:	0.7

more generally. The role of the right cerebral hemisphere in this regard has been documented recently in the human split-brain preparations (Gazzaniga, 1970) but deficits of this type had been identified earlier as a manifestation of right cerebral damage by Klove and Reitan (1958) and Wheeler and Reitan (1962).

When we return to the results on the patient first presented, it will be instructive to evaluate his performances with regard to the question of whether he shows any deficits in dealing with spatial configurations. Obviously we would not expect such deficits to be as pronounced as in the case of the present patient, but if specific pathognomonic errors were present, they might provide additional information with regard to the behavioral correlates of possible brain damage.

As a basis for further evaluation of the results on D. J., it would also be appropriate to look at the findings on a patient with a destructive lesion of the

FIG. 2. Examples of writing, calculating, and drawing done by L. B.

left cerebral hemisphere. Table 3 and Figure 3 present the findings on a
56-year-old woman, V. S., who had begun, about a month before our
examination, to have some difficulty with writing and in speaking. She had
shown progressive confusion in her work as a bookkeeper. An angiogram
demonstrated a mass in the left parietal area and a craniotomy was performed 1
week after psychological testing. At this time a partial removal of a glioblastoma
multiforme in the left parietal area was performed.

As shown in Table 3, this patient was seriously impaired in level of
performance on a considerable number of tasks. Her Verbal IQ was well below
the average level and she had an Halstead Impairment Index of 0.7, which falls
well into the brain-damaged range. She also had many specific difficulties in
dealing with language symbols and these are seen in patients with left as
compared with right cerebral damage (Wheeler & Reitan, 1962). When asked to
spell the word "square," she responded with "k-a-c-g." She made mistakes in
naming common objects, calling a picture of a fork a "knife." When asked to
read "7 SIX 2," she responded, "7 X 2." In simple reading she omitted words in
some instances and read words incorrectly in other instances. She was severely
impaired in her writing ability, not being able to form the letters appropriately

TABLE 3

Psychological Test Results for V. S., a 56-year-old Woman with a Left
Parietotemporal Glioblastoma Multiforme

| PATIENT: V. S. | AGE: 56 years | EDUCATION: 8 years |

Wechsler-Bellevue Scale (Form I)		Halstead's Neuropsychological Test Battery	
Verbal IQ	89	*Category Test*	86
Performance IQ	114	*Tactual Performance Test*	
Full Scale IQ	99	Right hand: 15.0 min.	
Verbal Weighted Score	30	(4 blocks placed)	
Performance Weighted Score	43	Left hand: 15.7 min.	
Total Weighted Score	73	(all blocks placed)	
Information	10	Both hands: 8.1 min.	
Comprehension	12	(all blocks placed)	
Digit Span	0	Total Time:	38.8 min.
Arithmetic	0	Memory:	5
Similarities	8	Localization:	1
Vocabulary	11	*Seashore Rhythm Test*	10
Picture Arrangement	8	Raw score: 19	
Picture Completion	9		
Block Design	10	*Speech-sounds Perception Test*	24
Object Assembly	11	*Time Sense Test* Memory:	211.8
Digit Symbol	5	Visual 287.9	
Trail Making Test		*Impairment Index:*	0.7
Trails A: 22 sec., 0 errors			
Trails B: 224 sec., 5 errors			

for the words she had in mind (see Figure 3). In addition, she had difficulty understanding verbal communication and easily became confused, apparently failing to understand the meaning of simple words. Finally, the patient demonstrated a tendency to become confused with respect to identification of her body parts. These deficits have been identified (Wheeler & Reitan, 1962) as ones that occur almost exclusively in association with left cerebral damage. Thus, in interpreting the results of D. J. with respect to possible manifestations of specific pathognomonic deficits, it would be worth reviewing his findings in terms of the possibility that he might show positive results of this type.

The next patient to be described was a 31-year-old man, G. Y., who was admitted to the hospital after having been found in a confused condition in a local hotel room. He obviously had been involved in some type of struggle,

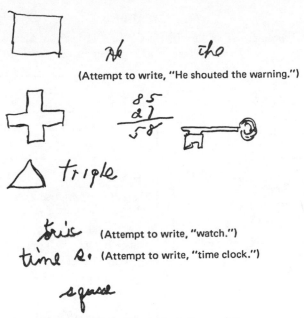

(Attempt to write, "He shouted the warning.")

(Attempt to write, "watch.")

(Attempt to write, "time clock.")

FIG. 3. Examples of writing, calculating, and drawing done by V. S.

having abrasions and bruises over much of his body. He was confused, and had very little memory for the several previous days. He complained only of a severe headache. Physical neurological examination was within normal limits. However, he had a laceration just anterior to the right ear with dark blood coming from it. A probe was inserted for several inches under the scalp. Skull x-rays showed a penetrating skull defect with in-driven fragments of bone, suggesting that the patient had sustained a bullet wound. However, the patient denied any knowledge of this injury. Carotid angiography showed marked elevation of the right middle cerebral artery. A few days after psychological testing, surgery was performed and a thick-walled abscess removed from the middle and anterior part of the right temporal lobe. The psychological testing had been done when the head injury was present, but neither the subject nor the examiner knew the nature of this injury at the time the testing was done. However, the results shown in Table 4 and Figure 4 were obtained on this patient who had an acutely destructive lesion of the right anterior temporal lobe.

The general level of this patient's intellectual performance appeared to be about normal. Our information indicated that he had completed 12 grades in school. The subject showed some depression of performance on the Digit Span subtest, but this is not unusual in hospitalized persons. The general level of performance shown by this patient was generally consistent with his occupation as a used-car salesman. However, the Performance subtests showed low scores on the Picture Arrangement and Block Design subtests. The patient performed

TABLE 4

Psychological Test Results for G. Y., a 31-year-old Man with a Right
Anterior Temporal Lobe Penetrating Injury

PATIENT: G. Y.   AGE: 31 years   EDUCATION: 12 years

Wechsler-Bellevue Scale (Form I)		Halstead's Neuropsychological Test Battery	
Verbal IQ	97	*Category Test*	68
Performance IQ	98	*Tactual Performance Test*	
Full Scale IQ	98	Right hand: 8.1 min.	
Verbal Weighted Score	44	Left hand: 10.1 min.	
Performance Weighted Score	44	Both hands: 5.0 min.	
Total Weighted Score	88	Total Time:	23.2 min.
Information	10	Memory:	5
Comprehension	8	Localization:	1
Digit Span	6	*Seashore Rhythm Test*	3
Arithmetic	9	Raw score: 27	
Similarities	11		
Vocabulary	8	*Speech-sounds Perception Test*	13
Picture Arrangement	4	*Finger Oscillation Test*	62
Picture Completion	12	Right hand: 62	
Block Design	6	Left hand: 37	
Object Assembly	12	*Time Sense Test* Memory: 200.6	
Digit Symbol	10	Visual: 60.3	
Trail Making Test		*Impairment Index:*	0.8
Trails A: 58 sec., 0 errors			
Trails B: 101 sec., 1 error			

Minnesota Multiphasic Personality Inventory

?	− 61	Pd	− 63
L	− 53	Mf	− 56
F	− 58	Pa	− 50
K	− 48	Pt	− 60
Hs	− 70	Sc	− 50
D	− 72	Ma	− 38
Hy	− 67		

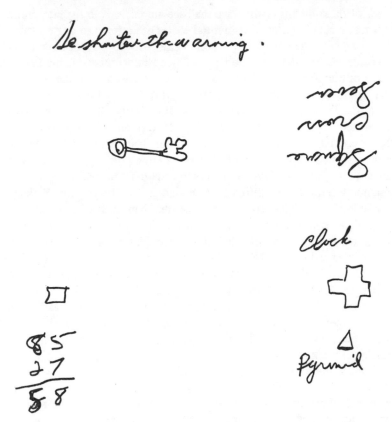

FIG. 4. Examples of writing, calculating, and drawing done by G. Y.

considerably more poorly on Halstead's Battery than would be predicted from his IQ values, earning an Halstead Impairment Index of 0.8. The tests that did not contribute to the Impairment Index were finger-tapping speed and the Memory component of the Time Sense Test. These are not, however, among the most sensitive tests in Halstead's Battery with respect to the condition of the cerebral hemispheres (Reitan, 1955a). Thus, level of performance on Halstead's Battery suggested that this patient had experienced some cerebral damage. The patient also performed somewhat poorly on Part B of the Trail Making Test and this finding would support a similar inference. The patient did not, however, show any specific signs of cerebral deficit either in terms of impaired language functions or in his attempts to copy simple spatial configurations. It is entirely possible that this patient may have had certain sensory-perceptual deficits which do not occur in subjects with normal brain functions, but the battery of sensory-perceptual tests was not routinely administered at the time this patient was examined.

The findings on these latter patients (L. B., V. S., and G. Y.) should also be evaluated with regard to information already reported in the literature. A number of these findings (which we shall see are relevant to the interpretation of D. J.'s test results) relate to differential scores or patterns among measurements. The patient with the destructive lesion of the posterior part of the right cerebral hemisphere (L. B.) demonstrated pronounced impairment on the Performance subtests of the Wechsler-Bellevue Scale in comparison with his results on the Verbal subtests. Conversely, the patient with the intrinsic tumor of the left cerebral hemisphere (V. S.) had a Verbal IQ of only 89 as compared with her Performance IQ of 114. The generality of differential levels of Verbal and Performance IQ values, with relation to lateralization of cerebral damage, was first documented by Andersen (1950) and Reitan (1955b). However, Fitzhugh, Fitzhugh, and Reitan (1962) also showed that in relatively chronic and longstanding lesions such differences tended not to be present. Patient G. Y., whose lesion was much more restricted in area than those of L. B. and V. S., did not show any significant difference between Verbal and Performance IQ values, but seemed to show specific deficits on the Picture Arrangement and Block Design subtests. In fact, Reitan (1955b) and Meier and French (1966a) have shown that with right anterior temporal lesions a rather specific deficit occurs on the Picture Arrangement subtest of the Wechsler Scale. These relationships suggest that it may be advantageous to inspect D. J.'s results regarding possible selective impairment on individual subtests of the Wechsler-Bellevue Scale, utilizing the prospect of differential scores as a basis for evaluating behavioral correlates of brain functions.

Finally, previous results (Reitan, 1958a) have shown that the comparative efficiency of the two sides of the body deviates from normal relationships in persons with lateralized cerebral damage. Patient L. B., with the right cerebral intrinsic tumor, was able to tap only 40 times with his left hand as compared with 54 times with his right hand, showing rather slow finger-tapping speed with his left hand. In addition, he performed quite poorly with his left hand as compared with his right hand on the Tactual Performance Test, being able to place correctly only two blocks in 12 min. with his left hand as compared with four blocks in 15 min. with his right hand, even though the performance with the left hand represented the second attempt at the task. Although our examination for sensory-perceptual functions was not administered in standardized form at the time that L. B. was examined, some tests of this type were given and the patient showed evidence of difficulty in tactile finger localization on his left hand and also seemed to be somewhat impaired in tactile form recognition on his left hand. In addition, the patient also showed a definite impairment in his ability to perceive tactile stimuli delivered to the left side of the body when comparable stimuli were administered to the right side of the body. Thus L. B., who had a right cerebral lesion, was definitely deficient on his left side in a number of respects as compared with his right side. V. S., who had a tumor of the left cerebral hemisphere, was not especially impaired in finger-tapping speed with her right hand, but she did perform very poorly with her right hand as compared with her left hand on the Tactual Performance Test.

In addition, she made no errors in perception of tactile stimuli to either the right hand or right face when the stimuli were given alone, but with competing simultaneous stimuli on both sides of the body she failed in every instance to report the stimulus given to her right side. The same type of phenomenon was presented with regard to auditory stimulation, although she did not show this type of perceptual deficit in perception of double simultaneous visual stimuli. In tests of finger localization she made a great many errors on her right hand but had relatively little difficulty with her left hand. She was only slightly better with her left hand than her right hand in fingertip number writing perception, but she had much more difficulty in tactile form recognition with her right hand than her left hand. It is important to observe that the deficiencies for this subject consistently occurred on the right side of the body, across from the cerebral hemisphere that contained the lesion. Turning to results on G. Y., his finger-tapping speed was excellent with his right hand but seriously impaired in his left hand. In addition, he required considerably more time with his left hand on the Tactual Performance Test than would have been predicted from the performance with his right hand. Additional sensory-perceptual tests were not performed, but the deficiency in finger-tapping speed and in psychomotor performance (Tactual Performance Test) with the left hand complemented the specific deficits shown on the Wechsler-Bellevue Scale (Picture Arrangement and Block Design) to implicate the right cerebral hemisphere and, more specifically, the right temporal lobe. (We believe that Block Design is especially sensitive to posterior right hemisphere involvement and especially to right parietal and occipital damage whereas Picture Arrangement is more sensitive to anterior right temporal lesions.) Thus, it is apparent from these examples that level of performance may not be an adequate criterion in its own right with respect to evaluation of behavioral deficits associated with brain lesions. It is also important to look for specific signs of cerebral damage, patterns and relationships among measurements, and differential performances on the two sides of the body. With this information in mind, we can turn back to the results for patient D. J. in an attempt to decide whether additional information regarding brain-behavior relationships is present in his test results.

Looking first for specific deficits, it appears that the cross shown in Figure 1 represents a mild deviation from expectation for a patient with the general ability of D. J. He appeared to distort the configuration on the left side to a mild degree. This becomes especially noticeable if one observes that the two vertical lines on the left side of the figure are not in the same plane. Even more specific indications of right cerebral dysfunction were shown in the patient's copy of a key. Patients with right cerebral lesions sometimes have difficulty with the mirror-image aspects of this figure. Along the stem of the key, for example, the patient failed to show symmetry on the two sides even though perfect symmetry is present in the picture he was copying. The patient also had difficulty of this type with respect to the teeth of the key. If one inspects this part of the figure it is possible to discern that the right-hand part essentially is represented by a vertically placed rectangle whereas the left side is represented by a horizontally placed rectangle. Deficiencies of this kind can have very definite significance even though the overall configuration may be fairly adequate. Thus, this patient did demonstrate in his drawing of simple objects the type of deficiency that is frequently seen in persons with right cerebral lesions. However, he did not have any language difficulties whatsoever and, therefore, no evidence was adduced to implicate the left cerebral hemisphere.

Inspection of the patterns and relationships among the test results was not very revealing. However, if one were to raise a question about the intactness of the right cerebral hemisphere one would inspect particularly the Performance subtests of the Wechsler-Bellevue Scale. This patient earned scores of 12, 13, or 14 on four of the subtests but a score of only 9 on the Picture Arrangement subtests. Considered by itself one could scarcely use this indication as a significant finding of brain dysfunction. Together with the other indications, however, it is entirely consistent and even contributory in postulating involvement of the right anterior temporal area.

The final method of inference, concerning the comparative functional efficiency of the two sides of the body, yielded very definite results for patient D. J. He was quite slow in finger-tapping with his left hand as compared with his right hand (usually a 10% difference in favor of the preferred hand is expected), and he required almost as much time with his left hand as with his right hand on the Tactual Performance Test in spite of the fact that postive practice-effect is expected on the second trial. Sensory-perceptual tests involving tactile, auditory, and visual functions had not been performed on this patient although available evidence (Wheeler & Reitan, 1962; Carmon & Benton, 1969; Reitan, 1970) indicate that such data is definitely of value.

These overall results indicate that patient D. J. showed definite deviations from normality even though his general level of performance was quite good. One would conclude, therefore, that the test findings presented evidence of cerebral dysfunction even though one would not conclude that a type of lesion was present which would cause serious or even significant deficits with respect to level of performance.

These illustrations of interpretations of psychological test results on individual subjects exemplify the complexity of psychological deficits associated with brain lesions in human beings. It is clear that we presently have the methodology to draw conclusions of specific relevance to individual subjects, but much more investigation is necessary to develop a rigorous procedure for this purpose. Boll (Ch. 5, this volume), discusses a specific investigation to assess the use of multiple methods of inference in an additive fashion (Boll & Reitan, 1970) and also calls attention to the recent effort by Russell, Neuringer, and Goldstein (1970) to apply a taxonomic procedure to this problem. Additional statistical methods may also be appropriate for this problem but, in any case, progress is urgently needed to replace the subjective decisionmaking processes in individual interpretation that presently are necessary.

3
CLINICAL NEUROPSYCHOLOGY OF CHILDHOOD: AN OVERVIEW[1]

Arthur L. Benton

In contrast to most of the chapters in this volume, my contribution to this symposium is of a general nature. I plan to present a brief survey of the field of the clinical neuropsychology of childhood and assess some of its achievements, its limitations, and its prospects.

First, a descriptive definition of this field is in order. The task of neuropsychology as a discipline is to elucidate the relations between behavior and the structure and functions of the nervous system. As a scientist, the clinical neuropsychologist pursues this aim, for the most part, by studying adults and children with damaged nervous systems. As a clinician, he applies the knowledge and insights gained from such study to the evaluation and treatment of children with behavioral disabilities and disturbances.

In comparison with his colleagues in the field of animal neuropsychology, the clinical neuropsychologist labors under some significant disadvantages. The animal neuropsychologist attempts to create a picture of brain-behavioral relations by producing controlled changes, reversible or irreversible, in the nervous systems of animals through electrical, chemical, and surgical techniques and studying the behavioral correlates of these changes; conversely, he studies the neural changes that may occur as a result of environment manipulation such as sensory or experiential deprivation. Since he can assess by autopsy examination the nature and extent of the irreversible neural changes produced by ablation, electrical or chemical destruction, or sensory deprivation, the

[1] The personal investigations mentioned in this chapter were supported by Research Grant NS-00616 and Program-Project Grant NS-03354 from the National Institute of Neurological Diseases and Stroke.

animal neuropsychologist is able to proceed on the basis of relatively precise knowledge of the central nervous system of the organism he is studying. The clinical neuropsychologist usually does not have the benefit of such complete knowledge of the status of the brains of his patients and he must rely on the less precise indications provided by various diagnostic and therapeutic techniques. In this respect, the neuropsychologist working with children is even more handicapped than his colleague who is working with adult patients since generally he has even less information about cerebral status at his disposal. As a consequence, a good deal of neuropsychological work has been done with children who are known to be brain-damaged but in whom the nature, extent, and locus of the damage are not known. More recently there has been considerable work with children in whom brain damage is a presumption or working hypothesis rather than an established fact (i.e., those designated as cases of learning disability or minimal brain damage).

Nevertheless, despite these handicaps, a fair amount of information about the behavioral characteristics of brain-damaged children has been gained during the past 15 years as a result of neuropsychological study in a number of areas—mental retardation, convulsive disorders, conduct problems, and learning disabilities. In addition, neuropsychologists have followed the approach (exemplified in the investigations of Reitan and others) of studying children with confirmed cerebral lesions independently of whether or not these children present behavioral or intellectual disabilities. Finally, in recent years, a start has been made in the neuropsychological study of normal children.

Considering first the approach represented by Reitan and his coworkers in this volume, a consistent finding has been that brain-damaged children show impressively lower IQs than normal children. As it happens, the same holds true for brain-damaged adults. Quite possibly the best single index of the presence of brain damage in adults, as well as in children, is a lower-than-expected total score derived from any reasonably comprehensive battery of tests (cf. Fogel, 1964). This fact that, on the evidence available, a single total score is probably as valid an indicator of acquired cerebral disease in adults as it is of early brain damage in children should make us wary about accepting without closer scrutiny the familiar proposition that the effects of brain damage are more generalized in children than in adults.

Another reason for caution is that comparative studies of brain-damaged and normal children, equated for age and IQ, have disclosed more or less specific defects in a significant proportion of the brain-damaged subjects, among these defects being impairment in visual memory, constructional performance, motor persistence, right-left discrimination, and finger recognition (cf. Benton, 1959, 1968c; Benton, Spreen, Fangman, & Carr, 1967; Clawson, 1962; Garfield, 1964; Rowley & Baer, 1961). Reitan's analyses of individual cases point in the same direction. Thus it appears that selective impairment in cognitive function certainly can occur as a consequence of cerebral disease in children.

Mental retardation is an area which, almost by definition, commands neuropsychological interest since the traditional concept is that the behavioral deficiencies shown by retarded children are a more or less direct expression of cerebral abnormality. The distinction between endogenous and exogenous types of mental retardation goes back many decades. A generation ago Strauss and Werner (1938, 1939, 1941) (Werner, 1945; Werner & Thuma, 1942a, 1942b) explored the behavioral implications of this distinction in a series of studies that left much to be desired from the technical standpoint and the results of which generally did not survive crossvalidation (cf. Benton, Hutcheon, & Seymour, 1951; Gallagher, 1957; Sarason, 1959). However, their work was of considerable stimulus value and, I think, was largely responsible for the recent development of the concepts of minimal brain damage and neurologically determined learning disability.

Mental retardation is both a potentially fruitful and a peculiarly difficult area for the neuropsychologist (cf. Benton, 1970). Since a significant proportion of these children surely have damaged brains, they would seem to be ideal subjects for study. But since the primary problem they present is of a social and educational nature, it is usually the case that nothing is known about their cerebral status. Added to this is the complication that such factors as experiential deprivation and emotional disorder contribute significantly to the clinical picture in a large number of cases. Consequently, most of the neuropsychological work in this area has been on a purely behavioral level.

One finds that, as with nonretarded brain-damaged children, a variety of specific deficits of a perceptual, linguistic, psychomotor, and somatosensory nature are brought to light by controlled studies involving comparisons of retardates with normal children of equivalent mental age (cf. Alley, 1969; Benton, 1955, 1959; Benton, Garfield, & Chiorini, 1964; Garfield, Benton, & MacQueen, 1966; Spreen, 1965). Investigations of defined subgroups have yielded some interesting results. For example, O'Connor and Hermelin (1962) have demonstrated a specific impairment in tactile recognition in mongoloids as compared to normal children and other types of retardates of equivalent mental age. But the neural determinants of this difference remain unknown. On the other hand, suggestive evidence of a relationship between the development of the parietal areas in retardates and their performance profile on a battery of verbal, perceptual, and visuomotor tests has been brought forth by Sylvester (1966) and Sylvester and Blundell (1967).

There have also been investigations of the psychological test characteristics of other genetically defined syndromes such as phenylketonuria, galactosemia, and Turner's syndrome. For example, Money (1963a, 1963b) and Shaffer (1962) have been able to demonstrate specific defects in spatial and form perception as well as in calculation in patients with Turner's syndrome. A recent study of a genetic condition that deserves mention because of its unusual findings is the report by Eldrige, Harlan, Cooper, and Riklan (1970) of an association between superior intelligence and recessively inherited torsion dystonia.

act of twisting — *abnormal tone of any tissue. Stretching power of contract-ed muscles*

Dyspraxia — inability to perform coordinated movements.

Neuropsychological study of epileptic children has a long history with attention being focused on such questions as intelligence level, specific defects, personality, and the influence of such factors as age of onset, frequency of seizures, and type of convulsive disorder. Until recently, however, the findings of these studies tended to be inconsistent and few valid conclusions could be drawn. With the development of electroencephalography and a more useful classification of epileptic disorders on the one hand, and the employment of more appropriate behavioral testing techniques on the other hand, a new era of investigation has begun and has yielded informative results. For example, Prechtl, Boeke, and Schut (1961), employing a reaction time task, have been able to demonstrate a temporal association between lapses of attention on the part of epileptic patients and flattening of their EEG record. A comparative study by Fedio and Mirsky (1969) of children with temporal lobe and centrencephalic epilepsy has disclosed distinctive patterns of intellectual impairment in different groups of patients. The children with convulsive disorders of centrencephalic origin showed maximal deficit in sustained attention and constructional performances; those with left temporal lobe abnormality showed maximal deficit in the learning and recall of verbal material while those with right temporal lobe abnormality showed maximal deficit in the learning and recall of nonverbal material (e.g., complex designs and random shapes). The results for the hemispherically damaged groups approximate those observed in adult patients with unilateral temporal disease. Thus, once again, the validity of the thesis that early brain damage causes global retardation is called into question. Finally, it should be noted that, as Fedio and Mirsky point out, differences in medication constituted an uncontrolled variable in their study and possibly could account for the observed differences between the centrencephalic and temporal lobe groups.

Turning to the areas of "minimal brain damage" and learning disability, we have to concede that at the present time this is truly a mare's nest. Some years ago Gomez (1967) equated "minimal cerebral dysfunction" with "maximal neurologic confusion" and he was surely on firm ground in doing so. The confusion is inherent in the term itself. A child is observed to show hyperactivity, distractibility, motor awkwardness, instability in behavior level, or perceptual handicap. These disabilities are relatively minor as compared to global retardation or frank cerebral palsy. Then, by a process of neurological mythmaking, the relatively minor behavioral manifestations are transformed into relatively minor brain abnormality. There is, of course, no justification for doing this. On the one hand, all these behavioral disabilities may have come about because of faulty nurture (using this term in its broadest sense). On the other hand, they may be the expression of major (not minimal) brain damage.

The term and concept of minimal brain damage are particularly unfortunate since—somewhat paradoxically—they tend to obscure the basic truth that cerebral damage or maldevelopment, which is not discernable by current infrabehavioral techniques, can be manifested in behavioral abnormality. This is one of the most fruitful fields in which the neuropsychologist can work, particularly in terms of his contribution to clinical evaluation. Admittedly, because of the lack of neurological support, he must be extremely critical in his assumptions and interpretations when studying these children. But such study, especially when it includes concurrent observations on children with confirmed brain damage and retarded children, should enable us to arrive at a valid conception of the reality represented by the misnomer, minimal brain damage. The isolation of a developmental agnosic-apraxic syndrome in otherwise normal children by Walton, Ellis, and Court (1962) is one example of the type of study which neuropsychologists could profitably undertake.

The area of learning disability is also one which the neuropsychologist can explore with promise of fruitful results. His first contribution here might well be of a definitional nature for, as of today, the term and concept are hopelessly vague. For many writers, "learning disability" appears to be equivalent to school failure in general, which is hardly a workable concept. Strict definitions in terms of performance profiles and psychological characteristics are a prerequisite for useful investigation of such problems as reading disability or specific arithmetic disability.

Here, as in other areas of clinical neuropsychology, more often than not, investigators have had to be content to do studies on a purely behavioral level since there has been no opportunity to explore brain-behavior correlations in any direct way. To date, little real headway has been made in understanding either the behavioral correlates or neurological background of specific reading disability. However, a number of studies have yielded results that offer leads for further investigation (cf. Bakker, 1966, 1967; Beery, 1967; Birch & Belmont, 1964; Bryden, 1970; Hughes & Parkes, 1969; Knott, Muehl, & Benton, 1965; Muehl, Knott, & Benton, 1965; Nielsen & Ringe, 1969; Walters & Kosowski, 1963; Zurif & Carson, 1970).

Finally, in recent years neuropsychological studies of normal children have been undertaken and some of these have been quite informative. For example, Doreen Kimura's application (1967) of the (dichotic) listening technique with both verbal and nonverbal material to preschool and young school children has provided us with indications of how hemispheric cerebral dominance develops in the early years of life. And Reed (1967) has been able to demonstrate relationships between lateralized patterns of finger recognition performance and reading skills in essentially normal school children.

Prospects for future developments in the area of the neuropsychology of childhood would appear to be reasonably bright. In order to make further advances, perhaps we should first make sure that we appreciate the complexities of the situation. Brain-behavior relations are not of a simple isomorphic nature and the search for direct, consistent associations between these two levels of events in individuals who differ in genetic makeup and environmental history can be expected to yield only imperfect results at best. Of course, neuropsychologists are well aware that many factors interact with cerebral damage to determine behavioral outcomes (or, to put it more specifically, test performances) and in their studies they try to control for some of these determinants such as age, sex, manual preference, and educational level. However, in addition to this approach that views the influence of these determinants as noise in the system, it may be advantageous to adopt the complementary approach and study individual differences as a topic of interest in its own right. Ghent (1961), Kimura (1967) and Lansdell (1962, 1964) have adduced evidence suggesting differences in the hemispheric organization of abilities in males and females and more studies along these lines are indicated. One cannot predict what the impact of investigative work of this nature would be. It might merely provide some interesting descriptive statistics or it might lead to new insights into the central problem. In any case, such a development would represent a broadening in the scope of our work that seems to be particularly desirable at this time.

4
PSYCHOLOGICAL EFFECTS OF CEREBRAL LESIONS IN CHILDREN OF EARLY SCHOOL AGE[1]

Ralph M. Reitan

Investigations have been made of a variety of behavioral disturbances thought to be associated with cerebral damage, including hyperactivity, impulsivity, emotional disturbances, learning disorders, behavioral disorders supposedly associated with some prior insulting condition of the central nervous system (e.g., postencephalitic behavior disorders), and conditions such as nutritional deficiencies or neonatal anoxia considered to be capable of producing brain dysfunction. Additional studies of children who demonstrate some type of physiological evidence of possible brain dysfunction, such as electro-encephalographic abnormalities, also have been done. Few extensive investigations, however, have focused on study of children with known cerebral lesions. Ernhart, Graham, Eichman, Marshall, and Thurston (1963) have discussed in detail the problem of generalizing regarding the effects of brain lesions under circumstances when classification criteria have been associated with brain damage to an unknown extent. For example, it is known that each of the above conditions occurs in perfectly normal children as well as in children with brain damage, but the differential frequency has not been perfectly established. Therefore, if one wishes to characterize the effects of cerebral damage it is desirable to select a group of children with known cerebral lesions in whom the criteria for selection relate to brain damage rather than to possible associated difficulties. In another sense the composition of brain-damaged groups should be independent of the behavior to be assessed, just as would be

[1] This research was supported in part by Grant HD 02274 to the Child Development and Mental Retardation Center of the University of Washington from the National Institute of Child Health and Human Development, National Institutes of Health.

the case with a comparison group of normal children. Following identification of the psychological correlates of known cerebral damage, it would be possible to compare and contrast such groups with groups of children in whom learning disorders, behavioral disturbances, specified nutritional deficiencies, etc., represented the criteria for identification. Ernhart et al. (1963), followed exactly such a procedure in their study of preschool children. Their identification of selection procedures and description of the necessary neurological findings for inclusion of subjects in the group with brain injury serves as an excellent example for additional work in this area. As they point out, however, their findings were based on children who were 3, 4, or 5 years of age. The results differed considerably from reported findings in the study of brain-damaged adults, a conclusion that also received general support from the study by H. B. C. Reed, Reitan, and Klove (1965) of children in the 10–14-year age bracket. Klonoff and his associates have performed extensive studies of older and younger children with both recent and longstanding brain lesions. Prior to the present volume, they had presented only preliminary results of their neurological, neuropsychological, and electroencephalographic findings (Klonoff, Robinson, & Thompson, 1969). This paper, therefore, is concerned with results obtained from extensive psychological examination of children in the 5–8-year age range with known cerebral lesions and comparisons with normally functioning children in the same age range.

METHOD

Subjects. Two groups of children ranging from 5 through 8 years of age were composed. In one group every subject had evidence of cerebral damage and in the other group each child was functioning normally. The subjects were matched in pairs on the basis of sex and chronological age. Each group consisted of 11 males and 18 females. Only three subjects in each group had not reached their 6th birthday so, in the main, the groups can be considered in the age range of the first 2½ grades in school. The brain-damaged subjects had a mean age of 84.93 months with a standard deviation of 10.50 months. The normal subjects had a mean age of 84.76 months and a standard deviation of 10.49 months. The normal subjects all came from a single school system and were volunteers. Participation was requested from parents with the only explanation being that psychological data were needed for research purposes. No interpretation of the test results was given to either subjects or parents, a condition which was made known when voluntary participation was requested. Neurological examinations were not performed on the normal subjects. However, in a previous investigation of comparable volunteer schoolchildren, complete histories and physical neurological examinations were performed on 56 consecutive subjects. The results on none of these subjects revealed significant positive findings, leading us to presume that the results on the present group also would be generally within the normal range.

An attempt also was made to avoid selecting the brain-damaged group of subjects because of special difficulties or complaints related to the behavioral manifestations rather than to known brain damage. The procedure in composing this group was to notify local neurologists and neurological surgeons that we wished to obtain psychological test data on children with known cerebral lesions. An explicit point was made that the purpose would *not* be to provide a clinical service but rather to obtain research data. Further, each physician who supplied patients for this study was told that unequivocal evidence of cerebral damage was necessary as a basis for qualifying each subject for inclusion. In order to supplement these screening requirements, a review of the history and neurological findings was made for each subject in order to be sure that positive evidence of cerebral damage had been obtained. Each brain-damaged child included in the study had been subjected to a detailed physical neurological evaluation by a qualified neurologist or neurological surgeon, a careful history had been obtained, and additional diagnostic procedures (such as electroencephalography and contrast studies) had been done as necessary in order to reach a firm neurological diagnosis. The 29 brain-injured children were heterogeneous with respect to etiology and fell in the following classifications: left infantile hemiplegia (or hemiparesis), 6; right infantile hemiplegia (or hemiparesis), 6; brain damage associated with encephalitis, 7; brain damage due to birth trauma, 2; accidental traumatic brain injury following birth, 7; and cerebral palsy, 1. Since 12 of the 29 subjects fall in the category of infantile hemiplegia, this category should be described briefly. Infantile hemiplegia refers to motor dysfunction on one side of the body, usually occurring during the first 3 years of life, that is a symptom of a wide variety of pathological states. In cases of infantile hemiplegia brain damage may well involve principally the cerebral hemisphere contralateral to the affected extremities although some generalized involvement is probably the rule rather than the exception. This condition frequently occurs as a complication of acute infectious disorders and the cerebral lesion is probably most often vascular in nature, even though the relationship of the hemiplegia to the infection is usually obscure in the individual instance. In this study, standardization of diagnosis of infantile hemiplegia was accomplished by the fact that the diagnosis was made in each instance by a single neurologist who was fully qualified and well experienced. Thus, variation in standards or criteria for this clinical diagnosis were probably relatively restricted in this study.

A careful review of the available evidence on each of the brain-damaged children indicated that 12 probably had sustained brain damage at birth or before; 7 within the first 2 years of life; 2 in each of the third, fifth, and sixth years; and 1, 2, and 1 additional subject in each of the seventh, eighth, and ninth years of life. The median age at which brain damage probably was sustained was 12 months. It is clear from this data that the group was fairly representative of brain-damaged children in terms of the age at which the lesion was sustained, since in most instances it occurred early in life; but in a few, as a result of adverse exogenous influences from illness or injury, it occurred not long before testing.

Measures of lateral dominance were performed in order to obtain information regarding handedness, footedness, and eyedness for each subject. Results on these tests were used not as dependent variables but rather as a basis for offering a more complete description of the groups. Evaluation of lateral dominance can be based on determination of the preferred side in performance of unimanual tasks or through comparison of the level of skill represented in performance of tasks on both sides. Our measures of handedness, eyedness, and footedness were based on assessment of the preferred side for unilateral performance. In determination of handedness, the subject was asked to perform seven tasks that included writing his name, throwing a ball, hammering a nail, cutting with a knife, turning a doorknob, using scissors, and using an eraser on a pencil. Footedness was evaluated through only two performances—kicking a football and stepping on a bug. Eyedness was evaluated with the Miles ABC Test of Ocular Dominance, a procedure that requires the subject to use uniocular vision for viewing a series of objects; most subjects are not aware that both eyes are not being used. These tests are scored by recording the hand, foot, or eye used for each trial.

Subjects were classified in this study as right- or left-handed in accordance with the hand preferred for writing. Among the 29 control subjects, 26 were classified as right-handed for writing and 3 as left-handed. Among the 29 brain-damaged subjects 19 used the right hand and 10 the left hand for writing. It is apparent that a considerably larger proportion of brain-damaged than control subjects were left-handed for writing. In each instance the subject was asked to write his name with each hand and both performances were timed in order to provide a comparison of the facility with which the task was performed. This information generally confirmed which hand the subject preferred for writing. With respect to the additional unimanual tasks, 21 of the 26 right-handed control subjects did all of these tasks with the right hand. Only 1 of the 3 control subjects who used the left hand for writing did all of the additional tasks with the left hand. Thus, 22 of the 29 control subjects were entirely consistent with respect to manual preference, whereas 7 of the subjects were not entirely consistent, distributing preference among both hands for the tasks involved.

While the brain-damaged subjects showed a greater incidence of left-handedness for writing, they also demonstrated a greater degree of consistency with respect to manual preference. All 19 of the right-handed subjects did all of the tasks with the right hand and 9 of the 10 left-handed subjects did all of the tasks with the left hand. These results would seem to suggest that the dominant hand, whether it is the right hand or left hand, is perhaps more consistently preferred for unimanual tasks among brain-damaged subjects than among control subjects.

Variables. Three test batteries were used: The Wechsler Intelligence Scale for Children, the Wide Range Achievement Test, and the Reitan-Indiana

Neuropsychological Test Battery. The Wechsler Intelligence Scale (Wechsler, 1949), an individually administered test for measurement of general intelligence, is widely known. The Wide Range Achievement Test (Jastak & Jastak, 1965) is a standard measure of academic ability in the areas of word recognition, spelling, and arithmetic. The Reitan-Indiana Neuropsychological Test Battery is composed of a series of tests in which an attempt has been made to measure the types of functions in children that are assessed in adults with the Halstead Neuropsychological Test Battery. A detailed description of the battery is presented in the Appendix of this volume.

The major purpose of this investigation was to evaluate abilities that fall in a variety of classifications and the tests that were used will be described within these categories. Classification of tests to these areas was based on precedent and face-validity rather than on any formal method such as factor analysis. Readers who are familiar with the tests used may wish to categorize the tests differently, and with this we would have no argument.

1. *Motor functions.* Tests used for evaluation of motor functions were the Finger Tapping Test, a measure of Strength of Grip, the Marching Test, and the Tactual Performance Test. These tests measure aspects of motor speed, motor strength, motor coordination, and motor problem-solving.

2. *Tactile-perceptual function.* While peripheral injury or damage of various types, including neuromuscular disorders, may impair motor functions on one side of the body or the other, it is probably less likely that tactile-perceptual functions would be unilaterally impaired in the absence of damage to the contralateral cerebral hemisphere. Consequently, several tests were included in a battery in this area including measures of tactile finger localization, fingertip symbol writing perception, and tactile form recognition.

3. *Academic ability.* Academic abilities were assessed through administration of the Wide Range Achievement Test. All three content areas, reading (word recognition), spelling, and arithmetic, were used.

4. A separate category was provided for Verbal, Performance, and Full Scale IQ values from the Wechsler Intelligence Scale for Children. It should be pointed out that these IQ values are summary measures and the individual tests on which they were based were included in other categories to be described.

5. *Verbal abilities.* Several tests were judged to provide measurements related rather specifically to verbal skills. These included the Information, Comprehension, Similarities, and Vocabulary subtests of the Wechsler Intelligence Scale for Children.

6. *Visual-spatial and sequential abilities.* This area was evaluated principally through the use of tests from the Wechsler Intelligence Scale for Children, including the Block Design, Picture Arrangement, Object Assembly and Mazes subtests. One additional test from the Reitan-Indiana Neuropsychological Test Battery, the Target Test, was also included in this category.

7. *Immediate alertness.* Three tests from the Wechsler Intelligence Scale for Children were considered to provide information concerning the immediate

alertness of the subject. These tests were the Digit Span, Picture Completion, and Coding subtests. The Digit Span subtest has often been thought of as a test of immediate memory, but it is clear that the subject must be alert to the stimulus material, register it properly, and be able to reproduce it in a short time interval. The Picture Completion test also requires alertness to visual-spatial configurations in terms of identifying the missing part. Finally, Coding requires alertness and efficiency in performance in terms of relating the code to the test material in a limited amount of time.

8. *Incidental memory.* After completion of the Tactual Performance Test (see motor functions above), the board and blocks were removed and the subject was given no opportunity to see them. He was asked to draw a picture of the board, putting as many of the blocks as he could recall in their proper positions. Since the subject had not been forewarned that he was going to have to draw a diagram of the board, the scores obtained on this measure were considered to be indications of incidental memory.

9. *Concept formation and reasoning ability.* Several tests were used to evaluate concept formation and the ability to apply organizing principles in performance of complex procedures. These were based on modifications of tests previously used to study the effects of brain lesions in adults. The Category Test represented a modification for use with younger children of the Halstead Category Test, and the Color Form Test and Progressive Figures Test were devised to simulate requirements of the Trail Making Test. The Matching Pictures Test was included as an abstraction measure utilizing pictures of everyday objects to complement the Category Test which uses abstract designs as stimulus material. The Arithmetic test of the WISC was also included in this category.

The Reitan-Indiana Neuropsychological Test Battery is customarily supplemented by the Reitan-Klove Lateral Dominance Examination, an examination for aphasia, and the Reitan-Klove Sensory-Perceptual Examination. These particular procedures were not included as dependent variables in this study.

Statistical procedures. Means and standard deviations based on raw socre distributions for each group were computed for all variables from the Wechsler Intelligence Scale for Children and the Wide Range Achievement Test. Because of the general familiarity with the interest in raw-score distributions for these variables, their descriptive statistics will be presented in the next section. However, most of the variables included in the Reitan-Indiana Neuropsychological Test Battery are not well known in terms of their raw-score distributions. Therefore, in the interest of space, raw-score distribution characteristics will not be presented for these variables.

Mean differences between the groups with and without cerebral damage were computed from normalized T-score distributions rather than from the raw-score distributions. A presumption of normality of distributions on the variables used in this study seems reasonable. Therefore, it seemed permissible to take advantage of this normalization procedure with respect to application of parametric statistical tests. Further, because the mean and standard deviations of the T-score distributions were composed so that the values were 50 and 10, respectively, direct comparison of the mean values of the two groups would be facilitated. The actual procedure involved pooling of both groups, transformation of raw scores to normalized T-scores for the combined groups, reconstitution of the separate groups, determination of T-score differences for matched brain-damaged and control pairs, and computation of t ratios to test the probability that the mean difference score for each distribution deviated significantly from zero. Mean T scores were also computed for each group in the nine areas of performance identified in the preceding section in order to provide possible evidence of differential levels of impairment in one area or another. To test this latter question, comparisons were made of all pairs of distributions of differences between brain-damaged and control groups in the nine areas in order to determine whether large and more consistent intergroup differences were present in some areas than in others. For example, we were interested in whether motor functions showed more impairment in the brain-damaged group, as compared to the controls, than did tactile-perceptual functions. Assuming that the shape of distributions of differences for matched pairs in each category reflected chance influences, we tested this question by computing t ratios that compared distributions of intergroup differences among all paired combinations of the nine areas.

RESULTS

In presenting the results, an attempt will be made to focus on comparisons between the normal and brain-damaged groups, and the possibility of reliable degrees of differences between the two groups in various functional areas will be considered.

Because of the general familiarity and interest in raw score IQ values, the distribution of WISC IQ values for each group is presented in Table 1.

It is apparent that variability among the brain-damaged subjects was much greater than among the normal subjects. In fact, the particular sampling of normal subjects resulted in a rather restricted range of IQ values as compared with normal expectation. The full range of IQ values is essentially represented by the brain-damaged subjects, but it is clear that there were considerably fewer in the average range than there were in the control group.

Table 2 presents more detailed quantitative information for the two groups on variables from the WISC and from the WRAT. The ranks assigned to each variable will be considered in more detail in Table 3, but for the present they may be identified as representing the magnitude of the t ratios obtained in comparing the two groups, numbered from largest to smallest among the 41 variables used in the study.

It is apparent that the IQ values for the control group fell essentially in the normal range, with a mean just a little above 100. Corresponding IQ values for the brain-damaged group, conversely, consistently were below the average level and fell at about the dividing point between the range of borderline mental

TABLE 1

Distribution of WISC IQ Values for Brain-damaged and Normal Groups

WISC values	Brain-damage			Normal		
IQ	Verbal IQ	Performance IQ	Full Scale IQ	Verbal IQ	Performance IQ	Full Scale IQ
115 and above	0	0	0	1	5	0
110–114	1	1	0	4	3	2
105–109	1	2	1	8	4	16
100–104	0	1	0	8	11	7
95–99	1	0	4	5	3	3
90–94	5	2	1	2	3	1
85–89	7	2	3	1	0	0
80–84	2	5	7	0	0	0
75–79	4	7	3	0	0	0
70–74	1	2	3	0	0	0
69 and less	7	7	7	0	0	0
Total	29	29	29	29	29	29

retardation and dull-normal intelligence. The ranks for the WISC variables (representing the magnitude of t ratios among all variables in the study) indicate that the 5 largest t ratios were based on WISC variables and 8 of the 10 largest t ratios were based on WISC variables. The WRAT scores indicated that the normal subjects had achievement levels which fell within the second-grade range. These results are about in line with expectation in consideration of the fact that the mean age was just beyond 7 years. The subjects with brain damage, however, had mean values that fell consistently below the first half of the first grade, indicating that their academic skills were quite limited. The magnitude of t ratios comparing means for the WRAT variables, however, was not as large as for the most sensitive variables from the WISC.

Table 3 presents information regarding mean values, t ratios, and comparative magnitude of t ratios for all of the 41 variables used in this study. The mean values in this instance are presented in T-score form in order to facilitate direct comparisons of the actual magnitude of differences between groups. With knowledge that the mean for the combined groups was 50 and the standard deviation 10, one can readily estimate the approximate position of the mean value for each group on each variable with respect to the overall distribution. The variables are listed in order from the one having the largest t ratio in comparing the two groups (WISC Full Scale IQ) to the variable showing the smallest t ratio (grip strength for the dominant hand). Table 3 makes it clear that highly significant differences existed between the two groups, with these differences being at statistically significant levels for all variables except strength of grip for the dominant hand. (We should note that an N of only 20 in each group was available for the WRAT variables, requiring use of a different number of degrees of freedom in interpretation of probability levels than for other variables.) Table 3 again indicates in the context of other variables that the WISC measurements tended to be among the most sensitive in differentiating the two groups. Detailed information is available in Table 3 with regard to the rank of each variable, but we would caution that any conclusion that one variable is more sensitive than an adjacent variable is hardly justified since the magnitude of

TABLE 2

Means and Standard Deviations on Wechsler Intelligence Scale for Children and Wide Range Achievement Test Variables for Matched Groups of Children With and Without Evidence of Cerebral Damage

Variables	Cerebral-damaged		Rank[a]	Normal	
	Mean	SD		Mean	SD
WISC variables					
Full Scale IQ	78.69	14.17	1	104.69	4.18
Mazes	5.93	0.20	2	10.14	0.21
Verbal IQ	82.07	13.14	3	103.48	7.64
Performance IQ	79.03	15.38	4	105.28	7.98
Object Assembly	7.21	0.25	5	10.93	0.22
Similarities	8.28	0.25	7	12.83	0.27
Information	6.79	0.26	8	10.45	0.18
Coding	6.24	0.29	9	10.86	0.28
Vocabulary	6.24	0.29	13	10.14	0.25
Picture Arrangement	6.83	0.27	14	10.69	0.29
Comprehension	6.90	0.25	20	9.66	0.26
Block Design	7.45	0.32	26	10.59	0.19
Arithmetic	6.93	0.30	27	9.97	0.17
Picture Completion	7.97	0.32	29	11.28	0.23
Digit Span	7.69	0.26	30	10.14	0.22
WRAT variables					
Reading	1.30	0.62	11	2.63	0.97
Spelling	1.14	0.66	16	2.22	0.78
Arithmetic	1.44	0.60	19	2.36	0.66

[a]The rank for each variable refers to the magnitude of the t ratio comparing the groups as it related to the total of 41 variables used in this study.

TABLE 3

T-Score Means and *t* Ratios Derived from Comparisons of Scores for Matched
Groups of Children With and Without Evidence of Cerebral Damage

Rank	Test	Mean values		*t* ratio
		Cerebral damage	Normal	
1	WISC Full Scale IQ	42.72	57.14	8.38
2	WISC Mazes	43.41	56.97	8.07
3	WISC Verbal IQ	43.21	56.62	6.95
4	WISC Performance IQ	43.17	56.69	6.90
5	WISC Object Assembly	43.83	56.07	6.88
6	Tactile Form Recognition (errors)—Left hand	43.97	54.00	6.64
7	WISC Similarities	43.69	56.24	6.24
8	WISC Information	44.03	56.00	6.20
9	WISC Coding	43.79	56.31	6.14
10	Finger-tapping—Nondominant hand	44.14	56.07	6.09
11	WRAT—Reading	44.00	56.20	5.84
12	Progressive Figures	45.14	55.10	5.54
13	WISC Vocabulary	44.21	55.69	5.47
14	WISC Picture Arrangement	44.38	55.62	5.33
15	Tactile Finger Recognition— Left hand	44.62	54.83	5.26
16	WRAT—Spelling	44.25	55.75	5.13
17	Marching—Coordination	44.62	55.45	5.13
18	Color Form	45.00	54.97	4.79
19	WRAT—Arithmetic	44.05	55.85	4.72
20	WISC—Comprehension	45.17	54.76	4.70
21	Marching—Dominant hand	44.66	55.31	4.68
22	Finger-tip Symbol Recognition— Left hand	45.38	54.28	4.68
23	Finger-tapping—Dominant hand	45.41	54.59	4.49
24	Tactile Form Recognition (errors)—Right hand	45.17	53.28	4.29
25	Category	44.86	54.93	4.27
26	WISC Block Design	45.10	54.62	4.07
27	WISC Arithmetic	45.28	54.76	4.00
28	Tactual Performance Test—non-dominant hand	45.00	55.10	3.98
29	WISC Picture Completion	45.00	55.00	3.98
30	WISC Digit Span	45.55	54.38	3.91

TABLE 3 (*continued*)

Rank	Test	Mean values		*t* ratio
		Cerebral damage	Normal	
31	Matching Pictures	45.07	54.69	3.89
32	Target	46.03	54.31	3.58
33	Tactual Performance Test—Both hands	45.41	54.69	3.50
34	Marching—Nondominant hand	45.62	54.62	3.46
35	Tactile Finger Recognition—Right hand	45.66	53.69	3.35
36	Grip Strength—Nondominant hand	46.69	53.38	3.22
37	Tactual Performance Test—Memory	46.72	53.35	3.20
38	Tactual Performance Test—Dominant hand	46.79	53.24	2.76
39	Finger-tip Symbol Recognition—Right hand	46.55	52.69	2.74
40	Tactual Performance Test—Localization	47.38	53.00	2.49
41	Grip Strength—Dominant hand	48.28	51.66	1.57

	t ratio[a]	*t* ratio[b]
$p < .001$	3.67+	3.92+
$p < .005$	3.05+	3.20+
$p < .01$	2.76+	2.88+
$p < .05$	2.05+	2.10+

[a]Degrees of freedom = 28.
[b]Degrees of freedom = 19. (WRAT: Reading, Spelling, and Arithmetic)

t ratios in this particular study is undoubtedly due in part to chance influences. While one might conclude that the WISC Digit Span subtest (occupying a rank of 30 among the 41 variables) was not as sensitive as the WISC Mazes subtest (occupying a rank of 2 among the variables), one would not be justified, on the basis of the present analysis, in drawing such a conclusion in comparison of WISC Block Design and WISC Digit Span. For inspectional purposes, however, it may be of interest to observe the comparative ranking of these various tests in general terms with relation to the magnitude of *t* ratios obtained in comparing the two groups.

An additional observation of interest may be derived from Table 3. Four variables reported results on the dominant and nondominant hands individually and three variables on the right and left hands. Dominant and nondominant hands were used for motor variables since prior evidence has indicated that the dominant hand customarily is more proficient in motor tasks than the nondominant hand in normal groups. With respect to the tactile-perceptual functions examined, however, no such evidence exists; so the procedure followed was to group data according to results based on the right and left hands. On three of the four variables reflecting motor functions, results with the nondominant hand showed considerably greater sensitivity in terms of the size of the *t* ratio than did results with the dominant hand. More specifically, *t* ratios were larger for finger-tapping, Tactual Performance Test, and strength of grip when comparing the nondominant performances of the normal and brain-damaged subjects than when comparing the same performances with the dominant hands. Only on the Marching Test was the relationship reversed. With respect to tactile-perceptual functions, comparisons of the left hands for the two groups yielded much larger *t* ratios in all instances. For example, tactile form recognition had a rank of 6 for the left hand but a rank of 24 for the right hand; tactile finger recognition had a rank of 15 for the left hand and 35 for the right hand; and fingertip symbol writing recognition had a rank of 22 for the left hand and 39 for the right hand. It would appear that comparisons of the left hand for tactile-perceptual functions provided considerably more sensitive differentiation of the groups with and without cerebral damage than comparisons of the same performances with the right hand. The differences in this regard seemed to reflect more striking differences between the tactile-perceptual measures (left versus right hands) than for the motor measures (nondominant versus dominant hands).

In accordance with the major aim of this study, Table 4 presents results for the groups with and without cerebral damage according to various areas of function or categories of measurement.

The *T*-score mean for each group, the difference between these means, and the overlap of the groups at the median score for the combined distributions is given. The groups with the larger mean differences tend also to have the smaller percentage of overlap, as would be expected. The range of overlap extends from 10.3% on the WISC Full Scale IQ to 30.0% on the measures of academic abilities based on WRAT scores. While these values may yield some comparative basis for assessing the particular areas of deficits shown by subjects with cerebral damage as compared with the normal subjects, certain cautions should be mentioned with respect to interpretation of the results. First, as would be expected without a cross-validation study, the results presented in Table 4 are subject to an unknown degree of chance variability. Second, and probably more important from a cautionary point of view, certain of the areas are represented by summary types of measures (e.g., WISC Full Scale IQ) whereas others are based upon single measurements. Further, some of the areas are represented by a number of scores derived from experimentally related or unrelated testing procedures, whereas other areas are based upon as little as one or two scores.

TABLE 4

Mean *T*-Scores for Matched Groups with and without Evidence of Cerebral
Damage Arranged According to Selected Areas; Proportion of Overlap
for Combined Groups Using the Median for Combined Groups as
the Cutoff Point

Category of function	Number of variables	Cerebral damage	Normal	Difference	% Overlap at median cutoff
Motor Functions	10	45.66	54.41	8.75	24.1
Tactile-perceptual Functions	6	45.22	53.79	8.57	19.0
Academic Abilities	3	44.10	55.93	11.83	30.0
WISC Full Scale IQ	1	42.72	57.14	14.42	10.3
Verbal Abilities	4	44.28	55.67	11.39	13.8
Visual-spatial and Sequential Relationships	5	44.55	55.52	10.97	13.8
Immediate Alertness	3	44.78	55.23	10.45	17.2
Incidental Memory	2	47.05	53.17	6.12	29.3
Concept Formation and Reasoning	5	45.07	54.89	9.82	24.1

Thus, interpretation of the various areas identified in Table 4, with respect to
the differences between subjects with and without cerebral damage, is open to
several qualifications. Nevertheless, the general trend is sufficiently pronounced
to merit certain comments. The subjects with cerebral damage performed poorly
on WISC Full Scale IQ, measures of Verbal Abilities, and the area of
Visual-Spatial and Sequential Relationships. A somewhat greater degree of
overlap in the groups occurred with respect to measures of Immediate Alertness
and Tactile-perceptual Functions. Motor Functions and Concept Formation and
Reasoning occupy the next positions, whereas measures relating to Incidental
Memory and Academic Abilities show the greatest amount of overlap in the two
groups. It is apparent that this analysis reflects, in substantial part, the sensitivity
of the WISC subtests to brain damage (as indicated in Tables 1, 2 and 3) since
these measures principally were represented in evaluation of verbal abilities and
visual-spatial and sequential relationships. In fact, even the fourth most sensitive
area, in terms of degree of overlap between the groups (Immediate Alertness)
was composed entirely of three subtests from the WISC. Thus, the various
abilities measured by the WISC appear to be among the most sensitive to the
effects of cerebral damage as indicated by the results of this study.
Tactile-perceptual Functions seemed possibly to be somewhat more sensitive
than Motor Functions. It is of particular interest to note that the area of

Concept Formation and Reasoning was among the less sensitive. This area of function in adult subjects has been identified as being one of the most sensitive to general effects of cerebral damage. The area of Incidental Memory also has been identified in studies of adults as being particularly sensitive (Halstead, 1947; Reitan, 1955a) although the present results may be a reflection of the fact that this category was based on only two measures. Finally, the relatively great amount of overlap in the groups with respect to scores reflecting academic achievement is somewhat surprising, particularly in consideration of the fact that the actual mean difference between the groups on this variable was next to the largest in absolute terms. It would appear, therefore, that while the subjects with cerebral damage sometimes showed very severe impairment of academic abilities, there were a number of instances in which comparatively good scores occurred among the subjects with cerebral damage and, as a result, there was less overlap in the two groups. It is possible that this area is singled out for remedial efforts and that a greater proportion of brain-damaged subjects are thereby elevated into the normal distribution.

Finally, statistical tests were made regarding the question of whether any differences existed in the degree of impairment shown by the brain-damaged subjects in the nine areas identified. Table 5 presents results in which differences between the normal and brain-damaged groups were compared for significance in each of the possible pairs of areas.

Table 5 is composed of t ratios in which comparisons of differences between groups in each area were made. It should be noted that the mean differences, on which the t ratios in Table 5 are based, were always in a consistent direction, with the brain-damaged subjects performing more poorly than the normal subjects in every area. Therefore, it is somewhat difficult for significant differences to occur between areas since the differences consistently deviated in the same direction. For example, while Motor Functions showed a somewhat greater overlap between the groups than Tactile-perceptual Functions (Table 4), Table 5 indicates that a t ratio of 0.21, was obtained in an actual comparison of the magnitude of the differences. Obviously no evidence was obtained, therefore, to indicate that Tactile-perceptual Functions were more significantly impaired than Motor Functions in the brain-damaged group. However, certain significant differences did occur. The WISC Full Scale IQ was significantly more impaired in the brain-damaged group, as compared with the normal subjects, than any of the other categories with the exception of Academic Abilities. The differences in these comparisons exceeded the .001 level of confidence for comparisons of WISC Full Scale IQ with Tactile-perceptual Functions and Incidental Memory; the .01 level for Motor Functions, Immediate Alertness, and Concept Formation and Reasoning; and the .05 level for Verbal Abilities and Visual-spatial and Sequential Relationships. The additional significant differences all involve Incidental Memory and this area seemed to be less impaired than others. More specifically, Verbal Abilities and Visual-spatial Sequential Relationships were more significantly impaired than Incidental

TABLE 5

t Ratios Comparing Differences in Extent to which Normal Subjects Exceeded Subjects with Brain Damage in Various Areas

Category of Function	1	2	3	4	5	6	7	8
1. Motor Functions								
2. Tactile-perceptual Functions	0.21							
3. Academic Abilities	1.00	1.49						
4. WISC Full Scale IQ	3.10**	3.99***	1.55					
5. Verbal Abilities	1.36	1.63	0.15	2.54*				
6. Visual-spatial and Sequential Relationships	1.35	1.84	0.27	2.34*	0.22			
7. Immediate Alertness	0.99	1.43	0.78	2.84**	0.56	0.42		
8. Incidental Memory	1.53	1.49	2.54*	4.80***	3.07**	3.36**	2.31*	
9. Concept Formation and Reasoning	0.59	1.03	1.03	3.10**	1.03	0.95	0.41	2.28*

*$p < .05$.
**$p < .01$.
***$p < .001$.

Memory ($p < .01$) whereas Academic Abilities, Immediate Alertness, and Concept Formation and Reasoning did not reach this level of statistical significance ($p < .05$).

It appears from these results that there are distinctly differential degrees of impairment shown by subjects with cerebral damage as compared with normals. It would be important, obviously, to repeat this kind of investigation in groups with more specific characterization of cerebral damage (possibly with respect to type, location, duration, age at which damage was sustained, etc.) before offering any final or even definitive statements. However, the present results would suggest that certain areas are more impaired than others and a great deal appears still to be learned about such phenomena.

DISCUSSION

The present results represent an extensive comparison of a broad range of intellectual and cognitive measurements and sensory-perceptual and motor functions in groups of brain-damaged and normal subjects. Except for presentation of preliminary results by Klonoff et al. (1969), the only other extensive evaluations and comparisons of this type have been done with preschool children (Ernhart et al., 1963; Graham, Ernhart, Craft, & Berman, 1963) and with older children (H. B. C. Reed et al., 1965). These investigations found that brain-damaged children were very generally impaired in all areas of measurement. H.B.C. Reed and coworkers (1965), for example, found that with comparisons on 27 measures, the differences between the groups were significant beyond the .005 level in 24 instances, and beyond the .02 level in the remaining three comparisons. The results of each of these investigations suggested that brain injury in children resulted in serious and widespread impairment, but that the brain-injured children were not equally impaired in all areas. Ernhart's group (1963) found that the brain-injured performed poorly in cognitive and perceptual-motor areas but were less impaired in the area of personality functioning. H.B.C. Reed et al. (1965) found that the major areas of deficit related to tests that were directly dependent upon facility in the use of language. In fact, results reported by Reed's group (1965) on children in the 10–14-year age range were extremely similar to those of the present study. Variables from the Wechsler-Bellevue Scale (Form 1) routinely showed the most consistent differences between the two groups, with measures of concept formation, immediate alertness, and motor functions not showing as striking differences.

These results are of interest with regard to the nature of psychological deficit resulting from injury or damage to the *young* versus the *mature* brain. Ernhart et al. (1963) make the point that the pattern of deficit customarily seen in adult subjects, involving relatively great impairment in perceptual-motor and conceptual abilities as contrasted with relatively mild impairment in vocabulary, was not found in their study of preschool children. We would point out that many detailed studies of specific neurological characteristics of brain lesions in adult subjects, as related to patterns of psychological deficit, have been made and the complexity of patterns of deficit are becoming increasingly known. Postulation of a single pattern for adults is hardly valid. However, the general conclusion appears to be justified. Previous studies, in fact, have shown that the Halstead Impairment Index is significantly more sensitive to the effects of cerebral lesions in adults than are measures on the Wechsler-Bellevue Scale (Reitan, 1959a). In the present findings, as well as those of H. B. C. Reed et al., (1965) with older children, the Wechsler IQ variables are clearly among the most sensitive in differentiating the groups.

Ernhart et al. (1963) have pointed out that a number of studies on animals (Benjamin & Thompson, 1959; Kennard, 1938, 1942) have demonstrated that brain lesions in young animals produce less motor and less sensory deficits than do comparable lesions in older animals. In this regard, it is of interest to note that measures of motor functions in the present study were not among the most sensitive to the effects of cerebral damage. This was true also of the findings of H. B. C. Reed et al. (1965) in studying older children. The problem is further complicated by preliminary evidence on adult patients with various types of lesions. For example, Reitan and Fitzhugh (1971) have recently found that motor deficits are very pronounced and more severe than deficits in higher level psychological functions in patients with cerebrovascular disease whereas in adult patients with traumatic injuries relatively less motor impairment is present. Thus, a generalization with respect to damage of the immature versus the mature brain is complicated by a variety of factors which makes specific interpretation difficult. Ernhart et al. (1963) had postulated, however, on the basis of their considerations in this respect that there might be an inverse relationship between age at the time of injury and vocabulary impairment, whereas a direct relationship might be present between age at the time of injury and perceptual-motor impairment. Our results do not seem to bear out any such contention. In fact, vocabulary functions and other types of verbal measures were consistently among the most sensitive to the effects of brain damage in the present study, results which were very similar to those obtained in older children by H. B. C. Reed et al. (1965). However, the particular findings with children, regarding patterns of psychological deficit, do suggest that the interaction of brain damage and the developmental process results in rather different psychological findings than occurs with adults. The extent of impairment in brain-damaged children has been quite pronounced in these studies of Ernhart et al. (1963), H. B. C. Reed et al. (1965), and the present findings. Ernhart et al. (1963) found that a composite index of impairment, based on their psychological measurements, correctly identified 72.7% of the brain-injured children and misidentified only 10.6% of the normal children. H. B. C. Reed et al. (1965) consistently found highly significant differences between the groups of older children, much as occurred in the present study. Thus, it would appear that brain-damaged children perform more poorly compared with normal children than is the general rule for brain-damaged adults compared with normal adults. The findings suggest that the general effects of brain damage in infancy or childhood limit the potential for normal development, resulting in some generalized depression of behavioral abilities. Thus, as contrasted with the results from animal studies relating to development of motor and sensory functions, damage of the immature brain appears generally to have more serious consequences with respect to higher level functions than does damage to the mature brain.

It should be recognized, however, that a number of factors may interact in determining psychological deficit resulting from cerebral damage sustained in infancy or childhood. While our results suggest that early damage has relatively severe consequences, it is possible that the plasticity of the immature brain may, in some instances, permit adaptation to the damage. Probably, however, the more frequent result is that damage to the immature brain imposes a limitation on the potential for acquisition of abilities in the developmental years of childhood. In adult subjects, cerebral functions may be relatively crystallized and specific cerebral lesions may result in rather discrete psychological deficits. In addition, in adult subjects who sustain cerebral lesions, the deficit involves loss of previously acquired abilities rather than also involving limitation of ability acquisition in the course of psychological development.

Recently Semmes (1968) has published a detailed analysis of comparative somatosensory functions of the two hands and has concluded that differences in results obtained indicate that capacities are more focally represented in the left cerebral hemisphere and more diffusely represented in the right cerebral hemisphere. This conclusion is of interest in consideration of the fact that comparisons of the brain-damaged and normal children in the present study rather consistently indicated more significant differences in comparison of the nondominant hand for skilled motor functions and the left hand for somatosensory functions than occurred for the dominant or right hand on corresponding measurements. Semmes proposed that focal representation of elementary functions in the left cerebral hemisphere would relate to integration of similar units and thus permit specialization of fine sensory-motor control such as manual skills and speech. She also felt that the diffuse representation of elementary function in the right cerebral hemisphere might lead to integration of dissimilar units and hence specialization of behavior relating to spatial abilities. Her findings of differential results in the two hands, therefore, prompted her to propose a "possible clue to the mechanism of hemispheric specialization." On the basis of the results of the present study we would be disinclined to offer such a profound rationale. First, the results are equivocal with respect to differential effects of lateralized cerebral damage in 6-, 7-, and 8-year-old children with regard to verbal and spatial abilities (Fedio & Mirsky, 1969; Pennington, Galliani, & Voegele, 1965) and verbal and spatial abilities do not seem to be closely related, on an intraindividual basis, to lateralized motor deficits (Reed, J. C., & Reitan, 1969). Of more significance, however, is the fact that when cerebral damage is present, it is likely to affect one cerebral hemisphere to a somewhat greater extent than the other. In children who have experienced some left cerebral damage, the right hand and arm may be somewhat impaired in their proficiency of functioning. Such children are likely to become left-handed. In fact, in previous studies based on adult subjects with cerebral damage dating back to infancy, approximately 50% of the subjects with left cerebral lesions have been found to be left-handed (Fitzhugh, Fitzhugh, & Reitan, 1962). Thus, it is likely that selective factors, relating to cerebral damage, may be influential in determining the handedness of the brain-damaged child. Under these circumstances the child is likely to perform somewhat better with his preferred hand (which still usually turns out to be the right hand) than with the nonpreferred hand. Inspection of the raw scores in this study lent support to an interpretation along these lines. The basis for the more significant differences between brain-damaged and normal groups on the nondominant hand (or left hand for somatosensory measures) related to a poor performance for the brain-damaged subjects on that side with relation to their own performances on the other side. Thus, it would seem that the explanation for this finding stems from the fact that brain-damaged subjects develop hand preference in accordance with the relative facility of the two upper extremities and, correspondingly, comparisons of the nonpreferred upper extremity with control subjects yields larger and more consistent differences because the nonpreferred upper extremity is more impaired with relation to the subject's own preferred hand.

Certain limitations of the present study should be noted. The groups presently compared were relatively small and were definitely heterogeneous with respect to characteristics of brain damage. It is entirely possible that differential relationships or patterns of psychological deficits to more detailed characteristics of cerebral damage may emerge as future work in this area progresses. Thus, the generalizations of the present study, which would apply to heterogeneous brain damage in children, may be subject to many qualifications as more detailed studies are made of recent versus more chronic injury or of damage to focal areas of the cerebral hemispheres.

It is even more important to point out explicitly that the approach to data analysis in the present paper is oriented exclusively toward level of performance and variability of measurements. The individual tests, and groups of variables, were evaluated in terms of the probability that mean differences had occurred on a chance basis. While this approach is conventional in statistical analysis and in published research, prior information has indicated that it scarcely represents an adequate model for inferring human brain-behavior relationships (Reitan, 1964b). In fact, a series of inferential methods for this purpose has been described in detail (Reitan, 1967a), and the test battery, on which the present results are based, was deliberately devised in such a way that each of these methods would be represented. The methods include not only level of performance but also evaluation of specific deficits or pathognomonic signs of cerebral damage, patterns and relationships among test scores that might have particular significance for involvement of one cerebral hemisphere or a particular area within a cerebral hemisphere, and comparisons of the functional efficiency of the two sides of the body in a subbattery of tests that includes sensory-perceptual, psychomotor, and motor performances. While it is necessary to determine comparative levels of performance for groups with and without cerebral damage, interpretation of results for individual subjects is greatly facilitated by simultaneous use of various methods of inference. In consideration of results on individual children similar to those used in this study (Reitan, 1967c), it appears, in fact, that a particularly powerful method of inference relates to comparisons of performances on the two sides of the body. Many children with cerebral lesions show deviations on the two sides that go well beyond normal expectations. These differences are not always limited consistently to a particular side. For example, a brain-damaged child may show serious impairment of finger-tapping speed with his left hand whereas tactile finger localization may be more impaired on the right hand than the left hand. While consistency of lateralization may provide a basis for drawing differential conclusions regarding the functional adequacy of the two cerebral hemispheres, the occurrence of intraindividual deviations themselves are often helpful in differentiating subjects with cerebral lesions from ones with normal brain functions. It is apparent that specification of a method of data analysis that is capable of simultaneously including these various methods of inference would be difficult to achieve. It is clear that it has not been achieved in this particular study and the results therefore, may be only of preliminary value with respect to clinical interpretation of results for individual subjects.

A discriminating technique for differentiating groups of adult subjects with and without cerebral lesions has been to devise a summary score such as was done by Halstead in developing his Impairment Index (Halstead, 1947). Previous findings (Reitan, 1955a; Wheeler, Burke, & Reitan, 1963; Wheeler & Reitan, 1963) reported that the Halstead Impairment Index differentiated groups of subjects with and without cerebral lesions at a high rate of efficiency, nearly equaling the percentage of correct classification achieved with linear discriminant functions based on 23 variables in one instance and 24 in another. In brief, a summary score of this type seems to have the advantage of showing typical levels of performance for individual subjects, deleting the significance of occasional good scores by persons with cerebral lesions and of occasional poor scores by persons without evidence of cerebral damage. It might seem, therefore, that employment of a similar technique would be advantageous in analyzing results obtained with children. We have been disinclined to develop such an index on the basis of findings in the present study for a number of reasons. First, the groups of subjects presently used were small and were not composed to serve as normative groups. Development of a summary score for identifying subjects with and without cerebral lesions necessarily presumes a practical orientation toward application and, therefore, groups of subjects should be more representative than the present ones necessarily were. Other considerations are of even more significance with respect to this question. A summary index is necessarily based on only one inferential method—level of performance. As mentioned above, the approaches to understanding the effects of brain lesions in individual children require other inferential methods as well. Thus, one might risk encouragement of application of an oversimplified approach to identification of children with brain damage by publication of a summary score scale and a cutting-point. Another consideration relates to identification of brain damage in children. It is apparent that firm and unequivocal diagnoses of cerebral damage are imperative as in the present study, in composing a group of brain-damaged children for comparison in a research context with normal children. However, this type of procedure undoubtedly requires exclusion of many children who have sustained brain damage but for whom definitive neurological diagnostic information is not or cannot become available. Thus, a brain-damaged group such as that used in the present study is probably far from inclusive of brain damage among children. Therefore, any specifically delineated method for identification of brain damage through psychological testing based on the present groups might well represent a premature closure and, correspondingly, cause some misdirection of future development in this area. In fact, it should be pointed out that the extreme differences between groups found in the present study represent differences in children with neurologically established brain damage as compared with normal children rather than children with milder types of brain deficiency and damage that may not be as readily subject to unequivocal neurological definition. It would seem that a more forward-looking approach to this problem would be one that did not risk underidentification of brain damage in children but, instead, pointed toward possibilities for future development in assessing brain-behavior relationships even in children with relatively mild brain damage or dysfunction. In order to achieve this aim, as well as to illustrate application of results obtained in the formal aspects of the study, a section is appended in which results are evaluated for individual children both in terms of their implications for the organic condition of the brain as well as for problems of adjustment arising from environmental demands or requirements.

RESULTS FOR INDIVIDUAL CHILDREN

This section will present results for individual children and will attempt to relate the findings to the intergroup comparisons previously presented. Four children were selected in order to illustrate a range of circumstances. Two of the children had cerebral lesions which were definitely established, and were the type of children who could have qualified on the basis of neurological findings for inclusion in the brain-damaged group used in this paper. The third and fourth children to be described very possibly may have sustained brain damage, but completely convincing evidence at the time of psychological examination was not available. Therefore, these children may be thought of as having possible brain damage and, in fact, at the time of neuropsychological examination were diagnostic problems. Thus, this section will present results on children with known brain lesions (one of whom was relatively intact in many respects whereas the other was rather generally impaired) and also will illustrate the contribution to clarification of diagnostic problems that may be made through neuropsychological examination. The two children with proved brain lesions represent one instance of recent damage and another of damage that had been present for some time. The two diagnostic problems were selected to represent one case in which a question of brain damage was the referring complaint and another in which behavioral changes prompted the evaluation.

An 8-year, 6-month-old girl with a postoperative left frontal lobe abscess. Two weeks before admission to the hospital this child had a mild febrile illness. She seemed to be improving until about 48 hr. before admission when she complained of numbness of the right face and arm and had an elevated body temperature. Weakness of the right arm and the right side of the face became apparent during the next 24-hr. period. When the patient was admitted to the hospital she was nauseated and vomited. She also had some unspecified speech difficulties at this time. Physical examination indicated clinical evidence of diminished breathing sounds in the right lung field, monoparesis of the right upper extremity, drooping of the right face, deviation of the tongue to the right, and venous engorgement in the optic fundi. Cerebrospinal fluid findings were in the normal range but 2 days after admission, total protein had risen sharply. Two electroencephalograms were performed and each indicated the presence of delta waves, Grade II, over the left frontotemporal area and dysrhythmia, Grade II, in the left temporoparietal area. Bilateral carotid angiography revealed the probable presence of a space-occupying lesion in the superior-posterior part of the left frontal lobe. Craniotomy was performed and needling of the superior part of the precentral gyrus produced a small amount of purulent material and necrotic brain tissue. A total of 15 cm^3 was evacuated and the pathological report indicated that the lesion was an abscess. The patient did well postoperatively and showed good recovery of strength in her right upper extremity and right lower face. Neuropsychological examination was performed 18 days after the craniotomy, when the patient was again able to be up and around, showing no signs of acute illness.

As shown in Table 6, the child had a Verbal IQ on the Wechsler Intelligence Scale for Children that fell at the upper end of the dull-normal range whereas her Performance IQ was 17 points higher and fell in the upper part of the normal distribution. Even though this child was definitely left-handed and had been left-handed before her illness, it is likely that her left cerebral hemisphere would be dominant for language functions (Penfield & Roberts, 1959). Thus, the disparity between the Verbal and Performance IQ values would be in the expected direction in consideration of the recently acquired left cerebral lesion.

TABLE 6

Psychological Test Results on an 8-year, 6-month-old Left-handed Girl with a Left Frontal Lobe Abscess

Wechsler Intelligence Scale for Children		Reitan-Indiana Neuropsychological Test Battery	
Verbal IQ	89	*Category Test*	8
Performance IQ	106	*Tactual Performance Test*	
Full Scale IQ	96	Left hand: 3.8 min.	
Verbal Weighted Score	41	Right hand: 10.9 min.	
Performance Weighted Score	54	Both hands: 1.6 min.	
Total Weighted Score	95	Time:	16.3 min.
Information	8	Memory:	5
Comprehension	6	Location:	5
Arithmetic	12	*Finger Tapping Test*	
Similarities	8	Left hand: 30	
Vocabulary	6	Right hand: 21	
Digit Span	9		
Picture Completion	7	*Target Test*	19
Picture Arrangement	14	*Matching Pictures Test*	17
Block Design	15	*Marching Test*	
Object Assembly	11	Coordination	71
Coding	6	Left hand: 16 sec.; 0 error	
Mazes	12	Right hand: 18 sec.; 3 errors	
		Progressive Figures Test— 44 sec.; 0 error	
		Color Form Test—21 sec.; 0 error	
		Tactile Finger Recognition	
		Left hand: 0 error	
		Right hand: 5 errors	
		Finger-tip Symbol Writing	
		Left hand: 1 error	
		Right hand: 2 errors	
		Tactile Form Recognition	
		Left hand: 1 error	
		Right hand: 1 error	

However, many children in whom definite evidence of cerebral damage is lacking may also show striking disparities between levels of Verbal and Performance IQ values. Consequently, it would be difficult to infer the presence of impairment of Verbal intelligence, specifically as a result of left cerebral damage, from the results on the Wechsler Intelligence Scale for Children. It is clear that the general level of intelligence for this child was not as deficient as occurred on the average for the brain-damaged group presented in this study. On a number of subtests of the WISC, the child's performances were actually well above the average level (e.g., Picture Arrangement and Block Design).

A review of the other areas of functioning included in the test battery is helpful in identifying the general level of performance shown by this child. In terms of motor functions, she was somewhat slow in finger-tapping speed with both hands. However, she did well on more complex coordinated and problem-solving motor functions as indicated by excellent scores on the Marching Test and the Tactual Performance Test. However, comparisons of the functions on the dominant and nondominant sides clearly indicated deficiencies on the nondominant (right) hand. The child was nine taps slower with her right hand than with her left hand, indicating greater impairment of motor speed on the right side than the left. She was just about as fast on the Marching Test with her right hand as with her left hand but not as accurate. She made three errors with her right hand but no errors with her left hand. Nevertheless, she was able to perform quite well in coordinated movements as required in the Marching part of the test. The child performed extremely well on the Tactual Performance Test with the dominant (left) hand as well as on the third trial when both hands were used. However, instead of showing positive practice-effect on the second trial while using the nondominant (right) hand, the patient required much more time than she had needed on the first trial. It is apparent, therefore, that this child performed very poorly with her right hand as compared with her left hand. Unfortunately the examination of this child failed to include measurements of strength of grip or of academic achievement. While this child would have qualified on neurological grounds for inclusion in the study reported above, she was not included because of this missing data.

The child performed relatively well on various measures of tactile-perceptual functions except, again, for indications of deficiencies on the right side. She made no mistakes in tactile finger recognition on her left hand but made five mistakes in 20 trials on her right hand. Fingertip symbol writing recognition also showed mild deficiencies on the right hand, with two mistakes occurring on that side as compared with one mistake when using the left hand. The patient made one mistake on each side in the test for tactile form recognition. These findings, even though indicating only mild impairment in certain aspects of higher level functions, suggest clearly that brain damage has occurred and the results again implicate the left cerebral hemisphere to a far greater extent than the right.

This child showed relatively impaired abilities, as compared with normal children, in the verbal area. This finding, in the battery of tests used, is essentially a reflection of the relatively low Verbal IQ mentioned above. However, the scores of this child were consistently above the average level for control children as well as for brain-damaged children on various tests of visual-spatial and sequential abilities. She performed excellently not only on various tests of this type from the WISC but also on the Target Test. This finding again, however, is largely a reflection of the difference in Verbal and Performance intelligence levels mentioned above. Additional areas of functioning indicated excellent performances in concept formation and reasoning abilities. The subject's score on the Category Test was well within the range for normal children and she also performed adequately on the Matching Pictures Test. She did very well on the Color Form and Progressive Figures Tests, indicating good flexibility in thought processes and ability to follow serial instructions as the nature of the task unfolded. She also did well on the Arithmetic subtest of the WISC.

Her good scores on the Memory and Localization components of the Tactual Performance Test suggest that this child was well able to reproduce aspects of this problem-solving situation even though her attention had not been specifically directed to this requirement. Thus, it appeared that her incidental awareness and memory were relatively intact. However, her scores were rather poor on measures of immediate alertness and efficiency of performance, as indicated by comparatively low scores on the Picture Completion and Coding subtests of the WISC.

It would appear from these findings that the abilities of this child are generally within the normal range. However, while she was above the average level on a number of tests, she was below the average level in Verbal intelligence and in certain measures of immediate alertness and efficiency of performance. Attribution of this pattern of test results specifically to cerebral damage would be difficult except for the indications of lateralized deficiencies derived from measures of motor and tactile-perceptual functioning. On these measures the nondominant (right) hand was clearly deficient with relation to the performances the child showed with her dominant hand. While the motor deficiencies on the right side were more pronounced than the tactile-perceptual deficits, the fact that both occurred lent support to the hypothesis that the limiting lesion was at the cerebral level rather than lower in the nervous system. Further, this evidence of damage of the left cerebral hemisphere (across from the right side of the body) was quite consistent with the pattern of higher level psychological functions which indicated impaired verbal ability. In fact, such selective impairment, accompanied by generally adequate levels of performance, is quite suggestive of relatively recent damage to the left cerebral hemisphere as contrasted with the more generalized deficits seen in children who have experienced longstanding influences of brain damage on their psychological development.

Severe traumatic brain injury 33 months before neuropsychological examination. This child was 7 years, 4 months of age at the time of neuropsychological examination and had been very seriously injured in an automobile accident at the age of 4 years, 7 months. Immediately following the injury she was admitted to the hospital in critical condition. She was essentially comatose and responded only with reflex reactions to painful stimuli. She also was having continuous focal seizures involving the left face and left upper extremity. Very shortly following the injury she had been partly conscious and her pupils had been equal in size and had reacted properly to light. However, at the time of admission her pupils were fixed and the right pupil was clearly larger than the left. She had a 6-cm. right frontal scalp laceration and skull films showed the presence of a linear skull fracture in the right frontal area. The patient was taken to surgery immediately and bilateral burr holes were made. The initial exploration was adjacent to the right frontal skull fracture where a small amount of epidural blood, but no significant hematoma, was found. However, a considerable degree of cerebral contusion was evident in both cerebral hemispheres. Extensive damage to the right temporal lobe was visible and right subtemporal decompression was carried out. For 24 hr. following the operation the patient remained comatose and in a state of decerebrate rigidity.

During the third week of hospitalization her level of consciousness began to show some improvement. It became apparent at this time that the child had a severe paralysis of her right face and limbs. She also was entirely mute, suggesting the possibility of severe aphasia. Electroencephalographic tracings had been done on repeated occasions following the operation and consistently showed the presence of generalized delta waves. About 6 weeks after the injury, the patient had improved sufficiently so that she could begin treatment in physical and speech therapy. She underwent such treatment for about 1 month before discharge. At the time of discharge she was able to stand and walk with some assistance and had some prehensile use of the right upper extremity. She had shown a definite improvement of speech functions during the last 2 weeks of hospitalization and seemed able to understand nearly everything but was able to speak only in short sentences. The final diagnosis was bilateral contusion of both parietal and temporal areas with residual paralysis of the right face and limbs, aphasia, and a right homonymous hemianopsia.

Neuropsychological examination indicated that this child was generally impaired. The Wechsler Intelligence Scale for Children yielded IQ values, as shown in Table 7, which fell in the range of mild-to-borderline mental retardation. We would estimate that there was no practical significance to the difference between levels of Verbal and Performance intelligence. Instead, the more meaningful conclusion would be that the child was impaired in both areas. As would be expected, she also was doing somewhat poorly with respect to academic progress. The child was presently repeating the first grade in school. Average achievement scores would have been 2.0 grade levels, but this child was performing only in the early part of the first grade in both reading (word recognition) and spelling abilities. However, her arithmetic skills were at the beginning of the second-grade level. It is often difficult to use academic achievement results as a basis for assessing the potential of a child for developing academic skills because of great variability in the degree of assistance and tutoring that may have been provided for any particular child. As noted in the

TABLE 7

Psychological Test Results on a 7-year, 4-month-old Left-handed Girl Who Had Suffered Traumatic Brain Injury 33 Months Earlier

Wechsler Intelligence Scale for Children		Reitan-Indiana Neuropsychological Test Battery	
Verbal IQ	76	*Category Test*	25
Performance IQ	69	*Tactual Performance Test*	
Full Scale IQ	70	Left hand: 7.4 min. (1 block placed)	
Verbal Weighted Score	31	Right hand: 7.4 min.	
Performance Weighted Score	28	Both hands: 6.6 min.	
Total Weighted Score	59	Time—Incomplete	
Information	8	Memory:	2
Comprehension	4	Location:	1
Arithmetic	5		
Similarities	5	*Finger Tapping Test*	
Vocabulary	8	Left hand: 34	
Digit Span	7	Right hand: 16	
Picture Completion	9	*Target Test*	7
Picture Arrangement	6	*Matching Pictures Test*	7
Block Design	5		
Object Assembly	5	*Marching Test*	
Coding	3	Coordination	0
Mazes	6	Left hand: 28 sec.; 0 error	
		Right hand: 48 sec.; 2 errors	
Wide Range Achievement Test		*Progressive Figures Test*—Discontinued at 185 sec.; 6 errors	
Reading	1.3	*Color Form Test*—94 sec.; 2 errors	
Spelling	1.3	*Tactile Finger Recognition*	
Arithmetic	2.0	Left hand: 0 error	
		Right hand: 2 errors	
		Finger-tip Symbol Writing	
		Left hand: 2 errors	
		Right hand: 0 error	
		Tactile Form Recognition	
		Left hand: 0 error	
		Right hand: 0 error	
		Strength of Grip	
		Left hand: 4.5 kg.	
		Right hand: 2.5 kg.	

previous section of this paper, a considerable degree of overlap in the groups with and without cerebral damage was present with regard to results on the Wide Range Achievement Test, even though the brain-damaged group consistently performed more poorly than the normal children. It is possible, therefore, that the Arithmetic achievement score of this child may have been a reflection of special tutorial assistance. However, again the more meaningful general conclusion would be one of impairment in academic progress.

The level of performance of this child indicated that she was impaired in most areas of function. Verbal abilities were at about the average for the brain-damaged group used in the first part of this study and visual-spatial and sequential abilities were even a little lower than the average for the brain-damaged group. Measures related to immediate alertness and incidental memory were also about comparable to the brain-damaged group. The child performed particularly well on the Category Test and achieved a score that was approximately at the average level for normal children. However, on other measures of concept formation and reasoning she performed very poorly. She was well below the average level even for brain-damaged subjects on the Matching Pictures Test. She had particular difficulty on the Color Form Test and performed much more poorly than the average brain-damaged child of her age. She was not able to complete the Progressive Figures Test and again performed much more poorly than most brain-damaged children of her age. She also did relatively poorly on the Arithmetic subtest of the WISC. Thus, it would appear that this child's general abilities were rather consistently impaired across a wide range of measurements.

The history of this child included definite evidence of traumatic brain injury which was observed and confirmed at surgery shortly following the injury. Thus the question of brain damage was clearly answered. However, it is of interest to evaluate behavioral examinations with respect to the basis they provide for drawing independent conclusions about the condition of the brain. The abilities of this child, reviewed above, certainly fell in the range characteristic of brain-damaged as compared with normal children, but it hardly would be defensible to conclude on this basis that this child was necessarily brain-damaged. Many other factors undoubtedly can contribute to poor ability levels in individual children. Tests of motor and tactile-perceptual functioning, however, suggested rather definitely that cerebral damage was a contributing factor with respect to the general psychological deficit. The child was presently left-handed but before the injury had been showing definite signs of developing right-handedness. The present results indicate that the child performed relatively well with her left hand on the Tapping, Marching, and Tactual Performance tests. She was somewhat low in strength of grip with both hands, but this measure is quite variable from one child to the next. The more significant finding related to the consistent evidence of poor performances with the nondominant (right) hand as compared to left hand. While only mild impairment was present in functions of the left hand, the child was consistently impaired on motor and psychomotor tests with her right hand. She performed particularly poorly with the right hand on the Tactual Performance Test and scarcely was able to make any progress whatsoever. Tactile-perceptual tests were performed better than motor and psychomotor tests, although the child had a little difficulty in tactile finger recognition with her right hand. However, she also had a little difficulty in fingertip symbol writing recognition with the left hand. The fact that these mistakes occurred, however, is a suggestive sign of cerebral damage even though the tactile-perceptual tests did not give differential lateralizing information.

In summary, measures of general intelligence and cognitive functions indicated that this child was seriously impaired in her level of abilities. These indications of impairment undoubtedly have serious consequences with respect to the potential of this child for eventual development. It is likely, for example, that a special educational-class placement will be necessary in order to achieve even the restricted potential that this child appears to have for academic development. Further, measures of motor and tactile-perceptual functions indicated quite clearly that the two sides of the body showed strikingly differential abilities, with the right side being impaired. In the context of general impairment of abilities, this finding suggests that the left cerebral hemisphere is more seriously involved than the right—a conclusion that is not inconsistent with the evidence of residual paralysis on the right side of the body at the time of discharge from the hospital shortly after the accident. It is likely, of course, that this child developed left-handedness because of impairment on the right side of the body. Serious impairment on the right side, however, probably has broader implications than those relating to handedness. The impairment on the right side probably reflects more significant involvement of the left than the right cerebral hemisphere. We have repeatedly observed instances of children with deficiencies on the right side of the body, across from the left cerebral hemisphere, who have particular difficulties in making adequate academic progress. This may not be unexpected in consideration of the fact that the left cerebral hemisphere customarily subserves language functions and related uses of symbols for communicational purposes. Thus, in the case of this particular child, we would recognize the need to be particularly alert in detecting possible deficiencies in academic progress as the child develops. In addition to showing a slowed rate of academic development, it is likely that this patient will need more frequent rehearsal and perhaps special conditions of positive reinforcement in order to sustain her interest and motivation and to avoid dropping further and further behind normal children of her own age.

A question of residual impairment following head trauma. The patient, a 5-year, 9-month-old boy, was struck by an automobile a few days after his fifth birthday and was immediately rendered unconscious. X-rays indicated a fracture of the midportion of the left clavicle and left pelvis, but skull films were normal. The boy seemed to make adequate progress for the first 6 days following injury but then he became more restless and lethargic and seemed to have increased movement difficulties on the left side. It was difficult to judge whether or not any significant degree of motor deficit was present in consideration of the fracture of the left clavicle. However, a definitely positive Babinski response was present on the left side. The child was in a varying state of consciousness for the first 6 days following the injury, but he failed to engage in verbal communication even when he appeared to be relatively alert. A right brachial angiogram was performed on the eighth day following the injury, but the procedure was judged to be unsatisfactory from a technical point of view. A brain scan performed 12 days after the injury showed some increased activity in the midline and to the right of the midline in the parietal area. A judgment was made that these overall results most likely indicated that some cerebral contusion had occurred. An electroencephalogram, performed on the same day as the brain scan, showed definitely abnormal tracings in the right frontal region. Immediately following these procedures the patient began talking and using his left extremities slightly. He showed steady improvement from this time until his discharge, almost 1 month after the injury. The diagnostic impression at this time was that the patient had sustained a closed head injury with contusion of the right frontal area and possibly of the posterior parts of each cerebral hemisphere. However, the child had shown substantial improvement and his physician doubted from the overall findings that any permanent brain damage had been sustained.

Neuropsychological examination was performed approximately 9½ months after the injury. The question at this time concerned whether or not any residual impairment was present. Neurological examination now yielded the impression that the child did have a very slight incoordination of the left arm and hand and that the left leg showed a mild diminution of motor strength as compared with the right leg. However, these deficiencies were judged as being extremely minimal and as representing scarcely any significant impairment.

The general intelligence of this child, as shown in Table 8, was well above the average level.

Inspection of the scaled scores showed a somewhat greater degree of variability than might normally be expected, but scores at the average level or above were earned on all subtests except for Comprehension and Coding. The Coding subtest oftentimes is poorly done by persons with even mild cerebral damage, but it would be difficult to discern from the results on the WISC, considered by themselves, that brain damage had been sustained.

This child also showed average or higher abilities in a number of other areas. Assessment of his verbal abilities and visual-spatial and sequential abilities all indicated average scores or somewhat above except for the Target Test. His general alertness seemed to be adequate and his incidental memory was as good as that of the average normal child. Arithmetical abilities, as indicated by WISC results, were extremely good. While the child performed at an average level on the Color Form and Matching Pictures Tests, he nevertheless manifested serious

TABLE 8

Psychological Test Results on a 5-year, 9 month-old Right-handed Boy Who
Had Been Struck by an Automobile 9 Months Eariler and in Whom a
Question Existed Regarding Possible Brain Injury

Wechsler Intelligence Scale for Children		Reitan-Indiana Neuropsychological Test Battery	
Verbal IQ	113	*Category Test*	45
Performance IQ	115	*Tactual Performance Test*	
Full Scale IQ	115	Right hand: 9.3 min.	
Verbal Weighted Score	60	Left hand: 10.2 min.	
Performance Weighted Score	61	Both hands: 1.8 min.	
Total Weighted Score	121	Time:	21.2 min.
Information	14	Memory:	4
Comprehension	8	Location:	4
Arithmetic	16	*Finger Tapping Test*	
Similarities	10	Right hand: 31	
Vocabulary	11	Left hand: 22	
Digit Span	13		
Picture Completion	10	*Target Test*	7
Picture Arrangement	12	*Matching Pictures Test*	14
Block Design	14	*Marching Test*	
Object Assembly	15	Coordination	52
Coding	8	Right hand: 34 sec.; 0 error	
Mazes	14	Left hand: 46 sec.; 4 errors	
		Progressive Figures Test—148 sec.; 2 errors	
		Color Form Test—36 sec.; 0 error	
		Tactile Finger Recognition	
		Right hand: 1 error	
		Left hand: 2 errors	
		Finger-tip Symbol Writing	
		Right hand: 1 error	
		Left hand: 0 error	
		Tactile Form Recognition	
		Right hand: 0 error	
		Left hand: 0 error	
		Strength of Grip	
		Right hand: 6.0 kg.	
		Left hand: 4.0 kg.	

impairment of certain aspects of concept formation and reasoning abilities as shown by very poor scores on the Category and Progressive Figures Tests. Thus, while the overall ability level of this child appeared to be at the average level or somewhat above, he performed poorly on certain tests. While these results might suggest the possibility of mild selective deficits in association with cerebral damage, there would be no way to infer definitely from the level of performance shown by this child that brain damage had occurred.

Evaluation of motor and tactile-perceptual functions, with special reference to the comparative performances on the two sides of the body, yielded significant information in regard to the question of brain damage. This child was consistently a little below the average in terms of level of performance on the various tests of motor function, but this result may be a reflection of his age. Of more significance was the indication of poor performances with the left hand as compared with the right hand. While neurological examination currently continued to indicate the presence of extremely minimal deficiencies on the left side, the deficits appeared more prominently in neuropsychological examination. Although measures of lateral dominance indicated that this child was strongly right-handed, right-footed, and right-eyed, his finger-tapping was quite slow with his left hand as compared with his right hand. Strength of grip was greater in the right (preferred) upper extremity as would be expected but, again, the left hand may have been just a little weak in comparison to the right hand. Results on the Marching Test clearly showed disparities in performance on the two sides. The left hand not only required more time to complete the task, but the patient made four errors when using his left hand and no errors with his right hand. Finally, the patient made no improvement on the Tactual Performance Test from the first trial (right hand) to the second trial (left hand), although he clearly was capable of improvement as shown by the excellent performance on the third trial when his right hand again was involved in the task. The child showed only relatively minor tactile-perceptual deficits but the fact that errors occurred at all on these tasks suggests the possibility of mild cerebral involvement.

These results suggested that the right cerebral hemisphere, across from the subject's left side, was mildly dysfunctional—a conclusion that would be perfectly consistent with the history and neurological findings shortly after the injury was sustained. It appeared, therefore, that the child had some mild but clear residual deficits which, in turn, suggested that the indications of selective impairment of certain higher level psychological abilities were also part of the overall picture of brain damage. Thus, while definite neurological evidence of cerebral damage was not available, it would appear from neuropsychological testing that this child had certain mild residual deficits due to brain damage. While we do not at this point know very much about specific recommendations that might be made in such an instance, it is entirely likely that the basic adaptive abilities of this child had been somewhat compromised, that special attention should be given to the possible occurrence of developmental deficits, and that every effort should be made to deal with the child in a consistent manner, recognizing the value of positive reinforcement in terms of shaping the child's behavior and in stimulating his motivation.

A question of brain damage as a basis for behavioral changes. Four months before the present examination this 6-year, 5-month-old boy was struck by an automobile. The bumper of the car hit the patient's leg, knocking him down and causing him to roll over several times. He was not thought to be completely unconscious from this blow, but he had bruises over his extremities and trunk. He also suffered a collapse of his left lung and developed fever and pneumonia. His recovery during hospitalization appeared to be entirely routine, but approximately 1 month after the injury, after his discharge, he began to have nightmares and episodes of sleepwalking. These occurred almost every night for nearly a 2-month period and not infrequently involved rather complex behavior. For example, his parents reported that one night he got out of bed, went out of the house, and climbed into the family station wagon. He spent some time climbing from one seat to the next and finally left the car by way of a window. At that point his mother asked him to return to the house, which he did. Although the patient was crying during all of this episode, he went directly to bed upon reentering the house and promptly fell asleep. On other occasions the patient awakened during the night screaming but did not get out of bed. Shortly after these episodes began, the patient developed severe headaches which were localized around the vertex and were worsened by physical activity. The patient also complained about visual peculiarities, noting that at certain times objects looked very small to him. His parents also noted general changes in his behavior. Whereas he previously had enjoyed playing outside of the house, he now preferred to stay inside and watch television. The patient's sleepwalking episodes had decreased in frequency during a several-week period and now occurred only about two out of every three nights. The parents were concerned that the child might have sustained some brain damage, which was now causing the behavioral changes, when he was struck by the automobile.

Because of these conditions the child was hospitalized again for several days for neurological and neuropsychological examination. The general physical and neurological examinations were entirely normal. Skull x-rays and an electroencephalogram were obtained and these also were normal. He was closely observed during 7 days of hospitalization and during this time demonstrated no unusual behavior.

Evaluation of lateral dominance indicated that this child had mixed-handedness although he was strongly right-footed and right-eyed. Although he used his left hand for writing, he tended to use his right hand for certain other unimanual tasks.

The Wechsler Intelligence Scale for Children yielded a Verbal IQ of 95, Performance IQ of 107, and Full Scale IQ of 101 (Table 9). Although the Performance IQ was 12 points higher than the Verbal IQ, inspection of the scaled scores for the individual subtests suggested that this difference may not

TABLE 9

Psychological Test Results on a 6-year, 5-month-old Left-handed Boy Who
Had Suffered a Mild Head Injury 4 Months Earlier and Who
Now Demonstrated Behavioral Changes

Wechsler Intelligence Scale for Children		Reitan-Indiana Neuropsychological Test Battery	
Verbal IQ	95	*Category Test*	16
Performance IQ	107	*Tactual Performance Test*	
Full Scale IQ	101	Left hand: 4.1 min.	
Verbal Weighted Score	46	Right hand: 4.5 min.	
Performance Weighted Score	55	Both hands: 2.4 min.	
Total Weighted Score	101	Time:	10.9 min.
Information	8	Memory:	6
Comprehension	8	Location:	0
Arithmetic	11		
Similarities	8	*Finger Tapping Test*	
Vocabulary	13	Left hand: 34	
Digit Span	7	Right hand: 36	
Picture Completion	13	*Target Test*	6
Picture Arrangement	9	*Matching Pictures Test*	15
Block Design	11	*Marching Test*	
Object Assembly	13	Coordination	7
Coding	9	Left hand: 31 sec.; 3 errors	
Mazes	11	Right hand: 24 sec.; 1 error	
		Progressive Figures Test—43 sec.; 0 error	
		Color Form Test—19 sec.; 1 error	
		Tactile Finger Recognition	
		Left hand: 2 errors	
		Right hand: 1 error	
		Finger-tip Symbol Writing	
		Left hand: 2 errors	
		Right hand: 0 error	
		Tactile Form Recognition	
		Left hand: 0 error	
		Right hand: 0 error	
		Strength of Grip	
		Left hand: 8.5 kg.	
		Right hand: 10.0 kg.	

have much practical significance. The range represented by the Verbal subtests was similar to that represented by the Performance subtests. Thus, it appeared that the general intelligence of this child was essentially within the average range.

Assessment of additional adaptive abilities suggested that the overall level of performance was approximately in the average range. Verbal abilities of this child were not very depressed and visual-spatial and sequential abilities were also at about the average level except for a somewhat low score on the Target Test. It appeared that the child's immediate alertness and efficiency on specified tasks may have been a little low, judging from the scores on the Digit Span and Coding subtests of the WISC. Incidental memory also was somewhat variable. He did very well in remembering the shapes on the Tactual Performance Test but performed poorly in recalling their proper location. The area of concept formation and reasoning ability seemed to be a little stronger than others. The child earned average scores on the Matching Pictures and Arithmetic tests whereas his performances on the Category and Color Form Tests were better than for most normal subjects. On the Progressive Figures Test he performed extremely well for a child of his age and readily comprehended and adapted to the changing clues provided in this test. Thus, in summary, some of his scores were well above average although most of them were at the average level or a little below. Under these circumstances it is conceivable that this child may have experienced some mild impairment as a result of brain damage, but the findings considered so far were hardly unequivocal in any such indication.

Results on motor and tactile-perceptual tests yielded fairly definite information suggesting that this child had experienced some generalized cerebral damage which involved the right cerebral hemisphere somewhat more than the left. He achieved approximately average scores, in terms of level of performance, in finger-tapping, strength of grip, and coordinated movements on the Marching Test with each hand individually considered. In each instance, however, he performed poorly with his left hand as compared with his right hand. Although this child showed evidence of mixed-handedness, the fact that he had developed writing skills with his left hand should have given that hand some advantage in these particular tasks. However, he was actually slower in finger-tapping speed with his left hand than with his right hand and had a strength of grip of only 8.5 kg. in his left upper extremity as compared with 10.0 kg. in his right upper extremity. On the Marching Test he not only required more time with his left than with his right hand but also made more errors. He also had a great deal of difficulty coordinating his hands with respect to the alternate movements required in the second part of the Marching Test, suggesting that he had some deficiency in motor coordination with his upper extremities. He did not have a great deal of difficulty on tactile-perceptual tasks but again made more mistakes with his left hand than his right hand. This was particularly significant with respect to fingertip symbol writing recognition inasmuch as he was able to perform perfectly with his right hand but made two mistakes with his left hand.

The only comparison of functional efficiency on the two sides of the body that deviated from this pattern occurred on the Tactual Performance Test. In this instance the child performed more poorly with his right hand than with his left hand and actually required more time on the performance with his right hand (second trial) than he had required with his left hand (first trial). This latter finding would suggest that cerebral dysfunction was not perfectly lateralized but that some left cerebral hemisphere dysfunction was present even though the right cerebral hemisphere seemed to be somewhat more involved.

These findings did not suggest that this child had any striking or serious impairment of brain functions or of corresponding intellectual and cognitive functions. However, they did suggest that the child had experienced some mild brain damage with corresponding behavioral deficits of a mild nature. In fact, the results were essentially in line with expectation, in consideration of the history, should positive evidence of brain damage have been discerned at all.

It is not possible to postulate a precise relationship between the behavioral disturbances of this child and the indications of very mild brain dysfunction. However, it is not unlikely that brain damage may reduce the threshold of an individual for inhibiting and controlling adverse emotional responses to stress-producing circumstances (Aita & Reitan, 1948). Considering the fact the etiology was traumatic in nature, improvement might very well be expected in time. Since mild brain damage may have been responsible for a reduction in the patient's ability to tolerate and resolve emotional problems, in comparison with his previous condition, it would seem to be important to provide additional emotional support in the child's environment (either through formal psychotherapy or through environmental adjustments or modifications) in order to avoid the development of problems which could conceivably themselves generate new difficulties of adjustment.

CONCLUDING COMMENTS

These illustrative instances provide evidence that it is possible to draw conclusions regarding brain-behavior relationships not only in children who have serious and general impairment of adaptive abilities but also for children who have relatively mild deficits. In fact, the results suggest that behavioral measurements may provide information for evaluation of the effects of brain damage in a considerably more sensitive manner than is customarily available through neurological evaluation. Further, information from anamnestic sources is frequently difficult to evaluate and some type of objective evidence is necessary in order to draw inferences regarding the possible role of brain damage in behavioral difficulties of individual children. It appears that neuropsychological testing, oriented toward evaluation of a broad range of abilities and considered within the context of the various methods of inference available for drawing conclusions about brain-behavior relationships, may provide such objective evidence. It should be clear from the illustrations presented that a method of evaluation oriented toward level of performance alone is not sufficient for developing a full understanding of the individual child. A great deal of information may be available through consideration of intraindividual relationships among the test results, both with regard to areas of function as well as to the two sides of the body. Thus, having studied children with known brain lesions to develop standards for neuropsychological inferences, one can apply the derived knowledge to children with suspected cerebral damage in a very profitable manner. Such an approach may eventually provide us with a sufficient understanding of the effects of brain lesions in individual children to permit development of training programs suited to the unique needs of children with particular constellations of deficits associated with brain damage.

5
BEHAVIORAL CORRELATES OF CEREBRAL DAMAGE IN CHILDREN AGED 9 THROUGH 14[1, 2]

Thomas J. Boll

SELECTIVE LITERATURE REVIEW

Much excellent work has been accomplished over the last 20 years in the area of human neuropsychology. Information has been provided about the relationship of many types and locations of brain impairment to adult adaptive abilities. The availability, for complementary use, of multiple inferential methods and a battery of tests providing behavioral data covering a wide range of human abilities of proven relevance to brain functions has made clinical application of this knowledge a rapidly growing practice (Parsons, 1970). With adequate training and experience a neuropsychologist can draw reliable inferences about the condition of the adult brain on the basis of a person's performance on a battery of behavioral measures. Such is not the case to a similar extent with children. In many individual instances, valid conclusions regarding cerebral damage can be reached. However, there remain a far larger

[1] The original research presented in this paper is based upon data collected at the Neuropsychology Laboratory, Indiana University Medical Center, under the direction of Dr. Ralph M. Reitan. The data collection was supported by Research Grants NB 02416, NB 05211, and NB 07178 (National Institute of Neurological Diseases and Blindness) to Dr. Reitan. The data analyses and preparation of the paper were supported by Grant HD 02274 to the Child Development and Mental Retardation Center, University of Washington, from the National Institute of Child Health and Human Development.

[2] The author assumes sole responsibility for the contents of this chapter. Nevertheless, this research has been built upon many of the conceptualizations of Dr. Ralph M. Reitan dealing with the neuropsychological evaluation of children's adaptive abilities. Therefore, a large portion of the credit for any knowledge and glimmerings of truth which can be gleaned from this report must go to Dr. Reitan without whose personal and scientific generosity this effort could not have been accomplished.

number of potentially interfering and confounding factors than is the case in work with adults. Such factors as age, general developmental rate and time of onset, and chronicity of disorder, while relevant for both adults and children, appear to play a far more crucial role in the latter group.

Within the literature relevant to children with known cerebral lesions, several reports stand out as important in more than one respect. Three such investigations will be considered individually and in some detail. In order of presentation below the three articles were authored by Ernhart, Graham, Eichman, Marshall, and Thurston (1963); Reed, Reitan, and Klove (1965); and Klonoff, Robinson, and Thompson (1969). These studies provide an amount of new knowledge unusual for single reports. The contribution of these articles, however, is not limited to reporting results on specific tests. They also discuss many problems and issues that must be dealt with along the road to an adequate understanding of brain-behavior relationships in children.

When Graham and Ernhart published their excellent monographs (Graham, Ernhart, Craft & Berman, 1963; Ernhart et al., 1963), the literature provided many sources of speculation with regard to the behavioral-personality concomitants of brain damage. The evidence behind such speculations was, and to a large extent continues to be, meager. When searching for previous work regarding intellectual-cognitive-perceptual abilities as they relate to known cerebral lesions, evidence had to be drawn primarily from work done with animals.

Graham and Ernhart were aware of the necessity of composing a battery of tests that tapped a wide sample of an individual child's adaptive abilities. Their procedures included measures of vocabulary, conceptual ability, perceptual-motor skill, and personality characteristics. A major limitation of this study relates to the time limit imposed on the testing procedures. "Selection and development of procedures were also influenced by the decision to limit testing to a period of less than one hour . . . " (Graham et al., 1963, p. 1). It is clear that no project can be free of limitations with respect to time, equipment, and subjects, among other crucial factors. However, as will be pointed out later, the adequate assessment of brain-behavior relationships is greatly enhanced by the use of a more comprehensive, albeit more time consuming, battery of ability measures.

The monographs by Graham, Ernhart, and their coworkers provided much informative discussion about such methodological issues as matching of subjects on variables which may or may not be independent of the condition under investigation. The difficulty in obtaining children for whom the diagnosis of brain damage was certain represented, then and now, a source of difficulty with regard to sample composition. The tendency for children with brain lesions to have low intellectual test scores made comparison with normal children with higher IQ problematic. This investigation did not solve all of these problems, even to the satisfaction of the authors. However, their careful consideration of these issues serves as an excellent source of information for any investigator who may be tempted to design a study without clearly appreciating the difficulties involved.

Despite limitations, these monographs provide much valuable and firmly documented data with regard to the psychological deficits experienced by children who have suffered brain impairment. Perhaps the most significant finding was that "no one of the tests selected a substantial number of brain injured" (Ernhart et al., 1963, p. 28). However, a composite index identified approximately 75% of the total brain-damaged group while misidentifying 10% of the normal group.

Results from this study indicated that children with brain damage were impaired in areas of language, concept formation, and perceptual motor ability, but showed relatively slight differences from normal children with respect to personality characteristics. Thus, the information derived was not consistent with previous, largely unverified, assumptions concerning personality chracteristics of brain-damaged children. The authors properly refrained from drawing a personality profile to fit "brain damage" as if it were a single entity and found that, at least in their sample, such frequently mentioned characteristics as the hyperkinetic syndrome were not typical.

They concluded that children and adults, when measured across a number of abilities, show differences in pattern of performance that could make the generalization of knowledge from one group to the other quite misleading. Children, as a group, tend to be impaired in vocabulary, concept formation, and perceptual-motor abilities. Adults show relatively greater impairment in conceptual and perceptual-motor functions while vocabulary level is less impaired.

Factors such as age at injury (Graham, Ernhart, Thurston, & Craft, 1962) or length of time since injury, with age at injury held constant (Teuber & Rudel, 1962), have been shown to influence not only level but also pattern of ability deficit. Such factors as type and location of lesion may well exert differential and ongoing influence on a child's rate and pattern of overall ability development. This developmental effect may in turn influence the type of life experiences each child encounters and also the manner and effectiveness with which they are handled. Such complex interactions have yet to be sorted out.

Work carried out during the last 20 years by Ralph M. Reitan and his associates has begun to shed some light on a limited number of these problems. Reitan first developed a battery of tests suitable for use with children. This battery utilized adaptations of and additions to the neuropsychological test battery developed for use with adults by Halstead (1947). Formal research with the battery developed by Reitan began in 1953, but it was not until 1965 that the first report of data from this extensive project was published by Reed et al. In their introduction, Reed et al. (1965) refer to the value of use of a large number of behavioral measures and the need for composition of groups of children who are not extremely heterogeneous with respect to their neurological condition. The fact that 12 years of well planned and actively pursued effort still left the latter of these two basic goals unfulfilled is a striking commentary on the size and complexity of the task of developing well-documented information in the area of brain-behavior relationships of children.

Reed et al. (1965) presented data derived from the use of 27 psychological-behavioral variables. This comparison of data on children (ages 9-14) with heterogeneous but firmly diagnosed brain damage versus a group who had normal brain functions served at least two major purposes. The first was a description, in a single article, of the types of tests utilized in a battery designed to be sensitive to the organic integrity of the brain. Of equal importance was the demonstration that these tests confirmed the conclusions drawn by Ernhart et al. (1963) with younger children. Reed et al. (1965) found that children with cerebral lesions were less adequate, on a wide variety of measures, than were children for whom there was no evidence or suspicion of neurological damage or disease. They also found that the brain-damaged children in this study performed more poorly on language-related or dependent tasks as compared with tasks that had a motor and/or problem-solving, nonlanguage requirement. Adults appear to be more impaired on tasks requiring current problem-solving ability and less impaired when able to rely on stored memory and experience. Using the data from Reed et al. (1965), Table 1 presents a ranking of the 27 tests based on size of mean difference scores obtained when the brain-damaged and normal children were compared. Of the 27 variables utilized in this study, the difference between the brain-damaged and non–brain-damaged groups was statistically significant beyond the .005 level in 24 instances. The differences between groups for the remaining three variables (Picture Completion; Tactual Performance Test, Memory; Finger Oscillation Test, dominant hand) reached significance at or beyond the .02 level. The significant difference between the two groups on each of these tests could be interpreted, by some, as indicating that Reed et al. had discovered 27 independent tests of brain damage. That the group data generated by any one test should not be applied to a single individual as an adequate measure of the status of his brain functions was made clear by Reed et al. (1965) in this same article. They demonstrated that the amount of overlap between the two groups on any single measure ranged from 4% (Digit Symbol Test) to 34% (Picture Completion Test). It is clear that application to a single individual of even highly reliable group data is a hazardous procedure. It is also apparent that no single test can adequately represent the behavioral consequences of widely variable cerebral lesions. Use of the entire battery, on the other hand, provides a far greater quantity of information with respect to an individual's adaptive-ability strengths and weaknesses. Thus, the measurements may be informative and clinically useful in describing the specific subject, whether or not a diagnostic classification of brain damage is made. The chances of understanding the psychological correlates of adequate brain functions are markedly increased when a more complete sample of brain-related behavior is elicited.

TABLE 1

Rank Order Distribution of Tests Used
by Reed et al., 1965, Based on Mean
Difference Scores of Brain-damaged
versus Control Children

Tests	Rank order
Wechsler Digit Symbol	1
Wechsler Total Weighted Score	2
Speech-sounds Perception Test	3
Wechsler Verbal Weighted Score	4
Trail Making Test (Total)	5
Wechsler Comprehension	6
Wechsler Vocabulary	7
Wechsler Similarities	8
Wechsler Information	9
Trail Making Test (Part A)	10
Trail Making Test (Part B)	11
Wechsler Performance Weighted Score	12
Wechsler Arithmetic	13
Time Sense Test (Visual)	14
Seashore Rhythm Test	15
Finger Oscillation Test (Dominant hand)	16
Wechsler Block Design	17
Wechsler Digit Span	18
Time Sense Test (Memory)	19
Tactual Performance Test (Localization)	20
Wechsler Object Assembly	21
Wechsler Picture Arrangement	22
Category Test	23
Tactual Performance Test (Total time)	24
Finger Oscillation Test (Nondominant hand)	25
Tactual Performance Test (Memory)	26
Wechsler Picture Completion	27

A final limitation on interpreting these data, mentioned by the authors, relates to their use of a single inferential method. As is true of almost all published psychological research dealing with group comparisons, level of performance (good versus poor) is the sole criterion used in deciding whether or not the two groups differ. While this method is a perfectly valid one, it does not exhaust the information the data can provide to the individual clinician. The combined use of several inferential methods is discussed in detail by Reitan (Ch. 2, this volume) and elsewhere by Reitan (1967a) and Russell, Neuringer, and

Goldstein (1970). An example of the complementary use of these methods in separating and identifying groups of children with and without brain damage was presented by Boll and Reitan (1972a) and will be discussed later in this chapter.

The many methodological issues in the field of brain-behavior relationships, while not all subject to solution at this time, alert us to the necessity of careful verification of hypotheses through well-designed experimentation if an organized body of knowledge rather than a system of fervently held beliefs is to be the result. Certain of the questions initially faced by Ernhart et al. (1963) and Reed et al. (1965) have recently been dealt with by Klonoff et al. (1969) in the first report of what promises to be a comprehensive and exceedingly valuable investigation of the behavioral consequences of brain damage in children. These authors address the problem of acute versus chronic neurological impairment in children under 9 years of age. The tests utilized in this study, while similar in large measure with those used in the previously mentioned studies, also include several other procedures described elsewhere (Benton, 1959; Benton & Spreen, 1963).

Klonoff et al. (1969) offer the first presentation, in one article, of results from a comprehensive evaluation of the effects of acute versus chronic brain damage in children aged 5 through 8. This fact alone gives the study considerable potential significance. It certainly underscores the disparity between the amount of speculation which has been published and the amount of firmly documented information upon which such speculations might be based. The method and design of the projected series of studies was dealt with in some detail and the neuropsychological tests employed were described. The paper placed an emphasis on the many methodological issues which can influence the adequate prosecution of such research. Such factors as potential sex differences, procedures for development of a scaling system for assessing severity of trauma, and methods for assessment of presence of neurological disorder received detailed consideration.

Children without past or present evidence of neurological or emotional disorders were evaluated to form a normative group and to provide information with respect to possible sex differences and the effect of age upon the tests used. Findings with respect to sex differences were sufficiently minimal to allow the authors to combine males and females into a single group for the purpose of comparison across age levels. As was predicted, a significant increase in ability level was noted with increasing age within the range of 3–8 years on the neuropsychological tests. No such age-related increase would be expected in IQ scores. The correlations between IQ and neuropsychological tests were significant in relatively few instances. The normal group (IQ = 113.38) exceeded the acute brain-damaged (IQ = 101.23) and the chronic brain-damaged group (IQ = 96.13) in measured intelligence and the difference was significant in both instances ($p < .01$). The neuropsychological findings were, in general, quite consistent with expectations. The differences between the normal and acute group reached statistical significance on 24 of the 32 variables. Discriminant analyses were applied to the data and revealed 91.64% of the children were correctly assigned to either normal or brain-damaged classification while 89.69% were correctly classified as having chronic brain damage, acute brain damage, or as normal. When discriminant analysis was applied by age levels, the degree of correct classification into normal, chronic, or acute groups increased from 79.63% for 3-year-old subjects to 96.43% or greater for subjects 6 years of age and older. When level of performance was examined, the chronic group was generally more severely impaired than was the acute group in relation to their respective matched normals. Multivariate relationships of neuropsychological test performance, as implied by the results of the discriminant analyses, were also distinctly different in the acute and chronic groups. Emphasis in this study was placed on the relationship of neuropsychological tests to other neurological diagnostic procedures. Findings from neurological examination and EEG consistently reached some degree of abnormality in the chronic group as did data from the neuropsychological tests. It was not felt that findings from the acute group could be used to predict residual EEG or physical neurological examination abnormalities. Followup testing, included in the overall plan of this research and reported in this volume, sheds further light on the course of human adaptive abilities after head trauma. In discussing the neurological, neuropsychological, and EEG parameters the authors conclude:

> Whereas the findings from the three disciplines were consistent in pointing to extensive impairment, statistical analyses failed to establish [un]equivocal relationships between the parameters regarding the details of impairment. There are a number of possible explanations for the absence of consistent relationships between the three variables, e.g., the neurological schemes were too global, the neuropsychological tests were not discriminating specific loss of function, or each discipline was measuring a somewhat different facet of biopsychological functioning (Klonoff et al., 1969, p. 210).

It would appear that the conclusions from an analysis of even the most careful and comprehensive studies leave one with far more new questions asked than old ones answered. Questions dealing with the influence upon adaptive abilities of such factors as type and location of lesion or disease process, age of onset of lesion, and nature of experiences and development prior to impairment remain unanswered (see Klonoff & Low, this volume; Klonoff & Paris, this volume).

These questions impose requirements with regard to subject availability which place significant progress in these areas beyond the scope of this paper. Instead, the remaining pages of this report will deal with new data providing a replication and extension of the study by Reed et al. (1965). Results will also be presented from a recently completed study dealing with the issue of the qualitative versus quantitative nature of ability deficit experienced by children with brain damage. In addition, an initial description of the comparative ability of selected individual tests to identify children with and without brain damage will be presented as will a method for complementary utilization of multiple inferential methods.

VALIDITY OF THE HALSTEAD NEUROPSYCHOLOGICAL TEST BATTERY FOR CHILDREN

Klonoff et al. (1969) and Reitan (Ch. 4, this volume) have described, in some detail, procedures involved in the neuropsychological evaluation of children of early school age. The tests included in the Halstead Neuropsychological Test Battery for Children as well as several other tests which are regularly used in many laboratories, including those at the Indiana University Medical Center and the University of Washington, have been described as a unit by Reitan and Heineman in 1968 (see also Appendix, this volume). Therefore, a separate section will not be devoted to detailed description of each test. However, some mention will be made of each, and tentative hypotheses as to the functions they tap will be included with the presentation of the statistical results. The primary purpose of presentation of this data is a replication and extension of the study by Reed et al. (1965), the first with this battery of tests for children aged 9–14 years. If such techniques are to be utilized with the degree of certitude hoped for from an empirically oriented discipline, such information is indispensable.

Methods of Procedure

Subjects. Twenty-seven brain-damaged children were matched for age, race, sex, and handedness with 27 children who had neither past nor present evidence of cerebral damage or disease. In each group there were 16 males and 11 females. The mean age of the brain-damaged subjects was 146.59 months (SD = 19.19) and the mean age of the control group was 143.15 months (SD = 18.92). The age differences between the groups did not approach statistical significance. The neurological diagnoses of the brain-damaged subjects included 3 instances of cerebral tumor, 10 of traumatic injury, 4 of congenital vascular anomaly, 6 of inflammatory disease, and 4 of perinatal lesions.

Tests. All of the tests were individually administered by thoroughly trained technicians. The technicians did not know the neurological diagnoses of the children nor were they aware of the purpose or design of the study.

The tests utilized and the publications in which they have been described include: the Wechsler-Bellevue (Form I) (Wechsler, 1944); the Wide Range Achievement Test (Jastak & Jastak, 1965); the Trail Making Test; and the Halstead Neuropsychological Test Battery for Children (Reed et al., 1965; Reitan, 1967a; Reitan & Heineman, 1968). The Halstead battery is composed of the Category Test, Tactual Performance Test, Rhythm Test, Speech-sounds Perception Test, Finger Oscillation Test, and Time Sense Test. Other tests described in detail elsewhere were the Tactile Finger Localization, Finger-tip Number Writing Perception, and the Reitan-Klove Tactile Form Recognition Tests (Reitan, 1967a). The strength-of-grip test utilizes the Smedley hand dynamometer and provides a measure of hand strength for both right and left sides of the body (Reitan & Heineman, 1968).

Three descriptive measures of lateral dominance were also administered to obtain information regarding handedness, footedness, and eyedness. Each subject was requested to perform seven unimanual tasks with his hand (throw, hammer, etc.) and two with his foot (kick and stamp) and the number of times each hand or foot was used was recorded. The Miles ABC Test of Ocular Dominance was used to provide information regarding eyedness. The subject was required to make 10 sightings through a V-shaped scope which allowed use of only one eye without the subject's awareness of this limitation. The number of times each eye was used constituted the subject's score.

Data analysis. The raw scores for both groups were combined, ranked, and converted to normalized T scores with a mean of 50 and a standard deviation of 10. T scores for subjects with and without brain lesions were then reassembled in their appropriate groups and the difference in means, for each of the variables, was analyzed by t ratios for statistical significance.

Results. The data presented in Table 2 clearly indicate that the level of performance of children with known brain damage, on a battery of psychological-behavioral measures, is less adequate than the performance of matched children with normal brain functions. The generalized decrease in ability seen in a group of children with heterogeneous brain damage is clear from the fact that 32 of the 40 variables significantly differentiated the brain-damaged and normal groups at or beyond the .05 level. In fact, differences between the groups reached significance at the .005 level for 19 variables and the .001 level for 11 of these.

Of the eight tests that failed to differentiate the distributions of children with and without cerebral lesions, five were measures of tactile-perception (Tactile Form Recognition—right and left hands; Finger-tip Number Writing Perception—right and left hands; and Tactile Finger Localization—left hand). Results on two tests of incidental memory (Tactual Performance Test, Memory and Localization scores) failed to differentiate the two groups. The Picture Completion subtest was the only Wechsler variable on which performance of brain-damaged and non-brain-damaged children did not differ significantly.

For purposes of discussion, the variables will be considered in 13 categories. These categories were composed to organize the total number of variables according to the types of abilities measured. The categories were formulated on the basis of clinical judgment and face validity rather than through use of statistical procedures such as factor analysis.

Category I   Verbal Tests of the Wechsler-Bellevue Scale (Form I) (Information, Comprehension, Digit Span, Arithmetic, Similarities, Vocabulary)

Each of the verbal subtests differentiated the children with and without brain damage at or beyond the .005 level except for Information ($p < .05$). The results of this study were consistent with the findings of Ernhart et al. (1963) and Reed et al. (1965). They indicated that children with brain damage experienced

TABLE 2

Raw Score and T-Score Means, t Ratio and Probability Level Based on Performance of Brain-damaged versus Control Children on the 40 Tests Utilized in This Investigation

Rank	Tests	Raw-score means		T-Score means		t	p
		Brain-damaged children	Controls	Brain-damaged children	Controls		
1	Name Writing (Nondominant hand)	48.56	23.56	43.41	56.60	6.58	.001
2	Trail Making Test (Part A)	38.26	16.22	44.04	55.95	5.77	.001
3	Performance IQ	87.56	109.96	44.86	55.13	5.23	.001
4	Comprehension	4.30	7.37	44.12	55.68	5.12	.001
5	Full Scale IQ	81.56	108.22	44.75	55.24	4.77	.001
6	Digit Symbol	5.33	8.44	44.40	55.67	4.69	.001
7	Trail Making Test (Part B)	106.33	32.67	44.37	55.62	4.59	.001
8	Name Writing (Dominant hand)	19.89	9.93	44.71	55.40	4.55	.001
9	Vocabulary	4.78	7.19	44.82	55.15	4.13	.001
10	Strength of Grip (Nondominant hand)	12.81	19.28	45.64	54.36	4.04	.001
11	Verbal IQ	79.78	104.89	44.89	55.10	3.96	.001
12	WRAT (Spelling)	3.87	6.03	45.16	54.85	3.92	.005
13	Block Design	6.19	9.67	45.35	54.71	3.88	.005
14	WRAT (Reading)	4.45	6.76	45.32	54.69	3.64	.005
15	Tapping (Nondominant hand)	24.89	33.96	45.58	54.48	3.58	.005
16	Time Sense Test (Visual)	307.51	114.54	45.39	54.66	3.44	.005
17	Speech-sounds Perception Test	18.19	8.89	45.66	54.27	3.29	.005
18	Similarities	6.15	8.78	45.54	54.31	3.17	.005
19	Arithmetic	3.81	6.70	46.05	54.17	3.08	.005
20	Seashore Rhythm Test	20.41	24.63	46.60	53.33	2.76	.025
21	Category Test	64.07	43.74	46.04	53.95	2.69	.025
22	Tactual Performance Test (Nondominant hand)	2.48	.57	46.85	53.14	2.67	.025
23	Picture Arrangement	6.26	8.85	46.76	53.38	2.61	.025
24	Information	5.00	7.37	46.21	53.79	2.58	.025
25	Digit Span	5.11	7.30	46.50	53.59	2.57	.025
26	Tapping (Dominant hand)	32.63	37.56	47.19	52.79	2.52	.025
27	Strength of Grip (Dominant hand)	16.50	21.17	46.86	53.14	2.51	.025
28	Tactile Finger Localization (Right hand)	2.89	1.19	47.45	53.40	2.45	.025
29	Time Sense Test (Memory)	557.90	303.87	46.64	53.39	2.27	.05
30	Object Assembly	6.93	9.04	47.21	52.71	2.20	.05
31	Tactual Performance Test (Both hands)	1.20	.33	47.10	52.89	2.14	.05
32	Tactual Performance Test (Dominant hand)	3.05	.82	47.05	52.94	2.07	.05
33	Tactile Finger Localization (Left hand)	3.37	1.44	47.94	52.86	2.05	.10
34	Tactile Form Recognition (Left hand)	.81	.07	48.92	52.51	1.95	.10
35	Picture Completion	7.19	8.37	47.78	52.23	1.77	.10
36	Finger-Tip Number Writing (Right hand)	4.52	2.52	47.54	52.23	1.73	.10
37	Tactual Performance Test (Localization)	2.33	3.15	48.07	52.10	1.54	.20
38	Finger-Tip Number Writing (Left hand)	4.22	2.96	49.03	50.45	.466	.70
39	Tactual Performance Test (Memory)	4.41	4.63	49.37	50.37	.412	.70
40	Tactile Form Recognition (Right hand)	.59	.33	50.24	51.16	.402	.70

considerable difficulty with tests requiring reliance upon past learning and experience, especially when a requirement for verbal expression was included.

Category II Performance Tests of the Wechsler-Bellevue Scale (Form I) (Picture Arrangement, Picture Completion, Block Design, Object Assembly, Digit Symbol)

These tests might be presumed to measure visual-perceptual problem-solving skills. Two of these tests (Block Design and Digit Symbol) differentiated the two groups at or beyond the .005 level of significance while two reached significance at the .05 level (Picture Arrangement and Object Assembly). The one performance test (Picture Completion) which failed to differentiate the two groups has neither a temporal, problem-solving, nor motor requirement. It appears, instead, to rely upon visual recognition skills and general environmental awareness and memory.

Category III Pure Motor Skill

Measures of finger-tapping speed (Finger Oscillation Test) and strength of grip (Smedley hand dynamometer) were obtained for the dominant and nondominant hand of each subject. Performance of the dominant hand ($p <$ .025) and nondominant hand ($p <$ .005) on each test produced differences between the two groups that attained statistical significance.

Category IV Motor Problem-solving

The Tactual Performance Test relies upon tactile and kinesthetic feedback, in the absence of visual cues, for the completion of this task. Speed of performance of the dominant and nondominant hands individually and both hands working together is obtained. Each of these three measures (dominant hand, nondominant hand, and both hands) produced significant differences in performance between the two groups ($p < .05$). However, differences significant at the .05 level reflect a high degree of overlap among the individual subjects in the two groups. In spite of the complex and unfamiliar demands of this test and its clinical usefulness when multiple inferential methods are employed (pattern and level of performance plus comparison of the right and left hands), the use of level of performance alone resulted in this test ranking among the less sensitive variables with respect to its ability to separate the two groups.

Category V Visual Motor Problem-solving

The Trail Making Test, Part A, requires the subject to locate numbers on a page and engage in rapid motor movements to connect the numbers in order from 1 to 25. Part B requires the subject to alternate numbers and letters connecting them in order, i.e., 1-A-2-B-3-C, etc. The requirement in Part B for the processing of both linguistic and numerical symbols is an additional factor as compared with Part A.

The results of this study confirmed the finding of Reed et al., (1965) that a group of heterogeneously brain-damaged children performed on both Part A and Part B of the Trail Making Test significantly less adequately than did a matched group with normal brain functions ($p < .001$).

Category VI   Tactile Perception

While children's perceptual abilities have received much attention, this attention has focused primarily upon vision and audition. Three measures of tactile-perceptual ability for each hand were obtained in this investigation. These included Tactile Finger Localization, Finger-tip Number Writing Perception, and Tactile Form Recognition. With the exception of Tactile Finger Localization—right hand ($p < .05$), the performance of the children with brain damage, while characterized by a larger absolute number of errors, failed to differ significantly from that of children without brain damage ($p > .05$).

Category VII   Academic Development

The Reading and Spelling sections of the Wide Range Achievement Test produced significant differences between the children with and without brain damage ($p < .005$). This test was not specifically designed to be sensitive to the organic integrity of the brain. The ability of this test to differentiate between these groups, while not necessarily reflecting more than the generalized disability seen in children with brain damage, nevertheless provides a type of specific information of clear significance for the individual patient.

Category VIII   Auditory Perception (Verbal and Nonverbal)

The Seashore Rhythm Test taps a person's ability to recognize, as same or different, two series of beats presented on a tape recorder. The difference between the groups on this test was statistically significant ($p < .025$). The Speech-sounds Perception Test requires both auditory perception and visual recognition of tape-recorded nonsense syllables. The language component of this test has been shown to present particular difficulties to aphasic adults (Reitan, 1960). Specific conditions of deficit in brain-damaged children which may relate to speech-sounds perception are not known, but in the present study the brain-damaged children did significantly less well than did the control children ($p < .005$).

Category IX   Visual Motor Reaction and Temporal Estimation

The visual component of the Time Sense Test, which requires the subject to stop a sweep second-hand at specific points, differentiated the two groups with a high degree of significance ($p < .005$). The memory component is a task which, on its face, would seem more demanding. It requires the subject to estimate an elapsed period of time. This task was also performed significantly less adequately by subjects in the brain-damaged group ($p < .05$). The control subjects obtained a much lower mean error score on the memory component than did the brain-damaged group but the degree of variability, and, therefore, overlap between the groups, was large. (Brain-damage mean error, 557.9; *SD*, 487.46; Control mean error, 303.87; *SD*, 254.3). Both aspects of this test produced significant differences between the groups here as well as in an earlier study with children (Reed et al., 1965) and with adults (Reitan, 1955a). The test has tended to produce a somewhat less striking separation between groups of adults with and without brain damage than the other measures within Halstead's battery. This factor, combined with the tedious and time-consuming aspects of its administration, has resulted in its omission by Reitan from the list of tests recommended for routine use. Despite the statistically reliable results obtained for groups of brain-damaged and normal children, a major difficulty for the clinical use of this test remains. The large intragroup variability makes the performance of an individual subject difficult to categorize as impaired or normal. For this reason, as well as for reasons relating to the tedious nature of the task, the Time Sense Test is no longer routinely included as part of the Halstead Neuropsychological Test Battery for Children.

Category X   Incidental Memory and Alertness

The memory and localization scores of the Tactual Performance Test measure the ability of a subject to benefit from aspects of a problem-solving experience to which his attention has not been specifically directed. The results in this study indicate that these measures were not sufficiently sensitive to the condition of the cerebral hemispheres to differentiate the two groups at the .05 level. In the Reed et al. study (1965) the memory and location components of the Tactual Performance Test ranked 26 and 20 respectively of the 27 tests. In this study they ranked 37 and 39 out of 40. The small difference between the groups in this study appears to result from the relatively good performance of the brain-damaged subjects rather than poor performance by the controls.

Category XI   Concept Formation

The Halstead Category Test has been found, in a large number of studies (Reitan, 1966b), to be very sensitive to impaired brain functions in adults. It appears to measure a person's ability to grasp the essential nature of problem situations and to postulate solutions indicating benefit from past trial and error. It requires flexibility and an ability to abstract and develop concepts, but does not require verbalized explanation nor even the ability to verbalize the bases of solution for the problems involved. The children with known brain damage performed significantly less well on this test ($p < .025$) than did children without evidence of cerebral impairment.

Category XII   Summary Intelligence Measures

The Verbal, Performance, and Full Scale Intelligence quotients derived from the Wechsler-Bellevue (Form I) provide, in summary form, an indication of general psychometric intelligence. When subjects, whether adult or children, are carefully matched on such non–brain-dependent variables as sex and age, the level of psychometric intelligence usually reflects significant differences between groups with and without brain damage (Reitan, 1959a; Reed et al., 1965). Considerable refinement of the relationship of aspects of IQ to location of lesion has been possible with adult patients (Andersen, 1950; Meier & French, 1966a). Similar types of relationships between the Verbal and Performance IQ and the two cerebral hemispheres are not as consistently well established for children (Pennington, Galliani, & Voegele, 1965; Fedio & Mirsky, 1969). However, the results from the present study are consistent with many others in indicating that Verbal, Performance, and Full Scale IQ were significantly different between the two groups ($p < .001$) with the brain-damaged subjects performing more poorly.

Category XIII Name Writing

The ability to write one's name is subject to considerable variation with respect to the age at which this task is learned. It is usually a well-practiced activity by age 10 or 11 even in children with brain damage. Despite its familiar nature, the rapidity with which this task is usually performed differs significantly between children with and without brain damage ($p < .001$). The children were not instructed to hurry and were allowed to write their own names in their accustomed manner. The time required by the brain-damaged patients was, on the average, over twice that required for their matched controls regardless of whether comparisons were made for the dominant or nondominant hands.

The results presented in Categories I through XIII confirm, in an overall manner, those obtained in the only other comprehensive evaluation of brain-damaged and normal children (Reed et al., 1965) within this age range (9–14) published prior to the present volume (see Ch. 6 and Ch. 7 by Klonoff and associates, this volume, for additional data). Several tests not utilized by Reed, et al. were reported upon here. Nevertheless, data on 26 measures used in common between the two studies are available and can be directly compared. As shown in Table 3, the order of the 26 tests used in both studies bears a statistically significant relationship ($p < .01$) when they are ranked according to the size of the mean-difference scores obtained from comparison of the brain-damaged and non–brain-damaged groups.

In both studies, 7 of 14 Wechsler-Bellevue variables were included among those tests whose ranks (based on mean-difference scores) fell from 1 through 10. The average rank of the verbal tests of the Wechsler-Bellevue (Form I) was 9.2 in the study by Reed et al. (1965) and 12.5 in the current study. The performance subtests achieved an average rank of 16.8 and 15.4 in the 1965 and current data, respectively. The Halstead variables ranked 16.64 in 1965 and 15.50 in this investigation. The comparability of results of these two studies performed on differing populations of normal and heterogeneously

TABLE 3

Rank Order Distribution of Tests, Based on
Mean-difference Scores for Groups of
Brain-damaged and Normal Children

Variables	Rank order	
	Reed et al., 1965	Current data
Wechsler Verbal IQ	4	8
Wechsler Performance IQ	11	2
Wechsler Full Scale IQ	2	3
Wechsler Information	8	18
Wechsler Comprehension	5	4
Wechsler Digit Span	17	19
Wechsler Arithmetic	12	14
Wechsler Similarities	7	13
Wechsler Vocabulary	6	7
Wechsler Picture Arrangement	21	17
Wechsler Picture Completion	26	24
Wechsler Block Design	16	9
Wechsler Object Assembly	20	22
Wechsler Digit Symbol	1	5
Trail Making Test (Part A)	9	1
Trail Making Test (Part B)	10	6
Category Test	22	16
Tactual Performance Test (Time)	23	23
Tactual Performance Test (Memory)	25	26
Tactual Performance Test (Localization)	19	25
Seashore Rhythm Test	14	15
Speech-sounds Perception Test	3	12
Finger Oscillation Test (Dominant hand)	24	20
Finger Oscillation Test (Nondominant hand)	15	10
Time Sense Test (Visual)	13	11
Time Sense Test (Memory)	20	21

brain-damaged children separated in time by 6 years suggests that reliable and valid information about brain-damaged children can be obtained when standardized procedures are consistently followed. It is through such procedures that the information necessary for an understanding of the behavioral correlates of brain damage in children will continue to develop. It should be noted, however, that the data for both of these studies were collected in the same laboratory which provided continuity of supervision and monitoring of standardized testing procedures.

QUALITATIVE VERSUS QUANTITATIVE CHANGES

A large gap continues to exist between the amount of empirical data reported concerning adult subjects and that available for children. It is possible now to present three studies designed to investigate somewhat more specific questions dealing with the adaptive abilities of children with proven brain lesions.

A recent investigation conducted in this laboratory (Boll & Reitan, 1972b) appears quite relevant to an issue first raised by Goldstein (1940, 1942) with respect to the type of psychological deficit (qualitative versus quantitative) caused by cerebral damage. It was his belief that brain-damaged persons suffered a decreased ability to assume an "abstract attitude" and this deficit reflected a qualitative alteration rather than merely a quantitative reduction in adaptive ability. The implication of this position was that brain-damaged persons were not subject to objective psychological-behavioral assessment and comparison with normal individuals. Reitan (1958c, 1959b) devised research designs to study whether or not the same abilities were being measured in patients with and without brain damage. His findings indicated a high degree of agreement between correlation matrices for groups with and without brain damage. He concluded that, while differing in level, the abilities of these two groups were essentially similar in kind. These data provided strong support for the efficacy of use of quantitative procedures in the study of brain-behavior relationships. The patients considered in Reitan's studies were adults. As evidence mounts that the behavioral correlates of cerebral lesions in children and adults are different in many respects, the need for investigation with children of many of the same issues on which data are available for adults, becomes more apparent. Toward this end, an investigation was designed to determine whether the interrelationship among test performances differs between groups of children with and without impaired brain functions.

The same 54 children (27 with proved brain damage and 27 without past or present indication of neurological damage or disease, matched in pairs on the basis of age, race, and sex) that were utilized in the previous study were employed in this investigation. The mean age for the brain-damaged children was 146.59 months and the mean age of the normal children was 143.15 months. There were 11 females and 16 males in each group.

Intercorrelations were obtained among 14 Wechsler-Bellevue (Form I) variables and 14 neuropsychological test variables including all of Halstead's tests plus a measure of strength of grip for each hand. All possible correlation coefficients were computed and then converted to Fisher's z values. The standard error of the difference for z was found and the pairs of coefficients (brain-damaged versus normals) were compared for statistically significant differences. For each group, 378 coefficients were computed and compared for intergroup differences; 61 of the paired coefficients (brain damage versus normal) differed to a degree that reached statistical significance ($p < .05$). This is over three times as many significant differences as would have been expected due to the operation of chance factors alone.

The correlation of each Wechsler-Bellevue (Form I) variable with all other Wechsler-Bellevue (Form I) variables was compared for the two groups. Of the 91 pairs (brain damage versus control) of coefficients, the differences among 16 pairs reached statistical significance. A second step compared the correlation of each neuropsychological test variable with all other neuropsychological test variables and yielded 91 pairs of coefficients. Differences among 14 of these pairs (brain damage versus control) of coefficients reached statistical significance. Finally, comparisons were made between each Wechsler-Bellevue variable and all neuropsychological test variables. This comparison yielded 196 paired coefficients. Of these, 31 differed significantly ($p < .05$).

The data from this investigation are quite consistent in indicating a greater-than-chance occurrence of significant differences among coefficients of correlation for groups of children with and without brain damage on a wide battery of psychological-behavioral measures when all possible intertest correlations were computed. Such results are in contrast to those found by Reitan (1958c, 1959b) in comparing groups of adult subjects. If the two sets of intercorrelations had been essentially similar, it would have been possible to conclude that the tests utilized were not measuring different kinds of abilities in persons with and without brain damage. The opposite inference is not as easily drawn from the results that were obtained. It is possible to conceive of a number of factors, such as differences in intragroup variability, which could operate to cause the correlations to differ while still not reflecting qualitative differences in ability structure among children in the two groups. Certainly, however, these results offer another occasion for a note of caution to be raised. The conclusions drawn by Reitan concerning the apparent general similarity in ability structure of brain-damaged and normal adults do not appear to be necessarily applicable to children. It may be that brain damage in children is complicated by factors other than those customarily present in adult subjects. The pattern of abilities and/or their development may be altered by various types of cerebral impairment. Further investigation of these problems is necessary to answer this important question.

USE OF MULTIPLE INFERENTIAL METHODS

The potential advantages of combined use of more than one inferential method as compared to reliance on level of performance, or any other single method alone, have been discussed by Reitan in this volume. A recent study (Boll & Reitan, 1972a) has attempted to demonstrate the value of joint use of three inferential methods (level of performance, specific or pathognomonic sign, and right-left comparisons) in the assessment of motor and tactile-perceptual abilities of children with and without cerebral lesions. The disadvantages of restriction to a "level-of-performance" approach in the presentation of group data has been pointed out by Reitan (1967a) and Russell et al. (1970). The fact remains, however, that research in the area of human clinical neuropsychology, as well as in most other areas concerned with animal or human behavior, is represented in published studies by an almost exclusive reliance upon this single inferential method.

Thirty-five children with proved cerebral lesions were matched for age, sex, and handedness with 35 children who had no evidence of neurological damage or disease. The mean age of the brain-damaged children was 141.26 months (SD = 20.65) and 141.23 months (SD = 18.39) for the non–brain-damaged children. Each subject was tested for motor and tactile functions individually, in a completely standardized manner, and was able to take all tests during a single session. The motor tests included in the study were the Finger Oscillation Test, Strength of Grip Test, and Tactual Performance Test. The tactile-perceptual tests were Tactile Finger Localization, Finger-tip Number Writing Perception, and Reitan-Klove Tactile Form Recognition. Each subject performed each task with the right and left hand.

All control subjects were able to complete each test with each hand while nine of the subjects in the brain-damaged group were unable to perform one or more of the required tasks. If the all or none (presence or absence of a specified behavior) criteria of the pathognomonic sign approach were applied to this data, nine brain-damaged subjects would have been correctly classified with no incidence of false positives. However, the fact that 26 of the 35 children with known brain damage were able to perform all tests demonstrated that the sign approach, by itself, is far from adequate for even the relatively limited goal of classifying subjects as brain-damaged or non–brain-damaged.

Use of level of performance to compare the two groups provided clear differences between them. In order to explore level of performance, the brain-damaged subjects who failed to perform one or more tests and their matched controls were removed for this analysis and together are referred to as "failure group." Using only subjects who could perform all tasks, intergroup comparison of performance of each hand for each test resulted in differences significant at or beyond the .01 level for 8 of the 12 variables. Performance on the Finger-tip Number Writing Perception Test and Tactile Form Recognition Test on either hand was not significantly different between the two groups ($p <$ .20). When the nine brain-damaged subjects who had failed at least one task and their matched controls were added to their respective groups, all but one intergroup difference reached significance at or beyond the .05 level.

The similarities between the results of this study and those reported in Table 2 should be noted. In both studies, which used the same tests but different subjects, the tests of Finger-tip Number Writing Perception and Tactile Form Recognition failed to significantly differentiate the brain-damaged and control groups. The other tests (Finger-tapping, grip strength, Tactual Performance, and Finger Localization) did produce performances by the two groups which differed at or beyond the .05 level in every instance but one (Tactile Finger Localization—left hand).

The comparative performance of the two sides of the body of subjects with and without brain damage was also investigated. The direction of difference between the two hands was considered to be equally as important as the magnitude of difference between them. A conversion table was developed which rated the relationship of the right versus left or dominant versus nondominant hand.[3] If the two hands performed in a manner judged from clinical experience to be optimal with respect to their relationship, a score of 10 was applied. If the relationship of the scores obtained by the two hands was judged to be less than optimal, a score ranging from 9 down to 0 was applied. It was hypothesized that a more deviant relationship between performances of the two hands would occur in the brain-damaged group.

The hypothesis was confirmed, although not for each measure nor with the degree of reliability noted for the other two methods (sign and level). While each group showed significant differences in the performance of the two hands, the relationship between the two hands was less optimal for motor than tactile-perceptual measures. The control subjects showed more optimal relationships between performance of the two hands than did the brain-damaged subjects on the Tapping, Tactual Performance, and Tactile Finger Localization Tests.

This study demonstrated a possible method for group comparisons utilizing three methods of inference which were shown to be complementary in their contribution to knowledge about the effect of cerebral impairment upon motor and tactile-perceptual functioning. Work of this type may aid in broadening the perspective of clinicians and researchers alike and serve as a step toward bridging the familiar gap between clinical and statistical inferential methods.

COMPARATIVE ABILITY DEFICITS

The last, in what could be thought of as a sampler of current research approaches, addresses itself to the question of differential effectiveness of the various individual measures that make up a battery of neuropsychological tests. Questions such as, "If I had to choose one test, which would be the best?" or, "If two tests yield seemingly contradictory results, which do you believe?", are not uncommonly heard among clinicians. Such questions have little meaning when posed outside a rather carefully specified context. If the question included a qualification such as "for patients with tumors of the left cerebral hemisphere" or "in children with head injury," the problem would be available to empirical investigation. However, as such investigations have yet to be accomplished, the

---

[3] This table was developed for another publication (Reitan, 1971a) and has been filed with the American Society for Information Science in Document NAPS-01582.

answer to even a most carefully phrased query could hardly be very satisfactory. An initial attempt to deal with such an issue was made in which children who had known cerebral lesions, of heterogeneous types, were compared with children with normal brain functions (Boll, 1972). It is rather widely held that brain damage and perceptual disorders are importantly related. Diagnoses of "minimal brain disorder" are often made on the basis of a child's difficulty with tasks requiring perceptual (especially visual-motor) skill. Data presented throughout this chapter make it fairly apparent that, when children with proved brain damage are considered as a group, their abilities in almost all areas compare poorly with children without such impairment. The presence of specified areas or types of psychological-behavioral disability, which may be more marked than others, has yet to be clearly demonstrated although clinical impressions have crystallized to the point that certain types of disturbances (e.g., hyperactivity) are sometimes equated with brain damage. It was the purpose of this initial investigation to compare tasks of perceptual, conceptual, and motor ability to determine the comparability of deficit in these areas experienced by children with known brain lesions. Twenty-seven children between the ages of 9 and 14 with proved brain damage were matched for age and sex with 27 children for whom there was no evidence of present or past neurological damage or disease. The average age at which brain damage occurred was 78.26 months. Each child was tested in a completely standardized manner and was able to complete all tasks within a single session. Areas of perceptual functioning tested were visual (Wechsler Block Design Test), auditory (Seashore Rhythm Test) and tactile (Reitan-Klove Tactile Form Recognition Test). The Halstead Category Test was employed as the measure of conceptual ability. The Halstead Finger Oscillation Test was used as a measure of motor speed.

The method for effecting these comparisons was devised by Reitan (1959a) and warrants detailed mention here. The purpose of this method was to determine whether any particular test was more effective than another in differentiating the brain-damaged from control subjects within matched pairs. Because difference scores vary in terms of scaling units across several tests, the difference scores (control minus brain damage) were rank-ordered for each variable on either side of zero. For example, if each control subject obtained a better score on a particular test than the matched brain-damaged subject, the rank order of difference scores would range from $+1$ to $+N$ (with N representing the number of pairs of brain-damaged and control subjects; in this study N was 27). If 10 brain-damaged subjects bested their matched control, and 17 controls did better than their matched brain-damaged subject, the range of ranked differences would be -10 to $+17$. In this way, plus scores indicate instances in which the performances of the controls were better than the brain-damaged subjects, and minus scores indicate the opposite relationship. A score of zero was reserved for tied scores. Raw difference score distributions for each variable were converted to this type of standard difference score distribution in which the rank orders indicated the magnitude and direction of difference in performance between pairs of subjects in each distribution. These distributions were then tested, by the Wilcoxon matched-pairs signed-ranks test (Siegel, 1956), in comparing variables to determine whether one variable showed greater effectiveness than another in differentiating between the groups.

The results of this study indicated that the Category Test was significantly more sensitive to the presence of impaired brain functions than any of the perceptual measures (visual, tactile, and auditory; $p < .006$). The measure of concept formation ability also separated the matched (brain damage versus control) subject pairs more reliably than did the measure of motor speed ($p < .001$).

The visual perception test (Wechsler Block Design) was significantly more sensitive to brain damage in this study than were the tests of tactile form perception ($p < .001$) or motor speed (Finger Tapping) ($p < .01$). Auditory perception (Seashore Rhythm) bested tactile form perception ($p < .001$). Motor speed was more sensitive to presence or absence of brain damage than was the measure of tactile form perception ($p < .004$). Measures of visual and auditory perception did not differ significantly from each other in their sensitivity to presence or absence of brain damage. Tests of auditory perception and motor speed did not demonstrate differential sensitivity to the presence or absence of cerebral damage ($p < .20$). The results, while obtained with a relatively small group of heterogeneously brain-damaged subjects, indicate that information about the effect of brain damage, when obtained from patients with definite cerebral impairment, may not fit certain popular conceptions obtained through examinations of children with primary difficulties in various areas of socioeducational adjustment. In fact, a phrase such as "conceptually handicapped" might be more accurate than is the term "perceptually handicapped" when describing the deficits of a group of children with a heterogenous mixture of cerebral lesions.

ILLUSTRATIONS WITH INDIVIDUAL SUBJECTS

The fact that many questions concerning the behavioral correlates of brain lesions in children remain to be answered does not indicate that knowledge of immediate clinical significance is unavailable. The purpose of the present section is to illustrate the application of knowledge derived from the group investigations reported in this paper. Essentially the same neuropsychological tests will be used to report results for two children who represented different types of clinical problems. Although skill in individual interpretation necessarily is a function, at least in part, of experience, it should be apparent from the illustrations that inferences can be drawn about both the organic integrity of the cerebral hemispheres and the adaptive strengths and weaknesses of the individual child. Further, the methods used permit evaluation of the relationships between these two important areas.

The reason for evaluation of the first child was the question of a possible brain tumor. The question in the case of the second child did not concern itself with his medical health. In this instance, the child's behavioral and academic difficulties were of primary interest. In each case, an understanding of the behavioral correlates of impaired brain functions was essential to providing an answer to the questions asked. The first case has been quoted from a series of illustrative examples privately published by Reitan (1967c).

CASE NO. 1.   Patient G. H.:   A question of a brain tumor in a 14-year, 5-month-old boy.

This child had developed essentially normally and without significant medical, psychological, or adjustive problems except that he had experienced four episodes of a tingling sensation in the right upper and lower extremities and right face, during the last 1½ years. He also had suffered rather frequent headaches during this period of time. The patient had experienced such an episode followed by vomiting and headaches a few days before admission. In addition, shortly before admission he had had a nocturanal grand mal convulsive seizure. The patient had no history of serious head trauma. However, he had been unconscious briefly after running into a tree approximately 2½ years prior to admission, and 2 years prior to admission he had been hit on the left side of his head by a baseball and had been stunned. At the time of admission, physical neurological examination was entirely negative. Ophthalmological consultation was obtained, and a conclusion was reached that the eye grounds of this patient gave evidence of early papilledema. An electroencephalogram indicated the presence of dysrhythmia, Grade I, generalized and delta waves, Grade I, of the left temporoparietal area. This evidence, together with the indication of probable increased intracranial pressure, considered in conjunction with the history, raised very definite concern about the presence of an intracranial tumor.

The Wechsler-Bellevue Scale (Form I) was administered, and the patient obtained a Verbal IQ well into the superior range and a Performance IQ in the lower part of the high-average range. Inspection of the weighted scores for individual subtests indicated that the patient performed somewhat poorly on the Picture Arrangement subtest, but one could hardly infer the presence of cerebral damage from the pattern of results obtained. If anything, one might raise a question concerning the functional integrity of the right anterior temporal lobe on the basis of the Picture Arrangement score, but in the absence of other evidence an inference of damage or dysfunction in this area from the Wechsler results alone would certainly have to be most tentative in nature. [See Table 4 and Figure 1.]

Neuropsychological examination indicated that this child had good basic adaptive abilities and, in terms of level of performance, could hardly be thought to have a significant brain lesion. In this instance, level of performance on certain critical tests was of great significance in consideration of the tentative diagnosis. The patient did extremely well on the Category Test, and such an excellent performance, in its own right, would almost certainly rule out the prospect of an intrinsic cerebral tumor. In addition, if neoplastic involvement of the left cerebral hemisphere were to be postulated because of the EEG results, the excellent Verbal IQ and the good score on the Speech-sounds Perception Test would argue strongly against this conclusion. The excellent score on Part B of the Trail Making Test would also be quite incompatible with an hypothesis of a cerebral neoplasm. Nevertheless, an hypothesis could be raised concerning the possible presence of much milder cerebral dysfunction. Finger-tapping speed possibly was a little slow with the right hand as compared with the left hand in this right-handed boy. In addition, he made one mistake in tactile finger localization on his right hand but made no mistakes on his left hand. Even more-pronounced lateralized disparities were present on the Finger-tip Number

TABLE 4

Psychological Test Results for G. H., a 14-year, 5-month-old Boy
with a Question of Left Cerebral Intrinsic Tumor

PATIENT: G. H.   AGE: 14-5   EDUCATION: 8 years

Wechsler-Bellevue Scale (Form I)		Halstead's Neuropsychological Battery for Children	
Verbal IQ	135	*Category Test*	11
Performance IQ	112	*Tactual Performance Test*	
Full Scale IQ	126	(8 Block Board)	
Verbal Weighted Score	69	Right hand: 6.1 min.	
Performance Weighted Score	56	Left hand: 5.3 min.	
Total Weighted Score	125	Both hands: 2.7 min.	
Information	12	Time:	14.1
Comprehension	13	Memory:	5
Digit Span	10	Localization:	3
Arithmetic	17		
Similarities	17	*Seashore Rhythm Test*	2
Vocabulary	12	Raw score: 28	
Picture Arrangement	8	*Speech-sounds Perception Test*	9
Picture Completion	14		
Block Design	12	*Finger Oscillation Test*	40
Object Assembly	12	Right hand: 40	
Digit Symbol	10	Left hand: 37	
		Time Sense Test Memory	428.8
		Visual: 19.3	
Trail Making Test for Children		Sensory-perceptual Examinations	
Trails A: 23 sec., 1 error		*Tactile:* RH 0 LH 0 Both: RH 0 LH 0	
Trails B: 23 sec., 0 errors		RH 0 LF 0 Both: RH 0 LF 1	
Dominance Tests		LH 0 RF 0 Both: LH 0 RF 0	
		Auditory: RE 0 LE 0 Both: RE 0 LE 0	
Visual Dominance: R 10 L 0		*Visual:* RV 0 LV 0 Both: RV 0 LV 0	
		Finger Recognition: RH 1 LH 0	
		Finger-tip Number Writing: RH 8 LH 2	
		Coin Recognition: RH 2 LH 2	

Writing Perception Test. The subject made 8 mistakes in 20 trials on his right hand but only 2 mistakes in 20 trials on his left hand. The patient showed no definite evidence of aphasia, but when he was asked to name the square, he first identified it as a rectangle and then spontaneously corrected himself. These results would be consistent in suggesting that the patient had experienced some mild disturbance of functions in the left cerebral hemisphere and could be considered to be compatible with the EEG findings. The test results also implied some very mild dysfunction of

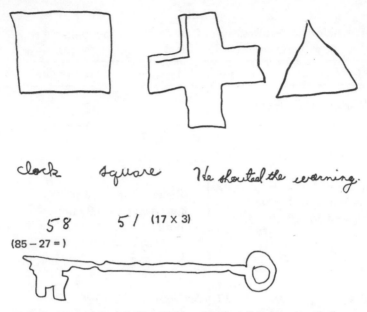

FIG. 1. Examples of spelling, writing, drawing of three geometric forms and a key, and arithmetic computation from patient G. H.

the right cerebral hemisphere. The patient showed a minimal tendency to fail to perceive a tactile stimulus to his left face when it was given simultaneously with one to the right hand. He also had some minimal difficulty in tactile coin recognition with his left hand as well as with his right hand. Finally, the speed of performance of the Tactual Performance Test was not quite as great with the left hand as one might have expected in consideration of the performance on the first trial with the right hand and with both hands on the third trial. However, all of these lateralizing indications had to be considered with relation to the level of performance as described above. While our results might have been indicative of mild cerebral dysfunction involving both the right and left cerebral hemispheres, we could hardly have concluded that the patient had an acute or progressive focal lesion of either cerebral hemisphere. We concluded in our interpretation that the patient had some very minimal impairment of brain functions that could be a residual of prior trauma or possibly of infectious disease involving the brain. The results, therefore, would be quite compatible with the history but hardly consistent with the conclusion of early papilledema.

Because of the evidence of papilledema it was felt that contrast studies should be performed. Angiographic findings were essentially normal, and a decision was made to follow this patient closely rather than to undertake additional diagnostic procedures or possible surgery. The ophthalmological findings remained constant during observation over a 2-month period, and the conclusion was finally reached that the peculiarities of the optic discs appeared to be within the range of normal variation and were subject to classification as pseudopapillitis rather than being indicative of intracranial hypertension. Treatment of this patient with anticonvulsant medication was begun, and he had no further sensory episodes or other complaints over the 3-month period during which he was followed. The final diagnosis, though tentative in nature, was that the patient had sensory seizures due to a possible static lesion in the left parietal area. Although the eventual diagnosis would certainly have been reached even if neuropsychological testing had not been done, in this instance the information indicating that this patient in all probability did not have a cerebral neoplasm was timely with respect to the development of the eventual understanding of the neurological complaints of this child and made a worthwhile contribution in his assessment. In other instances it is entirely possible that the results would not have been so strongly against a conclusion of a cerebral neoplasm, and neuropsychological findings would have been less helpful. It is worth bearing in mind, however, the psychological examination is entirely atraumatic and without danger in any physical sense; and, since the results might be helpful with respect to neurological diagnosis, this examination might well be indicated before using procedures that are not entirely without a certain element of risk.

CASE No. 2. Patient K. C.: A question of reasons for behavioral and academic difficulties. K. C. was a 12-year, 2-month-old boy referred by his parents and the school system who were equally unhappy with his poor academic record and his apparent inability to get along with other children. His parents indicated that, at age 4, he had complained of a bump on his head after a family car accident. When he was 3 he was rendered unconscious for a few seconds by a blow from a baseball bat. Nevertheless, physical and neurological examintion were reported to be within normal limits. He was described by his teacher as showing evidence of above average intelligence but very subnormal social consciousness.

The Wechsler Intelligence Scale for Children was administered and this boy obtained a Verbal IQ that fell in the range of borderline mental deficiency while his Performance IQ was within the range of average intellectual ability. It is not possible, relying upon the WISC alone, to conclude from even such a striking discrepancy in Verbal versus Performance intellectual functioning that the cause of these differences relate to impaired brain functions. It is possible to state that this boy's ability to deal with verbal problems and to benefit from the kinds of experiences most typically relied upon for adequate academic advancement are not sufficient to allow normal eductional progress. On the other hand, his ability to deal with visuospatial problem-solving types of tasks and to perform in a rapid and accurate manner in a situation with visual motor problem-solving requirements is quite adequate and falls within the normal range. [See Table 5 and Figure 2.]

The Wide Range Achievement Test was also given to this boy who, at the time of testing, had completed 5.7 years of education. He obtained grade level scores of 4.2 in Reading, 3.0 in Spelling, and 1.9 in Arithmetic. These scores indicated considerable academic retardation and made it clear that this boy was unable to compete successfully with his age mates in an academic setting. These results were quite consistent with his performance on the Wechsler Intelligence Scale for Children.

On an aphasia screening test K. C. showed marked difficulty in dealing with the symbolic aspects and the communicational significance of language symbols. He experienced difficulty naming simple objects and spelling words of a relatively simple nature. He also demonstrated considerable difficulty in reading, writing, and performing simple arithmetic computations. These difficulties were sufficiently severe to make understandable at least part of his problem in dealing with many of the verbal requirements of an academic situation. The kinds of difficulties he experienced are consistent with those seen in children who have suffered some degree of impairment of functioning of the left cerebral hemisphere. The findings on the WISC, while not themselves sufficient for implying organic impairment of the left hemisphere, may be viewed as consistent with that type of impairment, especially in the context of deficits of a specific nature in dealing with language and verbal symbols as determined in an examination for aphasia.

TABLE 5

Psychological Test Results for K. C., a 12-year, 2-month-old Boy with a
Question of Reasons for Behavioral and Academic Difficulties

PATIENT: K. C.	AGE: 12-2	EDUCATION: 5 years

Wechsler-Bellevue Scale (Form I)		Halstead's Neuropsychological Battery for Children	
Verbal IQ	76	*Category Test*	57
Performance IQ	103	*Tactual Performance Test*	
Full Scale IQ	88	(8 Block Board)	
Verbal Weighted Score	31	Right hand: 3.1 min.	
Performance Weighted Score	52	Left hand: 0.6 min.	
Total Weighted Score	83	Both hands: 1.0 min.	
Information	6	Time:	4.7
Comprehension	5	Memory:	5
Digit Span	7	Localization:	5
Arithmetic	7		
Similarities	8	*Seashore Rhythm Test*	10
Vocabulary	5	*Speech-sounds Perception Test*	7
Picture Arrangement	13		
Picture Completion	6	*Finger Oscillation Test*	42
Block Design	10	Right hand: 42	
Object Assembly	9	Left hand: 32	
Digit Symbol	14		

Trail Making Test for Children		Sensory-Perceptual Examinations	
Trails A: 15 sec., 1 error		*Tactile:* RH 0 LH 0 Both: RH 0 LH 0	
Trails B: 40 sec., 0 errors		RH 0 LF 0 Both: RH 0 LF 0	
		LH 0 RF 0 Both: LH 0 RF 0	
Jastak Wide Range Achievement Test		*Auditory:* RE 0 LE 0 Both: RE 0 LE 0	
		Visual: RV 0 LV 0 Both: RV 0 LV 0	
Reading: 4.2		*Finger Recognition:* RH 0 LH 1	
Spelling: 3.0		*Finger-tip Number Writing:* RH 0 LH 1	
Arithmetic: 1.9		*Coin Recognition:* RH 1 LH 1	
		Tactile Form Recognition: RH 0 LH 0	
Dominance Tests			
Hand Dominance: R 7 L 0			
Foot Dominance: R 2 L 0			
Visual Dominance: R 0 L 10			
Strength of Grip			
R: 28.5 kg. L: 18.5 kg.			

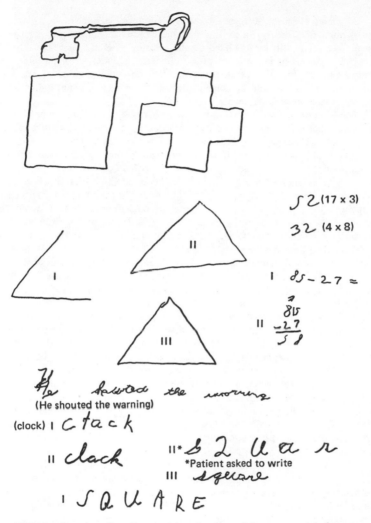

FIG. 2. Samples of spelling, writing, drawing of three geometric forms and a key, and arithmetic computation from patient K. C.

The Halstead Neuropsychological Test Battery for Children was administered and this boy's performance was at a level that fell mainly within the normal range. His least-adequate ability reflected some difficulty in grasping the essential nature of problem situations, postulating solutions to unfamiliar problems benefiting from past experience, and effectively organizing various aspects of his environmental situation (Category Test). On tasks requiring motor activity, either with or without a problem-solving component, this boy's performance was quite adequate. On an entirely unfamiliar task in which tactile and kinesthetic cues are required to solve a complex form board problem, he performed quite rapidly with both hands (Tactual Performance Test). Other tasks permitting motor performance were also performed in an above-average manner.

A battery of sensory-perceptual tests was administered and this boy demonstrated no significant difficulty on measures of tactile, auditory, or visual perception. He made one error with his left hand on the measure of tactile finger localization and one with his left hand on a measure of fingertip number writing while remaining error-free with the right hand. However, this very small number of errors can be considered to fall within the range of normal variation and is not indicative of any degree of functional impairment.

The level of this boy's performance was characterized by considerable variability, a finding that is frequently associated with damage to the cerebral hemispheres. His pattern of intellectual difficulties, coupled with specific problems in dealing with the communication significance of language symbols, implies that the left cerebral hemisphere functions less adequately than the right. Comparison of performance of the two sides of the body also yielded evidence of disparities which deviate from normal findings and suggests that the brain has suffered some generalized impairment. Despite evidence of strong right-handedness and right-footedness (but left-eyedness) derived from the Reitan-Klove Lateral Dominance Examination, and a generally good level of performance, K. C. required over three times as long with his right hand as he did with his left hand on the Tactual Performance Test. While this finding might imply some degree of left cerebral dysfunction, evidence for some mild impairment of the right hemisphere was derived from his performance on measures of motor speed (Finger Tapping) and strength (Strength of Grip). On each of these tests his performance with the left hand was considerably less adequate than would be expected when compared with his right hand. Thus, comparisons of lateralized performances complemented the earlier data from the WISC and aphasia examination in indicating the presence of mild cerebral damage. The overall evidence implicated both cerebral hemispheres rather than suggesting a single focal area of involvement. Further, the findings suggest the presence of a relatively stabilized condition of brain damage. A recent destructive lesion or a rapidly progressive brain disease would very likely have caused impairment which this child did not show. His relatively good scores on certain tests (e.g., Speech-sounds Perception; Tactual Performance Test—Total Time, Memory, and Localization; Trail Making Test), in the presence of the deficits described above, are suggestive of a stabilized condition of mild cerebral damage.

The ability to postulate some form of cerebral damage in this child, however, does not seem to represent the critical issue in attempting to shed some light on his difficulties of behavior and adjustment. This child's pattern of psychological test functioning was suggestive of the kind of child who experiences marked difficulty in understanding the rules and developing, either internally or externally, the verbalized explanations and controls necessary for organized behavior (WISC and aphasia examination). He also demonstrated a deficiency in his ability to organize his environment, understand the essential nature of complex interrelationships, and to modify his conceptualizations in accordance with positive and negative reinforcement (Category Test). At the same time, he demonstrated highly developed motor problem-solving and manipulatory skills (Tactual Performance Test). This is the kind of child, therefore, who tends to find contemplative and well-planned types of activities poorly reinforcing while rapid and impulsively carried out activities are usually done skillfully whether or not the end result is socially satisfactory to himself or others. The areas of deficit which were found with this battery of tests are entirely consistent with those described by his teacher who said, "K. seems to indicate complete lack of understanding of the problems he causes himself and others. He cannot talk realistically about it. He feels his peers don't like him, but he will not associate his behavior with their reactions." The type of difficulty experienced by this boy is not at all that seen in a child who is visually or otherwise perceptually handicapped. It is far more typical of that seen in children who are verbally and/or conceptually handicapped and who, while physically quite agile and able, are realistically unable to comprehend the demands of a situation, to relate their activities to the reactions of others and to formulate, either verbally or non-verbally, effective manners of interacting with the environment they perceive around them.

This child requires fairly specific academic remedial help in the areas of reading, writing, arithmetic, and spelling. The academic or classroom environment would constitute an extremely negative experience for this boy who has neither the current information nor the ability to compete adequately with his peers in an academic situation. It would be not at all surprising for his behavior to be characterized by many attempts to escape this very punishing type of experience. In addition to academic remediation, this boy should receive help in associating his behaviors, beginning with relatively simple and concrete examples, to their consequences and to the reactions that these behaviors might cause in others. He needs to develop the ability to benefit from past experience, to develop cues (either verbal or nonverbal) which allow him to understand the requirements of new and unfamiliar situations, and which allow him to utilize past experiences more effectively. He could benefit from instruction in which simple problems and relationships are presented. Solution of these problems should result in positive reinforcement. Emphasis needs to be placed on grasping the underlying principle of each problem. Initial verbal demands may need to be minimal and progression to a variety of more complex social and environmental concepts should be quite gradual. Such treatment, oriented toward his real and serious deficits, may prevent him from increasing what is probably already a high degree of anxiety and social discomfort as well as hostility and disappointment regarding the failure of his best attempts to meet with consistent social acceptance.

The preceding case examples represent two essentially different sets of problems and questions that can be directly addressed through the neuropsychological examination of an individual patient. The reliance on several inferential methods—including performance level, specific signs, patterns of ability strengths and weaknesses, and comparison of the performance of the right versus left side of the body—provide complementary types of evidence with respect to an individual's manner of functioning. Such evidence may be applied by an experienced neuropsychologist to evaluation of the presence of a possible life-threatening cerebral disease or to the relationship between problems of adjustment and adaptive abilities which are dependent upon brain functions. These considerations, however, are neither mutually exclusive nor exhaustive of the situations to which a neuropsychological evaluation can make a useful contribution.

The selective review of a number of investigations reported in this paper should illustrate the need for additional empirical investigation of the psychological correlates of cerebral lesions in children. The approaches that have been illustrated may be used for more extensive and intensive studies by clinical and research-minded psychologists alike. Clearly, until many of these very basic issues are better understood from a firm empirical viewpoint, significant clinical progress toward explanation and especially remediation of difficulties in adaptive ability due to cerebral damage or disease will remain discouragingly slow and uncertain. That they are, in large measure, open to investigation by those with the patience and support to pursue very long-range goals is the most exciting and encouraging aspect of the data and conclusions included in this report.

6

DISORDERED BRAIN FUNCTION IN YOUNG CHILDREN AND EARLY ADOLESCENTS: NEUROPSYCHOLOGICAL AND ELECTROENCEPHALOGRAPHIC CORRELATES[1]

Harry Klonoff and Morton Low

Disordered brain function can be evaluated by various means with varying degress of accuracy. The Halstead Neuropsychological Test Battery for Children (ages 9-14) and the Reitan-Indiana Neuropsychological Test Battery for Children (ages 5-8) have been shown to be sensitive to disordered brain function in children (Reitan & Heineman, 1968). Groups of brain-damaged children matched in terms of age have been compared with normal controls, with the brain-damaged groups showing consistently lower levels of neuropsychological functioning (Reed, 1963; Reed, Reitan, & Klove, 1965; Reed & Fitzhugh, 1966; Halstead & Rennick, 1966; Klonoff, Robinson, & Thompson, 1969; Boll, Ch. 5, this volume; and Reitan, Ch. 4, this volume). Research comparing brain-damaged and normal children matched on the basis of IQ, in contrast to some of the above results, found that the best discriminators were the motor and performance tests (Knights & Ogilvie, 1967). Factorial studies of these neuropsychological batteries have been done for each age group and have reported the minimum number of dimensions, composite scores reflecting these neuropsychological dimensions, and raw scores for each of the tests in the

[1] This research was supported by Grant 609-7-138, National Health Grants, Ottawa, Canada. The authors wish to express their appreciation to: Dr. C. D. Maclean and Dr. R. Paris, for examining the Chronic and Acute groups; Dr. A. McTaggart and Dr. R. Christie for examining the cerebral dysfunction group; Dr. G. Robinson and Dr. G. Thompson for their continued support; Mrs. B. Simpson, psychotechnician, for integrating the neuropsychological examination of patients; Mr. D. Crockett, for his invaluable assistance; Mr. J. Bjerring, Computing Centre, U.B.C., for his advice; and The Vancouver General Hospital and the Health Sciences Centre Hospital for providing the necessary research facilities.

respective neuropsychological batteries, as well as for the subtests of the WISC (Crockett, Klonoff, & Bjerring, 1969; Klonoff, 1971b).

Similarly, the electroencephalogram (EEG) is often altered in some way by disordered brain function, even without a demonstrable structural lesion. In many instances, the etiology of the disordered function can be identified, as in head injury. The electroencephalographic sequelae of head injury have been well documented. It is known that the EEG is very sensitive to even minor head injuries (Jasper, Kershmann, & Elvidge, 1945) and in the acute stage, that these changes may include a wide range of abnormality, but chiefly some degree of slowing and asymmetry (Dow, Ulett, & Raaf, 1944; Silverman, 1962; Bickford & Klass, 1966). Recent research has indicated that more severe injuries are not only generally accompanied by more seriously abnormal EEG findings but also that more severe injuries are associated with more rapid initial rate of recovery from EEG abnormalities (Kubala & Kellaway, 1967).

Many authors have emphasized the need for serial electrographic evaluation in attempting to use the EEG in prognosis. Virtually all agree that a single EEG taken several weeks or a month after injury is of very limited value in assessment, chiefly because of the difficulty in establishing a causal relationship between the remote head injury and a single abnormal tracing (Rodin, 1967; Kubala & Kellaway, 1967). While much is known regarding the usual evolution of EEG changes following head injury, the question remains open how well the EEG in such cases may serve as an indicator of the patient's neurological and psychological status after the acute period.

In other instances, the etiology of disordered brain function is more difficult to identify, as in minimal cerebral dysfunction (MCD). Early investigators found a significant number of abnormalities in the EEGs of children with "behavior disorders" (Jasper, Solomon, & Bradley, 1938; Knott, Platt, Ashby, & Gottleib, 1953; and Lindsley & Cutts, 1940). Chiefly, these abnormalities were occipital slow waves. Kahn and Cohen (1934) first reported EEG abnormalities in "organic driveness," a hyperkinetic, impulsive behavior pattern.

Since these initial reports, numerous studies have been done in attempts to define some specific pattern of electrographic abnormalities which would correlate with the minimal cerebral dysfunction syndrome. Authors have described various abnormalities as "most common" in children with this diagnosis, including slow occipital waves or paroxysmal slow bursts (Cohn, 1961; Major, 1967), diffuse slowing or "immaturity" (Corfariu, Szabo, Varilsy, & Rado, 1967; Polacek & Tresohlavova, 1969; and Predescu, Roman, Costiner, Cristian, & Oancea, 1968) and spike foci and 14 and 6 per second positive spike and wave activity (Kellaway, Crawley, & Maulsby, 1965).

Few investigators have attempted to predict EEG findings from psychological data, or vice versa, although Crawley and Kellaway in 1963 did state: "the EEG is a more reliable indicator of organic brain disease in children than in adults, since a disease which results in a personality or behavioral change in a child will almost always be associated with EEG changes," indicating that some correlation is to be expected.

Klove and White (1963), after studying 179 adult patients with verified brain damage (significant pathology such as abcess, traumatic epilepsy, hematoma) concluded that "in a well-defined patient population, it is possible to apply EEG criteria which have a rather striking differential relationship to performances of various groups on psychological tests." On the other hand, Stevens, Sachdev, and Milstein (1968) in their study of 120 children with behavior disorders, could achieve no better than chance predictability from the EEG to a psychological test using global ratings, but they did find some correlation with qualitative factors in the EEG and individual items in psychological testing.

The purposes of the present study were: (a) to compare the neuropsychological status of young children and early adolescents where the causation of brain damage is known and the duration varied (head trauma compared with meningitis, encephalitis, maternal rubella, and kernicterus) with matched control groups, and to determine the nature of neuropsychological change after a 1-year period; (b) to compare the neuropsychological status of young children and early adolescents where the specific etiology is unknown (minimal cerebral dysfunction) with a matched control group, and to determine the nature of neuropsychological change after a 1-year period; (c) to determine the nature of change in EEG functioning at the end of a 1-year period in children with known etiology (head trauma) as well as unknown etiology (minimal cerebral dysfunction); (d) to determine brain-behavior relationships in these groups of children with known and unknown etiology.

METHOD AND CLINICAL MATERIAL

Selection of Project Population

The project population included three main clinical groups, each containing two age levels, under 9 years and over 9 years. The subgroups have been designated as follows:

Acute I, aged 2 years, 8 months through 8 years, 11 months (131 children)

Acute II, aged 9 years, 0 months through 15 years, 10 months (100 children)

Chronic I, aged 2 years, 8 months through 8 years, 11 months (77 children)

Chronic II, aged 9 years, 0 months through 15 years, 11 months (39 children)

Minimal Cerebral Dysfunction I (MCD I), aged 4 years, 0 months through 8 years, 11 months (51 children)

Minimal Cerebral Dysfunction II (MCD II), aged 9 years, 0 months through 15 years, 6 months (44 children)

Each child in the six clinical groups was matched on age (within 3 months) and sex, generating six control groups:

Acute Control I, aged 2 years, 9 months through 8 years, 11 months (131 children)

Acute Control II, aged 9 years, 0 months through 15 years, 9 months (100 children)

Chronic Control I, aged 2 years, 11 months through 8 years, 11 months (77 children)

Chronic Control II, aged 9 years, 1 month through 15 years, 11 months (39 children)

MCD Control I, aged 4 years, 2 months through 8 years, 11 months (51 children)

MCD Control II, aged 9 years, 0 months through 15 years, 8 months (44 children)

The clinical and control groups were examined initially in order to obtain a neuropsychological baseline and reexamined 1 year later to determine the nature of neuropsychological change. The clinical groups were neurologically examined at time of intake and the Chronic group was reexamined 1 year later. The Acute and MCD groups received baseline EEGs and repeat EEGs 1 year later. The neuropsychological, neurological and EEG examinations and reexaminations were done independently.

Definition of Groups and Examination Procedure of Study

The study groups.   Acute groups I and II were comprised of consecutive admissions to the Health Centre for Children (Vancouver General Hospital) and St. Paul's Hospital, Vancouver, B.C., with diagnoses of head injury. The neurological, neuropsychological, and EEG examinations were arranged in temporal contiguity and as close to the time of discharge as possible.

The neurological assessment of degree of head injury was based on the type of injury and the extent of unconsciousness. Each child was graded for degree of neurological impairment according to the following schema:

   I. Minor, suspected but no proven loss of consciousness; no evidence of concussion
  II. Mild, suspected but no proven loss of consciousness; concussion (lethargy, vomiting, drowsiness, contusion, nausea, dizziness)
 III. Moderate, loss of consciousness for less than 5 min.; concussion
  IV. Severe, loss of consciousness for 5–30 min.; concussion; skull fracture
   V. Serious, loss of consciousness for more than 30 min.; concussion; skull fracture, depressed and/or compound; other sequelae (psychosis, aphasia, etc.)

Chronic groups I and II were selected from the records of seven hospitals and the 1957 British Columbia Registry for Handicapped Children and Adults. Only those children who met the criteria of the causal subgroups (meningitis, encephalitis, kernicterus, and rubella)[2] were included. Each child was rated for degree of neurological impairment (Table 1). Neurological and neuropsychological examinations were temporally contiguous.

MCD groups I and II included children who had been referred by any one of three child psychiatrists. Terms within the rating scheme were defined in advance, the ratings were independent and preceded the neuropsychological and electroencephalographic examinations. The child psychiatrists' rating of degree of cerebral dysfunction was based on the clinical examination (history from parents, examination of child, correspondence from referring physicians and school authorities, etc.). The schema included the following groups of behavioral signs and each sign was rated minimal, moderate, or severe: *Motor*—(a) hyperkinesis, (b) motor awkardness, (c) postural rigidity, (d) motor speech difficulties, (e) mixed dominance, (f) distractibility; *Intellectual*—(a) perceptual and/or conceptual difficulties, (b) academic or learning difficulties, (c) perseveration; *Personality*—(a) anxiety, (b) irritability or impulsivity, (c) difficulties in relating or social incompetence, (d) disturbed self-concept or body concept. A global rating of I (minimal), II (moderate) or III (severe) was then assigned to each child by the child psychiatrist. Only those children who exhibited positive signs in two of the three areas were selected. Children with disturbance in only the personality area or with histories of seizures were not included in this study.

Normal groups I and II consisted of children examined by any of six pediatricians in varying geographic areas in metropolitan Vancouver. Children were referred who met the following clinical criteria; (a) no neurological deficit; (b) no physical anomalies; (c) no profound signs of emotional disturbance; (d) normal school progress for those children attending school. The Normal groups provided: (a) normative data for the neuropsychological battery in terms of age levels and sex differences; (b) data regarding the relationships of IQ to the tests in the neuropsychological battery; (c) control groups for Acute, Chronic, and MCD groups, with respect to the neuropsychological batteries.

Neuropsychological test batteries. The neuropsychological examination for the children under 9 years included: the Reitan-Indiana Neuropsychological Test Battery for Children—14 tests and 28 variables; two of Benton's tests; a lateral dominance test; and the Stanford Binet, Form L-M for children under 5 years of age or the Wechsler Intelligence Scale for Children (WISC) for those aged 5 or over. The neuropsychological examination for children over 9 years included:

---

[2] Meningitis: The clinical diagnosis was confirmed by cell count and culture of CSF. Encephalitis: The clinical diagnosis was confirmed by cell count of CSF but viral studies were not available. Maternal rubella: The diagnosis was based on a history of a characteristic clinical syndrome during the first trimester of pregnancy, exposure to rubella, or evidence of spread to family members, and the presence of characteristic anomalies of this disease in the offspring. No viral studies were done. Kernicterus: The diagnosis was based on evidence of Rh or ABO isoimmunization and neonatal hyperbilirubinemia.

TABLE 1

Neurological Assessment of Degree of Damage
in Chronic Groups I and II

Degree of damage	Clinical signs
I. Minor	1 or 2 minor clinical signs
II. Mild	more than 2 minor clinical signs
III. Moderate	1 major clinical sign
IV. Severe	1 major clinical sign + 1 or more minor clinical signs
V. Serious	2 major clinical signs with or without minor clinical signs

Clinical signs — Minor	Clinical signs — Major

1. Impaired voluntary movement
   Poor balance
   Clumsiness
   Disdiadochokinesis
   Positive Romberg
   Hyper- and hypotonicity
   Cranial nerve lesion
   Mixed dominance
   Positive Babinski
   One-sided weakness
   Hypoactive reflexes
	1. Impaired voluntary movement
	   Pyramidal
	   Athetoid
	   Ataxic

2. Vision defect
   Strabismus
   Decreased visual acuity less
     than 20/200
	2. Vision defect
	   Greater than 20/200
	   Total field deficit 10° angle or
	     less

3. Deafness (mild)
   Less than 30 DB
	3. Deafness
	   Greater than 30 DB in 3 frequencies

4. Slow speech development	4. Severe speech delay
5. Delayed developmental milestones	5. Mental retardation
6. EEG abnormalities	6. Convulsions

7. Sensory abnormalities
   Position sense
   Vibration sense
   Astereognosis	

8. Other
   Head size
   Talipes equinovarus	

the above noted 18 tests which yielded 32 variables, and the Klove Motor Steadiness Battery, 5 tests and 16 variables, for a total of 48 variables. Test construction, scoring, and normative data have been reported by Reitan (1964a), Benton (1959), Knights (1966), and Klonoff et al. (1969). The tests are described in the Appendix of this volume.

The EEG. Initial and repeat EEG records were obtained from each child in the Acute and MCD groups. Hyperventilation for 3 min. and sleep (induced by chloral hydrate) were routinely used for activation (where there were no clinical contraindications). Recording techniques included the application of 19 scalp electrodes plus two ear electrodes in the International 10-20 positions. Both referential (ear) and bipolar montages were used, awake and asleep. All of the tracings were interpreted by the same electroencephalographer (MDL); he assigned a global rating of normal, borderline, minimally abnormal, moderately abnormal, or markedly abnormal according to the following schema:

NORMAL—1

Age 3 years (the lower end of the age distribution):
1. Awake: a well developed and symmetrical alpha rhythm of at least 8 cycles per second; some low voltage (less than 50 μv) 4-6-cycle-per-second activity in occipital and central leads with some lower voltage (less than 25 μv) 4-6-cycle-per-second activity in frontal leads; occasional 3-per-second waves less than 25 μv in amplitude in occipital and central leads.
2. Asleep: sigma activity present, symmetrical and synchronous; central transients present, symmetrical and synchronous.

Age 16 years (the upper end of the age distribution):
1. Awake: a symmetrical alpha rhythm of 8+ to 9+ cycles per second; no activity below 6 cycles per second in any region; some low voltage (less than 25 μv) and scattered 6-7-per-second waves centrally and anteriorly with only occasional low voltage fusing in the alpha rhythm.
2. Asleep: as above.

Between age 3 years and 16 years and over—records were classified as completely normal if they showed maturational changes appropriate for the patient's age both awake and asleep.

Hyperventilation response—at any age: a smooth buildup of generalized slow activity beginning posterior and becoming anterior dominant during hyperventilation; the record returns to resting level within 60-90 sec. following cessation of 3 min. of satisfactory hyperventilation (100 deep breaths); all persistent responses were repeated after glucose ingestion; no consistent asymmetry, no abnormal wave forms, i.e., spikes or spike and wave bursts, and no markedly episodic or persistent slowing.

BORDERLINE—$1\frac{1}{2}$

This category is used in the same sense that some previous investigators have used a "borderline" category. The records were not unequivocally or "ideally" normal, but showed some minor features such as minimal and inconsistent asymmetries, or minimal excesses of slow/fast activity which were near the limits of the normal range for the age.

MINIMALLY ABNORMAL—2

Records were categorized as minimally abnormal if they showed:
1. Nonparoxysmal and nonfocal slow activity (3-7 cycles per second), less than 70 μv in amplitude in posterior leads up to 10 years of age (the age of the patient was considered; the younger patients being allowed more slow frequency activity posteriorly);
2. Nonparoxysmal, nonpersistent and nonfocal slow activity 4-7 cycles per second, less than 70 μv in amplitude or 0.5-3 cycles per second, less than 30 μv in amplitude in any head region, depending upon the age of the patient;
3. Infrequent, nonsustained and nonfocal episodic 3-7-cycle-per-second activity greater than 50 μv in amplitude;
4. Slow activity persisting more than 90 sec. following cessation of hyperventilation;
5. Minor but consistent asymmetries of at least 20% but less than 50%;
6. Occasional fast spike and wave bursts (over 4 cycles per second).

MODERATELY ABNORMAL—3

Records were classified as moderately abnormal if they showed:
1. Diffuse, frontal dominant or posterior dominant slow activity 4-7 cycles per second greater than 70 μv, persistent or in brief paroxysms during the waking record, or 0.5-3 cycles per second greater than 30 μv scattered and nonsustained or appearing in brief bursts;
2. Asymmetries which were persistent, greater than 60% but less than 75%, with a background which was normal to moderately slow/fast;
3. Nonsustained, sporadic spike and wave bursts slower than 5 cycles per second with a normal to slightly slow background;
4. Isolated or sporadic spike or slow wave foci with normal or only slightly slow/fast background activity.

MARKEDLY ABNORMAL—4

Records were classified as markedly abnormal if they showed:
1. Persistent diffuse slow activity from 0.5-4 cycles per second greater than 30 μv in amplitude;

2. Constant asymmetries greater than 75% with moderate slow/fast background activity;

3. Continuous or nearly continuous spike and wave discharges;

4. Slow foci, spike foci, or spike and wave discharges arising from a moderately to markedly slow/fast background.

Analysis of Data

All statistical analyses reported were done on the IBM 360 computer, Computing Centre, University of British Columbia.

As children at the younger age levels could not complete all the tests, it was sometimes impossible to assign an exact raw score to a child's performance. In instances where the child was too young to do the test, the missing data was assigned the worst score (lowest or highest, depending on whether the test is scored in terms of correct or error/time) ± .20 of 1 SD for the respective age. This format was used for all statistical analyses. In the comparisons of low and high IQ Normal subgroups and in the discriminant analysis, the scores were then transformed to T scores (mean = 50, SD = 10) for each age level 4 through 15 years.

The discriminant analysis program used was UBC class M. multivariate analysis, BMDO7M stepwise discriminant analysis. Each discriminant analysis reported later in this chapter will consist of a classification matrix, i.e., the number of individuals correctly assigned to the designated classes. In arriving at this classification matrix, the significance of contribution of each variable (32 variables for the children under 9 years and 48 variables for the children over 9 years) to the prediction of class membership was computed at each step. The F probability for the significance of contribution to class membership varied from .05 to .25 among the respective discriminant analyses.

RESULTS

Demographic Factors; Duration of Brain Damage

Sex and age distributions, attrition of groups at reexamination. Table 2 summarizes the age and sex distribution of the six clinical groups and their respective matched normal groups at the time of initial examination as well as the sex distribution at subsequent reexamination 1 year later. Acute group children were the youngest in both age levels, followed by the Chronic and the MCD groups for the under-9-year level, with the order reversed for the over-9-year level. The mean age differences between the six clinical groups and their respective matched groups were nonsignificant in all instances.

The boys consistently outnumbered the girls in all of the clinical groups, the MCD groups having the highest ratio of boys compared to girls (3:1,5:1), followed by the Acute groups (8:5,2:1) and then by the Chronic groups (7:6,8:5).

Of the total of 884 children initially examined, 756 were reexamined 1 year later (Table 2), for an overall attrition rate of 14%.

TABLE 2

Age and Sex Characteristics of Population (Six Clinical Groups
and Respective Matched Control Groups) Examined Initially
and Numbers of Each Group Reexamined 1 Year Later

| Group | Examination | | | | | | Reexamination | |
| | Age[a] | | | Sex | | | Total | Attrition (%) |
	Mean	SD	Range	Boys	Girls	Total		
Acute I	5.87	1.76	2.67– 8.92	80	51	131	115	12
Acute Control I	5.89	1.77	2.75– 8.92	80	51	131	115	
Acute II	11.53	1.81	9.00–15.83	67	33	100	81	19
Acute Control II	11.59	1.78	9.00–15.75	67	33	100	81	
Chronic I	6.60	1.59	2.67– 8.92	40	37	77	70	9
Chronic Control I	6.43	1.54	2.92– 8.92	40	37	77	70	
Chronic II	12.03	1.88	9.00–15.92	24	15	39	36	8
Chronic Control II	12.01	1.82	9.08–15.42	24	15	39	36	
MCD I	7.22	1.29	4.00– 8.92	39	12	51	43	16
MCD Control I	7.15	1.31	4.17– 8.92	39	12	51	43	
MCD II	11.66	1.80	9.00–15.50	37	7	44	33	25
MCD Control II	11.65	1.80	9.00–15.66	37	7	44	33	
Totals				576	308	884	756	

[a] All differences between clinical groups and their matched controls in mean age were nonsignificant. Maximum $t = 0.98, p < .40$.

School grade of children, occupational status of fathers. None of the Acute or MCD clinical groups differed significantly from their matched control groups in mean grade placement. The mean grade for Acute group I was 2.03 (SD .87, range 1–4); for Acute Control group I it was 2.12 (SD .91, range 1–4). Acute group II had a mean grade placement of 5.79 (SD 1.96, range 3–10), while Acute Control group II averaged 6.05 (SD 1.87, range 3–10). The mean grade for MCD group I was 1.97 (SD .80, range 1–3); for MCD Control group I it was 2.17 (SD .96, range 1–3). MCD group II had a mean grade placement of 5.73 (SD 2.06, range 2–11) while MCD Control group II averaged 6.23 (SD 1.86, range 3–11). The Chronic groups, however, differed significantly from their matched normal control groups, in that 25 of the 77 children in Chronic group I and 24 of the 39 children in Chronic group II were in special class placement. Of the 51 children in MCD group I, 39 were in school, 11 were in preschool and 1 was in a special class. Of the 44 children in MCD group II, 3 were in special class placement. Ten of the matched normals were in preschool.

The occupational status of the fathers of the six normal control groups was consistently higher (skewed toward professional-managerial categories) than that of their respective clinical groups: Acute group I ($\chi^2 = 58.92, p < .01$); Acute group II ($\chi^2 = 20.88$ $p < .01$); Chronic group I ($\chi^2 = 28.16, p < .01$); Chronic group II (χ^2 = 38.64, $p < .01$); MCD group I (χ^2 = 21.69, $p < .01$); and MCD group II (χ^2 = 19.50, $p < .01$). These socioeconomic differences will be dealt with in a subsequent section of Results.

Duration of hospitalization, degree of chronicity. The mean length of hospitalization for Acute group I was 11.0 days, the median 5.3 days and the range 1 to 93. The mean length of hospitalization for Acute group II was 13.1 days, the median 6.3 days and the range 1 to 88 days. The median length of stay is a more representative reflection of severity of head injury as most instances of prolonged hospitalization were due to fractures and the need for traction.

For Chronic groups I and II, the distribution by diagnostic categories and the mean number of years between disease and the present examination were:

Disease	Group I		Group II	
	N	Years	N	Years
Meningitis	44	4.87	23	11.49
Maternal rubella	15	8.00	12	10.35
Kernicterus	10	7.30	3	11.17
Encephalitis	8	3.10	1	4.33

Summary[3]. In comparing the demographic characteristics of the three clinical groups, the Acute group was found to be the youngest and showed the highest level of educational achievement, while the MCD group contained the highest ratio of boys compared to girls. Occupational status of fathers was lower for the three clinical groups than for their respective matched normal groups. The mean length of hospitalization for combined Acute groups I and II was 11.9 days. The rank order of diagnostic categories in terms of numbers of children, for combined Chronic groups I and II was as follows: meningitis, maternal rubella, kernicterus, and encephalitis.

Normal Group–Neuropsychological Findings

Age differences. A number of methodological issues that entered into the standardization of the neuropsychological battery required clarification before turning to the evaluation of the neuropsychological findings of the clinical groups and their respective matched control groups.

The first question concerned the relationships between age and performance on the tests that comprised the neuropsychological battery. In order to assess these relationships, regression analysis was used. This analyses dealt with our pool of 333 Normal children under 9 years of age (Normal group I), and 197 Normal children over 9 (Normal group II) (Table 3). In the regression analysis of Normal group I data, scores were predicted from age for all of the variables

---

[3] As the Results section of this chapter contains considerable data, a summary has been included at the end of each section in the interest of continuity.

TABLE 3
Normal Groups I and II Age Comparisons: Regression Analysis, F Tests

Variable	Normal group I F $N = 333$		Normal group II F $N = 197$	
	Linear	Quadratic	Linear	Quadratic
Category Test (errors)	466.34****	5.30**	32.98****	
Tapping – Dominant (correct)	220.12****		140.76****	
Tapping – Nondominant (correct)	200.34****		168.03****	
Speech Perception (errors)	292.15****	38.66****	17.03****	
Trail Making A (time)	10.42****	19.27****	49.88****	
Trail Making B (time)	2.26	7.91****	38.96****	
Trail Making–Total (time)	2.70	9.55****	55.09****	
Matching Figures (time)	214.42****	20.34****	43.11****	
Matching Figures (errors)	165.35****	58.77****	2.05	
Matching V's (time)	82.84****		31.47****	
Matching V's (errors)	306.70****	10.41****	4.38*	
Star (correct)	29.57****	12.44****	1.43	
Concentric Squares (correct)	71.67****	29.67****	0.17	
Progressive Figures (time)	42.28****	43.73****	32.28****	9.63****
Color Form (time)	118.07****		43.91****	
Color Form (errors)	108.78****		1.94	
Target Test (correct)	269.67****	50.09****	22.25****	
Marching – Dominant (time)	278.23****	78.04****	20.65****	
Marching – Dominant (errors)	154.66****	71.37****	0.34	
Marching – Nondominant (time)	231.09****	61.01****	48.19****	
Marching – Nondominant (errors)	117.99****	63.00****	4.53*	9.38****
Tactual Performance Test–Dominant (time)	35.44****	36.32****	27.26****	4.37*
Tactual Performance Test–Nondominant (time)	40.51****	40.98****	20.96****	
Tactual Performance Test–Both (time)	46.88****	47.96****	29.72****	
Tactual Performance Test–Total (time)	50.76****	54.03****	41.73****	
Tactual Performance Test–Memory (correct)	50.95****	44.75****	2.21	
Tactual Performance Test–Location (correct)	38.03****	42.40****	11.39****	
Matching Pictures (correct)	334.20****	4.42*	0.13	4.38*
Sound Recognition	17.70****		21.37****	
Right–Left. Orientation (correct)	19.31****	24.68****	18.50****	
Lateral Dominance (correct)	40.70****		0.25	
Full Scale IQ	0.84		0.03	
Maze Coordination Dominant (time)			16.01****	
Maze Coordination Dominant (counter)			14.68****	
Maze Coordination Nondominant (time)			39.34****	
Maze Coordination Nondominant (counter)			34.13****	
Grooved Steadiness Dominant (time)			1.23	
Grooved Steadiness Dominant (counter)			0.63	
Grooved Steadiness Nondominant (time)			0.03	
Grooved Steadiness Nondominant (counter)			0.01	
Steadiness Dominant (time)			3.83*	
Steadiness Dominant (counter)			0.77	
Steadiness Nondominant (time)			2.45	
Steadiness Nondominant (counter)			2.08	
Grooved Pegboard Dominant (time)			16.77****	
Grooved Pegboard Nondominant (time)			19.25****	
Foot Tapping Dominant (score)			32.35****	
Foot Tapping Nondominant (score)			43.60****	

*$p < .05$.
**$p < .02$.
***$p < .01$.
****$p < .001$.

(significant *F* tests), except intelligence. For Normal group II, changes in scores with increasing age were also present on 24 of the variables, nonsignificant findings emerging for only 7 of them. The absence of significant findings for Full Scale IQ with the younger and older Normal groups is as predicted, in that intelligence levels were already age adjusted, whereas this was not true for the other variables. Prediction was not as high with the Motor Steadiness battery in that predictable changes occurred with only 9 of the 16 variables.

While the results indicate predictable changes with increasing age for a large proportion of the variables in the neuropsychological battery, the nature of the functions was distinctly different between the two age levels (Table 3). The functions in the younger group were most frequently both linear and quadratic (22 variables); followed by linear (7 variables) and then quadratic (2 variables). In examining these same 32 variables in the older group, it was found that: the most frequent functions were linear (20 variables); followed by both linear and quadratic (3 variables) and then quadratic (1 variable). The functions on the Motor Steadiness battery were exclusively linear for 9 of the 16 significant variables. It is evident, therefore, that the scores generally increase in a nonlinear manner with the younger group, become more linear with the older group, and in some instances the function has become asymptotic within the older group (no relationship between age and score).

Sex differences.   The second methodological question was the nature of sex differences on the various tests of the neuropsychological battery. Sex differences for the successive age levels of Normal group I were rare, as reported previously (Klonoff et al., 1969). Sex differences were also tested on 48 variables separately for each year age level from 9 to 15. Of these 336 comparisons, 58 found significance at .05 or better. However, these tests are not strictly independent because many of the variables share instrumental variance and others are otherwise correlated. Furthermore, the significant sex differences form no consistent or interpretable pattern. Therefore, sexes were pooled in subsequent analyses.

The relationships between IQ and tests in the neuropsychological battery. The third methodological question dealt with the relationships between differential levels of IQ and neuropsychological functioning. Only the Normal group included sufficiently large numbers of children to carry out such an analysis, after matching for age and sex. The results of the comparisons of children with lower IQs (90-109) with children with higher IQs (110-125) revealed the extent and nature of the associations of intelligence measurements and the neuropsychological battery scores for the two age levels (Table 4). For that portion of the battery common to both groups, comparisons of the groups with lower and higher IQ values showed that 8 of the 17 tests for the younger children and 9 of the 17 tests for the older children were significantly different. A number of the tests each yielded several variables. Of the 31 total variables common to both age groups, 13 were significantly different for the younger group and 14 for the older one. The relationships of intelligence to the other

TABLE 4

All Normal Controls: Comparison of Low Full Scale IQ (90–109)
with High Full Scale IQ (110–125) Subjects on
Neuropsychological Variables – t Tests

Variable	Younger normal controls (N=172)		Older normal controls (N=106)	
	Lower IQ	Higher IQ	Lower IQ	Higher IQ
Category Test (errors)	−32.00[a]	−27.42**	−44.91[b]	−37.15*
Tapping – Dominant (correct)	27.86	27.52	38.48	40.80
Tapping – Nondominant (correct)	25.46	24.52	34.81	35.75
Speech Perception (errors)	−20.52	−17.38	−6.21	−6.11
Trail Making A (time)	−39.14	−42.81	−22.64	−21.02
Trail Making B (time)	−90.80	−76.59****	−52.23	−36.74****
Trail Making Total (time)	−129.80	−119.30***	−74.87	−57.94****
Matching Figures (time)	−40.99	−39.97	−18.49	−18.34
Matching Figures (errors)	−0.99	−0.99	−0.17	−0.06
Matching V's (time)	−52.29	−47.31	−27.47	−24.72
Matching V's (errors)	−3.27	−2.81	−1.01	−0.40***
Star (correct)	6.61	8.20***	10.64	11.52***
Concentric Squares (correct)	8.35	10.50****	12.72	13.99***
Progressive Figures (time)	−102.00	−68.47****	−35.31	−25.12****
Color Form (time)	−54.36	−49.88	−16.21	−14.15
Color Form (errors)	−1.44	−1.43	−0.06	−0.06
Target Test (correct)	8.70	9.28	16.09	18.08****
Marching – Dominant (time)	−39.10	−32.86	−15.66	−16.45
Marching – Dominant (errors)	−1.67	−0.93*	−0.28	−0.26
Marching – Nondominant (time)	−44.92	−38.42	−18.60	−19.17
Marching – Nondominant (errors)	−2.04	−1.57	−0.77	−0.51
Tactual Performance Test–Dominant (time)	−8.40	−5.75****	−3.36	−2.92
Tactual Performance Test–Nondominant (time)	−6.62	−4.70****	−2.39	−1.74**
Tactual Performance Test–Both (time)	−4.55	−3.52***	−1.11	−0.89*
Tactual Performance Test–Total (time)	−19.71	−14.09****	−6.66	−5.55*
Tactual Performance Test–Memory (correct)	1.94	2.75****	4.32	4.83*
Tactual Performance Test–Location (correct)	1.03	1.29	3.13	3.96***
Matching Pictures (correct)	20.02	21.62	29.77	30.06
Sound Recognition	20.50	20.42	23.90	24.06
Right–Left Orientation (correct)	13.66	16.22*	24.96	28.26*
Lateral Dominance (correct)	13.14	13.04	14.57	14.42
Maze Coordination Dominant (time)			−2.25	−2.01
Maze Coordiantion Dominant (counter)			−23.17	−19.50
Maze Coordination Nondominant (time)			−5.89	−4.02****
Maze Coordination Nondominant (counter)			−47.43	−36.95***
Grooved Steadiness Dominant (time)			−3.26	−2.51
Grooved Steadiness Dominant (counter)			−24.48	−21.66
Grooved Steadiness Nondominant (time)			−3.96	−3.54
Grooved Steadiness Nondominant (counter)			−26.72	−25.27
Steadiness Dominant (time)			−11.82	−10.98
Steadiness Dominant (counter)			−99.11	−97.98
Steadiness Nondominant (time)			−19.04	−16.12*
Steadiness Nondominant (counter)			−129.50	−124.10
Grooved Pegboard Dominant (time)			−73.17	−66.57***
Grooved Pegboard Nondominant (time)			−76.04	−68.80***
Foot Tapping Dominant (score)			26.66	28.43
Foot Tapping Nondominant (score)			24.29	27.86***

[a] Reitan–Indiana Category Test.
[b] Halstead Category Test.
  *p < .05.
 **p < .02.
 ***p < .01.
 ****p < .001.

scores were remarkably similar for the younger and older groups in that 7 of the 9 tests where differences occurred were common to both age groups, whereas 11 of the 14 variables were common to both groups. In the extended battery (Motor Steadiness) for the older age group, 4 of the 5 tests and 6 of the 16 variables were significantly different. These results will accordingly be taken into consideration in explaining the relationships between intelligence and neuropsychological functioning. In the clinical-matched control group comparisons of neuropsychological functioning in this study, the statistical technique employed for controlling intelligence was analysis of covariance.

The relationships between occupational status of fathers and neuropsychological test results. The effect of socioeconomic status must also be reckoned with. Previous studies (Berelson & Steiner, 1964) have reported a positive relationship between IQ and social strata, and, accordingly, occupation, notwithstanding the controversy regarding interpretations of the relationship. The significant differences in occupation between the various clinical and matched control groups in this study is acknowledged, but the effect of occupational differences is in some measure controlled by the use of analysis of covariance where intelligence is parcelled out.

Summary. This section dealt with methodological problems and normal group data. The neuropsychological battery differentiated between age (maturational) levels. Sex norms are not required. In the comparison of groups of normal children differing in IQ levels, it was found that IQ was statistically significantly related to 33 of the 78 variables included in the battery for younger and older children. In later analyses of data in this chapter, therefore, analysis of covariance will be used to delimit the effects of intelligence and possibly occupational status, assuming the existence of a positive relationship between intelligence and occupational status.

Clinical and Matched Groups-IQ Findings

IQ—Initial examination. Data regrading IQ for the six clinical groups and their respective matched groups are presented in Table 5. There were significant differences between each of the clinical groups and their respective matched groups with respect to Full Scale IQ. The IQs of the Normal matched groups were consistently higher, the differences in Full Scale IQ between clinical and matched groups were as follows: Acute I—10.66; Acute II—9.80; Chronic I—19.78; Chronic II—20.62; MCD I—15.43; MCD II—7.61.

IQ—Initial examination and reexamination. There were no appreciable changes in the relative superiority of the normal groups compared with their respective clinical groups on retest. The overall between groups Fs were generally statistically significant (Table 6), while the groups x years interaction effects were generally nonsignificant. An exception to this generalization occurred, however, with Chronic group I which did not keep pace with their matched controls on Verbal and Performance IQs and four subtests during the interval between examinations.

TABLE 5

Full Scale IQ Means, Standard Deviations, Ranges and
t Tests for the Six Clinical Groups and
Their Respective Matched Normal Groups

Group	Mean	SD	Range	t
Acute I	101.88	14.25	46–135	7.82****
Acute Control I	112.54	9.70	90–135	
Acute II	104.50	14.25	58–136	6.62****
Acute Control II	114.30	9.31	91–131	
Chronic I	93.13	18.45	41–125	7.20****
Chronic Control I	112.91	9.71	91–130	
Chronic II	91.69	17.98	44–129	2.04*
Chronic Control II	112.31	6.93	94–124	
MCD I	98.86	10.93	78–125	9.21****
MCD Control I	114.29	8.10	94–129	
MCD II	101.09	10.68	72–130	3.02***
MCD Control II	108.70	9.59	90–128	

*$p < .05$.
**$p < .02$.
***$p < .01$.
****$p < .001$.

All children, with the exception of Chronic group II and their controls, showed some improvement between testings on one or more intelligence scores. For Acute groups I and II and their matched controls an improvement took place between years in a number of performance subtests, with the result that Performance IQs and Full-Scale IQs increased. Improvement at reexamintion was also noted for both MCD groups, although the pattern of change was somewhat different. MCD group I and their matched controls improved on Object Assembly and Mazes with a resulting increase in Performance and Full Scale IQs. However, while MCD group II and their controls also improved on two performance subtests between years there was no resulting increase in Performance or Full Scale IQs. Chronic group I along with their controls improved on only one performance subtest.

Summary. The IQs of each of the six clinical groups were significantly lower than those of their respective control groups, at initial examination as well as at reexamination 1 year later.

**Clinical versus Matched Control Group Differences
and Differences between Testing Occasions on
Neuropsychological Variables (Excluding
Intelligence Test)**

Initial examination and reexamination. This section deals with the evaluation of changes between initial examination and reexamination for the

TABLE 6
Clinical versus Matched Normal Control Group Comparisons on Wechsler Intelligence Scale for Children at Two Testing Periods, 1 Year Apart

Scale or Subtest	Acute I and Acute Control I (<9 yrs)			Acute II and Acute Control II (>9 yrs)			Chronic I and Chronic Control I (<9 yrs)			Chronic II and Chronic Control II (>9 yrs)			MCD I and MCD Control I (<9 yrs)			MCD II and MCD Control II (>9 yrs)		
	Overall between-groups F ratios	Between-years F ratios	Interaction group × year	Overall between-groups F ratios	Between-years F ratios	Interaction group × year	Overall between-groups F ratios	Between-years F ratios	Interaction group × year	Overall between-groups F ratios	Between-years F ratios	Interaction group × year	Overall between-groups F ratios	Between-years F ratios	Interaction group × year	Overall between-groups F ratios	Between-years F ratios	Interaction group × year
Full Scale IQ	86.81****	5.19*	0.00	41.34****	7.75***	1.44	95.71****	1.59	0.50	72.90****	0.98	0.10	123.71****	5.55**	1.27	10.79****	0.11	0.34
Verbal Scale IQ	83.92****	0.53	0.01	29.00****	1.35	0.87	38.24**	0.44	4.63*	131.97****	0.08	0.39	78.86****	0.71	0.90	9.52***	0.16	0.10
Performance Scale IQ	102.90****	4.56*	0.01	37.50****	13.39****	1.53	53.29****	0.02	6.64***	46.98****	1.46	0.07	99.65****	8.02***	0.33	3.48	0.00	0.75
Information	22.76****	1.44	0.12	25.10****	0.03	0.04	27.71****	0.74	7.03***	9.55***	0.57	0.76	29.52****	2.47	0.39	5.71**	1.07	0.63
Comprehension	2.36	0.31	0.04	15.32****	0.05	0.67	13.08****	0.50	4.40*	68.25****	2.24	0.85	17.94****	3.48	1.88	9.03****	1.89	0.77
Arithmetic	31.38****	0.14	0.11	13.86****	0.78	0.92	29.38****	0.13	3.08	46.52****	0.00	0.32	41.94****	3.49	0.87	6.67**	0.00	0.06
Similarities	21.89****	0.47	1.30	18.03****	3.00	4.51*	99.69****	0.42	8.72***	46.89****	0.03	0.65	27.13****	0.78	0.86	5.77**	1.04	0.05
Vocabulary	19.53****	1.30	2.41	19.43****	0.05	0.02	28.79****	0.27	1.44	124.22****	0.32	0.00	37.06****	0.00	0.10	4.59*	2.39	0.48
Digit Span	3.60	2.52	0.40	3.35	1.91	0.02	21.87****	0.12	1.11	72.83****	0.83	0.70	19.09****	0.79	2.27	0.13	0.18	0.00
Picture Completion	16.70****	0.25	0.09	3.62	4.90*	1.01	16.04****	1.22	3.25	16.64****	0.20	1.09	25.91****	0.36	0.67	0.16	0.71	0.92
Picture Arrangement	10.87****	0.37	0.00	6.83***	6.02**	1.39	44.29****	0.31	1.44	30.31****	1.08	0.87	13.99****	2.84	0.79	0.30	3.89*	0.88
Block Design	6.68***	0.98	1.15	18.40****	5.36*	0.06	15.61****	0.27	3.08	20.18****	1.18	0.06	46.81****	2.02	0.65	7.84***	1.57	0.16
Object Assembly	4.28*	4.40*	0.06	15.13****	11.10****	0.25	16.89****	4.69*	0.07	26.87****	2.62	0.01	39.52****	12.21****	0.00	0.58	6.09**	0.48
Coding	6.59**	6.21**	2.47	50.77****	6.66**	0.85	20.61****	1.71	2.29	26.27****	1.16	1.07	12.97****	2.38	2.95	7.52****	1.20	0.26
Mazes	8.05***	3.57	1.14	24.01****	4.12*	1.56	25.94****	1.61	4.54*	32.36****	0.04	2.15	26.80****	4.09*	0.00	2.23	0.69	0.75

*p < .05; **p < .02; ***p < .01; ****p < .001.

clinical and control groups (analysis of variance), and the evaluation of clinical versus control group differences and changes between examinations with intelligence controlled by means of analysis of covariance.

Table 7 summarizes the findings for Acute group I and their matched Normals. The Acute group children when compared with the control children exhibited generally lower scores (on 17 tests and 27 variables) across the two testing periods. On reexamination, however, both groups improved substantially (on 15 tests and 26 variables), with the Acute group exhibiting a significantly higher rate of improvement (on 3 tests and 3 variables). When intelligence was held constant, the pattern of differences between Acutes and Normals and between years still obtained, but with a reduction to 11 tests and 19 variables between groups and to 11 tests and 19 variables between years. With intelligence as the covariate, the Acute group was found to be bridging the gap in that they increased their range of differential improvement to 8 tests and 14 variables.

Table 7 also summarizes the findings for Acute group II and Acute controls II. The older Acute children, as the younger ones, exhibited a generalized decrement in scores during both examinations when compared to their respective matched controls (14 tests, 26 variables on the Halstead-Reitan-Benton battery and 10 variables on the Klove-Matthews battery). Both the older Acute group and their matched Normals showed significant improvement by reexamination (13 tests, 22 variables, and 3 tests and 7 variables of the Klove-Matthews battery). The Acute group, however, made significantly larger gains on 3 tests and 3 variables. The analysis of covariance produced some striking changes in the significance levels, in that the group differences were substantially reduced to 6 tests and 8 variables as well as 3 tests and 6 variables of the Klove-Matthews battery, with the year differences only slightly reduced to 9 tests and 17 variables and 2 tests and 6 variables of the Klove-Matthews battery. With intelligence held constant, the older Acute group was found to have made no strides in closing the gap with their matched Normals on those tests and variables where differences were noted.

Table 8 summarizes the findings for Chronic group I and Chronic control group I. Whereas the overall differences between the clinical and control groups were striking (17 tests and 30 variables), and while improvement in both groups occurred regularly on reexamination (15 tests and 25 variables), in no instance did Chronic group I close the gap when compared with their matched controls. With intelligence as the covariate, the group differences were radically reduced to 5 tests and 7 variables, while the improvement of both groups at time of reexamination was less affected (13 tests and 21 variables).

Table 8 also summarizes the findings for the older Chronic group and their matched controls. Overall differences were again striking (16 tests and 28 variables on the Halstead-Reitan-Benton battery along with 4 tests and 10 variables on the Klove-Matthews battery). Compared to the younger Chronic group, the improvement at time of reexamination was less striking (10 tests and 16 variables as well as 4 tests and 11 variables of the Klove-Matthews battery).

TABLE 7

Comparison of Acute Groups I & II With Their Matched Controls on Neuropsychological Variables at Two Testing Periods, 1 Year Apart

Variables	Analysis of Variance–Acute I			Analysis of Covariance–Acute I			Analysis of Variance–Acute II			Analysis of Covariance–Acute II		
	Overall between-groups difference	Between-years difference	Groups × years interaction	Overall between-groups difference	Between-years difference	Groups × years interaction	Overall between-groups difference	Between-years difference	Groups × years interaction	Overall between-groups difference	Between-years difference	Groups × years interaction
Category Test (errors)	11.00****	0.05	0.02	0.39	0.12	0.02	15.41****	16.34****	0.01	1.91	9.92***	0.17
Tapping–Dominant (correct)	6.00***	29.50****	0.01	0.38	27.22****	0.12	20.13****	22.53****	0.00	6.21**	16.29****	0.20
Tapping–Nondominant (correct)	3.35	27.33****	0.07	0.17	19.38****	0.10	11.42****	19.09****	0.08	2.13	13.42****	0.45
Speech Perception (errors)	21.88****	26.33****	0.08	6.64***	1.24	2.20	11.35****	5.80*	4.59**	0.36	2.35	3.22
Trail Making A (time)	0.97	0.24	0.40	4.58*	1.11	0.59	4.17*	6.80*	1.93	0.40	3.34	1.33
Trail Making B (time)	10.51****	1.40	0.11	6.85***	14.14****	0.00	8.83***	20.66****	0.65	0.00	13.20****	0.62
Trail Making–Total (time)	3.45	3.98*	0.06	0.20	1.77	0.34	10.99****	28.97****	1.38	0.01	20.64****	0.06
Matching Figures (time)	7.54***	24.53****	0.12	0.02	20.86****	5.05**	7.67***	7.33***	0.47	0.04	2.93	0.57
Matching Figures (errors)	5.40***	38.71****	0.27	9.30***	25.99****	2.01	3.65	0.00	0.15	0.55	0.18	0.23
Matching V's (time)	16.92****	23.42****	4.08*	1.35	11.51****	17.07****	7.97***	6.95***	0.09	0.14	2.04	1.25
Matching V's (errors)	17.26****	9.10***	0.78	28.15****	11.89****	2.72	1.36	2.12	0.86	0.80	0.34	0.52
Star (correct)	15.43****	9.69***	0.33	18.33****	4.00*	0.99	2.95	3.60	2.50	0.12	1.08	0.32
Concentric Squares (correct)	19.23****	8.39***	3.87	3.58	9.77****	0.45	4.72*	6.43**	0.26	1.40	4.53*	2.01
Progressive Figures (time)	50.09****	6.61**	2.06	2.22	0.98	9.41****	9.60****	14.88****	0.10	0.15	8.49***	0.00
Color Form (time)	22.19****	3.66	0.05	12.32****	1.04	8.10***	28.40****	3.56	0.01	7.20***	0.58	0.04
Color Form (errors)	18.39****	6.71***	0.13	2.32	8.04***	4.70*	10.95****	0.20	0.00	1.75	1.79	0.08
Target Test (correct)	10.66****	39.02****	1.00	5.59**	5.02**	6.63***	12.49****	20.36****	1.04	0.46	12.96****	0.29
Marching Test–Dominant (time)	6.51**	27.98****	2.00	12.98****	8.91****	15.08****	22.56****	14.04****	0.34	7.46***	8.97***	0.47
Marching Test–Dominant (errors)	7.97***	38.95****	0.90	11.01****	37.03****	15.94****	9.02***	0.06	0.47	1.67	0.25	0.08
Marching Test–Nondominant (time)	11.18***	31.45****	3.91	10.71****	11.01****	15.19****	21.18****	20.40****	0.30	7.72***	14.84****	0.14
Marching Test–Nondominant (errors)	19.32****	41.32****	2.41	19.39****	41.32****	0.11	9.41***	0.04	0.14	5.13*	0.01	0.45
Tactual Performance Test–Dominant (time)	17.88****	10.76***	5.51*	0.05	0.17	0.13	6.77**	15.60****	0.02	0.05	9.59***	0.01
Tactual Performance Test–Nondominant (time)	21.52****	15.33****	3.81	0.27	6.55***	8.67***	8.66***	21.30****	0.40	0.07	14.03****	0.02
Tactual Performance Test–Both (time)	16.03****	18.14****	2.88	8.97***	9.62***	26.14****	19.70****	22.17****	4.31*	3.93	14.71****	2.97
Tactual Performance Test–Total (time)	22.11****	4.32*	0.01	33.81****	0.00	4.74*	11.53***	24.23****	0.34	0.44	16.56****	0.01
Tactual Performance Test–Memory (correct)	0.07	17.85*	0.15	5.48**	28.25****	9.82****	21.63****	20.56****	0.40	2.83	12.93****	0.09
Tactual Performance Test–Location (correct)	11.46****	17.00****	0.06	9.93***	0.09	17.82****	23.79****	11.18****	0.46	7.33***	6.36**	0.00
Matching Pictures (correct)	8.50***	22.58****	0.22	7.30***	32.91****	0.64	2.44	5.38*	0.12	0.11	2.39	0.00
Sound Recognition	27.88****	31.40****	0.40	5.40**	36.28****	2.52	48.16****	17.03****	4.79**	23.87****	11.47****	3.63
Right–Left Orientation (correct)	15.02****	2.77	0.19	3.36	0.17	0.17	1.45	2.41	0.15	1.82	0.24	0.86
Lateral Dominance (correct)	10.46***	9.51***	4.05*	0.42	1.13	1.13	25.27****	0.34	0.11	18.54****	0.15	0.06
Maze Coordination Dominant (time)							18.21****	11.79****	0.80	7.65***	8.19***	0.42
Maze Coordination Dominant (counter)							31.41****	12.20****	2.10	16.80****	8.65***	1.49
Maze Coordination Nondominant (time)							33.74****	10.41****	2.29	16.87****	6.73**	1.58
Maze Coordination Nondominant (counter)							5.24**	7.77***	0.04	3.24	6.72**	0.07
Grooved Steadiness Dominant (time)							11.35****	0.16	0.12	3.10	0.07	0.00
Grooved Steadiness Dominant (counter)							3.22	0.94	0.15	0.60	0.30	0.04
Grooved Steadiness Nondominant (time)							2.96	0.01	0.12	0.08	0.55	0.01
Grooved Steadiness Nondominant (counter)							2.58	1.29	2.02	2.39	1.29	2.02
Steadiness Dominant (time)							12.51****	2.52	0.12	5.97***	1.37	0.03
Steadiness Dominant (counter)							0.23	0.45	0.56	0.05	0.32	0.49
Steadiness Nondominant (time)							7.13***	0.51	1.85	2.21	0.05	1.36
Steadiness Nondominant (counter)							1.67	1.18	0.15	0.08	0.43	0.04
Grooved Pegboard Dominant (time)							7.62***	5.66**	1.05	1.20	2.86	1.87
Grooved Pegboard Nondominant (time)							1.15	1.56	0.90	0.38	1.11	0.76
Foot Tapping Dominant (score)							19.13****	11.73****	1.42	9.94****	8.80***	1.97
Foot Tapping Nondominant (score)							14.37****	15.19****	0.76	8.67***	12.80****	0.99

*p < .05; **p < .02; ***p < .01; ****p < .001.

139

TABLE 8

Comparison of Chronic Groups I & II with Their Matched Controls on Neuropsychological Variables at Two Testing Periods, 1 Year Apart

Variables	Analysis of Variance—Chronic I			Analysis of Covariance—Chronic I			Analysis of Variance—Chronic II			Analysis of Covariance—Chronic II		
	Overall between-groups difference	Between-years difference	Groups × years interaction	Overall between-groups difference	Between-years difference	Groups × years interaction	Overall between-groups difference	Between-years difference	Groups × years interaction	Overall between-groups difference	Between-years difference	Groups × years interaction
Category Test (errors)	4.62*	4.41*	0.20	2.99	8.07***	0.67	3.61	13.50****	1.52	6.92****	13.76****	2.78
Tapping–Dominant (correct)	38.83****	3.75	0.00	17.85****	3.23	0.00	20.72****	6.11**	0.10	2.34	5.10**	0.20
Tapping–Nondominant (correct)	42.39****	3.13	0.01	9.71****	2.18	0.09	13.46****	4.84*	0.02	0.73	3.91*	0.00
Speech perception (errors)	62.29****	3.04	1.03	38.86****	2.17	0.58	51.84****	0.08	0.00	11.95****	0.01	0.03
Trail Making A (time)	24.79****	5.69**	0.03	1.74	6.07**	0.09	5.50**	4.11*	0.19	0.79	3.09	1.10
Trail Making B (time)	32.71****	0.88	2.30	19.33****	0.26	0.08	28.53****	8.68***	0.45	0.79	2.74	0.35
Trail Making–Total (time)	35.63****	1.18	2.58	21.87****	0.58	0.11	23.90****	8.79***	0.18	0.17	7.97***	0.09
Matching Figures (errors)	12.92****	1.11	0.13	0.40	0.52	0.02	12.59****	5.50**	1.47	0.00	8.12***	1.40
Matching V's (time)	12.31****	6.75***	0.02	0.09	5.23**	0.03	0.01	2.88	2.25	0.56	2.50	2.38
Matching V's (errors)	6.24**	8.64***	0.10	0.38	7.29***	0.36	6.13**	16.03****	0.00	0.79	15.33****	0.01
Star (correct)	20.97****	15.68****	0.06	0.96	14.08****	0.00	2.52	1.75	1.50	3.91*	0.96	0.79
Concentric Squares (correct)	21.93****	20.57****	0.72	2.51	18.36****	1.59	19.22****	1.75	0.44	0.35	0.28	1.44
Progressive Figures (time)	27.38****	12.90****	1.09	2.08	10.84***	2.73	6.40**	0.03	0.00	0.06	8.53***	0.03
Color Form (time)	23.47****	15.11****	0.01	0.77	16.29****	0.13	13.42****	9.59***	3.08	0.18	4.79*	3.08
Color Form (errors)	20.68****	11.90****	0.10	0.44	12.31****	0.69	24.92****	5.72**	0.46	0.19	0.04	0.35
Target Test (correct)	26.12****	8.77***	1.31	1.40	8.82***	0.76	12.60****	0.06	0.04	0.01	3.11	0.02
Marching Test Dominant (time)	19.37****	10.67***	1.44	1.42	9.35***	0.81	12.82****	4.04*	0.04	2.81	5.13**	0.23
Marching Test Dominant (errors)	14.69****	8.83***	0.27	0.20	6.89***	0.02	22.18****	6.16**	0.00	0.67	0.07	0.02
Marching Test Nondominant (time)	11.37****	4.04*	0.21	0.25	2.40	0.00	5.24*	5.24*	0.19	0.00	2.76	0.13
Marching Test Nondominant (errors)	15.81****	8.82***	0.04	0.55	6.19**	0.26	15.83****	3.74	0.47	0.10	0.13	0.82
Marching Test–Nondominant (errors)	16.20****	4.47*	0.54	0.60	2.36	0.03	9.41***	0.36	0.01	0.53	4.20*	0.00
Tactual Performance Test–Dominant (time)	15.37****	23.58****	0.42	0.23	24.00****	0.40	5.04*	5.24*	0.09	2.13	3.83*	0.03
Tactual Performance Test–Nondominant (time)	12.77****	13.49****	0.15	1.96	14.02****	0.99	7.61***	4.72*	0.33	5.28*	2.41	0.88
Tactual Performance Test–Both (time)	16.74****	19.48****	0.19	0.01	20.12****	0.23	15.62****	3.42	0.01	0.85	4.12*	0.01
Tactual Performance Test–Total (time)	13.45****	25.34****	0.00	0.02	25.47****	0.06	9.43***	4.99*	0.02	3.84*	7.98***	0.16
Tactual Performance Test–Memory (correct)	10.16**	17.89****	0.00	0.01	16.20****	0.26	13.88****	8.87***	0.02	0.04	0.31	0.00
Tactual Performance Test–Location (correct)	1.55	17.41****	0.39	0.52	15.75****	0.16	16.12****	0.87	0.77	0.09	2.44	1.26
Matching Pictures (correct)	23.31****	10.70***	1.20	2.24	9.15***	0.81	10.50***	3.41	1.03	0.22	0.51	0.94
Sound Recognition	39.58****	10.83***	2.55	17.44****	6.17***	0.73	5.62**	0.99	0.05	0.08	0.09	0.01
Right–Left Orientation (correct)	11.19****	4.13*	1.04	2.24	2.28	0.07	28.13****	0.11	0.14	0.12	6.84***	0.46
Lateral Dominance (correct)	14.03****	2.18*	1.00	7.29***	1.39	1.58	25.99****	0.00	0.63	6.33**	0.72	0.80
Maze Coordination Dominant (time)							16.61****	3.69	0.63	1.40	2.73	0.57
Maze Coordination Dominant (counter)							22.20****	11.12****	1.64	0.47	12.01****	1.91
Maze Coordination Nondominant (time)							17.60****	7.33***	0.58	1.76	7.18****	0.53
Maze Coordination Nondominant (counter)							16.73****	16.80****	0.19	0.26	17.70****	0.09
Grooved Steadiness Dominant (time)							6.76**	6.76**	3.43	0.62	5.71**	3.53
Grooved Steadiness Dominant (counter)							1.62	7.40***	3.90*	0.12	6.54***	3.77*
Grooved Steadiness Nondominant (time)							4.38*	6.92***	5.42**	1.02	5.86**	5.66**
Grooved Steadiness Nondominant (counter)							0.62	0.12	2.89	1.57	0.07	2.80
Steadiness Dominant (time)							5.11*	4.20*	0.42	0.03	3.43	0.34
Steadiness Dominant (counter)							2.20	12.20****	0.02	0.30	11.50****	0.01
Steadiness Nondominant (time)							8.62***	4.86*	2.36	0.11	3.94*	2.26
Steadiness Nondominant (counter)							0.12	12.68****	0.00	0.03	12.11****	0.01
Grooved Pegboard Dominant (time)							0.00	1.59	0.27	0.52	1.32	0.31
Grooved Pegboard Nondominant (time)							0.26	1.75	0.00	0.98	1.30	0.00
Foot Tapping Dominant (score)							13.16****	7.86***	0.56	1.16	6.84***	0.75
Foot Tapping Nondominant (score)							14.88****	1.15	0.09	2.16	0.72	0.05

* p < .05, ** p < .01, *** p < .001, **** p < .0001

With intelligence held constant, the group differences were drastically curtailed (5 tests and 6 variables), but the improvement at time of reexamination remained more or less the same (9 tests and 14 variables as well as 4 tests and 10 variables of the Klove-Matthews battery). The older Chronic group closed the gap with their matched normals on 1 test and 2 variables of the Klove-Matthews battery.

Table 9 summarizes the findings for the younger MCD group and their matched Normals. The number of overall differences between the younger MCDs and their normal controls across the two testing periods (13 tests and 23 variables) was below that noted for the other younger clinical groups and their respective controls. Significant changes were found in 12 of the tests and 21 of the variables between years for both the MCD and Control groups (due to learning and/or maturation). When intelligence was held constant, the pattern regarding group differences as well as changes over time was appreciably altered. Differences between groups were reduced to 2 tests and 2 variables, whereas improvement over time was noted in 8 tests and 11 variables.

Table 9 also summarizes the findings for the older MCD group and their control group (MCD II controls). In comparing the results of the older with those of the younger MCD group for the same battery of neuropsychological tests, one finds that across both testing periods the older MCD children differed less from their normal controls; i.e., on only 3 tests and 4 variables compared with 13 tests and 23 variables for the younger groups. Improvement between test periods was also less for the older compared with the younger groups, but only by 3 variables. When intelligence was controlled by analysis of covariance, the number of significant differences was radically reduced for the younger group. With the older groups, holding intelligence constant increased the number of significant differences; the group differences increased to 5 tests and 5 variables and the year differences increased to 13 tests and 21 variables.

On the Motor Steadiness battery, significant differences between MCD group II and their matched normals were found across test occasions on 1 test and 2 variables. For these older MCDs and their matched controls, all tests and 11 of the 16 variables discriminated between testing periods, but the groups showed no differential pattern of improvement on these variables over time. The findings were identical for the analysis of covariance compared to the analysis of variance.

Summary. Across both test periods, Chronic and then Acute groups, regardless of age level, showed the most marked neuropsychological impairment. The signs of deficit were somewhat less striking for the younger MCDs and greatly reduced for the older MCDs. At reexamination, all of the clinical and normal groups, but particularly the younger ones, exhibited significant improvement on various tests of the battery. But clinical-control group differences were still quite marked. When intelligence was controlled (analysis of covariance), the number of variables discriminating between clinical and control

TABLE 9

Comparison of MCD Groups I & II with Their Matched Controls on Neuropsychological Variables at Two Testing Periods, 1 Year Apart

Variables	Analysis of Variance—MCD I Overall between-groups difference	Between-years difference	Groups × years interaction	Analysis of Covariance—MCD I Overall between-groups difference	Between-years difference	Groups × years interaction	Analysis of Variance—MCD II Overall between-groups difference	Between-years difference	Groups × years interaction	Analysis of Covariance—MCD II Overall between-groups difference	Between-years difference	Groups × years interaction
Category Test (errors)	13.64****	7.73***	1.91	2.57	9.55***	2.40	0.16	4.83*	1.23	6.16***	7.96***	0.89
Tapping—Dominant (correct)	5.75**	21.13****	0.41	0.05	16.58****	0.87	0.00	7.07***	0.35	3.23	8.16***	0.12
Tapping—Nondominant (correct)	1.72	12.49****	0.14	0.80	9.18****	0.41	0.03	3.03	0.24	2.79	3.10	0.07
Speech Perception (errors)	12.11****	3.59	0.09	1.94	0.80	0.06	4.37*	2.71	2.61	1.91	2.58	2.31
Trail Making A (time)	13.98****	5.48**	3.63	0.04	2.73	2.63	5.52**	11.04****	2.13	2.82	10.93****	1.87
Trail Making B (time)	36.63****	4.70*	1.48	1.19	1.59	0.65	5.19**	2.67	0.23	2.13	2.55	0.41
Trail Making Total (time)	34.70****	5.78**	1.74	1.11	2.36	0.86	0.01	3.36	0.94	4.49	6.08***	0.60
Matching Figures (time)	0.49	2.58	0.04	2.93	1.02	0.01	0.00	2.72	0.64	4.76*	4.87*	0.32
Matching Figures (errors)	0.94	6.74**	0.04	2.25	4.06*	0.01	1.02	0.52	1.02	0.00	0.75	0.75
Matching V's (time)	0.01	6.01**	0.59	4.58**	3.65*	1.12	0.11	8.65***	0.17	2.65	10.88****	0.04
Matching V's (errors)	9.13***	4.92**	0.26	0.00	2.63	0.69	1.58	2.29	0.10	2.78	2.17	0.16
Star (correct)	13.74****	0.23	0.13	0.04	0.07	0.00	0.24	0.63	1.22	5.07**	1.90	0.93
Concentric Squares (correct)	10.14***	1.58	1.60	0.09	0.45	1.02	9.82***	0.39	0.25	5.46**	0.31	0.14
Progressive Figures (time)	27.01****	9.35***	1.39	0.30	5.07**	0.61	0.77	5.66**	0.52	3.25	6.59***	0.84
Color Form (time)	14.05****	6.89***	1.38	0.35	3.23	0.61	0.00	6.66**	0.41	2.19	8.93***	0.19
Color Form (errors)	17.21****	6.47**	0.79	0.01	3.17	0.26	0.04	5.38*	0.40	0.60	5.79**	0.55
Target Test (correct)	21.34****	9.43***	1.26	0.38	4.71**	0.43	0.00	7.30***	2.58	0.03	7.15***	2.45
Matching Test—Dominant (time)	9.94***	8.68***	1.54	0.96	4.66**	0.75	0.11	3.86*	0.23	3.29	6.86***	0.03
Matching Test—Dominant (errors)	3.08	2.29	1.09	0.09	1.47	0.83	0.72	1.37	0.05	2.10	3.05	0.03
Matching Test—Nondominant (time)	12.66****	8.38***	2.10	0.78	4.27**	1.14	0.43	2.50	0.68	3.23	5.41**	0.35
Matching Test—Nondominant (errors)	7.30***	2.40	0.08	0.88	0.59	0.01	0.24	5.74**	0.00	1.82	6.57***	0.03
Tactual Performance Test—Dominant (time)	7.66***	1.41	0.06	0.50	0.19	0.40	1.10	8.28***	1.70	0.00	9.81***	1.38
Tactual Performance Test—Nondominant (time)	18.58****	1.84	0.15	0.35	0.38	0.62	1.03	4.37*	1.22	0.00	5.26**	0.94
Tactual Performance Test—Both (time)	16.79****	10.04***	0.15	0.00	5.90**	0.72	0.68	6.12**	0.18	0.02	6.12***	0.07
Tactual Performance Test—Total (time)	21.76****	6.33**	0.01	0.19	3.00	0.30	1.23	18.76****	0.18	0.00	19.79****	0.06
Tactual Performance Test—Memory (correct)	29.91****	3.91*	0.02	1.23	1.37	0.37	0.51	6.39**	0.34	0.01	6.33***	0.56
Tactual Performance Test—Location (correct)	23.00****	10.28***	0.58	2.70	7.10***	0.25	1.57	0.67	0.00	0.10	0.56	0.03
Matching Pictures (correct)	1.94	6.36**	0.85	3.07	3.34	1.81	1.43	3.96*	0.02	7.34***	5.45**	0.01
Sound Recognition	0.80	2.51	0.24	4.26*	0.76	0.02	0.83	3.95*	0.83	1.39	4.08*	0.93
Right–Left Orientation (correct)	3.78	6.16**	0.00	2.05	3.10	0.20	0.15	5.98**	0.15	0.08	5.89**	0.13
Lateral Dominance (correct)	16.32****	3.75	0.01	0.00	1.30	0.10	1.51	0.35	0.08	0.44	0.43	0.03
Maze Coordination Dominant (time)							1.57	17.69****	0.07	0.35	17.68****	0.02
Maze Coordination Dominant (counter)							3.73	21.07****	0.71	1.77	20.99****	0.56
Maze Coordination Nondominant (time)							0.17	18.07****	0.70	0.01	17.81****	0.60
Maze Coordination Nondominant (counter)							0.46	17.11****	1.12	0.04	16.92****	0.96
Grooved Steadiness Dominant (time)							1.17	7.53****	1.01	0.56	7.36****	0.90
Grooved Steadiness Dominant (counter)							1.33	5.57**	1.12	0.90	5.46**	1.05
Grooved Steadiness Nondominant (time)							0.24	2.21	0.32	0.52	2.29	0.37
Grooved Steadiness Nondominant (counter)							0.52	0.73	0.37	1.17	0.81	0.47
Steadiness Dominant (time)							1.04	1.07	0.78	1.13	1.08	0.80
Steadiness Dominant (counter)							0.01	6.88***	1.82	0.02	6.81***	1.80
Steadiness Nondominant (time)							0.90	0.27	0.21	0.90	0.27	0.21
Steadiness Nondominant (counter)							0.03	0.16	0.71	0.01	0.15	0.69
Grooved Pegboard Dominant (time)							14.17****	26.38****	0.99	8.87****	26.72****	0.78
Grooved Pegboard Nondominant (time)							17.66****	16.34****	1.33	11.08****	16.51****	1.07
Foot Tapping Dominant (score)							0.57	10.75***	0.72	0.57	10.55***	0.61
Foot Tapping Nondominant (score)							0.00	8.99***	0.97	0.40	8.90***	0.77

groups and between test periods generally diminished. Stability of findings, with and without intelligence partialled out, was greatest for MCD group II, followed by Acute groups I and II, then Chronic groups I and II, and was least for MCD group I.

Normative Data for Normal, Acute, Chronic, and MCD Groups I and II

In order to provide investigators and clinicians with data that might be used for research purposes and for interpreting the presence or absence of neuropsychological impairment in relevant clinical work, normative tables have been prepared and included as Appendices to this chapter. In these normative tables, ages 2-5, 9-10, 11-12, and 13-15 were combined because of the relatively small number of children in the discrete age levels for some of the clinical groups. In order to facilitate comparisons between the normal and clinical groups, the same age levels were combined for the respective normative tables. An additional table (Appendix 9) was prepared for Normal group I for ages 2-3, 4, and 5; and another table (Appendix 10) for Normal group II for ages 9, 10, 11, 12, 13 and 14-15. The following normative tables, which include means and standard deviations for the initial examination, are included in the Appendices: Appendix 1-Normal group I, ages 2 through 8; Appendix 2-Normal group II, ages 9 through 15; Appendix 3-Acute group I, ages 2 through 8; Appendix 4-Acute group II, ages 9 through 15; Appendix 5—Chronic group I, ages 2 through 8; Appendix 6—Chronic group II, ages 9 through 15; Appendix 7—MCD group I, ages 2 through 8; Appendix 8—MCD group II, ages 9 through 15; and the age breakdowns referred to above for younger and older normal children (Appendices 9 and 10).

Neurological Ratings (Acute and Chronic Groups) and Cerebral Dysfunction Ratings (MCD Group)

Initial examination and reexamination data. The neurological ratings for the Acute and Chronic groups as well as the cerebral dysfunction ratings for the MCD group (the criteria for which were presented earlier in this chapter), are shown in Table 10. For younger Acute cases (I), the ratings were skewed with the bulk of cases at the severe-serious end of the continuum. There were however no within-group age ($\chi^2 = 3.20\,p < .60$) or sex ($\chi^2 = .84, p < .95$) differences in neurological ratings. For the older Acute cases (II), the ratings were more evenly distributed among the mild-moderate-severe-serious categories. There was an age difference ($\chi^2 = 8.32, p < .05$), with children over 12 showing more than the expected incidence of unequivocal abnormal ratings when compared with children 9 to 12. There was, however, no within-group sex difference ($\chi^2 = 2.02, p < .70$) in neurological ratings. Also for both younger and older (I and II) Chronic groups, the ratings were distributed more evenly throughout the continuum, but the mode in each instance was the severe category. There were no within-group age differences for either younger

TABLE 10
Initial Neurological Rating for Acute and Chronic Groups and Cerebral Dysfunction (Psychiatric) Rating for MCD Groups (Frequencies and Percentages)

Rating	Acute group I (N = 131)		Acute group II (N = 100)		Chronic group I (N = 77)		Chronic group II (N = 39)		MCD group I (N = 51)		MCD group II (N = 44)	
	No.	%	No.	%	No.	%	No.	%	No.	%	No.	%
Minor–1	2	2	1	1	12	16	5	13	20	39	22	50
Mild–2	26	20	23	23	23	30	7	18	18	35	17	39
Moderate–3	19	14	34	34	7	9	6	15	13	26	5	11
Severe–4	61	46	24	24	28	36	16	41				
Serious–5	23	18	18	18	7	9	5	13				

(χ^2 = 2.58, $p < .70$) or older (χ^2 = 1.01, $p < .90$) Chronic children. Nor were within-group sex differences found for younger (χ^2 = 3.33, $p < .50$) or older (χ^2 = .78, $p < .95$) Chronic children. The neurological reexamination of Chronic groups I and II resulted in a high degree of concordance with initial examination. Of the 70 younger children reexamined, ratings were reduced by 1 in four instances and by 2 in two instances, while of the 36 older children reexamined, ratings were reduced by 1 in four instances. The remainder of the ratings for these children did not change.

Disturbance in all three behavioral areas (motor, intellectual, personality) was recorded for 82% of MCD group I and 89% of MCD group II; disturbance in two areas was noted for 18% of MCD group I and 11% of MCD group II. The global ratings for both the younger and older MCD groups, but particularly for the older MCD group, were skewed with the mode toward the minimal end of the continuum. No within-group age differences emerged for either younger (χ^2 = 1.19, $p < .60$) or older (χ^2 = 1.03, $p < .60$) MCD children with respect to the global ratings. Nor were there any within-group sex differences in global ratings for younger (χ^2 = 2.17, $p < .40$) or older (χ^2 = 2.72, $p < .30$) MCD children.

Summary. As the rating schemes differ for the three clinical groups, inter-group comparisons are not warranted. The younger compared to older children in the Acute and MCD groups, and the older compared to the younger children in the Chronic group were rated as more impaired.

EEG Ratings and Qualitative Features (Acute and MCD Groups)

Initial examination and reexamination data. A detailed description of criteria used in classifying children to the EEG categories used in Tables 11 and 12 was presented earlier in this chapter. The results of the global EEG ratings are reported in Table 11 for both the older and younger Acute and MCD groups whereas the findings regarding changes in ratings between examination and reexamination are reported in Table 12. Only one significant age difference was recorded, i.e., the initial examination for Acute group II (χ^2 = 10.88, $p < .05$) where the children aged 9–10 exhibited more abnormal ratings. The remainder of the age differences were nonsignificant: initial examination Acute group I (χ^2 = .90, $p < .90$); reexamination Acute group I (χ^2 = 1.00, $p < .90$); reexamination Acute group II (χ^2 = 3.47, $p < .50$). The findings regarding sex differences were consistently nonsignificant: initial examination Acute group I (χ^2 = .96, $p < .90$); initial examination Acute group II (χ^2 = 3.75, $p < .50$); reexamination Acute group I (χ^2 = 1.56, $p < .80$); reexamination Acute group II (χ^2 = .59, $p < .98$).

Initial electrographic findings were unequivocally abnormal in 63% of the younger Acute patients. Twenty-two percent of records were definitely normal. For the older Acute children, the corresponding figures were 72% and 17% (Table 11). Table 13 shows the qualitative breakdown of EEG assessments. Diffuse slowing—both continuous and paroxysmal—asymmetries, and focal slow

TABLE 11

EEG Global Rating for Acute and MCD Groups
(Frequencies and Percentages)

Global Rating	Acute group I (<9)				Acute group II (>9)				MCD group I (<9)				MCD group II (>9)			
	Initial exam.		Re-exam.		Initial exam.		Re-exam.		Initial exam.		Re-exam.		Initial exam.		Re-exam.	
	No.	%	No.	%	No.	%	No.	%	No.	%	No.	%	No.	%	No.	%
Normal—1	28	22	35	31	17	17	37	48	14	30	19	51	26	68	22	73
Borderline—1½	19	15	23	21	11	11	15	19	14	30	9	24	2	5	2	7
Minimally abnormal—2	54	42	50	44	44	45	21	28	11	23	6	16	8	21	6	20
Moderately abnormal—3	26	20	5	4	25	25	4	5	6	13	2	6	2	6		
Markedly abnormal—4	1	1			2	2			2	4	1	3				
Total	128		113		99		77		47		37		38		30	

TABLE 12

EEG Global Rating Changes Between Initial Examination
(1st EEG) and Reexamination (2nd EEG) for Acute
and MCD Groups (Frequencies and Percentages)

EEG change	Acute group I (<9)		Acute group II (>9)		MCD group I (<9)		MCD group II (>9)	
	No.	%	No.	%	No.	%	No.	%
Return to 1, i.e., 1½-1, 2-1, 3-1, 4-1	17	15	25	32	11	31	3	10
Return to 1½, i.e., 2-1½, 3-1½, 4-1½	10	9	8	11	2	6	1	3
Return to 2, i.e., 3-2, 4-2	13	12	7	9	1	3		
Remained 1	17	15	12	16	7	20	19	64
Remained 1½	8	7	7	9	5	14	1	3
Remained 2	32	29	11	15	4	11	5	17
Remained 3	3	3	3	4	2	6		
Remained 4					1	3		
From 1-1½	5	4			1	3		
From 1-2	1	1	2	3			1	3
From 1½-2	3	3			1	3		
From 1-3	1	1						
From 2-3	1	1	1	1				
Total	111		76		35		30	
EEG not obtained	2		1		2			

abnormalities were the most common findings on initial examination for both age groups. Focal spikes were relatively uncommon on initial recording in the younger patients as were spike-wave discharges. The older patients showed more spike foci in the acute stage than did the younger ones (i.e., 15% versus 4.7%), but slightly less spike-wave abnormality (2% versus 4%).

TABLE 13

Specific EEG Abnormalities[a] (Awake and Asleep)—Initial Examination and Reexamination—for Acute Group I (<9) and Group II (>9) (Frequencies)[b]

EEG Abnormalities	Acute group I (<9)				Acute group II (>9)			
	Awake		Asleep		Awake		Asleep	
	Initial exam.	Re-exam.	Initial exam.	Re-exam.	Initial exam.	Re-exam.	Initial exam.	Re-exam.
Alpha asymmetry	2	5		1	5	1		
Slow	1							
Asynchrony	1				4		3	
Awake	1							
Asleep			1			1		1
Asymmetry	47	16	41	11	35	16	24	12
Depression	3	1	2	2				
Fast (13–17)	1	3	1	2			1	
Fast (18+)	1		1		1	1		
Fast and spindling			1				1	
Focus–slow								
Left anterior					2	1	1	
Left frontal	1		2					
Left central	3		2					
Left temporal	3	1	3			1		1
Left parietal		1						
Left occipital	1		1		1	1		
Right frontal	1		1	2	1	1	2	
Right central	1				1			
Right temporal	4	1	3	1	7	2	4	1
Right parietal	3	1	2					
Right occipital	2	1	1		2	1		
Right anterior	1		1		1		1	
Right posterior		1		1	4	1	1	1
Focus–Spike								
Left temporal						1		2
Right frontal					1			
Left posterior					1		1	1
Right anterior					2	2	2	2
Left central	1	1		1		1	1	3
Left parietal	1				1			
Left occipital		1		1	1			
Right central	2	1	1	2	1		2	1
Right temporal		2	1	2	2	1	1	1
Right parietal	1	1	1	1				
Right occipital		1		1	3		2	2
Left anterior		1		1	1		1	
Right posterior	1	1			2	2	1	2
Sharp waves (scattered)	6	4	7	4	1	1	3	
Slow waves (scattered)	7	4	5	6	1	2		1
Hyperventilation–abnormal	8	17			31	9		
Mixed slow and fast	2	3		2	1	1		
Occipital fusing	4	1			4			
Positive spikes			5	8			5	4
Slow								
Slight	39	33			25	16		
Moderate	11	11			19	6		
Marked	3				1			
Occipital dominant	11	1			18	2		
Paroxysmal–slow burst	7				3	1		
Paroxysmal generally slow	6	1			7	3		
Anterior–dominant slow	5	5			5	2		
Posterior–dominant slow	12	8			8	4		
Hemispheric–dominant slow	8	1			5			
Spike Wave								
Abortive				1			1	
Fast						1		1
Poly/spike	1		1				1	
Slow	1		1		1			2
3 per second	3	3	1	3				1
Temporal slow			1					

[a] Range of entries (awake and asleep) 1–12.
[b] Recorded frequencies not mutually exclusive.

Within the year between initial and followup studies, 24% of the younger Acute group EEGs returned to normal or near normal, while this figure was 43% for the older Acute children (Table 12). Ten percent of the under-9 Acute group and 4% of the over-9 Acute group became worse, with 32% of the younger patients' records and 19% of the older ones remaining minimally or moderately abnormal. Qualitatively, there tended to be persistence of spike foci and of minimal to moderate slowing, with all other abnormalities decreasing in occurrence between reexaminations (Table 13).

In the analysis of the global EEG ratings of the MCD groups, there were no sex differences at initial examination (χ^2 = .18, p < .90) or reexamination (χ^2 = 1.02, p < .60) when age levels were combined. There was only one age difference noted, i.e., for the group under 9 years at initial examination (χ^2 = 5.95, p < .05), the children aged 5-6 showing lesser ratings (1-1½) than the children aged 7-8 who exhibited more abnormal ratings (2-3-4). The findings regarding age differences were nonsignificant for the following: the reexamination for children under 9 (χ^2 = .01, p <.99); the examination for children over 9 (χ^2 = .02, p < .99); and the reexamination for children over 9 (χ^2 = .06, p < .99).

Of the 47 younger MCD (group I) patients on whom initial EEGs were done, 30% of the tracings were unequivocally normal, 30% were borderline, and 40% were unequivocally abnormal (Table 11). There was a variety of abnormalities (Table 14). The most common abnormality in this sample was some degree of diffuse slowing of the resting, waking record (24 patients or 51% of the total). Spike foci were relatively uncommon in the initial records (2 patients), and positive spikes (14 and 6) were found in only 2 patients. Asymmetries were more common than spike foci in this group (5 versus 2 patients). Focal slow activity was uncommon (2 patients). One year later, there was a considerably higher percentage of unequivocally normal records in this group (51% versus 30%). Only 2 patients showed more abnormality than on initial examination and these showed minimal global rating changes from 1 to 1½ and from 1½ to 2 (Table 12). Qualitatively (Table 14), the abnormalities on followup were somewhat different, with more-frequent occurence of spike foci (4%-22%) and of asymmetries (11%-24%) being the outstanding changes. Diffuse slowing was still the most common abnormality, but it was seen slightly less frequently, i.e., in 51% versus 41% of the records. One focal seizure discharge was recorded during sleep; the child had no clinical seizure manifestations during the recording, nor had he any history of seizures.

Initial examination of patients in the older MCD group (II) produced 68% normal records, only 5% borderline and 27% unequivocally abnormal records. Diffuse slowing (16%) was, again, a common type of abnormality, but focal spikes were equally common (16%) in this group (Table 14). There were 8% asymmetries, but no slow foci. Reexamination revealed only a 5% increase in unequivocally normal records, but none of the 20% abnormal tracings was more than minimally abnormal. The improvement qualitatively was accounted for chiefly by the disappearance of all spike foci.

TABLE 14

Specific EEG Abnormalities[a] (Awake and Asleep) — Initial Examination and Reexamination — for MCD Group I (<9) and Group II (>9) (Frequencies)[b]

EEG abnormalities	MCD group I (<9)				MCD group II (>9)			
	Awake		Asleep		Awake		Asleep	
	Initial exam.	Re-exam.	Initial exam.	Re-exam.	Initial exam.	Re-exam.	Initial exam.	Re-exam.
Alpha asymmetry	1	2			1	1		
Asynchrony	1		1	1				
Asymmetry	3	7	4	5	2		2	
Fast (13-17)					1	1	1	
Fast (18+)					2		2	
Focus -slow								
Right parietal	1	1						
Right occipital	1	1						
Focus–spike								
Left frontal					1		1	
Left central	1	2	1	2				
Left temporal					2		3	
Left parietal	1	2	1	2			1	
Right central		1		1	1		1	
Right parietal		2		2				
Right occipital		1		1				
Sharp waves (scattered)	3		3		4	1	2	
Slow waves (scattered)					4			
Hyperventilation–abnormal	5				5	2		
Mixed slow and fast		1			1	1		
Positive spikes			2	2				
Slow								
Slight	19	12			2	3		
Moderate	4	3			3	3		
Marked	1				1			
Occipital dominant	3	1			3	1		
Paroxysmal–slow burst			1			1		
Paroxysmal generally slow	1	1	1	1		1		
Anterior–dominant slow	2	3			2			
Posterior–dominant slow	4	1				1		
Hemispheric–dominant slow	1							
Spike wave								
Abortive					1	1	1	1
Slow	2		1					
3 per second		1						
Temporal slow	3		3		1		1	
Seizure record								
focal			1					

a Range of entries (awake and asleep) 1–8.
b Recorded frequencies not mutually exclusive.

Summary. The incidence of unequivocal EEG abnormalities during the initial examination and subsequent reexamination was as follows: Acute group I—63% and then 48%; Acute group II—72% and then 33%; MCD group I—40% and then 25%; and MCD group II—27% and then 20%. Changes in ratings from normal (1) or borderline (1½) to abnormal (2, 3, or 4) between initial examination and reexamination occurred as follows: Acute group I—6%; Acute group II–4%; MCD group I–3%; and MCD group II–3%. The most common specific EEG abnormalities noted during the initial examination and reexamination were as follows: Acute groups I and II–diffuse slowing, asymmetries, and focal slow abnormalities, and subsequently, persistence of spike foci and minimal to moderate slowing; MCD group I–diffuse slowing and to a lesser extent asymmetries, and subsequently, spike foci and asymmetries; and MCD group II–diffuse slowing and spike foci, and subsequently, diffuse slowing.

Stepwise Discriminant Analysis from Neuropsychological Data

Discrimination of clinical from control groups using neuropsychological data. Tables 15, 16, and 17 show the results of the discriminant analysis for each of the six clinical groups and their respective matched control groups, first generating weights from the neuropsychological data that derived from the initial examination, and subsequently, generating a new set of weights from neuropsychological data obtained during the reexamination. The levels of discrimination between clinical and matched groups were consistently high, i.e., varied from 76% to 85% correct identification with the initial examination data, and from 73% to 96% correct identification with the reexamination data.

Discrimination of neurological and cerebral dysfunction ratings from neuropsychological data. The neuropsychological data obtained during the initial examination were used to discriminate among three levels of neurological rating—minor and mild, moderate and severe, serious, and three levels of cerebral dysfunction rating—mild, moderate, severe (Table 18). Correct identification of neurological or cerebral dysfunction rating, in terms of three classes, was consistently higher for the older children in each of the three clinical groups (Acute, Chronic, and MCD). The overall correct assignments ranged from 57% to

TABLE 15

Discrimination of Acutely Brain-damaged Children from
Their Matched Controls Using Stepwise Discriminant
Analysis of Neuropsychological Battery at
Initial Examination and Reexamination 1
Year Later (% Correct to Two Assigned Classes)

Group	Acute group I (<9)				Acute group II (>9)			
	Initial exam.		Reexam.		Initial exam.		Reexam.	
	N	% Correct	N	% Correct	N	% Correct	N	% Correct
Normal	131	81	115	78	100	83	78	79
Acute	131	71	115	72	100	82	78	66
Overall % correct	262	76	230	75	200	83	156	73

TABLE 16

Discrimination of Chronically Brain-damaged Children
from Their Matched Controls Using Stepwise Discriminant
Analysis of Neuropsychological Battery at Initial
Examination and Reexamination 1 Year Later
(% Correct to Two Assigned Classes)

| Group | Chronic group I (<9) | | | | Chronic group II (>9) | | | |
| | Initial exam. | | Reexam. | | Initial exam. | | Reexam. | |
	N	% Correct	N	% Correct	N	% Correct	N	% Correct
Normal	77	84	70	94	39	92	36	97
Chronic	77	82	70	77	39	77	36	94
Overall % Correct	154	83	140	85	78	85	72	96

72% for the younger age level and from 61% to 82% for the older age groups. Among clinical groups, regardless of age, the lowest rate of correct prediction was with the Acute group, the highest with the Chronic or MCD groups. It should, however, be noted that the reported findings clearly exceed a chance level of correct assignment, which is $33\frac{1}{3}\%$ with the three classes used in the discriminant analysis.

Discrimination of EEG rating from neuropsychological data. The neuropsychological data were also used to discriminate among three levels of EEG rating—normal, borderline, abnormal (minimally, moderatley, markedly). The results of the discriminant analysis for the Acute and MCD groups are

TABLE 17

Discrimination of MCD Brain-damaged Children from
Their Matched Controls Using Stepwise Discriminant
Analysis of Neuropsychological Battery at Initial
Examination and Reexamination 1 Year Later
(% Correct to Two Assigned Classes)

| Group | MCD group I (<9) | | | | MCD group II (>9) | | | |
| | Initial exam. | | Reexam. | | Initial exam. | | Reexam. | |
	N	% Correct	N	% Correct	N	% Correct	N	% Correct
Normal	51	88	43	86	44	82	33	85
MCD	51	76	43	81	44	75	33	82
Overall % correct	102	82	86	84	88	78	66	83

TABLE 18

Concurrent Prediction of Neurological (Acute and Chronic Groups) and Cerebral Dysfunction (MCD Groups) Ratings from Neuropsychological Measures by Means of Discriminant Analyses
(% Correct to Three Assigned Classes)

Rating	Acute Group I (<9) N	% Correct	Acute Group II (>9) N	% Correct	Chronic Group I (<9) N	% Correct	Chronic Group II (>9) N	% Correct	Rating	MCD Group I (<9) N	% Correct	MCD Group II (>9) N	% Correct
Minor–Mild–(1-2)	28	64	32	63	35	54	12	83	Mild–1	20	70	22	82
Moderate–Severe–(3-4)	80	50	50	62	32	63	22	77	Moderate–2	18	78	17	88
Serious–(5)	23	74	18	56	10	90	5	80	Severe–3	13	62	5	60
Overall % correct	131	57	100	61	77	62	39	82		51	71	44	82

shown in Table 19. A separate analysis was undertaken with the initial examination neuropsychological and EEG data and then with the reexamination neuropsychological and EEG data for Acute group I as well as for Acute group II. Whereas separate discriminant analyses were also done for the younger and then the older MCD groups, the initial examination and the reexamination EEG and neuropsychological data were included in the same discriminant analysis. The combination of initial and reexamination data was necessitated by the small numbers in some of the EEG rating categories. The lack of statistical independence between observations would slightly bias the F test to be more significant, but this would not affect the percentages of classification. Using very small numbers in some of the EEG rating categories would, on the other hand, have produced artificially high discriminations. Notwithstanding the above, the discriminant analyses for the younger and older MCD groups should be interpreted with caution, in light of the lack of independence between observations.

Correct identification of EEG rating, in terms of three classes, was again consistently higher for the older children of the Acute and MCD groups. For the Acute groups, consistently higher levels of correct assignment were obtained with reexamination data. Better levels of prediction were made with the MCD groups where the rate of correct assignment varied from 50% to 82%, compared to the Acute groups where the rate of correct assignment varied from 52% to 74%. Here again the rate of correct classification in all instances clearly exceeded a chance level of accuracy, which is $33\frac{1}{3}$.

Summary.   The discriminant analyses involved prediction from neuropsychological data, and the overall percent of correct assignment was well beyond chance expectancy in all instances. The highest and most consistent prediction occurred with the discrimination of clinical from control groups (using initial examination and reexamination data); the rank order, generally considered, of rate of prediction was as follows: Chronic groups I and II; MCD groups I and II; and Acute groups I and II. The rate of prediction for the older groups approximated or was higher than the rate noted for the younger groups. Neurological and cerebral dysfunction ratings were predicted with a relatively high degree of success (using initial examination data); the rank order of rate of prediction, generally considered, was as follows: MCD groups I and II; Chronic groups I and II; and Acute groups I and II. In these instances the rate of prediction was consistently higher for the older children. A somewhat lower, but still well beyond chance expectancy, rate of prediction was obtained for the EEG global ratings (using initial examination and reexamination data). Correct identification of EEG ratings was somewhat higher for Acute group I compared to MCD group I, but higher for MCD group II compared to Acute group II. Here again rate of prediction was age-related within clinical groups, and in favor of the older children.

TABLE 19

Concurrent Prediction of EEG (Acute and Chronic Groups) Ratings from Neuropsychological Measures by Means of Discriminant Analyses (% Correct to Three Assigned Classes)

Rating	Acute group I (<9)				Acute group II (>9)				MCD group I (<9)		MCD group II (>9)	
	Initial exam.		Reexam.		Initial exam.		Reexam.		Initial & reexam.		Initial & reexam.	
	N	% Correct	N	% Correct	N	% Correct	N	% Correct	N	% Correct	N	% Correct
Normal—1	28	50	35	57	17	76	37	78	33	55	48	79
Borderline—1½	19	74	22	78	10	90	15	67	23	48	4	100
Abnormal (minimally, moderately, markedly)—2-3-4	81	48	56	52	72	71	25	68	28	46	16	88
Overall % correct	128	52	113	58	99	73	77	74	84	50	68	82

DISCUSSION

Yates (1966) pointed out that in the critical evaluation of tests of brain damage it is preferable to employ homogeneous criterion groups. Homogeneous brain-damaged groups in validity studies can be attained by adhering to factors such as the following: specified etiology—known or unknown; age or developmental stage of onset of disease; duration of disease; extent, distribution and focus of the damage. The present study set out to include homogeneous groups according to specific criteria. In the selection of the groups with known etiology, Acute and Chronic, criteria of age of onset of disease or trauma, and duration of disease or trauma, were met. Characteristics of damage, as a criterion, were not specified. The Chronic group would also serve to cross-validate any findings of neuropsychological impairment that might appear in the Acute or Minimal Cerebral Dysfunction (MCD) groups. While the absence of known etiology in the MCD group is acknowledged, the subjects in this group were selected according to designated criteria of minimal cerebral dysfunction. The inclusion of the MCD children enabled a comparison of known etiology groups with an unknown etiology group and also permitted the evaluation of MCD which in itself has great clinical relevance (Reitan, 1972).

Normative data were not available when this study was initiated in 1966. Hence, collection of appropriate data for the neuropsychological battery had to be undertaken before any evaluation could be made of its effectiveness in discriminating and differentiating brain damage. Age norms were accordingly evolved for a wide swath of the developmental range, from very young children aged 2 to 3 to early adolescents aged 15. Norms from ages 5 to 8 have been reported (Crockett et al., 1969), and Klonoff (1971b) subsequently published age norms on the neuropsychological battery for successive ages 9 to 15. Data for discrete age levels from 3 through 15 were then evaluated to determine the effects of maturation, i.e., do the tests of the neuropsychological battery discriminate between successive yearly intervals of age and what is the nature of the changes in scores that occur with age. Using a population of many hundreds of normal children, it was confirmed that the tests in the neuropsychological battery showed predictable changes with increasing age. The relatively minor effect of sex differences in the neuropsychological test battery at all age levels, from 3 to 15, obviated the necessity for sex norms. In the interest of precision, however, sex was retained as a variable in the design and controlled by matching. Because repeated measurements were to be obtained, the effects of learning also required specification or control. The effects of learning with five repeated administrations of the neuropsychological battery at yearly intervals, using our Normal population, are currently being evaluated. In the reporting of the present study, the effects of learning were controlled by comparison of the neuro-psychological functioning of the clinical groups with matched controls tested at the same intervals, and by isolation of testing occasion as a source of variance.

The relationships between IQ and neuropsychological test results were of focal interest to this study and also required clarification. First, in terms of the standardization procedure, the absence of significant IQ differences between successive age levels of the Normal group was a necessary condition of interpreting the neuropsychological test findings as reflecting age (maturational) differences. This condition was satisfied.

Second, it was necessary to specify the nature and extent of the relationships between intelligence and the tests of the neuropsychological battery. That measures of IQ and neuropsychological variables are not mutually exclusive was initially pointed out by Reitan (1956) in his study of brain-damaged adults and supported by Klonoff, Fibiger, and Hutton (1970) in their study of schizophrenic adults. Knights and Tymchuk (1968) in evaluating the Reitan-Indiana Category Test and the Halstead Category Test found that performance on them was significantly related to IQ. The relationships between IQ and the tests in the neuropsychological battery is accordingly not only of methodological import but also bears upon comparisons of the clinical and normal groups. The effect of IQ can be determined or controlled by: correlations between IQ and tests in the neuropsychological battery; matching of IQ between clinical and control groups; differences (*t* tests) in test scores between children with low and high IQs, after matching for age and sex; analysis of covariance between clinical and control groups.

Correlation analysis was previously used to document the relationships between IQ and tests in the neuropsychological battery for children under 9 years of age (Klonoff et al., 1969). This statistical technique at best provides a measure of relationship, but the matter of control of IQ remains unanswered. One means of determining and controlling for IQ would have been by matching on intellectual level as well as age and sex. This method of control would, however, have created an artifact for the Acute groups in that improvement in general neuropsychological status, including IQ, is anticipated with lapse of time after the trauma. Matching of IQ with the MCD but more particularly the Chronic group would have necessitated the inclusion in the control group of children of subnormal intelligence and in some instances retardates. Graham, Ernhart, Craft, and Berman (1963) question such a procedure of matching.

Another means of determing the role of IQ is that of comparing neuropsychological test scores that derive from children with low and high IQs. Comparisons of children with low and high IQs in any of the clinical groups in this study was precluded by the small numbers of pairs of children with low and high IQs after matching for age and sex. The Normal groups however included sufficiently large numbers of children to carry out such an analysis, after matching for age and sex. Test scores of 86 younger and 53 older Normal group children with lower IQs (90-109) were accordingly compared with test scores of equal numbers of younger and older Normal group children with higher IQs (110-125). The results of this analysis provide an estimate of independent neuropsychologic functioning as well as an estimate of the overlap between neuropsychological functioning and IQ.

Third, having determined that a relationship did exist between intelligence and tests in the neuropsychological battery for Normal children, analysis of covariance was employed to control intelligence in the comparative evaluation of clinical and matched control groups. The use of analysis of covariance in addition to analysis of variance resulted in a more definitive measure of neuropsychological functioning.

The IQs of all clinical groups, regardless of age level, were significantly lower when compared with their respective matched control groups. There were, however, selective differences between the clinical groups and within age levels for the three clinical groups. The Chronic group showed the greatest difference in IQ (in the order of 20 points), regardless of age, when compared with matched Normals. The Acute group differences in IQ when compared with matched Normals, were on the order of 10 points at both age levels, or approximately half of the analagous differences for the Chronic children. The older MCD group versus control group differences in IQ (7.61 points) were half as great as the younger MCD group versus control group IQ differences (15.43 points).

Evaluation of neuropsychological status, including intelligence, revealed striking differences between the clinical groups and their respective control groups, with the exception of the comparison of the older MCD and control groups. Neuropsychological impairment was marked and generalized for the younger and older Chronic groups and almost as pronounced for the younger and older Acute groups. The signs of deficit were somewhat less striking for the younger MCD group and greatly reduced for the older MCD group. The extent of neuropsychological impairment was not related to age in the Acute and Chronic groups, but definitely age related in the MCD groups. The striking differences between the younger and older MCD groups in neuropsychological status might accordingly be interpreted as reflecting intrinsic differences between these groups in terms of disordered brain function, in spite of similarity between the groups in terms of presenting symptoms. Corroborative evidence for this hypothesis derives from the electroencephalographic findings, in that here again the younger MCD children showed a higher incidence of unequivocal abnormalities. Another possibility is that the younger MCD children show a neuropsychological pattern found in other brain-damaged groups, compared to the older MCD children who may in fact be more similar to children who present with behavior disorders. Other explanations might include reconstitution which takes place over the years or developmental lag.

As might have been predicted, during the reexamination all of the clinical and matched groups showed improvement in a significant number of tests of the battery, due to maturation and practice. The younger clinical and control groups, in comparison with the older, did, however, reveal a greater degree of improvement. The absence of extra gains in scores for the Chronic group children at reexamination is quite understandable, as one expects relative stability in their neuropsychological status due to the chronicity of their condition and possibly to impaired potential for ability development. There is probably also little basis for expecting extra gains for the MCD group children. One might, however, have expected the Acute group children to compensate sharply in the year intervening between trauma and reexamination and accordingly close some of the gaps between their neuropsychological scores and those of the matched Normals. This did not occur in a dramatic manner, although a trend in this direction was recorded for both the younger and older Acute groups.

When intelligence was held constant by analysis of covariance, some rather interesting comparative findings resulted. Many of the significant differences obtaining when IQ was not controlled did vanish, attesting to the substantial relationship of intelligence to the other tests in the neuropsychological battery. But significant differences were still observed for all clinical-control group comparisons, including the younger MCD group where the number of significant differences dropped sharply. Stability in neuropsychological findings between the analysis of variance and analysis of covariance was highest for the older MCD group, followed by the Acute groups, then the Chronic groups, and finally by the younger MCD group. Even when intelligence was controlled, there still seemed to be a consistent relationship between the stability of neuropsychological findings and IQ level. That is, where IQ differences between clinical groups and their matched controls were smallest, analyses partialling out IQ were most similar to analyses in which IQ was not partialled out. Both Acute groups and the older MCD group, with lesser differences in IQ compared with their controls than was true for both Chronic groups and the younger MCD group, also showed the greatest similarity to their control groups on neuropsychological variables regardless of whether IQ was controlled by analysis of covariance. Improvement from initial examination to reexamination was still very much in evidence, but at a slightly reduced magnitude, with the exception of the older MCD group whose magnitude of improvement increased slightly. The younger Acute and Chronic groups, in comparison with the older, still revealed greater improvement. With the analysis of covariance controlling differences in IQ, the younger Acute children did exhibit a sharp gain over their matched controls.

Knights and Tymchuk (1968) reported a number of studies, including their own, as revealing a significant relationship between the Category Test and IQ. The findings in this study permit a more generalized inference regarding the relationship between the Category Test (Reitan-Indiana and Halstead) and IQ, namely, IQ is also significantly related to many other tests and variables of the battery. While performance on the neuropsychological tests studied here is positively related to IQ, our findings also lead to the conclusion that many of the variables in the neuropsychological battery employed are independently related to disordered brain function. This permits still another generalization, namely, neuropsychological assessment consists of comprehensive measures of adaptive functioning, and included among these measures are individual intelligence tests. Such intelligence tests, depending on their complexity and composite of abilities tapped, are nonetheless measures of a subset of adaptive functions deriving from neuropsychological assessment.

The initial neurological ratings for the Chronic group revealed a higher percentage of moderate, severe and serious ratings for the older compared to the younger children (69% versus 54%) and, as might have been predicted, there was almost no change in neurological status at reexamination 1 year after initial contact. Whereas the ratings for the Acute children, using the same descriptive categories, revealed higher percentages falling in the moderate to severe categories for both the younger and older groups (78% and 76%), the clinical signs which determined the ratings and the degree of neurological deficit were not the same for the Acute and Chronic groups. In terms of presenting symptoms, both younger and older MCD children, but particularly the older MCD group, were rated toward the minimal end of the continuum. The lesser evidence of positive neurological findings among the older MCD children might suggest that maturational influences have a differential effect on the neurological and behavioral concomitants of the condition. Our findings suggest that neurological disorders are more commonly associated with MCD among younger children but that these disorders may have disappeared among older MCD children, leaving behavioral difficulties as the basis for classification of many older children in the MCD group.

The EEG data for the Acute groups, including the qualitative findings and the changes from initial study to followup are consistent with those of many other authors (Dow et al., 1944; Frantzen, Harvald, & Haugsted, 1958; Marshall & Walker, 1961; Silverman, 1962; Enge, 1966; Weinmann, 1966; and others) and require no detailed discussion. It should be pointed out, however, that our initial EEG was done near the time of discharge from hospital, presumably after there had been some clinical (and EEG) improvement. Therefore the number of marked abnormalities would be expected to be relatively small, as was the case. This study also included a wide range of severity of head injury, with some cases of minor concussion, and these factors likely account for the relatively large number of normal or near-normal tracings found initially. Focal spikes and spike and wave discharges in the acute post–head injury period did not occur more frequently than would be expected in the general population, with the exception of the spike foci in the over-9-year age group. The persistence of spike foci in the patients studied, and the persistence of some degree of diffuse slowing (note particularly Table 12, item "Remained 2") may be due not to the effects of the head injury at all, but to some preexisting state of cerebral (dys)function.

Electrographic investigators of minimal cerebral dysfunction have reported a high incidence of EEG abnormality in clinical compared to control groups. The percentage of EEG abnormality in children with minimal cerebral dysfunction has varied from 40% to 65% (Polacek & Tresohlavova, 1969; Stevens et al.,

1968; and Misurec & Vrzal, 1969). Initial EEG examination in this study revealed that 34% of the combined younger and older groups exhibited unequivocal EEG abnormalities, with 19% showing borderline records. While the incidence of EEG abnormalities found in this study is below that reported by other investigators, a more precise comparison of findings in this study with published reports is not possible as the published reports have not specified detailed criteria for selection of their clinical groups nor the frames of reference for determining EEG abnormalities.

The results of this investigation support the concept of Kellaway et al. (1965), that there are no specific electrographic correlates of the MCD syndrome. However, unlike those of Kellaway et al. (1965), our findings do indicate that some degree of diffuse slowing is the most commonly encountered abnormality in the records of these children. Our studies did include a sleep trace; Kellaway's argument that spikes or other abnormalities would be proportionately greater if sleep tracings were obtained was not supported. Our findings are in very good agreement with those of Predescu et al. (1968), Polacek and Tresohlavova (1969), and numerous early investigators who reported a predominance of diffusely slow records in MCD children, ages 5–16 years.

The differences noted in demographic, neuropsychological variables and presenting symptoms for the older compared to the younger children with minimal cerebral dysfunction recorded in this study have also been observed in EEG studies. Predescu et al. (1968) noted that spike foci tended to disappear with age and that the older children in their series had fewer and less-severe EEG abnormalities than the younger patients. Our data support these observations. These findings emphasize the evanescent character of some focal EEG abnormalities, and their apparent dependence upon multiple factors, including maturational processes.

Our findings demonstrated a difference between the MCD and Acute groups with respect to the age-related incidence of spike foci. Specifically, the younger MCD patients had more spike foci than the older children, and none of the older MCD patients had spike foci on followup. By contrast, the incidence of spikes in the older head injury group was higher both initially and on reexamination than in the group of head-injury patients less than 9 years old and the MCD patients older than 9. It is possible that a "hard" spike focus, persisting into late childhood, has some type of relationship to the occurrence of head injury (aside from seizure production), and that many of these foci will not disappear with maturation as is expected with "soft" spike foci. The occurrence and persistence of spikes and other EEG abnormalities in both groups may, of course, be due in part to the effects of the head injury, but without a preinjury recording such a relationship cannot be established with certainty.

Children under 9 years of age, whether head-injured or MCD, show a remarkable similarity of changes in EEG ratings between initial and followup examination. Fifty-four percent of the patients in each group were assigned to the same category on the second examination as on the first. Thirty-six percent of the Acute group and 40% of the MCD group showed improvement, and ratings became worse in 10% of the Acute group and 6% of the MCD group. Only a slightly higher percentage (i.e., 78% versus 70%) of the head-injured patients under 9 years of age had abnormal or borderline EEGs on initial examination as compared to the MCD patients of the same age. There was, of course, a difference in the quality and degree of the abnormalities, with twice as many of the MCD children showing borderline EEG abnormalities.

That age (and/or maturational) factors interact with clinical condition in producing EEG changes is evident on examination of the changes in EEG ratings from initial to followup examination. Eighty-four percent of the MCD children over 9 years of age showed no change in EEG rating, as compared to 54% unchanged in the MCD group younger than 9. On the other hand, 52% of the head-injured children over 9 years of age showed EEG improvement from initial to followup study as compared to only 36% of the head-injured children under 9.

It would be expected that the EEG ratings of the head-injured patients would show some improvement from initial examination to followup study 1 year later. It is not so obvious, however, why the MCD children less than 9 should show such a significant trend toward improvement in EEG rating (40%) over a 1-year period. Only 13% of the EEGs in the MCD children over 9 years of age were considered to be improved after 1 year. It is possible that the head-injured and MCD children less than 9 years of age received their initial EEG and neurological evaluation in relatively close proximity to the etiologic factor(s) responsible for the EEG abnormalities. In the case of the head-injured children, the etiology presumably is known and in the MCD children the etiology, whatever it may be, produces its effect on the central nervous system within a limited time frame, and there is subsequent improvement in function both subjectively and objectively with the passage of more time. The rate of improvement as well as the expression of EEG abnormality may be both age and etiology dependent, as suggested by comparison of the percent improvement in EEG rating of the Acute and MCD groups greater and less than 9 years of age.

In addition, these findings suggest that traditional concepts of EEG evolution following head injury may require critical revision. It has been held to be nearly axiomatic (Gibbs & Gibbs, 1964) that the EEG abnormalities following head injury do evolve over time, and that this evolution is in the form of a function which is nearly a straight line from 100% abnormal to 0% abnormal over some period of time. However, Kubala and Kellaway (1967) have shown that the recovery curve is in fact hyperbolic, with a relatively large proportion of improvement within the first 3 months following head injury and a much slower evolution toward normal thereafter. Our findings[4] would support this concept, but we wish to emphasize the fact that in approximately half of our cases there was no change at all from initial study to followup 1 year later. This finding

---

[4] With extrapolation to points on the recovery curve obtained by continued followup studies done after the time of writing.

requires emphasis, since the above noted axiom is frequently invoked in the law courts by medical experts in determining whether or not certain EEG changes may be due to some previous head injury.

The fact that a very high percentage of the MCD patients over 9 years of age show no change at all from initial to followup EEG examination (84% showed no change and 64% were normal on both tests) raises the possibility that minimal cerebral dysfunction in these older children may be "different" from minimal cerebral dysfunction in younger children. The very large percentage of normal records in the older patient and a very small percentage of change in either direction over the 1-year period suggests either that the "cerebral dysfunction" is not reflected in recognizable EEG changes, or that the EEG has become fixed at a given point of function/maturation, a factor which might indicate a worse prognosis for clinical improvement in these patients.

Methodologically, this study could have been improved by the inclusion of EEG data from "normal control" children. This was not done chiefly because of the logistical problems involved in performing EEGs on a large group of asymptomatic children. To our knowledge, there have been no long term prospective studies reported anywhere specifically to define normality in EEG terms. Such a project constitutes a major undertaking by itself, irrespective of concern for defining correlates of disease or states of dysfunction. Acknowledging this defect, we have referred our data to reports in the literature, chiefly those of Cobb (1963), Stevens et al. (1968), Misurec and Vrzal (1969), and the Normative EEG Data Reference Library (Kellaway, 1966), describing an incidence of EEG abnormality in "normal" controls of 5% to 15%. Qualitatively, these abnormalities may include all types of EEG patterns, i.e., focal, diffuse, paroxysmal, and continuous. Our incidence of abnormality, in Acute and MCD children over 9 and under 9, both on initial study and at followup, was considerably higher than 15%.

The percentage of correct discriminations of clinical group children from their respective matched normal controls using neuropsychological data was consistently high, while the proportion of correct discriminations was significantly larger for the older than for the younger children. Correct identification of EEG status from neuropsychological data was comparable with identification of neurological or cerebral dysfunction status from neuropsychological data, and in each analysis higher rates of class assignment were derived for the older compared to the younger groups. The higher rate of prediction for the older compared to the younger group might be explained in terms of greater neuropsychological and neurophysiological plasticity and, hence, greater variability among the younger age group.

The significant relationship between neuropsychological and EEG status as demonstrated by our findings would accordingly enable prediction of one from the other. In fact, our findings support the concept that prediction of EEG from neuropsychological measurements can be consistently achieved with a hit rate which clearly exceeds a chance level of accuracy. The lack of success of Stevens et al. (1968) in predicting from EEG to psychological test results might have been due to the nature of the psychological test data and not to a necessary absence of relationship between the electrophysiological and behavioral realms.

It may, therefore, be concluded that there is reasonably good agreement between the behavioral, as measured by this neuropsychological battery, and the electrophysiological, as measured by the EEG state of the patient following head injury. These findings indicate that many of the head-injured children have not returned to status quo ante. With further passage of time, reconstitution will in all probability continue in neuropsychological as well as electrophysiological status. Furthermore, with repeated examinations the agreement between neuropsychological and electroencephalographic data may prove to be even better, as attrition over the years will maximize differences between the normal and abnormal categories.

SUMMARY

Three clinical groups of children—231 head-injured (Acute), 116 brain-damaged (Chronic), and 95 with minimal cerebral dysfunction (MCD), each comprised of two age levels (under 9 and over 9 years of age)—were compared with 442 normal children matched on an individual basis (in terms of sex and age within 3 months of age). Of the 884 children, 756 were reexamined 1 year later. The initial neuropsychological examination of all groups provided a baseline, the second examination 1 year later provided a measure of neuropsychological change. The clinical groups were initially rated with respect to neurological status or degree of cerebral dysfunction. The Acute and MCD groups received EEGs to provide a baseline and repeat EEGs 1 year later to determine the nature of electrographic change. Relationships between neuropsychological status and neurological/MCD ratings and neuropsychological status and EEG ratings were determined by discriminant analysis.

Using analysis of variance, the neuropsychological battery discriminated between each of the six clinical groups (three groups at two age levels) and their respective matched normal groups. IQ was positively related to performance on many variables in the neuropsychological battery. However, while the levels of discrimination between clinical and matched control groups decreased with IQ partialled out, many of the variables of the neuropsychological battery were independently related to disordered brain function. Electrographic findings were unequivocally abnormal in 63% of the head-injured children on initial examination and in 42% on reexamination, and in 34% of the MCD children on initial examination and 22% on reexamination. Qualitative EEG findings were presented for the respective clinical groups. Prediction of neurological rating, MCD rating, and EEG rating from neuropsychological status occurred with a high degree of success.

Differential age-etiology interaction patterns emerged in the neuropsychological, neurological, and EEG data. The younger MCD group revealed comparatively greater neuropsychological deficit than did the older MCD group. All younger groups, clinical as well as control, showed a greater incidence of neuropsychological improvement at time of reexamination than did their etiologically analogous older groups. The younger Acute and MCD groups when compared with their respective older groups were rated as showing more pronounced neurological and cerebral dysfunction at time of examination. The younger Acute group exhibited a higher incidence of unequivocal EEG abnormalities than the older Acute group at time of reexamination, while the younger MCD group revealed a higher incidence of unequivocal EEG abnormalities on initial examination as well as on reexamination than did the older MCD group. Age was also a critical factor in the prediction of neurological or cerebral dysfunction ratings as well as encephalographic ratings from neuropsychological data, except that in these instances the higher percentages of correct identification occurred with the older clinical groups. The findings that derived from this investigation were then compared with relevant studies in the literature that have dealt with head injuries and cerebral dysfunction.

APPENDICES TO CHAPTER 6

APPENDIX 1

Means and Standard Deviations for All Neuropsychological Variables for Younger Normals on Initial Examination — Ages 2-5 ($N = 154$), 6 ($N = 54$), 7 ($N = 60$), and 8 ($N = 65$)

Variable	2-5 years		6 years		7 years		8 years	
	M	SD	M	SD	M	SD	M	SD
Category Test (errors)[a]	-38.66	11.10	-24.76	11.16	-18.94	10.80	-13.09	6.39
Tapping—Dominant (correct)	24.31	4.83	28.15	3.48	29.78	4.72	33.75	5.09
Tapping—Nondominant (correct)	22.14	4.11	25.36	3.01	26.82	4.17	29.86	4.71
Speech Perception (errors)	-27.76	16.77	-13.76	5.60	-12.03	4.94	-8.86	5.20
Trail Making A (time)	—	—	-79.07	27.20	-34.45	9.88	-29.59	11.88
Trail Making B (time)	—	—	—	—	-94.78	40.49	-70.02	28.64
Trail Making–Total (time)	—	—	—	—	-129.10	43.82	-99.98	34.12
Matching Figures (time)	-59.78	34.10	-31.44	9.55	-30.73	15.86	-22.97	8.06
Matching Figures (errors)	-1.98	2.26	-0.71	1.10	-0.39	1.17	-0.18	0.51
Matching V's (time)	-59.71	30.17	-41.59	12.29	-40.52	13.75	-35.68	14.32
Matching V's (errors)	-4.83	2.53	-2.09	2.08	-1.42	1.90	-0.85	1.23
Star (correct)	4.42	4.47	9.03	3.14	10.36	2.26	10.63	2.07
Concentric Squares (correct)	5.53	3.51	12.28	7.44	12.03	2.88	12.40	3.05
Progressive Figures (time)	-113.72	38.59	-79.52	43.86	-66.44	39.69	-43.95	18.92
Color Form (time)	-86.74	52.99	-35.94	17.06	-28.91	12.78	-22.15	7.80
Color Form (errors)	-3.34	2.44	-0.62	1.04	-0.42	0.71	-0.29	0.63
Target Test (correct)	4.62	3.20	10.41	4.53	12.64	3.28	14.79	2.78
Marching Test–Dominant (time)	-51.26	32.07	-24.88	6.82	-27.46	14.67	-21.56	9.75
Marching Test–Dominant (errors)	-2.29	2.85	-0.72	0.99	-0.47	0.79	-0.42	0.66
Marching Test–Nondominant (time)	-60.74	41.61	-30.44	9.32	-30.36	10.15	-24.47	8.50
Marching Test–Nondominant (errors)	-2.87	2.96	-1.02	1.03	-0.95	1.08	-1.12	1.21
Tactual Performance Test–Dominant (time)	-7.10	3.86	-6.33	3.83	-5.39	2.87	-4.28	1.89
Tactual Performance Test–Nondominant (time)	-5.84	4.20	-5.71	3.56	-4.10	2.14	-3.26	1.85
Tactual Performance Test–Both (time)	-5.37	4.33	-3.82	2.56	-2.44	1.42	-1.91	1.15
Tactual Performance Test–Total (time)	-18.29	5.62	-15.84	8.69	-11.93	4.14	-9.40	3.79
Tactual Performance Test–Memory (correct)	0.88	0.82	2.94	1.90	3.33	1.63	3.92	1.35
Tactual Performance Test–Location (correct)	0.21	0.44	1.26	1.52	1.77	1.76	2.48	1.63
Matching Pictures (correct)	15.90	7.46	25.38	8.42	27.06	3.85	28.35	4.16
Sound Recognition	19.63	7.07	22.52	2.55	22.63	1.55	21.97	2.40
Right-Left Orientation (correct)	11.06	5.10	12.88	8.96	15.25	8.31	21.44	9.09
Lateral Dominance (correct)	12.10	3.00	13.40	2.27	13.98	2.35	14.03	2.16
IQ	111.71	10.17	113.27	9.44	112.32	8.92	113.79	8.96

Note.–Minus signs preceding scores indicate those variables on which a high score represents a poor performance, i.e., errors or time. The dash (–) indicates no score was obtained, as child was too young to do the test.
[a] Reitan-Indiana Category Test.

APPENDIX 2

Means and Standard Deviations for All Neuropsychological Variables for Older Normals on Initial Examination — Ages 9-10 ($N = 77$), 11-12 ($N = 70$), and 13-15 ($N = 53$)

Variable	9-10 years		11-12 years		13-15 years	
	M	SD	M	SD	M	SD
Category Test (errors)[a]	−49.47	17.70	−35.97	14.86	−30.88	14.30
Tapping–Dominant (correct)	35.82	5.12	41.22	4.81	46.18	5.89
Tapping–Nondominant (correct)	31.86	4.43	36.67	4.08	42.11	5.41
Speech Perception (errors)	−7.27	4.10	−5.01	2.76	−4.79	1.90
Trail Making A (time)	−23.71	8.64	−20.39	6.64	−15.46	4.36
Trail Making B (time)	−53.75	24.30	−39.60	17.52	−31.33	9.41
Trail Making–Total (time)	−77.47	29.19	−60.13	20.51	−46.79	11.10
Matching Figures (time)	−21.16	8.75	−17.49	5.27	−13.92	4.35
Matching Figures (errors)	−0.05	0.17	−0.08	0.32	−0.07	0.24
Matching V's (time)	−28.70	12.63	−23.61	9.80	−18.75	6.72
Matching V's (errors)	−0.77	1.21	−0.55	1.11	−0.35	0.76
Star (correct)	10.99	1.81	11.31	0.87	11.15	1.19
Concentric Squares (correct)	13.34	2.61	14.19	2.46	13.52	1.98
Progressive Figures (time)	−36.31	20.64	−25.90	9.56	−20.43	10.48
Color Form (time)	−17.62	8.18	−14.31	5.73	−10.35	3.37
Color Form (errors)	−0.08	0.27	−0.01	0.05	0.00	0.00
Target Test (correct)	16.68	2.57	17.66	1.84	18.33	1.94
Marching Test–Dominant (time)	−16.75	3.51	−15.09	3.90	−14.10	3.50
Marching Test–Dominant (errors)	−0.25	0.52	−0.24	0.65	−0.14	0.40
Marching Test–Nondominant (time)	−20.73	4.70	−17.25	4.28	−16.08	4.44
Marching Test–Nondominant (errors)	−0.81	0.95	−0.33	0.64	−0.50	0.73
Tactual Performance Test–Dominant (time)	−3.62	1.87	−2.66	1.19	−2.35	0.73
Tactual Performance Test–Nondominant (time)	−2.43	1.56	−1.79	0.97	−1.40	0.67
Tactual Performance Test–Both (time)	−1.18	0.55	−0.91	0.49	−0.71	0.29
Tactual Performance Test–Total (time)	−7.28	2.83	−5.36	2.04	−4.49	1.32
Tactual Performance Test–Memory (correct)	4.67	1.17	4.79	1.04	5.00	0.95
Tactual Performance Test–Location (correct)	3.38	1.69	4.16	1.33	4.27	1.25
Matching Pictures (correct)	29.61	3.50	30.49	2.89	30.42	3.15
Sound Recognition	23.72	2.01	24.30	1.52	25.06	1.21
Right-Left Orientation (correct)	25.52	8.34	28.64	6.83	30.44	4.76
Lateral Dominance (correct)	14.68	2.35	14.42	2.26	14.60	1.75
IQ	112.51	10.15	113.43	9.25	112.40	8.84
Maze Coordination Dominant (time)	−2.62	2.18	−1.83	2.54	−1.51	1.38
Maze Coordination Dominant (counter)	−25.35	19.90	−16.60	8.84	−14.83	9.71
Maze Coordination Nondominant (time)	−5.97	3.07	−4.03	2.58	−2.49	1.56
Maze Coordination Nondominant (counter)	−49.48	21.53	−37.21	21.27	−24.76	9.96
Grooved Steadiness Dominant (time)	−3.55	2.81	−2.94	2.36	−2.19	1.83
Grooved Steadiness Dominant (counter)	−28.11	24.73	−19.95	17.72	−17.54	12.61
Grooved Steadiness Nondominant (time)	−4.42	3.88	−4.89	4.48	−3.08	3.17
Grooved Steadiness Nondominant (counter)	−28.54	23.73	−27.10	21.86	−21.20	20.80
Steadiness Dominant (time)	−13.68	6.94	−5.33	5.13	−8.63	4.98
Steadiness Dominant (counter)	−108.22	34.08	−92.74	35.98	−82.44	33.95
Steadiness Nondominant (time)	−19.62	9.70	−14.43	7.10	−13.16	5.87
Steadiness Nondominant (counter)	−136.54	42.54	−114.85	39.37	−102.78	37.21
Grooved Pegboard Dominant (time)	−75.43	13.57	−66.81	8.22	−62.70	9.04
Grooved Pegboard Nondominant (time)	−78.98	13.98	−69.50	9.80	−65.37	8.51
Foot Tapping Dominant (score)	24.28	5.91	28.05	8.22	35.48	7.92
Foot Tapping Nondominant (score)	23.25	7.97	26.88	7.46	33.60	8.08

Note—Minus signs preceding scores indicate those variables on which a high score represents a poor performance, i.e., errors or time.

[a] Halstead Category Test.

APPENDIX 3

Means and Standard Deviations for All Neuropsychological Variables for Younger Acutes (I) on Initial Examination — Ages 2–5 (N = 74), 6 (N = 14), 7 (N = 22), and 8 (N = 21)

Variable	2–5 years		6 years		7 years		8 years	
	M	SD	M	SD	M	SD	M	SD
Category Test (errors)[a]	-44.71	14.23	-26.21	11.64	-20.64	10.48	-19.57	9.80
Tapping–Dominant (correct)	21.72	3.92	26.10	3.01	27.04	3.92	30.13	3.33
Tapping–Nondominant (correct)	20.54	3.31	23.08	4.47	24.79	3.54	27.09	3.67
Speech Perception (errors)	-41.65	19.42	-14.14	2.91	-17.64	13.67	-10.60	5.48
Trail Making A (time)	—	—	-76.09	49.50	-37.05	11.95	-42.10	25.99
Trail Making B (time)	—	—	-103.00	22.43	-88.54	28.06	-67.01	26.13
Trail Making–Total (time)	-76.88	43.04	-179.07	35.20	-125.56	38.37	-109.11	39.38
Matching Figures (time)	—	—	-34.14	13.54	-27.50	11.69	-26.00	11.49
Matching Figures (errors)	-3.35	2.99	-2.50	1.46	-0.82	1.43	0.40	0.82
Matching V's (time)	-70.37	32.87	-55.93	24.34	-38.90	18.04	-48.62	28.05
Matching V's (errors)	-5.96	2.31	-2.82	2.74	-1.40	1.56	-0.99	1.79
Star (correct)	1.87	2.35	8.07	3.80	10.91	2.23	9.70	2.37
Concentric Squares (correct)	3.09	2.72	8.04	4.88	11.45	3.52	12.38	3.49
Progressive Figures (time)	-146.37	36.62	-139.10	84.39	-68.09	31.68	-52.65	28.91
Color Form (time)	-87.04	33.78	-43.78	19.05	-27.77	12.42	-31.24	15.46
Color Form (errors)	-3.72	1.58	-1.25	1.74	-0.45	0.80	-0.90	1.55
Target Test (correct)	2.41	3.18	8.79	4.35	13.19	3.74	14.10	3.32
Marching Test–Dominant (time)	-63.63	33.61	-34.43	10.97	-26.10	6.58	-22.50	5.21
Marching Test–Dominant (errors)	-3.78	2.87	-1.29	0.91	-0.73	0.78	-0.45	0.59
Marching Test–Nondominant (time)	-73.72	32.78	-41.15	22.00	-35.00	15.35	-32.85	16.89
Marching Test–Nondominant (errors)	-5.04	2.95	-2.38	1.98	-1.73	1.45	-1.50	1.53
Tactual Performance Test–Dominant (time)	-10.22	1.14	-5.87	2.18	-8.33	5.29	-4.64	1.75
Tactual Performance Test–Nondominant (time)	-8.92	0.85	-4.70	1.73	-6.06	3.62	-4.21	2.51
Tactual Performance Test–Both (time)	-3.59	0.23	-3.13	1.83	-3.84	2.14	-2.69	1.85
Tactual Performance Test–Total (time)	-22.70	1.78	-13.67	3.70	-18.47	10.51	-11.56	5.54
Tactual Performance Test–Memory (correct)	0.50	0.74	2.62	1.60	3.18	1.99	3.26	1.37
Tactual Performance Test–Location (correct)	0.79	0.16	1.08	1.14	1.05	1.29	1.42	1.28
Matching Pictures (correct)	12.96	7.07	22.73	4.57	23.64	5.40	25.24	4.91
Sound Recognition	17.32	5.22	20.86	3.18	20.36	3.35	20.48	3.30
Right–Left Orientation (correct)	5.14	4.30	11.92	9.65	15.55	11.09	17.76	8.15
Lateral Dominance (correct)	10.36	3.81	13.07	3.02	14.10	2.14	14.62	1.47
IQ	99.73	15.87	103.86	15.11	105.32	9.63	104.48	10.66

Note—Minus signs preceding scores indicate those variables on which a high score represents a poor performance, i.e., errors or time. The dash (−) indicates no score obtained, as child was too young to do the test.
[a] Reitan-Indiana Category Test.

APPENDIX 4

Means and Standard Deviations for All Neuropsychological Variables for
Older Acutes (II) on Initial Examination — Ages 9-10 (N = 42),
11-12 (N = 34), and 13-15 (N = 24)

Variable	9-10 years		11-12 years		13-15 years	
	M	SD	M	SD	M	SD
Category Test (errors)[a]	−54.39	16.71	−40.94	17.59	−44.33	19.93
Tapping—Dominant (correct)	34.82	5.20	37.16	6.13	43.03	6.86
Tapping—Nondominant (correct)	31.33	5.09	33.93	6.27	38.64	5.09
Speech Perception (errors)	−9.69	5.48	−8.15	6.61	−8.13	5.92
Trail Making A (time)	−25.54	9.48	−20.50	6.82	−19.05	6.74
Trail Making B (time)	−73.42	44.11	−41.82	19.74	−33.36	10.60
Trail Making—Total (time)	−98.84	48.25	−62.03	23.82	−52.23	13.24
Matching Figures (time)	−26.14	17.10	−17.94	5.69	−18.71	15.59
Matching Figures (errors)	−0.27	0.44	−0.09	0.43	−0.10	0.25
Matching V's (time)	−35.43	17.41	−23.94	8.04	−23.50	18.58
Matching V's (errors)	−1.44	1.01	−0.63	0.81	−0.46	0.91
Star (correct)	10.46	2.42	11.17	2.05	10.85	1.37
Concentric Squares (correct)	12.94	2.20	12.22	3.39	12.67	2.67
Progressive Figures (time)	−55.01	41.27	−29.18	17.73	−34.46	32.69
Color Form (time)	−24.38	15.93	−17.48	11.36	−14.88	10.78
Color Form (errors)	−0.06	0.14	−0.02	0.07	−0.02	0.04
Target Test (correct)	15.99	3.09	17.12	2.67	16.96	3.18
Marching Test—Dominant (time)	−21.64	9.54	−18.66	5.29	−16.70	4.00
Marching Test—Dominant (errors)	−0.53	0.71	−0.56	1.10	−0.30	0.46
Marching Test—Nondominant (time)	−25.07	10.85	−19.87	5.10	−19.81	7.20
Marching Test—Nondominant (errors)	−0.72	0.81	−0.53	0.70	−0.57	0.63
Tactual Performance Test—Dominant (time)	−3.60	1.94	−3.59	3.14	−2.86	1.87
Tactual Performance Test—Nondominant (time)	−2.68	1.27	−2.41	1.53	−2.46	2.39
Tactual Performance Test—Both (time)	−1.65	0.85	−1.27	0.80	−1.49	1.52
Tactual Performance Test—Total (time)	−7.91	3.42	−7.08	4.93	−6.81	5.63
Tactual Performance Test—Memory (correct)	3.95	1.34	4.21	1.34	4.36	1.43
Tactual Performance Test—Location (correct)	2.33	1.45	3.03	1.36	3.59	1.46
Matching Pictures (correct)	27.69	4.32	29.85	3.53	29.67	3.77
Sound Recognition	22.26	3.40	22.76	2.22	22.96	2.29
Right-Left Orientation (correct)	23.67	9.91	28.24	7.09	28.67	7.33
Lateral Dominance (correct)	13.38	3.00	13.74	2.31	14.30	1.92
IQ	102.78	16.03	102.67	14.49	100.75	17.01
Maze Coordination Dominant (time)	−5.68	4.49	−4.94	3.30	−2.27	0.84
Maze Coordination Dominant (counter)	−43.27	27.16	−33.38	14.75	−23.27	5.79
Maze Coordination Nondominant (time)	−10.14	6.00	−5.84	2.25	−4.24	1.53
Maze Coordination Nondominant (counter)	−70.48	31.22	−52.33	17.85	−38.67	9.89
Grooved Steadiness Dominant (time)	−4.30	1.13	−3.40	2.51	−3.60	1.27
Grooved Steadiness Dominant (counter)	−35.18	14.57	−33.73	8.94	−33.00	15.24
Grooved Steadiness Nondominant (time)	−4.63	2.28	−4.30	1.69	−3.88	2.10
Grooved Steadiness Nondominant (counter)	−33.10	13.08	−27.83	10.06	−24.59	16.63
Steadiness Dominant (time)	−16.78	5.08	−10.14	3.33	−8.62	4.66
Steadiness Dominant (counter)	−121.73	28.61	−99.27	23.11	−79.50	32.12
Steadiness Nondominant (time)	−27.85	10.16	−16.19	3.77	−11.84	6.47
Steadiness Nondominant (counter)	−148.90	32.92	−120.50	15.31	−96.43	39.19
Grooved Pegboard Dominant (time)	−80.14	11.16	−72.89	15.84	−60.75	4.85
Grooved Pegboard Nondominant (time)	−94.86	20.19	−79.43	18.28	−73.54	5.91
Foot Tapping Dominant (score)	21.17	3.73	26.72	4.29	27.78	4.85
Foot Tapping Nondominant (score)	18.99	3.76	23.53	3.34	28.85	5.47

Note—Minus signs preceding scores indicate those variables on which a high score represents a poor performance, i.e., errors or time.

[a] Reitan-Indiana Category Test.

APPENDIX 5

Means and Standard Deviations for All Neuropsychological Variables for Younger Chronics (I) on Initial Examination – Ages 2-5 (N = 26), 6 (N = 14), 7 (N = 16), and 8 (N = 21)

Variable	2-5 years		6 years		7 years		8 years	
	M	SD	M	SD	M	SD	M	SD
Category Test (errors)[a]	-45.54	15.66	-30.79	14.27	-22.06	9.45	-23.19	17.59
Tapping—Dominant (correct)	21.04	7.76	24.63	4.06	28.19	4.41	27.32	3.64
Tapping—Nondominant (correct)	18.93	7.60	22.31	4.52	24.90	3.68	23.94	6.75
Speech Perception (errors)	-40.71	18.77	-21.91	17.50	-17.78	6.25	-27.20	12.96
Trail Making A (time)	–	–	-70.40	58.95	-48.91	21.63	-55.73	14.13
Trail Making B (time)	–	–	-154.24	87.03	-122.45	59.84	-79.58	8.01
Trail Making—Total (time)	–	–	-224.60	102.67	-171.34	65.98	-135.32	7.64
Matching Figures (time)	-61.52	38.02	-34.64	13.96	-34.00	10.81	-34.71	18.02
Matching Figures (errors)	-3.15	3.29	-2.98	2.26	-1.88	2.12	-0.83	1.41
Matching V's (time)	-55.51	20.18	-51.21	20.04	-52.75	30.46	-46.95	19.75
Matching V's (errors)	-5.47	2.68	-4.35	2.27	-2.38	1.88	-1.57	0.83
Star (correct)	1.04	2.38	4.21	3.60	9.47	3.72	7.90	4.81
Concentric Squares (correct)	2.02	3.13	6.25	3.98	9.97	3.16	9.79	5.25
Progressive Figures (time)	-148.89	38.44	-133.69	42.58	-79.22	42.17	-78.33	40.97
Color Form (time)	-103.85	48.44	-81.81	50.20	-39.00	17.64	-34.42	23.67
Color Form (errors)	-4.11	1.83	-2.73	2.24	-1.19	1.60	-1.05	1.02
Target Test (correct)	3.10	3.44	8.00	5.25	11.93	3.60	11.75	5.37
Marching Test—Dominant (time)	-60.72	30.21	-32.75	15.34	-28.19	11.28	-33.15	18.92
Marching Test—Dominant (errors)	-3.54	3.97	-1.09	1.78	-0.56	0.63	-0.54	0.67
Marching Test—Nondominant (time)	-62.53	20.08	-51.56	28.88	-34.31	10.85	-35.05	17.82
Marching Test—Nondominant (errors)	-4.22	3.05	-1.73	1.30	-1.19	1.33	-1.49	1.84
Tactual Performance Test—Dominant (time)	-11.72	2.86	-9.39	4.91	-5.45	1.96	-5.54	2.51
Tactual Performance Test—Nondominant (time)	-6.14	0.58	-4.93	1.78	-4.56	2.06	-3.86	1.43
Tactual Performance Test—Both (time)	-6.01	0.99	-4.17	1.79	-3.06	1.65	-3.12	1.55
Tactual Performance Test—Total (time)	-23.69	3.37	-18.16	6.40	-13.05	4.13	-12.48	4.54
Tactual Performance Test—Memory (correct)	0.56	0.80	1.97	1.49	3.00	2.07	2.48	1.83
Tactual Performance Test—Location (correct)	0.13	0.26	0.29	0.47	1.63	1.86	1.38	1.69
Matching Pictures (correct)	13.88	7.73	16.29	7.03	22.45	8.81	23.93	7.43
Sound Recognition	14.57	7.17	19.00	4.37	19.07	3.09	16.64	4.86
Right-Left Orientation (correct)	6.00	5.82	6.50	7.79	13.36	9.77	12.08	9.29
Lateral Dominance (correct)	9.46	4.04	11.64	3.65	12.56	3.41	11.81	3.34
IQ	99.38	18.10	96.36	23.51	100.31	12.06	87.95	18.82

Note.—Minus signs preceding scores indicate those variables on which a high score represents a poor performance, i.e., errors or time. The dash (–) indicates no score obtained, as child was too young to do the test.
[a] Reitan-Indiana Category Test.

APPENDIX 6

Means and Standard Deviations, for All Neuropsychological Variables for Older Chronics (II) on Initial Examination — Ages 9-10 (N = 10), 11-12 (N = 18), and 13-15 (N = 11)

Variable	9-10 years		11-12 years		13-15 years	
	M	SD	M	SD	M	SD
Category Test (errors)[a]	−53.20	29.76	−51.11	20.75	−42.36	24.63
Tapping–Dominant (correct)	33.36	5.79	32.71	7.01	40.16	7.99
Tapping–Nondominant (correct)	29.29	6.37	29.88	7.18	37.22	8.04
Speech Perception (errors)	−9.80	2.02	−8.00	2.90	−5.33	1.39
Trail Making A (time)	−43.00	24.99	−28.88	14.83	−24.27	14.48
Trail Making B (time)	−85.25	44.96	−78.03	42.39	−52.64	38.84
Trail Making–Total (time)	−128.09	66.07	−106.86	52.01	−76.91	50.45
Matching Figures (time)	−32.37	16.44	−21.61	9.10	−22.91	8.63
Matching Figures (errors)	−1.00	2.83	−0.28	0.78	−0.27	0.65
Matching V's (time)	−34.19	11.07	−35.39	18.45	−27.55	13.81
Matching V's (errors)	−1.70	2.75	−0.86	1.14	−0.65	0.90
Star (correct)	8.39	3.80	9.81	2.84	10.23	2.87
Concentric Squares (correct)	12.00	3.16	13.08	2.44	13.41	3.71
Progressive Figures (time)	−71.50	45.60	−70.56	83.02	−41.27	36.47
Color Form (time)	−24.23	14.67	−26.11	16.61	−23.10	18.79
Color Form (errors)	−0.10	0.32	−0.06	0.21	−0.04	0.17
Target Test (correct)	14.00	3.59	16.33	1.94	16.91	4.85
Marching Test–Dominant (time)	−23.67	8.94	−20.72	8.70	−19.70	7.10
Marching Test–Dominant (errors)	−0.67	0.67	−0.67	1.08	−0.40	0.66
Marching Test–Nondominant (time)	−26.22	5.35	−23.06	11.44	−20.00	6.65
Marching Test–Nondominant (errors)	−1.28	0.79	−1.00	1.03	−1.20	1.40
Tactual Performance Test–Dominant (time)	−4.98	2.84	−2.58	1.45	−2.67	2.08
Tactual Performance Test–Nondominant (time)	−2.79	1.14	−2.07	1.40	−1.90	0.73
Tactual Performance Test–Both (time)	−2.49	2.01	−1.12	1.01	−1.55	1.36
Tactual Performance Test–Total (time)	−10.26	5.83	−5.77	3.51	−5.91	2.54
Tactual Performance Test–Memory (correct)	3.25	1.62	4.39	1.58	4.45	1.21
Tactual Performance Test–Location (correct)	1.37	1.49	3.78	1.86	3.00	1.84
Matching Pictures (correct)	26.40	7.03	25.82	6.74	27.72	4.43
Sound Recognition	20.50	3.51	22.67	2.76	24.50	0.74
Right–Left Orientation (correct)	18.25	8.04	19.76	12.10	23.36	14.40
Lateral Dominance (correct)	11.60	2.84	13.06	3.10	13.18	2.79
IQ	92.10	17.12	91.06	17.21	92.45	22.37
Maze Coordination Dominant (time)	−7.52	4.15	−5.88	2.59	−5.09	3.13
Maze Coordination Dominant (counter)	−44.80	19.52	−45.56	23.98	−39.91	27.00
Maze Coordination Nondominant (time)	−11.31	2.49	−10.67	9.76	−8.17	4.42
Maze Coordination Nondominant (counter)	−85.60	20.44	−70.17	31.87	−47.27	35.06
Grooved Steadiness Dominant (time)	−9.12	6.48	−7.33	6.36	−4.97	2.58
Grooved Steadiness Dominant (counter)	−39.80	20.86	−39.50	28.79	−35.64	25.70
Grooved Steadiness Nondominant (time)	−8.48	5.43	−7.95	6.84	−4.47	2.13
Grooved Steadiness Nondominant (counter)	−49.40	20.14	−40.00	20.09	−38.18	14.42
Steadiness Dominant (time)	−21.45	4.53	−20.20	12.22	−12.76	8.57
Steadiness Dominant (counter)	−121.20	29.01	−109.09	39.71	−105.00	34.02
Steadiness Nondominant (time)	−33.44	5.43	−27.66	14.06	−18.20	13.26
Steadiness Nondominant (counter)	−146.80	21.49	−133.17	36.74	−116.55	55.78
Grooved Pegboard Dominant (time)	−84.20	10.05	−75.27	15.28	−73.00	16.82
Grooved Pegboard Nondominant (time)	−84.80	6.61	−80.26	14.40	−73.09	19.77
Foot Tapping Dominant (score)	22.80	9.13	26.14	3.49	28.75	7.40
Foot Tapping Nondominant (score)	22.42	9.09	25.40	3.76	26.87	9.43

Note–Minus signs preceding scores indicate those variables on which a high score represents a poor performance, i.e., errors or time.

[a] Reitan-Indiana Category Test.

APPENDIX 7

Means and Standard Deviations for All Neuropsychological Variables for Younger MCDs (I) on Initial Examination — Ages 2-5 (N = 8), 6 (N = 14), 7 (N = 10), and 8 (N = 19)

Variable	2-5 years		6 years		7 years		8 years	
	M	SD	M	SD	M	SD	M	SD
Category Test (errors)[a]	-45.00	4.69	-35.43	11.26	-20.70	13.84	-16.79	11.36
Tapping–Dominant (correct)	20.90	1.97	27.00	3.64	28.69	3.77	29.83	3.54
Tapping–Nondominant (correct)	20.03	2.15	24.67	3.49	26.21	3.54	28.25	4.16
Speech Perception (errors)	-32.25	18.20	-22.28	11.30	-21.10	14.94	-14.58	9.99
Trail Making A (time)	–	–	-96.55	56.98	-69.83	48.71	-35.95	13.83
Trail Making B (time)	–	–	-106.51	21.30	-106.42	43.76	-110.03	67.69
Trail Making—Total (time)	–	–	-203.07	20.31	-176.20	61.00	-145.98	79.40
Matching Figures (time)	-60.00	14.37	-40.29	13.64	-21.70	5.03	-27.53	10.66
Matching Figures (errors)	-2.43	2.12	-0.79	1.23	0.45	1.29	-0.16	0.38
Matching V's (time)	-63.13	28.55	-47.86	17.96	-49.50	44.08	-36.21	11.16
Matching V's (errors)	-5.12	2.29	-3.71	2.16	-1.80	2.04	-1.48	1.82
Star (correct)	1.60	2.70	6.46	3.74	8.40	4.18	10.37	2.25
Concentric Squares (correct)	2.50	1.77	8.07	3.23	9.50	3.90	12.63	3.21
Progressive Figures (time)	-145.00	63.42	-141.78	71.66	-81.23	35.17	-67.37	37.91
Color Form (time)	-68.98	42.40	-65.60	49.46	-39.02	15.07	-23.47	8.36
Color Form (errors)	-3.89	0.77	-2.12	1.79	-0.62	0.54	-0.53	0.23
Target Test (correct)	1.00	2.07	6.93	4.73	8.00	4.24	13.00	3.71
Marching Test—Dominant (time)	-73.89	27.26	-39.29	16.95	-35.70	32.79	-22.79	5.95
Marching Test—Dominant (errors)	-5.32	2.26	-1.00	1.18	-0.70	1.25	-0.58	0.77
Marching Test—Nondominant (time)	-83.00	41.27	-43.86	16.85	-38.70	19.00	-25.89	6.27
Marching Test—Nondominant (errors)	-4.31	2.52	-2.36	1.86	-0.90	0.99	-0.79	0.63
Tactual Performance Test—Dominant (time)	-7.17	1.26	-6.77	3.02	-4.45	1.26	-4.92	2.53
Tactual Performance Test—Nondominant (time)	-4.98	2.04	-5.22	2.22	-3.79	0.66	-4.45	2.11
Tactual Performance Test—Both (time)	-4.40	2.00	-4.08	2.01	-2.67	1.09	-2.33	1.11
Tactual Performance Test—Total (time)	-16.53	6.02	-16.04	3.99	-10.90	2.25	-11.69	4.71
Tactual Performance Test—Memory (correct)	0.75	0.98	1.79	1.63	2.20	1.75	3.32	1.34
Tactual Performance Test—Location (correct)	0.20	0.65	0.36	0.63	0.50	0.53	1.58	1.54
Matching Pictures (correct)	14.88	4.09	22.79	5.01	28.15	5.27	26.89	5.44
Sound Recognition	19.88	3.76	21.08	3.08	20.10	4.09	22.05	2.80
Right–Left Orientation (correct)	3.33	3.49	7.86	8.18	10.50	8.11	17.74	8.32
Lateral Dominance (correct)	10.63	4.93	11.14	2.74	10.70	4.06	13.32	2.71
IQ	91.88	8.74	97.79	9.25	99.00	11.79	102.74	11.80

Note.–Minus signs preceding scores indicate those variables on which a high score represents a poor performance, i.e., errors or time. The dash (–) indicates no score was obtained, as child was too young to do the test.

[a] Reitan-Indiana Category Test.

APPENDIX 8

Means and Standard Deviations for All Neuropsychological Variables for
Older MCDs (II) on Initial Examination — Ages 9-10 (N = 18),
11-12 (N = 15), and 13-15 (N = 11)

Variable	9-10 years		11-12 years		13-15 years	
	M	SD	M	SD	M	SD
Category Test (errors)[a]	−60.61	22.08	−46.93	14.98	−45.82	13.96
Tapping−Dominant (correct)	34.13	9.37	41.69	5.11	42.85	4.50
Tapping−Nondominant (correct)	31.49	8.44	36.57	5.86	40.31	4.69
Speech Perception (errors)	−11.44	5.67	−9.40	6.05	−8.82	10.19
Trail Making A (time)	−29.94	12.43	−24.20	7.99	−21.91	14.12
Trail Making B (time)	−69.39	40.31	−51.80	16.06	−33.82	11.26
Trail Making−Total (time)	−99.33	42.51	−76.13	21.86	−55.73	21.16
Matching Figures (time)	−23.61	12.32	−20.20	5.25	−17.82	5.65
Matching Figures (errors)	−0.06	0.24	0.04	0.09	−0.05	0.15
Matching V's (time)	−31.50	13.57	−26.53	8.94	−29.82	12.85
Matching V's (errors)	−1.22	1.64	−0.53	0.92	−0.63	1.05
Star (correct)	10.89	1.53	10.53	1.52	11.55	0.82
Concentric Squares (correct)	14.08	1.98	14.27	1.88	14.23	1.75
Progressive Figures (time)	−40.54	18.20	−31.60	10.12	−29.45	17.55
Color Form (time)	−25.67	20.53	−19.00	8.05	−14.45	3.75
Color Form (errors)	−0.09	0.15	−0.02	0.06	−0.02	0.09
Target Test (correct)	14.94	4.47	16.20	3.41	17.55	2.30
Marching Test−Dominant (time)	−19.22	5.98	−18.67	6.32	−14.50	2.39
Marching Test−Dominant (errors)	−0.61	0.92	−0.27	0.46	−0.33	0.60
Marching Test−Nondominant (time)	−22.11	5.54	−21.53	8.77	−16.87	2.82
Marching Test−Nondominant (errors)	−0.89	0.96	−0.60	0.91	−0.60	0.94
Tactual Performance Test−Dominant (time)	−3.72	1.64	−3.82	1.38	−2.89	1.61
Tactual Performance Test−Nondominant (time)	−3.83	2.21	−2.34	1.54	−1.86	1.06
Tactual Performance Test−Both (time)	−1.50	1.19	−1.15	0.64	−1.06	0.62
Tactual Performance Test−Total (time)	−9.00	4.46	−7.13	2.72	−5.82	2.14
Tactual Performance Test−Memory (correct)	4.22	1.00	4.60	1.55	4.64	1.29
Tactual Performance Test−Location (correct)	2.94	1.83	3.47	1.81	3.27	2.00
Matching Pictures (correct)	26.72	5.86	28.73	3.49	29.18	3.43
Sound Recognition	21.18	5.34	23.53	2.23	24.64	2.25
Right−Left Orientation (correct)	21.39	9.84	27.53	5.42	25.45	8.47
Lateral Dominance (correct)	14.06	1.98	14.00	3.70	14.45	2.91
IQ	102.83	12.54	99.40	9.07	101.45	10.91
Maze Coordination Dominant (time)	−6.07	3.80	−3.25	2.55	−2.28	1.33
Maze Coordination Dominant (counter)	−42.87	24.89	−23.47	13.53	−24.18	15.61
Maze Coordination Nondominant (time)	−8.80	4.34	−5.34	5.01	−4.54	3.33
Maze Coordination Nondominant (counter)	−64.67	23.58	−43.18	28.01	−38.27	23.20
Grooved Steadiness Dominant (time)	−5.51	3.83	−3.16	2.42	−3.67	2.80
Grooved Steadiness Dominant (counter)	−35.60	23.55	−27.91	16.84	−23.80	21.71
Grooved Steadiness Nondominant (time)	−5.43	3.92	−4.21	3.37	−3.79	3.41
Grooved Steadiness Nondominant (counter)	−32.80	21.28	−28.00	25.97	−26.18	14.50
Steadiness Dominant (time)	−17.82	7.54	−13.46	4.73	−8.40	4.49
Steadiness Dominant (counter)	−115.53	27.40	−119.40	43.39	−80.55	45.90
Steadiness Nondominant (time)	−25.15	9.10	−18.59	7.17	−14.75	8.17
Steadiness Nondominant (counter)	−144.53	22.90	−124.13	33.24	−107.82	39.91
Grooved Pegboard Dominant (time)	−85.00	10.10	−76.27	13.60	−71.45	12.32
Grooved Pegboard Nondominant (time)	−84.56	10.15	−80.47	18.75	−73.27	14.91
Foot Tapping Dominant (score)	24.28	8.47	26.17	7.62	32.66	7.88
Foot Tapping Nondominant (score)	23.00	6.34	22.62	9.75	29.89	8.07

Note—Minus signs preceding scores indicate those variables on which a high score represents a poor performance,
i.e., errors or time.

[a] Reitan-Indiana Category Test.

APPENDIX 9

Means and Standard Deviations for All Neuropsychological Variables for Younger Normals (I) on Initial Examination – Ages 2-3 ($N = 39$), 4 ($N = 52$), and 5 ($N = 63$)
(Breakdown of Data in Appendix 1)

Variable	2–3 years		4 years		5 years	
	M	SD	M	SD	M	SD
Category Test (errors)[a]	−46.97	10.53	−41.19	8.43	−32.53	6.41
Tapping–Dominant (correct)	22.28	5.36	23.23	3.48	26.98	5.14
Tapping–Nondominant (correct)	20.15	4.01	21.79	4.18	23.99	4.18
Speech Perception (errors)	−44.08	15.61	−26.46	15.59	−23.42	15.11
Trail Making A (time)	−	−	−	−	−	−
Trail Making B (time)	−	−	−	−	−	−
Trail Making–Total (time)	−	−	−	−	−	−
Matching Figures (time)	−75.64	38.57	−63.07	24.88	−55.10	26.06
Matching Figures (errors)	−3.82	2.68	−2.04	2.01	−0.89	1.10
Matching V's (time)	−66.77	26.42	−55.91	19.00	−65.79	27.98
Matching V's (errors)	−6.17	2.29	−5.73	2.01	−3.77	2.46
Star (correct)	−	−	−	−	4.42	4.47
Concentric Squares (correct)	−	−	−	−	5.53	3.51
Progressive Figures (time)	−	−	−	−	−113.72	38.59
Color Form (time)	−	−	−120.99	63.12	−55.83	21.55
Color Form (errors)	−	−	−4.35	2.31	−2.22	1.55
Target Test (correct)	−	−	2.23	2.34	6.78	3.69
Marching Test–Dominant (time)	−87.00	43.02	−45.52	14.35	−35.42	13.87
Marching Test–Dominant (errors)	−5.24	3.63	−2.01	2.13	−0.82	1.03
Marching Test–Nondominant (time)	−101.42	59.96	−56.04	21.66	−40.63	12.10
Marching Test–Nondominant (errors)	−5.64	3.88	−2.57	2.05	−1.51	1.57
Tactual Performance Test–Dominant (time)	−	−	−	−	−7.10	3.86
Tactual Performance Test–Nondominant (time)	−	−	−	−	−5.84	4.20
Tactual Performance Test–Both (time)	−	−	−	−	−5.37	4.33
Tactual Performance Test–Total (time)	−	−	−	−	−18.29	5.62
Tactual Performance Test–Memory (correct)	−	−	−	−	0.88	0.82
Tactual Performance Test–Location (correct)	−	−	−	−	0.21	0.44
Matching Pictures (correct)	11.92	6.03	15.54	6.52	18.21	5.45
Sound Recognition	16.97	13.49	19.87	2.72	21.24	2.13
Right–Left Orientation (correct)	−	−	−	−	11.06	5.10
Lateral Dominance (correct)	10.91	3.55	12.25	2.55	12.65	2.88
IQ	112.05	10.56	113.44	10.49	110.00	9.53

Note—Minus signs preceding scores indicate those variables on which a high score represents a poor performance, i.e., errors or time. The dash (−) indicates no score obtained, as child was too young to do the test.

[a] Reitan-Indiana Category Test.

Means and Standard Deviations for All Neuropsychological Variables for Older Normals (II) on Initial Examination — Ages 9 ($N = 35$), 10 ($N = 42$), 11 ($N = 38$), 12 ($N = 32$), 13 ($N = 21$), and 14–15 ($N = 32$) (Breakdown of Data in Appendix 2)

Variable	9 years		10 years		11 years		12 years		13 years		14 and 15 years	
	M	SD	M	SD	M	SD	M	SD	M	SD	M	SD
Category Test (errors)[a]	−50.77	16.62	−48.38	18.68	−37.97	15.47	−33.50	13.93	−32.00	14.46	−28.39	13.59
Tapping—Dominant (correct)	33.90	4.12	37.37	5.43	40.90	4.79	41.61	4.89	45.97	5.80	46.32	6.04
Tapping—Nondominant (correct)	30.20	3.27	33.20	4.86	36.48	4.75	36.89	3.88	42.01	4.58	42.18	5.45
Speech Perception (errors)	−7.11	4.73	−7.40	3.54	−4.62	2.59	−5.50	2.92	−5.29	1.31	−4.45	2.17
Trail Making A (time)	−25.09	10.50	−22.57	6.63	−20.92	6.28	−19.73	7.11	−16.76	5.41	−14.58	3.29
Trail Making B (time)	−54.94	22.00	−52.76	26.29	−40.51	16.10	−38.47	19.36	−30.95	7.29	−31.58	10.71
Trail Making—Total (time)	−80.02	28.09	−75.31	30.42	−61.43	20.33	−58.18	22.67	−47.68	10.29	−46.08	13.04
Matching Figures (time)	−21.40	8.71	−20.96	8.89	−18.70	5.19	−16.00	5.06	−14.95	4.85	−13.23	3.90
Matching Figures (errors)	−0.03	0.12	−0.05	0.19	−0.05	0.33	−0.10	0.32	−0.07	0.24	−0.07	0.24
Matching V's (time)	−29.26	11.40	−28.24	13.70	−24.65	9.73	−22.33	9.89	−19.14	6.77	−18.48	6.79
Matching V's (errors)	−0.80	1.13	−0.73	1.29	−0.51	1.14	−0.60	1.07	−0.38	0.80	−0.32	0.75
Star (correct)	10.90	1.49	11.00	2.07	11.22	0.97	11.42	0.71	11.19	1.19	11.19	1.19
Concentric Squares (correct)	13.35	2.21	13.32	2.93	14.35	2.45	13.98	2.49	13.40	1.77	13.94	2.07
Progressive Figures (time)	−40.54	23.14	−32.79	17.82	−28.14	11.19	−23.13	6.17	−19.40	5.50	−20.74	12.73
Color Form (time)	−19.09	8.99	−16.40	7.34	−14.72	4.98	−13.80	6.58	−9.86	2.31	−10.68	3.94
Color Form (errors)	−0.08	0.28	−0.07	0.26	−0.02	0.05	−0.01	0.03	−0.00	0.00	−0.00	0.00
Target Test (correct)	16.17	2.44	17.12	2.62	17.59	1.72	17.73	1.99	18.19	1.81	18.42	2.05
Marching—Dominant (time)	−17.37	3.73	−16.24	3.27	−15.08	4.12	−15.10	3.69	−15.05	2.92	−13.45	3.75
Marching—Dominant (errors)	−0.25	0.50	−0.24	0.53	−0.24	0.68	−0.23	0.63	−0.14	0.36	−0.15	0.40
Marching—Nondominant (time)	−21.77	4.91	−19.86	4.38	−17.78	4.81	−16.60	3.49	−18.14	5.06	−14.68	3.38
Marching—Nondominant (errors)	−0.97	1.09	−0.67	0.79	−0.38	0.72	−0.27	0.52	−0.57	0.68	−0.45	0.77
Tactual Performance Test—Dominant (time)	−3.84	2.21	−3.33	1.19	−2.76	1.11	−2.52	1.28	−2.41	0.75	−2.31	0.72
Tactual Performance Test—Nondominant (time)	−2.17	1.08	−2.57	1.67	−1.92	0.81	−1.64	1.12	−1.56	0.74	−1.30	0.61
Tactual Performance Test—Both (time)	−1.22	0.55	−1.14	0.54	−0.91	0.58	−0.81	0.34	−0.71	0.30	−0.71	0.28
Tactual Performance Test—Total (time)	−7.11	2.91	−7.00	2.65	−5.68	2.12	−4.96	1.90	−4.75	1.61	−4.33	1.07
Tactual Performance Test—Memory (correct)	4.63	1.14	4.72	1.21	4.79	0.97	4.73	1.08	5.20	0.92	4.87	0.96

APPENDIX 10

Means and Standard Deviations for All Neuropsychological Variables for Older Normals (II) on Initial
Examination – Ages 9 (N = 35), 10 (N = 42), 11 (N = 38), 12 (N = 32), 13 (N = 21), and 14-15 (N = 32)
(Breakdown of Data in Appendix 2)–Cont'd.

Variable	9 years M	9 years SD	10 years M	10 years SD	11 years M	11 years SD	12 years M	12 years SD	13 years M	13 years SD	14 and 15 years M	14 and 15 years SD
Tactual Performance Test–Location (correct)	3.29	1.71	3.45	1.69	4.27	1.36	4.03	1.30	4.05	1.28	4.42	1.23
Matching Pictures (correct)	29.09	3.88	30.05	3.13	30.65	2.62	30.30	3.21	30.14	3.07	30.68	3.24
Sound Recognition	23.51	2.34	23.90	1.69	24.38	1.34	24.20	1.73	24.90	1.09	25.16	1.29
Right–Left Orientation (correct)	24.94	8.72	26.00	8.08	28.00	7.40	29.43	6.08	29.29	6.02	31.23	3.58
Lateral Dominance (correct)	14.49	2.52	14.83	2.20	14.86	2.23	13.87	2.19	13.81	2.27	15.13	1.02
IQ	114.70	10.31	110.70	10.92	115.90	9.84	112.40	9.12	111.40	8.34	112.90	9.33
Maze Coordination–Dominant (time)	-2.81	2.08	-2.42	2.44	-2.36	4.00	-1.41	0.98	-2.08	1.85	-1.13	1.02
Maze Coordination–Dominant (counter)	-27.37	18.24	-23.39	20.76	-18.30	9.59	-14.66	8.45	-15.89	9.52	-14.14	10.94
Maze Coordination–Nondominant (time)	-6.62	3.31	-5.33	3.30	-4.62	3.16	-3.35	1.83	-3.10	1.95	-2.10	1.35
Maze Coordination–Nondominant (counter)	-55.66	22.90	-43.48	22.75	-41.76	27.03	-32.03	13.38	-25.06	7.90	-24.57	12.16
Grooved Steadiness Dominant (time)	-3.83	3.66	-3.27	2.35	-2.55	2.26	-3.37	2.64	-2.80	2.83	-1.80	0.94
Grooved Steadiness Dominant (counter)	-28.66	23.93	-27.58	23.79	-19.03	17.04	-20.55	18.63	-20.78	18.18	-15.46	8.97
Grooved Steadiness Nondominant (time)	-4.81	4.80	-4.04	3.62	-4.56	2.26	-5.40	6.09	-4.04	4.72	-2.45	1.99
Grooved Steadiness Nondominant (counter)	-30.16	28.92	-26.97	22.84	-26.12	20.68	-27.17	22.32	-23.78	22.35	-19.54	18.59
Steadiness Dominant (time)	-14.37	6.39	-13.01	8.59	-9.97	5.21	-9.80	5.57	-9.29	4.89	-8.23	5.00
Steadiness Dominant (counter)	-112.20	36.11	-104.30	33.90	-92.42	34.56	-93.10	36.84	-86.00	28.67	-80.29	40.95
Steadiness Nondominant (time)	-20.57	10.36	-18.69	9.53	-14.44	8.05	-14.42	6.69	-14.63	4.39	-12.26	7.17
Steadiness Nondominant (counter)	-136.10	41.85	-137.00	42.78	-110.20	43.25	-120.10	38.23	-114.60	28.73	-95.61	44.55
Grooved Pegboard Dominant (time)	-79.00	17.84	-71.97	10.18	-68.82	8.24	-64.52	8.46	-59.78	6.10	-64.57	11.03
Grooved Pegboard Nondominant (time)	-81.66	17.23	76.39	12.75	-71.64	10.76	-67.07	9.07	-64.39	9.64	-66.00	8.79
Foot Tapping Dominant (score)	24.02	6.00	24.53	6.93	26.20	9.63	30.13	6.64	31.84	8.01	37.81	7.92
Foot Tapping Nondominant (score)	20.85	4.98	25.58	10.75	25.51	8.58	28.43	6.52	30.64	8.98	35.51	7.93

Note—Minus signs preceding scores indicate those variables on which a high score represents a poor performance, i.e, errors or time.

7

IMMEDIATE, SHORT-TERM AND RESIDUAL EFFECTS OF ACUTE HEAD INJURIES IN CHILDREN: NEUROPSYCHOLOGICAL AND NEUROLOGICAL CORRELATES[1]

Harry Klonoff and Robert Paris

Major gaps exist in our knowledge regarding the short-term and long-term effects of head injuries in children. Systematic studies of head-injured children are rare, particularly where the sample is followed for a number of years after trauma and where relationships are sought between behavioral or neuropsychological and neurological sequelae. The epidemiology of head injuries in children as well as predisposing factors, accident conditions, accident proneness, and sequelae have been reported previously (Klonoff & Robinson, 1967; Klonoff, 1971a). Studies that have been concerned with the nature and/or extent of sequelae of head injuries in children include those of Rowbotham, Maciver, Dickson, and Bousfield (1954), Burkinshaw (1960), Dencker (1960), Dillon and Leopold (1961), Richardson (1963), Hendrick, Harwood-Hash, and Hudson (1964), and Hjern and Nylander (1964). There are no studies, apart from the present one being reported, which have examined and then reexamined the relationships between neuropsychological and neurological variables in a group of head-injured children.

For comparative purposes, one might also look to studies of head injuries in adults. The epidemiology of head injuries in adults was reported previously (Klonoff & Thompson, 1969). Other reports have described recovery rates,

[1] This research was supported by Grant 609-7-138, National Health Grants, Ottawa, Canada. The authors express their appreciation to Drs. M. Low, G. Robinson, and G. Thompson for their continued support; to Mrs. B. Simpson, psychotechnician, for integrating the neuropsychological examination of patients; to Mr. D. Crockett for his invaluable assistance; to Mr. J. Bjerring, Computing Centre, U.B.C., for his advice; to the Vancouver General Hospital and the Health Sciences Centre Hospital for providing the necessary research facilities.

179

residual disability, and permanent sequelae, often in veteran populations (Hillbom, 1959; Auerback, Scheflen, Reinhart, & Scholz, 1960; Miller, 1961; Norrman & Svahn, 1961; Gurdjian & Thomas, 1965; Lishman, 1966; Fahy, Irving, & Millac, 1967; Hay, 1967; and Walker & Erculei, 1969).

The present investigation derives from one of the groups of children reported in the previous chapter by Klonoff and Low (this volume), but deals with another facet of the natural history of head injuries in children. The purposes of the present study were: (*a*) to determine immediate accident effects; (*b*) to evaluate the nature and extent of sequelae 1 year after trauma and then 2 years after trauma; (*c*) to determine the relationships between sequelae and demographic factors, premorbid status, immediate, short-term and residual accident effects; and (*d*) to determine the relationships between neuropsychological and neurological variables.

METHOD AND CLINICAL MATERIAL

Selection of Population

The population included two age groups designated as follows: Acute I, aged 2 years, 8 months through 8 years, 11 months (131 children); Acute group II, aged 9 years, 0 months through 15 years, 10 months (100 children). The groups were comprised of consecutive admissions to the Health Centre for Children (Vancouver General Hospital) and St. Paul's Hospital, Vancouver, British Columbia, with diagnoses of head injury, during the period April 1966–September 1969.

Acute group I will henceforth be referred to as the younger group or younger children, Acute group II as the older group or older children.

Medical-neurological Examination

All children were examined by the same pediatrician (R. Paris) immediately prior to discharge from the hospitals. Data reflecting the following variables were recorded: (*a*) demographic; (*b*) retrograde amnesia; (*c*) anterograde amnesia; (*d*) loss of consciousness; (*e*) site of head injury; and (*f*) skull fractures. Hospital records were available and a neurosurgeon acted as consultant to the project.

The same pediatrician reexamined the head-injured children and interviewed a parent 1 year after the trauma. The following variables were recorded at the time of first reexamination: (*a*) developmental progress; (*b*) premorbid status; (*c*) complaints following head injury; (*d*) head wounds and residual defects; (*e*) educational achievement; (*f*) relationship at school; (*g*) relationship at home; (*h*) relationship with peers; (*i*) reactions of children to head injury; (*j*) reactions of parents to head injury; (*k*) assignment of blame by parents of head-injured children; and (*l*) sequelae (nature of sequelae).

The same pediatrician reexamined the head-injured children and interviewed a parent 2 years after trauma. Changes in status during the intervening year were recorded for variables (*c*) to (*l*).

Neuropsychological Examination

Details regarding the neuropsychological test battery for groups of younger and older children, and administration procedures were reported in the previous chapter. Medical-neurological and neuropsychological examinations and reexaminations were temporally contiguous.

Discriminant analysis was used to determine the relationships between neuropsychological data and the following medical-neurological variables: (a) initial examination—retrograde amnesia, anterograde amnesia, loss of consciousness, site of injury, presence and type of fracture; (b) reexamination 1 year after trauma—complaints, sequelae; and (c) reexamination 2 years after trauma—complaints, sequelae.

Analysis of Data

Medical-neurological variables were analyzed by means of chi square (χ^2), taking into account: sex factors within the two age groups for the respective reexaminations, 1 year and then 2 years after trauma; and age factors (younger versus older children) for the respective reexaminations.

In addition to the analysis of the variables at time of trauma and subsequently (1 year after trauma and then 2 years after trauma), relationships were determined between the presence or absence of sequelae and the following: demographic factors; developmental progress; premorbid status; extent of amnesia—retrograde and anterograde; extent of unconsciousness; presence of skull fracture; educational achievement; relationships—at school, at home, with peers; reaction to head injury—by children and parents; and assignment of blame by parents.

Details regarding the discriminant analysis program were reported in the previous chapter.

RESULTS

Age, Sex, School Grade of Patients; Occupation of Fathers; Attrition of Sample

Table 1 summarizes the age and sex distribution of younger and older groups at time of trauma as well as the sex distribution during subsequent reexaminations 1 and 2 years after trauma.

Of the 131 younger children, 115 or 88%, were reexamined 1 year later and 97 or 74% of the original sample were reexamined 2 years later. Ninety five of the 131 younger children were reexamined during two consecutive years. Of the 100 older children, 81% were reexamined 1 year later and 66% of the original group were reexamined 2 years later. Sixty-five of the 100 older children were reexamined at both 1 and 2 years after the initial examination.

Educational placement for the younger group was as follows: regular class (60); preschool (15); too young (56). All of the children in the older group were

TABLE 1

Age and Sex Characteristics of Head Injured Groups at Time of Trauma and Sex Distribution 1 Year and 2 Years After Trauma

Group	Time of trauma — Age Mean	SD	Range	Time of trauma — Sex Boys	Girls	Total	1 Year after trauma — Sex Boys	Girls	Total	2 Years after trauma — Sex Boys	Girls	Total
Younger children	5.87	1.76	2.67–8.92	80	51	131	73	42	115	63	34	97
Older children	11.53	1.81	9.00–15.83	67	33	100	58	23	81	49	17	66

in school and in regular class. The occupational status of fathers was distributed as follows: *professional*—younger group (8%), older group (11%); *managerial*—younger group (10%), older group (11%); *sales/technical/clerical*—younger group (18%), older group (25%); *skilled*—younger group (26%), older group (16%); *semiskilled*—younger group (14%), older group (15%); and *unskilled* or *unemployed*—younger group (24%), older group (22%).

Immediate Accident Effects

Table 2 summarizes the details regarding retrograde and anterograde amnesia. In total, retrograde amnesia was found in 15% of the younger group and 22% of the older one. There were no sex differences for the younger ($\chi^2 = .79, p < .40$) or older ($\chi^2 = .14, p < .70$) groups. Nor was there any age difference ($\chi^2 = 1.73, p < .20$). Anterograde amnesia was recorded for a high proportion of the total number of younger children (47%) but even more so for the older children (72%). Here again there were no sex differences ($\chi^2 = 1.81, p < .20$ and $\chi^2 = .13, p < .70$), but there was an age difference ($\chi^2 = 15.02, p < .01$) with the older group showing a significantly higher incidence of anterograde amnesia. There was a striking difference in the overall incidence of anterograde (58%) compared to retrograde (18%) amnesia.

Table 3 summarizes the data regarding loss of consciousness. A high proportion of both groups experienced periods of unconsciousness, i.e., 53% of the younger group and 68% of the older group. There were no significant sex differences ($\chi^2 = .97, p < .40; \chi^2 = .51, p < .50$), nor age differences ($\chi^2 = .93, p < .40$). The overall incidence of unconsciousness (60%) was slightly higher than that noted for anterograde amnesia.

Prolonged periods of amnesia (1 hr. or more) and unconsciousness (30 min. or more) were recorded as follows for the combined groups: retrograde (4%); anterograde (22%); and unconsciousness (10%).

TABLE 2

Incidence of Retrograde and Anterograde Amnesia

Degree	Retrograde amnesia				Anterograde amnesia			
	Younger children ($N = 131$)		Older children ($N = 100$)		Younger children ($N = 131$)		Older children ($N = 100$)	
	Boys	Girls	Boys	Girls	Boys	Girls	Boys	Girls
	Percent							
Not known or none	83	88	80	76	48	60	28	31
Not proven or momentary	15	8	6	12	8	4	1	3
Less than 1 hr.	0	2	10	3	29	18	40	39
1–12 hr.	1	2	4	3	9	10	22	15
More than 12 hr.	1	0	0	6	6	8	9	12

TABLE 3

Incidence of Loss of Consciousness

Degree	Younger children (N = 131)		Older children (N = 100)	
	Boys	Girls	Boys	Girls
	Percent			
Not known or none	50	40	34	28
Not proven or momentary	15	24	9	18
Less than 30 min.	29	20	48	45
30 min.–1 hr.	1	2	4	3
1 hr.–24 hr.	1	10	1	0
More than 24 hr.	4	4	4	6

Table 4 summarizes the site of head injury. A significant number of injuries for both groups occurred in the frontal as well as in the posterior (occipital and parieto-occipital) areas. There were no significant sex differences ($\chi^2 = .27, p < .60; \chi^2 = 1.78, p < .20$). There was, however, a significant difference between age groups, with the younger children showing a higher incidence of injuries in the frontal and occipital/parieto-occipital areas, when compared with the older children ($\chi^2 = 17.08, p < .01$). This result may have been due in part, however, to a greater proportion of unknown sites in the older group.

TABLE 4

Site of Head Injury

Site	Younger children (N = 131)		Older children (N = 100)	
	Boys	Girls	Boys	Girls
	Percent			
Frontal	28	24	19	13
Occipital, parieto-occipital, vertex, temporoparietal	39	42	28	30
Temporal, posterior fossa, basal	12	12	13	6
Frontal-temporal	5	4	4	3
Facial, head contusions, and unknown site	16	18	36	48

TABLE 5

Incidence of Skull Fractures by Type

Fracture	Younger children ($N = 131$)		Older children ($N = 100$)	
	Boys	Girls	Boys	Girls
	Percent			
None	50	45	64	76
Simple linear	25	27	22	15
Basal	14	8	6	6
Depressed	11	20	8	3

Table 5 summarizes the incidence and type of skull fractures. Fractures were classified as: simple linear; basal; or depressed. The rank order in many respects indicates degree of seriousness, in terms of complications. Basal fractures in particular are more often associated with complications such as posterior fossa hematomas. Fractures were recorded for 52% of the younger group and for 32% of the older group. There were no sex differences for either group regarding the incidence of fractures ($\chi^2 = 2.68$, $p < .50$; $\chi^2 = 1.73$, $p < .70$) or type of fracture ($\chi^2 = 2.33$, $p < .50$; $\chi^2 = .02$, $p < .99$). Whereas the younger group had a significantly higher incidence of fractures ($\chi^2 = 10.47$, $p < .02$), there was no age difference regarding type of fracture ($\chi^2 = 1.43$, $p < .70$).

Developmental Progress and Premorbid Status

Table 6 summarizes developmental progress. Positive findings in developmental history were recorded for 17% of the younger group and 12% of the older one. There was a significantly higher incidence of developmental anomalies for boys compared to girls ($\chi^2 = 5.29$, $p < .05$) in the younger group, but not in the older group ($\chi^2 = .04$, $p < .85$). There was, however, no significant difference between the groups ($\chi^2 = .53$, $p < .50$) with respect to the frequency of developmental anomalies.

Table 7 summarizes the findings regarding premorbid status. There were positive premorbid factors for 23% of the younger group and 36% of the older one. Here again sex differences were recorded for the younger group, i.e., higher incidence for boys ($\chi^2 = 5.80$, $p < .05$), but not for the older group ($\chi^2 = .01$, $p < .90$). No significant difference was found between the younger and older groups ($\chi^2 = 2.55$, $p < .15$) with respect to premorbid status.

Complaints, Headaches, and Head Wounds

Table 8 summarizes the incidence and types of complaints. These complaints were elicited by interview of the parents and reexamination of the injured children 1 year after the accident, and subsequently 2 years after the accident.

TABLE 6

Incidence of Developmental Anomalies and
Types of Developmental Slowness

Development	Younger children (N = 115)		Older children (N = 81)	
	Boys	Girls	Boys	Girls
	Percent			
Incidence of developmental anomalies				
Normal	77	93	88	87
Slow in milestones	23	7	12	13
	Frequency			
Types of developmental slowness				
Motor slowness	8	2	4	2
Speech slowness	9	2	4	2
Mental slowness	3	1	3	2

Note.—Categories of types of developmental slowness are not mutually exclusive.

TABLE 7

Incidence of Premorbid Factors and
Types of Factors

Premorbid factor	Younger children (N = 115)		Older children (N = 81)	
	Boys	Girls	Boys	Girls
	Percent			
Incidence of premorbid factors				
None	68	91	64	65
Present	32	9	36	35
	Frequency			
Types of premorbid factors				
Learning (intellectual) difficulties	5	1	17	5
Emotional problems	3	2	3	2
Developmental anomalies	17	3	9	5

Note.—Categories of types of premorbid factors are not mutually exclusive.

TABLE 8

Incidence of Complaints and Types of Complaints[a]
Following Head Injury

Complaint	1 Year after trauma				2 Years after trauma			
	Younger children (N = 115)		Older children (N = 81)		Younger children (N = 97)		Older children (N = 66)	
	Boys	Girls	Boys	Girls	Boys	Girls	Boys	Girls
	Percent							
Incidence of complaints								
No complaints	46	52	40	35	48	71	53	71
Complaints	55	48	60	65	52	29	47	29
	(56)	(55)	(65)	(69)	(52)	(27)	(47)	(31)
	Frequency							
Types of complaints								
Poor memory and/or concentration	6	5	6	2	5	2	8	1
Learning difficulties	15	7	16	3	12	2	9	1
Intellectual changes	1	2	8	1	1	0	1	0
Irritability	16	2	12	3	11	0	3	0
Personality changes	23	13	17	8	15	5	10	2
Fatigability	15	9	8	5	4	2	2	3
Difficulty with sleep	2	2	5	2	6	0	5	0
Speech problems	2	0	0	0	4	0	1	0
Tics	1	0	0	0	1	0	0	0
Dizzy spells (vertigo, giddiness)	3	4	15	7	3	0	7	2
Headaches	19	9	19	10	12	4	10	3
Visual or auditory defect	6	5	9	4	7	4	6	1
Impaired voluntary movements	4	3	5	2	5	1	4	0
Paralysis	2	1	3	1	2	1	3	0
Seizures	4	2	3	2	2	2	0	1

Note.—Incidence of complaints in parentheses include only those children reexamined at both 1 and 2 years after the initial examination.

[a] Types of complaints are not mutually exclusive.

Dys---: abn. deceased, impaired
faulty

The data recorded 1 year after the accident reflect complaints for the period intervening between the hospitalization and the reexamination or complaints still present at time of reexamination. The data recorded 2 years after the accident reflect complaints for the period intervening between the initial and the second reexamination. At initial reexamination complaints were elicited for 52% of the younger children (N = 115) and 62% of the older group (N = 81)[2]. The incidence of complaints for the combined groups was 56%. There were no significant sex (χ^2 = .31, $p <$ .60; χ^2 = .01, $p <$ .90) nor age (χ^2 = 2.51), $p <$ .15) differences. At subsequent reexamination 2 years after trauma, complaints were elicited for 44% of the younger (N = 97) and 42% of the older children (N = 66). The incidence of complaints for the combined groups decreased to 44%. At this point in the natural history of recovery, sex differences did appear among the younger children, with girls showing a precipitous and significant drop in complaints since the initial reexamintion (χ^2 = 3.84), $p <$ .05). There were still no sex differences (χ^2 = .95, $p <$ .30), nor age differences (χ^2 = .01, p $p <$ .90) for the older children.

In order to rule out sampling artifact among the attrition group, the complaint data were reanalyzed and only the children reexamined both 1 year and 2 years after trauma were included in the analysis. (In Table 8 and certain ensuing tables such results will be enclosed by parentheses.) For these 95 younger children, total complaints 1 year after trauma were slightly increased from 52% (N = 115) to 56% (N = 95), while total complaints 2 years after trauma remained relatively constant, i.e., 44% (N = 97) and 43% (N = 95). (Data given in Table 8 reflect the same percentages but are further broken down in each age range by sex.) The same pattern of slight changes in percentages was noted for the boys as well as for the girls for the respective reexaminations. Using the complete reexamination data for the same sample reveals that the younger girls had slightly fewer complaints than the younger boys in the year intervening between trauma and reexamination, but that the symptoms giving rise to these complaints subsided for a significant number of the girls 2 years after trauma.

Of the 60 younger children with complaints, more than one complaint was listed for 48 children, and five or more complaints were listed for 15 children. Multiple symptoms were still noted 2 years after trauma in 43 of the 97 children with complaints; more than one complaint was recorded for 23 children and five or more complaints for 6 children. The most frequent complaints in terms of rank order elicited 1 year after trauma were: personality changes, headaches, fatigue, learning difficulties, irritability, poor memory and/or concentration, and visual or auditory defects. The same pattern of complaints with some change in rank order was elicited 2 years after trauma, namely, personality changes,

[2] In the discussion of the data presented in the tables, we will attempt to present additional information, based on total groups for example, rather than to repeat the figures already given in the tables themselves.

Akinetic: loss of muscular sense or sense of movement

Dyskinesia: abn. a disordered movement (occurs c phenothiazine intoxication

headaches, learning difficulties, irritability, visual or auditory defects, and poor memory and/or concentration.

Of the six younger children with complaints of seizures during the year after trauma the following was noted: one child experienced a focal cerebral seizure 45 min. after the injury with no subsequent seizures; one child had a grand mal seizure 7 days after the head trauma with no subsequent seizures; one child experienced akinetic seizures for a period of months after the injury, but the seizures subsided before the reexamination; one child was still experiencing posttraumatic petit mal seizures at time of reexamination; one child was experiencing episodes of shaking during the night which might be nocturnal seizures; one child was experiencing staring spells during the day which might be petit mal. During the subsequent reexamination 2 years after trauma, complaints of seizures were elicited from only three of the six children, but one additional child with no history of seizures reported blackouts for the first time 2 years after trauma, possibly grand mal, but this is yet to be validated.

Sampling artifact was also ruled out in the older group by reanalyzing the complaint data for the same 65 children reexamined 1 year and then 2 years after trauma. For these 65 older children, total complaints 1 year after trauma changed from 62% ($N = 81$) to 66% ($N = 65$), while total complaints 2 years after trauma remained the same, i.e., 42% ($N = 66$) and 43% ($N = 65$). In contrast to the younger group, the percentage of complaints for the older children decreased for the boys as well as for the girls, but the decrease was much more notable for the girls.

Of the 50 older children with complaints, more than one complaint was recorded for 37 children, and five or more complaints for 14 children. Multiple symptoms were still noted 2 years after trauma in 28 of the 66 children with complaints; more than one complaint was recorded for 11 children and five or more complaints for 4 children. The rank order of the most frequent complaints elicited 1 year after trauma was: headaches, personality changes, dizzy spells, learning difficulties, irritability, fatigue, and visual or auditory defects. Two years after trauma, the rank order remained the same for headaches, personality changes, dizzy spells, and learning difficulties, followed by poor memory and/or concentration, visual or auditory defects, and fatigue.

Of the five older children with complaints of seizures during the year after trauma, the following was noted: two children experienced grand mal seizures shortly after the injury with no subsequent seizures; one child experienced blank, staring spells which might have been petit mal seizures; one child experienced "blackout" spells, which might have been akinetic seizures; one child experienced episodes of weakness and drowsiness followed by sleep, which might have been grand mal variants. During subsequent reexamination 2 years after trauma, complaints of seizures were found in only one child, namely, the girl who presented with episodes of weakness and drowsiness, initially described as a possible grand mal variant.

The complaint of headaches was examined in greater detail and the findings

Akinetic seizure: an epileptic seizure marked by sudden loss of motor power... seizure is usually brief w/ no post ictal confusion, stupor, or sleep are summarized in Table 9. A history of headaches before the injury was noted (no change—headache present) and differentiated from headaches ascribed to the injury. One year after trauma, headaches were recorded for 24% (28 children) of the younger and for 36% (29 children) of the older group in both categories of change. There were no sex differences for the younger (χ^2 = .16, $p <$ .70) or older (χ^2 = .77, $p <$ .40) groups. Nor was there any age difference (χ^2 = 2.64, p < .15) regarding the incidence of headaches. By 2 years after the accident the incidence of headaches in the younger group had decreased from 24% to 16%, the extent of decrease being comparable for boys as well as girls (χ^2 = .40, $p <$ .50). The same pattern of decrease during the second reexamination was found with the older children, the incidence of headaches decreasing from 36% to 23%. Here again, there were no sex differences regarding the incidence of headaches (χ^2 = .09, $p <$ .80), nor age differences (χ^2 = .88, $p <$ .40).

Table 10 summarizes the status of head wounds, involving verified bone damage, at the time of initial and subsequent reexaminations. Head wounds were sustained by 17% of the younger group and by 6% of the older group. The younger girls sustained a disproportionately high number of head wounds and had a significantly greater number of defects in healing 1 year later (χ^2 = 6.80, p < .05). There were no significant sex or age differences regarding head wounds for the older group. Two years after trauma, girls as well as boys of both age groups continued to make strides in the healing of head wounds but residual defect was still most evident in the girls of the younger group.

Educational Achievement and Range of Relationships

Educational achievement 1 year and then 2 years after the injury is summarized in Table 11. Academic difficulties increased slightly for only the older group, i.e., the younger group showed about the same incidence (14%) of

TABLE 9

Incidence of Headaches

Headache	1 Year after trauma				2 Years after trauma			
	Younger children (N = 115)		Older children (N = 81)		Younger children (N = 97)		Older children (N = 66)	
	Boys	Girls	Boys	Girls	Boys	Girls	Boys	Girls
	Percent							
None	74	79	67	57	81	88	78	76
No change—headaches present	3	0	5	4	3	0	2	0
Change—headaches present	23	21	28	39	16	12	20	24

TABLE 10

Incidence of Head Wounds (Bone Damage)

Head wounds	1 Year after trauma				2 Years after trauma			
	Younger children (N = 115)		Older children (N = 81)		Younger children (N = 97)		Older children (N = 66)	
	Boys	Girls	Boys	Girls	Boys	Girls	Boys	Girls
	Percent							
None	88	74	93	96	96	88	94	94
Fully healed, no defect	7	5	2	4	2	0	0	0
Defect	5	21	5	0	2	12	6	6

academic difficulties at successive reexaminations, but for the older group the incidence of 11% recorded 1 year after trauma increased to 17% 2 years after trauma. There were no sex differences regarding educational achievement for either the younger (χ^2 = .26, p < .70) or older (χ^2 = .60, p < .50) groups at

TABLE 11

Incidence of Change Regarding Educational Achievement and
Relationships at School, at Home, and with Peers

Education and relationships	Change	1 Year after trauma				2 Years after trauma			
		Younger children (N = 115)		Older children (N = 81)		Younger children (N = 93)		Older children (N = 66)	
		Boys	Girls	Boys	Girls	Boys	Girls	Boys	Girls
		Percent							
Educational achievement	Normal	84	89	86	96	80	94	80	94
	Decline	9	3	9	4	18	6	16	0
	Failed grade	7	8	5	0	2	0	4	6
Relationships at school	No change	95	100	95	96	97	100	100	94
	Change (deterioration)	5	0	5	4	3	0	0	6
Relationships at home	No change	89	100	88	87	94	100	96	94
	Change (deterioration)	11	0	12	13	6	0	4	6
Relationships with peers	No change	90	100	97	96	90	100	98	100
	Change (deterioration)	10	0	3	4	10	0	2	0

Note.—Nineteen children who were not of school age were excluded from the educational achievement and school relationships comparisons.

initial reexamination. By the second year after trauma, the boys of both groups showed an increase in the decline-failed-grade categories while the girls exhibited an increase in the normal category, but the sex difference in educational achievement remained nonsignificant, (χ^2 = 2.24, p < .15; χ^2 = 1.21, p < .25). There were also no significant differences in educational achievement between the younger compared to the older groups at either reexamination (χ^2 = .31, p < .60; χ^2 = 1.21, p < .30).

Table 11 also summarizes the changes (deterioration) noted in three categories of relationships. For the younger group, the rank order of changes 1 year after trauma was: at home (8%), with peers (7%), at school (3%). Two years after trauma there was a slight improvement from 1 year post trauma in all categories of relationships and the rank order changed to: with peers (6%), at home (4%), and at school (2%). For the older group, the rank order of change at initial reexamination was: at home (12%), at school (6%), and with peers (4%). Two years after trauma the incidence of deterioration in relationships decreased compared with 1 year post trauma, but the rank order remained the same, namely, at home (5%), at school (2%), and with peers (2%). Whereas the boys did show a consistently higher incidence of change (deterioration) at time of both reexaminations in terms of relationships at school, at home and with peers, the sex differences did not appear to be significant. Nor were there any age differences in school, home and peers changes either 1 year (χ^2 = .24, p < .70; χ^2 = 1.13, p < .30; χ^2 = .41, p < .60), or 2 years after trauma.

Psychological Reactions to Trauma

The reactions of the children to the head injury at time of reexaminations are summarized in Table 12. The data derive from the interview of parents and reexamination of injured children 1 year after trauma. Reactions were rated as follows: change in self concept (e.g., shame); change in relationships with others (e.g., greater dependency, use of injury for attention); change in response to potential dangers (e.g., is now more cautious); and denial (little or no concern). For the younger group, denial was by far the most common reaction both at initial reexamination (70%) and subsequently (67%), followed by change in response to potential dangers 1 year after trauma (25%) and the subsequent year (28%). There was a negligible incidence of change in relationships with others—greater dependency (4% and then 3%) or change in self concept—shame (1% and then 2%) at either reexamination. The pattern of response was somewhat different for the older group although the consistency of reactions upon reexaminations was very similar, i.e., denial (65% and then 68%), change in response to potential dangers (15% and then 17%), change in self concept (15% and then 12%), and greater dependency (5% and then 3%). There were no sex differences for either the younger (χ^2 = 1.97, p < .40; χ^2 = .54, p < .80), or older (χ^2 = 2.99, p < .30; χ^2 = .49, p < .50) groups at either reexamination. The younger children, however, reacted differently to the head injury both 1 year and 2 years after the accident than did the older ones (χ^2 = 11.63, p < .01;

TABLE 12

Reaction of Child to Head Injury

Reaction	1 Year after trauma				2 Years after trauma			
	Younger children (N = 115)		Older children (N = 81)		Younger children (N = 97)		Older children (N = 66)	
	Boys	Girls	Boys	Girls	Boys	Girls	Boys	Girls
	Percent							
Change in self concept	1	0	10	26	3	0	12	12
Change in relationships with others	5	2	5	4	3	3	4	0
Change in response to potential dangers	22	31	17	9	27	29	19	12
Denial	72	67	68	61	67	68	65	76

χ^2 = 6.41, p < .05); the younger children became more sensitive to potential dangers while the older children exhibited a more profound change in self concept.

The reactions of the parents to head injury at time of reexaminations are summarized in Table 13. Reactions were rated as follows: persistent or continued anxiety (e.g., still fearful of, or feels there is, permanent damage); anxiety dissipated (e.g., earlier concern has disappeared, feels child is now normal); change in treatment of child (e.g., more protective and cautious, fear another accident); cause of parental and familial strife; and denial (e.g., no present concern, no mention of earlier concern or other concerns). For parents of the younger group, the psychological responses to the aftermath of the accident were very similar at initial and subsequent reexaminations. Dissipation of anxiety (48% and then 51%) was the most common reaction. Other reactions were more or less evenly distributed: change in treatment of child (18% and then 20%); persistent anxiety (17% and then 20%); and denial (16% reduced to 8%). A negligible portion (3% and then 2%) reported that the injury of the child led to parental or familial strife. The pattern of reaction for parents of the older group was almost identical at both reexaminations; the rank order of reaction for parents of the older group was dissipation of anxiety (47% and then 45%), denial (27% and then 20%), persistent anxiety (19% and then 27%), change in treatment of child (5% and then 8%), and cause of parental or familial strife (2% and 0%). There were no sex differences at either reexamination for parents of either the younger (χ^2 = 2.80, p < .50; χ^2 = .53, p < .95) or older groups (χ^2 = 2.09, p < .60; χ^2 = 2.64, p < .30). The parents of the younger children did however respond differently at both reexaminations to the head injury than did

TABLE 13

Reaction of Parents to Head Injury

Reaction	1 Year after trauma				2 Years after trauma			
	Younger children (N = 115)		Older children (N = 81)		Younger children (N = 97)		Older children (N = 66)	
	Boys	Girls	Boys	Girls	Boys	Girls	Boys	Girls
	Percent							
Persistent or continued anxiety	17	17	22	9	19	20	33	12
Anxiety dissipated	45	50	41	61	49	53	41	59
Change in treatment of child	22	12	5	4	24	12	8	6
Cause of parental and familial strife	1	5	2	4	0	6	0	0
Denial	15	16	30	22	8	9	18	23

the parents of the older ones (χ^2 = 8.85, $p < .02$; χ^2 = 8.64, $p < .02$). The parents of the younger children exhibited changes in treatment of children, being more protective and concerned about the possibility of another accident, whereas the parents of the older children made a greater use of denial of past or present concern.

Assignment of blame by parents was more or less the same at both reexaminations (Table 14). Only 50% and on subsequent reexamination 54%, of the parents of the younger group did not assign blame for the accident; others (26% and then 23%) were often blamed, and the injured child (24% and then 23%) was also a frequent target of blame. Parents of the older group at both reexaminations were even more inclined to assign blame: no blame assignment being 40% and then 32%; followed by others (33% and then 41%); and followed by blame of child (27% and then 27%). There were significant differences in blame assignment by parents of the girls compared to parents of the boys of the younger group at both reexaminations (χ^2 = 10.12, $p < .01$; χ^2 = 8.82, $p < .02$), the parents of the younger girls assigning blame to others much more frequently. There were also sex differences in blame assignment by parents of the older group at both reexaminations (χ^2 = 8.28, $p < .02$; χ^2 = 11.98, $p < .01$). Whereas there was no difference between parents of the younger and older groups in blame assignment one year after trauma (χ^2 = 2.35, $p < .40$), parents of the older group did show a significant decrease in blame assignment 2 years after trauma (χ^2 = 8.74, $p < .02$).

Sequelae

Incidence of sequelae as well as the nature of sequelae 1 year and then 2 years after trauma are summarized in Tables 15 and 16. The medical-neurological status of the child 1 year after the injury and then 2 years after injury was derived from the interview of parent(s) and reexamination of the child. Sequelae were categorized as follows: no sequelae, equivocal findings, sequelae. The equivocal category was included to allow for sequelae that might be related to premorbid complaints or factors; the equivocal category was accordingly combined with the no-change category in the evaluation of injury effects. Ratings of sequelae were based on arithmetically weighted scores of the following: neurological signs; subjective complaints; personality changes; intellectual changes.

At the time of initial reexamination sequelae were found in 37% of the younger group, with an increase to 40% 2 years after trauma (Table 15). In contrast to the younger group, sequelae for the older group decreased from 44% 1 year after trauma to 38% 2 years after trauma. The incidence of sequelae for the combined younger and older groups was 40% 1 year after trauma, and this was only slightly reduced to 39% 2 years after trauma. For the younger group, the incidence of sequelae was significantly higher for the boys (45% and then 49%) compared to the girls (21% and then 23%) at both reexaminations (χ^2 = 4.61, $p < .05$; χ^2 = 5.05, $p < .05$). There were, however, no differences between the boys (45% and then 41%) compared to the girls (43% and then 29%) of the

TABLE 14
Assignment of Blame by Parents

Blame	1 Year after trauma				2 Years after trauma			
	Younger children (N = 115)		Older children (N = 81)		Younger children (N = 97)		Older children (N = 66)	
	Boys	Girls	Boys	Girls	Boys	Girls	Boys	Girls
	Percent							
None	56	36	42	35	61	41	39	12
Child	28	21	34	4	25	18	33	12
Other, personal (friend or relative of parents)	4	7	3	4	3	6	2	0
Other, impersonal (person unknown to parents)	12	36	19	57	11	32	26	76
Child and other, impersonal	1	0	2	0	0	3	0	0

TABLE 15

Incidence of Sequelae

	1 Year after trauma				2 Years after trauma			
Sequelae	Younger children (N = 115)		Older children (N = 81)		Younger children (N = 97)		Older children (N = 66)	
	Boys	Girls	Boys	Girls	Boys	Girls	Boys	Girls
	Percent							
No sequelae	49 (50)	74 (70)	48 (47)	57 (50)	48 (48)	71 (73)	53 (53)	71 (69)
Equivocal	6 (5)	5 (6)	7 (6)	0	3 (4)	6 (6)	6 (6)	0
Sequelae	45 (45)	21 (24)	45 (47)	43 (50)	49 (48)	23 (21)	41 (41)	29 (31)

Note.—Incidence of sequelae in parentheses include only those children examined at both reexaminations.

older group regarding sequelae (χ^2 = .15, $p <$ .70; χ^2 = .07, $p <$ .80) at either reexamination. Nor were there any age differences in sequelae either 1 year or 2 years after trauma (χ^2 = 2.42, $p <$ .15; χ^2 = .26, $p <$ .60).

Sequelae data were reanalyzed in the same manner as complaint data in order to rule out sampling artifact attributable to attrition. When the incidence of sequelae among the 95 children of the younger group who were examined at both reexaminations was compared with that of the 115 children reexamined 1 year after trauma and that of the 97 of these 115 children reexamined 2 years after trauma, no appreciable changes were noted. Specifically, sequelae changed from 37% (N = 115) to 38% (N = 95) at first reexamination and from 40% (N = 97) to 39% (N = 95) at the second reexamination. The changes for the boys and the girls were both negligible.

The same pattern was noted when the 65 older children who were examined at both reexaminations were compared with 81 children reexamined 1 year after trauma and the 66 of these 81 children reexamined 2 years after trauma. Specifically, sequelae changed from 44% (N = 81) to 48% (N = 65) at first reexamination and from 38% (N = 66) to 38% (N = 65) at second reexamination. The changes for the boys and the girls were both negligible.

Positive signs in two or more areas, or the presence of neurological signs, were recorded for 27 of the 42 younger children with sequelae at initial reexamination and for 22 of the 39 children with sequelae at second reexamination (Table 16). Whereas the proportion of younger children with sequelae increased somewhat, the severity of sequelae in terms of areas affected decreased somewhat. Among the older children the incidence of positive signs in two or more areas, or neurological signs, was 22 of the 36 children with sequelae 1 year after trauma and 14 of the 25 children with sequelae 2 years after trauma. Decrease in severity of sequelae over time was much more dramatic with the older than with the younger children.

The rank order of areas of sequelae was very similar between age groups, regardless of time of reexamination; namely, subjective complaints, personality changes, neurological signs, and intellectual changes in that order. The only change in rank order occurred between the subjective and personality categories of the younger group.

Antecedent Factors Related to Immediate, Short-term, and Residual Effects

The children with and without sequelae in the younger and older age groups were compared in order to determine which factors might be useful in prediction or management. Age at time of injury proved to be a significant variable for the younger group, with children aged 6 to 8 showing a significantly higher incidence of sequelae compared with children aged 3 to 5 ($\chi^2 = 11.74, p < .05$).

TABLE 16

Types of Sequelae at Each Reexamination

Nature of sequelae	1 Year after trauma				2 Years after trauma			
	Younger children (N = 115)		Older children (N = 81)		Younger children (N = 97)		Older children (N = 66)	
	Boys	Girls	Boys	Girls	Boys	Girls	Boys	Girls
	Frequency							
Change								
1 area, 1 sign excluding neurological	12	2	7	3	11	3	7	2
1 area, 2 or more signs	1	0	3	1	3	0	2	0
1 neurologic sign	3	1	1	0	3	1	3	1
2 areas	10	3	9	3	10	0	3	1
3 or 4 areas	7	3	6	3	4	4	5	1
Areas								
Neurological signs	13	3	8	3	9	5	7	2
Subjective complaints	21	6	18	8	16	5	13	4
Personality changes	17	6	15	7	17	5	9	2
Intellectual changes	11	3	10	1	9	1	7	1

Note.—Areas of complaint include only complaints present at reexamination and are not mutually exclusive categories.

Age at time of injury was noncontributory for the older children ($\chi^2 = 3.65, p <$ .70). No differences were found between children with sequelae and those without with respect to occupational status of fathers for either the younger ($\chi^2 =$ 8.01, $p < .15$) or older ($\chi^2 = .98, p < .98$) children. Neither were significant relationships found between sequelae and developmental history among the younger ($\chi^2 = .02, p < .90$) or the older ($\chi^2 = .01, p < .90$) children or between sequelae and premorbid factors among the younger ($\chi^2 = 2.06, p < .20$) or older ($\chi^2 = .01, p < .90$) children.

An examination of relationships between immediate accident effects and sequelae revealed no significant findings for either age groups, regarding retrograde amnesia ($\chi^2 = 3.33, p < .10$ for the younger group; $\chi^2 = .68, p < .50$ for the older group), or anterograde amnesia ($\chi^2 = 6.89, p < .10$ for the younger group; $\chi^2 = 3.69, p < .20$ for the older group), or for the younger group regarding loss of consciousness ($\chi^2 = 3.32, p < .20$). However, among the older children, those with sequelae experienced more pronounced periods of unconsiousness compared with the children without sequelae ($\chi^2 = 10.53, p <$ .02). There was also a differential pattern regarding skull fractures for the sequelae and nonsequelae children of the younger and older groups; older children with sequelae had a significantly higher incidence of skull fractures ($\chi^2 = 7.87, p < .01$) compared to the younger group in which no such differences were found between the children with and without sequelae ($\chi^2 =$ .55, $p < .50$).

An examination of short-term and residual accident effects revealed a consistent patterning regarding educational achievement. At both reexaminations all of the children who showed a decline in academic achievement or failed a grade, regardless of whether they were in the younger or older groups, showed postinjury sequelae. There were no significant findings relating relationships at school and presence or absence of sequelae in either the younger ($\chi^2 = 2.35, p <$ .15) or older ($\chi^2 = 1.61, p < .25$) groups at either reexamination. Whereas among the younger children a difference in relationships at home was observed at the initial reexamination between the children with and those without sequelae ($\chi^2 = 9.63, p < .01$), this difference disappeared at the second reexamination ($\chi^2 = .86, p < .40$). The same pattern was noted for the older group where relationships at home were initially significantly impaired ($\chi^2 =$ 7.78, $p < .01$), but improvement was noted with few exceptions two years after the accident. Relationships with peers at initial reexamination were significantly poorer for younger children with sequelae compared to those without ($\chi^2 =$ 7.77, $p < .01$), but by the following year the difference was nonsignificant ($\chi^2 =$ 3.22, $p < .10$). Among the older children, presence versus absence of sequelae was unrelated to peer relationships at both first ($\chi^2 = .92, p < .40$) and second reexaminations.

At initial reexamintion the younger children with sequelae reacted to their head injuries differently from similarly aged children without sequelae ($\chi^2 =$ 4.82, $p < .05$), but by the second year after trauma these differences in reaction disappeared (χ^2 = .52, p < .80). Among the older children there were no differences in reactions to head injury between children with and those without sequelae at either reexamination (χ^2 = .40, p < .90; χ^2 = 3.15, p < .10). The reactions of parents of the younger group with sequelae at first reexamination were also different from those of the parents of the younger group without sequelae (χ^2 = 12.27, p < .01), and this difference was sustained at second reexamination (χ^2 = 9.88, p < .02). But among parents of the older children there were no differences in reactions between those whose children had sequelae and those whose children did not at either reexamination (χ^2 = 5.14, p < .20; χ^2 = 5.46, p < .10). Regarding assignment of blame by parents, there were no significant differences between the children with sequelae compared to those without at either reexamination for either the younger (χ^2 = .35, p < .90; χ^2 = 1.19, p < .60) or older (χ^2 = 1.74, p < .50; χ^2 = .02, p < .90) groups.

Relationships between Neuropsychological and Medical-Neurological Data

This portion of the chapter is concerned with the documentation of quantitative relationships between different conceptual realms of data, by means of stepwise discriminant analysis. In all instances medical-neurological variables were predicted from neuropsychological variables. The neuropsychological data used for this purpose were described in detail in the preceding chapter. In those instances where the comparisons related to immediate effects, the neuropsychological data were obtained at initial examination, i.e., while the children were in hospital recovering from the trauma sustained. Comparisons relating to short-term effects concern neuropsychological data obtained at first reexamination, i.e., 1 year after trauma. Comparisons relating to residual effects concern neuropsychological data obtained at second reexamination, i.e., 2 years after trauma.

Discrimination of immediate effects from neuropsychological data. The neuropsychological data obtained during the initial examination were used to discriminate among two levels (absence or presence) of retrograde amnesia, anterograde amnesia, and loss of consciousness. The findings are summarized in Table 17. The levels of discrimination, in terms of total percent of correct assignment, were consistently high in all instances, varying from 65% to 85%. Chance level of prediction is 50% with two classes. The rank order of discrimination was: anterograde amnesia, retrograde amnesia, and loss of consciousness. Correct identification of retrograde amnesia from the neuropsychological data was higher for the younger compared to the older group (81% and 69%), but the percentages of correct predictions of anterograde amnesia were higher for the older than the younger group (85% and 71%). No difference was present between age levels with respect to loss of consciousness (65% and 67%).

Prediction of site of injury, in terms of five classes, from neurological data was well above the chance expectancy of 20% (Table 18). Here, a somewhat higher

TABLE 17

Prediction of Absence or Presence of Retrograde Amnesia, Anterograde Amnesia and
Loss of Consciousness from Neuropsychological Measures by
Means of Discriminant Analyses
(% Correct to Two Assigned Classes)

Amnesia and loss of consciousness	Retrograde amnesia				Anterograde amnesia				Loss of consciousness			
	Younger children		Older children		Younger children		Older children		Younger children		Older children	
	N	% Correct	N	% Correct	N	% Correct	N	% Correct	N	% Correct	N	% Correct
Absence	118	80	79	72	76	74	28	86	65	63	34	68
Presence	13	92	21	57	55	67	72	85	66	67	66	67
Total	131	81	100	69	131	71	100	85	131	65	100	67

rate of correct classifications occurred with the older group (54%) compared to the younger one (46%). When the category—facial, head contusions, unknown—was excluded from the discriminant analysis, the rate of correct classification rose to 63% and 72% for the younger and older groups, respectively. Table 19 presents the findings for the prediction of absence versus presence of skull fractures from neuropsychological data. The relationships in this instance were more striking, i.e., 68% and 76% correct assignment (total) for the respective younger and older age groups, and significantly higher than chance prediction of 50%. Again, a somewhat higher level of correct prediction was noted for the older age group.

Discrimination of short-term and residual effects from neuropsychological data. The neuropsychological data obtained 1 year after trauma were used to discriminate among two categories (absence or presence) of complaints as well as two categories (absence or presence) of sequelae. Separate discriminant analyses, using the same categories, were done for the neuropsychological data obtained 2 years after injury (Table 20). Total percent of correct assignment was consistently high in all analyses and well above the chance level of 50%. The rank order of rate of prediction (basing rank order on the data from the first reexamination) was as follows: older group, predicting complaints, 85% at first reexamination, and 78% at second; older group, predicting sequelae, 83% at first reexamination, 84% at second; younger group, predicting sequelae, 78% at first, and also 78% at second; younger group, predicting complaints, 75% at first

TABLE 18

Prediction of Site of Injury from Neuropsychological Measures
by Means of Discriminant Analysis
(% Correct to Five Assigned Classes)

Site	Younger children		Older children	
	N	% Correct	N	% Correct
Frontal	34	50	16	63
Occipital, parieto-occipital, vertex tempero-parietal	53	38	29	52
Temporal, posterior fossa, basal	16	69	10	50
Frontal-temporal	6	50	5	60
Facial, head contusions, and unknown site	22	41	40	53
Total	131	46	100	54

TABLE 19

Prediction of Absence or Presence of
Skull Fractures from Neuropsychological
Measures by Means of Discriminant Analysis
(% Correct to Two Assigned Classes)

Fracture	Younger children		Older children	
	N	% Correct	N	% Correct
None	63	70	68	77
Fractures	68	66	32	75
Total	131	68	100	76

reexamination, 81% at second. Separate discriminant analyses were done on the data of the reduced sample of those younger and older children reexamined during two consecutive years. Percentage of correct discrimination (based on data from the first reexamination) remained higher for the older compared with the younger children.

DISCUSSION

In order to provide a frame of reference for understanding the natural history of head injuries in children, the following seven areas will be discussed: causation with particular emphasis on vulnerability; clinical signs and behavioral measures; the necessary conditions for interpreting complaints, sequelae, and prognosis; patterning and remission of complaints; nature of sequelae; comparison of children with and without sequelae; and the relationship between neurological data and neuropsychological functioning. Whenever applicable, children in the present study who sustained severe head injuries will be compared with a previous study which dealt with children who incurred slight head injuries (Klonoff, 1971a). This will then be followed by a discussion of relevant findings that have derived from studies of head injuries in adults.

Vulnerability to head injury has been shown to be age related, young children being the most susceptible to head injuries (Read, Bradley, Morison, Lewall, & Clarke, 1963; Klonoff, 1971a). The findings relating sex to vulnerability are also unequivocal; boys invariably having been shown to be more predisposed to head injuries than girls, probably because of their role and activity level (Burkinshaw, 1960; Partington, 1960; Read et al., 1963). The increased susceptibility to head injuries of boys compared to girls was borne out in the present study, by a ratio of 12:7. Furthermore, a comparative study which was concerned with slight head injuries in 298 children recorded an identical ratio of boys compared to girls (Klonoff, 1971a).

The more prominent clinical signs associated with head injuries include loss of consciousness and amnesia. Impact also frequently results in skull fracture. Clinical signs, when compared with the detection of skull fractures, are more difficult to determine with any degree of reliability, particularly if the duration is transient, and especially with young children. Skull fractures on the other hand can be demonstrated radiographically. Little documented information exists regarding the comparative incidence of clinical signs in severely versus slightly head-injured children; the present study and the prior investigation, which dealt with slight head injuries (Klonoff, 1971a), provide such comparative data.

TABLE 20

Prediction of Absence or Presence of Complaints and Sequelae from Neuropsychological Measures by Means of Discriminant Analyses
(% Correct to Two Assigned Classes)

Complaints and sequelae	1st Reexamination				2nd Reexamination			
	Younger children		Older children		Younger children		Older children	
	N	% Correct	N	% Correct	N	% Correct	N	% Correct
Complaints								
Absence	55	75	31	84	54	87	38	76
	(44)	(68)	(23)	(78)	(54)	(85)	(37)	(76)
Presence	60	75	50	86	43	74	28	82
	(51)	(73)	(42)	(78)	(41)	(78)	(28)	(82)
Total	115	75	81	85	97	81	66	78
	(95)	(71)	(65)	(78)	(95)	(82)	(65)	(78)
Sequelae								
Absence	73	80	45	80	58	86	41	83
	(59)	(73)	(34)	(82)	(58)	(88)	(40)	(83)
Presence	42	76	36	86	39	67	25	83
	(36)	(67)	(31)	(87)	(37)	(70)	(25)	(83)
Total	115	78	81	83	97	78	66	84
	(95)	(71)	(65)	(84)	(95)	(81)	(65)	(84)

Note.—Entries in parentheses include only those children examined at both reexaminations.

Whereas the incidence between the two studies of retrograde amnesia was similar, the differences in incidence of anterograde amnesia were striking, i.e., 58% of children in the present study experienced periods of anterograde amnesia in contrast to only 19% of the children in the slight head-injury study (Klonoff, 1971a). The same pattern obtained regarding loss of consciousness in that a significantly higher incidence of loss of consciousness was recorded for children in the present study (60%) compared with those in the slight head-injury study (28%). There were also quantitive differences between the two studies regarding the duration of disturbed consciousness, in that children in the present study experienced more pronounced periods of amnesia and unconsciousness.

The relationship between age and incidence of clinical signs of disturbed consciousness in children with severe head injuries is worthy of note. In the present study, the older group when contrasted with the younger one exhibited consistently higher frequencies of amnesia (retrograde and anterograde) and periods of unconsciousness, but the differences were significant only with respect to anterograde amnesia.

The overall incidence of skull fractures in this study was 43% for the combined younger and older groups of children. This incidence of fractures is significantly higher than that reported by other investigators (Burkinshaw, 1960; Hjern & Nylander, 1964; and Hendrick et al., 1964). Whereas children in the older group experienced significantly longer periods of amnesia, the younger children sustained a significantly higher incidence of skull fractures. Age differences regarding incidence of skull fractures would in all probability be accounted for in terms of agent of injury. That is, for the younger group, falls from heights were the most common agents of injury, and the force of impact was generally great due to such falls. In comparing the slight and severe head-injury studies, it was found that skull fractures were almost invariably associated with the more severe head injuries of the present study; such fractures seldom occurred (i.e., less than 3% of cases) among children who sustained slight head injuries (Klonoff, 1971a).

The presence of impairment in behavior, as measured by neuropsychological tests, has been reported in detail by Klonoff and Low in the previous chapter.

Complaints and sequelae deriving from head injuries as well as prognosis can be interpreted with a higher degree of reliability and validity if certain conditions are specified. The initial condition is methodological and includes: specification of time interval between trauma and the appearance of symptoms or the presence of sequelae; specification of the reexamination procedure, e.g., hospital records, questionnaire, interview of parent(s), or direct examination of child; and accounting for interexaminer (physician) differences during followup reexaminations. The present study met the methodological considerations by standardization of time intervals for all children reexamined, i.e., annually; a parent, invariably the mother, accompanied the child; and the same physician interviewed the parents and reexamined the children.

The second condition relates to the premorbid status of children sustaining head injuries. Interpretation of symptoms should be within the context of the child's premorbid status, taking into account developmental anomalies. The incidence of developmental anomalies was almost identical in the present severe (15%) and the previous slight (14%) head-injury studies. Premorbid factors, including developmental anomalies, were recorded for 29% of the severe head-injured group. This incidence of premorbid factors is consistent with the findings of Fabian and Bender (1947) in whose study 22% of the head-injured group had predisposing factors, and with those of Harrington and Letemendia (1958) who reported that 29% of one of their groups showed emotional disorders before the accident. But there are no directly relevant published studies nor information regarding the incidence of developmental anomalies in the general population that might be used for comparative purposes. Developmental anomalies, however, seem age and sex related; in the present study the boys when contrasted with the girls of the younger group showed significantly higher frequencies of developmental anomalies and other premorbid factors. While increased vulnerability to head injuries may well be related to differences in roles and activities of boys compared to girls, younger boys with developmental anomalies and other premorbid factors may well be most vulnerable to head injuries.

The third condition relates to the differentiation of immediate accident effects, complaints, and sequelae, and this may be most readily met by using a time perspective. Disturbance of vital signs, such as unconsciousness, amnesia, and certain other symptoms are associated with the acute and semiacute phases of head injury (hours or days after the injury). Some of these symptoms and new symptoms may also be found during the recovery phase (months after the injury). In the present study, complaints referred to those symptoms present any time between the subacute phase and the first reexamination 1 year after injury, or between the first and second reexaminations. These symptoms were elicited by direct examination of the child and interview of the parents. Symptoms that lingered on or appeared many months after the trauma were then referred to as sequelae, if these symptoms were not present before the injury occurred and were elicited at time of reexamination. In the present study short-term sequelae referred to symptoms elicited at time of reexamination 1 year after trauma, taking into account the premorbid status of the child; residual sequelae referred to symptoms elicited 2 years after trauma, again in the context of the child's premorbid condition.

We will now turn from the conditions necessary for interpretation of complaints to the patterning and remission of complaints observed in the present study. Complaints were recorded for more than half (56%) of the present study group 1 year after trauma with a reduction to 44% 2 years after trauma. But the reduction was due to the subsiding of complaints in the older children, and more particularly among the older girls. In contrast, the incidence of complaints among children with slight head injuries (Klonoff, 1971a) was only 10%. The pattern of complaints during the first year after trauma was, however, similar in both studies. The rank order of complaints for the presently reported severe head-injury study was: personality changes, headaches, learning difficulties, fatigue, irritability, dizzy spells, visual or auditory defects, and memory and/or concentration difficulties. The rank order of complaints for the previously reported slight head-injury study was: headaches, personality changes, memory and/or concentration difficulties, irritability, learning difficulties, dizzy spells, and visual or auditory defects.

This study sheds additional light on a number of other complaints, including seizures, educational difficulties, disturbed relationships and adverse reaction to trauma, that have been cited as resulting from head injuries in children. In the present study, the incidence of seizures was low, while the rate of remission of seizures was high. Decline in educational achievement occurred infrequently during the first year after trauma, but a slight increase in academic difficulties was noted for the boys during the second year after trauma. The girls on the other hand continued to compensate. Change in range of relationships—at school, at home, and with peers was noted infrequently during the first year after trauma, and improved between the first and the second year post trauma. Considering psychological reactions of children to head injury 1 year after trauma, the children with severe head injuries examined in this study as well as the children with slight head injuries previously reported (Klonoff, 1971a), exhibited identical and high frequencies of denial (68%). The severe head-injured group showed a slight decrease in the use of denial 2 years after trauma; comparable data are not available for the slight head-injured group. The psychological reactions of the parents were more varied, anxiety and then dissipation of anxiety being the most common reactions. In contrasting the present study of severe head injuries with the previous one of slight head injuries with respect to assignment of blame by parents 1 year after the trauma, the differences were very striking; blame was assigned to the child or others almost four times as frequently by parents of severely head-injured children (55%) compared to the parents of children with slight head injuries (15%). No significant change in blame assignment by parents of children with severe head injuries was noted 2 years after trauma, compared with that recorded at 1-year posttrauma.

Sequelae (defined as involving one or more of the following areas—neurological signs, subjective complaints, personality changes, and intellectual changes) were recorded for 40% of the combined younger and older groups 1 year after trauma, and this figure was only slightly reduced to 39% 2 years after trauma. This incidence of sequelae is less than the incidence of complaints, as complaints include symptoms that had subsided before the reexaminations. The incidence of sequelae changed only slightly for both the younger and older age groups between successive years of reexamination (increase of 3% for the younger group and decrease of 6% for the older group).

There were, however, more substantial within-age-group sex differences and between-age-group sex differences, namely, the boys (45%) compared with the girls (21%) of the younger age group exhibited a significantly higher incidence of sequelae 1 year after trauma, and this significant difference was retained 2 years after trauma (49% for the boys and 23% for the girls). On the other hand, for the older group the incidence of sequelae was more or less equivalent for girls and boys 1 year after trauma; 2 years after trauma sequelae were approximately as numerous as they had previously been for the boys but decreased, though not significantly, for the girls. The complexity of sequelae, in terms of areas of functioning affected, did however, decrease for both the younger and older age groups, particularly for the latter. Other investigators have reported figures on the incidence of sequelae following head injury in children which bracket the figure obtained in the present study. Burkinshaw (1960) reported sequelae in 52% of his head-injured group; however, the followup interval was variable and the data were derived from questionnaires mailed to the mothers of the head-injured children. Rowbotham et al. (1954), on the other hand, reported a lesser incidence of sequelae than found in the present study.

Apart from age and sex, factors correlated with vulnerability to head injuries remain poorly defined. Furthermore, the relationship between immediate head-injury effects, and short- and long-term effects has seldom been documented in a standardized manner. The literature and clinical practice have been cited as supporting extent and type of amnesia, and presence of skull fractures as reliable indices for predicting course of recovery and sequelae. A post-hoc comparison of children with and without sequelae would provide information regarding the validity of such relationships. Such a comparison in the present study yielded no significant findings in terms of antecedent factors, apart from a higher incidence of sequelae among children aged 6–8. There were, however, significant relationships among the older children with sequelae and immediate accident conditions, specifically, length of unconsciousness and fractures.

Effects on adjustment subsequent to head injury and the nature of remission might also be clarified by a post-hoc comparison of children with and without sequelae. In the present study, the presence of sequelae was associated with a drop in school achievement, recorded 1 year after trauma and sustained 2 years after trauma. Regardless of age, deterioration in relationships at home was noted on first reexamination but there was a substantial improvement 2 years after trauma. For the younger group only, relationships with peers were adversely affected during the first year after trauma, but the incidence of this difficulty decreased by the second year after trauma. The younger children with sequelae became more sensitive to potential dangers, but this sensitivity subsided by the second year after trauma. The parents of these younger children engaged in changes in child-rearing, possibly becoming more protective, and these changes were sustained 2 years after trauma.

The manner in which differential immediate effects from head injuries relate to behavior or neuropsychological functioning would add to our understanding regarding the natural history of head injuries in children. This analysis was accordingly undertaken in the present study. Significant relationships were found between neuropsychological functioning and retrograde amnesia, anterograde amnesia, loss of consciousness, fractures, and to a lesser extent, site of injury. Establishing the nature of the relationships between clinical data, (which leads one to infer sequelae), and neuropsychological functioning would be extremely beneficial in the management of and the planning for children who sustain head injuries. This study established that such relationships can be demonstrated, in that the presence or absence of sequelae were predicted with a reasonably high degree of success from the neuropsychological data, the scope of prediction often being higher for older compared to the younger head-injured children, and also improving with subsequent reexaminations.

The relationship between duration of unconsciousness and subsequent psychological test performance has received attention in the literature, but the conclusions have been conflicting. Ruesch (1944) who studied head injuries in adults and Dencker (1960) whose study included children as well as adults, reported no relationship between disturbances of consciousness and psychological test scores. Dailey (1956) on the other hand did report a relationship between duration of posttraumatic amnesia and impairment on tests of memory and intelligence. Smith (1961) surveyed the literature on duration of unconsciousness and also concluded that increased duration of unconsciousness was associated with increased cognitive impairment. Klove and Cleeland (1967) in their study of head-injured adults were able to present a more precise statement regarding the nature of the relationship:

> Duration of unconsciousness may contribute to the prediction of posttraumatic neuropsychological impairment, if impairment is measured during the first three months following head injury. Thereafter, the predictive contribution of this variable seems negligible.

In this same study the authors concluded that the presence of a skull fracture adds little predictive information regarding psychological status of adults who sustain head injuries. If generalization from children to adults is warranted, the results of this investigation support the conclusion of Klove and Cleeland (1967) regarding the relationship between unconsciousness and neuropsychological status. However, unlike those of Klove and Cleeland, our findings do indicate a predictable relationship between skull fractures and neuropsychological status.

In order to place sequelae within a developmental perspective, it might be useful to compare some of the findings that emerged from the present study with results of head injuries in adults reported in the literature. Studies reporting sequelae might be divided in terms of those providing quantitative versus qualitative findings for nonveteran and veteran groups. Studies dealing with the general population have included: Gurdjian and Thomas (1965) who reported that 88% of their patients made an apparent or satisfactory recovery; Selecki, Hay, and Ness (1967) who found that 9% of their patients showed neurological deficit; and Fahy et al. (1967) who reported that, of 32 patients, few survivors escaped permanent sequelae. Studies dealing with veteran populations include: Walker & Jablon (1959) who noted that 9 months after injury, 60% of the patients complained of neurological symptoms; and Walker and Erculei (1969) who reported that only 50 of 249 men examined 15 years after injury had no abnormality of neurological function. Unfortunately, the methodology in these studies has been so varied that cross-comparisons may or may not be meaningful. All that may be concluded is that the range of sequelae seems to be as variable with adults as with children.

In conclusion, the present study provides data that may assist the researcher and clinician in evaluating the immediate, short-term and residual effects of head injuries in children. Evaluation of the long-term effects of head injuries of the children included in this study as well as the nature of the relationship between neuropsychological status and long-term effects must await the passage of time.

SUMMARY

This study dealt with 231 children ranging in age from 2.7 to 15.8 years, divided into one group under 9 years of age and a second group over 9 years of age, who were admitted to hospital with head injuries. Followup data were obtained for 196 of the original sample 1 year later, and for 163 of the 231 children 2 years later. Immediate, short-term and residual effects of injury were determined and then related to neuropsychological status shortly after trauma, 1 year later, and then 2 years later.

The mean age of the younger group was 5.9 years, of the older group 11.5 years; the boys: girls ratio was 8:5 and 2:1 for the respective groups and 12:7 for the combined groups. At reexamination 1 year after trauma, sex differences were noted primarily among the younger children and as follows: a higher incidence of developmental anomalies, positive premorbid factors and sequelae for the boys; and a higher incidence of head wounds and assignment of blame to others for the girls. During reexamination 2 years after trauma, sex differences were again noted primarily with the younger group and as follows: a higher incidence of complaints and sequelae for the boys; and a higher incidence of blame assignment to others for the girls. The only sex difference noted at consecutive reexaminations with the older group was more-frequent assignment of blame to others by the parents of the girls compared to boys. The younger children when compared with the older ones showed a significantly different patterning in some of the immediate accident effects, for example, regarding site of head injury, and a higher incidence of skull fractures. The older children on the other hand, had a higher incidence of anterograde amnesia. One year after trauma, the younger children showed a heightened sensitivity to potential dangers while the older children responded to their head injury with a more profound change in self concept. One year after trauma the parents of the younger children were more protective, in contrast to parents of the older children who made greater use of denial. These age-related differences were sustained 2 years after trauma, and in addition, the parents of the older children showed a significant decline in blame assignment.

Incidence of sequelae 1 year and then 2 years after the accident was as follows: 37% and then 40% for the younger group; 44% and then 38% for the older group; and 40% and then 39% for the combined groups. When the groups with and without sequelae were compared, the following variables discriminated younger children with sequelae from those without sequelae 1 year after trauma: age (a higher incidence of sequelae for children aged 6 to 8 compared with children aged 3 to 5); academic achievement (declined); relationship at home (deteriorated); relationship with peers (deteriorated); reaction of child to head injury (heightened sensitivity to potential dangers); and reaction of parent to head injury (increase in overprotective attitudes). Two years after trauma only academic achievement and reaction of parent remained significantly different. The following variables discriminated older children with sequelae from those without sequelae 1 year after trauma: loss of consciousness (more prolonged); skull fractures; academic achievement (declined); and relationship at home (deteriorated). Two years after trauma only academic achievement remained significantly different.

Using discriminant analysis, immediate effects (specifically, retrograde amnesia, anterograde amnesia, loss of consciousness, site of injury, and skull fractures) were predicted from neuropsychological data with a degree of success well exceeding chance expectancy. Short-term effects 1 year after trauma and residual effects 2 years after trauma (specifically, complaints and sequelae) were also predicted from neuropsychological status with even a higher degree of success. The findings that derived from this investigation were then compared with relevant studies in the literature that have reported on head injuries in children as well as head injuries in adults.

8
VALIDATION STUDIES IN ADULT CLINICAL NEUROPSYCHOLOGY

Hallgrim Klove

A basic assumption in clinical neuropsychology is that systematic measurement of intellectual, motor, and sensory functions with an appropriate and standardized battery of tests provides a basis from which inferences may be made regarding the organic integrity of the brain. A considerable body of scientific knowledge is presently available to support this assumption. This chapter will review validation studies of the Halstead Battery of Neuropsychological Tests as well as the relationship between brain and intelligence as measured by the Wechsler-Bellevue Scale.

The Halstead Neuropsychological Test Battery grew out of the work of Ward C. Halstead at the University of Chicago. Halstead's laboratory, which was established in 1935, was the first laboratory dedicated to full-time research in human neuropsychology. Over the years a large number of publications came from this laboratory, the most important of which is Halstead's book (1947), *Brain and Intelligence: A Quantitative Study of the Frontal Lobes.* Chapman and Wolff (1959) regarded this publication as a "major step forward in human cerebral physiology. Halstead selected, devised and standardized procedures of greater sensitivity to cerebral injury than any previously developed" [p. 371].

In this chapter several validation studies will be reviewed which demonstrate the striking sensitivity of Halstead's Neuropsychological Test Battery to the organic integrity of the cerebral hemispheres. Being fully aware of the wide range of brain-behavior research conducted by scientists in this country and abroad, it should be emphasized that this review will selectively concern itself with tests from the Halstead Battery rather than attempting to review the wide range of other psychological techniques which have been shown to have varying degrees of relevance to the organic condition of the brain. Emphasis will be placed upon results relating to clinically useful test methods which have been well researched and which are currently in general use. The temptation to comment on many additional important and significant studies will have to be resisted. The first part of this chapter will limit itself to reviewing those tests from the Halstead Battery that have been widely used by clinical neuropsychologists.

Based on factor analysis of 13 tests developed in his laboratory, Halstead (1947, 1951) proposed the concept of "biological intelligence". Halstead (1947) summarized the nature of these factors as follows:

1. A central integrative field factor C. This factor represents the organized experience of the individual. It is the ground function of the "familiar" in terms of which the psychologically "new" is tested and incorporated. It is a region of coalescence of learning and adaptive intelligence. Some of its parameters are probably reflected in measurements of psychometric intelligence which yield an intelligence quotient.

2. A factor abstraction A. This factor concerns a basic capacity to group to a criterion, as in the elaboration of categories, and involves the comprehension of essential similarities and differences. It is the fundamental growth principle of the ego.

3. A power factor P. This factor reflects the undistorted power factor of the brain. It operates to counterbalance or regulate the affective forces and thus frees the growth principle of the ego for further ego differentiation.

4. A directional factor D. This vector constitutes the medium through which the process factors, noted here, are exteriorized at any given moment. On the motor side it specifies the "final common pathway," while on the sensory side it specifies the avenue or modality of experience [p. 147].

STUDIES OF THE HALSTEAD NEUROPSYCHOLOGICAL TEST BATTERY

The significance of Halstead's four-factor theory of biological intelligence as a theoretical framework for neuropsychological research is presently uncertain. Nevertheless, it cannot be disputed that the tests themselves have provided the methodological impetus for a large amount of research which has increased our knowledge of brain-behavior relationships and which has led to significant advances in clinical human neuropsychology.

Halstead concluded that his test battery was more sensitive to lesions in the frontal than in the posterior parts of the hemispheres. This conclusion is in part based on the findings which are reflected in Table 1. Halstead's results indicated that a group with nonfrontal lesions generally performed more poorly than the group without cerebral damage, but that the frontal group was more seriously impaired on most of the tests than either the nonfrontal or control group. It has been difficult to confirm Halstead's findings in this regard. Reitan (1964b) has reported findings indicating that statistical analysis of results obtained on groups with frontal versus nonfrontal lesions failed to reveal significant differences, and clinical analysis of the data suggested that prediction of the localization of a

TABLE 1

Mean Scores and Probability Levels Based on Intergroup Comparisons for Selected Tests as Reported by Halstead (1947)

Test	Controls $N = 30$	Frontal lesions $N = 28$	Nonfrontal lesions $N = 22$	1-2	1-3	2-3
Category Test	37.22	94.50	72.30	.001	.006	.033
Tactual Performance Test (TPT)	10.56	21.70	16.10	.001	.006	.046
Memory Component	8.17	4.90	7.30	.001	.007	.001
Localization Component	5.92	2.50	5.20	.001	ns	.001
Seashore Measures of Musical Talent	20.88	37.80	26.90	.001	.070	.022
Speech-sounds Perception Test	10.36	20.40	18.90	.001	.005	ns
Finger Tapping Test— Dominant hand	54.92	43.90	48.40	.001	.006	.054
Time Sense Test— Memory component	198.90	609.70	256.10	.016	ns	.062
Impairment Index	0.1	0.8	0.3	.001	.002	.001

lesion was actually more accurate with posterior than frontal locations. In a later publication (Shure & Halstead, 1958) the conclusion based on Halstead's 1947 studies was modified to indicate that only tests having to do with the capacity to elaborate abstractions were performed significantly less well by patients with frontal lesions. Chapman and Wolff (1959) reevaluated Shure and Halstead's (1958) data and maintained that destruction of an equivalent mass of cerebral tissue in nonfrontal areas resulted in as great or greater impairment of abstraction ability as was noted in subjects with frontal lobe lesions. In reassessing Shure and Halstead's findings, Chapman and Wolff concluded that the apparent greater loss of cognitive function in Halstead's frontal lobe subjects represented an artifact since larger amounts of cerebral tissue had been removed in the frontal than in the nonfrontal cases. Chapman and Wolff, however, did confirm the Halstead Battery's great sensitivity to the organic condition of the brain. Their analysis revealed that the degree of impairment, as measured by the Halstead Battery, appeared to be directly related to the mass of brain tissue removed regardless of whether this removal was in the anterior or posterior areas of the brain. Among often-quoted validation studies of Halstead's Test is one by Reitan (1955a) in which 50 pairs of subjects (brain-damaged versus non-brain-damaged) were compared. This study did not evaluate the relative sensitivity of the tests to anterior or posterior location of brain damage, but did confirm Halstead's original findings regarding the general sensitivity of the tests. Reitan's data analyses indicated that each of Halstead's tests, with the exception of two measures based on critical flicker fusion, yielded significant differences between the groups. In fact, the probability that the distributions differed on a chance basis was shown to be extremely minimal for most of the tests.

(Raw-score means for Reitan's groups are presented in Ch. 10, this volume, by Matthews.)

In a well-designed cross-validation study of the Halstead Test Battery, Vega and Parsons (1967) compared 50 brain-damaged and 50 control subjects. The results are summarized in Table 2. The authors noted the somewhat lower levels of performance for their control group than those obtained by the control populations in other studies and ascribed cultural factors as a possible explanation. However, this did not seem to have any detrimental effect on the test battery's ability to discriminate between the brain-damaged and non–brain-damaged groups. It should also be noted that Vega and Parsons' control group consisted primarily of patients hospitalized on a neurological ward for disorders other than brain damage. The authors cited this factor as an important consideration in evaluating the clinical utility of the test battery.

The studies by Halstead and Reitan referred to above sampled a Midwestern population; Chapman and Wolff (1959) sampled a population from a large Eastern metropolitan area (New York City); and Vega and Parsons (1967) sampled a population from a Southwestern geographic location. In order to pursue the cross-validation studies further, a natural step would be to compare results obtained in examination of Americans and other nationality groups. Klove and Lochen administered the Halstead Battery to groups of Norwegian control and Norwegian brain-damaged subjects and groups of Wisconsin control and Wisconsin brain-damaged subjects. Descriptive statistics regarding age, education, and IQ for each of these groups are shown in Table 3. The data on

TABLE 2

Mean Values for Brain-damaged and Control Groups on Selected Halstead Tests and Probability Levels of Differences as Reported by Vega and Parsons (1967)

Test	Brain-damaged $N = 50$	Controls $N = 50$	p
Category Test	81.3	59.4	<.001
Tactual Performance Test (TPT)	32.4	20.6	<.001
Memory Component	4.5	6.6	<.001
Localization Component	1.4	2.9	<.001
Seashore Rhythm Test			
(Raw score)	20.4	23.3	<.001
Speech-sounds Perception Test	16.9	9.5	<.001
Finger Tapping Test—			
Dominant hand	35.5	44.6	<.001
Time Sense Test—			
Memory component	476.2	320.4	ns
Impairment Index	.83	.57	<.001

TABLE 3

Means and Standard Deviations for Age, Education, and IQ in American and
Norwegian Groups with and without Brain Damage

Variable	Group							
	Controls				Brain-damaged			
	Americans		Norwegians		Americans		Norwegians	
	Mean	SD	Mean	SD	Mean	SD	Mean	SD
N	22	na	22	na	33	na	33	na
Age in years	31.6	16.5	32.1	16.4	41.6	15.0	42.5	15.7
Education in years	11.1	2.21	12.2	2.60	11.2	2.24	11.2	2.20
IQ	109.3	13.1	111.9	15.4	99.3	9.9	100.8	12.9

the Norwegian subjects were obtained from the National Hospital (Rikshospitalet) at the University of Oslo School of Medicine, and the Wisconsin population was studied at the Neuropsychology Laboratory, University of Wisconsin Medical Center. The neurological criterion information for the Wisconsin and the Norwegian groups was obtained independently by different neurologists in two separate geographic and language environments. It should be pointed out that while good matching was obtained for the two control groups and for the two brain-damaged groups on age and education variables, the mean age difference between the two control groups and the brain-damaged groups is approximately 10 years, the brain-damaged groups being older. Reports by Reitan (1955d, 1967b) suggest that there is little systematic age-related influence on results obtained with the Halstead Battery in the range from 15 to 45 years. Thus, this age discrepancy probably had no major effect on the results.

Inspection of the results in Table 4 demonstrates a high degree of discrimination between the controls and the brain-damaged groups and this level of discrimination is maintained in both international and intranational comparisons. Thus, it appears that factors such as different language background and to some degree different cultural background have little influence on the discriminative power of these tests.

Wheeler, Burke, and Reitan (1963) applied a discriminant function technique to 24 behavioral indicators including the Halstead Neuropsychological Test variables. Based on independent neurological criterion information, 140 subjects were divided into the following four groups: no cerebral damage, left cerebral damage, right cerebral damage, and diffuse cerebral damage. The groups were comparable in regard to sex distribution, handedness, age, and education. The distribution of summed weighted scores in each intergroup comparison, resulting from the discriminant function analysis, was inspected for the point of minimum overlap. The individual's weighted score categorized him as belonging to one group or the other depending on whether it fell above or below the established point. These assignments, when compared with the neurological criterion

TABLE 4

Mean Scores and Probability Levels in Comparing American and Norwegian Groups with and without Organic Cerebral Damage

Variable	All controls	p	All brain-damaged	Norwegian controls	p	American brain-damaged	American controls	p	Norwegian controls	American brain-damaged	p	Norwegian brain-damaged	Norwegian controls	p	Norwegian brain-damaged	American controls	p	American brain-damaged
Category Test	39.9	.001	65.7	45.5	.001	59.2	34.6	ns	45.5	59.2	.01	71.8	45.5	.001	71.8	34.6	.001	59.2
Tactual Performance Test Total Time	14.1	.001	20.4	13.7	.001	21.3	14.0	ns	13.7	21.3	ns	19.4	13.7	.001	19.4	14.0	.001	21.3
Memory Component	7.3	.001	6.1	7.5	.001	5.9	7.2	ns	7.5	5.9	ns	6.4	7.5	.01	6.4	7.2	.03	5.9
Localization Component	4.7	.001	3.2	5.2	.001	3.1	4.3	ns	5.2	3.1	ns	3.4	5.2	.003	3.4	4.3	.08	3.1
Seashore Rhythm Test (Raw score)	25.2	.001	22.9	24.7	.002	22.6	25.7	ns	24.7	22.6	ns	23.0	24.7	.05	23.0	25.7	.02	22.6
Finger Tapping Test – Dominant hand	45.8	.09	42.7	48.5	.05	40.3	43.0	.01	48.5	40.3	ns	44.2	48.5	.05	44.2	43.0	ns	40.3
Impairment Index	.34	.001	.63	.34	.001	.62	.35	ns	.34	.62	ns	.64	.34	.001	.64	.35	.001	.62

assignments of the subjects to groups, were expressed as percentages of correct predictions as indicated in Table 5. In a similar study by Wheeler and Reitan (1963), the weightings based on linear discriminant function analyses from the previous study were applied to 23 behavioral test scores, including the Halstead tests, derived from examination of 304 subjects. The subjects had been classified, on the basis of thorough neurological evaluations, into groups without evidence of cerebral damage, left cerebral damage, right cerebral damage, and bilateral, or diffuse, brain damage. The groups with left and right cerebral lesions did not have as pronounced neurological evidence of unilateral cerebral damage as did the corresponding groups in the previous study. The results of this cross-validation study, when compared to the study just mentioned, demonstrated 10 to 20% reduction in accuracy for all comparisons except for the right-damage versus bilateral-damage groups where the discrimination on cross validation was essentially no better than chance. The reduction in accuracy of classification was probably attributable, in part, to the relaxation of criteria, as noted above, for lateralization of cerebral damage.

Klove (1963) examined the prospect of a complementary relationship between neuropsychological test performance and the neurological examination by studying one group without cerebral damage, one with negative findings on the physical neurological examination, and one with positive findings on the physical neurological examination. Each group consisted of 35 subjects. Intergroup comparability with regard to age and education is shown in Table 6. The group with normal physical neurologic status had unequivocal evidence of brain disease or injury as derived from other sources of information. The diagnoses in these cases were established on the basis of history, laboratory studies, radiologic studies, electroencephalographic findings, and in some cases, craniotomy. The findings based on physical neurologic examination were, for the purpose of this study, defined to include reflex status, sensory status, coordination, locomotion, and cranial nerve status. Ophthalmoscopy and auscultation of the head were also included as part of the objective physical neurologic examination. The two groups with brain lesions were also matched

TABLE 5

Correct Predictions of Subjects to Groups, Based on
Discriminant Function Analyses
(Wheeler, Burke, & Reitan, 1963)

Group comparisons	Percentage
Controls vs. all brain-damaged subjects	90.7
Controls vs. left hemisphere damage	93.0
Controls vs. right hemisphere damage	92.4
Controls vs. diffuse damage	98.8
Right hemisphere vs. left hemisphere damage	92.9

TABLE 6

Descriptive Information for Control Group and Two Brain-damaged Groups who Differed with Regard to Results Based on Physical Neurologic Examination

Group	N	Sex		Mean age	SD	Range	Mean education	SD	Range
		Female	Male						
Control	35	2	33	39.40	11.02	20–62	10.40	2.64	4–19
Brain-damaged: Negative neurological examination	35	9	26	39.80	13.41	19–72	10.14	3.13	3–17
Positive neurological examination	35	4	31	38.60	16.27	17–70	11.00	3.15	3–17

TABLE 7

Diagnostic Categories of Patients in Two Brain-damaged Groups
Who Differed With Regard to Results Based on
Physical Neurological Examination

Diagnosis	Negative neurological examination	Positive neurological examination
Cerebrovascular accident	9	9
Epilepsy	4	4
Head injuries		
Penetrating	2	2
Closed	5	5
Intrinsic tumor	12	12
Vascular malformation	3	3
Total	35	35

for diagnostic categories as shown in Table 7. Analysis of the data obtained for these groups indicated that the presence or absence of cerebral pathology was decisive in determining presence or absence of behavioral impairment while the presence or absence of abnormal neurologic findings had no significant effect on the test results. The results shown in Figure 1 may be heavily dependent upon having held the type of pathology constant in the two brain-damaged groups. However, when given this condition, it does not follow that patients with abnormal findings on the neurologic examination are more likely to demonstrate cognitive impairment than are patients with normal neurologic status, nor does it follow that patients with normal neurologic status are less likely to demonstrate cognitive impairment than are patients with abnormal neurologic findings. One is clearly tempted to draw the conclusion that the neuropsychological examination is considerably more sensitive to the organic integrity of the cerebral hemispheres than is the physical neurological examination, even when competently performed. Such a conclusion, however, would depend upon results obtained in the converse experiment; namely, one in which impaired and relatively normal neuropsychological findings represented the independent variables which differentially defined two matched brain-damaged groups, and results of the physical neurological examination represented the dependent variable. One would postulate that most subjects with relatively normal neuropsychological findings would also show nonspecific or normal findings on the physical neurological examination. However, this experiment should be done before a definite conclusion is drawn regarding the comparative sensitivity of the physical neurological and neuropsychological examinations. Table 8 shows the mean raw scores and the probability levels for the differences between the three groups on selected Halstead tests. The control group consistently performed

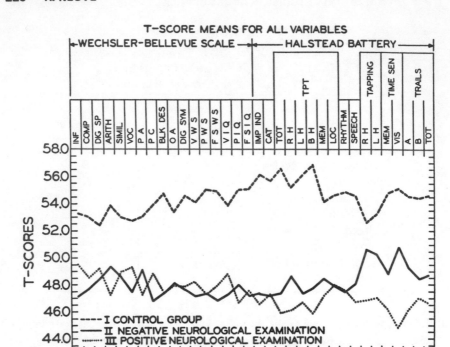

FIG. 1. Graphic presentation of results on behavioral measures for a group without cerebral damage and two groups with cerebral damage who differed with regard to positive or negative findings on the physical neurological examination.

TABLE 8

Raw-score Means and Probability Levels for Differences between Means on Selected Halstead Tests in Control Group and Two Brain-damaged Groups Who Differed with Regard to Results Based on Physical Neurological Examination

| Test | Control N = 35 | Neurological examination | | 1–2 | 1–3 | 2–3 |
		Negative N = 35	Positive N = 35			
Category Test	42.97	66.70	59.73	.001	.001	ns
Tactual Performance Test						
Total Time	16.10	26.48	29.99	.001	.001	ns
Memory Component	6.57	5.23	4.86	.05	.005	ns
Localization Component	3.34	1.91	2.03	.001	.005	ns
Seashore Rhythm Test (Raw score)	24.23	20.43	20.03	.001	.005	ns
Speech-sounds Perception Test	8.94	13.49	15.14	.01	.005	ns
Finger Tapping Test–Dominant hand	47.22	45.14	39.22	ns	.02	ns
Time Sense Test–Memory component	272.89	557.46	540.33	.01	.001	ns
Impairment Index	0.44	0.69	0.71	.001	.001	ns

better than either brain-damaged group but the brain-damaged groups showed no significant differences between them.

In another series of studies from the Neuropsychology Laboratory at the University of Wisconsin, Matthews and Booker (1972) investigated the relationship between certain aspects of pneumoencephalographic findings and a wide range of behavioral indicators, including tests from the Halstead Battery. The first of these studies demonstrated that a relationship exists between the size of the cerebral ventricular system and behavioral indicators. From a pool of 50 patients who had received a technically satisfactory pneumoencephalogram and complete neuropsychological evaluation, the 15 patients with the smallest cerebral ventricles and the 15 patients with the largest cerebral ventricles were compared. Figure 2 shows the results of this study. On only 3 of the 24 dependent variables did the group with the largest ventricles obtain higher mean scores than the group with the smallest ventricles and in none of these instances was the difference more than marginal. On the contrary, the group with the smallest ventricles achieved a better performance in 21 of the 24 comparisons, 6 of which were at the 5% probability level. While it should be noted that a relationship exists between the size of the ventricular system and performance on the neuropsychological tests, this relationship became evident only when the extremes of the distribution were compared. This qualification is of considerable importance, in order to impose proper restrictions on predicting or assuming behavioral deficits on the basis of pneumoencephalographic findings alone.

Another study in this series by the same authors reported differences between two subgroups drawn from the same pool of 50 patients which represented the 15 cases with the largest right over left ventricle measurement ratios and the 15 cases with the largest left over right ventricle measurement ratios. Raw scores were converted to T scores for the combined groups and the direction of the conversions was determined so that higher T scores would reflect, at least hypothetically, more impairment of the right cerebral functions and lower T scores would represent poorer left cerebral functions (see Figure 3). The comparative positions of the groups, in accordance with ventricular size, corresponded with laterality of cerebral impairment on 17 of 20 motor and sensory variables. Although, as shown in Figure 3, most of the differences were not statistically significant, the consistency of association between unilateral ventricular dilatation and lateralized neuropsychological deficits provided evidence of the validity of the measurements with relation to impaired brain functions. Some of the comparison variables, such as the Category Test, were considered for the purpose of analysis of this study to show no differential sensitivity to unilateral cerebral damage. Confirmation of this postulate is reflected in the mid position of the Category score in Figure 3, demonstrating the lack of difference between the right and the left groups on this variable.

A study by Doehring and Reitan (1962) has also demonstrated that impairment on the Category Test is unrelated to laterality of brain damage.

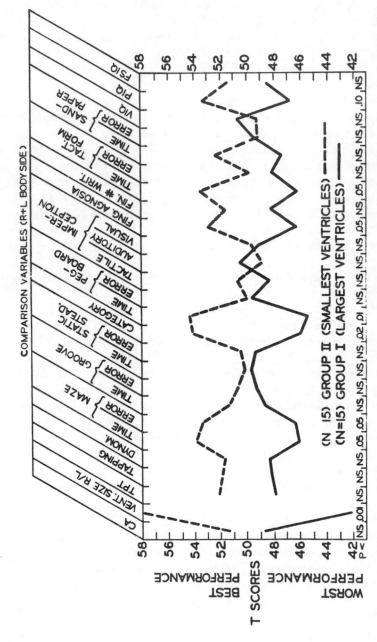

FIG. 2. Graphic presentation of neuropsychological results in groups selected for small and large lateral ventricles on the basis of pneumoencephalographic findings.

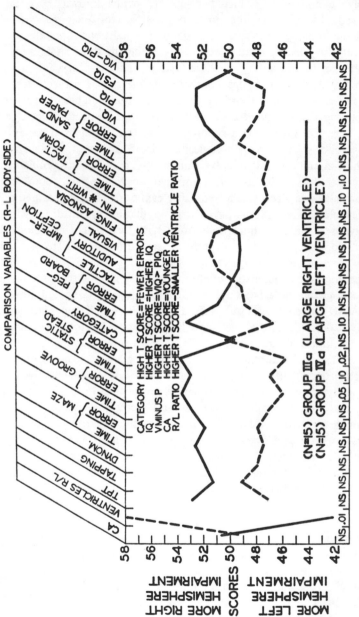

FIG. 3. Graphic presentation of neuropsychological results comparing groups with disparities in the sizes of the lateral ventricles.

The control groups used in many of the studies reviewed in this chapter were deliberately composed to include subjects with known physical and psychological disability at the time of testing (for example, paraplegia, peripheral neuropathy, medical and surgical conditions unrelated to the cerebrum, and psychiatric disturbances). A recurring question is raised in studies of this type as to the ability of these tests to achieve significant intergroup separation if the control groups consisted exclusively of subjects who were hospitalized for psychiatric disorders. Further, the question has been repeatedly raised regarding the ability of these tests to separate institutionalized patients with diagnoses of "chronic brain syndrome" and institutionalized patients with "chronic psychosis." The methodological problems associated with such studies are complicated and difficult to solve. Among the more obvious problems is the circumstance that in institutions with both neuropsychological laboratories and active neurological services, access frequently cannot readily be obtained to both chronic neurologic and chronic psychiatric populations. Institutions with both of these types of patient populations often have insufficient neurological and neuropsychological capability to perform scientifically satisfactory studies. However, several studies investigating the question of differential neuropsychological characteristics of chronic brain syndrome groups and chronic schizophrenic groups have been published. A group of Veterans Administration Hospital (VAH) psychologists published a study (Watson, Thomas, Anderson, & Felling, 1968) in which they attempted to separate by means of statistical analysis and clinical interpretation of the Halstead test data, one group labeled "schizophrenics" from another group labeled "organics." The results of this study as reported by the authors, can be summarized as follows: Neither the statistical analysis nor the clinical evaluation of the test protocols succeeded in separating the two groups. However, several methodological problems were present which must be considered in evaluating the negative outcome of this study. First, neurological examinations were not given at the time of the study, but all patients had received a neurological evaluation at the time of admission from the admitting physician. This procedure implies an apparent failure to realize that there is a distinct difference between a *clinically useful* diagnosis on the one side and a *scientifically adequate* diagnostic classification on the other side. A clinical admitting diagnosis may be neither objectively nor scientifically correct in spite of the fact that the same neurological admission evaluation may be adequate for the purpose of responsible clinical disposition of the case. A second problem associated with this particular study is that only about half of the "organic" group had received expert neurological examination, and these cases were represented by those patients who had been transferred to St. Cloud, Minnesota, VAH from the Minneapolis VAH which is a University-connected hospital with a neurology service. None of the "schizophrenics" had received an expert neurological examination and the argument justifying this was that referral for such an examination would imply a suspicion of brain damage, and that suspicion of brain damage would be a basis for excluding a patient from the schizophrenic group (Watson et al., personal communication, 1970). Another methodological difficulty in this study was that about 20% of the "schizophrenics" included in the study had received electroconvulsive shock treatment at one time or another and virtually all of the "schizophrenics" and some of the "organics" included in this study were on phenothiazine medication. No reference, however, was made to data regarding the effects of phenothiazine or electroconvulsive shock treatment on the particular measures that were used.

These points raise serious questions about the methodological adequacy of this investigation and demonstrate its deficiencies in controlling relevant variables. The absence of information regarding neurological findings such as EEG, brain scan, spinal fluid examination, neuroradiological studies, and a failure to obtain expert neurological evaluation of both the neurologic and schizophrenic groups would, in addition to the other factors mentioned, lead inescapably to the conclusion that the question raised remains unanswered. One should understand, however, that this study was designed to evaluate the utility of this neuropsychological test battery for differentiating between patients with chronic brain syndrome and schizophrenia in a neuropsychiatric setting, and as the authors themselves point out (Watson et al., personal communication, 1970):

> It would therefore have been inappropriate to exclude schizophrenics on phenothiazines. Drug-free patients are a rare and atypical breed and their exclusion would have precluded the development of clinically useful findings. After all, if these tests cannot separate the real life organics from schizophrenics in such a setting, they are of questionable utility.

One can hardly argue with the authors' good intentions in addressing themselves to a very practical question. The purpose of discussing their findings is to point out the many difficulties which face competent and conscientious researchers tackling these kinds of problems.

The question of the test battery's ability to differentiate between patients with organic brain damage and patients who are not brain damaged but whose presenting signs and symptoms suggest the possibility of organic brain damage represents an interesting and challenging problem. Heilbrun (1962) has stated the issue as follows:

> The major clinical contribution which the psychologist could make would be to make valid inferences regarding brain status in persons where the symptoms are much more subtle and the ability of neurologists to agree considerably less than standard research methodology has required. A crucial study would be one in which the neurological group is made up entirely of subjects for whom neurologists disagree as to diagnosis or are unable to make a diagnostic statement at all at the time the psychological measures are obtained and for whom retrospective diagnosis is possible [p. 513].

Addressing themselves to this general problem, Matthews, Shaw, and Klove (1966) employed a methodology and, in part, diagnostic classifications of patients similar to those proposed by Heilbrun. All the subjects used in this study were referred either because of known or suspected brain damage. The neuropsychological test battery was administered to each subject without regard for either provisional diagnostic impressions or differential diagnostic or evaluative questions posed by the referral sources. Two groups of patients were composed, each consisting of 32 patients. One group was labeled "brain-damaged" and the other was labeled "pseudoneurologic." The "pseudoneurologic" group consisted of patients who had been admitted to University Hospitals because of symptoms strongly suggestive of organic brain damage. Typical symptoms in this group included headache, nausea, paresthesia, motor weakness and/or incoordination, gait disturbances, visual and auditory difficulties, and ictal episodes suggestive of epilepsy. All had been examined extensively by expert neurologists and all had been given one or more EEG examinations and had been studied by other neurologic diagnostic methods including pneumoencephalography, angiography, radioactive brain scan, and spinal fluid analysis. Chest and skull films were also obtained for each patient. Results of these examinations had been, without exception, negative. Because of the persistence of somatic complaints in these patients, a consultation by the Department of Psychiatry was obtained and in all instances a psychiatric diagnosis was assigned as listed in Table 9. The "brain-damaged" group consisted of a stratified random sample of patients with unequivocal evidence of brain damage. This group was selected from a population of approximately 1,000 patients using a three-way stratification system to control for age, sex, and years of education. Thus, each member of the "pseudoneurologic" group was matched with an individual in the "brain-damaged" group who closely corresponded to him in terms of these three variables. The diagnostic classifications for the "brain-damaged" group are also given in Table 9. The results for these two groups were analyzed and compared statistically. The raw-score means and probability levels based on intergroup comparisons are presented in Table 10. It should be emphasized that a large number of significant differences were found in this study even though the groups were deliberately composed to attenuate rather than maximize the differential performance levels, e.g., matching on age, sex and education, exclusion of subjects with Full Scale IQs below 80, and the presence of neurologiclike symptoms in both groups of patients. These selection factors would seem to underscore the specific sensitivity of the comparison variables employed to the neurologic conditions and the potential contribution to the difficult differential diagnostic problem posed by patients presenting with neurologic as opposed to "pseudoneurologic" symptomatology. In addition, these results were based upon comparisons of level of performance alone, and did not include the additional methods of inference, as described in other chapters in this volume, which contribute greatly to interpretations of results for individual subjects.

TABLE 9

Age, Education, and Diagnoses for Brain-damaged and Pseudoneurologic Groups

| Variable | Groups | | | | | |
| | Brain-damaged | | | Pseudoneurologic | | |
	Range	Mean	*SD*	Range	Mean	*SD*
Age	16–51	31.19	11.32	16–50	31.25	11.73
Education	7–16	11.69	2.24	6–16	11.66	2.93
Diagnosis			*N*			*N*
Epilepsy			15			
Grand mal (6)						
Psychomotor (2)						
Mixed seizures (7)						
Posttraumatic encephalopathy			3			
Multiple sclerosis			7			
Cerebral arteriosclerosis			1			
Parkinson's disease			2			
Huntington's chorea			2			
Postencephalitic encephalopathy			3			
Conversion reaction						6
Tension headache						3
Personality trait disturbance						5
Personality pattern disturbance						2
Character disorder						2
Neurotic reaction						9
Schizophrenic reaction						3
Situational reaction						2
Totals			32			32

THE WECHSLER–BELLEVUE SCALES AND BRAIN DAMAGE

Birren (1951) and Cohen (1952) independently published factor analyses of the Wechsler-Bellevue Scale. Both found factors composed of verbal subtests only and of performance subtests only. Subsequent studies have identified additional factors, but Birren and Cohen's studies are of interest because they seem to provide a reasonable theoretical framework for the many studies relating differential intellectual impairment as measured by the Wechsler-Bellevue Scales to differentially lateralized cerebral pathology. The relationship between lateralized brain damage and patterns of differentiated impairment on the

TABLE 10

Raw-score Means and Standard Deviations for Selected Halstead Tests and
Probability Levels Comparing the Brain-damaged and
Pseudoneurologic Groups

Variable	Brain-damaged		Pseudo-neurologic		p
	Mean	SD	Mean	SD	
Category Test	63.66	27.66	44.53	24.63	<.01
Tactual Performance Test					
Total Time	27.60	13.55	14.79	6.32	<.001
Memory Component	6.44	1.86	7.56	1.41	<.05
Localization Component	3.16	2.38	4.38	2.34	<.05
Finger Tapping Test—Dominant hand	37.78	10.04	43.90	9.15	<.01
Seashore Rhythm Test (Raw score)	22.53	4.44	25.94	2.76	<.001
Speech-sounds Perception Test	8.25	4.06	6.25	4.00	<.05
Impairment Index	.63	.21	.32	.18	<.001

Wechsler Scales was first reported by Andersen (1950, 1951). Since Andersen's publications, a large number of studies have appeared, most of which have confirmed that the Verbal subtests on the Wechsler-Bellevue Scale tended to be suppressed in patients with left hemisphere damage and the Performance subtests tended to be suppressed in patients with right hemisphere damage. Reitan (1955b) published the following findings:

> Thirteen of the 14 patients with left-sided lesions had lower verbal than performance total weighted scores. Fifteen of the 17 patients with right-sided lesions, however, had a higher Verbal than Performance total. The patients with diffuse lesions were approximately evenly distributed with respect to higher Verbal or Performance averages [p. 477].

Reitan's findings have been confirmed in a series of subsequent papers. Klove (1959a) demonstrated the same pattern in the distribution of the Wechsler-Bellevue scores in a study using electroencephalographic criteria for composing the lateralized and diffuse groups. The patients with electroencephalographic abnormality maximized over the left hemisphere had a significantly lower Verbal than Performance IQ; the patients with electroencephalographic abnormality maximized over the right hemisphere had a lower Performance than Verbal IQ. No differences were found between Verbal and Performance IQ in the group with bilateral EEG changes or in the brain-damaged group with normal EEG, although the Wechsler scores for this latter group were somewhat higher than for the other groups. It is of interest to note that in this study Halstead's Impairment Index was in the impaired range for the four brain-damaged groups and showed no statistically significant intergroup differences. The important point with respect to the validity of the

Impairment Index was that the groups, all of which were brain damaged, showed impairment of a comparable degree even though one of the groups had normal EEG findings. Mean IQ results for each of the four groups are presented in Table 11. In another study, Klove (1959b) found that unilateral and bilateral sensory imperception had a systematic influence on Wechsler scores. Patients who failed to perceive stimuli on the right side under conditions of bilateral simultaneous stimulation (right sensory imperception) had a relative deficit on the Verbal Scale as compared to the Performance Scale. Patients with left sensory imperception demonstrated relative deficit on the Performance as compared to the Verbal subtests. Patients with bilateral sensory imperception failed to demonstrate differentiated intellectual impairment and brain-damaged patients whose perceptual responses of this type were normal also failed to show evidence of differentiated impairment.

In still another study, using EEG as a criterion for composing the groups, Klove and White (1963) demonstrated that electroencephalographic criteria which reflected the degree, rather than laterality of abnormality were related to results obtained on the Wechsler Scale. In this study, a control group, without past or present evidence of cerebral damage, and four brain-damaged groups were used. One of the brain-damaged groups had normal EEG tracings, but the other groups demonstrated EEG abnormalities. Specific criteria were used to compose these groups of subjects with mild EEG abnormalities, moderate EEG abnormalities, and severe EEG abnormalities. No evidence of differential Verbal and Performance levels were found on the Wechsler-Bellevue Scale. Halstead's Impairment Index significantly identified the control group as clearly better than the experimental groups and did this with much less intergroup overlap than did the Wechsler-Bellevue Scale. The Impairment Index also classified the brain-damaged group with normal electroencephalograms with the groups having abnormal electroencephalograms, thus indicating the sensitivity of the Impairment Index to the organic condition of the brain even when the electroencephalogram was normal. As will be noted in Figure 4, the control

TABLE 11

Mean Values for Four Brain-damaged Groups Who Differed with Regard to EEG Findings

Item	EEG			
	Right N = 37	Left N = 42	Diffuse N = 45	Normal N = 61
Verbal IQ	99.79	88.43	93.46	100.75
Performance IQ	87.82	98.43	93.15	102.62
Full Scale IQ	93.88	92.69	92.61	101.88
Impairment Index	.65	.70	.63	.61

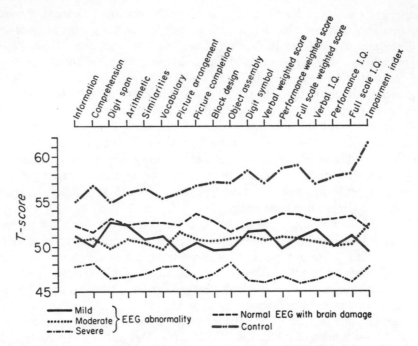

FIG. 4. *T*-score means for Wechsler-Bellevue and Impairment Index shown by a control group with normal functions and four brain-damaged groups ranging from normal EEGs to severe EEG abnormalities.

group had the best mean score on each of the variables used in the study and the group with severe EEG abnormalities had the poorest mean score on each measure. While many of the individual mean comparisons between adjacent groups were not significant, Figure 4 clearly shows the general trend for poorer scores to be associated with progressively more severe EEG abnormalities.

Klove and Reitan (1958) studied the relationship of organic language deficits (dysphasia) and difficulties in copying the spatial configuration of a Greek cross (spatial distortion) to Wechsler-Bellevue results. The results indicated that the group with spatial distortion was clearly impaired on the Performance section of the Wechsler-Bellevue Scale while the patients with dysphasia were significantly impaired on the Verbal subtests. A third group in which both dysphasia and spatial distortions were present gave results on the Wechsler-Bellevue Scale that approximated the most impaired levels for each of the other groups. These findings are in agreement with similar results reported by Critchley (1953) and Hécaen (1962).

In a study by Doehring, Reitan, and Klove (1961), brain-damaged groups were composed according to the presence or absence of homonymous visual field defects. In this study patients with right homonymous field defects obtained a lower mean Verbal than Performance IQ, patients with left homonymous field defects obtained a higher mean Verbal than Performance IQ, and brain-damaged patients without field defects failed to demonstrate differentiated intellectual impairment, although all the brain-damaged groups obtained significantly lower scores on the Verbal, Performance, and Full Scale IQ measures than did the control group. Figure 5 summarizes the principal results of this study. The studies reviewed above have been based on results obtained with the Wechsler-Bellevue (Form I), but for a number of years the Wechsler-Adult Intelligence Scale (WAIS) has been in common use. Thus, in a practical sense, it would be important to know whether or not similar relationships were obtained with the WAIS. Klove (1965) essentially repeated Reitan's study (1955b) in comparing groups with lateralized and generalized cerebral lesions. His findings demonstrated that the WAIS results were quite similar to the Wechsler-Bellevue (Form I) patterns for groups with lateralized and diffuse encephalopathy. The group with left hemisphere damage had a Verbal IQ smaller or equal to the Performance IQ in 28 of 40 comparisons, and the right hemisphere group had a Verbal IQ equal to or larger than the Performance IQ in 30 of the 35 comparisons. There was no difference between the Verbal and Performance IQ for the diffuse group. The IQ values for the three groups of this study are given in Table 12.

As part of a larger study by Satz (1966), the distribution of WAIS scores was related to the laterality of brain damage and the following hypotheses were confirmed:

1. Verbal IQ would be lower than Performance IQ in cases of left hemisphere lesions.

2. Verbal performance would be higher than nonverbal performance in cases of right hemisphere lesion.

3. Verbal performance would be no different than nonverbal performance in cases of indeterminate hemisphere lesions.

4. Verbal IQ would be no different than Performance IQ in the control population.

The mean Verbal and Performance IQ for each of the four groups are given in Table 13.

Parsons, Vega, and Burn (1969) suggested that the Verbal Scale has consistently been found to be depressed with left cerebral lesions but that right cerebral damage has not been as consistently reported to impair the Performance subtests. In analysis of their data, these investigators found that a comparison of two selected subtests, namely Vocabularly and Block Design, yielded highly consistent differences between groups with lateralized cerebral lesions. The group with left cerebral lesions had significantly lower Vocabulary than Block Design scores and was significantly lower than the group with right cerebral lesions on Vocabularly. Exactly the opposite relationships, again at statistically significant levels, were obtained in analyzing results for their subjects with right cerebral lesions.

Fields and Whitmyre (1969) also investigated the relationship of WAIS results to lateralized encephalopathy. They examined 23 patients with right hemisphere

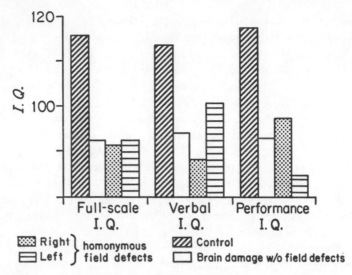

FIG. 5. Mean Full Scale IQ, Verbal IQ, and Performance IQ values on the Wechsler-Bellevue Intelligence Scale for a control group and three brain-damaged groups who varied with respect to their visual field defects.

damage and 18 patients with left hemisphere damage and concluded that deficits in verbal functioning were related to impaired integrity of the left cerebral hemisphere, and deficits in performance functioning were related to damage of the right hemisphere.

The results from the studies cited above can be summarized as follows: Both the Wechsler-Bellevue Scale (Form I) and the Wechsler Adult Intelligence Scale reflect differential intellectual impairment in cases of lateralized brain damage. The Verbal Scale tends to be impaired in cases of left hemisphere damage and the Performance Scale tends to be impaired in cases of right hemisphere damage.

TABLE 12

IQ Values Derived from the Wechsler Adult
Intelligence Scale for Groups with
Right, Left, and Diffuse Cerebral Damage

Variable	Cerebral damage		
	Right $N = 35$	Left $N = 40$	Diffuse $N = 31$
Verbal IQ	101.51	86.10	92.96
Performance IQ	89.68	92.35	89.35
Full Scale IQ	96.28	88.15	90.93

TABLE 13

WAIS Verbal and Performance IQ for Control and Brain-damaged Groups

Variable	Laterality of lesions			Control
	Left	Right	Indeterminate	
Verbal IQ	94.92	107.22	90.21	100.03
Performance IQ	105.17	99.78	87.00	97.09

A summary of results obtained in four of these studies (Reitan, 1955b; Klove, 1959a; Klove, 1965; Fields & Whitmyre, 1969) is given in Table 14 which presents the percentage incidence of Verbal levels being better than Performance levels in relationship to laterality of brain damage as well as comparative results for the combined groups. In regard to diffuse and bilateral encephalopathy, a significant discrepancy between the Verbal and Performance levels may occur in individual cases. This most likely reflects the asymmetry of the organic involvement in cases of bilateral and diffuse brain damage. It is noteworthy, however, that the studies cited above failed to demonstrate a systematic impairment of either Verbal or Performance scores in the diffuse brain damage classifications.

In rather sharp contrast to this group of studies is a report by Smith (1966) in which his results were summarized as follows:

> Reports of systematic differential effects of acute lateralized brain lesion on Wechsler-Bellevue Verbal and Performance weighted score sums were tested by comparison of individual and group scores and IQs for 48 patients with left-sided, 51 with right-sided and 21 with bilateral tumors, the locus and presence of which were established by surgery and/or autopsy. The hypothesis that with few exceptions non-aphasic and aphasic patients with left hemisphere lesions will show lower verbal than performance aggregate scores was not supported despite the inclusion of 12 aphasics in the 48 patients with left hemisphere tumors. Mean IQ and Verbal and Performance weighted scores sums also failed to show marked differences as a function of laterality [p. 522].

TABLE 14

Incidence of Directional Differences in Verbal and Performance Results in Groups with Left and Right Cerebral Lesions, Results of Four Studies

Cerebral damage	Wechsler-Bellevue (Form I)		Wechsler Adult Intelligence Scale		Combined data	
	Reitan (1955a)	Klove (1959a)	Klove (1965)	Fields & Whitmyre (1969)		
	VWS>PWS	VIQ>PIQ	VIQ>PIQ	VWS>PWS	V<P	V>P
Right	88%	78%	84%	78%	18%	82%
Left	7%	19%	35%	39%	75%	25%

A few other studies have reported negative or only partial confirmation of the general findings summarized above, (Heilbrun, 1956; Meyer & Jones, 1957) but these studies are not directly comparable to those studies we have reported. Heilbrun used the verbal part of the Wechsler-Belleuve Scale, but included only some of the Wechsler variables among his nonverbal (spatial) tests. This may be one factor in explaining his failure to find differences in the groups with lateralized lesions on the spatial (or nonverbal) tests. It should be noted, however, that among the intragroup differences on verbal and spatial performances, Heilbrun's group with right cerebral lesions had the largest difference (with spatial scores being lower than verbal scores) of any of the groups used. The groups with lateralized lesions showed within-group patterns in the expected directions according to the hemisphere involved and the difference between patterns was statistically significant. In regard to the study by Meyer and Jones (1957), its limitation in this context is that it used a very selected patient population consisting exclusively of patients with temporal lobe epilepsy. The patients were tested before and after surgery and they found that patients with right-sided lesions did not score lower on the nonverbal than the verbal subtests. It is generally accepted that uncomplicated temporal lobectomy does not yield specific or differentiated impairment on the Wechsler-Bellevue Scale.

Smith's findings are difficult to explain. The mean age of his group tends to be somewhat higher than in the other studies, but whether this factor alone represents an adequate explanation for the differences in results is uncertain. However, the fact that the evaluation of the verbal-performance differences are based on mean verbal and mean performance score sums may be of relevance in that Smith's population with a mean age of approximately 46–47 years consistently showed lower mean performance weighted score sums than mean verbal weighted score sums. It is well known that the performance scales when not age corrected will fall off at a fairly rapid rate after approximately age 40 (Wechsler, 1944), and Smith gave no indication in his study of control of this age-related variation in scores. Smith's groups consisted of 120 right-handed patients in whom locus and type of tumor had been verified by surgery or autopsy. In spite of the mention of surgery and autopsy criteria, no information is given in regard to tumor classification. Clinical experience and research findings indicate that differentiated deficits on the Wechsler-Bellevue Scales are typically not present in "extrinsic" as opposed to "intrinsic" brain tumors. Reed (1962) demonstrated that differentiated impairment did not occur with lateralized meningiomas, and only mildly differentiated impairment on the Wechsler Scale occurred when laterality was ascertained by neurological methods in cases of lateralized infiltrating tumors. While location of lesions within the hemisphere has not been a controlled variable in any of the previously cited studies in which a predictable relationship between the Wechsler-Bellevue patterns and the lateralization of brain damage was found, there is good clinical evidence indicating that the differential impairment is most pronounced in posterior rather than anterior location of the lesion. It is conceivable that factors relating to the anterior-posterior location of the lesion and the type of neoplasms may play a role in explaining Smith's findings.

A few studies have addressed themselves to the effects of acute versus chronic brain damage. Klove and Fitzhugh (1962) demonstrated absence of differential intellectual impairment in a chronic epileptic population which had been subdivided into four EEG groups (maximal right, maximal left, bilateral, and normal EEG), using the same EEG criteria which were used in a previously cited study (Klove, 1959a). This absence of differential impairment is compatible with the conclusions reached in a study by Fitzhugh, Fitzhugh, and Reitan (1962) in which differential impairment on the Verbal and Performance portions of the Wechsler-Bellevue Scale was demonstrated for groups with lateralized lesions of recent onset but no such impairment was demonstrated in groups with chronic encephalopathy. With the noteworthy exception of Smith's findings (1966), the general conclusion from many studies seems to be that acute and lateralized brain damage results in differential intellectual impairment on the Wechsler-Bellevue Scale, the type of impairment being dependent upon the lateralization of the brain damage. In cases of slowly developing or chronic static lesions such differential impairment does not seem to result.

It should be emphasized that in clinical analysis of individual subjects, differential impairment on the Wechsler-Bellevue Scales *alone* cannot ordinarily be accepted as evidence of lateralized brain damage. Many conditions have been demonstrated to result in differential intellectual impairment. Such factors include psychiatric conditions, educational and social factors, very possibly vocationally developed skills, and asymmetric bilateral cerebral lesions. Thus, the Wechsler-Bellevue Scales should be viewed as an adjunct in the overall assessment of lateralized or focal brain dysfunction. Differential impairment on the Wechsler Scales takes on specific meaning only when the findings are supported by other more direct indicators of lateralized cerebral dysfunction as is demonstrated by the presentation of results on individual subjects in other chapters in this book.

9
NEUROPSYCHOLOGICAL STUDIES OF PATIENTS WITH EPILEPSY[1]

Hallgrim Klove and Charles G. Matthews

A number of excellent reviews have been published of research and clinical reports regarding psychological studies of patients with epilepsy. In the interests of a reasonably brief exposition of our findings, earlier studies will not be reviewed in any detail; the reader is referred to surveys such as those by Rodin (1968), Lennox (1960), and Reitan (in press).

During the past several years, a major emphasis in our neuropsychology research program has been upon patterns and level of cognitive impairment in variously composed groups of epileptic patients (Klove & Matthews, 1966, 1969; Matthews & Klove, 1967, 1968). Our approach to studying this complex problem has been to investigate patterns of cognitive impairment in a series of increasingly refined classifications of patients with epilepsy. The first psychological test comparisons to be presented were based upon quite broadly defined patient categories (i.e., between patients with epilepsy of known versus unknown etiology). In the second study to be reviewed, neuropsychological test comparisons were made between groups of patients with epilepsy of known and unknown etiology which were further subdivided into major motor, psychomotor, and mixed seizure disorder classifications. The third study in the series is concerned with the relationships between age at onset of epilepsy and behavioral deficits as measured by the same neuropsychological test battery utilized in the first two studies to be described.

The basic question posed in the first study was: Which is more important in determining behavioral deficits associated with epilepsy, the seizures themselves

[1] The research reported in this chapter was supported by Grant NB 03360 from the National Institute of Neurological Diseases and Blindness, United States Health Service.

or the underlying cause of the seizures? Table 1 presents descriptive information on the four groups which were composed in an attempt to provide a preliminary answer to this question.

Group 1 was composed of subjects without history or clinical evidence of brain damage. Group 2 was composed of subjects with a diagnosis of brain damage or disease, but without history of epilepsy. Group 3 was composed of subjects with definite neurological diagnoses of brain damage and unequivocal evidence of epilepsy, presumed to be secondary to the brain damage. Group 4 was composed of patients matched as closely as possible with members of Group 3 in regard to type of seizures (Table 3). However, in Group 4, no etiology for the epilepsy could be determined after a thorough study of neurological, neuroradiological and case history findings.

In order to make meaningful comparisons between these four groups, an effort was made to control for type of cerebral pathology in Groups 2 and 3. Inspection of Table 2 shows the close correspondence achieved between these groups on this matching variable.

In addition to matching the groups on age, education, and type of pathology, the distribution of seizure types within Group 3 (verified brain damage with epilepsy) and Group 4 (epilepsy of unknown etiology) was made as comparable as possible. These comparisons are presented in Table 3.

The psychological test variables on which the four groups were compared are shown in Table 4.

Variables 1, 2, and 3 are Verbal, Performance, and Full Scale IQ scores on the Wechsler Adult Intelligence Scale. The remaining comparison variables listed in Table 4, except the Trail Making Test, are from Halstead's Neuropsychological Test Battery (Halstead, 1947) and can be viewed as measures of cognitive and adaptive abilities, including concept formation ability, complex psychomotor

TABLE 1

Sex, Age, and Education for Control Group, Brain-damaged Group without Epilepsy, and Two Groups with Epilepsy

Group	N	Sex		Mean age	SD	Mean education	SD
		Male	Female				
1. Control	51	31	20	33.49	10.09	11.53	2.74
2. Verified brain damage without epilepsy	51	41	10	34.88	13.24	10.63	2.62
3. Verified brain damage with epilepsy	51	43	8	34.65	10.37	10.51	2.87
4. Epilepsy of unknown etiology	51	32	19	31.67	9.62	11.23	3.53

TABLE 2

Types of Brain Damage Characterizing Group without Epilepsy (Group 2)
and Group with Epilepsy (Group 3)

Diagnosis	Group 1[a]	Group 2	Group 3	Group 4[b]
Closed head injury	–	22	21	–
Chronic brain lesion	–	11	11	–
Cerebrovascular accident	–	10	11	–
Penetrating head injury	–	4	4	–
Arteriovenous malformation	–	2	2	–
Multiple sclerosis	–	1	1	–
Abscess	–	1	1	–

[a]No history or clinical evidence of brain damage.
[b]No etiology for epilepsy but closely matched with Group 3 in regard to type of seizures.

problem-solving skills and attention and verbal-symbolic functioning. The Trail Making Test has been described and validated by Reitan (1958b).

DATA ANALYSIS

In order to facilitate group comparisons, raw scores from all four groups on each variable were pooled and ranked from poorest to best performance. These ranks were converted to normalized standard scores (T scores) which were then reclassified according to their groups of origin. The direction of ranking was adjusted so that higher T scores always represented more adequate test performances. Analysis of variance was performed for each variable, and F ratios were determined. In those instances in which the F ratios were significant at $p <$ .05, the probability that intergroup mean differences on each variable were attributable to chance were determined by Student's t test. In order to present the psychometric test data in a conventional form, mean Verbal, Performance,

TABLE 3

Epileptic Seizure Types in Subjects with Known (Group 3) and Unknown
(Group 4) Etiology

Seizure type	Group 1[a]	Group 2[b]	Group 3	Group 4
Major motor	–	–	30	29
Major motor and psychomotor	–	–	10	10
Psychomotor	–	–	9	9
Mixed	–	–	2	3

[a]Control group.
[b]Diagnosis of brain damage or disease; no history of epilepsy.

TABLE 4

Psychological Test Variables Used for Comparison of Control Group,
Brain-damaged Group without Epilepsy, and Epileptic Groups of
Known and Unknown Etiology

Variable
1. Wechsler Adult Intelligence Scale Verbal IQ
2. Wechsler Adult Intelligence Scale Performance IQ
3. Wechsler Adult Intelligence Scale Full Scale IQ
4. Mean time per block on Halstead's Tactual Performance Test
5. Memory component of Halstead's Tactual Performance Test
6. Localization component of Halstead's Tactual Performance Test
7. Seashore Rhythm Test
8. Halstead's Speech-sounds Perception Test
9. Mean finger oscillation speed for dominant hand on Halstead's Finger-tapping Test
10. Trail Making Test, Part A
11. Trail Making Test, Part B
12. Trail Making Test, Part A plus Part B
13. Halstead's Category Test
14. Halstead's Impairment Index

and Full Scale IQ scores and standard deviations for these means were computed.

RESULTS

Means and standard deviations of Verbal, Performance, and Full Scale IQ scores for the four groups are presented in Table 5.

Figure 1 presents the T score means and probability levels associated with mean group differences in comparison of all variables listed in Table 4.

TABLE 5

Means and Standard Deviations for Wechsler Adult Intelligence Scale
IQs in the Four Groups

Group	Verbal IQ		Performance IQ		Full Scale IQ	
	Mean	SD	Mean	SD	Mean	SD
1. Control	108.16	13.59	108.88	12.53	109.14	13.27
2. Brain damage without epilepsy	93.88	15.34	91.69	16.07	92.89	15.28
3. Brain damage with epilepsy	97.27	14.56	94.94	12.22	96.04	12.90
4. Epilepsy of unknown etiology	100.45	16.13	100.29	14.11	100.39	15.31

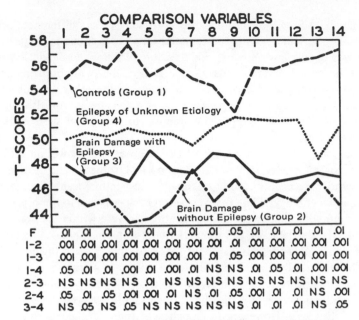

FIG. 1. *T*-score means and probability levels associated with 14 comparison variables in epileptic and nonepileptic groups.

Inspection of the data shown in Figure 1 indicates that the control group achieved significantly better performances than the three experimental groups in 40 of 42 possible comparisons. The two instances in which significant differences were not present were between controls and subjects with epilepsy of unknown etiology on the Speech-sounds Perception Test and on the Finger Tapping Test. However, in 10 of 12 other comparisons between controls and patients with epilepsy of unknown etiology, intergroup differences in favor of the control subjects were significant beyond the .01 level, and in the remaining two comparisons (Verbal IQ, Trail Making Test-Part B) a confidence level of $p <$ .05 could be assigned to the mean differences.

Mean performances of the group with epilepsy of unknown etiology (Group 4) exceeded the scores of Groups 2 and 3 in each instance, although statistically significant differences occurred more frequently between the group with epilepsy of unknown etiology and the brain-damaged group without epilepsy than between the group with epilepsy of unknown etiology and the group with verified brain damage with epilepsy. Analysis of the test performances of the two groups matched for type of pathology in which one group also had epilepsy (Group 3) while the other did not (Group 2), failed to yield significant intergroup differences in 13 of 14 measures.

The results of this study support a conclusion that the presence of epileptic seizures is associated with significantly lower psychometric and adaptive ability levels than those found in control subjects. These test score differences occurred both in epileptic subjects with verified cerebral pathology and in subjects whose epilepsy was of unknown etiology and in whom physical neurological status was judged to be within normal limits. Comparison of the two groups matched for type of pathology, one of which had seizures while the other did not, failed to show additional significant impairment in the seizure group although both groups performed at levels generally inferior to the group with epilepsy of unknown etiology.

Many previous studies have emphasized the absence of significant differences on psychological test variables between normal subjects and patients with epilepsy who have been variously classified as idiopathic, cryptogenic, essential, or of unknown etiology. While the Wechsler IQ values found in the present study for the group with epilepsy of unknown etiology were within the average range (Full Scale IQ X = 100.39), the mean Halstead Impairment Index of this group was 0.56 as opposed to an Impairment Index of only 0.32 in the controls ($p <$ .001). The statistically significant difference on the Impairment Index between controls and patients with epilepsy of unknown etiology indicates that this group of epileptic subjects is clearly distinguishable from controls in terms of adaptive ability level. However, the Impairment Index of the unknown etiology group was lower (i.e., better) than the group with verified brain damage without epilepsy ($p <$ .001) or the group with verified brain damage with epilepsy ($p <$ .05). These results provide support for previously reported conclusions stating that patients with epilepsy of unknown etiology show less cognitive impairment than do patients with epilepsy associated with known etiology, but it is important to note that the group with epilepsy of unknown etiology was clearly impaired in comparison to subjects without epilepsy and without history or current evidence of brain damage.

In summary, the results of the first study in this series indicate that epileptic manifestations, whether or not associated with known etiology, result in significant impairment of adaptive abilities in comparison to control subjects. However, the findings also show that in those epileptic patients in whom verified lesions were present, the ictal episodes per se did not result in significant additional cognitive impairment when such patients were compared to nonepileptic patients matched for age, educational level, and type of cerebral pathology.

It is immediately apparent that a number of interpretative restrictions must be imposed upon the results obtained in this first study because several variables, which in all likelihood have a direct bearing upon the results, were uncontrolled. These variables include age at onset of seizures, seizure frequency, and seizure type. While in the first study the two groups of patients with seizures were equated as closely as possible with respect to equal numbers of subjects with the same clinical seizure classification, a number of different seizure types were present in each group.

The second study that we shall review was concerned with performances on the same battery of neuropsychological tests used in the initial study, but the seizure classifications employed were further refined in an effort to minimize confounding seizure type with seizure etiology. Thus, the aim of the second study was to investigate the relationship between seizure types and psychological performance within categories of epilepsy of known and unknown etiology.

Data regarding sex, age, and education distributions are given for each group in Table 6 and indicate the general comparability of the groups.

Two control groups were used, one composed of nonneurological subjects and one composed of patients with verified brain damage but wihout epilepsy. Three categories of patients with seizures of known etiology and three categories of patients with seizures of unknown etiology were also composed. Within each general category of known and unknown etiology, subgroups of patients with major motor seizures, psychomotor seizures, and mixed (i.e., major motor and psychomotor) seizures were identified. Clinical and etiological classifications were based upon detailed medical history, EEG, neurological examinations, and,

TABLE 6

Sex, Age, and Education for Non-Brain-damaged Control Group, Nonepileptic Brain-damaged Control Group, and Epileptic Groups with Known and Unknown Etiology

| Group | N | Sex | | Age | | Education | |
		Male	Female	Mean	SD	Mean	SD
Control							
1. Nonneurological	51	31	20	33.49	10.09	11.53	2.74
2. Verified brain damage without epilepsy	48	35	13	33.31	12.01	11.06	2.76
Known etiology							
3. Major motor seizures	23	20	3	32.43	10.81	10.30	2.57
4. Psychomotor seizures	22	12	10	29.00	9.60	10.82	2.54
5. Mixed (major motor and psychomotor) seizures	20	16	4	30.10	8.69	10.80	2.17
Unknown etiology							
6. Major motor seizures	29	15	14	30.69	10.93	11.31	2.98
7. Psychomotor seizures	22	17	5	28.27	8.50	11.82	2.67
8. Mixed (major motor and psychomotor) seizures	18	10	8	26.94	9.12	10.11	2.70

in most instances, angiography, pneumography, and brain scan. Physical neurological status was within normal limits for each subject in Groups 6, 7, and 8 (epilepsy of unknown etiology), although EEG abnormalities were common in these patients. In none of these subjects, however, could a neurological diagnosis be assigned explaining the presence of epilepsy and the seizures were, therefore, classified as being of unknown etiology.

An effort was made to control for type of cerebral pathology as closely as possible. Table 7 demonstrates the close matches which were achieved for the brain-damaged group without epilepsy (Group 2) and the three groups (3, 4, 5) with major motor, psychomotor, or mixed seizure disorders associated with known cerebral pathology.

The groups were compared on the same battery of tests that was employed in the initial study (see Table 4).

Table 8 shows means and standard deviations for Verbal, Performance, and Full Scale IQ scores in the eight groups.

Mean scores on all 14 variables, and probability levels based on intergroup mean comparisons of Groups 1 and 2 (controls, brain damage without epilepsy) and the two categories of patients with major motor seizures (one of known etiology and the other of unknown etiology) are presented in Figure 2.

Both groups with major motor seizures were clearly inferior to the normal control subjects. The major motor group of known etiology was significantly lower than the controls on all measures except for Variable 9 (Finger Tapping) and the major motor group of unknown etiology performed more poorly ($p <$ .01) than the controls on 9 of 14 measures, with suggestive differences ($p < .05$) found on two additional test comparisons. Comparison variables failing to yield

TABLE 7

Diagnostic Classifications of Verified Brain-damaged Groups

Diagnosis	Group[a]							
	1	2	3	4	5	6	7	8
Total N	51	48	23	22	20	29	22	18
	Percent							
Closed head injury	—	46	30	41	45	—	—	—
Chronic brain lesion	—	25	26	27	30	—	—	—
Infiltrating tumor	—	13	17	27	15	—	—	—
Penetrating head injury	—	8	4	0	5	—	—	—
Arteriovenous malformation	—	4	13	5	5	—	—	—
Multiple sclerosis	—	2	4	0	0	—	—	—
Abscess	—	2	4	0	0	—	—	—

[a]As identified in Table 6.

TABLE 8

Means and Standard Deviations for Wechsler Adult Intelligence Scale IQs in
Non–Brain-damaged and Brain-damaged Control Groups and Groups with
Epilepsy of Known and Unknown Etiology

Group	Verbal IQ		Performance IQ		Full Scale IQ	
	Mean	SD	Mean	SD	Mean	SD
Control						
1. Nonneurological	108.16	13.59	108.88	12.54	109.14	13.27
2. Verified brain damage without epilepsy	95.38	14.02	91.10	14.07	93.19	12.92
Known etiology						
3. Major motor seizures	95.00	14.75	92.22	14.91	93.43	14.06
4. Psychomotor seizures	96.27	17.63	93.91	13.31	95.05	14.98
5. Mixed (major motor and psychomotor) seizures	97.65	12.54	95.20	12.09	96.65	12.24
Unknown etiology						
6. Major motor seizures	98.48	15.99	96.14	11.90	97.24	14.04
7. Psychomotor seizures	105.59	17.49	105.32	14.93	105.91	16.70
8. Mixed (major motor and psychomotor) seizures	95.28	14.53	93.28	14.77	94.06	15.15

significant differences between controls and subjects with major motor seizures
of unknown etiology were Speech-sounds Perception, Finger Tapping speed, and
Part B of the Trail Making Test. The intergroup comparisons reported in Figure
2 for Groups 3 and 6 show that on each variable the group with major motor
seizures of unknown etiology showed better performances than did the group
with major motor seizures of known etiology although only 5 of 14 comparisons
were significant at $p < .05$.

Comparisons between the groups with psychomotor seizures of known and of
unknown etiology are shown in Figure 3.

The control group attained higher scores on each of the 14 measures than did
the group with psychomotor epilepsy of known etiology, with 11 of 14
differences being significant at $p < .01$. In contrast to these results, the group
with psychomotor epilepsy of unknown etiology performed essentially at the
same levels as the normal controls. On only 2 of 14 comparison variables were
even suggestively significant differences ($p < .05$) found in favor of the control
subjects, and inspection of the figure shows that on 7 of 14 measures the mean
score of the psychomotor group of unknown etiology equaled or exceeded the
score of the controls. The group with psychomotor epilepsy of known etiology

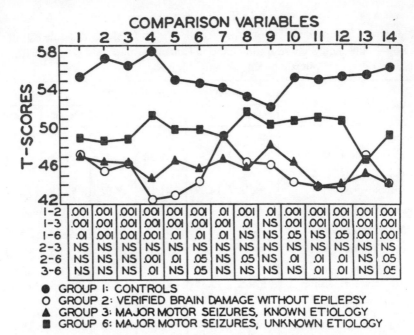

FIG. 2. *T*-score means and significance of differences between nonneurological controls, brain-damaged subjects without epilepsy, and groups with major motor epilepsy of known and of unknown etiology on 14 psychological tests.

performed at consistently lower levels than the psychomotor epilepsy group of unknown etiology, with 5 of 14 comparisons being significant at $p < .01$.

Figure 4 was prepared to facilitate comparison of results found between groups that were presented separately in Figures 2 and 3.

This figure shows that the two most divergent groups are represented by psychomotor seizures of unknown etiology in which the highest test scores were obtained, and by major motor seizures of known etiology, in which the poorest performances were consistently present. Groups 4 and 6 (psychomotor seizures of known etiology and major motor seizures of unknown etiology) performed at almost identical levels with none of the intergroup comparisons being significant at $p < .05$.

Table 9 summarizes the results of the second study by presenting the ranking of the eight groups from best to worst performance, with the rankings based upon the mean Halstead Impairment Index of each group. The Impairment Index, which represents the best single estimate of overall performance on the test battery, was computed for each subject by summing the number of Halstead variables on which the subject's score fell within the range that has been found in previous research (Shure & Halstead, 1958; Reitan, 1955a, 1959a) to be characteristic of brain-damaged as opposed to control subjects.

The data reported in Table 9 indicate that the nonneurological control subjects showed the lowest (i.e., best) Impairment Index, and this group was found to be significantly better on this composite estimate of test performance than all groups other than the group with psychomotor seizures of unknown etiology. The two most divergent epilepsy groups were represented by the group with psychomotor seizures of unknown etiology and the group with major motor seizures of known etiology. Significantly poorer Impairment Index rankings ($p < .05$) were found in patients with major motor seizures of known than of unknown etiology and in patients with psychomotor seizures of known than of unknown etiology. Both major motor seizure groups performed more poorly on the Impairment Index score than did either group with psychomotor epilepsy. Comparison between psychomotor seizures of known etiology and major motor seizures of unknown etiology failed to yield a difference significant at $p < .05$. All additional comparisons of paired groups are shown in Table 9.

Although the intergroup comparisons made in our initial study indicated that epileptic seizures, whether of known or of unknown etiology, were associated with significantly lower psychometric and adaptive ability levels than those found in control subjects, a necessary caveat was imposed on these conclusions because a number of different seizure classifications were included in the two epileptic groups that were compared. The results of the second study, which included the additional matching variable of type of seizure within categories of epilepsy of known and of unknown etiology, demonstrates the need for cautious

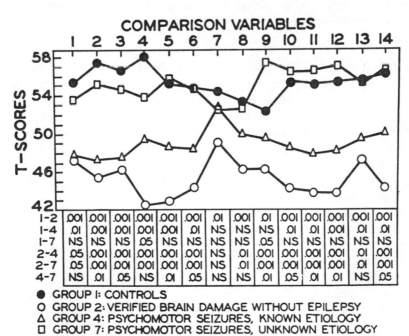

FIG. 3. T-score means and significance of differences between nonneurological controls, brain-damaged subjects without epilepsy, and groups with psychomotor epilepsy of known and unknown etiology on 14 psychological tests.

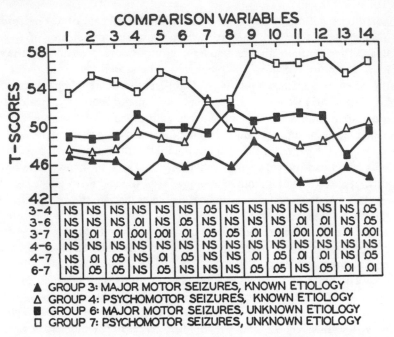

	1	2	3	4	5	6	7	8	9	10	11	12	13	14
3-4	NS	NS	NS	NS	NS	NS	.05	NS	NS	NS	NS	NS	NS	.05
3-6	NS	NS	NS	.01	NS	.05	NS	NS	NS	NS	.01	.01	NS	.05
3-7	NS	.01	.01	.001	.001	.01	.05	.05	.01	.01	.001	.001	.01	.001
4-6	NS	NS	NS	NS	NS	NS	NS	NS	NS	NS	NS	NS	NS	NS
4-7	NS	.01	.05	NS	.01	.05	NS	NS	.01	.05	.01	.01	NS	.05
6-7	NS	.05	.05	NS	.05	NS	NS	NS	.05	.05	NS	.05	.01	.01

▲ GROUP 3: MAJOR MOTOR SEIZURES, KNOWN ETIOLOGY
△ GROUP 4: PSYCHOMOTOR SEIZURES, KNOWN ETIOLOGY
■ GROUP 6: MAJOR MOTOR SEIZURES, UNKNOWN ETIOLOGY
□ GROUP 7: PSYCHOMOTOR SEIZURES, UNKNOWN ETIOLOGY

FIG. 4. *T*-score means and significance of differences between major motor and psychomotor epileptic groups of known and of unknown etiology on 14 psychological tests.

interpretation of the more general findings reported in the initial investigation. Patients with either major motor or with mixed (major motor and psychomotor) seizures of unknown etiology, performed more poorly than did normal controls, but the patients with psychomotor seizures of unknown etiology did not. Not only were the test performances of the psychomotor group closely comparable to those found in normal controls, but they were significantly better in terms of the Impairment Index than any other epilepsy group or the brain-damaged group without epilepsy. Reviewing the rankings in Table 9 indicates that, with the single exception of the psychomotor group of known etiology (which ranked immediately below the psychomotor group of unknown etiology) the rankings proceeded from normal control to psychomotor to mixed to major motor seizures of unknown etiology, followed by mixed seizure and major motor seizure classifications of known etiology. This ranking suggests that a major consideration in predicting impairment of adaptive abilities in patients with various classifications of seizures is the independent identification by means other than electroencephalography of cerebral pathology associated with the seizure condition. This conclusion appears to be in general accord with the findings reported by Winfield (1951). However, the present findings indicate that there is little test performance difference between psychomotor and major motor seizure groups when etiology is known, but that psychomotor patients perform at substantially higher levels than do patients with major motor seizures when etiology in both groups is unknown (Figure 4).

The results of our study do not appear to agree with conclusions by Collins and Lennox (1947) and Lennox (1960) who stated that patients with mixed seizure disorders show greater intellectual impairment than do patients with a single type of seizure. The rankings in Table 9 suggest that the group with major motor seizures of known etiology performed more poorly (although not at statistically significant levels), than did the group with mixed seizures of known etiology. This same relationship was found in comparing the groups with major motor versus psychomotor seizures in the two mixed seizure classifications in this second study; however, it seems likely that the somewhat better test performance levels found in the mixed seizure groups than in the groups with major motor seizures might be attributed to a larger proportion of the total seizure activity in the mixed classifications expressing itself clinically as psychomotor epilepsy. If substantially different proportions of major motor and psychomotor seizures were present in the mixed seizure groups than have been

TABLE 9

Mean Halstead Impairment Indexes for Non–Brain-damaged and Brain-damaged Non-Epileptic Control Groups and for Six Epileptic Groups

	Group	Mean Impairment Index
Best	1. Nonneurological.	.32
	7. Psychomotor seizures of unknown etiology.	.34
	4. Psychomotor seizures of known etiology.	.54
	8. Mixed (major motor and psychomotor) seizures of unknown etiology.	.58
	6. Major motor seizures of unknown etiology.	.58
	5. Mixed (major motor and psychomotor) seizures of known etiology.	.63
	2. Verified brain damage without epilepsy.	.72
Worst	3. Major motor seizures of known etiology.	.75

Levels of significance on intergroup comparisons

Paired groups	$p <$	Paired groups	$p <$	Paired groups	$p <$	Paired groups	$p <$	Paired groups	$p <$
1–2	0.001	1–8	0.01	2–8	(0.05)	4–5	ns	5–8	ns
1–3	0.001	2–3	ns	3–4	(0.05)	4–6	ns	6–7	0.01
1–4	0.01	2–4	0.001	3–5	ns	4–7	(0.05)	6–8	ns
1–5	0.001	2–5	ns	3–6	(0.05)	4–8	ns	7–8	(0.05)
1–6	0.001	2–6	(0.05)	3–7	0.001	5–6	ns		
1–7	ns	2–7	0.001	3–8	(0.05)	5–7	0.01		

studied by other investigators, this would represent a reasonable basis for the apparent discrepancy between our findings and those of other workers.

The dedicated reader may recall that in our initial study, the group with epilepsy of known etiology achieved slightly better performance levels than did the brain-damaged group without epilepsy, whereas in the second study the group with brain damage without epilepsy obtained test scores slightly higher than the group composed entirely of major motor seizures of known etiology. It would seem that the most likely explanation for this apparent lack of agreement in the two studies is again related to the mixed composition of the epilepsy group in the first investigation. Since both psychomotor and major motor seizures were represented in this group, the better ability levels of the patients with psychomotor seizures would tend to raise the overall performance level of this mixed group above that of the group with verified brain damage without epilepsy.

Were sufficient numbers of subjects available for comparing optimal groups, one ideally would match three separate brain-damaged groups without epilepsy on type and location of lesion with the three separate classifications of epilepsy of known etiology that were composed for the second study. While the nonepileptic group with brain damage was adequately matched on age and education variables with all other groups, matching for type of pathology could be effected only in the general sense of providing comparable proportions of known diagnostic classifications in the four groups with verified brain damage (Table 7). This design limitation obviously fails to control for possible relationships between the seizure classifications and the type, extent, and localization of epileptogenic lesions. It seems reasonable to assume, for example, that lesions in the temporal areas more often are associated with psychomotor epilepsy than with major motor seizures and, conversely, that psychomotor seizures occur less frequently with epileptogenic lesions located in areas other than in the temporal lobes. Thus, the better performances found in the second study in psychomotor epileptics than in the other seizure classifications might be related in part to the characteristics of the lesions associated with temporal lobe epilepsy. The difficulty in identifying appropriate controls with respect to the design problem just discussed may be related to the possibility that only a limited number of patients with nonepileptogenic chronic-static lesions of the temporal lobe exhibit clinical symptomatology sufficient to prompt neurological referral and examination, thus making this type of nonepileptic brain-damaged control subject infrequently available for systematic study.

A third study in our series was concerned with the effect of age at onset of epilepsy upon performance on the same battery of psychological tests employed in the first two investigations. Because of the complex interrelationships between seizure type and test performance level demonstrated in the first and second studies, subjects in the third study were limited to patients with major motor seizures of known and of unknown etiology. Table 10 presents age, sex, and education information on three groups with major motor seizures of

TABLE 10

Sex, Age, and Education of Major Motor Seizure Groups of Known and
Unknown Etiology and of Group with Brain Damage but without
Epilepsy, According to Age at Onset

| Group | Etiology | Age at onset (in years) | N | Sex | | Mean age | Mean education |
				Male	Female		
1. Major motor	Unknown	0–5	16	11	5	26.00	8.94
2. Major motor	Unknown	6–16	16	8	8	22.38	10.75
3. Major motor	Unknown	17–50	16	8	8	21.19	11.50
4. Major motor	Known	0–5	16	10	6	27.06	9.06
5. Major motor	Known	6–16	16	11	5	23.88	10.00
6. Major motor	Known	17–50	16	14	2	22.88	11.69
7. Brain damage	No epilepsy	0–5	16	14	2	29.00	10.50
8. Brain damage	No epilepsy	6–16	16	13	3	30.06	10.88
9. Brain damage	No epilepsy	17–50	16	11	5	27.38	12.50
Total			144	100	44		

unknown etiology, three groups with major motor seizures of known etiology, and three groups of brain-damaged patients without epilepsy. One group in each of these major categories had onset age of neurological symptoms or complaints between 0 and 5 years, one had onset age between 6 and 16 years, and one had onset age between 17 and 50 years.

Table 11 presents information on the distribution of the diagnostic classifications of all subjects in Groups 4 through 9. Inspection of the table shows that reasonable success was achieved in an effort to match pairs of subjects with and without epilepsy, not only on age at onset but also for general types of pathology.

Table 12 summarizes the relationships found between age at onset and the level of test performance in these nine groups of patients.

The table presents for each group its overall ranking based upon the mean rank order of each group on 11 tests from the battery (Full Scale IQ, Trails total, and Impairment Index were excluded from this tally to avoid redundancy among measures). The column adjacent to the mean ranking shows the mean Impairment Index for the same groups. Inspection of Table 12 shows that within each of the three major groups (major motor seizures of unknown etiology, major motor seizures of known etiology, and brain damage without epilepsy) the best performances were associated with the group with the latest onset (i.e., 17–50 years). These best scores in each major category are indicated by the superscript a.

The rankings presented on the right side in Table 12 represent the rank-order scores for the major combinations of groups. The comparisons made in Table 12,

TABLE 11

Distribution of Diagnoses in Groups with Major Motor Seizures of Known
Etiology and Brain Damage without Epilepsy,
According to Age at Onset

Diagnosis	Age at onset (in years)					
	0-5	6-16	17-50	0-5	6-16	17-50
	Group					
	4[a]	5[a]	6[a]	7[b]	8[b]	9[b]
Head injury	4	7	9	4	10	9
Perinatal	5	1	–	4	–	1
Intracranial neoplasms[c]	–	4	4	–	2	4
Postinfectious	3	3	–	1	4	–
Developmental anomalies	1	1	–	5	–	–
Anoxia	2	–	1	–	–	–
Hemiatrophy-cerebral palsy	1	–	–	1	–	–
Atrophy-degenerative disease	–	–	1	1	–	1
Multiple sclerosis	–	–	1	–	–	1
Total	16	16	16	16	16	16

[a]MM seizures, known etiology.
[b]Brain damage, no epilepsy.
[c]Meningioma (3); abscess (1); cholesteatoma (1); pinealoma (2); neurofibroma (3);
astrocytoma (3); craniopharyngioma (1).

for example, show that the brain-damaged subjects without epilepsy (Groups 7,
8, 9) had the best performance level with age at onset of all groups included in
the analysis. Statistical comparisons of intergroup mean differences in these
Impairment Index rankings showed no significant difference between adjacent
Impairment Index groups, but a significant difference ($p < .05$) was found
between the combined group with major motor epilepsy of unknown etiology
(Groups 1, 2, 3) and the combined brain-damaged group without epilepsy
(Groups 7, 8, 9). The comparisons shown in Table 12 represent mean rank
orders for the groups classified according to age at onset. Again, the groups with
the latest age at onset (Groups 3, 6, 9) demonstrated the best performance
levels, while less satisfactory performances were associated with onset of
epilepsy or neurological impairment or disease earlier in life. Statistical analysis
of the Impairment Index rankings for these combined groups showed a
significant difference ($p < .05$) between 0-5-year onset group and the
17-50-year onset group, and between the 6-16- and 17-50-year onset groups.
No difference was found between the 0-5- and the 6-16-year classifications on
the Impairment Index variable.

To illustrate the summary test battery relationships reported in Table 12 in terms of scores achieved by the nine groups on a specific test variable, Full Scale WAIS IQ data for each group are presented in Figure 5.

It is apparent from inspection of the IQ values for the nine groups shown in Figure 5 that the lowest scores were associated with the major motor seizures of unknown etiology and this difference was present in each age-at-onset category. When the three groups with major motor seizures of unknown etiology were collapsed across age-at-onset classifications, their Full Scale IQ was significantly lower than the combined brain-damaged groups without epilepsy ($p < .01$). Similarly, when the Full Scale IQ of the three groups with onset age of 0–5 years was compared with the Full Scale IQ of the groups with 6–16-year onset age and with 17–50-year onset age, only the youngest and oldest age-at-onset comparisons were significant ($p < .05$).

The preliminary results of this third study suggest that, in general, the earlier the age at onset of major motor seizures of unknown or of known etiology, the greater is the impairment of adaptive abilities in adulthood. However, a linear relationship between age at onset and adaptive ability performance may be present only in the group with major motor seizures of known etiology. It is unclear why the 6–16-year onset group with major motor seizures of unknown etiology performed at a slightly lower level than the 0–5-year onset group of unknown etiology. The differences between the unknown and known etiology groups of patients in this regard may reflect any number of as-yet-uncontrolled variables, including frequency of seizures, temporal differences regarding the time of the last seizure prior to neuropsychological examination, medication variables, the influence upon test results of possible genetic factors, differential social-economic and educational experience variables, or other sampling differences associated with the limited number of

TABLE 12

Mean Rank Orders by Etiology and Age at Onset

Group	Etiology	Age at onset (in years)	Mean rank on 11 tests	Mean Impairment Index	Groups	Mean rank on 11 tests	Mean Impairment Index
1. Major motor	Unknown	0–5	7.64	.74	1,2,3	6.55	.70
2. Major motor	Unknown	6–16	8.27	.76	4,5,6	4.97	.61
3. Major motor	Unknown	17–50	3.73[a]	.60[a]	7,8,9	3.49[a]	.55[a]
4. Major motor	Known	0–5	7.18	.69	1,4,7	6.15	.66
5. Major motor	Known	6–16	6.18	.66	2,5,8	6.18	.67
6. Major motor	Known	17–50	1.55[a]	.48[a]	3,6,9	2.67[a]	.54[a]
7. Brain damage	No epilepsy	0–5	3.64	.54			
8. Brain damage	No epilepsy	6–16	4.09	.59			
9. Brain damage	No epilepsy	17–50	2.73[a]	.53[a]			

[a]Best performance.

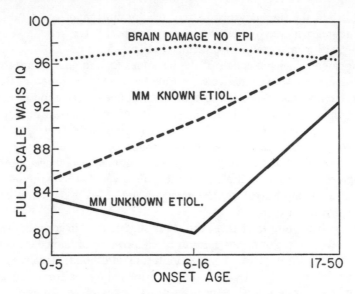

FIG. 5. WAIS Full Scale IQs in nine groups composed according to age at onset, brain damage without epilepsy, and epilepsy (major motor seizures) of known and unknown etiology.

subjects in each group. A number of significant interaction effects between etiology and age at onset remain to be analyzed, but even in their preliminary form, the results of the present study raise important issues regarding the significance of age at onset of epilepsy as a predictive variable for determining later level of neuropsychological impairment.

ILLUSTRATIVE PATIENTS

In order to illustrate in specific instances some of the findings reported in the present chapter, neurologic background information and neuropsychological test scores and reports are presented on four subjects. Two of these patients had major motor epilepsy (one of known and one of unknown etiology) and two patients had psychomotor epilepsy (one of known and one of unknown etiology).

It should be emphasized that the neuropsychological examination as such does not give any explicit clues to presence or absence of epilepsy but rather reflects the organic integrity of the brain whether epilepsy is present or not. Epilepsy must be viewed as a symptom of brain dysfunction, and in neuropsychological terms there is no specific "epileptic test pattern." It is our firm conviction that specific attempts to rule epilepsy in or out on the basis of neuropsychological test data of the type presented in this book are likely not to be successful. The test patterns reflect the underlying etiology, and the cases presented are intended to represent ones that are reasonably typical for the four diagnostic classifications cited above. The diagnosis of epilepsy is most often a clinical diagnosis and the combination of electroencephalography and appropriate clinical experience and skill are the primary requisites for making this diagnosis. Sometimes the diagnosis is easy to make; at other times it is very difficult to make. In either event, the neuropsychological test data are not likely to contribute significantly to questions relating to the diagnosis of epilepsy as such. However, one exception may be related to differential diagnostic inferences between pseudo seizures and bona fide epilepsy with definite pathophysiological correlates.

Patient with Grand Mal
Seizures of Unknown Etiology

This patient was admitted to the University Hospitals because at age 23, during her first pregnancy, she developed grand mal seizures. Past medical history and family history were noncontributory. Physical and neurological examinations were within normal limits. The patient was in her sixth month of pregnancy. X-rays revealed normal skull findings. Routine EEG, sleep EEG, and provoked EEG studies were all within normal limits. The diagnosis was grand mal seizures of unknown origin. The patient was referred for neuropsychological testing to determine whether the findings might reveal any evidence of a focal brain lesion.

Neuropsychological summary. Halstead's tests yielded an Impairment Index of 0.5, indicating mild impairment of adaptive abilities dependent upon organic brain function. In spite of clear left-sided motor preference shown in the Lateral Dominance examination, the patient performed more slowly with the left than right hand on the Finger Tapping Test and the left hand was also slightly weaker than the right on the dynamometer test. It was also noted that the patient had a slight tendency to make finger-tip number writing errors on the left hand and not on the right hand. However, other tests of sensory function failed to give supporting evidence of lateralized sensory deficits. The indications of possible left-sided motor impairment were not paralleled by differential functioning levels on the Verbal and Performance sections of the WAIS nor were distortions noted in her reproductions of geometric figures. The patient's IQ values were in the lower part of the average range and analysis of the pattern of subtests was noncontributory with respect to either lateralized or focal encephalopathy. The patient showed no evidence of aphasia.

In summary, the overall pattern of test results obtained by this patient would be consistent with a picture of relatively mild impairment of organic brain functions which has resulted in a decline in abstraction and concept formation ability (Category Test) and in ability to maintain attention to auditory discrimination tasks (Speech-sounds Perception and Rhythm Tests). The level and pattern of test results obtained would be highly atypical for progressive or recently developed brain disease, but would be quite consistent with mild

TABLE 13

Neuropsychological Test Results for a 26-year-old Left-handed Woman with Grand Mal Seizures of Unknown Etiology

PATIENT:　C. H.　　　　AGE:　26 years　　EDUCATION:　12 years

Wechsler Adult Intelligence Scale		Halstead's Neuropsychological Test Battery	
Verbal IQ	93	*Category Test*	60
Performance IQ	94		
Full Scale IQ	93	*Tactual Performance Test*	
Verbal Weighted Score	54	Left hand:　3.8 min.	
Performance Weighted Score	45	Right hand: 1.5 min.	
Total Weighted Score	99	Both hands: 1.1 min.	
Information	7	Total time:	6.4 min.
Comprehension	9	Memory:	8
Arithmetic	7	Localization:	6
Similarities	13	*Seashore Rhythm Test*	10
Digit Span	10	Raw score:　20	
Vocabulary	8	*Speech-sounds Perception Test*	13
Digit Symbol	10		
Picture Completion	10	*Finger Oscillation Test*	35
Block Design	8	Left hand:　35	
Picture Arrangement	8	Right hand: 37	
Object Assembly	9	*Impairment Index*	0.5

Trail Making Test	
Trails A: 24 sec.	
Trails B: 61 sec.	

MMPI				Motor Steadiness Battery		
					Dom.	Nondom.
?	50	Pd	53	*Maze Coordination*		
L	60	Mf	41	timer	1.02	1.13
F	48	Pa	47	counter	7	5
K	57	Pt	56			
Hs	44	Sc	49	*Vertical Groove*		
D	63	Ma	45	timer	0.0	0.0
Hy	49	Si	53	counter	0	0

Tactile Forms:	RH = 24	*Steadiness Test*	
	LH = 27	timer	9.62　　19.73
Sandpaper:	RH = 36	counter	72　　　82
	LH = 31		

Wide Range Achievement Test	*Grooved Pegboard*
Reading Grade = 11.3	Dom.　　62(0)
Spelling Grade = 10.0	Nondom.　74(0)
Arithmetic Grade =　8.5	Total　　136(0)

Dynamometer
RH　=　28.0 kg.
LH　=　27.5 kg.

chronic and static dysfunction which has had only relatively minor effects upon psychometric intelligence. The personality inventories that were administered gave no evidence of significant affective disturbance.

Comments. The patient's neuropsychological test findings, as summarized by the Halstead Impairment Index, indicated the presence of mild cognitive deficits. Detailed analysis of the motor and sensory tests gave evidence of mild deficits on certain tests on the left (preferred) side, but striking evidence was not present of differentiated lateralized motor and sensory dysfunction or differentiated intellectual impairment. With most of the cognitive and motor-sensory levels being within the average range for the patient's age, it was concluded that the neuropsychological examination failed to give evidence for lateralized or focal encephalopathy.

Followup evaluation of this patient also failed to give evidence of active neurological disease. This test pattern characterized by mild but definite impairment of adaptive functions without evidence of lateralized or focal deficits is a quite typical finding in patients with grand mal epilepsy in whom no definite etiology has been established.

Patient with Focal Epilepsy Secondary to a Left Temporal Lobe Lesion

This 33-year-old woman was admitted to the hospital for evaluation of a seizure disorder which had been present for approximately 17 years. The patient had an aura which is described as a tense and "quivery" feeling and by a sensation that her right hand was in an "unknown position." Head and eyes would often turn toward the right and the right hand and thumb would jerk progressively. At this point the patient would lose consciousness and have a grand mal seizure. The frequency of these seizures varied from one in 2 or 3 months to as many as two or three a week.

Significant findings on the neurological examination included nystagmus on lateral gaze bilaterally, a positive Babinski sign on the right, and diminished two-point discrimination on the right forearm. Skull x-rays were normal. A pneumoencephalogram was performed which showed an increase in the subarachnoid space around the Island of Reil on the left side, indicating an atrophic lesion in that location. A left carotid arteriogram was negative. Electroencephalograms showed generalized abnormalities. The neurological diagnosis was focal epilepsy secondary to an atrophic lesion in the left temporal lobe. Neuropsychological examination was requested to obtain evidence regarding the question of whether the lesion was chronic or might possibly represent a progressive type of condition.

Neuropsychological Summary. This subject demonstrated difficulties in naming common objects and in simple spelling on our aphasia examination indicating the presence of possible mild dysnomia and spelling dyspraxia. Halstead's Neuropsychological Test Battery yielded an Impairment Index of 0.7, indicating moderate impairment of abilities dependent upon organic brain functions. The patient demonstrated definite impairment of abstraction and

TABLE 14

Neuropsychological Test Results for a 33-year-old Left-handed Woman with
Focal Epilepsy Secondary to a Left Temporal Lobe Lesion

PATIENT: V. B.   AGE: 33 years   EDUCATION: 12 years

Wechsler Adult Intelligence Scale		Halstead's Neuropsychological Test Battery	
Verbal IQ	80	*Category Test*	74
Performance IQ	93		
Full Scale IQ	85	*Tactual Performance Test*	
Verbal Weighted Score	41	Left hand: 5.8 min.	
Performance Weighted Score	44	Right hand: 12.0 min.	
Total Weighted Score	85	Both hands: 4.6 min.	
Information	6	Total time:	22.4 min.
Comprehension	6	Memory:	9
Arithmetic	10	Localization:	5
Similarities	6	*Seashore Rhythm Test*	10
Digit Span	6	Raw score: 17	
Vocabulary	7		
Digit Symbol	8	*Speech-sounds Perception Test*	16
Picture Completion	8	*Finger Oscillation Test*	
Block Design	9	Left hand: 44	44
Picture Arrangement	6	Right hand: 28	
Object Assembly	13	*Impairment Index:*	0.7
Trail Making Test			
Trails A: 33 sec.			
Trails B: 45 sec.			
MMPI			

?	50	Pd	50
L	60	Mf	49
F	70	Pa	65
K	49	Pt	60
Hs	56	Sc	69
D	61	Ma	65
Hy	59	Si	67

concept formation skills. The Lateral Dominance examination revealed
preference for the left hand. However, the Tactual Performance Test and the
Finger Tapping Test consistently demonstrated a relative deficiency on the right
as opposed to the left body side. There was evidence of mild tactile
imperception of stimuli to the right hand, and the patient also made an error in
tactile form discrimination when using the right hand. Mild bilateral impairment
of tactile finger recognition was present, more pronounced on the left than the
right hand and fingertip number writing perception was mildly impaired bilaterally.

The WAIS showed moderate, differentiated impairment with the Verbal IQ being 13 IQ points lower than the Performance IQ. These findings and the lateralized sensory-motor findings indicated quite consistently that the left hemisphere functions on a lower level than the right, although it would be difficult to state that the results definitely imply a clearly focal area of brain dysfunction. The tests suggest that the underlying lesion seems to be maximized in the frontotemporal area of the left hemisphere and is most likely essentially static in nature. The consequences for the patient's intellectual functioning seem to be a mild to moderate depression of abilities which are related to verbal and symbolic functioning. There is evidence that this patient's speech function is subserved by the left hemisphere.

Comments. This patient's neuropsychological examination showed moderate impairment of cognitive functioning. A pattern of mildly differentiated intellectual impairment in the WAIS with deficiency in the verbal subtests was associated with motor-sensory deficits more pronounced in the right than the left body side. This constitutes quite a typical pattern for lateralized cerebral dysfunction. The dysfunction would seem to be relatively widespread involving parietal as well as temporal areas. There are deficits both in simple motor functions (finger tapping) and more complex psychomotor functions (Tactual Performance Test). This would suggest that the dysfunction is maximized in the middle part of the hemisphere. The aphasic symptoms elicited in this patient were mild and mainly restricted to problems with spelling. However, the general suppression of verbal-symbolic skills might indicate that the temporal area would be the site of maximal involvement. The only definite independent evidence of a brain lesion in this patient was obtained from the pneumoencephalogram which showed an atrophic lesion in the left anterior temporal area. The patient's EEGs were nonfocal and it was never demonstrated with certainty that the patient's seizure condition had a relationship to the cerebral atrophy. It is, however, very likely that the neuropsychological deficits are directly related to the pneumoencephalographic findings.

Neuropsychological evidence of focal and/or lateralized cerebral dysfunction is frequently found in seizure conditions where the etiological factors have been reasonably well identified. Bilateral findings may also be present if the etiology is related to infection, trauma, or conditions which by their nature would imply widespread effects.

Patient with Psychomotor
Seizures of Unknown Etiology

This patient had a few episodes of febrile convulsions in infancy when he was about 16 months of age. At approximately age 17 years he started to have seizures which were described as beginning with a sour taste in his stomach and profuse sweating. He would then stare and become motionless for several minutes and this, in turn, would be followed by a confused state.

The patient's general physical neurological examinations had been consistently within normal limits although EEG showed generalized dysrhythmia (Grade II to III) with focal abnormalities in the right temporal area. The patient's mother, brother, and sister all had febrile convulsions as children but these family members have not developed epilepsy later in life. Neuroradiological studies including brain scan, skull x-ray, pneumoencephalogram, and angiograms all have been within normal limits. The patient has graduated from college and is a music teacher. He has not been able to function as a teacher and has had to take jobs far below his educational level. He has had a long history of depressive episodes and general difficulties related to interpersonal relations. The neurological diagnosis was psychomotor seizures of unknown etiology. He was referred for neuropsychological testing to see if evidence was forthcoming to suggest the presence of structural changes in the right cerebral hemisphere that would correspond with the EEG findings.

Neuropsychological summary. Although this patient obtained an Impairment Index of 0.2, suggesting that the overall integrity of organic brain functions was within the normal range, the patient did give evidence of a decline in psychometric intelligence and in facility in reading, spelling, and arithmetic that was well below expectation with relation to his educational level (Wide Range Achievement Test grade equivalency scores: Reading = 11.3, Spelling = 10.0, Arithmetic = 8.5). The specific referral question addressed itself to the possibility of neuropsychological evidence of a right anterior temporal lobe lesion in this patient. Although the neuropsychological test results did not give strong evidence of lateralized or focal encephalopathy, the mild slowing of the left hand in finger-tapping speed and the relative slowness of the left as compared to the right hand on the Tactual Performance Test, in conjunction with a low score on the Picture Arrangement subtest of the Wechsler Scale, represents a constellation of findings that could be compatible with maximal dysfunction in the right temporal lobe. In addition, the test results also gave indications of mild bilateral dysfunction.

Comments. The neuropsychological test pattern in this patient represents reasonably typical findings in patients with psychomotor seizures without demonstrable etiology. Neuropsychologically, these patients are characterized by relatively little impairment and the studies described earlier in this chapter demonstrate that there indeed are no consistent differences in level of performance between control groups and patients falling within the diagnostic classification of psychomotor epilepsy without known etiology. It is important to bear in mind, with respect to interpretation of results for individual subjects, that complementary methods of inference must be used to derive a more complete understanding of brain-behavior relationships as Reitan pointed out earlier in this volume (Ch. 2). In fact, as indicated in the report, this patient did demonstrate some evidence of mild dysfunction which would point toward involvement of the right temporal area. It should be pointed out that the overall level of test results is quite good although the patient's psychometric levels and

TABLE 15
Neuropsychological Test Results for a 30-year-old Right-handed Man with Psychomotor Epilepsy of Unknown Etiology

PATIENT: W. H.   AGE: 30 years   EDUCATION: 16 years

Wechsler Adult Intelligence Scale		Halstead's Neuropsychological Test Battery	
Verbal IQ	98	*Category Test*	26
Performance IQ	99		
Full Scale IQ	99	*Tactual Performance Test*	
Verbal Weighted Score	59	Right hand: 3.0 min.	
Performance Weighted Score	49	Left hand: 2.9 min.	
Total Weighted Score	108	Both hands: 1.6 min.	
Information	7	Total time:	7.5 min.
Comprehension	10	Memory:	9
Arithmetic	10	Localization:	5
Similarities	12		
Digit Span	10	*Seashore Rhythm Test*	6
Vocabulary	10	Raw score: 25	
Digit Symbol	8		
Picture Completion	10	*Speech-sounds Perception Test*	4
Block Design	13		
Picture Arrangement	7	*Finger Oscillation Test*	45
Object Assembly	11	Right hand: 45	
		Left hand: 37	
		Impairment Index	0.2

Trail Making Test			Motor Steadiness Battery		
Trails A: 30 sec.				*Dom.*	*Nondom.*
Trails B: 71 sec.			*Maze Coordination*		
			timer	0.49	0.00
MMPI			counter	4	0
?	50	Pd	67	*Vertical Groove*	
L	53	Mf	59	timer	0.69	1.11
F	53	Pa	70	counter	3	9
K	53	Pt	81			
Hs	65	Sc	61	*Horizontal Groove*	
D	77	Ma	73	timer	0.00	4.07
Hy	76	Si	52	counter	0	23
Foot Tapping			*Steadiness Test*		
Dom. = 39; Nondom. = 47			timer	10.99	14.23
			counter	101	88
Tactile Forms: RH = 15(0)			*Resting Steadiness*		
LH = 15(0)			timer	0.00	1.25
Sandpaper: RH = 22(2)			counter	0	8
LH = 23(2)			*Grooved Pegboard*		
			Dom. 81(1) Nondom. 75(0) Total 156(1)		

Wide Range Achievement Test levels certainly are incompatible with his education and vocational history. The patient's MMPI profile would support the impression often repeated in his hospital chart of psychoneurotic manifestations and a high anxiety level.

Patient with Psychomotor Seizures Secondary to a Right Temporal Lobe Astrocytoma

This patient was admitted for neurological evaluation with a 1-year history of psychomotor seizures. Neurological examination was within normal limits. Skull x-rays were normal but a pneumoencephalogram demonstrated a right temporal lobe mass. Following histological examination of tissue removed at surgery, a diagnosis was made of psychomotor seizures secondary to an astrocytoma, Grade II, right temporal lobe. The operation involved removal of the right anterior temporal lobe. The patient was referred for neuropsychological examination to evaluate evidence of lateralized or focal cerebral damage. The patient was examined prior to the radiological studies and craniotomy.

Neuropsychological report. The neuropsychological examination yielded an Halstead Impairment Index of 0.3 which is ordinarily considered in the normal to borderline normal range with respect to adequacy of organic brain functions. Analysis of the pattern of test results, however, indicates with considerable consistency that the right hemisphere functions on a lower level than the left. Evidence for this impression came from the relative deficiency of dynamometer grip strength in the left hand, and the significantly lower Performance than Verbal IQ on the WAIS. Absence of sensory-perceptual deficits of a tactual and visual nature would argue against involvement of the right parieto-occipital area. Tactile finger recognition, fingertip number writing perception, tactile form recognition, and perception of bilateral simultaneous stimuli through the tactile and visual avenues were all within normal limits. Thus it was felt that the most likely area of involvement was in the right temporal area. This localization inference was supported by a finding of moderate left-sided impairment in perception of bilateral simultaneous auditory stimuli (two imperceptions with the left ear, none with the right). The Picture Arrangement score on the WAIS was quite good and this was viewed as possible evidence against a rapidly developing or highly malignant lesion in the right temporal lobe. It was felt that the discrepancy between the very adequate Category Test score and the impairment on Part B of the Trail Making Test might represent additional evidence for a temporal location of cerebral dysfunction. The very good Category score would also argue against a major structural lesion in the frontal area. While the exact location of involvement in the right hemisphere was somewhat difficult to infer from the neuropsychological test data obtained on this patient, the test pattern yielded very striking evidence of dysfunction in the right hemisphere and this evidence, in turn, was considered strong enough that efforts should be made toward ruling out neoplastic brain disease.

TABLE 16

Neuropsychological Test Results for a 32-year-old Right-handed Man Prior
to Surgery for a Right Temporal Lobe Lesion

PATIENT: D. I.   AGE: 32 years   EDUCATION: 12 years

Wechsler Adult Intelligence Scale		Halstead's Neuropsychological Test Battery	
Verbal IQ	117	*Category Test*	15
Performance IQ	108	*Tactual Performance Test*	
Full Scale IQ	114	Right hand: 6.3 min.	
Verbal Weighted Score	78	Left hand: 2.7 min.	
Performance Weighted Score	56	Both hands: 1.8 min.	
Total Weighted Score	134	Total Time:	10.7 min.
Information	11	Memory:	8
Comprehension	15	Localization:	2
Arithmetic	13		
Similarities	11	*Seashore Rhythm Test*	3
Digit Span	16	Raw score: 27	
Vocabulary	12		
Digit Symbol	7	*Speech-sounds Perception Test*	5
Picture Completion	13	*Finger Oscillation Test*	41
Block Design	12	Right hand: 41	
Picture Arrangement	13	Left hand: 34	
Object Assembly	11	*Impairment Index*	0.3

Trail Making Test			Motor Steadiness Battery		
Trails A: 17 sec.				*Dom.*	*Nondom.*
Trails B: 102 sec.			*Maze Coordination*		
MMPI			timer	3.71	4.16
			counter	22	26
?	50	Pd 71	*Vertical Groove*		
L	53	Mf 43	timer	0.07	0.46
F	53	Pa 47	counter	1	2
K	61	Pt 50			
Hs	52	Sc 50	*Steadiness Test*		
D	58	Ma 50	timer	5.07	6.11
Hy	58	Si 52	counter	42	40
Tactile Forms: RH = 30			*Grooved Pegboard*		
LH = 27			Dom. 92(1)		
Sandpaper: RH = 41			Nondom. 104(1)		
LH = 35			Total 196(2)		
Dynamometer					
RH = 48.5 kg.					
LH = 36.0 kg.					

Comments. This patient demonstrated the problem that often exists in differentiating between static lesions and slowly developing low-grade astrocytomas on the basis of neuropsychological findings. The main difference between this patient and the immediately preceding patient was related to the evidence of differentiated WAIS impairment in this patient as opposed to absence of such findings in the prior case. The finding of auditory imperception on the left also contributed to the regional localization inference. It should be pointed out, also, that this patient's physical neurological examination had been entirely normal at the time of neuropsychological evaluation. Nevertheless, the neuropsychological test data revealed consistent motor impairment on the left as compared to the right body side. Findings of this type may be viewed as a demonstration of the clinical significance implicit in precisely quantified measures of a wide range of motor and sensory-perceptual functions.

SUMMARY

Results of three studies investigating neuropsychological test performances in selected classifications of epileptic patients support the following general conclusions:

1. In groups of epileptic patients in whom type of seizure is not further specified, known organic etiology of epilepsy appears to be of more significance for impaired level of neuropsychological functioning than are the seizure manifestations themselves, although patients with epilepsy of unknown etiology demonstrate psychological performance levels which are significantly below those of nonepileptic control subjects.

2. When age at onset of epilepsy is not taken into account in comparing groups, major motor seizures of known etiology appear to be associated with more serious impairment of psychological abilities than do major motor seizures of unknown etiology, as do psychomotor seizures of known as opposed to unknown etiology. Psychomotor seizures of unknown etiology yield test levels which are closely comparable to normal controls and that are significantly better than levels found in either the major motor classification or in the psychomotor group of known etiology.

3. Determination of the impairment levels of groups with major motor seizures of unknown as opposed to known etiology appears to be dependent upon the inclusion of an age-at-onset variable in the experimental design.

When age at onset of major motor seizures was not controlled (as in Study 2), better performances were found in the unknown than in the known etiology group. When similar classifications of patients were composed with age at onset of seizures included in the analysis, better overall test level was associated with the known etiology classification of major motor seizures. Preliminary analysis of these latter data suggest that early onset of major motor seizures of unknown etiology is associated with greater impairment of later psychological functioning than that found with early onset of major motor seizures of known etiology or of neurological symptoms without epilepsy.

It should be mentioned that an extensive literature is available on behavioral effects associated with surgical removal of epileptogenic foci. This literature is particularly rich in regard to the effects of temporal lobectomy. In order to appreciate fully the nature of the cognitive deficits associated with various forms of epilepsy, it would be essential for the reader to study those reports which are explicitly concerned with focal epilepsy and the psychological sequelae associated with removal of well-defined epileptogenic areas of the brain. It should be emphasized that while much has been learned about the relationship of cognitive functions to lateralized and regional surgical lesions in epileptic patients, there is, nevertheless, little to suggest that there are specific types or patterns of cognitive impairment which are unique to epilepsy. The determinants of intellectual deficits are related to many factors such as the location of the epileptogenic lesion, the lesion's pathological characteristics, the type of seizure produced by the lesion, the patient's age at onset of the illness, and the frequency of seizures.

Finally, of perhaps equal pertinence is the range and complexity of psychological defenses and coping mechanisms and the unique interaction of social and personality variables in each patient with epilepsy.

10

APPLICATIONS OF NEUROPSYCHOLOGICAL TEST METHODS IN MENTALLY RETARDED SUBJECTS[1]

Charles G. Matthews[2]

If one accepts for working purposes a definition of clinical neuropsychology as the study of brain-behavior relationships in human beings, it is immediately apparent that exploration of potential applications of clinical neuropsychological methods of assessment in mental retardation is a hazardous undertaking. Severe empirical and theoretical constraints and uncertainties limit both the brain and the behavior components of the definition as applied to mental retardation. The controversy regarding the presence, nature, and incidence of cerebral dysfunction in retardates, especially in those classified psychometrically as falling within the mild to borderline ranges, is matched only by the level of dissatisfaction with methods now employed to measure problem-solving and adaptive abilities of subjects so described. Also, the current Zeitgeist in mental retardation does not appear to be particularly supportive of research orientations which are perceived as being preoccupied with sterile concerns of etiology, impairment and adaptive failure rather than upon investigations of social-environmental variables, reinforcement, and behavior-shaping methods and attitudinal-motivational factors which may be susceptible to correction and change.

[1] The work reported in this chapter was supported in part by National Institute of Neurological Diseases and Stroke Grant 03360-09.
[2] The author wishes to thank the administrative and psychology department staffs at the Fort Wayne State Hospital and Training Center, Fort Wayne, Indiana, and acknowledge their sustained support and active participation in the neuropsychology program described in this chapter. A specific acknowledgement is made to Iona C. Hamlett, Ph.D., and Raymond J. Clausman, Ph.D., of the Department of Psychology, and to Leo J. Davis, Ph.D., former research psychologist at the Fort Wayne State Hospital and Training Center, for their contributions to this ongoing project.

A large and influential sector of psychology and special education has shown a growing indifference to research efforts concerned with the demonstration of psychological test patterns which are purported to be of differential diagnostic significance. Much current work in behavioral modification and operant conditioning procedures with retardates and other subjects with learning disabilities seems to view psychological test data or etiology as offering little help either for predictive or planning purposes. Sidman and Stoddard (1966) for example, offer the following prescription for behavioral evaluation: "Don't test, teach. Tests tell us what a person has already learned. They may say very little about what a person is capable of learning" [p. 159]. To emphasize their position, the authors then give an account of teaching a circle versus ellipse discrimination to a 40-year-old microcephalic of IQ less than 20.

A major factor contributing to disenchantment with research in differential diagnosis, particularly of such elusive entities as the minimally brain damaged child, the "Strauss syndrome," and the like is a growing awareness that much of the conventional wisdom concerning the behavioral and educational characteristics of such children rests upon a very insecure empirical base. Birch (1964) has commented on the stereotyped syndrome of hyperactivity, distractibility, and perceptual disturbance that has come to characterize children with brain damage. He says:

> One major obstacle to knowledge has been the tendency to consider the problem of the "minimally brain-damaged" child as a problem in the singular. The essential inadequacy of the term "brain damage" for purposes of classification derives from the contradiction between its singular form and the plurality of content which it seeks to embrace. . . . Brain damage may vary with respect to etiology, extent, type of lesion, locus, duration of damage, rate at which damage has been sustained, time of life and developmental stage at which the injury has occurred, and the syndromes of dysfunction that may result. In point of fact there is not *a* minimally brain-damaged child but rather many varieties of brain-damaged children [p. 6].

Gallagher (1957) concluded his careful study of groups of brain-injured versus familial retarded subjects with a complementary observation. Following a discussion of certain differences (and, more importantly, a great many similarities) between these groups on measures of perception, learning aptitude, intellectual scatter, language development, quantitative ability, and personality characteristics, he asks:

> Do these differences imply the need for drastically modified educational and training programs or merely slight modifications in existing programs? Here the answer is less clear and depends to a large degree on which brain-injured child you are talking about. The range of different problems and the lack of problems within the brain-injured group is large enough to cast considerable doubt on the notion that plans can or should be made for brain-injured children as though they were a homogenous group [p. 65].

Studies which are concerned with the identification of specific test patterns and/or behavioral characteristics of children who have been categorized into brain-damaged versus non–brain-damaged groups impose a burden on diagnostic neurological criterion information which is frequently unwarranted. Werry (1972) has reviewed a large number of studies of relationships between cerebral dysfunction and behavior in children. Of particular interest in the present context is Werry's discussion of neurological criterion problems in pediatric neurology and the paradox of identifying brain injury by means of so-called soft or minimal neurological signs, the significance of which remains largely unknown. He also gives well-deserved attention to the preoccupation with severely retarded brain-damaged groups in psychological studies of test validation, the distressing degree of overlap in test scores found between brain-damaged and control subjects, and the mutual overvaluing of neurological findings by psychologists and of psychological findings by neurologists.

Comparable difficulties characterize present diagnostic and classification systems used with mentally retarded subjects. Sanders (1970) provides a succinct summary of the terminology-classification problems in mental retardation and documents the need for further development and refinement of the American Association of Mental Deficiency (AAMD) classification (Heber, 1961) which is probably the most comprehensive and widely used system at this time. Sanders concludes his review by stating:

> The assumption involved in the AAMD classification is that the retarded can be differentiated into mutually exclusive classes or groups. That this assumption is not satisfied is apparent in practice and in the literature. The medical section with its rule of etiology generates a large number of cases of unknown or presumed causes and placement within a category is dependent upon discriminating between overlapping symptoms and frequently inadequate histories. The behavioral classification with its intellectual and adaptive criteria provides at best indices for administrative groupings but fails to give sufficient information for individual decisions [p. 302].

It hardly need be noted that even when subjects are assigned to a specified diagnostic category such as cultural-familial mental retardation, no satisfactory etiological closure or resolution has been attained (Hayes, 1962; Zigler, 1967).

The paucity of information regarding the presence, type, and incidence of demonstrable brain pathology in retardates and the effects of any such lesions upon behavior has placed heavy explanatory and extrapolative demands upon brain-behavior studies in animals. The advantages of animal neuropsychological investigations with respect to precise control of site and type of experimental lesions and of environmental manipulation of sensory, motivational, and other variables are well known, as are the limitations and restrictions upon the range and type of behavioral variables, as mentioned in a previous chapter by Reitan (Ch. 2), which are of direct interest and applicability in the study of humans. Although many of the basic assumptions and premises of comparative psychology are being subjected to extremely critical scrutiny (Lockard, 1971), comparative psychology and the study of mental retardation share a number of common concerns. As stated by Turkewitz and Birch (1970),

> The first of these is the identification of the mechanisms underlying behavior. Such an identification is basic to an understanding of both the levels of behavioral

organization in different species and the differential diagnosis and planning of rehabilitation in mentally subnormal individuals. Second, both disciplines are concerned with an understanding of the factors that lead to the development of competence in dealing with environmental demands. In the study of mental retardation, this concern expresses itself in the search for etiologic factors in the production of mental subnormality; in comparative psychology, it is expressed in an attempt to define the conditions which are necessary for the development of normal and abnormal behavior. Finally, both comparative psychology and the study of mental retardation share a concern with methods for producing alterations in behavior [p. 14].

Rosvold (1967) has reviewed a number of neuropsychological studies in animals which are relevant to mental retardation. Included in his review are descriptions of work by Rosenzweig, Krech, and Bennett (1960) demonstrating correlations between maze performance and cholinesterase activity in rats; the effects of hypophysectomy on learning in rats (Stone & Obias, 1955); and effects of asphyxia at birth on learning in guinea pigs (Windle & Becker, 1943) and in the monkey (Ranck & Windle, 1959). Rosvold also discusses a series of animal studies which indicate that removal of large masses of tissue from the infant animal brain appears to have little effect upon adult performance, even though comparable removals from adult animals have striking effects. Such investigations include studies by Lansdell (1953) with infant rats, and by Harlow, Akert, and Shiltz (1964) who showed that massive prefrontal lobe damage in monkeys in the first 150 days of life did not impair learning of a delayed response habit, whereas similar damage in the adult monkey resulted in complete loss of the habit.

The same issue of the differential behavioral effects in human beings of lesions incurred early versus later in development is not at all clear, although there is an emerging body of findings which is in essential accord with the observations of Teuber and Rudel (1962) that, depending upon the nature of the test employed, it can be shown that early injury may be less disabling, equally disabling, or more disabling than the same injury in the adult. Studies concerned with this topic of differential behavioral effects of early as opposed to later-occurring lesions in children have been critically reviewed by Werry (1972) and by Reitan (this volume, Ch. 4).

NEUROPSYCHOLOGICAL METHODS

Benton (1970) has described potential contributions of clinical neuropsychological approaches to an increased understanding of brain-behavioral relationships in the mentally retarded. Benton discusses several of the methodological and criterion problems relating to neuropsychological study of the mentally retarded described above, but he suggests that it is, nonetheless, feasible to investigate a variety of language, psychomotor, somesthetic and other behaviors in retardates, to compare the findings with those observed in patients with well-defined, acquired lesions and, on the basis of analogy from what is known about brain-behavior relationships in neurological patients, to speculate about the state of affairs with respect to brain-behavior relationships in the retarded.

The battery of neuropsychological tests originated by Halstead (1947) and extended and modified by Reitan (1959c, 1966b) has been widely used in investigations of brain-behavior relationships in human subjects. Validation studies conducted in a variety of laboratory settings have demonstrated the sensitivity of these measures to the presence of central nervous system dysfunction in adults (Reitan, 1955a; Matthews, Shaw, & Klove, 1966; Vega & Parsons 1967; and in this volume: Boll; Klonoff & Low; Klove; Reitan). Relationships have also been shown between lateralized and focal brain disease as identified by various neurological, neurosurgical, and neuroradiological criterion information and patterns of psychometric, other cognitive and motor-sensory impairment on this test battery. Detailed accounts of such studies are given by Reitan (1962, 1964b) and Reitan has discussed some of the interpretative strategies and principles which permit specific inferences to be derived from these data regarding type, lateralization, localization, and recency versus chronicity of cerebral dysfunction or deficit in adults (Reitan, 1959c) and in children (Reitan & Heineman, 1968; and in this volume, Boll; Klonoff & Low; Reitan). The validity of these clinical-inferential methods has been recently confirmed by computer analysis techniques devised by Russell, Neuringer, and Goldstein (1970).

A number of studies have appeared which have been concerned with the performance of variously composed groups of retardates on this battery of tests (Matthews, 1963; Matthews & Reitan, 1963; Davis & Reitan, 1967). Although Black and Davis (1966) in a study using many of the subjects employed here, presented results on finger agnosia, fingertip symbol recognition and finger-tapping speed in 245 Ss classified according to four IQ ranges, no report has been made of scores achieved by fairly large groups of retardates on the entire battery. Because of the continuing interest in improved methods of differential diagnostic assessment of the retarded, both for etiological and vocational-predictive purposes, and the potential contribution of neuropsychological testing to clinical evaluative problems, normative data are reported on 81 subjects examined with the Halstead Neuropsychological Test Battery for Children (age range, 9–14 years), the Wechsler Scales, and a number of additional tests, and on 286 subjects examined with similar tests for the adult age range (15 years and older) at the Fort Wayne State Hospital and Training Center (FWSH & TC). Test results obtained on several individual patients will also be presented in order to illustrate interpretation of the findings.

Subjects and Methods

Detailed descriptions of the neuropsychology batteries for both adults and children, including administration and scoring procedures, are given by Reitan (1959c; 1969) and additional data are presented in this volume in several of the chapters. Knights (1966) and Spreen and Gaddes (1969) provide normative data on children aged 6 through 14 years. Table 1 identifies the measures used in the present report and the nature of the scores reported in the tables to follow. Table 1 and subsequent tables include results on conventional psychometric and academic achievement measures which are administered as part of the test

TABLE 1
Description of Measures in Neuropsychological Test Battery

Variable description	Scoring procedure
W-B or WISC	Full Scale IQ, Verbal IQ, Performance IQ
Peabody Picture Vocabulary (PPVT)	IQ
Wide Range Achievement Test (WRAT)	Grade score equivalents
Trail Making Test, Part A (children, 15 circles; adults, 25 circles)	Seconds to complete
Category (children, 168 items; adults, 208 items)	Number of errors
Tactual Performance Test (TPT) (children, 8 blocks; adults, 10 blocks)	Average time per block (3 trials)
Memory	Number of shapes reproduced
Localization	Number of shapes located
Boston Speech Perception[a]	Number correct in 72 trials
Dynamometer grip strength (right hand plus left hand)	Mean score in kg. (2 trials each hand)
Finger-tapping speed (right hand plus left hand)	Mean number of taps in 10 sec. (5 trials each hand)
Tactile, auditory, and visual imperception testing (right and left body sides)	Number correct in 24 trials (tactile); in 8 trials (auditory and visual)
Tactile finger recognition (right hand plus left hand)	Number correct in 40 trials
Finger-tip number writing (right hand plus left hand)	Number correct in 40 trials
Tactile form recognition (right hand plus left hand)	Number correct in 16 trials

[a]Pronovost and Dumbleton (1953).

battery. The Boston University Speech-Sound Discrimination Picture Test (Pronovost & Dumbleton, 1953) consists of 36 cards, each showing three subsets of pictures; e.g., *cat-cat, cat-bat, bat-bat*. The subject listens to a tape recorder which directs him to point to the picture which is like the words he just heard. This test is used with FWSH & TC subjects to circumvent the reading requirements of the nonsense syllable tasks given for assessment of speech-sound discrimination ability when using the Halstead Speech-sounds Perception Test.

Each subject was individually tested by a neuropsychology technician. Typical administration time totaled 6 to 7 hours. Although the sample was unselected for etiological diagnosis, 73% of the subjects had been given one of the following major AAMD diagnoses (Heber, 1961) by the FWSH & TC diagnostic staff: Ninety-eight subjects were classified in prenatal, natal, or postnatal infection or injury groups (AAMD code number 11, 12, 29, 31, 32, 33, 34); 91 subjects were classified as cultural-familial mental retardation (code number 81), and 79 were classified as "mental retardation, other, due to uncertain cause, with the functional reaction alone manifest" (code number 89). The remaining 99 subjects had been variously classified under other AAMD diagnostic codes.

RESULTS

Table 2 reports the sex and age characteristics of the 81 children and the 286 adult subjects who were examined. Mean scores and standard deviations are shown for each group on each test variable.

In accord with the general Wechsler-Bellevue test pattern expectation for mildly retarded, institutionalized subjects (Gunzburg, 1965), higher mean Performance than Verbal IQ scores were found in both groups. The sample of children had a mean Verbal IQ of 59.23 (*SD* 12.39) and a Performance IQ of 63.69 (*SD* 15.44). Mean Verbal IQ in the adult sample was 60.58 (*SD* 9.10) and mean Performance IQ was 65.27 (*SD* 16.67). Although most of the scores shown for the two groups in Table 2 are derived from identical test tasks, the Category Test and Trail Making Test for Children contain fewer items than the adult forms of these tests (see Table 1); hence, the substantial raw-score differences in favor of the younger group on these tests.

The only additional analysis of the data shown in Table 2 was to determine correlations between the Wechsler Verbal, Performance, and Full Scale IQ scores and scores achieved on each additional test variable in the two groups. Correlations significant at $p < .05$ are shown in Table 3.

With the exception of Tactual Performance Test (TPT) time, dynamometer grip strength, auditory and visual imperception errors and finger-tapping speed, all measures for the children were significantly correlated ($p < .05$) with Full Scale IQ. Finger-tapping speed was significantly correlated with Performance IQ. In the adult group correlations of $p < .05$ were found between Wechsler-Bellevue Full Scale IQ and other measures in the battery with the exception of Trail

TABLE 2

Performance Level of Subjects on Neuropsychological Test Batteries for
Children and Adults

Variable	Children (9–14 years) N = 81 (M 54, F 27)		Adult (15 years and over) N = 286 (M 183, F 103)	
	Mean	SD	Mean	SD
Chronological age	12.37	1.56	22.42	9.36
Full Scale IQ	57.09	13.43	58.83	12.91
PPVT	69.40	12.54	61.51	13.43
WRAT: Reading	1.78[a]	1.00	2.74[a]	2.01
Spelling	1.54[a]	.85	2.43[a]	1.72
Arithmetic	1.94[a]	1.08	2.47[a]	1.24
Trail Making Test, Part A	57.68[b]	43.73	86.45[b]	60.83
Category	81.78[c]	25.64	97.20[c]	25.56
TPT: Time per block	1.57[d]	3.44	2.20[d]	2.60
Memory	3.36[e]	2.02	4.36[e]	2.21
Localization	1.60[f]	1.76	1.18[f]	1.47
Speech Perception (72 items)	58.44[g]	9.85	58.63[g]	11.43
Hand Dynamometer total	38.97[h]	18.34	53.58[h]	21.33
Finger Tapping total	62.40[i]	12.31	67.81[i]	17.12
Tactile Imperception (sum = 24) total	19.98[g]	3.10	19.80[g]	4.23
Auditory Imperception (8 trials)	7.11[g]	1.42	6.85[g]	1.54
Visual Imperception (8 trials)	7.62[g]	1.11	7.37[g]	1.38
Tactile Finger Recognition (40 trials)	31.42[g]	6.18	32.11[g]	6.54
Finger-tip Number Writing (40 trials)	30.33[g]	7.55	33.47[g]	7.04
Tactile Form Recognition (16 trials)	14.16[g]	1.53	14.76[g]	2.16

[a]Grade score equivalent. [d]Minutes. [g]Number correct.
[b]Seconds to complete. [e]Number of blocks recalled. [h]Kilograms.
[c]Number of errors. [f]Number of blocks located. [i]Number of taps in 10 sec.

Making A, dynamometer, finger-tapping speed, and tactile finger recognition. In each of these instances, however, scores in the adult sample were significantly correlated with Performance IQ. Fingertip number writing perception, and the number of errors in auditory and visual imperception, were not significantly correlated with any IQ measure in the adult group.

Table 4 presents means and standard deviations for children on neuropsychological measures in three WISC Full Scale IQ groups: IQ 40–54 ($N = 29$), IQ 55–69 ($N = 31$), and IQ 70–84 ($N = 14$).

In general, performances on the test variables shown in Table 4 were ordered according to IQ classification and, with the exception of dynamometer grip and

TPT time scores, those tests in which poorer scores were associated with one of the two higher IQ groups yielded very few errors in any of the three IQ categories (e.g., auditory and visual imperception testing).

Table 5 reports performance levels found in adult subjects composed according to three Wechsler Full Scale IQ ranges: 40-54 (N = 91), 55-69 (N = 121), and 70-84 (N = 49). All measures other than finger-tapping speed and fingertip number writing perception yielded mean score values ordered in accord with adjacent IQ classifications.

Table 6 shows test scores achieved by adult retardates, control subjects without cerebral lesions, and subjects with acquired brain lesions. The retarded group (N = 64) is a right-handed subsample drawn from the adult battery group of 286 described in Table 2. Each subject in the subsample made seven right-handed choices on a seven-item lateral dominance test. It should be noted that the scores reported on several variables in Table 6 differ in format from that used in previous tables in order to permit direct comparisons between retardates and published data on control and neurological subjects (Reitan, 1955a, 1958b).

TABLE 3
Correlations ($p < .05$) between Wechsler IQ Scores and Selected Neuropsychological Variables

Variable	Children N = 81			Adult N = 286		
	Verbal IQ	Perform-ance IQ	Full Scale IQ	Verbal IQ	Perform-ance IQ	Full Scale IQ
Full Scale IQ	.85	.83		.77	.93	
Verbal IQ		.55	.85		.55	.77
PPVT MA	.56	.43	.55	.53	.42	.52
PPVT IQ	.65	.48	.63	.49	.34	.42
WRAT: Reading	.44	.40	.44	.59	.25	.43
Spelling	.41	.39	.44	.55		.39
Arithmetic	.51	.55	.57	.60	.43	.54
Trail Making Test, Part A	−.33	−.48	−.46		−.31	
Category	−.33	−.28	−.29	−.31	−.41	−.41
TPT: Time	−.26				−.38	−.34
Memory		.48	.40		.54	.38
Localization		.44	.32		.43	.47
Speech Perception	.25	.39	.40	.28	.29	.32
Hand Dynamometer					.26	
Tapping		.36			.31	
Tactile Imperception		.34	.25	.31	.34	.37
Tactile Finger Recognition	.26	.40	.36		.30	
Finger-tip Number Writing	.40		.36			
Tactile Form Recognition			.28		.32	.34

TABLE 4

Performance Levels of Children Aged 9 through 14 Years on the
Neuropsychological Battery in Three IQ Ranges

Variable	IQ					
	40-54		55-69		70-84	
	N = 29 (M 20, F 9)		N = 31 (M 17, F 14)		N = 14 (M 11, F 3)	
	Mean	SD	Mean	SD	Mean	SD
Chronological Age	13.04	1.09	12.32	1.60	12.43	1.18
Full Scale IQ	48.42	3.55	60.32	3.96	73.79	8.66
PPVT IQ	63.35	6.99	68.50	14.33	82.93	11.91
WRAT: Reading	1.63	.78	1.74	.95	2.52	1.18
Spelling	1.40	.57	1.54	.83	2.19	1.00
Arithmetic	1.58	.52	2.13	1.29	2.79	.99
Trail Making Test, Part A	80.65	54.50	41.50	37.02	24.93	16.69
Category	92.04	23.63	78.57	26.56	63.21	16.70
TPT: Time	2.26	5.60	1.03	.65	1.35	2.43
Memory	2.96	1.72	3.50	2.35	4.50	1.68
Localization	1.31	1.73	1.75	1.94	2.64	1.59
Speech Perception	56.23	11.39	59.36	8.66	63.36	6.96
Hand Dynamometer	41.68	17.73	36.22	19.36	44.31	18.98
Tapping Total	58.92	10.71	64.75	12.63	68.00	12.29
Tactile Imperception	18.96	3.25	19.82	3.49	22.14	1.96
Auditory Imperception	6.85	1.63	7.39	.94	7.36	.81
Visual Imperception	7.77	.58	7.68	.85	7.36	.35
Tactile Finger Recognition	30.85	4.63	31.61	7.03	33.00	6.76
Finger-tip Number Writing	28.88	7.01	31.14	7.60	31.36	6.55
Tactile Form Recognition	14.69	1.79	14.14	3.66	14.36	3.15

While Reitan (1955a) reported much of these data originally in standard-score form, he supplied raw-score data for use in Table 6.

The data shown in Table 6 are presented for orientation purposes; namely, to generate a comparative set of general test score expectancies for mildly retarded institutionalized subjects vis-à-vis normal controls and adult neurological patients who had sustained significant cerebral damage after an extended period of relatively normal growth and development. The table illustrates the need for normative data which reflect performance variability within variously composed psychometric and etiologic classifications of retardates, since the application of cutoff scores which have been derived for control and adult neurological subjects would yield entirely predictable decisions of "impaired" neuropsychological functions in most retarded subjects.

Because of the importance in neuropsychological assessment of identifying motor and/or sensory-perceptual asymmetries in performance on the two body sides, Table 7 shows right and left body side scores obtained by the retarded subsample on several motor and sensory-perceptual measures.

Inspection of the scores in Table 7 shows the same relationship between preferred and non-preferred hand performances on motor tasks (tapping, dynamometer) that has been reported for nonretarded subjects. Because of the

TABLE 5

Performance Levels of Adult Subjects on the Neuropsychological Battery in
Three IQ Ranges

Variable	IQ					
	40-54 $N = 91$ (M 51, F 40)		55-69 $N = 121$ (M 84, F 37)		70-84 $N = 49$ (M 34, F 15)	
	Mean	SD	Mean	SD	Mean	SD
Chronological Age	19.98	5.18	22.72	8.84	26.90	14.24
Full Scale IQ	47.41	4.11	61.71	4.30	75.14	4.19
PPVT IQ	54.80	12.02	62.51	12.61	71.31	10.87
WRAT: Reading	1.77	1.17	3.15	2.13	3.79	2.13
Spelling	1.67	.93	2.79	1.83	3.30	2.05
Arithmetic	1.73	.83	2.76	1.22	3.42	1.00
Trail Making Test, Part A	106.12	70.04	77.97	45.87	67.59	48.56
Category	108.96	19.48	94.93	20.92	82.53	27.43
TPT: Time	2.31	1.84	1.64	1.41	1.09	.92
Memory	3.49	2.05	4.62	1.85	5.53	2.06
Localization	.71	1.20	1.26	1.38	1.92	1.70
Speech Perception	56.39	11.48	60.60	9.87	62.39	10.35
Hand Dynamometer	48.66	19.89	55.50	20.03	58.21	24.10
Tapping Total	63.40	16.30	71.31	16.23	69.88	17.51
Tactile Imperception	18.26	3.79	20.84	3.63	21.20	4.76
Auditory Imperception	6.84	1.43	6.93	1.55	7.06	1.41
Visual Imperception	7.18	1.35	7.47	1.48	7.65	.94
Tactile Finger Recognition	29.96	7.47	33.02	5.37	34.24	6.07
Finger-tip Number Writing	33.58	6.29	33.82	7.05	33.59	7.50
Tactile Form Recognition	14.20	2.68	15.12	1.48	15.49	1.37

TABLE 6

Comparative Neuropsychological Test Data on Control, Brain-damaged, and
Retarded Adult Subjects

Variable	Controls[a]		Brain-damaged[a]		Retardates	
	$N = 50$ (M 35, F 15)		$N = 50$ (M 35, F 15)		$N = 64$ (M 48, F 16)	
	Mean	SD	Mean	SD	Mean	SD
Chronological Age	32.36	10.78	32.32	10.61	20.94	6.73
Education	11.58	2.85	11.56	3.03	3.36[c]	2.31[c]
Full Scale IQ	112.64	14.28	96.16	19.68	64.23	11.15
Verbal IQ	110.82	14.46	98.40	19.05	63.64	9.16
Performance IQ	112.18	14.23	94.12	19.41	72.73	14.01
Category	32.28	12.62	61.98	21.82	103.84	27.06
Finger Tapping (dominant hand)	50.74	7.29	45.58	7.32	39.87	9.03
TPT: Total minutes	12.59	5.20	25.19	12.67	29.46	10.80
Memory	7.65	1.41	5.92	1.75	5.20	2.31
Localization	5.29	2.12	1.88	1.74	1.52	1.48
	Controls[b]		Brain-damaged[b]		Retardates	
	$N = 84$ (M 71, F 13)		$N = 200$ (M 167, F 33)		$N = 64$ (M 48, F 16)	
	Mean	SD	Mean	SD	Mean	SD
Chronological Age	33.45	11.16	34.88	10.87	20.94	6.73
Education	11.19	3.43	10.56	2.99	3.36[c]	2.31[c]
Trail Making Test, Part A (seconds)	32.32	11.80	64.28	29.60	78.42	70.74
Trail Making Test, Part B (seconds)	74.29	26.32	189.80	95.28	228.24[d]	120.33[d]

[a]Reitan, 1955a.
[b]Reitan, 1958b.
[c]WRAT Reading score equivalent.
[d]$N = 42$.

slower tapping rate bilaterally in the retarded sample, the average tapping speed discrepancy between the two hands is approximately three taps per 10 sec. rather than the 5–7-tap difference usually found in adult controls. However, consistent deviations from the expected pattern of preferred hand superiority on motor measures or deviations from the expected pattern of essentially comparable scores bilaterally on sensory discrimination tasks would appear to lend themselves to the kinds of inferences regarding the relative integrity of the cerebral hemisphere contralateral to the motor and/or sensory-perceptual deficit that have been repeatedly validated in patients with acquired right or left hemisphere lesions.

Individual Test Protocols

Results obtained on three subjects examined with the Adult battery are presented in Table 8. Consideration of the variability in pattern and level of test performance within specified diagnostic categories of mental retardation, even when age, sex, and IQ matches are imposed, should make it unnecessary to emphasize that the three sets of test scores do not purport to illustrate specific test patterns which can be considered to be typical, much less pathognomic of the particular category to which the subject had been assigned. Nevertheless, presentation of results on individual subjects may complement the data based on groups of subjects which were previously presented.

Patient A, a microcephalic with major motor seizures and a generalized EEG dysrhythmia maximized in the left hemisphere, was chosen because the test results obtained appear to be in reasonable accord with available criterion information, and also because there is little question that brain damage is prominent in the etiology of the retardation. Patient B and Patient C were selected because each had been classified as cultural familial retardation but show quite divergent test patterns, one of which (Case C) appears to support neuropsychological inferences which are at substantial variance with this diagnosis as conventionally defined.

Patient A. The patient attended regular school classes for 6 years plus 2 years of special education. He was referred to the University of Wisconsin Department of Neurology because of acting-out behavior and a poorly controlled seizure disorder. In addition to confirmation of the presenting diagnosis of microcephaly, neurological study found a generalized EEG

TABLE 7

Lateralized Comparisons on Motor and Sensory-perceptual Measures in Right-handed Retarded Subsample ($N = 64$)

Measure	Right hand		Left hand	
	Mean	*SD*	Mean	*SD*
Finger Tapping[a]	39.87	9.03	36.66	7.96
Finger Recognition[b]	2.33	1.28	2.91	2.91
Finger-tip Number Writing[b]	4.69	4.34	4.95	3.88
Tactile Form Recognition[c]	0.34	0.77	0.34	0.75
Dynamometer Grip Strength[d]	33.10	10.07	30.10	9.22

[a]Number of taps in 10 sec.
[b]Number of errors in 20 trials.
[c]Number of errors in 8 trials.
[d]Kilograms (mean of two trials).

TABLE 8

Test Results on Three Patients Examined with Adult Battery

Variable	Patient A (Microcephaly, major motor seizures, CA 19, Sex male, U.W. Medical Center)		Patient B (Cultural-familial mental retardation, CA 16, Sex male, FWSH & TC)		Patient C (Cultural-familial mental retardation, CA 21, Sex male, FWSH & TC)	
Verbal IQ	68		75		66	
Performance IQ	76		80		88	
Full Scale IQ	70 (WAIS)		75 (W-B-I)		74 (W-B-I)	
PPVT IQ	ng[a]		71		78	
WRAT: Reading	1.7		3.4		3.0	
Spelling	1.6		3.1		3.0	
Arithmetic	2.5		4.8		3.5	
Category—errors	99		70		87	
Boston Speech—errors	9		6		12	
Trail Making Test, Part A (seconds)	80		66		43	
Trail Making Test, Part B (seconds)	cnd[b]		163		cnd[b]	
TPT: Time RH	10.0 (0 in)		8.2		15.0 (6 in)	
LH	10.0 (4 in)		6.4		14.2	
BH	10.0 (5 in)		5.2		10.6	
Total	30.0 (9 in)		19.8		39.8 (26 in)	
Memory	3		7		4	
Localization	0		2		1	
	Right	Left	Right	Left	Right	Left
Lateral Dominance—eye (ABC)	9	1	10	0	2	8
Lateral Dominance—hand	7	0	7	0	9	1
Tapping Speed	29	28	47	41	42	44
Dynamometer	29	35	36	29	44	44
Imperception errors:						
Tactile RH LH	2	0	0	0	1	1
RH LF	1	0	0	0	2	0
RF LH	0	0	0	0	1	0
Auditory RE LE	0	0	0	0	0	0
Visual OD OS	2	0	0	0	0	0
Tactile Finger Recognition—errors	7	8	1	2	3	1
Finger-tip Number Writing—errors	13	11	2	0	5	5
Tactile Form Recognition—errors	2	0	0	0	2	1

[a]Not given.
[b]Could not do.

dysrhythmia which was maximized over the left cerebral hemisphere. Physical neurological examination failed to demonstrate reflex asymmetries or other evidence of lateralized neurological dysfunction. The patient's neuropsychological test scores were considered to be compatible with bilateral and diffuse impairment. He performed very poorly on both right and left hands in a variety of simple motor and sensory tasks (e.g., finger-tapping speed and tactile finger recognition) and in more complex psychomotor problem-solving tasks as well, making little progress on either right- or left-hand trials of the Tactual Performance Test. In spite of number-letter recognition skills sufficient for the task, he was unable to complete Part B of the Trail Making Test and he had considerable difficulty identifying and maintaining the abstraction principles needed for solution of the Halstead Category Test. While the overall level and pattern of test scores suggested bilateral impairment, several of the comparisons between right and left body side performances supported an inference of maximal dysfunction of the left hemisphere. The patient was only marginally faster on the preferred right hand in finger tapping; he showed a definite reversal on dynamometer grip strength with the right hand weaker than the left; and he accumulated a number of right-sided but not left-sided errors in tests for tactile and visual imperception. The neuropsychological test summary postulating moderate, bilateral impairment of abilities dependent upon adequacy of brain function, but maximized in the left cerebral hemisphere, is in reasonable accord with the diagnosis of microcephaly and the left hemisphere lateralization of the EEG findings in this patient.

The lower Verbal than Performance IQ found on the WAIS is consistent with the left hemisphere lateralization inference but would not weigh heavily in this decision were the WAIS pattern not supported by the motor and sensory findings. As was noted by Klove (this volume, Ch. 8) in his review of data relating lateralization of cerebral functions to Wechsler-Bellevue Verbal and Performance IQ values, cerebral lesions that are longstanding in duration and date back to infancy or early childhood do not show a very consistent relationship to Verbal and Performance IQ values even though one hemisphere may be more involved than the other. It should be noted, however, that Patient A was given the Wechsler Adult Intelligence Scale, which was found by Fisher (1960) not to share the low Verbal-high Performance bias associated with Wechsler-Bellevue scores in retarded subjects. Thus, the lower Verbal than Performance IQ in subject A may be of greater significance than the same pattern had it been based on Wechsler-Bellevue data.

Patient B.   This was a 16-year-old male admitted at age 12 to the FWSH & TC. He had attended special education classes for 5 years prior to admission. Institutional placement was requested because of acute dissolution of a chronically unstable family unit and alleged abuse of the patient. Family history of mild mental retardation was present in three of four siblings and in his mother. Physical examination was within normal limits; perinatal history and acquisition of major developmental milestones were unremarkable, other than delay in expressive speech skills. The FWSH & TC staff reached a diagnosis of cultural-familial mental retardation.

Neuropsychological test findings in the subject show psychometric intelligence to be within the borderline range. The patient's verbal-symbolic limitations are evident from the VIQ of 75 and from the third-grade levels in reading and spelling subtests on the Wide Range Achievement Test. Inspection of the remainder of the test score array shows fairly good performances on a number of adaptive ability tasks. The error score of 70 on the Category Test is relatively good in relation to IQ peers, as are the memory and incidental learning (localization) scores on the Tactual Performance Test. Of particular interest is the excellent total time score on the Tactual Performance Test and the model relationship found between performances on the right, left, and both hand trials. The expected superiority on the right hand in finger-tapping speed and dynamometer grip strength measures is also present. Imperception testing was entirely within normal limits, and the errors made on finger recognition and finger-tip number writing tasks were infrequent and were distributed approximately equally on the two hands.

Regardless of one's preference for "defect" or for learning and motivational orientations toward cultural-familial retardation (Zigler, 1967), the above array of test scores would not appear to do serious violence to either theoretical bias. The important consideration from a neuropsychological test point of view would seem to be that Patient B shows mild impairment on a variety of psychometric, academic achievement, and other measures of adaptive ability but gives no evidence of motor or sensory asymmetries. Thus, the results do not permit a confident inference of structural damage in either cerebral hemisphere as a basis for the mild psychological deficit. The results illustrate the importance, in individual interpretation, of deriving positive findings, which have complementary significance, from more than one inferential approach before drawing a conclusion that cerebral damage is present.

Patient C. This 21-year-old male resident of the FWSH & TC was admitted at CA 14, following 7 years' attendance in a special class program. Institutional placement was prompted by chronic truancy, disruptive behavior, and poor achievement in school, and by community pressure on the family because of stealing and "malicious destruction of property." Mild mental retardation was reported in several siblings. Available birth and developmental history was unremarkable. Physical examination on admission was within normal limits. The diagnostic formulation reached by the staff was cultural-familial mental retardation.

The Wechsler-Bellevue Scale (Form I) yielded a Full Scale IQ within the borderline retardation range. The composite Full Scale IQ score was based upon sharply differentiated performances in the verbal (IQ–66) and in the nonverbal (PIQ–88) scales of this instrument. Verbal-symbolic difficulties were also attested to by very poor performance on the Boston Speech Perception Test and by his inability to make any progress on the number-letter sequences in Part B of the Trail Making Test. To postulate that his poor performances on these measures primarily reflect his history of language and other experiential impoverishment and his episodic participation in formal school programming would seem to be congruent with the available history and the diagnosis of cultural-familial retardation that was assigned. Scores obtained on additional measures in the battery, however, strongly suggested that an alternate hypothesis should be considered. Although measures of lateral dominance indicated that the subject was right-handed, he was unable to complete the Tactual Performance Test when using the right (dominant) hand; finger-tapping rate was slower with the right than with the left hand, and the expected superiority with preferred hand on grip strength testing was not present. In testing for perception of bilateral sensory stimulation, he made four errors on the right side but only one on the left side and he also made more errors on right than left hand trials of finger identification and tactile form recognition tasks. Taken together, these results provide a reasonable basis for postulating that, to a significant if not primary degree, his verbal deficits and other ability limitations may be related to neurological dysfunction which is maximized in the left cerebral hemisphere.

DISCUSSION

The present paper provides initial normative data for adolescent and adult institutionalized retardates on a test battery which has been widely employed in investigations of brain-behavior relationships in patients with verified neurological disease or damage. The barriers to extending such neuropsychological inquiries from neurological patients to retarded subjects are impressive ones, particularly considering the relative infrequency with which lateralized or focal lesions in this population are identified by current neurological diagnostic methods. Further, the fact that whatever neurological dysfunction which may be present in retarded subjects is, by definition, chronic and in most instances static, represents an additional difficulty in identifying behavioral deficits of the kind associated with specified cerebral damage in adult nonretarded subjects. A number of studies, for example, have shown that recently acquired lesions of the left hemisphere are associated with lower Verbal IQ and similar lesions of the right hemisphere tend to be associated with decrements in Performance IQ. However, Fitzhugh, Fitzhugh, and Reitan (1962) found that, while these Wechsler IQ patterns were confirmed in their groups with acute lesions, the same patterns were present only in highly attenuated form in groups with chronic, lateralized hemispheric lesions.

Consideration must also be given to the more general issue of the lack of specificity of impairment which is believed by many investigators to characterize the adaptive ability structure of the mentally retarded, since this viewpoint would appear to have serious implications for utilizing the neuropsychological test battery described here.

Rosvold's (1967) review of animal studies pertinent to mental retardation includes a cumulative series of investigations into the behavioral effects of selected experimental lesions in many different cortical and subcortical areas of the monkey. Rosvold summarizes these findings as follows:

Taken together, our studies of brain function indicate that the damage responsible for the general impairment of the mental retardate is not likely to be found in any one part of the cortex nor in any one of the related subcortical structures. Rather, such localized damage is more likely to result in specific disabilities. What, then, do these studies suggest for the problem of the physiological basis of mental retardation? They suggest that the agent which has been responsible for the brain changes in the retardate has a very diffuse effect capable of altering the functions of structures throughout the whole brain [p. 178].

Rosvold then presents data obtained on brain-damaged and non–brain-damaged human subjects, including retardates, on the Continuous Performance Test and concludes that this type of measure of attention is not only sensitive to brain damage in children and adults of normal intelligence, but also in retardates as well. Based upon additional data on this test in subjects with verified damage to centrencephalic structures which are known to have a very diffuse distribution to the brain and to affect the general activity of the brain, Rosvold says:

The supposition is that impairments on this test are related to disturbances of alertness and attention. Such results as these suggest that at least some types of mental retardation may be due to dysfunctions in the activation pattern of the brain. Early in the life of the organism this could so attenuate the effectiveness of environmental stimuli as to lead to retardation in mental development [p. 181].

In the résumé and discussion of his Ability Structure Project in mental retardation, Clausen (1966) offers a similar formulation.

It appears that the "General Ability" type of retardates may be a result of more or less slight impairment of the ARAS (ascending reticular activating system) resulting in hypofunction. It is assumed that slight impairment of the ARAS would make a less efficient arousal mechanism resulting in generally impaired performance on all tasks [p. 180].

Although the major conclusion of both Rosvold's and Clausen's studies is one of generality of impairment of adaptive abilities in retardates, this does not necessarily imply that measures of the kind sampled in the neuropsychological battery reported here are inappropriate or without potential applicability to this population. As an alternative to his proposal that the general behavioral limitations in retardates are the result of damage to one structure with many diffuse interconnections, Rosvold suggests that the impairment may be the result of damage to many structures. Clausen reported that neurological examination and EEG criterion information did permit the identification of certain impairment patterns in his retarded groups even though etiological classifications did not, and that motor measures seemed to be especially sensitive to such indices of cortical impairment. Thus, measures which sample a wide variety of motor, sensory, abstraction, memory, attention, and other abilities, as in the test battery reported here, should permit systematic inquiry into many of these complex interrelationships.

The demonstrated sensitivity of this test battery to effects of known cortical lesions in neurological patients suggests that these tests may also lend themselves to the identification of more specific areas of cortical impairment which may be present in an unknown number of subjects who are presently viewed as globally or diffusely impaired. However, caution must be exercised to avoid the perseverative application of a particular set of measures which works well in one population to another population, even when parallel goals are involved. Review of the individual test protocols which supported divergent neuropsychological inferences in the two patients diagnosed as cultural-familial retardation (Patients B and C) raises several questions regarding the employment of the entire test battery as presently constituted with retardates. Patient B did perform at better levels on a number of the more complex problem-solving measures, including the Category Test and Tactual Performance Test, than did Patient C in which lateralized brain damage was inferred. While the better scores found in Subject B on these measures are in general keeping with the results of several studies to be described below, it is nonetheless apparent that the consistency with which relative impairment in motor and in sensory discrimination tasks was found on the right body side in Patient C represented the more important consideration in the differential interpretation that was offered for these two sets of test data. The possibility certainly must be entertained that performance on a number of the measures in the present battery may be so heavily dependent upon psychomotric level that more specific cognitive deficits will not be identified in many retarded subjects. It would therefore seem that particular effort must be directed to the further development and validation of motor and sensory measures which permit detailed comparison of performances on the two body sides.

The extremely poor performances found on a number of the tests of more complex problem-solving ability, particularly in the lowest IQ groups and in the younger subjects (e.g., the larger standard deviation than mean score found for the TPT in the adolescent IQ 40–54 group) suggests that some of the measures may be so difficult for this population that their differential diagnostic yield does not warrant the time required for their administration. Other measures, such as the Continuous Performance Test described by Rosvold (1967) may prove to be of equal or greater utility. Another possible approach to modification of the present battery is now under investigation with FWSH & TC subjects; namely to determine the level and range of scores found in adult retardates on the less-demanding versions of the Category Test and TPT which were used in the examination of children ages 5 through 8 years and reported by Reitan in this volume (Ch. 4).

Several studies suggest that, even as presently composed, the battery has some classificatory potential, at least within rather broadly defined exogenous-endogenous categories of presumed etiology of mental retardation. Matthews

(1963) reported intergroup comparisons on 26 tests in the present battery in four diagnostic categories of retarded subjects (cultural-familial, brain-damaged, undifferentiated and undifferentiated accompanied by psychotic or personality disorder). The tests were ranked on a continuum from tests judged to be most dependent upon immediate problem solving ability to tests judged to be most dependent upon experiential background for task success. The results showed that the familial group performed significantly better than the other three categories on tests within the problem-solving half of the continuum and that the familial group performed significantly more poorly than the other three groups on measures within the experiential background half of the distribution. In two other studies (Matthews & Reitan, 1961, 1962), retardates were found to show significantly greater proportional or relative improvement rates than subjects with known cerebral lesions on tests within the problem solving half of the continuum (e.g., Category Test, Tactual Performance Test). Thus retardates scored well on tests which permit demonstration of immediate learning and improved performance as a function of practice, even though they had poorer absolute or initial test scores. These results suggest that similar analyses of such test performance characteristics between various diagnostic classifications of retardates might profitably be conducted.

The research by analogy strategy described by Benton (1970) has been utilized in several studies using selected aspects of the test battery with retardates. Davis and Reitan (1967) showed that Wechsler Verbal and Performance IQs could be ordered by behavioral criteria (dysphasia or constructional dyspraxia) which have been found in other studies (e.g., Wheeler & Reitan, 1962) to be related to the functioning of the left and right hemispheres, respectively. An investigation by Matthews, Folk, and Zerfas (1966) into the relationship between lateralized finger localization deficits and Wechsler Verbal-Performance patterns in retarded subjects yielded results which seemed explicable within the framework of previously reported studies of the significance of finger localization deficits in patients with verified cerebral pathology.

Windle's monograph (1962) on prognostic factors carefully documents the limited state of our knowledge concerning the relative importance and differential contribution of psychometric performances and of emotional-personality variables associated with successful as opposed to unsuccessful vocational-social outcomes in retarded subjects. The current emphasis in neuropsychological research with subjects at the FWSH & TC is directed to this problem. Test battery results are being obtained in addition to a variety of vocational tests, personality measures, and behavioral rating data on mildly retarded subjects who have been enrolled in an intensive vocational assessment, training, and job placement program. Approximately 150 subjects have completed the training and placement sequence at the time of this writing, and have been categorized according to five outcome groups ranging from failure (i.e., return to the regular institutional program with on-the-grounds vocational training assignments) to successful job placement and independent living in the community for 6 months or greater duration. This study should permit conclusions to be derived regarding the motor-sensory and general ability functioning levels associated with the five outcome groups, and the predictive utility of these measures vis-à-vis case history and other behavioral-adjustmental data obtained on subjects in each category.

SUMMARY

A battery of neuropsychological tests, including tests devised by Halstead, Wechsler, and others, was administered to 367 institutionalized retardates aged 9 through 14 years ($N = 81$) and 15 years and older ($N = 286$). Mean scores and standard deviations obtained on each measure were presented for three WISC and three Wechsler-Bellevue Scale IQ groups: 40-54, 55-69, and 70-84. Test results obtained on several individual patients were also reported. Methodological-clinical problems and potential contributions of neuropsychological investigations in mental retardation were discussed in terms of previous studies employing this test battery, both with neurological subjects and with retarded groups. Although the theoretical and applied yield of neuropsychological investigations of retarded subjects using this test battery must be considered to be still minimal and uncertain, findings to date warrant further studies of test performance characteristics of retardates with these or similar measures.

11
SOME CHALLENGES FOR CLINICAL NEUROPSYCHOLOGY[1]

Manfred J. Meier[2]

This paper is designed to examine some of the challenges confronting adult clinical neuropsychology during this decade. Clinical neuropsychology is defined here as that component of the human neuropsychological enterprise which emphasizes the use of objective psychological methods in the assessment of higher cortical functions. It is recognized that such restriction in the use of this term is somewhat arbitrary. By defining clinical neuropsychology in terms of objective test application, it is intended to provide a frame of reference for establishing a perspective on recent developments within neuropsychology more broadly conceived, especially as these developments may have implications for clinical or applied neuropsychology. Since appropriate literature reviews are available for each of the areas to be discussed, an exhaustive analysis of related developments converging upon clinical neuropsychology will not be provided. Instead, an attempt will be made to outline these developments. Selected arguments and illustrative data will then be introduced in the framework of this outline.

Neuropsychology will be regarded as consisting of three major research styles or approaches to the scientific study of brain-behavior relationships in man.

[1] Preparation of this paper was supported by Research Career Development Award NS-18,539 from the National Institute of Neurological Diseases and Stroke. The research of the Neuropsychology Laboratory, University of Minnesota, cited in this paper was supported by a number of sources including Grant NS-03394 from the National Institute of Neurological Diseases and Stroke, NIH; the Graduate School (University of Minnesota); the Lyle A. French Fund; and the A. B. Baker Fund for Research in Clinical Neuropsychology.

[2] Special acknowledgement is expressed to Leslie Arthur for her assistance in data collection and to Dr. Milton Ettinger of the Hennepin County General Hospital for his continued collaboration in this area of research.

These include clinical neuropsychology (as defined above), human physiological psychology, and behavioral neurology. Other areas which might be meaningfully included, but lie outside the purview of this discussion are speech pathology and the evolving area of applied psycholinguistics. These areas, of course, can be seen to overlap appropriately in the context of specific problems. This discussion is directed to issues involving the convergence of related developments in human physiological psychology and behavioral neurology upon clinical neuropsychology. It is prompted by recognition of a conceptual and methodological lag between these areas and clinical neuropsychological test applications. This is reflected particularly in conspicuous deficiencies in the validity of even the more established test batteries and the unduly constraining nature of the cross-sectional or diagnostic framework in which such batteries are usually applied.

The specific objectives of this paper involve an examination of (*a*) the current status of objective psychological methods in relation to the clinical question of lesion localization, (*b*) selected developments in human physiological psychology and behavioral neurology which might be incorporated into future applied research, and (*c*) previously neglected clinical assessment problems and external criteria in neuropsychological test validation.

CLINICAL NEUROPSYCHOLOGY

Antecedent Considerations

Much of the clinical neuropsychological literature documents a succession of investigations in search of the universal test of "organicity" (Spreen & Benton, 1967). As a tradition within clinical psychology, these efforts appear to have been guided by the diagnostic need in psychiatric settings to differentiate between organic and psychotic states. The primary methodological input was given by the "mental testing movement" which produced a wide range of standardized tests for which normative data were available. These were assessed in terms of their empirical relationship to global external criteria of cerebral involvement. Such criteria were derived from ratings or judgments of neurological involvement which irregularly included specific reference to objective neurological deficits. In later studies, criterion development incorporated special confirmatory neurological data provided by EEG, pneumoencephalography, angiography, and brain scanning techniques.

The appeal to clinical psychologists of a unitary concept of "brain damage" as a model for criterion development in test validation may be related to the empirical and relatively atheoretical emphasis of applied psychology, particularly in the Midwest where much of this work was done. Also, the broadening role of clinical psychology in World War II precipitated an interest in techniques which provided an easily scored and definitive answer to a large array of clinical questions. Since clinical psychologists worked primarily in psychiatric settings, the organic diagnostic question typically was posed to them in dichotomized form: presence versus absence of cerebral involvement. Since only a validated cutting score was needed to give a professionally effective response, the reinforcement schedule for entrenchment of this criterion model was established.

Recognition of the rich variability in the nature and magnitude of psychological deficits resulting from cerebral lesions emerged more from the work of psychologists who entered the neurological setting. These were variously trained in clinical or physiological psychology. Modern clinical neuropsychology utilized the unitary organicity model only as a point of departure and gradually replaced it with the localization model which prevailed in the neurological setting. In a specific sense, Halstead's battery (1947), as extended and applied by Reitan (1955b), gave impetus to this liberation from the organicity model (Reitan, 1962). Similarly, Benton introduced a variety of carefully constructed and validated tests to the clinical neuropsychological community. His interest in language disorders quite naturally prompted him to adopt the concepts and descriptive criteria of classical behavioral neurology as well as a more deliberate emphasis on theory than is characteristic of the clinical neuropsychological group as a whole (Benton, 1963, 1967b, 1968b).

The major external criterion for this approach was lesion localization usually given by neurological diagnosis, with or without explicit listing of objective focal neurological or neurosurgical supporting findings. This cross-sectional criterion guided the development of psychological test batteries directed at yielding a substantive and comprehensive account of the behavioral consequences of any focal or diffuse cerebral lesion. It was assumed that the pattern of test outcomes associated with such lesions would provide a basis for inferring the presence, laterality localization, cephalocaudal localization, extent, etiological conditions, and progressive course of the underlying neuropathological process (Reitan, 1964b). Progressive refinements led to acknowledgment of the many interactions between such factors as etiology, age at onset, and laterality manifestations of focal lesions. These interactions accounted for the wide variability in test outcomes but also obscured, in a vexing way, the meaning of individual scores. Furthermore, elaborate test interpretation required extensive knowledge of neurological disease and diagnostic criteria. Generation of such multifaceted inferences also required extensive acquaintanceship with the inferential strategies of the specific battery user. One consequence of these considerations is that there is no way of estimating the extent to which clinical test batteries are being misused. To the more naive user, a set to infer the presence of a localized lesion may well lead to overinterpretations. These can prove to be awkward and embarrassing, particularly if they induce the referring medical service to do additional and potentially harmful diagnostic tests which turn out to be negative. This kind of complication can develop even if deliberate emphasis is placed on the probabilistic aspect of the actuarial statements utilized in communication of conclusions.

The entire battery approach seems to be at issue here. Since this volume is representative of the current status of the clinical neuropsychological track in neuropsychology, it seems reasonable to ask where this approach has fallen short of its previous objectives, what urgent problems it has not pursued, and what contributions it might make in the future.

Localization: Laterality Axis

Batteries incorporate both psychological (cognitive, memory, perceptual-motor) and neurological (sensorimotor, sensory suppression) levels of analysis in their methodology. Detection and laterality of a focal lesion often constitute the primary diagnostic questions being asked by the referral source. A given inferential "hit" might be derived exclusively from a sensorimotor measure. Not surprisingly, such measures are among the most valid for lateralizing focal cerebral lesions (Costa, Vaughn, Levita, & Farber, 1963). Insofar as neurologists have emphasized sensorimotor phenomena in the diagnosis of cerebral involvement, clinical neuropsychologists should perhaps be more concerned with the development of cognitive measures, since our most cogent contribution to diagnosis is likely to be made in the *absence* of objective neurological findings. This is not to suggest that sensorimotor functions are less important to the neuropsychologist, but rather that the localization of a lesion on the sole basis of the sensorimotor measurements may be trivial at the point in the diagnostic process at which the neuropsychologist makes his contribution. Therefore, it seems reasonable to evaluate deliberately the validity of our most frequently used cognitive measures and contrast them with the sensorimotor changes which are often conspicuous to even casual clinical observation.

Recent observations (Reitan, 1970) of the presence of greater cognitive impairments in patients with impaired sensorimotor functions do not appear to alter these implications for cognitive assessment in neuropsychological batteries. As indicated, his sensorimotor impaired group consisted largely of patients with vascular lesions while the intact group was similarly overrepresented by younger, traumatic cases. It would be of greater interest to find differences in cognitive deficits as a function of sensorimotor impairment within disease categories. But the differences may not appear in such analyses. For example, cerebrovascular accidents which produce a Broca's (expressive) aphasia almost always are associated with severe right hemiparesis. However, these patients retain remarkably high levels of verbal comprehension, presumably because the lesion lies anteriorly and, thereby, spares the language processing areas in the posterior temporo-parieto-occipital juncture (Geschwind, 1965). Similarly, infarctions involving the posterior language systems produce severe verbal deficits while leaving motor abilities relatively intact (Benson, 1967).

An example of a marginal cognitive measure in neuropsychological applications is the VIQ-PIQ discrepancy, derived from the Wechsler Scales, to patients with known focal cerebral lesions. Much of the literature bearing on the validity of this measure for lateralizing focal cerebral lesions has been reviewed by Klove in this volume (Ch. 8), and by Parsons (1970). As these authors have shown, some studies have confirmed the validity of the discrepancy at diagnostically meaningful levels. There is considerable evidence that WAIS discrepancy measures should be used judiciously in clinical application.

Findings which raise additional questions regarding the use of such measures for inferring lateral involvement are the absence of WAIS changes after unilateral prefrontal (Milner, 1964) and anterior temporal lobe (Meier & French, 1966a) ablations in patients with focal, atrophic, epileptogenic lesions in these regions. In the latter study, right anterior temporal lobectomy was associated with prolonged reduction (up to 5 years) on the Picture Arrangement subtest score, consistent with previous clinical reports of such selective subtest relationships (Reitan, 1955c, 1959c). Thus, the only persisting subtest mean change after unilateral temporal lobectomy involved a circumscribed nonverbal function. Compatible with this outcome is a report of more consistent selective impairment of nonverbal WAIS functions after cerebrovascular accident, both in Japanese and U.S. samples (Meier & Okayama, 1969). Such findings highlight the fact that unilateral prefrontal or anterior temporal lobe lesions are difficult to detect, either with neurological or quantitative neuropsychological approaches.

Recent attempts to confirm the validity of WAIS measures in lateralization have examined specific subtest score differences (Parsons, Vega, & Burn, 1969). These investigators reported greater differentiation of left from right hemisphere lesions on the basis of Vocabulary-Block Design (Voc–BD) subtest score discrepancy in an etiologically mixed group of patients with focal cerebral lesions. While they obtained more clearcut within-group Voc-BD differences in the right hemisphere group, the discrepancy reached only .05 (one-tail test) within the left hemisphere group. In one subsample, the controls also scored significantly lower on Vocabulary.

The *diagnostic* application of WAIS measures for lesion lateralization would appear to be increasingly open to question even when the presence of a lesion is known. A meaningful evaluation of such measures would appear to require their application to patients with disturbances in higher cortical function which are not expressed unequivocally through objective neurological changes. In this direction, we applied a number of WAIS measures obtained from patients with focal cerebral lesions selected on the basis of a relative absence or paucity of focal neurological findings, in an effort to determine the relative merits of each of these measures for lateralizing such lesions. First, the VIQ-PIQ discrepancy was examined as a laterality estimator. In addition, a Verbal Deviation Quotient (VDQ)-Perceptual Organization Deviation Quotient (PDQ) discrepancy was analyzed as an alternative to the VIQ-PIQ since DQ discrepancies are based on factor scores derived from subtest combinations carrying higher constituent factor loads on the verbal and nonverbal dimensions tapped by the WAIS (Tellegen & Briggs, 1967). The IQ and DQ results have been reported elsewhere (Meier, 1970a). As a third lateralizing device, the Voc–BD discrepancy was examined since this measure appeared to have greater validity in lateralization, at least when applied to a focal lesion sample unselected with respect to the presence or absence of sensorimotor findings.

This selected sample of patients with minimal focal neurological findings was drawn from our files of focal cerebrovascular and neoplastic patient groupings. The cerebrovascular episode patients had exhibited an abrupt onset of focal neurological symptoms but without prolonged motor residuals. The neoplastic group was tested after neurosurgical removal of histologically confirmed neoplastic tissue. Again, only those with minimal or no motor impairments were included. Twenty left hemisphere, 20 right hemisphere, and 20 age- and education-equivalent normal controls provided the data found in Table 1.

It can be seen that the *between* group discrepancies for the Voc and BD differences are consistent with expectation, though the verbal measures are less powerful in differentiating the groups ($p < .05$). The within-group differences need to be examined more carefully, however, since clinical predictions are made by applying cutting scores or judgmental criteria to *intraindividual* discrepancies. Here the left hemisphere group discrepancies failed to reach statistically acceptable levels for any of the three measures under examination. By contrast, the right hemisphere group differences were significant at the .01 level, consistent with previous reports. Within-control-group discrepancies were not significant, as expected.

Collectively, these studies suggest that lower WAIS performance measures emerge more consistently with right cerebral involvement than do corresponding selective changes in verbal measures after left hemisphere lesion. Such inconsistencies with expectation probably are related to differential effects on verbal behavior of deeper lesions as contrasted with lesions of the cortical mantle in focal left hemisphere disease. For example, a small infarct involving the internal capsule produces severe focal neurological deficits but would not be expected to produce definitive or lasting changes in verbal functioning clinically (Bonhoeffer, 1914). Furthermore, lesions of the left cerebral hemisphere which lie outside the classical speech areas can produce transient aphasias,

TABLE 1

Vocabulary-Block Design Discrepancy Data of the "Silent" Lesion Groups

Within groups				Between groups		
Group	Mean Vocab	Mean BD	*t*	Group	*t* Vocab	*t* BD
LH	8.65	9.35	1.17	LH–RH	2.63*	2.81**
RH	10.05	7.75	4.02**	LH–C	4.26**	3.81**
C	10.90	11.35	0.55	RH–C	1.65	6.66**

*$p < .05$.
**$p < .01$.

"nonaphasic" syndromes due to isolation of the speech areas from sensory input systems (Dejerine, 1914; Geschwind & Kaplan, 1962), and partial aphasic syndromes. The likelihood that such WAIS-derived discrepancies would reveal consistent changes across this multitude of determining conditions and outcomes seems low, particularly when the factorial irregularity of the verbal subtests is considered. Many clinicians, in recognition of these limitations, have adopted an approach which emphasizes the use of conjoint inferential methods and complementary data (as illustrated by Reitan in the second chapter of this volume), rather than to attempt to depend upon one variable such as verbal and performance WAIS differences. It is not surprising that some of the most valid actuarial test score (sign) applications in lesion laterality determination involve the use of aphasia screening procedures (Wheeler & Reitan, 1962).

The lesion laterality question can be attacked through behavior changes that arise between the cognitive and sensorimotor levels of analysis. It might be hypothesized that focal lesions that fail to produce consistent WAIS VIQ–PIQ discrepancies or unequivocal (perhaps subclinical) sensorimotor changes will become manifest behaviorally under conditions of conflicting intersensory input during motor performances. This formulation was translated operationally into application of closed-circuit television techniques in an effort to augment or facilitate the expression of subclinical impairments of perceptual-motor functioning of the contralateral hand in the above series of patients. This investigation (Meier, 1970a) was designed to compare relationships between lesion laterality and differences between the right and left hands on the Seguin-Goddard Formboard under various conditions of televised self-monitoring during performance. Conflict between visual feedback and the movement-produced somatosensory (proprioceptive and kinesthetic) cues during performance was produced by reversing or inverting the image on the television monitor (Smith, K. U., & Smith, W. M., 1962). This can be accomplished by means of special circuitry in the television camera.

As indicated above, the discrepancy between WAIS verbal and visuospatial measures failed to discriminate within the left cerebral hemisphere group consistently, nor did the greater differentiation achieved with such measures reach levels of diagnostic significance in the right hemisphere group. Presence of mild, equivocal, or no pyramidal tract findings in these patients was reflected in the minimal differences between left- or right-hand performance times under direct nontelevised visual feedback. Each televised reafference condition decreased performance speed bilaterally, but increased the performance time differences between the two hands, characteristically slowing performance speed of the hand contralateral to the involved hemisphere more than the hand ipsilateral to the side of the lesion. Such relative increase in contralateral performance time was maximal under the reversal condition, particularly in the right hemisphere subgroup.

The maximally sensitive condition appears to be reversal of visual feedback, since variability of response time was quite high under the inversion condition.

This outcome was evident particularly in some ratios which were derived from the basic measures of difference in response time between the hands and measures of the separate response times of the hand contralateral as well as ipsilateral to the lesion. Thus, ratios of the average difference in response time between the hands, relative to the ipsilateral and contralateral response times, were separately computed. Maximal ratio values were obtained with the ipsilateral hand time as a reference in both lesion groups since, of course, those times were relatively shorter than the contralateral hand times. By contrast, utilization of the contralateral hand time as a reference in the denominator of the ratio resulted in a highly stable mean ratio value which approached "0" for the lesion groups, as did all mean ratio values, irrespective of which hand was used as a reference, of the controls.

The chance (or questionably higher) differentiability of the WAIS discrepancies when applied to the left hemisphere subgroup was also characteristic of the hand-difference measure of response time with direct confrontation formboard placements when the median was utilized as a cutting score. WAIS measure applications yielded a 60% accuracy of differentiation of the left hemisphere group while the confrontation measure identified 50% of this group accurately. The reversal and inversion conditions, in turn, yielded approximately 75% accuracy of identification in the left hemisphere group. Interestingly, the right hemisphere-control separations reached the 90% level under reversal condition, compared with 68-75% on the WAIS discrepancy measures.

Thus, the introduction of a conflict between visual and somatosensory feedback appeared to augment the expression of a contralateral impairment during reafference, perhaps as a consequence of transcortical effects which lie outside the pyramidal tract. Although the apparent diagnostic utility of such measures would appear to exceed those of the WAIS, it should be noted that like the WAIS measures, their relative sensitivity to right is selectively greater than to left hemisphere lesions. Taking into consideration the anticipated attenuation of inferential accuracy of the televised measures with cross validation, these measures may not hold their advantage over the WAIS in relation to left cerebral lesions, where the televised procedures similarly fall short of the optimal levels of discriminability required of diagnostic measures. It remains to examine test formats which involve the manipulation of verbal materials under conditions of reafference, but the rational derivation of verbal tests in this framework is not clear. Disturbances in writing, reading, and repetition are prevalent in language disorders of central origin. Facilitation of subtle verbal deficits might be accomplished by means of *delayed* visual (or auditory) feedback amplifying such deficits where, for example, aphasia screening procedures provide only marginal or suggestive indications of language impairment in patients with left hemisphere lesions.

Localization: Cephalocaudal Axis

Even this cursory examination of the laterality localization issue suggests that interhemispheric differences in function are not being sampled optimally in clinical neuropsychological application, particularly in the diagnosis of left cerebral hemisphere lesions. The need for development of objective neuropsychological methods with effective sensitivity to subtle verbal changes might well be met by future research that incorporates procedures for measuring cerebral dominance and aphasia. These will be discussed more appropriately in the outline of related developments in human physiological psychology and behavioral neurology. Although this literature could well be cited here, it bears so much upon the localization of lesions along the cephalocaudal or anterior-posterior axis that a prior evaluation of the current status of the test battery approach for determining behavioral correlates of lesions along this dimension seems warranted.

Problems encountered in attempts to apply neuropsychological test batteries to the differentiation of anterior from posterior lesions are exemplified by the efforts of Reitan (1964b). He used results from Halstead's tests, the Wechsler-Bellevue Scale, and other measures to generate inferences for individual patients regarding location along both dimensions (left anterior, left posterior, right anterior, right posterior), extent of lesion (focal, diffuse), and lesion etiology (cerebrovascular disease, tumor, trauma, multiple sclerosis). Inferences were derived exclusively from knowledge of test scores, age, and education. Classifications based on these inferences were then compared with independently derived neurological classifications along these variables. Significant agreement was consistently present between the neuropsychological and neurological inferences. Agreement levels were uniformly high for the focal versus diffuse classifications, for the laterality of lesions located posteriorly (but not as high for those located anteriorly), and for identifying type of lesion (with the exception of extrinsic tumors). Reitan was careful to interpret these concordance data in the framework of his earlier (1962) emphasis upon the complexity of behavioral changes and their relationship to underlying neuropathological conditions. The study pointed up the difficulty experienced in specifying those features of the neuropsychological measurements which influence the determination of specific inferences. His work in this volume is directed particularly to this issue.

While the above classifications were based on evaluation of neuropsychological and neurological results for individual patients, Reitan also analyzed the statistical relations between the entire set of Halstead measures, the Wechsler-Bellevue (Form I), and the Trail Making Test. The findings revealed the particular difficulty encountered in localizing along the anterior-posterior dimension. Of 192 possible specific intergroup (test-criterion) comparisons between the focal lesion groups (laterality and cephalocaudality simultaneously), only 25 reached acceptable confidence levels statistically. These were limited relatively to the Tactual Performance and Finger Tapping tests which sample, at least in part, behavior at the sensorimotor level of analysis.

Returning to the individual classifications, effective differentiation of focal from diffuse lesions was achieved validly. Reitan did not test the statistical reliability of differences in proportions of correct classifications in the four localization groups, but the frequencies themselves indicated that frontal lesions were more frequently misclassified and were associated with a relatively high frequency of false negatives. Apparently this was due to the presence of less conspicuous neuropsychological deficits in patients with anterior lesions. This seems to pinpoint the essence of the cephalocaudal localization problem: anterior lesions are typically rather elusive regarding adequate quantitative behavioral analysis, although the clinical literature abounds with qualitative descriptions of behavioral change in such patients (Luria, 1966). By contrast, posterior lesions, particularly those involving the temporo-parieto-occipital juncture, often produce dramatic and profound behavioral changes which probably can be detected and described by means of procedures that are sufficiently broad to elicit subsequent disturbances of verbal comprehension after left hemisphere and constructional activity after right hemisphere involvement (Critchley, 1953; Wheeler & Reitan, 1962; Geschwind, 1965).

Reitan's analysis also revealed that his inferential accuracy in inferring localization of left posterior lesions was *lower* than his corresponding accuracy level for right posterior lesions (11 of 16 patients as compared with 15 of 16 patients correctly classified), consistent with the WAIS and televised feedback results reviewed above. Although the anterior inferential classifications (both left and right) were almost equally divided between correct and incorrect congruence with the neurological classifications, Reitan exhibited a tendency toward a higher "hit" rate in the left anterior group (9 of 16 patients as compared with 7 of 16 patients). Although this minor difference cannot be considered as statistically reliable, it may have been associated with the mild, detectable, dysphasic disturbances which are sometimes observed in prefrontal lesions, even with sparing of Broca's area (Borkowski, Benton, & Spreen, 1967). However, the statistical analysis revealed few quantitative differences between anterior and posterior lesions within the same hemisphere while lateralized differences were primarily a function of visuomotor and blindfolded performance decrements in the hand contralateral to the lesion. This area of application would appear to require further validation of specific tests as well as the objectification of decision rules in the inferential process. A preliminary attempt to objectify the inferential process has recently been published by Russell, Neuringer, and Goldstein (1970).

Localization: Vertical Axis

Clearly, if valid anteroposterior localization is considered a desirable outcome of objective neuropsychological test application, even the established batteries may be incapable of consistently yielding such specificity in their present form. This appears to hold not only for applications involving the separation of prefrontal from posterior lesions but for the detection and isolation of anterior temporal lobe lesions as well. Since these regions are relatively "silent," in the sense that gross sensorimotor deficits do not appear when they are involved, their localization may be less accessible to corresponding components of neuropsychological test batteries. Chapters by Reitan (Ch. 2) and Klove (Ch. 8) in this volume explicitly demonstrate the types of findings that imply the presence of anterior temporal lobe lesions. Similarly it is generally accepted that suppression phenomena, language and visuospatial deficits, and other changes in higher cortical function are not as readily demonstrated with involvement of these regions as contrasted, for example, with lesions of the posterior temporoparietal area. Unlike the posterior temporoparietal association area, both prefrontal and anterior temporal lobe structures have direct extensive connections with deeper and phylogenetically older structures (MacLean & Delgado, 1953). Like the posterior temporoparietal region, they participate in transcortical networks (Crosby, Humphrey, & Lauer, 1962). The expected interactions between these regions and deeper structures with which they are connected may well provide a basis for the development of objective behavioral methods to detect lesions in these regions.

Since prefrontal and anterior temporal lesions do not produce the readily measured gross changes in behavior observed with more posterior involvement, they may provide a neural reserve for restoration of the more debilitating disturbances of higher cortical function associated with posterior lesions. This points up an urgent clinical neuropsychological problem area which may have been neglected by earlier preoccupation with diagnostic localization—namely, the actuarial and behavioral prediction of spontaneous recovery of impaired higher cortical functions.

Examination of behavioral outcomes in terms of lesion localization along the cortical-subcortical and transcortical axes might contribute to the development of empirically more sensitive test batteries in the cross-sectional, diagnostic framework and foster a concern with new clinical problems such as the longitudinal course of behavioral recovery under differing etiological and disease conditions. The search for such improved measures may be necessary for the continuation of a meaningful clinical neuropsychological role in the neurological and neurosurgical settings. Such expansion would appear to include selected progressive modification of the test battery approach through (a) application of assessment strategies provided by recent developments in behavioral neurology and human physiological psychology and (b) investigations of clinical problems which transcend the localization issue in appropriate etiological contexts, such as the recoverability of higher cortical functions after cerebrovascular infarction.

RELATED DEVELOPMENTS

Developments in behavioral neurology and human physiological psychology can be seen as outgrowths of three general theoretical orientations with respect to the organization of higher cortical functions. Primary differences among these theories involve the assumptions regarding the characteristics of the neural substrate underlying the generation of behavioral change in cerebral disease and the differentiation of function in the development of behavior. Insofar as they provide a convenient frame of reference for examining related developments in the behavioral neurosciences they will be summarized here. More extensive treatments are available elsewhere (Hebb, 1949; Meyer, 1960; Luria, 1966; Rosner, 1970).

Modern Behavioral Neurology

The "strict localization" position assumes that higher cortical functions are localized discretely in the cerebral hemispheres. In the extreme, this class of postulates is derived from direct connectionistic or "switchboard" models of the neuronal systems subserving specific functions. To the extent that such systems are regarded as organized in a relatively static or stereotyped manner, adherents to this viewpoint have tended to ignore the plasticity of CNS organization and, thereby, the question of functional restoration. This approach evolved from 19th century European neurology, based largely upon data obtained by means of strategies applied during clinical neurological examination. Since language disturbances are among the most dramatic changes to occur in focal cerebral disease, and are readily amenable to behavioral analysis at the bedside, attention understandably was directed to the aphasias, apraxias, and agnosias. Extremely innovative and imaginative evaluative strategies were brought to bear on these problems. The resulting findings added impetus to the entire neuropsychological effort and yielded considerable knowledge of behavioral change in patients with focal cerebral lesions.

A major reason that psychologists became involved in a quest for localizing devices might be reflected in the casual incorporation of higher cortical assessment approaches into clinical diagnosis on the part of American neurologists. With some notable exceptions (Bender & Teuber, 1946; Denny-Brown, 1958; Horenstein & Casey, 1963; Joynt & Benton, 1964) behavioral neurology was primarily a European interest until Geschwind (1965) integrated this literature and, thereby, stimulated further expansion of this approach in American neurology.

Previously, language assessment in this country was primarily the concern of speech pathologists who had established a wide assortment of techniques, reviewed by Osgood and Miron (1963). A brief assessment of language deficits in clinical neuropsychological evaulations has utilized the Halstead-Wepman Aphasia Screening Test (Halstead & Wepman, 1949) as modified by Reitan. Recent efforts to quantify language disturbances seem directly relevant to clinical objectives. The construction of formal aphasia batteries, of course, was pioneered by Hildred Schuell (1950, 1957) and her coworkers, (Schuell & Jenkins, 1959; Schuell, Jenkins, & Jimenez-Pabon, 1964) before her untimely death. Similarly, Jones and Wepman (1961) provided more psychometric (e.g., quantifiable) operations for obtaining analyzable data within the complex domain of language. Although still research instruments, these hold considerable promise as additions to the test armamentarium of the clinical neuropsychologist. Benton (1967b) has reviewed problems of quantitative aphasia test construction and described an effort to devise a battery which yields a graphic representation of the profile of scores obtained (Spreen & Benton, 1968). Efforts of the Boston Veterans Administration Hospital Aphasia Unit (Goodglass & Kaplan, 1972) have utilized Geschwind's systematized account of the behavioral neurological approach and the localization doctrine as bases for constructing an extensive aphasia battery. Further attempts to measure language disturbances (as contrasted with qualitative characterization and tabulated descriptions) involve the Porch Index of Communicative Ability (Porch, 1967) and the Functional Communications Profile (Taylor, 1965).

The more refined orientation toward localization of modern behavioral neurology and the collection of methods emerging from the interdisciplinary efforts of aphasiologists generally would appear to provide rich resources for improving existing test batteries. The need for added sophistication in the areas of language assessment and behavioral neurology is related to the apparent weaknesses of current clinical neuropsychological assessment approaches in lesion lateralization and in lesion localization within the affected cerebral hemisphere.

As indicated above, exclusive focus upon the localization issue has created the kind of overemphasis which restricts disciplinary effort unduly. An opposing theoretical orientation which also evolved from 19th-century neurology discounts the strict localization doctrine and holds that association cortex is organized dynamically as a generalizable system in which any given region is equally capable of participating in functions which are normally subserved by either adjacent or remote cortical areas (Lashley, 1929; Goldstein, 1934). At its extreme, this view postulates that the extent of impaired function is related proportionately to the amount of association cortex destroyed. The nature of the function, therefore, is minimized in accord with the notion of mass action. The importance of this view is reflected in the emphasis on regional equipotentiality of function and on neuronal systems which are capable of contributing to multiple representation of higher cortical functions. Although regional differentiation of function was underestimated by the equipotential position, it prompted neuropsychological investigators to acknowledge major shortcomings of the strict localization model. However powerful that model has become for predicting the rather unique and "pure" syndromes produced by lesions which lie within the classical speech areas, or for isolating these language processing fields from sensory input channels, it provides no conceptual guidelines to account for the reorganization and restitution of higher cortical functions. In addition, the localization position does not account for the presence of impaired adaptive capacities which do not clearly fall into the area of the language or constructional deficits. It was the presence of such nonspecific deficits in brain-damaged patients that prompted Goldstein to incorporate measurement of the ability to maintain or shift, as environmental conditions require, a set or attitude (Goldstein & Scheerer, 1941). This view contributed to the development of sorting tasks (Weigl, 1927) for measuring conceptual thinking (Grant & Berg, 1948). Current theoretical formulations in human neuropsychology generally coalesce the more valid components of the localization and equipotentiality positions. The resulting general theory can be referred to as the "regional localization" position which recognizes the complexity of interactions among differentiated but functionally overlapping cortical zones (Luria, 1966). This position attempts to account for the facts relating to zonal differentiation; variability of behavioral outcomes associated with cerebral lesions over time; and the hierarchical re-representation and multiple control of function through learning and sensory experience (Hebb, 1949; Luria, 1963; Rosner, 1970).

This theoretical view begins with Jackson 1931–1932 who recognized early the capability for re-representation of function in successively higher and phylogenetically newer levels of the central nervous system. He based his formulations on observations of "release" phenomena in epilepsy and argued that higher structures can have inhibitory influences on lower structures which subserve more stereotyped and primitive behavior. Evidence from research in neurophysiology supports the presence of such autoregulatory systems which place higher functions simultaneously under both afferent and efferent control (Anokhin, 1935, 1956; Moruzzi & Magoun, 1949; Luria, 1966).

The evidential basis of the dynamic regional localization position extends the domain of the localization issue into the "silent" cortical zones where lesions do not produce the extensive and more easily detected changes in language behavior which arise with involvement of Broca's area anteriorly or the association cortex posteriorly (temporo-parieto-occipital juncture). In addition, this position postulates that even remote regions can participate, through relearning and experience, in the restoration of impaired function that a particular region would not otherwise subserve, either in normal development or as preferred modes of adaptive behavior (Rosner, 1970). Therefore, it provides at least tentative guidelines for extending clinical neuropsychological assessment from the cross-sectional bounds of the localization issue to the longitudinal prediction and evaluation of recovery changes.

Human Physiological Psychology

Laterality axis. Many of the experimental-physiological investigations of higher cortical function in man have explored functional asymmetries between the cerebral hemispheres. It is now well established that the dominant (usually left) cerebral hemisphere primarily subserves verbal intellectual functions, while the nondominant (usually right) cerebral hemisphere mediates the integration of visuospatial and temporal-spatial relationships (Meyer, 1960; Reitan, 1962; Piercy, 1964; Luria, 1966).

The extensive documentation of lateral asymmetries in function between the cerebral hemispheres has been confirmed by investigations of the relationship between response of a single hemisphere to the selective sensory inputs achieved after sectioning of the forebrain commissures in man (Sperry, 1961; Gazzaniga,

1965, 1970). These studies have demonstrated the selective capability of the left hemisphere for expressive speech and comprehension of more elaborate verbal constructions. Interestingly, the right hemisphere in the adult has been shown to be capable of processing concrete nouns, as evidenced in matching maneuvers executed with the left hand. However, the right hemisphere is incapable of any expressive communicability, as indicated by the absence of naming in response to commands introduced within the left visual half-field. Correspondingly, left-hand (right hemisphere) Block Design constructions and figure drawings were superior to those of the right hand (left hemisphere).

These characteristic test outcomes after commissurotomy in adults were at variance with comparable results in a 12-year-old boy with a history of seizures dating to age 3. Butler and Norrsell (1968) report that prolonged exposure of the right hemisphere to words presented in the left half-field yielded a naming response from that hemisphere. Restrictive stimulation of that hemisphere was controlled by means of electronic elimination of the stimulus when saccadic eye movements signalled a break in fixation. Assuming that the patient did not fixate beyond the central point in the plane of the field, thereby bringing the verbal stimulus into the right visual half-field and left hemisphere, it was concluded that the patient's right hemisphere could subserve some expressive speech. Presumably, this capability could be derived from bilateral representation of language at earlier ages. Also, early damage to the left hemisphere might be expected to be associated with a developmental reorganization of language function in both hemispheres, such as has been observed in the development of language in (right) infantile hemiplegia (Basser, 1962). Such age-dependent effects point up a potential source of individual differences in the organization of selected functions within each cerebral hemisphere and in the behavioral manifestations of specific interactions between the hemispheres.

Individual differences in cerebral organization of function appear to be related to genetic, racial, and cultural factors. Genetic factors have been implicated in studies of lateral dominance in identical twin pairs and families (Satz, 1968). Although manual preferences and performance asymmetries are examined frequently in clinical test batteries, individual variation in such asymmetries has been incorporated into inferences only arbitrarily, since data bearing on their significance in relation to test outcomes are as yet insufficient for direct application except for a few measures, such as manual preference, speed, and strength where the associations are relatively firm and consistent.

Systematic efforts to examine lateral dominance by means of the dichotic listening method (Broadbent, 1954; Kimura, 1961) have provided a supplementary tool for evaluating such individual differences. Strategies which assess concordance between manual performances and asymmetries in the processing of simultaneously introduced auditory and visual stimuli may yield more valid behaviorally derived estimates of lateral dominance. Such quantitative, multichannel estimates of the relative organization of overlapping stimulus processing systems might have direct implications for future assessment efforts in the prediction of recovery potential and estimation of lesion localization. It is evident that the question of cerebral dominance can no longer be assessed by means of motor function alone and that even family prevalence data might provide a significant input to the multivariate determination of lesion outcomes (Satz, 1970).

Cultural (and perhaps even racial) variables may contribute to the organization of CNS function. Porteus Maze Test performances appear to be affected much less by cerebrovascular infarctions in Japanese than in comparable American stroke patients. Even when matched for lesion laterality, degree of neurological involvement, WAIS Full Scale IQ, age, education, and sex, a Japanese (Kyushu) sample of such patients scored at levels approaching the U.S. norm while the matched U.S. (Minnesota) group scored at levels comparable to those observed acutely after prefrontal lobotomy (Meier & Okayama, 1969; Meier, 1970b). These data suggest that cultural factors may play a particularly strong role in the cerebral representation of cognitive style and the more elusive related changes in behavior following lesion of the so-called "silent" areas of the cortex.

Cephalo-Caudal Axis

Prefrontal area. Functional asymmetry of the prefrontal areas does not seem to be as differentiated as that observed between the posterior association regions of the cerebral cortex. Conflicting findings with respect to the behavioral effects of prefrontal lesions have not resolved the earlier controversies posed by the frontal lobotomy literature (Willett, 1960). Gross quantitative reductions in global intelligence do not appear consistently after lobotomy, topectomy (Mettler, 1949), or unilateral lobectomy (Hebb, 1949; Milner, 1964). Consistent with clinical observation, there is growing evidence, after removal of dorsolateral prefrontal cortex on either side, of a decline in the integrity of purposive, goal-directed behavior involving the execution of serially organized visuomotor behavior. Detailed investigations (Milner, 1964) of the effects of unilateral prefrontal lobectomy introduced to remove an atrophic epileptogenic lesion, have implicated especially the Wisconsin Card Sorting Test (WCST), a task designed to measure flexibility in the strategic application of concepts. Abstract reasoning deficits had been shown earlier to arise from frontal lobe lesions (Grant & Berg, 1948). Among the tests in current application within the clinical test battery framework, the Halstead Category Test, which also taps conceptual behavior, has been reported to be selectively sensitive to frontal lobe involvement (Halstead & Shure, 1954). That the related deficit appears to involve an impaired regulation of sequentially organized motor behavior is reflected in presence of perseveration and conceptual inflexibility in related performances. Such deficits may have contributed to poor Porteus Maze Test performances after prefrontal lobotomy (Porteus, 1959; Smith, 1960).

Another approach to assessing behavioral deficits in frontal lobe disease has been the measurement of visual exploration. Luria (1966) has monitored graphically the rate and direction of active scanning movements during prolonged examination of objects. He reports a lowering of spontaneous visual exploration in selected patients with frontal lobe disease, though his data do not allow conclusions with respect to the effects of unilateral lesions of the lateral convexity on such behavior. A related deficit appeared in a report of reduced speed of visual search in the contralateral field in the absence of impairment of lateral gaze or of visual field defects in patients with unilateral penetrating missile wounds of the frontal lobes (Teuber, Battersby, & Bender, 1949; Teuber, 1964). Field-of-search test procedures (Poppelreuter, 1917) involved the presentation in random array of 48 visual patterns. In response to presentation of one of the patterns in a circular central area, the patient was required to identify the matching pattern in the array with full use of active scanning movements. Application of the Aubert Task to these same patients suggested some prefrontal lobe participation in setting a luminous line to the vertical, particularly under conditions of conflicting visual and postural feedback (Teuber & Mishkin, 1954). Seated in a tilted chair, an upright baseline measure did not differentiate frontal from parietal lesion groups. When the body was tilted in either direction, thus producing a between-modality cue conflict, subjects with frontal lesions made more exaggerated errors in setting the luminous rod from a tilted to an estimated or judged vertical position. By contrast, setting the line to the vertical in the presence of a striped visual background, but without body tilt (within-modality conflict), was done less accurately by parietal lobe group. Others in Teuber's group (Cohen, 1959) have reported unexpected results in a comparison of groups with unilateral versus bilateral frontal involvement on measures of the rate of expressed reversals in a double Necker cube. While the unilateral subgroup communicated (by means of tapping response during reversal monitoring) the fewest number of reversals over a standardized time period, the bilateral group produced the greatest number. Posterior lesion groups fell between the extremes presented by the frontal subgroups. Teuber (1964) suggests that the bilaterals may have less orbital frontal or deeper and more medial involvement. He attempts to explain the scattered and sometimes perplexing results on the basis of disrupted transcortical transmission of motion-produced physiological responses in oculomotor zones of the prefrontal cortex to the posterior receptor fields of the parieto-occipital region. This "corollary discharge" is considered to be involved in a physiological mechanism which presets the posterior cortical fields for receiving the visual inputs subsequent to the oculomotor tracking movements (Bizzi, 1967, 1968; Bizzi & Schiller, 1970). These regulatory mechanisms might generalize to other forms of sensorimotor coordination on the basis of cortical-subcortical interactions, i.e., anatomical relationships along the vertical axis of CNS structure, about which more will be said later.

The subtle and mild nature of the measurable deficits associated with unilateral frontal disease obviously make the localization of such lesions difficult to establish on psychometric grounds alone. The relative difficulty encountered by Reitan (1964b) in lateralizing and localizing anterior cerebral lesions is entirely consistent with the outcomes of unilateral prefrontal ablations in more controlled physiological psychological research in this area. The problem of frontal lobe assessment is compounded by the paucity of lateralized effects resulting from unilateral frontal lesions. Milner's work on the Wisconsin Card Sorting Test, probably the most definitive data available in relation to the effects of unilateral prefrontal involvement, suggests that conceptual inflexibility follows somewhat more consistently after left-sided ablation. Selective impairment of verbal fluency has been observed after dorsolateral prefrontal ablations (Milner, 1964). Similarly, patients with left frontal lesions performed more poorly than those with right frontal lesions on a measure of verbal associative fluency (Borkowski et al., 1967). Patients with right frontal lesions showed greater impairment of three-dimensional constructional performances (Benton & Fogel, 1962; Benton, 1968b), consistent with similar deficits in copying Visual Retention Test patterns (Benton, 1963). However, posterior cerebral lesions produce such deficits as well (Critchley, 1953).

Some of these studies do not include neurosurgical criteria of the location and extent of involvement. When localization criteria are derived from clinical diagnosis, the resulting samples usually consist of cerebrovascular accident and tumor patients. Cerebrovascular accidents are identified by history, relying especially on the sudden onset of hemiparesis and/or language disturbance. If the hemiparesis is not associated with a visual field cut, the lesion is inferred to be located anteriorly. However, this may not be a sufficient basis for concluding that only the frontal lobe is involved. In addition, edematous changes in the acute poststroke period may give rise to more extensive dysfunction. Neoplastic disease presents other complications for building localization criteria, including the well-established secondary or remote effects of a growing tumor. Differential rates of growth among various types of intrinsic cerebral tumors, and the extent of their involvement of brain tissue, are additional variables which complicate if not confound determination of precise localization.

Construction of new tests for prefrontal involvement can only proceed tentatively from the conflicting literature. The most productive area of concentration would appear to involve the utilization of serial visuomotor operations and conceptual flexibility test paradigms. Perhaps the deficits arising from prefrontal lesions cannot be meaningfully understood without reference to possible cortical-subcortical interactions and their disruption (Meier & Story, 1967). An understanding of the anatomical-physiological interactions subserving the motivational component in the impulsive behavior predispositions suggested in the Wisconsin Card Sorting Test performances and in the personality change observed in such patients might yield more efficacious test strategies for eliciting frontal lobe dysfunction.

Anterior temporal region. Recent research into the behavioral effects of unilateral anterior temporal lobectomy suggests that this region is more differentiated in terms of laterality than is the prefrontal area. In turn, the effects of unilateral anterior temporal lobe ablation appear to be relatively more subtle than comparable effects of posterior temporoparietal involvement, at least in patients with static, atrophic lesions. Therefore, chronic and stabilized temporal involvement produces behavioral changes which are clinically inconspicuous, except for the periodic occurrence of psychomotor seizures. Specialized testing procedures, however, have revealed that anterior temporal structures participate in memory, learning, and perceptual processes, with the nature and extent of the deficit depending upon lesion laterality and the particular structures involved. Furthermore, personality disturbances have also been observed with bilateral and deeper lesions of the temporal lobe.

The major impairments arising out of unilateral temporal lobectomy involve acquisition and short-term retention of visual and auditory information. These deficits in learning and memory are material-specific, since systematic differences appear in the effects of left as compared to right temporal lobectomy. Characteristically, impairment of verbal learning and retention occurs after left temporal lobectomy (Meyer & Yates, 1955; Milner & Kimura, 1964). Comparable deficits for nonverbal stimulus materials have been reported after right temporal lobectomy (Corkin, 1965; Milner, 1965). These deficits arise as a function of the stimulus material used and do not appear to be related to the particular sensory channel into which the information is introduced. Although such deficits are present preoperatively in patients selected for temporal lobectomy, presumably as a result of a specific lesion which has produced intractible psychomotor seizures, they increase significantly following temporal lobectomy and may disappear over time.

Perceptual processing of information fed into the two ears (Broadbent, 1954), in which different digits are presented simultaneously, is only mildly impaired after temporal lobe removals (Kimura, 1961). For this reason, the characteristic memory losses resulting from left temporal removals (Milner & Teuber, 1968) appear to transcend immediate memory span and the perception of stimuli. This is also evidenced by the relative insensitivity of span tests to the presence of amnestic disorders such as Korsakoff's syndrome (Talland, 1965). The importance of the time interval between presentation and recall is reflected in the severe retention losses exhibited by patients with temporal removals when testing involved a 1-hour delay between initial oral presentation (Milner, 1964), or visual presentation (Milner, 1968) and subsequent recall of short prose passages.

This deficit appears to be related to the extent and kind of tissue removed. Indications of a functional interaction between the hippocampus and the temporal neocortex are evident (Milner, 1967). Neuropathological correlates of the global amnestic disorder implicate the hippocampus, mamillary bodies, and fornix which lie in the mesial temporal distribution of the posterior cerebral artery (Adams, 1969; Brion, 1969). A broad array of memory testing procedures have been collated from the literature (Barbizet & Cany, 1969; Barbizet, 1970). The usual clinical neuropsychological test battery includes mostly tests of immediate recall for assessing memory functioning. A rich theoretical and empirical basis for specific test applications would appear to warrant expansion of memory test representation in neuropsychological batteries.

Bilateral functional relationships between hippocampus and temporal neocortex may also subserve the transfer of symbolic learning from one hemisphere to the other. Meier and French (1965a) have reported a selective deficit with the right hand, after previous learning with the left hand, of an inverted alphabet printing task after left, as compared with right, temporal lobe ablation. Another mechanism underlying this transfer deficit may be the development of cortical inhibitory effects, accumulated by means of the habituation which develops in repetitive learning tasks (Eysenck, 1955). Such inhibitory effects may dissipate less rapidly in verbal learning after left temporal excisions and in nonverbal learning situations after right temporal lobe excisions. Predispositions to generate increased cortical inhibition within corresponding zones may be introduced if the lesion, for example, interrupts the interrelations between the temporal lobe and the information consolidation and/or storage mechanism of the hippocampus and related structures.

The corresponding impairments for nonverbal materials resulting from right anterior temporal lobectomy relate particularly to complex visual and auditory stimuli (Milner, 1970). The wide range of procedures utilized in previous research provides a ready source of nonverbal materials for developing clinical tests of functions subserved by medial temporal lobe structures. As with verbal short-term memory tests, clinical test batteries do not attempt to sample such functions routinely. These impairments have been elicited with recognition and recall tests and have been shown to involve variously the recognition of irregularly patterned stimuli (Kimura, 1963); recall of faces (Milner, 1968); delayed recognition in nonsense figures (Kimura, 1963); and the progressive learning of both visually or proprioceptively guided stylus mazes (Corkin, 1965; Milner; 1965).

Collectively, these data implicate the medial temporal lobes in the consolidation phase of new learning, but subtle perceptual defects may also contribute significantly to the measured deficits. For example, discrimination of fragmented concentric circular patterns is more impaired after right, as compared to left, temporal lobectomy (Meier & French, 1965a). Moreover, prolonged selective reduction of Picture Arrangement subtest mean scores has been reported after right temporal lobectomy, in the absence of a corresponding decrement on any other WAIS performance subtest (Meier & French, 1966a). Such losses are similar to the visual discrimination deficits produced in monkeys after bilateral excision of the inferior and basal temporal cortex (Chow, 1950; Mishkin & Pribram, 1954) and support the view that the temporal lobes provide an extrastriate focus for visually guided behavior. More recent neurophysiological evidence adds further support to this interpretation (Gross, Bender, & Rocha-Miranda, 1969). The Seashore Tests of Musical Talent (Saetveit, Lewis, & Seashore, 1940) have also been used to identify auditory deficits following right anterior temporal lobectomy. Discrimination of tonal patterns, tone quality or timbre, and tonal memory have been implicated (Milner, 1962). These deficits appear to be relatively permanent and are not contingent upon removal of the primary auditory projection cortex (Milner, 1967).

There is considerable evidence for the participation of the hippocampus in these material-specific memory disorders (Milner, 1970) in right as well as left temporal ablations. In general, more extensive removals of the hippocampus and parahippocampal gyrus have been associated with accentuated impairment of stylus maze learning (Corkin, 1965; Milner, 1965), and subsequent recognition of unfamiliar photographed faces (Milner, 1968). By contrast, no relationship has been found between extent of hippocampal removal and memory for nonsense figures or complex designs (Milner, 1970).

The McGill group has been applying an assortment of memory tasks in search of neocortical hippocampal effects in short-term retention. Procedures derived from techniques developed in experimental psychology (Peterson & Peterson, 1959) involve recall of verbal trigrams after a short interval of interpolated activity (counting backwards) to prevent rehearsal. Corsi (1969) has shown that extent of left hippocampal destruction is related to impairment on this task. Similarly, Crosi is obtaining right hippocampal effects in the visual localization of position after an interval of distracting activity between stimulus presentation and recall (Milner, 1970). The more profound effects of bilateral hippocampal involvement have been carefully studied and reported (Milner, 1967, 1970).

Evidence for the development of more severe behavioral disburbances with bilateral temporal lobe involvement can be derived from studies of personality change associated with focal lesions and ablations. Interactions between vertically organized anatomical and physiological systems of the central nervous system have been recognized to be of fundamental significance to emotional and motivational patterns of behavior in animals (Klüver & Bucy, 1938; Bard & Mountcastle, 1948; MacLean & Delgado, 1953; Brady, 1958; Olds, 1958; Ruch, 1961). It has become apparent that efferent projections from the hippocampus and cingulate cortex lead to the midbrain reticular formation. In turn, reciprocal interconnections exist between the midbrain and the nonspecific intralaminar nuclei of the thalamus (Johnson, 1953). These nuclei have been shown to inter-act anatomically with limbic system structures in both ascending and descending manner (Nauta, 1953, 1956) and, along with the midbrain reticular formation, project to the neocortex (Morison & Dempsey, 1942; Moruzzi & Magoun, 1949). The limbic system, in addition to the temporal pole and deeper subcortical structures, includes portions of the frontal lobe, specifically the orbital frontal surface and the cingulate cortex (Ramón y Cajal, 1909; Lorente de Nó, 1934). This system therefore includes both frontal and temporal lobe components, including the hippocampus, amygdala, and insula, to form a vertically organized system. Relationships within these structures are maintained through the uncinate fasciculus (Kendrick & Gibbs, 1958).

As has been noted elsewhere in this paper, the usual horizontal model and the somewhat arbitrary zonal topography used by clinical neuropsychologists in criterion development are not sufficiently comprehensive to accommodate the known organization of the central nervous system. This is rather pointedly evident in the frontal and temporal lobe literature cited above and becomes even clearer when personality changes in central nervous system disease are considered. In this context there is some indirect evidence that personality disturbances, as measured by the Minnesota Multiphasic Personality Inventory (MMPI), develop with combined involvement of the temporal neocortex and limbic system (Meier & French, 1964; 1965b; Meier, 1969). Bilateral EEG abnormalities, especially bitemporal EEG spike foci, are associated with greater MMPI elevations on the schizoadaptive (Pa, Sc) and affective disorder scales (D, Ma), than are unilateral EEG abnormalities in patients with temporal lobe lesions. MMPI Scale configurations suggest the presence of anxiety, depression, guilt feelings, social withdrawal, feelings of alienation and isolation, somatic concern, and schizophreniclike ideational disturbances in such patients. These manifestations contrast with indications of anxiety-reduction, blandness of affect, and a hysteroid outlook suggested in profiles of patients with frontal lobe disease (Friedman, 1950; Williams, 1952; Willett, 1960). These findings imply that intrinsic pathophysiological variables affecting limbic system function can contribute to personality disturbances. This conclusion is supported amply by the observed effects of thalamic and limbic system stimulation in man (Ervin, Mark, & Stevens, 1969). Stimulation effects in the nonspecific intralaminar thalamic nuclei (dismay and aversion), the anterior hypothalamus (relaxation), and particularly the amygdala (variable and sometimes profound affective changes) bear a strong resemblance to the inferred correlates of these MMPI profiles. Bilateral hippocampal stimulation produces total amnesia for coincident events, while unilateral stimulation can produce lesser memory defects and sometimes dysphoric and hallucinatory subjective content.

Obviously, additional investigations with objective personality tests might yield related manifestations of deeper temporal lobe involvement. Since many extrinsic factors can contribute to personality changes, the application of such measures will necessarily be indirect in the assessment of temporal lobe involvement. They might also provide a link in the establishment of more effective approaches for detecting frontal lobe lesions and their subtle behavioral effects. This conclusion is also related to the apparent alterations in cognitive *style* implied in the impaired performances on the Wisconsin Card Sorting Test in Milner's patients, combined with the known effects of frontothalamic disconnections on personality functioning; namely, increases in judgmental lapses and impulsivity and decreases in anxiety and internal discomfort. Test strategies designed to measure cognitive abilities to the exclusion of cognitive style may continue to fall short of detecting the subtle and elusive reductions in adaptive functioning associated with "silent" area lesions.

Temporo-parieto-occipital juncture. The more sharply lateralized and clinically conspicuous behavioral disturbances associated with involvement of the posterior association cortex have been thoroughly documented in the voluminous clinical and experimental literature. These definitive deficits probably account for the relative success of screening procedures in detecting and lateralizing lesions in this area. Profound and prolonged verbal intellectual and paraphasic speech impairments occur with involvement of the posterior portion of the superior temporal gyrus (Wernicke's area), and the supramarginal and angular gyri (inferior parietal lobule) of the left cerebral hemisphere (Critchley, 1953; Geschwind, 1965). There is evidence that the anatomical complexity of the rich crossmodal connections of this region is greater in the dominant cerebral hemisphere (Geschwind & Levitsky, 1968). Equally profound, though perhaps less dramatic in their overt manifestations, are deficits in visuo-constructive and visuospatial abilities which arise with involvement of the corresponding cortical zone in the right or nondominant cerebral hemisphere.

The various etiological contributing conditions frequently produce significant somatosensory, motor, inattention, and suppression phenomena, so that a broad array of impaired functions has become amenable to analysis. These have been incorporated into empirically robust screening procedures whose application (beyond a simple lateralization criterion) requires knowledge of the classical neurological literature.

In addition to the more sophisticated descriptions and inferences regarding lesion localization such knowledge would yield for the individual clinician, more rational strategies for building quantitative methods can be expected to emerge. Indeed, attempts to integrate the qualitative classifications of clinical description and the quantitative rigor of the neuropsychological testing approach have provided new test designs and knowledge with respect to the measurement of deficits resulting from posterior lesions (e.g., Arrigoni & DeRenzi, 1964; DeRenzi & Faglioni, 1965, 1967; DeRenzi, Pieczuro, & Vignolo, 1966, 1968; Costa, Vaughan, Horwitz, & Ritter, 1969). Recent applications involving the measurement of binocular depth perception by means of random-dot stereograms (Julesz, 1964) suggest that right posterior lesions produce extensive *selective* impairment of stereopsis (Carmon & Bechtoldt, 1969; Benton & Hécaen, 1970). Methods for evaluating the varied disorders of perception which arise with posterior cerebral disease can be made to meet the shorter time requirements of screening procedures. These can be supplemented with use of visuomotor and drawing tasks (Warrington, James, & Kinsbourne, 1966). Contralateral adaptation to televised reversal and inversion of visual feedback was impaired maximally in the parietal lobe subgroup of our series (Meier, 1970a). Similarly, Butters and Barton (1970) reported that involvement of the right or left parietal lobes was associated selectively with impairments on tasks requiring the performance of reversible operations in space.

A separate volume could be devoted to a detailed account of the many methods of potential clinical use now available in the general neuropsychological literature for selective enrichment of clinical batteries in the context of lateralized posterior cerebral involvement. Future methodological refinements might well incorporate growing knowledge of interhemispheric interactions elucidated by the split-brain work cited above and related conceptual formulations involving reciprocal interhemispheric inhibitory effects during selective attention to verbal or nonverbal stimuli (Kinsbourne, 1969). These recent efforts might well provide conceptual models of cortical-subcortical as well as interhemispheric interactions bearing on the organization of function in the posterior regions.

Nevertheless, standardized and validated tests for evaluating the behavioral effects of prefrontal and anterior temporal lobe lesions are perhaps more urgently needed since lesions in these areas produce relatively subtle changes. Furthermore, recovery from the more severe language and visuospatial impairments associated with nonprogressive posterior lesions might well depend upon the integrity of the more "silent" cortical zones and the amount of residually intact tissue surrounding such lesions. If valid, such an expectancy would require a more integrated conceptual approach to longitudinal assessment than has been characteristic of previous clinical neuropsychological preoccupation with the localization issue.

LONGITUDINAL APPLICATIONS

While previous research has contributed heavily to knowledge of higher cortical functions subserved by association cortex, the longitudinal course or restitution of higher cortical function in focal lesions and the predictability of recovery changes should be examined. In previous ablation research, lesions were introduced in areas which produced epileptogenic disturbances on a chronic basis, usually as a result of injury sustained early in life, before higher cortical functions have achieved their genetically and developmentally preferred modes of organization. The ablations, therefore, did not involve removal of normal or recently involved cortical regions. Such lobectomized focal epileptic samples may not be the most suitable for investigation of the natural course of neurological and psychological recovery after acute cerebral involvement. Naturally occurring lesions in patients with acute cerebral infarction due to cerebrovascular occlusion may provide more appropriate baseline data for monitoring the longitudinal course of recovery, particularly if this baseline can be established early in the recovery period, before spontaneous changes have arisen (Meier, 1970b).

Evaluation of individual differences in outcome over time will require: (*a*) more precise operational criteria for identifying clinical populations, and (*b*) the introduction of longitudinal assessment strategies. The latter are also needed to identify and replicate patterns of neuropsychological deficit and recovery of higher cortical functions in selected neurological groups. The resulting prognostic estimations might help delineate the boundary conditions within which behavioral modification and rehabilitation procedures can be introduced. Intervention strategies could then be designed systematically in order to accelerate spontaneous recovery changes. (While intervention research appropriately might be introduced here, this subject extends beyond the purposes of this paper. Furthermore, substantive treatment of rehabilitation approaches are given elsewhere (Darley, 1970; Diller, 1970).)

Pluripotentiality of the neural reserve in the regional localization framework is assumed to provide the anatomical and physiological basis for subsequent recovery. Since the location and extent of intact cortical tissue can be inferred from the assessment of function, it is hypothesized that a careful sampling of a hierarchy of adaptive capacities, as measured by neuropsychological tests, may provide an empirical basis for predicting recovery. The limiting conditions within which such recovery will occur are likely to involve a multivariate group of determinants including such factors as the specific etiology, location, and size of lesion; premorbid cerebral status; areas of intact association cortex; presence of bilateral cerebral changes; and age at onset.

The restoration of function is likely to be related to individual variation in two kinds of recovery (Luria, 1963; Rosner, 1970).

1. Restitution or reestablishment: The functioning of a structurally intact region of the cortex may be disorganized on the basis of disruptive effects arising from more remote sources. Among such sources can be included widespread biochemical and edematous changes associated with an acute cerebral lesion. In addition, direct physiological effects from an adjacent (or more remote) anatomically linked area of involvement can reversibly interrupt or disrupt the functioning of an intact area. Under some etiological circumstances, such as acute cerebrovascular infarction, these effects may dissipate at variable rates, depending upon the function being examined, and result even in complete restitution or reestablishment of function. Under other conditions, such as the emergence of a malignant neoplasm, these effects can increase progressively and, thereby, mask potential functional levels of a related but structurally intact region. As such lesions progress, of course, they may envelop previously uninvolved regions. Restitution is then no longer at issue and any subsequent recovery is dependent upon the availability of some neural reserve whose functions can be modified, by the presence of a latent capacity to subserve the impaired functions. Enlistment of such a neural reserve in retraining involves a process of reorganization. This process may affect in varying degree the areas of primary involvement and any interrelated regions, either adjacent or remote.

2. Reorganization: Even with direct involvement of a cortical zone, interrelated regions which are partly or wholly intact may assume the affected function at near-normal levels or in somewhat modified form. This would represent redundant representation of a psychological capacity in an

incompletely destroyed cortical zone. In the more extreme instance, an area which might otherwise participate minimally becomes involved, through retraining and/or experience, in the multiple control of remote damaged areas. Neural configurations participating in such reorganization would be expected to include bilaterally paired centers at the level of the cerebral hemispheres, areas which influence a common pathway, and zonal interactions which introduce the capabilities of adjacent or even remote areas of association cortex.

A sufficiently broad neuropsychological test battery should provide measures which are sensitive to individual variation in these limiting conditions and objectively document the changes themselves. Resulting test batteries could include predictor and outcome measures. A predictor battery would be derived from investigation of empirical relationships between these tests and outcome measures. In addition, correlations between tests within the battery may provide an account of the functional hierarchy across sensorimotor, perceptual, cognitive, and language functions as neuropsychological recovery changes occur in varying order of progressive return.

We have embarked on an extended investigation of neurological and behavioral recovery during the acute and subacute phases of cerebrovascular occlusions and associated cerebral infarction. Our early efforts were directed at the isolation of objective neuropsychological test predictors of subsequent neurological change, as rated from comparisons of repeated neurological examinations before and after a 14-day evaluation period during the first month after symptom onset. The resulting tests were then applied to predict subsequent neurological change along a three-point scale after 1 year. The resulting followup study, reported in detail elsewhere (Meier, 1970b), yielded a predictability of overall outcome at about 75%. However, the neurological outcome rating, although acceptably reliable, reflected global changes where specific patterns of change involving sensorimotor, perceptual, language, and visuospatial functions were obviously occurring. Encouraged by this general linear relationship between selected neuropsychological test variables and rated outcome, we have continued this investigation by introducing initial behavioral evaluations earlier and by reassessing a wide range of higher cortical functions at 30, 60, and 180 days after symptom onset. Of the approximately 25 patients followed with this more-intensive approach, the general predictive efficiency of the earlier efforts is being maintained at 70–75%. Of even greater interest, perhaps, are the emerging *patterns* of behavioral changes observed over time. A few protocols will serve to illustrate the inferred interactions between extent of involvement and capacity for re-representation or multiple control of impaired functions.

These patterns of change often reflect differing rates of recovery for different behavioral functions. A large number of patients will need to be evaluated longitudinally before multivariate statistical analyses can be done. The complexity of the inferred relationships between neuropathological variables and the ultimate degree of rerepresentation or recovery of function achieved can be illustrated by means of selected test battery protocols. Before examining some of these data, distinctions between current "predictor" and an "outcome" battery should be made.

Predictor Battery

This sub-battery consists of tests which were shown to yield significant correlations with global ratings of neurological recovery changes after acute cerebral infarction (Meier & Resch, 1967). Since these correlations were still present after a 1-year followup period, the battery would appear to have some potential application in outcome prediction. The tests in this sub-battery consist of the Porteus Maze Test (Porteus, 1959), a modification of the Trail Making Test (Reitan, 1958b), the Seguin-Goddard Formboard which represents a procedural modification of the Halstead Tactual Performance Test, and the Visual Space Rotation Test (Meier & French, 1966b). The principal modifications of procedure include administration of the Trail Making Test through use of demonstration, and visually guided practice before the "blindfolded" performance of the Tactual Performance Test. A priori, this battery is expected to be sensitive to the extent of residually intact association cortex and to the presence of bilateral cerebral dysfunction, largely on the basis of the known sensitivity to cerebral dysfunction of some of these tests. These kinds of validity should favor the potential utility of this sub-battery for predicting to objective outcome criteria.

Outcome Criteria Battery

This battery was devised to provide objective measures of behavioral outcome across a broad range of functions. Some of these measures will probably turn out to have predictive validity as well, to the extent that they may be sensitive to the underlying neuropathological and pathophysiological determinants which favor or disfavor positive outcomes. This battery can be subdivided in terms of the level of function being assessed. For purposes of discussion, emphasis will be placed upon sensorimotor tests. However, some measures of cognition will also be included.

1. Abbreviated Wechsler Adult Intelligence Scale (WAIS): Age-corrected subtest scores can be selectively combined to yield factor scores with maximal loadings on the primary intellectual functions measured by this well-known test (Tellegen & Briggs, 1967). Comprehension and Vocabulary scores can be combined to measure the Verbal Comprehension factor (Verbal Deviation Quotient or VDQ), while the Block Design and Object Assembly subtests form the empirical basis for quantifying a Perceptual Organization factor (Perceptual Deviation Quotient or PDQ). Testing time is proportionately reduced without effect on the validity of these quotients for lateralizing focal cerebral lesions (Meier, 1970a). VDQ should undergo longitudinal changes as a function of improved language function. PDQ, a quantitative measure of constructional

ability, may well improve dramatically in patients identified by the predictors as having relatively smaller lesions in the nondominant cerebral hemisphere. The PDQ, of course, is reduced by lesions of the nondominant cerebral hemisphere so that frequently observed PDQ reductions in left hemisphere disease may also reflect transient, reciprocal, inhibitory effects of the dominant (onto the nondominant) cerebral hemisphere (Kinsbourne, 1969).

2. Aphasia Screening Test (AST) (Wheeler & Reitan, 1962): For the present discussion, a simple tabulation of the error count for the 32 items was made. An error was defined as any incomplete or distorted response. No effort was made to separate verbal from nonverbal items.

3. Dynamometer: A dynamometer calibrated in kilograms of force is used for measuring maximal hand grip strength for each hand taken from the best of two alternating trials.

4. Grooved Pegboard Test: The patient is required to place 25 small identically keyed pegs into a set of randomly oriented openings with each hand separately and a performance time is recorded for each hand.

5. Index Finger Tapping: Utilizing a standard key-driven counter (Halstead, 1947) tapping speed of the right and left index fingers is measured.

6. Ballistic Arm Tapping (Meier, Story, French, & Chou, 1966): Patient taps each end of a 24-in. board with a stylus with the board lying perpendicular to the axis of the patient's body and a speed score is obtained for each arm.

7. Modified Tactual Formboard Test: The well-known formboard, used by Halstead, yielded measures of predictive utility in the pilot phase of these investigations. It is included here to illustrate how a test can be used as an outcome measure as well. Blindfolded testing was preceded by a direct confrontation placement procedure, unlike Halstead's procedure in which the subject is begun blind. Preliminary results (unpublished) suggest that the validity of this modification for lateralizing cerebral lesions is not affected significantly.

As a preliminary step in predictor test validation, the sub-battery which correlated with neurological ratings of change is of particular interest. Since these ratings were based primarily on indications of objective neurological changes, the predictor battery should be related to the sensorimotor outcome measures above. An additional preliminary question would involve the relative capability of the same battery to predict subsequent WAIS and AST changes, for example. An outline of the neurological outcome criteria, specific test predictor signs, and predictions of the initial study is given in Table 2.

The notations ±, +, and ++ are used to denote neurological outcomes in the initial study, in order of degree of functional recovery. Test signs (pass-fail) are based on error scores for each part of the Trails and performance of the hand ipsilateral to the lesion on the modified formboard. The three testing conditions of the Visual Field Rotation (90°, 180°, 270°) are also treated in terms of a Pass-Fail score, but one failure (300 sec. time limit) is allowed (i.e., two of three (2/3) are sufficient to yield a "pass" sign). Application of these signs then

TABLE 2

Neurological Outcome Ratings, Individual Predictor Test
Signs, and Outcome Prediction Criteria

Neurological outcome ratings		
± No definite neurological recovery		
+ Significant improvement, major residuals		
++ Considerable improvement, minor residuals		

Individual test signs	Pass	Fail
Trails A (Errors)	0	≥ 1
Trails B (Errors)	0	≥ 1
Formboard (#) (Ipsilateral hand)	10	< 10
Visual Field Rotation (90°, 180°, 270°)	2/3	0 or 1/3
Porteus Test Age	Quantitative	

Outcome predictions (2/3 signs)		
(±)		
Porteus TA < 6		
Fail Trails A *and* B		
Fail Formboard		
(+)		
Porteus TA 6–8		
Pass Trails A *or* B		
Pass Formboard		
(++)		
Porteus TA > 8		
Pass Trails B *and* Formboard		
Pass Visual Space Rotation		

follows actuarial specifications, derived empirically as previously described. These are listed under the prediction which conformed most frequently to the test signs listed. If a given patient's performances fulfill two of the three signs under a prediction he would be so classified for subsequent cross validation of the original series.

For this discussion, such predictions are generated merely to illustrate some of the relationships between expectancies based on these predictions and subsequent test battery performance changes. This is designed to make an examination of representative patient protocols more meaningful and, hopefully, bring some of the difficulties in this area of research into focus. Protocols were selected on the basis of the presence of a severe hemiparesis on admission and fulfillment of the criteria for cerebrovascular accident (Loewenson, 1969). Although emphasis here is placed on the recovery of sensorimotor functions, some mention will be made of language and intellectual changes as well.

Table 3 shows the predictor and outcome data for a 72-year-old male who was tested on Day 1 following admission and again at approximately Days 30 and 180. He presented with a dense right hemiparesis and clinically conspicuous

TABLE 3

Comparison of Prediction and Outcome in a Patient with (±) Negative
Outcome Test Characteristics at Admission

Predictor	Yield	Prediction
Porteus Test Age: 3	±	
Trails A & B: Pass, Fail	+	
Formboard: Fail	±	±
Trails B & Formboard: Fail, Fail	±	
Visual Field Rotation: Fail, Fail, Fail	±	

Outcomes	Day				
	1	5	10	30	180
WAIS VDQ	115			109	112
WAIS PDQ	65			83	72
Aphasia (AST)–Errors	12			2	6
Dynamometer (kg.)					
Right	0			3	6
Left	23			32	26
Grooved Pegboard–Time (#)					
Right	300 (0)			300 (0)	
Left	300 (12)			176 (25)	
Finger Tapping–#					
Right	0			3	3
Left	26			33	24
Ballistic Tapping–#					
Right	0			0	0
Left	29			46	44
Formboard–Time (#)					
Right	300 (0)			300 (0)	300 (0)
Left	300 (0)			300 (1)	300 (1)

language disturbance. Initial predictor test findings consistently yielded ± outcome signs. Examination of the outcome measures reveals persisting severe contralateral impairments on the motor measures as would be predicted. The remarkably high VDQ and paradoxically low PDQ are noteworthy for a left cerebrovascular infarction. The poor visuoconstructional abilities suggested by these data may have been due to severe motor apraxia with relatively mild losses of verbal comprehension. Such behavioral characteristics are often found in conduction aphasias, for example (Geschwind, 1965). Comprehensive cognitive assessment here should include complete language evaluation. Although the reduction in AST error score simply totals the verbal *and* constructional errors, it probably reflects some improvement in language function over time.

In most of the protocols of left cerebral hemisphere involvement in which outcome predictions were derived to date, the extent of language and general intellectual impairment is much greater than is seen here. Atypical cerebral organization of function may have been present premorbidly, perhaps in relation to reversed cerebral dominance. Estimation of premorbid cerebral dominance from motor testing is difficult in the presence of severe motor impairments contralateral to the hemisphere of primary involvement. For lesions lying outside the temporal lobe or deeper white matter lesions, dichotic listening evaluations might contribute to additional understanding of the relative premorbid participation of the two hemispheres in language processing. Relevant familial history for handedness should be included in these evaluations. Self-report of right handedness was confirmed by other informants in this instance, but any discordance between such report and measures of cerebral dominance derived from dichotic listening studies might reveal the presence of higher order interactions or suppression variables in predicting patterns of outcomes in individual patients. Specific laterality effects, of course, would need to be taken into account in the interpretation of dichotic listening data.

An example of a (+) prediction and associated outcomes can be found in Table 4.

Clinical findings for this 86-year-old female were consistent with a cerebrovascular accident in the distribution of the right middle cerebral artery, including a dense left hemiparesis. Predictor battery test results yielded two + level characteristics: a Test Age of 7 on the Porteus and errorless performance on Trails A. Examination of the motor data reveals some return of motor function at 30 and 180 days, particularly for the proximal movements measured by ballistic arm tapping. A small infarct deep in the white matter of the frontal lobe might account for this recovery pattern. The expected VDQ-PDQ discrepancy did not appear, again reflective of a deeper lesion, perhaps one that spared the cortical mantle. The most clearcut indication of motor changes appeared on the grooved pegboard, suggesting that fine manipulative skills recovered relatively more than hand grip strength and index fingertapping speed. This outcome could again reflect the considerable sparing of cortical tissue suggested in the intellectual data.

TABLE 4

Comparison of Prediction and Outcome in a Patient with (+) Intermediate
Outcome Characteristics at Admission

Predictor	Yield	Prediction
Porteus Test Age: 7	+	
Trails A & B: Pass, Fail	+	+
Formboard: Fail	±	
Trails B & Formboard: Fail, Fail	±	
Visual Field Rotation: Fail, Fail, Fail	±	

Outcomes	Day				
	1	5	10	30	180
WAIS VDQ	89			88	85
WAIS PDQ	105			103	100
Aphasia (AST)–Errors	4			4	3
Dynamometer (kg.)					
Right	17			21	19
Left	0			5	9
Grooved Pegboard–Time (#)					
Right	102 (25)			96 (25)	126 (25)
Left	300 (0)			300 (6)	218 (25)
Finger Tapping–#					
Right	36			36	28
Left	0			8	6
Ballistic Tapping–#					
Right	66			69	54
Left	0			37	42
Formboard–Time (#)					
Right	300 (8)			300 (5)	300 (5)
Left	300 (0)			300 (3)	300 (2)

Even this superficial examination of longitudinal changes begins to reveal the
rich variety of recovery patterns resulting from cerebrovascular infarctions. A
favorable (++) outcome protocol is shown in Table 5. Positive Day 1
performance levels appeared on three relevant ++ outcome predictors: a Test
Age of 14.5 on the Porteus and completion of the drawings with the ipsilateral
hand within the time limits on at least two of the three rotation conditions of the
Visual Space Rotation Test (all three in this instance). Clinical picture of this

62-year-old male involved a dense left hemiparesis of abrupt onset, again consistent with right hemisphere infarction.

Outcome test data at each of five periods, including three assessments during the first 10 days after symptom onset, were obtained. Excellent subsequent recovery of motor functions was observed over the 180-day period on all

TABLE 5

Comparison of Prediction and Outcomes in a Patient with (++) Good Recovery Test Characteristics at Admission

Predictor	Yield	Prediction
Porteus Test Age: 14.5	++	
Trails A & B: Pass, Fail	+	
Formboard: Pass	+	++
Trails B and Formboard: Fail, Pass	+	
Visual Field Rotation: Pass, Pass, Pass	++	

Outcomes	Day				
	1	5	10	30	180
WAIS VDQ	97	97	103	94	100
WAIS PDQ	95	111	116	111	125
Aphasia (AST)— Errors	4	5	1	1	1
Dynamometer (kg.)					
Right	33	29	34	31	38
Left	0	0	9	23	28
Grooved Peg- board—Time (#)					
Right	82 (25)	78 (25)	90 (25)	75 (25)	65 (25)
Left	0	0	300 (3)	100 (25)	90 (25)
Finger Tapping—#					
Right	24	21	25	23	34
Left	0	0	9	22	29
Ballistic Tapping—#					
Right	63	57	65	56	70
Left	0	17	31	49	63
Formboard— Time (#)					
Right	173 (10)	90 (10)	138 (10)	155 (10)	128 (10)
Left	300 (0)	300 (0)	300 (1)	213 (10)	267 (10)

TABLE 6

Comparison of Prediction and Outcomes in a Patient with (++) Good
Recovery Test Characteristics at Admission

Predictor	Yield	Prediction
Porteus Test Age: 13	++	
Trails A & B: Pass, Fail	+	
Formboard: Fail	±	++
Trails B & Formboard: Fail, Fail	±	
Visual Field Rotation: Pass, Pass, Pass	++	

Outcomes	Day				
	1	5	10	30	180
WAIS VDQ	75	75	72	61	100
WAIS PDQ	84	75	84	97	114
Aphasia (AST)–					
Errors	14	10	14	7	4
Dynamometer (kg.)					
Right	0	0	0	0	0
Left	16	20	19	23	24
Grooved Peg-					
board–Time (#)					
Right	300 (0)	300 (0)	300 (0)	300 (0)	300 (0)
Left	152 (25)	152 (25)	110 (25)	80 (25)	77 (25)
Finger Tapping–#					
Right	0	0	0	0	0
Left	18	18	17	18	31
Ballistic Tapping–#					
Right	0	0	0	0	0
Left	35	38	37	51	63
Formboard–					
Time (#)					
Right	300 (0)	300 (0)	300 (0)	300 (0)	300 (0)
Left	300 (4)	300 (4)	300 (6)	300 (5)	288 (10)

outcome tests. Performances approached age-equivalent norms (not shown here)
for these measures, but clearly some mild selective left-sided asymmetries of
performance were suggested on most measures (other than Ballistic Tapping).
The latter measure was the first to undergo recovery changes (Day 5). The
remaining motor test outcomes exhibited only a brief lag in recovery when

substantial changes appeared on Day 10. The greatest recovery lag appeared to involve Grooved Pegboard and Formboard performances. These functions may require the participation of larger areas of association cortex than do the other motor tests.

A possible relationship between recovery lag (where recovery can occur at all) and elaboration of organization in the cerebral cortex is reflected in the predictor and outcome data obtained from a 61-year-old female who presented with a dense right hemiparesis and aphasia of sudden onset, due to a cerebrovascular infarct in the left cerebral hemisphere (Table 6). The ++ outcome prediction was based on the combined criterion of high Porteus level and Visual Space Rotation adaptability. However, the predicted contralateral motor changes did not appear across the entire 180-day followup period. Selectively greater reduction of the WAIS VDQ on admission was consistent with left cerebral hemisphere involvement, but the other WAIS measures suggested generalized intellectual impairment. Of particular interest was the *increase* in PDQ at Day 30, without corresponding increase in VDQ. Meanwhile, the Aphasia Screening Test error level dropped at Day 30, as compared with Day 10. By Day 180, the VDQ increased from 61 to 100. WAIS PDQ also continued to increase. Four AST errors, combined with the WAIS changes suggested considerable recovery of language and cognitive functioning. Recovery lags for these functions were greater than observed for motor performances in the previous patient whose test results were shown in Table 5.

It remains to account for the absence of motor recovery in this patient. End-artery occulsions which affect the blood supply to the internal capsule might produce a permanent hemiplegia and initial reduction in cognitive functions subserved by the involved hemisphere. The cognitive alterations would be expected to resolve with time since the cortical mantle can be minimally involved in such instances. The cognitive recovery rate following cortical lesion might be slower than the corresponding motor recovery rate in a comparable lesion of the cortical mantle which produces a similar immediate outcome pattern consisting of a dense hemiparesis and residual behavioral levels meeting (++) predictor test requirements.

It should be obvious that these illustrations provided only tentative, fragmentary, and isolated clues regarding re-representation and hierarchical return of function. Development of valid test strategies for monitoring and predicting the nature and extent of recovery changes should be an interesting challenge to clinical neuropsychology. Selection of the functional domain and specific methods for new test construction, might be guided by the converging interdisciplinary developments of behavioral neurology and human physiological psychology. Assimilation of the theoretical and methodological sophistication of these expanding areas of scientific effort into the research style of clinical neuropsychology may provide the major impetus for future growth.

12
CURRENT STATUS OF CLINICAL NEUROPSYCHOLOGY[1]

Leslie A. Davison

The practical problems which generate activity in clinical neuropsychology were described in some detail in the first chapter of this volume. Briefly, they are (*a*) Differentiation among diagnostic possibilities, given a particular presenting problem; and (*b*) specification of patterns of adaptive deficits and abilities in order that rational behavioral management, disposition, and treatment may be instituted, so that the outcomes of treatments or the natural progression of pathological conditions may be evaluated, and so that a basis for compensation can be established. We have chosen to divide the content of clinical neuropsychology into child clinical neuropsychology and adult clinical neuropsychology. The state of development in these two domains differs considerably, much more currently being known about adults than children in this respect (Benton, Ch. 3 and Reitan, Ch. 4, in this volume). We will now attempt to appraise the status of each of these domains in the light of the data presented in this volume and in relation to the two basic practical problems confronting the field.

CHILD CLINICAL NEUROPSYCHOLOGY

Reitan (this volume, Ch. 2) notes that the clinical tasks in which we are interested demand the production of knowledge relevant to the understanding of individual cases. Only with great difficulty, imprecision, and enormous margin of error can most of the data of psychology, which is cast in general terms, be

[1] I am indebted to Ralph M. Reitan for the many helpful suggestions he made when I wrote this chapter.

applied to individual cases. If one takes seriously the need to produce neuropsychological data useful for clinical tasks, the first step, Reitan notes, is to "formulate some kind of statement of an adequate set of psychological measurements (test battery) to reflect the behavioral correlates of brain functions [ibid., p. 21]."

In the domain of child clinical neuropsychology we are clearly in the midst of developing such a battery or batteries of measures. The careful reader will have noted that the batteries used in the different studies of children reported in this volume, while possessing considerable overlap in terms of variables used, differ not only as a function of the age level of the children studied, but also as a function of the investigator. In some cases the same test may be used by two or more investigators, but each will focus on a somewhat different set of variables generated by the test. For example, compare the list of variables reported by Reitan for his sample of children under 9 (this volume, Ch. 4), and those reported by Klonoff and Low for their younger children (this volume, Ch. 6). Reference to Table 1, prepared primarily for a different purpose, will facilitate comparison of the children's studies reported in this volume with respect to variables used. A blank in the intersect of a column defined by an investigator's name and a row defined by the name of a variable indicates that that variable was not reported by that investigator, while a numerical entry in the intersect means that the variable was reported by that investigator. In some cases the variation reflects data collection at different points in time. For example, when the data reported by Boll (this volume, Ch. 5) for himself and for Reed, Reitan, and Klove (1965), were collected a number of tests reported by Reitan and by Klonoff and Low in this volume were not yet in general use. The differences in variables reported primarily reflect the developing state of this field.

Despite this variation, the data from these studies present an opportunity for evaluating which of the variables reported show most power as discriminators of groups of brain-damaged from groups of matched control children. We may also be able to ascertain whether the classifications of the subjects, younger (< 9) versus older ($\geqslant 9$) and chronic versus acute are related to the discriminating power of the variables. One way of comparing the discriminating power of variables across studies is to rank the variables in each study according to the values of the t tests, or other statistics, reflecting separation of brain-damaged from normal control groups. Reitan (this volume, Ch. 4) ranked his variables in this fashion, and Boll (this volume, Ch. 5) did the same, both for his own data and those of Reed et al. (1965). Table 1 recapitulates these rankings and also shows the ranking of the variables used by Klonoff and Low (this volume, Ch. 6) derived from their tables comparing the test behavior of their Acute and Chronic brain-damaged groups with matched controls. Data on their minimal cerebral dysfunctional groups were not tabled since the purpose of summarizing these various studies is here limited to evaluation of these variables with diagnosed brain damage. The numerical values in the table are percentile ranks reflecting the relative power of each variable in each study. The larger the percentile rank, the larger was the separation of brain-damaged from control children by that variable in that study. The first column under a study heading ranks all variables used in that study while the second column shows the ranking of the 19 variables used in every one of these studies, compared only with each other. The column on the far right shows the mean percentile rankings of the variables across studies.

Before discussing what this table shows, some limitations of these data must be emphasized. As Reitan (this volume, Ch. 4) has cautioned, the conclusion that one variable is is more or less sensitive than one adjacent to it in such rankings is not justified due to sampling error affecting the magnitude of the t ratios on which the rankings are based. On the other hand, substantial differences in percentile ranks probably do reflect reliable differences in sensitivity. Another caution has to do with the fact that other methods of comparing the sensitivities of the variables might produce somewhat different results. Both Reitan (this volume, Ch. 4) and Boll (this volume, Ch. 5) also compared some of their variables or groups of variables by methods which permit direct comparisons of the discriminating power of variables. With Boll's data it is possible to compare the relative ranking of four of his tests according to their t ratios separating brain-damaged from controls with their relative rankings generated by this different direct comparison. They are not identical; in the first case the relative rankings are (a) Block Design, (b) Seashore Rhythm, (c) Category Test, (d) Tactile Form Recognition, while in the second case they are: (a) Category Test, (b) Block Design, (c) Seashore Rhythm, and (d) Tactile Form Recognition. Another caution has to do with the fact that what are listed in this table as the same variables for different studies are in fact merely *similar* variables. The Wechsler Bellevue, Form I was the intelligence test used in the studies reported by Boll, while Reitan, and Klonoff and Low reported results using the Wechsler Intelligence Scale for Children. Even with the same test, different investigators sometimes reported different variables. Boll, for example, reported IQs while Reed's group reported sums of weighted scores. Variables other than IQ measures, though subsumed under the same name, sometimes also differ somewhat from one study to another. Where these variables seemed comparable, despite some differences, they were included in the table as the same variable, however, in cases of the same test producing incomparable variables these were listed separately. Such differences across studies should tend to reduce consistency in the findings so that the consistencies observed are likely to be even more stable under conditions of more standardized measurement.

Another caution has to do with varying levels of certainty to be attached to conclusions drawn from this summary depending upon the amount of cross validation involved. We shall be quite certain about generalizations which apply to all seven of the groups tabled, and proportionately less certain about findings which present inconsistencies, or concerning which some groups provide no relevant information.

While group comparisons of this kind are certainly useful, they are not sufficient for identification of an efficient and comprehensive battery for clinical application. Such comparisons are no test of a variable's unique contribution to a battery. Reitan (this volume, Ch. 2 and Ch. 4) and Boll (this volume, Ch. 5) have both noted, and demonstrated in their analyses of individual cases, that variables useful in arriving at inferences in individual cases may not show much power in group comparisons. It is not necessary or appropriate to recapitulate Reitan's sophisticated and thorough treatment of this issue (this volume, Ch. 2) to which the reader is again referred. However, it may be worthwhile to emphasize some conditions under which clinically useful variables may show little or no power to discriminate a group of brain-damaged individuals from a group of normal controls.

One such circumstance pertains to pathognomonic signs which have a very low base rate of occurrence, but nearly invariant association with brain pathology when they do occur; such variables can easily be discarded by certain methods of statistical comparison. Another concerns the case of variables which have little discriminating power by themselves, but which may aid clinical interpretation substantially when evaluated in relation to the pattern of scores on other variables in a battery. Such patterns are somewhat amenable to statistical evaluation, for example, by means of "O"-type cluster or factor analysis, but such methods of identification are not entirely satisfactory with this sort of material since they exclude variables which contribute unique variance to a matrix and tend to exclude variables with peculiar distributions. Group comparisons on individual variables do not address the point at all. Furthermore, a variable which shows little diagnostic power in group comparisons may, nevertheless, be quite valuable in describing individual cases so as to make optimal dispositional recommendations. Personality tests, academic achievement and interest tests, together with the clinical interview, are frequently added to the clinical battery for this purpose even though they may have little or no power to detect brain damage (Matthews, Ch. 10 and Meier, Ch. 11, in this volume). Composing a battery useful for localizing lesions and for distinguishing among different etiologies of brain damage requires study of finely differentiated pathological groups. When this is done, one sometimes finds that variables useless in discriminating brain-damaged individuals in general from normal controls may be useful in separating individuals with particular brain pathologies from others and from normals. Spreen and Benton (1967) review some data indicating that this can be so, and some of the findings presented in Table 1, and shortly to be discussed, suggest that this is the case with children belonging to different age groups and suffering from different types of brain damage.

Different sets of variables may also be appropriate to different groups of subjects. The division of children into two age groups, 5-8 and 9-14, for the purpose of battery construction may not be sufficiently refined to span adequately the developmental range of interest, as is suggested by Klonoff and

Low's analysis of the relationships between age and performance on the variables in their batteries (this volume, Ch. 6). And with children younger than 5 (they included children as young as 2 years, 8 months) they had to devise a method of assigning scores when children could not take a test. Other modifications of particular tests have been made by Matthews (this volume, Ch. 10) and Meier (this volume, Ch. 11), and they have proposed yet additional changes in order to meet the particular needs of special study groups, such as the mentally retarded, or specialized prediction problems, such as prediction of recovery. With respect to our data on children contained in Table 1, this point bears on the possibility that failures of group discriminations may derive from inadequate refinement of measurement.

Now let us turn our attention to the contents of Table 1. We will find it convenient to group the variables in clusters possessing some internal homogeneity. Both Reitan (this volume, Ch. 4) and Boll (this volume, Ch. 5) presented systems of organizing the variables they studied into groups possessing definable communalities. The following discussion utilizes a synthesis of their two systems with some modifications to encompass all the variables involved.

Pure Motor Skill

Finger tapping; foot tapping; strength of grip; the Marching Test; and the Klove Maze Coordination, Static Steadiness, and Grooved Steadiness tests were considered in this category. Fore-Finger Tapping was reported for all groups. Both dominant and nondominant hand scores ranked quite high in comparison with other variables in one or more groups, both performing especially well with the Klonoff and Low Chronic groups. The nondominant hand score was considerably superior to the dominant hand score in the Reitan and Boll groups, while the reverse obtained for the Reed et al. (1965) subjects and for the two Klonoff and Low Acute groups. In every group one or both of these scores approached or exceeded median discriminating power compared with all other variables used. Foot tapping was reported only for the older Klonoff and Low subjects. Both dominant and nondominant scores performed excellently with the acutes, but neither score did as well relative to other variables with the Chronics, and there the dominant measure did not attain statistically significant discriminating power. The Marching Test was reported for Reitan's subjects and by Klonoff and Low for all four of their groups. One or more of the five variables generated by this test (time and error scores for dominant and nondominant hands, and coordination) achieved median or higher ranking in every group. However, a variable of relative potency in one group, always appeared among the least discriminating in some other (except for coordination which was reported only by Reitan). Time scores were consistently superior to error scores among the older subjects. Nondominant-hand scores were more discriminating than the corresponding dominant hand scores in 5/9 of such comparisons.

TABLE 1

Power of Variables in Discriminating Brain-damaged Children from Non-Brain-damaged Controls in Studies Reported by Reitan,[a] Boll[b] (Reed et al.[c] and Boll data) and Klonoff and Low[d]

Younger children (< 9): Reitan N = 41; Klonoff & Low N = 46 (Acute, Chronic). Older children (≥ 9): Reed et al. N = 27; Boll N = 40; Klonoff & Low N = 62 (Acute, Chronic).

Variable[e]	Reitan N=41		K&L N=46 Acute		K&L N=46 Chronic		Reed et al. N=27		Boll N=40		K&L N=62 Acute		K&L N=62 Chronic		Mean percentile ranks	
W Full Scale Score	99	97	88	76	97	97	95	92	89	87	94	97	31	18	85	81
W Verbal Score	94	92	90	82	92	87	87	87	74	71	81	82	99	97	88	86
W Performance Score	92	87	92	87	62	50	59	61	94	97	93	92	91	71	83	78
W Information	82	71	66	61	75	61	69	66	41	34	80	76	20[f]	13[f]	62	55
W Comprehension	52	45	23	18	12	18	80	82	91	92	43	13	06[f]	03[f]	44	39
W Arithmetic	35	24	55	40	88	76	54	55	54	50	59	40	94	82	63	52
W Similarities	84	76	71	71	03[f]	03[f]	72	71	56	55	73	71	93	76	65	60
W Digit Span	28	13	64	55	71	55	35	40	39	29	23	03	96	87	51	40
W Vocabulary	70	55	97	97	95	92	76	76	79	76	62	45	98	92	82	76
W Digit Symbol/Coding	79	66	95	92	49	40	98	97	86	82	91	87	77	55	82	74
W Picture Completion	30	18	42	24	10	13	02	03	14[f]	13	46	18	40	29	26	17
W Block Design	38	29	68	66	25	24	39	45	69	66	56	29	67	50	52	44
W Picture Arrangement	67	50	58	45	84	66	20	24	44	40	65	55	40	29	54	44
W Object Assembly	89	82	23	18	60	45	24	29	26	18	72	66	64	45	51	43
W Mazes	96		77		31						75		88		73	
Finger Tapping, D	45	40	49	29	90	82	43	50	36	24	57	34	83	66	58	46
Finger Tapping, ND	77	61	14	08	86	71	09	13	64	61	31	08	78	61	51	40
Category	40	34	51	34	34	34	17	18	49	45	49	24	09[f]	08[f]	36	28
TPT Memory	11	08	08	03	27	29	06	08	04[f]	03[f]	64	50	46	34	24	19
TPT Localization	04	03	62	50	05[f]	08	28	34	09[f]	08[f]	70	61	54	40	33	29
TPT, D	09		86		14				21		27		36		32	
TPT, ND	33		29		01[f]				46		44		30		30	
TPT, Both hands	21		99		81				24		69		22[f]		53	
TPT, Total time			38		18		13				48		44		32	
Trails A			16		51		65		96		09		57		49	
Trails B			03[f]		79		61		84		33		86		58	
Trails Total (A+B)			05		77		83				40		85		58	
Speech Perception			60		99		90		59		60		90		76	
Time Sense, Visual							50		61						56	
Time Sense, Memory							31		29						30	
Strength of Grip, D	01[f]								34						18	
Strength of Grip, ND	13								76						44	
Finger-Tip Number/Symbol Writing, R	06								11[f]						08	
Finger-Tip Number/Symbol Writing, L	48								06						27	
Finger Localization, R	16								31						24	
Finger Localization, L	65								19[f]						42	
Tactile Forms, R	43								01[f]						22	
Tactile Forms, L	87								16[f]						52	
Lateral Dominance			45		58						30		10		36	
Name Writing, D									81							
Name Writing, ND									99							
Seashore Rhythm							46		51						48	
Matching Figures, E			12		23						06[f]		04[f]		11	
Matching Figures, T			10		42						22		62		34	
Marching, D E			01[f]		40						19		33		23	
Marching, ND E			75		47						04[f]		38		41	
Marching, D T	50		25		38						78		72		53	

TABLE 1 (*Cont.*)

Variable[e]	Younger children (< 9)			Older children (> 9)				Mean percentile ranks
	Reitan N = 41	Klonoff & Low N = 46		Reed et al N = 27	Boll N = 40	Klonoff & Low N = 62		
		Acute	Chronic			Acute	Chronic	
Marching, ND T	18	27	73			67	52	47
Marching, Coordination	60							
Progressive Figures	72	84	64			51	59	66
Matching Pictures	26	40	36			15	60	35
Color Form E		81	53			38	56	57
Color Form T	57	47	71			77	69	64
Target	23	18	53			36	49	36
Star		73	16			07[f]	14[f]	28
Concentric Squares		79	08[f]			43	01[f]	33
Matching V's E		36	45			10	15[f]	26
Matching V's T		34	21			36	27[f]	30
Left-Right Orientation		53	29			02[f]	81	41
Sound Recognition		31	66			86	28[f]	52
Maze Coordination, D E						98	78	88
Maze Coordination, ND E						28	73	50
Maze Coordination, D T						90	70	80
Maze Coordination, ND T						99	75	87
Peg Board, D						54	02[f]	28
Peg Board, ND						96	07[f]	52
Static Stead., D T						52	35	44
Static Stead., ND T						88	65	77
Static Stead., D E						17	20[f]	18
Static Stead., ND E						12	12[f]	12
Grooved Stead., D T						25	48	26
Grooved Stead., ND T						01[f]	43	22
Grooved Stead., D E						14	23[f]	18
Grooved Stead., ND E						20	17[f]	18
Foot Tapping, D						83	23[f]	53
Foot Tapping, ND						85	52	68
WRAT Spelling	62			71				66
WRAT Reading	74			66				70
WRAT Arithmetic	55							

Note.—First column for each study gives percentile rank of variable compared with all other variables in that study. Second column gives percentile rank of variables used in all studies (N = 19). Percentile ranks are based on size of *t* ratio discriminating brain-damaged Ss from controls except for Reed et al. where they are based on magnitude of mean differences. Klonoff and Low data are taken from their initial examination comparisons only.

[a] This volume, Ch. 4.
[b] This volume, Ch. 5.
[c] 1966.
[d] This volume, Ch. 6.
[e] Abbreviations: Wechsler = W; dominant hand/foot = D; nondominant hand/foot = ND; Tactual Performance Test = TPT; right hand, right = R; Left hand, left = L; errors = E; Time = T; Wide Range Achievement Test = WRAT; Steadiness = Stead.; Trail Making Test = Trails; Speech-sounds Perception = Speech Perception.
[f] Underlined percentile ranks indicate that the variable failed to discriminate brain-damaged from control children at $p \leq .05$ in the study indicated.

Klove Maze Coordination, Static Steadiness, and Grooved Steadiness were reported for the older Klonoff and Low subjects. Maze coordination was a very potent variable in both groups, exceeding the 70th percentile rank, with only one exception, with all four variables (time and errors for both dominant and nondominant hands) and for both groups. Nondominant-hand steadiness time showed excellent discriminating power in both groups. However, the remaining three steadiness variables performed poorly relative to the other variables used in these studies, especially the two error scores which did not even achieve statistical significance in the Chronic group. Grooved Steadiness generally performed less well than Static Steadiness, two of the four variables, again the error scores, failing to achieve statistical significance with the Chronic subjects, and nondominant time failing to achieve significance with the Acutes. However, both dominant- and nondominant-hand time scores approached median discriminating power with the Chronics.

Strength of grip was reported by Reitan and by Boll. It achieved relatively high discriminating power only in the case of the nondomiant-hand measure with the older Boll subjects. Dominant-hand strength was consistently inferior to nondominant strength, and did not achieve statistically significant discriminating power for brain damage in Reitan's study.

Overall, there were 32 cases in which a dominant member motor variable could be compared with a comparable measure obtainted from the nondominant member. The relative power of dominant and nondominant measures in discriminating brain damage was equal in this respect, each achieving superior ranking compared with the other in exactly half the comparisons.

Tactual Perceptual Measures

Tactile finger localization, Tactile Form Recognition, and Finger-tip Symbol (younger children) or Finger-tip Number Writing (older children) are the measures included in this category. They were reported only by Reitan and by Boll. These were more potent variables among the younger children reported by Reitan than among the older reported by Boll. In fact, in the older group the best of the six measures, right and left hands for each of the three tests listed above, attained a percentile rank of only 31 and the other five did not discriminate significantly, while for the younger children the left-hand measures consistently discriminated well even though right hand fingertip symbol writing and finger localization did poorly relative to the other variables used in that study. Left-hand measures were better discriminators than analogous right-hand measures in 4 out of 6 instances. Whether these right-versus-left and age differences will be generalizable must await replication.

Immediate Alertness

After Reitan (this volume, Ch. 4) this seems to be a useful category even though only two variables, Wechsler Digit Span and Picture Completion can be placed here and each of these tests, of course, involves much more than immediate alertness alone. Digit Span proved to be a fairly high ranking variable for both the Chronic and Acute Klonoff and Low younger subjects, and was a very potent variable for the Klonoff and Low older Chronics. However, it did not rank in the upper half of the variables in other groups including the Klonoff and Low older Acutes. The discriminating power of Picture Completion was insufficient to place it in the upper half of the distribution of variables in any group, and for three of the groups it was among the very least discriminating (percentile rank < 20) of variables.

Auditory Perception

This category includes three tests: Speech-sounds Perception, Seashore Rhythm, and Benton Sound Recognition. Rhythm was reported only by Reed et al. and by Boll. In each case it fell near the median in discriminating power compared with the remaining variables. Benton Sound Recognition was used by Klonoff and Low with both older and younger children. It performed quite variably, achieving a percentile rank as high as 86 for the older Acutes, but as low as 28 for the older Chronics. Its power was not systematically related to age or to chronicity. Speech-sounds Perception was reported for all groups except Reitan's. Its power was consistently above the median compared with other variables used in these studies, and in three of the groups it achieved the 90th percentile rank or higher. It was especially potent with both the older and younger Chronics of Klonoff and Low and in Reed's group. These findings with Speech-sounds Perception appear to bolster Reitan's and Boll's observations concerning the saliency of language deficits among chronically brain-damaged children.

Tactual-motor Problem Solving

The Halstead Tactual Performance Test's perceptual-spatial-motor components (time scores) seem sufficiently unique to warrant separate categorization. Unlike other perceptual motor tasks in these batteries, the TPT sensory motor performances involve only tactual and kinesthetic perceptual cues, vision being deliberately excluded. The TPT was reported by all investigators but the variables reported differed somewhat. The score for both hands together was a moderately potent variable relative to others with the older Acute group, while it was the most potent discriminator of brain damage for the younger Acutes. It was quite a potent variable also for the Klonoff and Low younger Chronic group. On the other hand, it performed relatively poorly compared with the other variables used in the Reitan, Boll, and Klonoff and Low older Chronic groups, in the latter case failing to achieve statistical significance. Dominant-hand performance was also a powerful variable for the younger Acute group, but this variable did not perform impressively relative to other variables for the other groups in which it was used. Nondominant-hand performance did not achieve a median ranking in any list of variables, though it approached this position with the Boll and older Acute groups. TPT total time also did not achieve median relative power in any group's ranking of variables, but approached this status for the two older Klonoff and Low groups. Dominant- and nondominant-hand performances were equal in their frequency of achieving greatest discriminating power compared with one another.

Visual-Spatial and Visual-Sequential Abilities

A large number of variables were included in this category: Five Wechsler variables—Block Design, Picture Arrangement, Object Assembly, Mazes, and Digit Symbol; five Reitan-Indiana battery variables—Target Test, Star Drawing, Concentric Squares drawing, Matching V's, and Matching Figures; Trails A; and the Grooved Pegboard Test, for 12 tests and 15 variables in all. Digit Symbol, or Coding, discriminated very well in most groups. It was the most potent variable of all in the Reed et al. study and approached or bettered the 80th percentile in all groups except the Klonoff and Low younger Chronics where it approached the median of all variables. Block Design, while consistently producing significant discriminations, did not surpass the 70th percentile rank in any group, and failed to surpass the median ranked variable in three of them. Picture Arrangement performed more variably, achieving percentile ranks as high as 84, but as low as 20. For both Block Design and Picture Arrangement, the variation seemed unrelated to chronicity or subject age. Object Assembly performed even less consistently. It was an extremely discriminating variable in Reitan's study and ranked very high in the Klonoff and Low older Acute group. However, for three of the groups it fell around the 25th percentile. WISC Mazes discriminated extremely well in all cases in which it was employed except for the younger Chronic group of Klonoff and Low. It was the second most potent variable out of 41 in Reitan's study.

The Target Test was reported for five groups, Reitan's and the four Klonoff and Low groups. It showed close to median potency with the two Chronic groups, but less than that in the remaining three comparisons. The Star and Concentric Squares drawing tasks and the Matching Figures and Matching V's Tests were reported for the four Klonoff and Low groups. The Matching Figures Time score ranked near the median of all variables used in the Chronic groups, but achieved only relatively low discriminating power in the Acute groups. Matching Figures Error scores did not achieve high ranking in any group. Neither the Matching V's Time or Error scores surpassed the median in any comparison. Both the Star and Concentric Squares drawing discriminated well compared with other variables for younger Acutes, but except for Concentric Squares approaching median relative discriminating power among older Acutes, these drawing tasks did not otherwise perform well relative to the other variables included in these studies.

Trail Making Test, Part A was reported for all groups but Reitan's (see his discussion, in this volume, Ch. 4, of the replacement of Trail Making Test, Parts A and B, in the younger children's battery with the Progressive Figures and Color-Form Tests). It was the second most discriminating variable in Boll's study. It performed relatively well in all other groups except for the young and old Acute groups for which it was a relatively poor discriminator of brain damage.

The Grooved Pegboard Test which requires fine visual-motor and tactual-motor coordination and efficiency (speed) was reported only for the older Klonoff and Low subjects. Both dominant-hand and nondominant-hand scores were good discriminators in the older Acute group, especially the nondominant-hand score. However, both of the variables were among the very poorest discriminators for the older Chronics, neither achieving statistical significance. Compared with each other, the nondominant-hand score was consistently superior to the dominant.

There are indications in the above of interactions between type of visual-spatial, visual-sequential measure on the one hand and both chronicity and age on the other. In agreement with Boll's conclusion (this volume, Ch. 5), perceptual-motor deficits and perceptual deficits (see sections on Tactual Perceptual measures and on Auditory Perception above) can hardly be said to be the most outstanding or consistent characteristics of brain-damaged children. On the other hand, certain perceptual and visual-spatial, visual-sequential (perceptual-motor) variables are among the most sensitive measures of brain damage for certain groups of children. However, the suggested interactions between such variables, age, and chronicity must await replication before we can consider them firmly established, while solid understanding of them, if they hold up, depends on yet further analysis and study.

Verbal Abilities

Four Wechsler variables—Information, Comprehension, Similarities, and Vocabulary—constitute this class. Vocabulary discriminated consistently well. It was the second best variable in both the Klonoff and Low younger Acute and older Chronic groups, and the third most discriminating in the Klonoff and Low younger Chronic group. It attained or surpassed a percentile rank of 60 in all other groups. While the remaining three verbal measures each performed extremely well (at or above 80th percentile rank) with one or more groups, they each also showed relatively poor performance with one or more groups. Both Information and Comprehension performed poorly with the older Chronic group, while Comprehension also performed poorly with both Klonoff and Low younger groups. Similarities performed very poorly (percentile rank of 03) with the younger Chronic group. However, despite these occasional relative failures, the performance of these Wechsler verbal measures is very impressive in view of the comparative insensitivity of such measures to the effects of brain damage (considered generally without regard to location or type) in adults. Vocabulary, at least, is consistently among the most sensitive reflectors of brain damage in children, regardless of age and chronicity, with other expressive verbal measures showing similar but not as consistent sensitivity. And this generalization is quite at odds with generalizations concerning the effects of brain damage on such abilities in adults. See Reitan (this volume, Ch. 4) for a discussion of this finding which may now be considered to be well established.

Incidental Memory

TPT Memory and Localization scores were reported for all seven groups of children. These variables performed relatively poorly with most groups, exceptions occurring for the younger Acutes and both Klonoff and Low older groups with the Localization component, and for these two older groups for the memory component. Again, this is contrary to findings with adults among whom TPT Localization is one of the more sensitive variables to brain damage in general.

Summary IQ Measures

Benton (this volume, Ch. 3) has noted that the best single discriminator of brain damage in children or adults is a lower than expected total score on any reasonably comprehensive battery of tests, including IQ tests. However, with adults a composite of neuropsychological variables, the Halstead Impairment Index, has repeatedly been shown to be more discriminating than IQs (Klove, this volume, Ch. 8; Reitan, 1959a). In the studies of children reported here, the three summary Wechsler IQ measures, Full Scale, Verbal, and Performance scores were, with one exception, Full Scale WISC IQ in the older Chronic group of Klonoff and Low, at or above median discriminating power compared with other variables employed. With but four exceptions out of the total of 21 comparisons involved, these composite variables achieved percentile ranks in the 80s and 90s. For every group, one or more of these three variables fell among the top five in terms of discriminating power. Two groups showed only moderate relative discriminating power for Performance IQ (or Performance total weighted score), while the Verbal and Full Scale scores (except for the one anomalous finding with the latter) produced consistently superior performance.

Concept Formation, Reasoning, Organizational Ability, and Flexibility in Applying Principles

The Category Tests, Color-Form Test, Progressive Figures Test, Matching Pictures Test, Wechsler Arithmetic, and Trail Making Test, Part B, are considered under this rubric. The Category variable only once fell in the upper half of any distribution of variables, but only the older Klonoff and Low Chronic group produced an extremely low percentile rank for this test; it did not achieve statistically significant discriminating power in that group. The Color-Form Test performed better, with most groups showing above median rankings on both time and error scores. Progressive Figures was better yet, all groups providing above median rankings for this variable. It seemed to perform best with younger subjects. Matching Pictures, on the other hand, produced only one ranking above the median and two quite low relative rankings in five comparisons. Differential performance of this variable appeared unrelated to age and chronicity. Wechsler

Arithmetic produced very high relative discriminations for both Chronic groups, and above median relative discriminations for all other groups except Reitan's in which it ranked below all other variables in this category with the exception of Matching Pictures. Trail Making Test, Part B, reported for all groups but Reitan's, showed good relative discrimination in all comparisons except the Klonoff and Low younger and older Acutes.

The above findings appear to require modification of the implications of Reitan's discussion of the findings of his study (this volume, Ch. 4) that measures of concept formation, reasoning, organizational ability, and flexibility in applying principles are among the least sensitive classes of variables in discriminating brain damage in children. Some of the variables are among the most consistently potent discriminators, though none of them rivals the composite IQ measures or the Wechsler Vocabulary or Digit Symbol/Coding subtests in power. Perhaps a composite of the better variables in this category would be as potent as these IQ variables. Reitan (this volume, Ch. 4) has already suggested that the relative weakness of this category of variables in his study may have been due to its being represented by few variables.

Academic Ability

The WRAT variables were reported for only the Reitan and Boll groups of subjects, and Boll did not report WRAT Arithmetic. These variables consistently achieved above median rankings, but did not perform as well as the better Wechsler variables.

Miscellaneous Variables

Trail Making Test, total score; name writing; Left-Right orientation; Halstead's Time Sense Test; and lateral dominance could not easily be classed with other variables. Trail Making Test, total score, is rather arbitrarily relegated to this category because Trail Making Test, Parts A and B, were each assigned to different categories. Trails total showed an almost identical pattern of performance to that of Trails B. Only one of the five groups for which it was reported yielded low relative discriminating power for this variable. This was the younger Acute group. The older Acute group also yielded a below median relative power score. In the remaining three groups the relative power of this variable was quite high. All three Trails scores appear to be relatively insensitive to acute brain damage. Surprisingly, nondominant name writing was the most powerful variable in Boll's study, while dominant name writing also achieved high relative power. This was the only group for which these variables were reported. See Reitan's discussion (this volume, Ch. 2) of name writing as a neuropsychological variable; he found this to be a powerful variable with younger children as well (Reitan, 1971a, 1971b). Left-right orientation was reported for the four Klonoff and Low groups. It showed extreme variability of power, apparently unrelated in any linear fashion to age or chronicity. Lateral dominance was also presented for the four Klonoff and Low groups where it showed moderate relative discriminating power for the younger groups, but performed less well relative to other variables with the older groups. Reitan (this volume, Ch. 4) found that his brain-damaged subjects showed greater incidence of left-handedness for writing, but also demonstrated greater consistency of manual preference than did their normal controls. Halstead's Time Sense Test was reported only by Boll and by Reed et al. The Visual component ranked at or above the median of all variables in discriminating power in both studies, but the memory component did relatively poorly. Boll advocates abandoning this variable on grounds of excessive tediousness and time required for administration, especially relative to its contribution. This variable has generally been dropped from the adult battery. However, if it could be shown that these scores added something unique to a battery it would be worth attempting to design more efficient means of eliciting this behavior. Petrie (1952) found time estimation to be impaired by bilateral prefrontal lobotomy in neurotics. The visual component involves reaction time. Reaction time, otherwise measured, is routinely used by some European investigators (Faglioni, Spinnler, & Vignolo, 1969) as a measure of, and control for, severity of brain damage in comparing different groups of subjects.

An overall comparison of all measures, regardless of category, which provided separate scores for left and right or dominant and nondominant members produced 46 instances in which dominant or right and nondominant or left measures could be contrasted in discriminating power with comparable measures from the opposite side of the body. Nondominant or left measures were superior to dominant or right measures in over half (25) of these comparisons. While this is not grounds for concluding that nondominant or left measures are generally superior, particularly in view of the lack of consistency across studies in this respect, it is grounds for addressing more careful attention to left-side or nondominant measures than has sometimes been the custom.

In all, 45 different tests yielding 79 different variables were used in these studies of brain-damaged children. With one or more groups, all of these variables showed some power to detect brain damage in children by the test of group discriminations. The above discussion has evaluated the relative discriminating power of the variables in relation to the various groups with which they were used. It is of further interest to summarize the overall sensitivity of the most powerful of these variables. Although averaging percentile ranks is a questionable statistical procedure, and the number of groups entering into such averages differs from one variable to another, ranking the variables according to their mean percentile ranks across groups provides us with a rough preliminary index of the overall sensitivity of the variables to brain damage in children. Of the variables which were used with both older and younger subjects, the 27 achieving above median overall discriminating power were, with their ranks: Wechsler Verbal score (1); Wechsler Full Scale score (2); Wechsler Performance score (3); Wechsler Vocabulary (4.5); Wechsler Digit Symbol/Coding (4.5); Halstead Speech-sounds Perception (6); Wechsler Mazes

(7); Wide Range Achievement Test, Reading (8); Reitan-Indiana Progressive Figures (9.5); Wide Range Achievement Test, Spelling (9.5); Wechsler Similarities (11); Reitan-Indiana Color-Form time (12); Wechsler Arithmetic (13); Wechsler Information (14); Halstead Finger Tapping, dominant hand (16); Trail Making Test, Part B (16); Trail Making Test, total A + B (16); Reitan-Indiana Color-Form errors (18); Wechsler Picture Arrangement (19); Halstead Tactual Performance Test, both hands (20.5); Reitan-Indiana Marching Test, dominant-hand time (20.5); Wechsler Block Design (23); Reitan-Klove Tactile Forms, left hand (23); Benton Sound Recognition (23); Wechsler Digit Span (26); Halstead Finger Tapping, nondominant hand (26); and Wechsler Object Assembly (26). The list includes measures of pure motor skill; tactual-perceptual discrimination; immediate alertness; auditory perception; tactual-motor problem solving; visual-spatial and visual-sequential abilities; verbal abilities; summary psychometric intelligence; concept formation, reasoning, organizational ability, and flexibility in applying principles; and of academic ability. Of our a priori categories of variables, only incidental memory did not produce a high-ranking variable in terms of overall discriminating power. Of course, our definition of high ranking is arbitrary, but the intermixture of variables from the various categories in terms of rank order of overall sensitivity emphasizes the diverse effects of brain damage in children.

The above data are insufficient by themselves for the composition of a clinically useful battery. A number of other criteria must be utilized in the selection of variables. One of these is the power to make an independent contribution to the clinical tasks of interest. Klonoff and Low have also provided us with data showing which of their variables reliably discriminate brain-damaged from normal children with the variance between the groups accounted for by Full Scale IQ partialled out (their analyses of covariance data). Since IQ, by itself, is such a potent discriminator of brain damage, variables sensitive to brain damage independently of IQ make an important contribution to the battery. These data also answer a question, sometimes asked by individuals just becoming acquainted with clinical neuropsychology, whether neuropsychological variables contribute anything independent of IQ.

Variables showing overall (across both testing occasions) statistically significant between groups differences in analysis of covariance with Full Scale IQ as the covariate are listed here, ranked from that with the largest F ratio to that with the least. The Acute groups yielded many more of these measures independent of IQ than did the Chronic subjects. For the younger Acutes they were: TPT memory; Star drawing; TPT, dominant time; Progressive Figures; Trails B; Marching, dominant errors; Matching Pictures; Matching V's time; TPT total time; Benton Sound Recognition; Marching, nondominant time; Trail Making Test (Trails) total; Speech-sounds Perception; Marching, dominant time; TPT Localization; right-left orientation; and Trails A. The older Acute subjects showed a few less discriminators of brain damage independent of IQ than did their younger counterparts. These were Benton Sound Recognition; lateral dominance; Maze coordination, nondominant time; Maze coordination, dominant errors; Foot Tapping, nondominant; Marching, nondominant time; Maze coordination, dominant time; Marching, dominant time; TPT Localization; Color-Form time; Finger Tapping, dominant; and Static Steadiness, dominant time. Sound recognition; Marching, dominant and nondominant time; and TPT Localization appear in both lists, providing some cross validation for these variables, while the Color-Form test contributed to both lists, though with different variables. The Marching test showed particular potency, contributing both error and time variables to the list for younger subjects, while its time scores also appeared on the list for older subjects. Some of the variables appearing in the list for older subjects had no opportunity to do so with the younger ones, since they were not used with them. It seems particularly noteworthy that some measures of categorizing, reasoning, and cognitive flexibility discriminated brain damage independently of IQ. These were the Progressive Figures and Color-Form tests.

The younger Chronic subjects produced seven variables sensitive to their brain damage independently of IQ. These were: Speech-sounds Perception; Trail Making Test (Trails) total time; Trail Making Test, Part B; Finger Tapping, dominant; Benton Sound Recognition; Finger Tapping, nondominant; and lateral dominance. For the older Chronics the list was: Speech Sounds Perception; Category; lateral dominance; TPT, nondominant; Matching V's errors; and TPT total. Only lateral dominance overlapped the two groups, but note that Benton Sound Recognition, Speech-sounds Perception, Trails B, Trails total, TPT total, and Finger Tapping, dominant were also discriminators independent of IQ for one or the other or both of the Acute groups. Again, a measure of categorizing, reasoning, and cognitive flexibility, this time the Category Test, showed discrimination of brain damage independently of IQ.

The fact that Chronic subjects showed many fewer discriminators of brain damage independent of IQ than did Acutes seems to support Reitan's argument (this volume, Ch. 4; see also Matthews, Ch. 10) concerning the probable deficits in acquisition of adaptive behaviors resulting from brain damage in children and eventuating in generalized adaptive impairment with the passage of time. A direct test of this hypothesis would be to relate time since acqustion of brain damage to the pattern of deficits observed. At the time of this writing, Boll had studies in process which support this hypothesis (R. Reitan, personal communication, 1972). The differences between Chronic and Acute groups in the Klonoff and Low study may be more a reflection of differences in the type of brain damage sustained than of the processes which have occurred over time since the injuries were sustained (chronicity). All of their acutely brain-damaged subjects were head injury cases.

Other data relevant to the evaluation of variables' contributions to these batteries independent of the variance accounted for by IQ is to be found in Klonoff and Low's comparison of high and low IQ subgroups among their Normal controls on the variables of their batteries (this volume, Ch. 6) and in

Matthew's correlations between IQ scores and selected neuropsychological battery variables (this volume, Ch. 10). However such comparisons and correlations are not of as direct relevance to the selection of variables to compose a battery as are the data reviewed above on the separation of brain-damaged from control groups by such variables with IQ partialled out. Therefore they will not be summarized here; the interested reader is referred to the appropriate portions of this volume.

Again, it may be necessary to remind the reader that group discriminations produced by individual variables are merely one test of the contribution of a measure to a diagnostic battery. It is indefensible to leap to the conclusion that one could compose an adequate children's battery or batteries with the WISC plus those measures listed above as discriminators of brain damage independent of IQ. See Reitan's chapter (this volume, Ch. 2) and paragraph 4 ff of this chapter for discussions of the issues involved.

We seem to have assembled a set of variables which can provide a fairly comprehensive description of adaptive functioning related to the organic integrity of the brain in children. However, the set, at least the large sets used by Klonoff and Low, are clearly very time consuming and expensive. They were assembled for research purposes: to study differences between groups, to accumulate norms, and to determine which of these variables showed greatest promise for incorporation into a clinically useful battery. Before considering how these sets might be trimmed, we must first, however, address another question; are these sets empirically comprehensive enough to permit assignment of subjects to groups with little margin of error?

One approach to this task was that employed by Wheeler, Burke, and Reitan (1963) and Wheeler and Reitan (1963) (See Klove's discussion in this volume, Ch. 8). This method requires the establishment of criterion groups and the employment of discriminant analysis to obtain the best linear combination of variables in a battery for the purpose of predicting criterion group membership. If the method involves cross validation of the variable weights obtained, as was done by Wheeler and Reitan, one may acquire convincing evidence, as they did, for the adequacy of a battery to produce the diagnostic discriminations asked of it. Examination of the weights assigned to the variables in the different discrimination problems also permits identification of the variables contributing to different diagnostic decisions.

Klonoff and Low have here applied discriminant analysis to the variables in their batteries to predict the criteria: (*a*) brain damage versus no brain damage; (*b*) for the Acute and Chronic brain-damaged, three levels of rating of neurological impairment—minor and mild, moderate and severe, and serious; (*c*) for the minimal cerebral dysfunctionals (MCDs), three categories of rated cerebral dysfunction—normal, borderline, and abnormal. Initial and repeated neuropsychological test data were evaluated separately to make concurrent predictions with discriminant weights determined independently in each analysis. Overall percent correct assignment to brain damage versus control groups varied between 73 and 96% with little difference between initial and followup examination results. Acutes were predicted less accurately than were Chronics or MCDs. Prediction of neurological impairment ratings, and for the MCDs, rated cerebral dysfunction, was made only with initial examination data. Overall correct assignment to classes varied from 57% with the younger Acutes to 82% for both older Chronics and older MCDs. EEG ratings were predicted with hit rates varying from 50% for the younger MCDs on reexamination to 84% for these same younger MCDs on initial examination.

Klonoff and Paris, in the followup study of their traumatically injured Ss, also employed discriminant analyses of the neuropsychological batteries applied at initial examination to predict: (a) impairment of consciousness and memory—(i) retrograde amnesia, (ii) anterograde amnesia, and (iii) loss of consciousness; (b) site of injury—(i) frontal; (ii) occipital, parieto-occipital, vertex, temporo-parietal, (iii) temporal, posterior fossa, basal, and (iv) facial, head contusions, and unknown site; and (c) presence versus absence of skull fractures. Impairment of consciousness and of memory was predicted with overall hit rates varying from 65% (loss of consciousness for younger children) to 85% (anterograde amnesia for older children). Site of injury was predicted with hit rates of 46% for the younger and 52% for the older children, improved to 63% and 72%, respectively, when the catchbasket category, "facial, head contusions, and unknown site," was eliminated. Presence versus absence of skull fractures was predicted with hit rates of around 70%. Separate discriminant analyses were also performed on the neuropsychological data 1 year postinjury and those obtained 2 years postinjury to make concurrent predictions of: (a) presence versus absence of complaints, and (b) presence versus absence of sequelae. Hit rates varied from 75% for 1 year postinjury data, predicting complaints for the younger subjects, to 85% for 1 year postinjury data, predicting complaints for the older subjects.

In all cases, correct assignment of subjects in these problems was above chance expectancy, though obviously hit rates as low as 50%, even when use of multiple prediction categories reduce chance expectancy well below 50%, have little practical utility for most prediction problems. While the neuropsychological batteries thus show statistically significant power to assign these subjects to classes based on diverse criteria related to brain damage, their power, even for the criterion they were designed to predict, presence versus absence of brain damage, was not as great as that of the adult battery in making similar predictions (Klove, this volume, Ch. 8). Since the batteries showed consistent above-chance assignment of subjects to categories determined by a variety of criteria, all of which are independently related to brain damage, the variables included in them are in that sense cross validated. However, the weights obtained were not cross validated. Obviously, the problem of performing such predictive studies with children is in some respects much more difficult than with adults, which is itself difficult enough. With children, weights assigned to variables are bound to be less than optimal due to developmental influences which are, in many cases, nonlinear (Klonoff & Low, this volume, Ch. 6). The collection of the data presented by these authors was a huge, one is tempted to say, heroic, task by itself: The collection of data for cross validation was beyond the scope of their effort and probably beyond their means. Furthermore, the diagnostic criteria used by Klonoff and his coworkers related to head trauma, and other indirect indicators of brain damage, rather than to direct evidence of brain damage per se; this also may have limited the predictive power of the neuropsychological variables in these studies. Reitan and his coworkers, in their discriminant analysis studies of adults, found it possible to select specific, well-defined instances of cerebral damage from among the thousands of cases in Reitan's files in order to reduce diagnostic ambiguity to a minimum. Klove feels that the shrikage in percent correct classifications experienced by Reitan and Wheeler in cross validation was significantly influenced by having to relax stringent diagnostic criteria in order to amass sufficient numbers of cases for cross validation.

We wish to take nothing from these discriminant anslyses with children. They are quite promising with respect to the adequacy of these batteries to assign cases to diagnostic categories. The relationships with neurological examination ratings, ratings of degree of cerebral dysfunction among MCDs, classes of severity of EEG abnormalities, site of injury, presence versus absence of skull fractures, and presence versus absence of complaints and sequelae contribute additional evidence that the neuropsychological variables included, consistently reflect brain function, and probably do so in a fairly comprehensive fashion.

Yet we are left with many important questions, some of which could be answered, at least tentatively, through further analysis of these data or by presentation of data which were the byproducts of the analyses already performed. Which variables entered into the various prediction equations? What were their relative weights? How much consistency was there in the selection of variables and their weightings across prediction problems? How accurately can subsequent neurological, academic, social, and adaptive functioning criteria be predicted from earlier neuropsychological examinations? It is to be hoped that Klonoff and his colleagues will continue to mine their rich lode for answers to questions such as these. Such examinations of these and other data yet to be collected will be required in order to cull these impractically huge batteries, and perhaps, to identify areas of measurement required but not presently covered.

Klonoff and Low's inclusion of the minimal cerebral dysfunctional groups in their study was enlightening. This diagnostic category is, as yet, poorly defined, but neuropsychological investigations of minimal brain dysfunction may be of considerable significance in clarifying the nature of this condition (Reitan, 1972; Benton, this volume, Ch. 3). Future studies of this currently focal topic should use a similar paradigm to that employed by Klonoff and Low with respect to: (a) concurrent study of children with this type of deficit and of children with definitely diagnosed brain damage along with appropriate normal controls; (b) comprehensive neuropsychological measurement, social and academic measures, and physical neurodiagnostic procedures; and (c) longitudinal study. Although Klonoff and Low did not make direct statistical comparisons between their MCD samples and like-aged children with known brain damage, they did make some comparative generalizations concerning performances on measures of adaptive competency, and EEG ratings. It is also possible to make some observations regarding their rated degree of impairment. In all three respects, the younger MCDs resembled like-aged children with diagnosed brain damage to a much greater degree than did the older MCDs. Considering the paucity of variables reliably distinguishing the older MCDs from their matched controls, compared with other groups (7 Wechsler variables out of 15, and only 5 other variables out of 47), the success of the discriminant analyses of the battery in correctly distinguishing them as to severity of EEG abnormalities (hit rate of 82% overall), and with respect to ratings of severity of their cerebral dysfunction (overall hit rate of 82%) is surprising. These percentages of correct classification are comparable to or exceed those achieved for the other groups. Again, it might be of some heuristic value to learn what variables entered into the various discriminant analyses.

The differences between the younger and older MCDs, favoring the older group in all categories studied (psychiatric ratings of severity, EEG abnormalities, and performance on the measures of adaptive functioning) are intriguing but unexplained, and probably inexplicable from these data. Are these differences a result of positive maturational changes? An answer to this question may require an extended longitudinal study of an MCD group identified at an early age employing the same multifaceted measurement of neurological, neuropsychological, and psychiatric status, and adding personality and ambient adjustment, social, and academic variables.

The chapter by Klonoff and Paris (this volume, Ch. 7) is a valuable contribution to clinical neuropsychology in another respect. The rather comprehensive presentation of data on the natural history of traumatic brain injury in children follows Benton's suggestions for studying such problems (this volume, Ch. 3). It provides background data for evaluating individual cases; the clinical picture in individual cases becomes clearer when evaluated against the background of base-rate occurrence of complaints, sequelae, neuropsychological test scores (Klonoff & Low, this volume, Appendices 1-10, Ch. 6) social functioning, academic achievement, EEG findings, neurological findings, antecedents, and the interrelationships among these classes of variables. Clinical work would be aided greatly by similar longitudinal studies of other classes of brain damage in adults as well as in children.

Consideration of other possibly fruitful endeavors in the clinical neuropsychology of children will be deferred until we have examined the state of the field of adult clinical neuropsychology. The two fields share many of the same problems and potentially fruitful avenues of approach to them.

ADULT CLINICAL NEUROPSYCHOLOGY

The chapters of this volume addressed to problems in the field of clinical neuropsychology of adults can be seen to reflect a different state of development from that of the children's field. It is not yet possible to write a succinct survey of validation studies concerning child clinical neuropsychology as was done in this volume by Klove (Ch. 8) for validation studies with the Halstead Neuropsychological Test Battery for Adults. Basic data, such as that presented for children in this volume, have been presented elsewhere for adults and may now be summarized, as was done here by Klove. In the adult field we are now turning our attention to the study of particular clinical groups such as epileptics (Klove & Matthews, this volume, Ch. 9) and the mentally retarded (Matthews, this volume, Ch. 10) and focusing on as-yet-unresolved diagnostic difficulties (Klove, Ch. 8 and Meier, Ch. 11, in this volume), and methodological problems (Reitan, this volume Ch. 2).

The studies reviewed by Klove address a number of points frequently raised by those first becoming acquainted with clinical neuropsychology. The sensitivity of the battery to brain damage in general and under a variety of special circumstances has been demonstrated. These variables have the power to discriminate brain damage even in the presence of a negative neurological examination. They can also discriminate pseudoneurologic from neurological cases. The cross-cultural validity of the battery is also supported, at least in certain other western cultures, such as Norway. In linear combination, these variables have demonstrated impressive power to allocate adequately diagnosed subjects to the categories: brain-damaged versus non–brain-damaged, and among the brain damaged, to separate right from left hemisphere damage, and each of these from diffuse damage.

However, a number of concurrent validity problems continue to lack satisfactory solutions. One of these is the problem, examined by Klove in this volume (Ch. 8), of discriminating brain-damaged from schizophrenic subjects among inpatients, particularly psychiatric inpatients. Some studies comparing the performance of hospitalized brain-damaged and schizophrenic subjects on the Halstead Neuropsychological Test Battery for Adults have found much greater overlap between these groups than has been the case with validity studies concerning other differential diagnostic applications of this battery (Watson, Thomas, Anderson, & Felling, 1968; Lacks, Harrow, Colbert, & Levine, 1970). The Watson et al. study showed no useful discrimination between their brain-damaged and schizophrenic subjects on group comparisons using individual variables of the Halstead Battery or by means of battery interpretation by neuropsychologists.

A number of variables appear to be relevant to this problem. One is the condition of schizophrenia per se, the onset of which typically is accompanied by some impairment of intellectual functioning. A second is the condition of hospitalization, which with schizophrenics has some relationship to severity of adaptive impairment and which tends to be associated with impaired performance of control subjects on some measures of adaptive functioning. A third is chronicity, chronic schizophrenics displaying impairment more similar to that of brain-damaged subjects than do acute schizophrenics. A fourth is the process-reactive dimension in schizophrenia; the process end of this dimension has been shown to be associated with decrements of performance on some tests of brain damage independently of chronicity (Lilliston, 1970).

The degree of chronicity of the schizophrenics used in the studies reporting negative or relatively negative findings with respect to separation of schizophrenics and brain-damaged patients appears to be the most important contributor to these results. Weiner (1966) in his excellent volume, *Psychodiagnosis in Schizophrenia,* reviews considerable literature comparing chronic with acute schizophrenics and with brain-damaged subjects on a wide variety of tests and experimental procedures. He concludes,

> It has generally been demonstrated that chronic schizophrenics, as distinguished either by duration of disturbance or by one of the criteria reviewed in the previous pages [criteria generally referring to malignant premorbid factors], exhibit to a greater degree than acute schizophrenics most of the identifying features of schizophrenic ego impairment.... With certain specific exceptions..., chronic schizophrenics deviate more from normal persons than do acute schizophrenics in their abilities to maintain cognitive focus, reason logically, form concepts at appropriate levels of abstraction, perceive realistically, employ adaptive defenses, utilize constitutionally determined potentials, and integrate their personality functioning [p. 243].

As would be expected from this generalization, empirical findings concerning the performance of chronic schizophrenics on the Halstead Battery have shown them to be fairly severely impaired on these measures of adaptive functioning. A study evaluating chronic schizophrenics who had been psychotic at least 8 years, both inpatient and outpatient, with and without brain damage (Klonoff, Fibiger, & Hutton, 1970) found that these chronic schizophrenics, hospitalized or not, were markedly impaired on the Halstead Neuropsychological Test Battery for Adults and on some other neuropsychological tests, including the Trail Making Test. On the other hand, a study by Small, Small, Millstein, and Moore (1972) of acutely psychotic hospitalized schizophrenics, manic-depressives, and patients with mixed manic-depressive and schizophrenic symptomatology yielded scores (with the single exception of the Finger Tapping Test) on the normal side of brain damage cutting scores on tests of a neuropsychological battery which included a number of Halstead and Reitan-Klove tests. It is of particular note that these patients were tested after they had been off antipsychotic medication for 1 month and while most of them were manifesting overt psychotic symptomatology. Stack and Phillips (1970) compared schizophrenics with relatively brief hospitalization (average of 8.1 months) with samples of hospitalized brain-damaged and medical patients on the Halstead variables: Category Test, Tactual Performance Test (TPT) total time, TPT Localization,

TPT Memory, Speech-sounds Perception, Rhythm, Tapping, and the Halstead Impairment Index; and the Trail Making Test. The brain-damaged subjects were significantly differentiated from the medical controls on all variables except Rhythm, and from the schizophrenics on all variables except the Category Test, TPT Localization, and Rhythm. Overall, the schizophrenics were not differentiated from the medical controls, though the individual variables, Category errors, TPT Time, and Trails B did separate these two groups significantly. These investigators also found that clinical psychologists could significantly discriminate the brain-damaged from schizoprhenic subjects on the basis of their performance on these tests. Their clinicians correctly diagnosed 72% of the combined schizophrenics and brain-damaged subjects. However, while they were able to diagnose almost all brain-damaged subjects correctly, they made many false positive judgments of brain damage with the schizophrenics. The major problem in the Watson et al. (1968) and the Lacks et al. (1970) studies was also that of excessive false positives for brain damage among the schizophrenics (and sometimes other non–brain-damaged subjects). In this connection, Stack and Phillips (1970) point out that an unknown number of their "false positives" may in fact have been true positives since the screening procedures they used could not insure elimination of all brain-damaged individuals from their schizophrenic subsamples. In a very well designed recent study Levine and Feirstein (1972) compared groups of schizophrenics, brain-damaged, and medically hospitalized patients which were equated on duration of hospitalization (moderate duration: group means were 22–27 months) as well as on the more commonly employed control variables: age, education, and IQ measures. The test battery included the Category, Tactual performance, Tapping, Speech Perception, and Rhythm Tests from the Halstead Battery as well as the Bender-Gestalt, Trail Making Test (Trails), and two WAIS subtests. All of the variables employed with the exception of TPT Memory and Localization discriminated the brain-damaged from medical controls, while none of them significantly discriminated the schizophrenics from the controls. Ten of their 16 variables significantly discriminated the brain-damaged from schizophrenic subjects, including the Tapping and Rhythm tests and Impairment Index of the Halstead Battery. A simple additive combination of equally weighted summary variables from each of their major sources of data: the Halstead Battery, the Trail Making Test, the Bender-Gestalt, and the WAIS, correctly diagnosed 78% of the brain-damaged, 67% of the schizophrenics, and 78% of the medical control patients.

Although Watson et al. (1968) distinguished two levels of chronicity in both their brain-damaged and schizophrenic samples, their definition of chronicity was duration of hospitalization at their facility, not time since first disability-related hospitalization, nor time since onset of disabling symptoms. Even with their definition, the mean chronicity of their least chronic sample of schizophrenics was over 1 year. Furthermore, their schizophrenic and brain-damaged subsamples were not equated on their measure of chronicity, the schizophrenics exceeding the brain-damaged in chronicity by a considerable margin (mean duration of hospitalization was 4.3 and 60.9 months for the least and most chronic brain-damaged subsamples, 13.9 and 134.0 months for the least and most chronic schizophrenic subsamples). They used no control for this difference between the two diagnostic groups even though their own data show a significant relationship between chronicity and the Halstead Impairment Index across diagnostic samples (see Levine & Feirstein, 1972, for an excellent critique of this aspect of the Watson et al. (1968) study). These uncontrolled differences in duration of hospitalization (chronicity) between the schizophrenics and brain-damaged subjects in the Watson et al. (1968) study could by themselves, account for these investigators' failure to discriminate between the two groups on neuropsychological variables (Levine & Feirstein, 1972). However, there are other important variables which may have contributed to the negative findings of some investigators attempting to discriminate schizophrenics from brain-damaged patients by means of the Halstead Battery.

Psychotic manifestations, acute and chronic, can also lead to inability to cooperate in testing, at least temporarily. Small et al. (1972) trained their psychotic subjects to cooperate in evaluations and did not test them when they were unable to cooperate. DeWolfe (1971) interrupted testing when psychotic subjects could not cooperate, resuming it when they could. Levine and Feirstein (1972) eliminated from their sample, schizophrenic subjects who could not cooperate in assessment. Stack and Phillips (1970) selected schizophrenic subjects in part on their ability to complete the Minnesota Multiphasic Personality Inventory. Since some investigators, including Watson et al. (1968), do not comment on this problem; failure to deal with it may have contributed to the poor scores obtained by schizophrenics in some of these studies.

As Klove points out, a further difficulty with the Watson et al. (1968) study, a difficulty which is shared by a number of other studies concerned with discriminating brain-damaged from schizophrenic subjects, is inadequate or inadequately specified diagnostic criteria. Watson et al. stated simply that their brain damaged subjects "displayed strong clinical and/or laboratory evidence of cerebral lesions [p. 680]," and that they eliminated diagnostically ambiguous cases and those whose records suggested both brain damage and schizophrenia by carefully screening the clinical records. Many of the patients in psychiatric inpatient facilities actually lack scientifically defensible diagnoses even though their charts may reflect little diagnostic ambiguity (Klove, this volume, Ch. 8). If the goal is to compare clearly distinguished groups, this state of affairs requires that all patients be diagnosed by adequate and consistent procedures. The degree to which this has been accomplished appears to vary considerably from one study to another; the success of these studies in discriminating brain-damaged from schizophrenic subjects appears to be positively related to the adequacy of diagnostic criteria employed.

The above summarized findings on the differentiation of schizophrenics from brain-damaged subjects with the Halstead Neuropsychological Test Battery for

Adults show that schizophrenics of slight to moderate chronicity can be discriminated from brain-damaged subjects of equal chronicity with these techniques. They also show that schizophrenics of considerable chronicity produce levels of performance on the variables of this battery similar to those obtained by brain-damaged subjects, though no data appear to be available concerning the comparative performances of such chronic schizophrenics and equally chronic brain-damaged subjects.

These findings that chronicity in schizophrenia, and perhaps the process-reactive dimension independently of chronicity (Lilliston, 1970), is related to impaired performance on most neuropsychological tests and that some groups of chronic schizophrenics perform as poorly as brain-damaged subjects on these neuropsychological tests require interpretation. They raise questions concerning what the neuropsychological tests measure and, conversely, what underlies the chronic schizophrenics' maladaptive performances. Some may conclude that these tests are not specifically sensitive to impairment of adaptive functions dependent upon the organic integrity of the brain, but are also quite sensitive to the particular, presumably psychogenic, adaptive impairment labeled chronic schizophrenia. However, it is equally defensible to conclude that these findings support the hypothesis of physiological brain malfunction underlying the adaptive deficits of chronic schizophrenics (Klonoff et al., 1970). As Weiner (1966) observes,

> It may be that chronic schizophrenia, or perhaps all schizophrenic disturbance, is based on certain kinds of cerebral dysfunction. . . . In other words, although it has been pointed out above that brain damage and chronic schizophrenia may be phenotypically similar but genotypically different, it is equally reasonable to hypothesize that organic and schizophrenic conditions may be phenotypically different, though sharing certain common genotypic features [p. 242].

A second issue concerns the remaining diagnostic questions, the differentiation of chronic and process schizophrenia from chronic brain damage, improvement of the differentiation of acute schizophrenics from brain-damaged subjects, and the detection of recently acquired brain damage in chronic and process schizophrenics. These questions have important treatment implications regardless of the underlying causes of the behavioral deficits in schizophrenia. Schizophrenics tend to respond favorably to antipsychotic medication (Klein & Davis, 1969), while brain-damaged patients tend to react adversely to such medication. While no controlled study supporting the latter generalization could be found, it is supported by the clinical experience and practice of clinicians who deal with large numbers of brain-damaged and schizophrenic patients at this medical center. Concerning recently acquired brain damage in schizophrenics, detection of this condition is necessary for appropriate neurological and/or neurosurgical treatment.

While chronic schizophrenics and brain-damaged patients tend to produce similar levels of performance on most neuropsychological variables, it does not follow that these conditions are not otherwise distinguishable. Some evidence suggests that level of performance on certain neuropsychological variables may be capable of distinguishing brain damage from chronic schizophrenia, or even of detecting chronic brain damage in chronic schizophrenics. Klonoff et al. (1970) found that two neuropsychological variables, Trails B and Benton Sentence Repetition, did significantly discriminate their chronic schizophrenics with brain damage from those without. However, most of their brain-damaged chronic schizophrenics had frontal lobe damage; other types of brain damage in chronic schizophrenics might not produce these results. These findings also require cross validation.

A number of investigators have presented evidence that schizophrenics arrive at *levels* of performance similar to those of brain-damaged individuals by different processes and that these different processes can be identified for diagnostic application. As in distinguishing one type of brain damage from another, relationships or variables which are not generally valid for distinguishing brain-damaged patients from non–brain-damaged controls may be valid for making specific discriminations, in this case distinguishing brain-damaged subjects from chronic schizophrenics. Based on clinical experience, Goldstein and Neuringer (1966) hypothesized that qualitative analysis of Trail Making Test performances would discriminate hospitalized schizophrenics from brain-damaged patients, though previous research had shown no useful discrimination of these groups by means of the time scores. Most of their specific predictions were confirmed. Eighty-three percent of their schizophrenics but only 29% of their brain-damaged subjects, produced "schizophrenic" signs: error-free performance, illogical performances with bizarre or random-appearing patterns, or giving up. Seventy percent of the brain-damaged subjects, but only 17% of their schizophrenics, produced one of their two "brain-damage" signs, sequence binding, the following of a letter or number series only. Though the chronicity of these patients was not reported by Goldstein and Neuringer, these results do illustrate that specific criteria designed to distinguish brain-damaged from schizophrenic patients on neuropsychological tests can be developed even though the customary scores derived for other purposes might not be effective. Similarly, and more to the point, since the schizophrenics employed were chronic, having been hospitalized for at least 7 years preceding the study, DeWolfe (1971) identified WAIS patterns which on cross validation correctly classified 76% of his brain-damaged patients and 68% of his chronic schizophrenics. Davis, DeWolfe, and Gustafson (1972) obtained and cross validated different WAIS subscale patterns for process and reactive schizophrenic groups and for brain-damaged subjects. They concluded that similar levels for the brain-damaged and process schizophrenic groups on Digit Symbol were arrived at by employment of different abilities reflected in different patterns for these two groups over other subtests. Parsons and Klein (1970) reviewed some studies which found process schizophrenics and brain-damaged subjects to arrive at similar levels of performance on concept formation tasks by different methods. Weiner (1966) presents voluminous data characterizing the performance of chronic schizophrenics; many of their psychological test performances cited by him are distinctly unlike those of most brain-damaged subjects.

Thus, while chronic and process schizophrenics have been shown to perform at levels of impairment comparable to brain-damaged subjects on many neuropsychological variables and other measures of adaptive behavior, various findings also indicate distinctions between their performance characteristics and those of most brain-damaged subjects, both on measures of adaptive functioning including neuropsychological tests, and on personality measures. In clinical practice, the differential diagnosis of chronic or process schizophrenia versus brain damage relies not only upon level of performance on neuropsychological variables, but on other methods of inference described by Reitan (1967a) and by Russell, Neuringer, and Goldstein (1970), as well as upon personality testing and historical data.

However, the entire problem of distinguishing schizophrenia, particularly chronic schizophrenia, from brain damage requires considerably more investigation. The detection of recently acquired brain damage in chronic schizophrenia seems to have received no systematic study. However, it would appear to be a less difficult task than that of distinguishing chronic schizophrenia from chronic brain damage, since recently acquired lesions, even in such cases, should produce more distinctive effects on neuropsychological variables than is the case with longstanding brain damage.

A research strategy which has seldom been applied to such problems, probably because of the practical difficulties involved, is to study, longitudinally, and in great detail, the subgroups lacking definitive diagnoses, obtaining complete neurological evaluations, including all physical tests which are clinically permissible and indicated; determining the course of the conditions by actual outcome; evaluating response to treatment; and relating the differential outcomes, including autopsies, to comprehensive neuropsychological, neurological, historical, personality, and social data obtained at the time the diagnostic questions were raised.

Another diagnostic difficulty is touched upon by Klove's mention (Ch. 8) of the Vega and Parsons (1967) results, and is addressed explicitly by Meier (Ch. 11) in this volume. This is the problem of relationships between cultural and, perhaps, racial factors and performance on neuropsychological tests. Vega and Parsons' controls performed very poorly on the Halstead tests, obtaining mean scores on the brain-damage side of cutting scores on a number of the variables for an average Impairment Index of .57. Vega and Parsons (1967) suggested that these impaired performances could be attributable to cultural factors leading to lessened motivation to perform on such tests. Clinical experience also suggests that a number of ethnic minorities tend to obtain rather poor scores on these tests, and of course, there is abundant evidence that Blacks and Chicanos score significantly less adequately than whites on a variety of measures of adaptive functioning (Jensen, 1969; Killian, 1971). Other ethnic groups may perform better than American whites on certain tests sensitive to brain damage. Meier reported, it may be recalled, that the Porteus Maze performance of Japanese stroke patients was superior to that of comparable White Americans (Meier & Okayama, 1969; Meier, 1970b). These ethnic differences in level of performance, particularly generally depressed or elevated performance, present no problem when the test battery provides convincing lateralizing or localizing data. However, they do present a problem when one is faced with an array of moderately depressed scores without a localizing or lateralizing pattern and one of the diagnostic possibilities is static or slowly progressive generalized cortical impairment.

Of course, a number of approaches to the solution of this problem may be invoked. One is to obtain norms for these measures on non–brain-damaged members of the relevant minority groups. Another would be to relate neuropsychological test scores in such groups to independent measures of adaptive functioning, and neurological status, and to etiological factors such as degree of environmental deprivation, history of injury, childhood and fetal malnutrition, etc. Such studies could document the etiology and significance with respect to brain function and adaptive sufficiency of these cultural-racial differences.

Meier (this volume, Ch. 11) also raises a number of other concurrent validity problems so far lacking satisfactory solutions. One has to do with the detection of other than acutely destructive or very extensive lesions in the prefrontal and anterior-temporal regions of the brain. As Meier summarized, objective research shows the battery to be less sensitive to frontal than to nonfrontal lesions. In working with clinical cases with well-diagnosed extensive lesions of the frontal areas one sometimes finds only a generalized reduction in level of performance rather than specific deficits. As Meier notes, even under such circumstances, the distinctive "frontal" personality characteristics of these patients are sometimes as striking as their paucity of specific adaptive deficits. In other cases, presumably of less-extensive frontal lesions, the characteristic "frontal" personality features may be entirely lacking or so subtle that they do not constitute reliable diagnostic indicators.

Another difficult problem discussed by Meier is detection of similar small or nonacutely destructive lesions of the anterior temporal lobes. Many patients are referred for differential diagnosis with clinical pictures including apparent psychomotor seizures. The presence or absence of hysterical personality features and hysterical neurotic defenses in such cases is an unreliable diagnostic indicator of an emotional basis for the patient's symptoms. Persons with such hysterical features do sometimes have brain lesions, certain kinds of brain lesions can apparently facilitate the development of hysterical personality features, and individuals without hysterical features can develop psychogenic "hysterical" pseudoneurologic symptoms. Reitan, (this volume, Ch. 2) and Klove and Matthews (this volume, Ch. 9) presented cases with similar diagnostic problems in order to illustrate the methods of inference required for individual clinical evaluation of such patients. In part, the problem encountered in inferring the presence of such lesions may reflect the tendency toward heavy reliance upon reduction of level of performance to identify neuropsychological impairment, as certainly is true of most of the research literature. Reitan's and Klove and Matthew's cases illustrate the need for multiple methods of inference in these cases, as is also true of most other neuropsychological diagnostic problems.

Meier makes a number of suggestions, based on various studies, for additions to the battery of variables which might add power for the detection of subtle prefontal and anterior temporal lesions. Most of these procedures so far lack convincing cross-validational work and adequate norms for clinical application. However, they do present some useful leads which, it is to be hoped, will generate the necessary research to evaluate their potential usefulness. For maximal generalizability and subsequent utility new procedures such as this should be studied in the context of the paradigm outlined by Reitan in Chapter 2, particularly with respect to the simultaneous collection of data on the tests of the Reitan revised and extended Halstead Neuropsychological Test Battery for Adults.

A general problem in evaluating battery profiles for subtle evidence of brain dysfunction is that performance on a number of tests in the battery is related to factors independent of brain damage. Some of these factors are well established in terms of presence of relationships, for example, premorbid level of intellectual functioning and age (Reitan, 1967b; Reitan & Shipley, 1963). For others there are scattered reports of relationships between the premorbid or concurrent patient characteristics and performance on the tests of the battery, or tests similar enough to present presumptive evidence for relationships, for example, race and culture, education and occupational experience, proficiency with the English language, and various situational stresses, emotional factors and psychiatric symptomatology. In practice, one accumulates subjective norms for these factors, but at best, this involves an indeterminate margin of error, and at worst, can lead to very erroneous conclusions. As Meier notes, there is no way to "play safe" with such diagnostic problems; both under- and overinterpretations generate hazards for the patients concerned.

The general problem would appear to fit the conceptual model of an array of multiple prediction equations in which the various factors related to performance on neuropsychological tests constitute the predictors and the individual neuropsychological variables constitute the dependent variables. Each neuropsychological variable would have a prediction equation which could be used to generate a confidence interval for an expected value on the variable, once the values of the predictors were known. A method similar to this has been used by Benton (1963) with his Visual Retention Test, permitting age and estimated premorbid IQ to generate expected values for the scores of this test.

Meier has also devised some techniques, and suggested others, which involve the principle of discordant feedback to make evident, subtle deficits due to brain damage. These and other techniques for eliciting evidence for subtle impairments through nervous system overload, as used by Luria (1966) deserve systematic investigation. Meier's preliminary results and Luria's observations suggest that such research will be fruitful.

Both Matthews (this volume, Ch. 10) and Meier (this volume, Ch. 11) suggest the addition of comprehensive personality and social assessment to improve battery power. There has so far not been much published on the interrelated application of comprehensive personality-social and comprehensive neuropsychological measurement. However, personality testing has sometimes contributed to the diagnosis and understanding of the behavioral effects of brain damage, suggesting that complementary neuropsychological and personality-social measurements merits systematic development. Hall, Hall, and Lavoie (1968) found interesting differences between right- and left-hemisphere-damaged patients on a variety of Rorschach variables. Recently, Overall and Gorham (1972) found that a combination of variables from the Wechsler Adult Intelligence Scale and from the Holtzman Inkblot Technique was more successful in discriminating aged from chronic brain syndrome subjects than the best combinations of variables from either test alone. The report of Matthews' study of employment outcome with mental retardates is eagerly awaited in this connection, since it involves personality measurement and behavioral ratings together with comprehensive neuropsychological evaluation. Vocational fitness appraisal of this group is a pressing social problem to which clinical neuropsychologists are frequently asked to bring their services, but about which adequate predictive data are lacking.

This leads to a more general consideration. Researchers in clinical neuropsychology have tended to concentrate on neuropsychological description of classical neurological syndromes or on the development of tests or batteries aimed at concurrent differential diagnostic questions (Meier, this volume, Ch. 11). A second class of questions has to do with specification of the adaptive deficits and assets in a particular case; this has received less systematic published attention. A number of distinguishable issues are involved. One is the application of group data to individual cases. The reader is again referred to Reitan's detailed consideration of this problem (this volume, Ch. 2). Another has to do with the need for different data bases and different methods of data collection for different kinds of clinical problems. Utilization of a standardized battery, particularly when it is administered by someone other than the neuropsychologist who will interpret it, presents great advantages for research in that the objective data can be evaluated without contaminating influences, and all subjects secure scores on the same variables. However, the method also presents great liabilities for *some* clinical diagnostic problems, among them adequate specification of an individual's characteristics for the purpose of predicting behavior in his ambient existence. For this purpose the data collector must have a clear idea of the practical problem to which he is predicting and the freedom, knowledge, and ingenuity to add tests to the battery for individual cases and to *improvise* individualized assessment when necessary. The clinical problems of individual patients, whether or not they have brain lesions, always contain unique elements; the clinician must recognize his responsibility not simply for addressing the referral problem, but toward the patient as a whole.

Meier has presented preliminary data on pioneering efforts in what promises to be one of the most stimulating and challenging areas in adult clinical neuropsychology, the prediction of spontaneous recovery from the behavioral deficits produced by cerebral insult and related problems of management and rehabilitation of such cases. Reitan (personal communication, 1972) has recently initiated a similar longitudinally organized project to evaluate outcome (recovery) in patients who have sustained brain trauma. The rate and nature of neuropsychological changes in individual patients following brain injury or disease need study in many other neurological conditions. Ability to predict extent and type of recovery will facilitate the counseling of patients and their families and the making of recommendations concerning disposition and treatment. Related problems are specification of the limits and nature of disability so that rehabilitation efforts can be tailored to the individual patient, and the design of appropriate rehabilitation approaches (Reitan, 1973). Meier's data are, so far, encouraging with respect to prediction of recovery. His approach underlines the point that measurement suitable for concurrent prediction may not be appropriate to prediction of later-maturing criteria.

Except for rehabilitation of motor and speech deficits, little practical knowledge appears to have been developed concerning rehabilitation of adaptive behavior following brain damage. A wide variety of approaches has been tried (Luria, 1963; Birch, 1964), many more with children than with adults. The large number of competing theories and methods for correcting deficits of adaptive functioning in children eloquently testifies to the limitations of understanding which remain. Despite the success of some approaches which have used detailed analysis of deficits to generate tailored remedial training programs (Morrison & Pothier, 1972), many attempts to deal with the problem have been handicapped by conceptual limitations which lead to considering brain damage as an undifferentiable condition, particularly with respect to deficits of higher cortical functions (Davison, Ch. 1; Benton, Ch. 3 and Matthews, Ch. 10, in this volume). Remediation of adaptive deficits in children variously diagnosed as having minimal cerebral dysfunction, minimal brain damage, brain damage, cerebral palsy, and mental retardation, is in a state of limited development despite relatively great attention to the problem. The analagous problem with adults has received comparatively little attention. The obvious deficits of brain-damaged adults, speech and movement disorders, receive remedial attention primarily because they are obvious, whereas more subtle deficits such as impairment of judgment and reasoning ability, even though of critical significance for functional re-adaptation, tend to be neglected.

NEUROPSYCHOLOGICAL ASSESSMENT
AS A STUDY TECHNIQUE

The two chapters in this volume concerned with specific adult problems involving brain damage, Chapter 9 by Klove and Matthews dealing with epilepsy, and Chapter 10 by Matthews, addressed to mental retardation, provide clinically useful information on these topics and illustrate the application of clinical neuropsychological assessment as a study technique. In each case, epilepsy and mental retardation, a significant content area defined by social and historic-medical factors, is revealed to contain differentiable cases with respect to adaptive functioning dependent upon the organic integrity of the brain. Further differentiation of these groups to the benefit of improved understanding of the conditions and improved case handling could well result from attempts to identify different categories in terms of neuropsychological functioning and personality-social characteristics within traditional groupings of these conditions.

Klove and Matthews' study of epilepsy already shows that different epileptic conditions are associated with different degrees of adaptive impairment. In one case, a generally accepted notion that patients with mixed seizures show more intellectual impairment than those with a single variety of seizure was not supported by their data. More strikingly discrepant from common belief was the finding of impairment of adaptive functions of patients with major motor seizures of unknown etiology. They further found that taking account of age at onset of seizures or neurological impairment showed a greater association between age at onset and degree of impairment in the group with major motor seizures of unknown etiology than among those with major motor seizures of known etiology or those with neurological impairment without epilepsy. The explanation of this finding is not apparent, but the implication is clear that individuals with major motor seizures of unknown etiology suffer impairment of adaptive functions which is more pronounced the earlier the onset of the seizures. Beside providing much needed background data for dealing with clinical cases, the findings may stimulate further investigation which could ultimately lead to understanding of the impairment of brain function involved in these cases. The individual cases presented illustrate these investigators' point that patterns of functioning on the neuropsychological battery are related to the condition of the brain and not to the presence of seizures per se.

Matthews' study of mental retardates provides much-needed interpretive reference material for this group. In evaluating an individual case, for example, it is useful to know how his pattern of scores compares with means for like-aged institutionalized mental retardates. The individual cases presented eloquently demonstrate that this classification of behavior pathology, and even the subclassifications within it, contain individuals differing not just in level of adaptive functioning, but in patterns of adaptive functioning which are understandable in terms of what is known about the effects of lesions in various parts of the brain. The variances of the measures listed in Table 6 of Matthews' chapter are instructive on this point (see Table 2, this chapter).

As expected, IQ scores were more variable among the normals, since the mental retardates were held to a restricted range of IQ (40-84). According to conceptions supported by studies which did not include comprehensive neuropsychological data, the mental retardates are afflicted with a general reduction of adaptive capacity (see Matthews' discussion, this volume, Ch. 10). If this were true, we would expect their scores on the neuropsychological ability measures to be restricted in variability compared with normals. However, the opposite is the case. Their scores on the neuropsychological tests are more variable in every case except for TPT Localization in which instance their very low mean (1.52 compared with 5.29 for normals) greatly truncates the distribution in the lower direction. With five of the seven neuropsychological variables the variance of the mental retardates is significantly larger by two-tailed test than that of this normal group. The data support the notion of varying patterns of adaptive deficit, measured by appropriate means, among these individuals of low IQ and restricted range of IQs. Of course, these data are merely suggestive. This normal group was not composed to be a control group for these mental retardates. Ages and many other factors are not comparable. Still, these data agree with those from the case studies, those cited by Matthews from Clausen's work, and those cited by Benton, (this volume, Ch. 3) that mental retardates are individuals not merely of low adaptive ability in general, but are acutely suffering from many different patterns of adaptive insufficiency.

TABLE 2

Comparison of Variances of Mental Retardates and Controls on IQ Scores and Selected Neuropsychological Variables

Variable	Control[a] group variance	Mentally retarded[b] group variance	F	p
Full Scale IQ	203.92	124.32	1.64	ns
Verbal IQ	209.09	83.91	2.49	< .002
Performance IQ	204.49	196.28	1.04	ns
Category Test	159.26	732.24	4.60	< .001
Finger Tapping	53.14	81.54	1.53	ns
TPT: Total Time	27.04	116.64	4.31	< .001
Memory	1.99	5.34	2.68	< .002
Localization	4.49	2.19	2.05	< .02
Trails A	139.24	5,004.15	35.94	< .001
Trails B	692.74	14,479.31	20.90	< .001

Note.—Adapted from Matthews (this volume, Ch. 10).
[a] $N = 50$.
[b] $N = 64$ except for Trails B where $N = 42$.

Presumably, these patterns have implications both for understanding and treatment of this class of individual. It would be instructive to analyze all the protocols, as Matthews has done for the three he presents, to determine how many contain patterns of relatively high and low scores which would support inferences of areas of more or less adequate brain tissue. Another means of analyzing such data would be to subject them to "O"–type cluster or factor analysis to determine what patterns of adaptive functioning exist in this group.

We can expect that a number of other socially and clinically important subgroups of individuals suffering from behavior pathology could be investigated with profit through the simultaneous employment of comprehensive neuropsychological, personality, and social measurement. Chronic alcoholism, drug abuse, aging, and learning disabilities, as suggested by Benton (this volume, Ch. 3), are only some of the more obvious categories.

CLINICAL-INDIVIDUAL VERSUS GENERAL KNOWLEDGE

Study of the chapters in this volume addressed to the clinical neuropsychology of adults can easily lead to some mistaken impressions. In none of these chapters was the full range of variables included in the adult battery presented or considered. There is a more-or-less standardized adult neuropsychological test battery (see Appendix, this volume, for descriptions of the tests used). Reitan's modification of the Halstead Neuropsychological Test Battery for Adults is employed by many workers in the field. This includes five of the original Halstead tests which generate seven variables entering into the Halstead Impairment Index plus some others which are used for other purposes: the Category Test,[2] the Tactual Performance Test (dominant hand time, nondominant hand time, both hands time, total time,[2] Memory,[2] and Localization[2]), the Speech-sounds Perception Test,[2] the Seashore Rhythm Test,[2] and the Finger Tapping Test (dominant hand score,[2] nondominant hand score). The Wechsler Adult Intelligence Scale, administered in its entirety, has replaced the Wechsler Bellevue, Form I, although Reitan is continuing to use the W-B I in his laboratory to maintain continuity of data collection. Klove reviews some studies performed by him and others to determine whether the WAIS can be used in the same manner as the W-B I for making diagnostic inferences, concluding that it can. Reitan's modification of the Halstead-Wepman Aphasia Screening Test is an integral part of the battery. So is the Reitan-Klove sensory-perceptual examination, which includes: tests of visual, tactual, and auditory suppression with bilateral simultaneous stimulations; finger agnosia or finger localization tests; fingertip number writing; and tactile coin recognition. The Reitan-Klove Tactile Form Recognition Test is used. A lateral dominance inventory, including the Miles ABC visual dominance examination, is commonly

---

[2] Variables entering into the Halstead Impairment Index.

employed, although for most purposes, preferred hand for signature writing is considered to indicate neurospychologically significant manual dominance. The other lateral dominance tests provide data concerning consistency of dominance versus mixed dominance which can aid interpretation in some cases. Strength of grip is measured bilaterally, usually with the Smedley hand dynamometer. The Trail Making Test, Parts A and B, is an integral part of the battery. In addition, the Minnesota Multiphasic Personality Inventory is routinely employed as part of the battery in order to provide information on emotional factors, personality characteristics, and psychopathology. Some MMPI configurations have some association with brain damage (Marks & Seeman, 1963; Meier, 1969), but not enough to base diagnosis on this alone, while others are associated with pseudoneurologic symptoms.

Many uses of the basic battery delete one or more tests or variables, while, more commonly, a number of favorite or experimental tests are added. Frequently it is desirable to add additional personality measurement; interest measurement; and especially, direct measurement of socially important behaviors such as the Wechsler Memory Scale, especially with 1-hour delayed recall of prose and designs portions (Milner, 1958), reading, spelling, and calculational tests, and the Vineland Social Maturity Scale.

No validational study has ever taken account of all of the variables and interrelations of variables employed in interpreting the "standard" battery described above. The closest approaches to utilizing all of the battery's variables simultaneously with adults were those of Wheeler et al. (1963), Wheeler and Reitan (1963), and Russell et al. (1970). This is, of course, excluding validation studies such as those of Reitan (1964b) which employed clinical judgment by expert neuropsychologists of the results of the "standard" battery.

Despite the success of those studies and those employing discriminant analyses in categorizing brain-damaged subjects, a cursory review of unsolved problems in the area of adult clinical neuropsychology might give the impression that knowledge in this field is so limited that little of practical value can be accomplished. This is far from the case. The reader is reminded of the difficulties of casting in scientifically acceptable terms knowledge gained from exposure to many different kinds of cases under many different conditions which was discussed by Reitan in Chapter 2 (this volume). The reader is also reminded of the various individual cases presented in this volume. Although the qualitative and configural information provided in case descriptions has been attacked as a chimera invented to cover the failures of clinical research, such information provides the bulk of data collected by some investigators in this field (Luria, 1966), and was encouraged for inclusion in this volume by its editors in the conviction that such information is essential to clinical practice.

Still we are far from having produced a systematic case book. Learning about this field would be very much facilitated if an adult clinical neuropsychology manual were available. At this writing there is none in generally available published form. The closest things to such a manual are Luria's *Higher Cortical*

Functions in Man (1966), the applied portions of which have little direct applicability to the use of a standardized neuropsychological test battery, and Russel et al. *Assessment of Brain Damage* (1970), which also presents its own difficulties as a manual. We will return shortly to this latter important contribution to the field. However, let clinical neuropsychologists acknowledge that they owe practitioners and students a good clinical manual. Such manuals as those for the Wechsler batteries, Rappaport, Gill, and Schafer's *Diagnostic Psychological Testing* (1945, 1946), and the various excellent manuals for the Rorschach Technique did much to popularize the techniques involved and to elevate their application to professionally defensible levels.

One resistance to the production of such a manual by those clinical neuropsychologists capable of doing so is reluctance to impose premature closure on a developing field. Another is that such a work would require great time and energy which would necessarily be diverted from more scientific (as contrasted with applied) pursuits. In the meantime, the student and practitioner suffer a rather severe handicap. Privately published (mimeographed) interpretive monographs, which fulfil some of the functions of a manual in combination with similarly produced battery administration and scoring manuals, documents usually obtained as a byproduct of attendance at neuropsychology workshops conducted by Reitan, are treasured by those that have them, since they are not easily replaceable and are necessary for employment of the neuropsychological batteries described in this volume.

A general handicap to the development of adequate information for clinical work has been the adoption of an inappropriate model of data collection, a byproduct of which is the denigration of naturalistic observation. Frequently, we move to a level of hypothesis testing related to theory before adequate naturalistic observation has been performed upon which to construct adequate theory and from which to derive sensible hypotheses (Scriven, 1969). In addition to systematic presentation of case material along with the reasoning leading to various descriptions of and inferences based upon these data, as was done with individual cases presented in this volume, we require further appraisal of the methods and steps of inference involved in clinical decisions. Group statistical methods are not appropriate to reflect or evaluate the information contained in comprehensive batteries of variables such as the modified Halstead Neuropsychological Test Battery for Adults (Reitan, this volume, Ch. 2). (We have considered various methods which attempt to get at combinations of variables and their configurations in relation to specific data evaluation problems.) Reitan (1967a) has described the methods of interference and their complementary use involved in appraisal of the results of such a battery. A very impressive pioneering effort to make explicit and objective the reasoning involved in the analysis of the results of this battery is the work by Russell et al. (1970). In this work, based upon the PhD dissertation of Russell, the authors explicate the decision rules involved in arriving at determinations of: brain damage versus no brain damage; left versus right, and each of these versus diffuse brain damage; and categorizations of acute, static, or congenital brain damage. The rules were evaluated by assessing agreement between classification of patients by these rules versus neuropsychologists' categorizations of the patients based on the same protocols and neurological examinations aimed at the same categories. The level of agreement was impressive. This work was handicapped by the fact of having to adopt rather arbitrary values for some of the decision rules since relevant empirical data were not available; because for rules based on clinical experience, the base of experience was not as broad as optimal; and because, despite the impressive complexity of detail of this work, the complete range of data, decision processes, and types of decisions encountered in this work was not encompassed. Nevertheless, this is a model for a type of investigation which could make this enterprise more objective and more teachable.

We look forward to the appearance of a clinical neuropsychology manual and the continuation of this promising work of Russell and his associates. These efforts should go far to advance this complex but very gratifying field.

APPENDIX
DESCRIPTION OF PSYCHOLOGICAL
TESTS AND EXPERIMENTAL
PROCEDURES

Psychological tests and procedures that have been studied with relation to brain functions have come to be known as neuropsychological tests. Some of these tests have been developed specifically to evaluate brain functions whereas others have been developed for other purposes. Many of the authors in this volume have used the same tests and, in some instances, modifications of standard procedures have been used. In order to organize and clarify the situation for the reader, the tests on which data was reported are listed in Table 1 by authors and chapters. Columns in Table 1 indicate the tests used for data reporting in each chapter whereas the rows indicate the chapters in which any particular test, procedure, or battery was studied.

Some of the procedures listed in Table 1 are generally well known whereas others are less well known. Rather than to present descriptions of tests and procedures in each chapter individually, which would have been unnecessarily repetitive, the methods used for data collection are described below. When a number of tests have been composed for conjoint use for a particular purpose, we have listed them under the heading of test batteries. Although some tests are described in more detail than others, we have not tried to present adequate information to serve as the basis for standarized administration of any of the tests. The reader who wishes to give any of the tests should refer to the appropriate instructions for administration and scoring.

TABLE 1
Test Batteries, Individual Tests, and Data Collection Procedures on which Data is Reported in this Volume

	Chapters							
	Authors							
	2	4	5	6	8	9	10	11
	Reitan	Reitan	Boll	Klonoff & Low	Klove	Klove & Matthews	Matthews	Meier
General Intelligence Batteries								
Wechsler-Bellevue Scale (Form I)	X		X		X		X	X
Wechsler Adult Intelligence Scale		X		X	X	X	X	
Wechsler Intelligence Scale for Children				X				
Stanford-Binet (Form L-M)								
General Neuropsychological Batteries								
Halstead's Neuropsychological Test Battery for Adults	X	X						
Halstead's Neuropsychological Test Battery for Children			X					
Reitan-Indiana Neuropsychological Test Battery				X	X	X		
Specialized Neuropsychological Test Batteries								
Reitan-Klove Sensory-Perceptual Examination		X	X	X	X	X	X	X
Klove-Matthews Motor Steadiness Battery				X	X	X	X	
Reitan-Klove Lateral Dominance Examination			X					
Additional Test Batteries								
Wide Range Achievement Test	X	X	X			X	X	
Minnesota Multiphasic Personality Inventory	X					X		
Individual Tests and Experimental Procedures								
Aphasia Screening Test	X							
Ballistic Arm Tapping								
Benton Right-Left Orientation Test		X	X	X				X
Benton Sound Recognition Test		X	X	X				X
Boston University Speech-sounds Discrimination Test								
Dynamometer				X	X	X	X	
Index Finger Tapping			X		X	X	X	X
Klove-Matthews Sandpaper Test			X		X			X
Modified Tactual Formboard Test								
Peabody Picture Vocabulary Test							X	X
Porteus Maze Test								
Reitan-Klove Tactile Form Recognition Test	X	X	X	X	X	X	X	X
Trail Making Test for Adults		X			X	X	X	
Trail Making Test for Children		X	X				X	
Visual Space Rotation Test								X

364

TEST BATTERIES

GENERAL INTELLIGENCE TEST BATTERIES

Wechsler-Bellevue Intelligence Scale [Form I]
(Wechsler, 1944)

The Wechsler Scales of Intelligence are the most widely used tests for individual (as opposed to group) evaluation of adult intelligence. The Wechsler-Bellevue Scale has been superseded by the Wechsler Adult Intelligence Scale, but both sets of tests are very similar in content, scoring, and interpretation. Six Verbal subtests and five Performance subtests are included. The Verbal subtests include Information (a test of general information), Comprehension (understanding of statements that have a certain degree of complexity or social significance), Digit Span (repetition of series of digits in both a forward and backward order), Arithmetic (solution of arithmetical problems presented orally and in written form), Similarities (explanations of the common category or meaning of pairs of words), and Vocabulary (definition of words). Among the Performance tests, the Picture Arrangement Test requires the subject to arrange pictures in a proper sequence to tell a meaningful story (much like arranging comic strip squares that had been placed in an improper sequence). The Picture Completion Test requires the subject to identify a missing part in each of a series of pictures. Block Design requires the subject to duplicate spatial configurations shown on cards using a set of colored blocks. The Object Assembly Test is similar to a jigsaw puzzle in which the subject is required to put the parts together to complete a whole figure. The Digit Symbol Test requires the subject to substitute symbols for numbers, using a code that is presented together with the test. Both a Verbal and Performance IQ, as well as a Full Scale IQ, may be computed from the subtest results.

Wechsler Adult Intelligence Scale [WAIS]
(Wechlser, 1955)

The WAIS, as mentioned above, is very similar to the Wechsler-Bellevue Scale [Form I]. The normative tables, however, are based on a more extensive sample.

Wechsler Intelligence Scale for Children [WISC]
(Wechsler, 1949)

The WISC grew logically out of the Wechsler-Bellevue Intelligence Scales, with most of the items being from Form II of these tests. In addition, some easier items were added and the WISC covers an age range from 5 to 15 years. The WISC consists of 12 tests, divided into Verbal and Performance groups. The Verbal tests include Information, Comprehension, Arithmetic, Similarities, Vocabulary, and Digit Span; the Performance tests are Picture Completion, Picture Arrangement, Block Design, Object Assembly, Coding, and Mazes.

Stanford-Binet Intelligence Scale [Form L-M]
(Terman & Merrill, 1960)

This is a widely used test of general intelligence that is especially useful with young children. In this volume, data on the Stanford-Binet were reported only by Klonoff and Low.

GENERAL NEUROPSYCHOLOGICAL
TEST BATTERIES

Halstead's Neuropsychological Test Battery for
Adults (Halstead, 1947; Reitan, 1969)

As Halstead indicated in his book, *Brain and Intelligence* (1947), he employed a battery of 27 behavioral measures in his studies of the effects of brain lesions. However, the 10 measures that he selected to contribute to the Halstead Impairment Index have come to be known as his test battery. Reitan (1955a) found that 3 of these 10 measures were not particularly effective in differentiating subjects with and without brain lesions. These tests were the Time Sense Test-Memory component, Critical Flicker Frequency, and Critical Flicker Frequency Deviation Score. In most instances investigators contributing to this volume have omitted data on these three tests. Other tests in Halstead's Battery are the Category Test, the Tactual Performance Test (Time, Memory, and Localization components), the Seashore Rhythm Test, the Speech-sounds Perception Test, and the Finger Oscillation Test. The Visual component of the Time Sense Test is determined as part of the procedure in obtaining the score for the Memory component. Finally, the Halstead Impairment Index may be determined from scores on the individual tests in Halstead's Battery.

Category Test. This test utilizes a projection apparatus for presentation of 208 stimulus figures on a milk-glass screen. An answer panel for use by the subject is attached to the test apparatus and is located at a convenient level below the screen. The answer panel contains four levers which are numbered from 1 to 4. The subject is told that he should inspect each stimulus figure when it appears on the screen and depress one of the four levers, depending upon which answer he thinks may be correct. Depression of any of these levers will cause either a bell or buzzer to sound depending upon whether or not the lever selected is the "right" or "wrong" answer. Only one response is allowed for each item. Before the test begins, the subject is told that the test is divided into seven groups of pictures and that each group has a single principle running through the entire group from beginning to end. On the first item in any group, the subject can only attempt to guess the right answer, but as he progresses through the items of the group, the sound of the bell or buzzer with each response indicates whether his guesses are correct or incorrect. In this way, the test procedure permits the subject to test one possible principle after another until an hypothesis is hit upon which is positively reinforced consistently by the bell.

The subject is never told the principle for any group regardless of the difficulty he might encounter, but the first and second groups are nearly always easily performed even by persons with serious brain lesions. The first group requires only the matching of Arabic numerals above each of the answer levers with individual Roman numerals that are shown on the screen. In the second group, the subject must learn to press the lever which has a number corresponding to the number of items appearing on the screen, regardless of their content. For example, the answer would be "2" if two squares appeared, "4" if four letters of the alphabet composed an item, etc. The examiner announces the end of each group and tells the subject that he is ready to proceed to the next group. Before each group of items is begun the examiner points out that the principle might be the same as it has been or that it might be different and that the task of the subject is to try to discern the principle. The third group of items is based on a uniqueness principle. Four figures appear in each item, and the subject must learn to depress the lever corresponding with the figure which is most different from the others. Although this group begins rather simply, it progresses to items in which one figure may differ from the others in three or more respects (such as size, shape, color, solidness of figure), while the rest of the figures differ from each other in only two respects. For example, an earlier item may be made up of four identical triangles except that the third triangle is large and the others are equally small. In this case the "correct" answer would be "3" with the determinant of uniqueness having been size. On a later item all four figures may differ in shape and color, be the same size, with the first figure being solid while the other three figures are formed only by an outline. Uniqueness in this case could not be determined by shape, color, or size since these determinants were entirely variable or entirely constant. The answer would be "1" since the first figure was the only one that was solid.

The fourth group uses identification of one of the four quadrants of each figure as the basis for the correct response. The upper left quadrant is associated with "1" as the correct answer and "2," "3," and "4" correspond with a clockwise progression of quadrants. The first six items omit one quadrant or another in each item, but the three quadrants present in these items are identified by Roman numerals. The relationship between number and quadrant is, of course, constant throughout the entire group of items. After the first six items the Roman numerals identifying quadrants are no longer present even though one quadrant or another is omitted in each item. At this point the subject is told that the principle is the same, even though the numbers are no longer present. Some normal subjects do not remember the correct answer for each quadrant, particularly confusing quadrants 3 and 4. However, the bell and buzzer soon provide them with the necessary information. Subjects with cerebral lesions, however, frequently persist in misidentification of quadrants (especially 3 and 4) even though the buzzer makes it perfectly clear that their answers are wrong.

The fifth group of items is organized according to a principle based on the proportion of the figure that is composed of solid versus dotted lines. If one-quarter of the figure is solid the answer is "1" and so on to an answer of "4" for a completely solid figure. Even though varied stimulus figures are used, the principle remains constant throughout the group. As with other groups, the examiner announces the end of the group and states that the next group may be based upon the same principle or it may use a new principle. Group six is based on the same principle as group five, the only instance in the test where use of the same principle occurs in an ensuing group.

The seventh group is not based on a single principle because it is a review group that makes use of items and principles that have been used previously in the test. The subject is told this and instructed to try to remember the correct answer for each item.

The Halstead Category Test has several characteristics that make it somewhat different from many tests. It is a relatively complex concept formation test which requires fairly sophisticated ability in noting similarities and differences in stimulus material, postulating hypotheses that appear reasonable with respect to recurring similarities and differences in the stimulus material, testing these hypotheses with respect to positive or negative reinforcement (bell or buzzer), and adapting hypotheses in accordance with the reinforcement accompanying each response. While the test is not particularly difficult for most normal subjects, it would seem to require competence in abstraction ability especially, since the subject is required to postulate possible solutions in a structured rather than permissive context. Since positive or negative reinforcement (bell or buzzer) follows each response, the test in effect presents a learning experiment to each subject in the area of concept formation, rather than the usual situation in psychological testing which requires solution of an integral problem situation. While this aspect of the test may well reflect an important approach in the study of human brain-behavior relationships, it also represents a serious complication with respect to determining the reliability of the procedure as a single psychological test. The essential purpose of the test is to determine the ability of the subject to profit from both negative and positive experiences as a basis for altering his performance, and the precise pattern and sequence of negative and positive reinforcement is probably never exactly the same throughout the test for any two subjects. Since every item in the test may be presumed to have an effect on the subject's response to ensuing items, and the pattern of positive and negative reinforcement is different for each subject (or for the same subject upon repetition of the test), the usual approaches toward determintion of reliability indices may be confounded. The essential nature of the test, as an experiment in concept formation, is nevertheless fairly clear.

Tactual Performance Test (Time, Memory, and Localization components). The Tactual Performance Test utilizes a modification of the Seguin-Goddard form board. The subject is blindfolded before the test begins and is not permitted to see the form board or blocks at any time. His task is to fit the blocks into their proper spaces on the board using only his preferred hand. After having completed this task and without having been given prior warning, he is asked to perform the same task using his nonpreferred hand only. Finally, he is asked to do the task a third time using both hands. The time recorded for each trial provides a comparison of the efficiency of performance of the two hands, but the time score for the test is based on the total time needed to complete the three trials. After the board and blocks have been put out of sight, the blindfold is removed; and, the subject is asked to draw a diagram of the board representing the blocks in their proper spaces. This drawing is scored according to Memory and Localization components. The Memory component is based upon the number of blocks correctly reproduced in the drawing, and the Localization component is based on the number of blocks approximately correctly localized.

The Tactual Performance Test undoubtedly is a complex test in terms of its requirements. Ability in placing the variously shaped blocks in their proper spaces on the board depends upon tactile form discrimination, kinesthesis, coordination of movement of the upper extremities, manual dexterity, and visualization of the spatial configuration of the shapes in terms of their spatial interrelationships on the board.

Rhythm Test. The Rhythm Test is a subtest of the Seashore Tests of Musical Talent. The subject is required to differentiate between 30 pairs of rhythmic beats which are sometimes the same and sometimes different. This test would appear to require alertness to nonverbal auditory stimuli, sustained attention to the task, and the ability to perceive and compare different rhythmic sequences.

Speech-sounds Perception Test. The Speech-sounds Perception Test consists of 60 spoken nonsense words, the beginning and ending consonant sounds of which vary while their "ee" vowel sound remains constant. The test is played from a tape recorder with the intensity of sound adjusted to meet the subject's preference. The subject's task is to underline the spoken syllable, selecting from the four alternatives printed for each item of the test form. This test requires the subject to maintain attention through 60 items, to perceive the spoken stimulus-sound through hearing, and to relate the perception through vision to the correct configuration of letters on the test form.

Finger Oscillation Test. This test is a measure of finger-tapping speed using a specially adapted, mounted manual tapper. Precise characteristics of this apparatus (tension of the arm, angle of the arm, position on the board, etc.) have been maintained in order to ensure comparability of data between subjects and between various investigators. Measurements are made first with the subject using the index finger of the preferred hand, and a comparable set of measurements are obtained with the nonpreferred hand. The subject is given five consecutive 10-sec. trials with the hand held in a constant position in order to require movements of only the finger rather than the whole hand and arm. Every effort is made to encourage the subject to tap as fast as he possibly can. This test would appear to be rather purely dependent upon motor speed.

Time Sense Test (Visual and Memory components). The Time Sense Test requires the subject to depress a key which permits a sweep-hand to rotate on the face of a clock. The subject's task is to allow the hand to rotate 10 times and then to stop it as close to the starting position as possible. After 20 trials during which the subject observes the rotation of the sweep-hand on the face of the clock, the face of the clock is turned away; and, the subject is asked to duplicate the visually controlled performance as closely as possible. After 10 "memory" trials, series of 10 visual and 10 memory trials are interspersed to represent a total of 40 visual trials and 20 memory trials in the entire test. The score, recorded separately for each procedure, represents the amount of error made. This test is used in identical form for both adult subjects and older children. The visual component of this test requires the subject to maintain alertness and coordinate counting from 1 to 10 with the rotation of the clock's sweep-hand. Rather discrete visual-motor coordination (a type of reaction time measure) is required to stop the hand's rotation in the correct position. The memory component requires estimation of the duration of time necessary for the hand to make 10 revolutions, using the subject's initial perception of this interval as the reference point. In a prior validation study (Reitan, 1955a) results on this test did not reach the very highly significant levels of differentiation of groups with and without cerebral lesions that characterized most of the other tests.

Critical Flicker Frequency and Critical Flicker Frequency Deviation. In this test an electronic instrument (Strobotac) with a short flash duration is used to provide intermittent light at variable frequencies. The Strobotac is housed in a specially constructed soundproof apparatus. The test involves the determination of the point at which a variably intermittent light fuses into the appearance of a steady light. The subject is required to adjust a knob until the flashing rate of the light is increased to the point where fusion is reached and the light appears to be steady. The frequency of intermittency, in terms of cycles per second, is recorded. An additional score is obtained as an expression of deviation from this point for the subject on five successive trials. Our prior results (Reitan, 1955a) using this apparatus have not shown significant differences in groups with and without cerebral lesions.

Halstead Impairment Index. The Impairment Index is a summary value based upon the 10 tests in the Halstead Battery (omitting the Visual component of the Time Sense Test in the 11 tests described above). It is determined for an individual subject merely by counting the number of tests on which the results fall in the range characteristic of the performance of brain-damaged rather than normal subjects. Criterion values for the Impairment Index have been established only for adult subjects.

The Halstead Neuropsychological Test Battery for Children (Reitan, 1969)

The developmental research for this battery of tests was performed from 1951 to 1953 by Reitan. The Halstead Battery for adults has already been found satisfactory for use with persons 15 years of age and older but it appeared that certain modifications would be needed for younger persons. The first step was to administer the adult battery to a sample of normal children below the age of 15 years in order to determine the types of changes that needed to be made. It appeared that relatively minor changes were necessary. These were made and a new group of children were then tested to evaluate the changes in actual practice. The modifications that were made represented simplification of the tests rather than any basic change in content or procedure. We found that essentially the same instructions used for adults could be used for older children. The next developmental step represented testing children from 14 years of age and downward in order to determine the lower age limit at which the tests could validly be administered. It appeared that the tests could consistently be given to 9-year-old children, whereas a number of children younger than 9 years found the complexity level of certain tests too great. The developmental research and standardization of procedures was completed in 1954 and this battery has been in standard research and clinical use since that time for evaluation of children aged 9 through 14 years.

Changes in the battery were made only for the Category Test, the Tactual Performance Test, and the Speech-sounds Perception Test. The Halstead Critical Flicker Fusion Test was omitted.

Changes in the *Category Test* included reorganization of some of the items in order to achieve a more orderly evolution of the principles in various subtests. Further, because we had previously had some difficulties in reproducing colored items in the test, the colors were dropped and only black and white was used. Finally, the fourth group of items was omitted entirely. This group, in the adult version of the test, was based on identification of one quadrant or another as a basis for the correct response. We found that normal children tended to have difficulty with this concept. Omission of this group of 40 items reduced the test in length from 208 items in the adult version to 168 items. As with the adult version, the last group of items was not based on any particular principle but rather represented items that had been presented previously in the test.

The *Tactual Performance Test* was changed from the adult form by omission of four of the figures. These figures were the star, circle, triangle, and the elongated six-sided figure. Familiarity with the placement of figures in the adult test would serve as a basis for recognition that these four figures were located at the top, bottom, and the two sides. The modification was effected merely by omission of these figures in the board, leaving the six remaining figures in their exact places as compared with the adult form of the test. The size of the blocks and spaces, as well as the outside dimensions of the board, remained the same.

The *Speech-sounds Perception Test* remained the same in terms of the tape recording, but the answer form was modified. This modification was effected by reducing the number of alternatives for each item from four to three. Selection of the alternative for deletion was made by using a table of random numbers to identify one of the three incorrect alternatives for each item.

It is apparent from these changes that the essential requirements of the tests were not altered. The changes represented only simplifications or abbreviations of the tests as they existed in the adult form. As mentioned above, the instructions have remained essentially the same. As with adult subjects, it has been our practice to attempt to communicate the requirements of the testing situation to the subject in giving the instructions so that every subject has an understanding of what is being asked of him. In attempting to achieve this aim, it becomes clear that comprehension of the instructions does not represent part of the test, as tends to be true with some projective tests and in certain testing techniques.

Reitan-Indiana Neuropsychological Test Battery for Children (Reitan, 1969)

The developmental research for this battery of tests was begun in 1955 after enough experience had been achieved with the Halstead Battery for Children aged 9 through 14 to assure us that promising results were forthcoming. Essentially the same type of program was followed as in the modification of the adult battery for older children. First, we obtained initial insights into needed changes by administering the Halstead Neuropsychological Test Battery for Children to youngsters below the age of 9 years. As had been found in our previous developmental research, a significant number of children below the age of 9 years had difficulties with at least certain parts of this test battery. Therefore, modifications were necessary for a considerable number of the tests and, in some instances, it was necessary to develop entirely new tests. Several criteria were observed in composing the entire battery, including the composition of a group of tests that would permit the conjoint and integrated use of the various methods of inference concerning the effects of brain lesions in human beings, coverage of a broad range of abilities from simple motor and sensory-perceptual functions to complex cognitive and intellectual functions, and development of a group of tests that would seem to have promise of holding the interest of the subject.

Category Test. In modifying the Category Test we realized the younger children would not be able to respond differentially to the symbolic connotations of numbers. A decision was made to use the same apparatus but to identify the four answer buttons by red, blue, yellow, and green lights. The colors were permitted to vary not only in wavelength but in other dimensions as well in order to minimize the possible disadvantage of color blindness or color weakness in some subjects. We have found it possible to administer this test quite successfully to completely colorblind persons. Thus, it is clear that stimulus characteristics other than hue are sufficient to subserve an excellent performance and we can conclude that color blindness is not necessarily a limiting factor in the performance of this test. Nevertheless, color blindness cannot be ruled out as a possible disadvantage at least for certain subjects. The test also has been considerably shortened from either the adult version or the test for older children. The test in total consists of 80 items. The first subtest is 10 items in length, followed by three 20-item subtests and a final subtest that is

10 items in length. We attempted to develop the test in such a way that it used essentially the same principles as did the version for older children and adults. For example, the first group of items, instead of requiring the subject to match numbers, requires the subject to match colors. Therefore, if a red figure appears on the screen the subject's task is to respond by depressing the "red" lever. The second group of items in the test for older children and adults is based upon the idea of quantity. For example, if three circles appear on the screen, the answer is Lever #3. This principle was adapted in the test for younger children by requiring a response in terms of the predominant color on the screen. Thus, if a large red square and a small blue square appear in a particular item, the answer is in terms of the color that predominates in area or size. The third principle in the test for older children and adults is based upon a uniqueness or oddity concept. The subject responds to the number of the figure that is most different from the others, with differences being based on color, shape, size, and solidness or emptiness of the figure. The corresponding group of items in the test for young children is also based upon an oddity principle with color, of course, being eliminated as one of the differentiating characteristics. However, one item or another differs from the rest with respect to size, shape, or solidness or emptiness of the figure. Thus, if an item consists of four squares in which three are identical in size but the red square is larger than the rest, the answer would be the "red" lever. The fourth group of items requires the subject to respond to the particular color that is less prominently displayed than the others. For example, if a figure is represented by equal parts of the three colors, green, yellow, and blue, but by a lesser part of the color red, the response would be the "red" lever. Items of this kind make up the first 10 items of this group. Following this, the test consists of items that make use of only three colors and the subject's task is to respond to the *missing* color. As with the tests for older children and adults, the subject is never told the principle but instead must develop an understanding of this for himself in accordance with information given by the bell and the buzzer. The fifth group, which consists of 10 items, is a summary group as is also true of the last group in the tests for older children and adults. This group is made up of items that the subject has already seen and he is instructed to try to remember the right answer and to give the same answer again.

Tactual Performance Test This test is administered in essentially the same way to younger children as to older children. However, the board is placed in a horizontal position rather than a vertical position. More specifically, the board is so placed that the cross is in the upper left-hand corner. Thus, smaller children in the age range from 5 through 8 years are not required to reach as high as are older children and adults in placing the blocks in their proper spaces. In terms of procedure, including blindfolding of the subject before the task is begun, the task is the same as for older children and adults. While some younger children need reassurance before being blindfolded, we are regularly successful in being able to follow this procedure. However, this test is usually not administered until the subject and examiner have shared experiences with other tests and thereby have developed a personal relationship in the testing situation.

Finger Tapping Test. The finger-tapping apparatus was modified from the version used for older children and adults. We found that children in the 5–8-year age range often had fingers that were somewhat small for proper use of the adult apparatus. Therefore, another version of the test was developed that used an electronic counter and a tapping key that did not traverse as wide an arc as that used for older children and adults. The procedure, however, is essentially the same, including determination of finger-tapping speed with both hands.

Marching Test. While measurement of finger-tapping speed represents a basis for evaluation of fine motor functions, we felt also that the battery should include a procedure for evaluating more gross skeletal muscular function. For this purpose the Marching Test was developed. This test consists of a practice page and five legal-size pages for the test itself. On each page there are a series of circles on the left side and another set on the right side. These circles are connected by a line, indicating the progression from one circle to the next. On the practice page the circles are arranged in a perfect vertical manner and the subject's task is to proceed from the circle nearest him to the circle at the top of the page. Crayons are used so that the movements made by the subject are clearly recorded. Further, the time required to accomplish the coordinated movements is measured. The first part of the test requires the subject merely to "march" up the page as quickly as possible, being sure to hit each circle with his crayon. The task is done first with the preferred hand and then repeated on the other side of the page with the nonpreferred hand. When the examiner is sure that the subject understands the procedure on the practice page, the test is performed for the preferred and the nonpreferred hand on each of the next five consecutive pages. Procedures for administration of the test and recording of errors are noted in the test instructions. Following the use of the hands individually, another aspect of the test is attempted. Sometimes this aspect of the test is too difficult for certain children. However, an attempt is made to determine the subject's ability to march up the page using both hands. The examiner places her index fingers on the circles and requests the subject to march up the page with his index fingers, following her alternation of movements from one hand to the other. The subject's right hand follows the sequence of circles on the right side of the page and the left hand must follow the sequence of circles on the left side of the page. The marching progresses at the approximate rate of one move per second. The test is scored by recording the total number of circles the subject is able to complete.

Color Form Test. Several tests were devised in the attempt to provide measurements regarding organizational ability, abstraction, concept formation, and flexibility in thinking processes. Two of these attempted to use the requirements of the Trail Making Test as a starting point. These tests are called the Color Form Test and the Progressive Figures Test. The Color Form Test uses stimulus material of various colors and shapes. The subject's task is to follow a sequence of moves from one figure to another on an $8\frac{1}{2}'' \times 11''$ page, making the first move on the basis of shape, the second move on the basis of color, etc. Thus, the patient moves from the initial figure to one having the same shape even though the color is different, then proceeds to a figure that is different in shape but has the same color, and continues to alternate in this fashion. Essentially, the test requires the subject to make progess from the beginning to the end of the test, alternating form and color criteria in much the same way that Part B of the Trail Making Test requires alternation between numbers and letters.

Progressive Figures Test. This test has turned out to be somewhat more difficult than the Color Form Test. This test also is presented on a $8\frac{1}{2}'' \times 11''$ sheet of paper on which are printed eight stimulus figures. Each stimulus figure consists of a large outside figure (such as a circle) and a smaller figure of another shape inside (such as a square). The subject's task is to use the small inside figure as the clue for progressing to the outside shape of the next stimulus figure. For example, if the subject is located at a large circle enclosing a small square, the small square would indicate that the next figure to move to would be the one having a large square. If the large square enclosed a small triangle, the small triangle would serve as a cue for the next move. In this way the subject progresses from inside figure to outside figure, moving from one stimulus complex to the next. Each of these tests is scored in terms of the time required to complete the test. The instructions for each test are given to the subject not only verbally but also by example, using a practice page.

Matching Pictures Test. Another simple abstraction or concept formation test is represented by the Matching Pictures Test. This test consists of five pages, the first of which includes practice items. In general, the task requires the subject to match items from the top of the page to those listed at the bottom of the page. The practice items require only matching of identical figures. This is true also of the first page of the test. The second page, however, begins to require a limited degree of generalization. For example, among various available figures a woman must be used to match the stimulus figure of a man. A horse matches a cow, a chicken matches a rooster, etc. The test progresses through somewhat more complex items. Obviously this test requires the subject to be able to respond in terms of categories in order to do the test correctly. The score is reported as the number of correct responses in the total of 19 items.

Target Test. Several tests were also developed to tap the important area related to reception and expression of visual-spatial relationships. The Target Test consists of a stimulus figure that is affixed to the wall in front of the subject. This figure is $18'' \times 18''$ in size and contains nine large black dots that are arranged in the form of a square. The subject's answer form consists of 20 similar nine-dot figures arranged on an $8\frac{1}{2}'' \times 11''$ sheet of paper. The test itself consists of 20 items. The examiner, using a pointer, taps out a design on the stimulus figure for each item in the test. The subject is required to watch this performance and after a 3-sec. delay to attempt to draw the figure on his answer sheet. Thus, this test requires a delayed response in addition to a reproduction of a visual-spatial configuration. The test proceeds through the 20 items from simple items to ones that are more complex and is scored as the number of items correctly reproduced.

Individual Performance Test. Several rather simple tasks concerned with receptive and expressive aspects of visual-spatial relationships are included in a test called the Individual Performance Test. The first of these tests, called Matching V's, requires the subject to match stimulus figures in accordance with the size of the angles involved. A card is placed in front of the subject on which Vs representing a small angle extend from the left side to Vs representing a wider angle on the right side. The subject is presented with a number of small blocks on which Vs of various angles appear and is asked to place the Vs on each of these small blocks under the V on the stimulus card that has the same angle. The task is scored in terms of the time required to complete it and the number of errors made. Following this the subject is asked to copy the figure of a six-sided star. It is pointed out to the subject that this figure consists of two overlapping triangles and he is instructed to draw them in this way, positioning one triangle properly on top of the other. After the instructions are given the patient is told to start and the test is scored in terms of the number of seconds required to complete the drawing. An accuracy score is also obtained by counting the number of angles (or points of the star) protruding to the outside of the drawing isolated by a straight line in the figure. The Matching Figures Test is very similar to the Matching V's Test. In this case, however, the figures to be matched range from ones that are rather simple in their configuration to ones that are more complex. The subject must match each of the individual stimulus figures with its appropriate figure on the stimulus card. In order to accomplish this task without error, it is necessary that rather close attention be paid to the details of the design. This test also is scored in terms of the number of seconds required to complete the task and the number of errors made. Finally, among the four tests of the Individual Performance Test, the subject is asked to copy a figure made up of concentric squares. The instructions require that the subject be told that the figure is made up essentially of three boxes placed inside of each other and that he should proceed to try to draw them in this way. The drawing is scored in terms of the number of seconds required for completion and an accuracy score is obtained by counting the number of angles that touch outside lines.

SPECIALIZED NEUROPSYCHOLOGICAL TEST BATTERIES

A number of neuropsychological test batteries, rather specialized in content, have been developed to supplement and complement the more general batteries.

Reitan-Klove Sensory-Perceptual Examination
(Reitan, 1969)

It became apparent to Reitan in the course of trying to predict type and location of cerebral lesions in individual patients that Halstead's Battery and the Wechsler-Bellevue Scale needed to be supplemented by additional measures of a simple nature that reflected the adequacy of sensory-perceptual performances on the two sides of the body. Klove contributed to the development of this battery both in terms of its content and scoring procedures. The tests used are certainly not original since they have been investigated, particularly in neurological studies, for many years. However, their use in conjunction with tests of higher brain functions of an intellectual and cognitive nature greatly augments their clinical significance.

Tactile, Auditory, and Visual Imperception. This procedure attempts to determine the accuracy with which the subject can perceive bilateral simultaneous sensory stimulation after it has already been determined that his perception of unilateral stimulation on each side is essentially intact. The procedure is used for tactile, auditory, and visual sensory modalities in separate tests. With respect to tactile function for example, each hand is first touched separately in order to determine that the subject is able to respond with accuracy to the hand touched. Following this, unilateral stimulation is interspersed with bilateral simultaneous stimulation. The normal subject is able to respond accurately to stimulation of the right hand, left hand, or both hands. Subjects with lateralized cerebral lesions are often able to identify unilateral stimulation correctly but sometimes fail to respond under circumstances of bilateral simultaneous stimulation to the hand contralateral to the damaged hemisphere. Contralateral face-hand combinations are also used with single or double simultaneous stimulation as part of our standard procedure. Testing for auditory imperception makes use of an auditory stimulus produced through lightly rubbing the fingers together very quickly and sharply. Essentially a similar procedure is applied in visual examination with the examiner executing discrete movements of the fingers while the subject focuses on the examiner's nose. Our standard procedure calls for as minimal a stimulus as is necessary to achieve consistently correct responses to unilateral stimulation. The test for perception of bilateral simultaneous stimulation is, of course, obviated if the patient has a serious lateralized tactile, auditory, or visual loss and is not able to respond correctly to unilateral stimulation on the affected side. Such unilateral impairment is rarely encountered in the tactile and auditory modalities but is not infrequently seen in the visual modality (homonymous hemianopia). Lateralized deficiencies, of course, may have significant implications for nervous system disorders even though they obviate use of a test for perception of bilateral stimuli. The score is recorded as the number of errors.

Tactile Finger Recognition. This procedure tests the ability of the subject to identify individual fingers on each hand following tactile stimulation of each finger. Before the examination begins, the examiner must work out a system with the patient for reporting which finger was touched. Customarily, the patient will report by number, but sometimes patients prefer to identify their fingers in other verbal terms. Although the test itself is given without the subject's use of vision for identification, it is sometimes necessary to give the patient practice with his eyes open in order to be sure that he is able to report reliably. When the patient is not able to give a reliable verbal report, he is asked to point to the finger touched using his other hand. Four trials are used for each finger on each hand, yielding a total of 20 trials on each hand. The score is recorded as the number of errors for each hand.

Finger-tip Number Writing Perception. This procedure requires the subject to report numbers written on the fingertips of each hand without the use of vision. Standard numbers are used and written on the fingertips in a standard sequence, with a total of four trials being given for each finger on each hand. The score is represented by the number of errors for each hand. This procedure has generally been found to be satisfactory for persons 9 years and older, but tactile recognition of numbers is often difficult for younger children. Therefore, for children aged 5 through 8 years, "X" and "O"s are used as the stimulus figures rather than numbers.

Tactile Coin Recognition. This test requires the subject to identify through touch alone, pennies, nickels, and dimes, in each hand tested separately. The subject is not told even that coins are to be used, but is asked merely to identify the object placed in his hand. The two hands are first tested alternately in successive trials following which the hands are tested in simultaneous tactile discrimination. The score is the number of errors made on each hand. This test is used clinically only for persons 9 years of age and older because younger children are sometimes not familiar with coins.

Klove-Matthews Motor Steadiness Battery

This battery includes a group of tests to measure motor coordination and tremor.

Maze Coordination. A maze is used (Lafayette Instrument Company, #2706A) modified so that blind alleys have been eliminated. The maze is placed on a stand in a vertical position directly in front of the subject. The subject is required to go through the maze with an electric stylus, trying not to touch the sides. The stylus is attached to a time clock and counter. Cumulative time of contact with the sides of the maze and cumulative error (number of contacts) scores are recorded for the two right and two left hand trials.

Vertical Groove Steadiness. A groove steadiness apparatus (Lafayette Instrument Company #4605B) is placed in a vertical position directly in front of the subject. The groove width is set at 4 mm. Using a stylus, the subject is required to proceed from the bottom to the top of this groove and return to the starting point, trying not to touch the sides. Total cumulative time of contact and number of contacts are recorded for two right-hand and for two left-hand trials.

Horizontal Groove Steadiness. The apparatus and scoring procedure are identical with that described above. The apparatus is presented with the groove in a horizontal position and the subject proceeds from left to right and returns to the starting point. Two trials are given using each hand.

Static Steadiness. The subject is required to insert a stylus into a conventional hole-type steadiness test (Lafayette Instrument Company, #4605C). The subject must keep the stylus in each hole for 15 sec. and is not allowed to brace or rest his arm. Cumulative timer (total time of contact) and counter (number of contacts) scores are obtained for each hand.

Resting Steadiness. The same apparatus is used as above. The subject is required to insert the stylus into hole #6 (in terms of decreasing size) for 15 sec. In this procedure the subject is permitted to rest his hand against the examining table. If no errors are made with either hand, the task is discontinued. If errors are made, three trials are given using each hand. Cumulative timer and error scores are obtained.

Grooved Pegboard. This is a manipulative dexterity task which uses a pegboard containing 25 holes with randomly positioned slots (Lafayette Instrument Company, #4202). The pegs, which have an edge along one side, must be rotated to match the holes before they can be inserted. The time required and number of pegs dropped are recorded for each hand.

Foot Tapping. A foot-tapping apparatus is connected to an electric power source and the counter used in the other tests of the Motor Steadiness Battery. The subject is instructed to tap as rapidly as possible and the number of taps for each trial is recorded. Trials are alternated between the right and left feet. The mean tapping rate is recorded for each foot as the average of the three highest scores obtained in five trials.

Reitan-Klove Lateral Dominance Examination

This test is given to obtain information regarding handedness, footedness, and eyedness. Lateral dominance can be evaluated either in terms of the side used for a task or the comparative skill on the two sides of the body. The set of procedures in this battery utilizes only tasks that can be performed with one side of the body or the other. Other tests on which data is reported in this volume, such as the Halstead Finger Oscillation Test, measurements of strength of grip, and the Halstead Tactual Performance Test, provide information on the comparative functional efficiency of the upper extremities.

Handedness is determined by having the subject perform a series of simple unimanual tasks. First he is asked to write his name in his normal manner and the hand used as well as the time required is recorded. Then he is asked to write his name in the same manner using his other hand. He is then asked to perform a series of other tasks which include throwing a ball, hammering a nail, cutting with a knife, turning a doorknob, using a pair of scissors, and using a pencil eraser. Visual or ocular dominance is determined by having the subject first look through a telescope and next aim a gun at the tip of the examiner's nose. The

Miles ABC Test of Ocular Dominance (Psychological Corporation) is also used for determining eyedness. The subject is required to look through a V-shaped scope at stimulus materials held by the examiner. Three scopes are used and the subject is required to change scopes for each trial in order to avoid developing a postural set. The scopes require the subject to use monocular vision even though most subjects do not realize that this is the case. The examiner holds the stimulus material directly below his own eyes so that he is able to look through the end of the scope (which is being held by the subject) and determine which eye the subject is using to look at the stimulus material. The test itself is described to the subject as a procedure for evaluation of visual acuity and no mention is made of the fact that the actual purpose is to determine which eye the patient uses for sighting. Results are recorded as the number of times, in 10 trials, that the subject uses each eye.

Footedness is briefly evaluated by having the subject show how he would kick a football and by having him pretend that there is a bug on the floor on which he is to step. Results are recorded by indicating which foot is used.

ADDITIONAL TEST BATTERIES

The Wide Range Achievement Test
(Jastak & Jastak, 1965)

This is a widely used test for evaluation of academic achievement and consists of three parts: Reading (word recognition), Spelling, and Arithmetic. The test yields grade equivalents representing the child's performance in each part.

Minnesota Multiphasic Personality Inventory
[MMPI] (Hathaway & McKinley, 1967)

This is a well known procedure that consists of 550 items. The subject is instructed to read each item and answer True, False, or Cannot Say. The test includes several validity scales as well as scales for evaluation of the patient's emotional status. Investigators who reported results on the MMPI in this volume routinely used the following scales: Hypochondriasis, Depression, Hysteria, Psychopathic Deviate, Masculinity-Feminity, Paranoia, Psychasthenia, Schizophrenia, and Hypomania. A number of additional scales have been developed and, in some instances, additional scales were used in this volume.

INDIVIDUAL TESTS AND EXPERIMENTAL
PROCEDURES

A number of individual tests were studied in this volume, in several instances by a number of investigators. Descriptions of these tests and procedures are given below.

Aphasia Screening Test (Wheeler & Reitan, 1962)

This test represents Reitan's modification of the Halstead-Wepman Aphasia Screening Test (Halstead & Wepman, 1949). The test was not devised to provide continuous distributions that reflect a range of responses on the individual items. Instead, the test is intended as a procedure to identify failures of performance and specific deficits. The test provides quite an extensive survey of possible aphasic and related deficits. The subject is required to name common objects, spell simple words, identify individual numbers and letters, read, write, calculate, enunciate, understand spoken language, identify body parts, differentiate between right and left, and copy simple shapes. The test is so organized that these various performances are examined, to some extent, in terms of the particular sensory modalities through which the stimuli are perceived. In addition, the receptive and expressive components of the test, as differentially required by various items, provide an opportunity to judge whether the limiting deficit for a particular subject is receptive or expressive in character. Since the performance of the subject is judged in terms of specific deficits in his performance, rather than being subject to scoring in the usual sense, the examiner must necessarily have experience with the test in order to be able to discern milder instances of deficiency in performance. This limitation is more of a problem with children than adults because of the variation in rates of acquisition of abilities among normal children.

Ballistic Arm Tapping (Meier, Story, French, & Chou, 1966)

A 24-in. board is used that lies perpendicular to the axis of the subject's body and the subject taps each end of the board with a stylus. The score for each arm is represented by the best performance in two alternating 30-sec. trials.

Benton Right-Left Orientation Test (Benton, 1959)

Form C of this test was used in the data reported by Klonoff and Low. The test consists of 32 items and requires the child to: (a) identify single lateral body parts and to execute crossed and uncrossed commands; (b) point to lateral parts on a schematic front view representation of a person and execute crossed and uncrossed commands; (c) name on command lateral body parts on the schematic representation; and (d) name on command hand and body parts on another schematic representation which depicts crossed and uncrossed localizations. The test is scored as the number of correct responses.

Benton Sound Recognition Test

This test was used by Klonoff and Low for data presented in the present volume. Children under 7 years of age were presented with cards that contained four choices for each of 26 stimuli, and were asked to point to or name the stimulus. Children over 7 years were asked to identify and record each of the 26 stimuli. The test was scored as the number of stimuli correctly identified.

Boston University Speech-sounds
Discrimination Test

This test consists of 36 cards, each showing three subsets of pictures; e.g., cat-cat, cat-bat, bat-bat. The subject listens to a tape recorder which directs him to point to the picture that is just like the words he just heard. The score is recorded as the number of correct identifications.

Dynamometer

Measurements of grip strength were made with each hand for each subject. The dynamometer (Smedley Hand Dynamometer) was adjusted for the size of the hand of each subject. Alternating trials were given for the preferred and nonpreferred hands, with two trials in total for each hand. Average scores for each hand were reported in all chapters except for Meier's, who used the best recording for each hand.

Index Finger Tapping

The standard apparatus of the Finger Oscillation Test in the Halstead Neuropsychological Test Battery was utilized by Meier for measuring this variable. However, the procedure used by Halstead and Reitan was somewhat modified. The right and left index fingers were used and two alternating 10-sec. trials were given for each finger. The score was the best performance of the two trials for each hand.

Klove-Matthews Sandpaper Test

This test was devised to evaluate the subject's tactile sensitivity to texture rather than form. After a visual trial that is part of the test instruction, the subject is blindfolded and then required to arrange four blocks, each covered with a different grade of sandpaper, in order, from smoothest to roughest. The subject is asked to perform the task as quickly as possible with trials alternating between the dominant and nondominant hands. The time needed to complete the task and an accuracy score is derived for each hand.

Modified Tactual Formboard Test

The same board and blocks were used by Meier in this test as those used in the Halstead Tactual Performance Test. In order to reduce time as well as frustration associated with failure, Meier introduced some procedural modifications to make the test were suitable for the older subject with cerebrovascular disease. The patient was first allowed to see the board while placing the forms, using separate trials with each hand and when using both hands simultaneously. Following these practice trials, the patient was blindfolded and instructed to place the forms with each hand separately.

Performance time of each hand constituted the measure used. Failure to complete the task on either trial in a 5-min. period is scored as "fail". The number of blocks placed was also recorded. We have listed this test separately here because the procedure differs from that used with the Halstead Tactual Performance Test.

Peabody Picture Vocabulary Test (Dunn, 1959)

This test measures vocabulary by requiring the subject to identify the picture named by the examiner. The test is applicable to subjects with mental ages covering a very wide range.

Porteus Maze Test (Porteus, 1959)

This test consists of a series of paper-and-pencil mazes which vary in difficulty and extend on an age scale from 3 to 17 years. Performances on the test yield scores for "test age" and "test quotient."

Reitan-Klove Tactile Form Recognition Test

This procedure for examination of tactile form recognition makes use of flat, plastic shapes (cross, square, triangle, and circle) which, when placed in the subject's hand, must be matched against a set of stimulus figures that are visually exposed. This test has been found to be suitable for use with persons 5 years of age and older. Klove initiated measurement of time of response whereas previously only correct and incorrect responses had been recorded. Thus, time measurements are made for each trial and the total time required for four trials for each hand is determined. The total number of errors for each hand is recorded as a separate score.

Trail Making Test for Adults (Reitan, 1958b)

The Trail Making Test consists of two parts, A and B. Part A consists of 25 circles distributed over a white sheet of paper and numbered from 1 to 25. The subject is required to connect the circles with a pencil line as quickly as possible, beginning with the Number 1 and proceeding in numerical sequence. Part B consists of 25 circles numbered from 1 to 13 and lettered from A to L. The subject is required to connect the circles, alternating between numbers and letters as he proceeds in sequence. The scores obtained are the number of seconds required to finish each part. This test would appear to require immediate recognition of the symbolic significance of numbers and letters, ability to scan the page continuously to identify the next number or letter in sequence, flexibility in integrating the numerical and alphabetical series, and completion of these requirements under the pressure of time.

Trail Making Test for Children (Reitan, 1971c)

This test is identical with the Trail Making Test for Adults except that only the first 15 circles are used in both Parts A and B. The instructions, procedure for administration, and scoring are the same as for the adult form.

Visual Space Rotation Test
(Meier & French, 1966b)

This procedure uses two Dove prisms, mounted in a tube, through which the subject can view his thumb and forefinger in a 2-in. field. The subject's task is to draw an X in a $\frac{3}{4}$-in. square on electroconductive paper under three conditions of rotation of the field (90°, 180°, and 270°). If the patient fails to complete the test in 5 min., a "fail" score is assigned and the task is attempted under the next rotation condition. When the patient is able to complete the task within 5 min. at a given rotation condition, four additional trials are run and the trial contact and noncontact durations are recorded by means of electronic timing devices. Thus, the basic measure derived from the readaptation data is the number of rotation positions failed (maximum of 3; minimum of 0). In addition, quantitative separations of the total time for task execution into contact and noncontact components are obtained for those patients who can perform the task within the time limits.

REFERENCES

Adams, R. D. The anatomy of memory mechanisms in the human brain. In G. A. Talland & N. D. Waugh (Eds.), *The pathology of memory*. New York: Academic Press, 1969.

Aita, J. A., & Reitan, R. M. Psychotic reactions in the late recovery period following brain injury. *American Journal of Psychiatry*, 1948, **105**, 161-169.

Alley, G. R. Comparative constructional praxis performance of organically impaired and cultural-familial mental retardates. *American Journal of Mental Deficiency*, 1969, **74**, 279-282.

Andersen, A. L. The effect of laterality localization of brain damage on Wechsler-Bellevue indices of deterioration. *Journal of Clinical Psychology*, 1950, **6**, 191-194.

Andersen, A. L. The effect of laterality localization of focal brain lesions on the Wechsler-Bellevue subtests. *Journal of Clinical Psychology*, 1951, **7**, 149-153.

Anokhin, P. K. *Problems of center and periphery in the physiology of nervous activity*. Gorki [U.S.S.R.]: Gosizdat, 1935.

Anokhin, P. K. General principles of compensation for disturbed functions and their physiological basis. *Proceedings of a Conference on Problems in Defectology*. Izdatel'stvo Akademiya Pedagogicheskikh Nauk RSFSR, Moscow, 1956.

Arrigoni, G., & De Renzi, E. Constructional apraxia and hemispheric locus of lesion. *Cortex*, 1964, **1**, 170-197.

Auerbach, A. H., Sheflen, A. E., Reinhart, R. B., & Scholz, C. K. The psychological sequelae of head injuries. *American Journal of Psychiatry*, 1960, **117**, 499-505.

Baker, G. Diagnosis of organic brain damage in the adult. In B. Klopfer, et al., (Eds), *Developments in the Rorschach technique*. Vol. 2. New York: World Book Company, 1956.

Bakker, D. J. Sensory dominance in normal and backward readers. *Perceptual and Motor Skills*, 1966, **23**, 1055-1058.

Bakker, D. J. Temporal order, meaningfulness, and reading ability. *Perceptual and Motor Skills, 1967*, **24**, 1027-1030.

Barbizet, J. *Human memory and its pathology*. San Francisco: Freeman, 1970.

Barbizet, J., & Cany, E. A psychometric study of various memory deficits associated with cerebral lesions. In G. A. Talland & N. C. Waugh, (Eds.), *The pathology of memory*. New York: Academic Press, 1969.

Bard, P., & Mountcastle, V. B. Some forebrain mechanisms involved in expression of rage with specific reference to suppression of angry behavior. *Association for Research in Nervous and Mental Disease, Research Publications*, 1948, **135**, 187-195.

Basser, L. S. Hemiplegia of early onset and the faculty of speech with special reference to the effects of hemispherectomy. *Brain*, 1962, **85**, 427-460.

Beery, J. W. Matching of auditory and visual stimuli by average and retarded readers. *Child Development*, 1967, **28**, 827-833.

Bender, M. B., & Teuber, H.-L. Phenomena of fluctuation, extinction, and completion in visual perception. *Archives of Neurology and Psychiatry*, 1946, **55**, 627-658.

Benjamin, R. M., & Thompson, R. F. Differential effects of cortical lesions in infant and adult cats on roughness discrimination. *Experimental Neurology*, 1959, **1**, 305-321.

Benson, D. F. Fluency in aphasia: Correlation with radioactive scan localization. *Cortex*, 1967, **3**, 373-394.

Benton, A. L. Right-left discrimination and finger localization in defective children. *Archives of Neurology and Psychiatry*, 1955, **74**, 583-589.

Benton, A. L. *Right-left discrimination and finger localization: Development and pathology*. New York: Hoeber, 1959.

Benton, A. L. *The revised Visual Retention Test: Clinical and experimental applications*. (3rd ed.) Iowa City: The State University of Iowa (Distributed by the Psychological Corporation, New York), 1963.

Benton, A. L. Constructional apraxia and the minor hemisphere. *Confinia Neurologica*, 1967, **29**, 1-16. (a)

Benton, A. L. Problems of test construction in the field of aphasia. *Cortex*, 1967, **3**, 32-58. (b)

Benton, A. L. Differential behavioral effects in frontal lobe disease. *Neuropsychologia*, 1968, **6**, 53-60. (a)

Benton, A. L. La praxie constructive tri-dimensionnelle. *Revue de Psychologie Appliquée*, 1968, **18**, 63-80. (b)

Benton, A. L. Right-left discrimination. *Pediatric Clinics of North America*, 1968, **15**, 747-758. (c)

Benton, A. L. Neuropsychological aspects of mental retardation. *Journal of Special Education*, 1970, 4, 3-11.

Benton, A. L., & Fogel, M. L. Three dimensional constructional praxis: A clinical test. *Archives of Neurology*, 1962, 7, 347-354.

Benton, A. L., Garfield, J. C., & Chiorini, J. C. Motor impersistence in mental defectives. *Proceedings of the International Copenhagen Congress on the Scientific Study of Mental Retardation*, 1964, 746-750.

Benton, A. L., & Hécaen, H. Stereoscopic vision in patients with unilateral cerebral disease. *Neurology*, 1970, 20, 1084-1088.

Benton, A. L., Hutcheon, F., & Seymour, E. Arithmetic ability, finger-localization capacity and right-left discrimination in normal and defective children. *American Journal of Orthopsychiatry*, 1951, 21, 756-766.

Benton, A. L., & Spreen, O. *A social recognition test for clinical use*. Iowa City: University of Iowa, Neurosensory Center and Departments of Neurology and Psychology, 1963.

Benton, A. L., Spreen, O., Fangman, M. W., & Carr, D. L. Visual Retention Test, Administration C: Norms for children. *Journal of Special Education*, 1967, 1, 151-156.

Berelson, B., & Steiner, G. A. *Human behavior*. New York: Harcourt, Brace & World, 1964.

Bickford, R. G., & Klass, D. W. Acute and chronic findings after head injury. In W. F. Caveness & A. E. Walker (Eds.), *Head injury: Conference proceedings*, University of Chicago, 1966.

Birch, H. G. *Brain damage in children—the biological and social aspects*. Baltimore: Williams & Wilkins, 1964.

Birch, H. G., & Belmont, L. Auditory-visual integration in normal and retarded readers. *American Journal of Orthopsychiatry*, 1964, 34, 852-861.

Birren, J. E. *A factorial analysis of the Wechsler-Bellevue Scale given to an elderly population*. The University of Chicago Psychometric Laboratory, 1951, (No. 73).

Bizzi, E. Discharge of frontal eye field neurons during eye movements in unanesthetized monkeys. *Science*, 1967, 157, 1588-1590.

Bizzi, E. Discharge of frontal eye field neurons during saccadic and following eye movements in unanesthetized monkeys. *Experimental Brain Research*, 1968, 6, 69-80.

Bizzi, E., & Schiller, P. H. Single unit activity in the frontal eye fields of unanesthetized monkeys during eye and head movement. *Experimental Brain Research*, 1970, 10, 151-158.

Black, A. H., & Davis, L. J. The relationship between intelligence and sensorimotor proficiency in retardates. *American Journal of Mental Deficiency*, 1966, 71, 55-59.

Boll, T. J. Conceptual vs. perceptual vs. motor deficits in brain-damaged children. *Journal of Clinical Psychology*, 1972, 28, 157-159.

Boll, T. J., & Reitan, R. M. Motor and sensory-perceptual deficits in brain-damaged children. Paper presented at the meeting of the Midwestern Psychological Association, Cincinnati, May 1970.

Boll, T. J., & Reitan, R. M. Motor and tactile-perceptual deficits in brain-damaged children. *Perceptual and Motor Skills*, 1972, **34**, 343-350. (a)

Boll, T. J., & Reitan, R. M. Comparative ability interrelationships in brain-damaged and normal children. *Journal of Clinical Psychology*, 1972, **28**, 152-156. (b)

Bonhoeffer, K. Klinischer und anatomischer Befund zur Lehre von der Apraxie und der "motorischen Sprachbahn". *Monatsschrift der Psychiatrie und Neurologie*, 1914, **35**, 113-128.

Borkowski, J. G., Benton, A. L., & Spreen, O. Word fluency and brain damage. *Neuropsychologia*, 1967, **5**, 135-140.

Brady, J. V. The palecortex and behavioral motivation. In H. F. Harlow & C. N. Woolsey (Eds.), *Biological and biochemical bases of behavior*. Madison: University of Wisconsin Press, 1958.

Brion, S. Korsakoff's syndrome: Clinico-anatomical and physio-pathological considerations. In G. A. Talland & N. C. Waugh (Eds.), *The pathology of memory*. New York: Academic Press, 1969.

Broadbent, D. E. The role of auditory localization in attention and memory span. *Journal of Experimental Psychology*, 1954, **47**, 191-196.

Bryden, M. P. Laterality effects in dichotic listening: Relations with handedness and reading ability in children. *Neuropsychologia*, 1970, **8**, 443-450.

Burkinshaw, J. Head injuries in children. *Archives of Disease in Childhood*, 1960, **35**, 205-213.

Butler, S. R., & Norrsell, U. Vocalization possibly initiated by the minor hemisphere. *Nature*, 1968, **220**, 793-794.

Butters, N., & Barton, M. Effect of parietal lobe damage on the performance of reversible operations in space. *Neuropsychologia*, 1970, **8**, 205-214.

Carmon, A., & Bechtoldt, H. P. Dominance of the right cerebral hemisphere for stereopsis. *Neuropsychologia*, 1969, **7**, 29-39.

Carmon, A., & Benton, A. L. Tactile perception of direction and number in patients with unilateral cerebral disease. *Neurology*, 1969, **19**, 525-532.

Chow, K. L. Effects of partial extirpation of the posterior association cortex on visually mediated behavior in monkeys. *Comparative Psychological Monographs*, 1950, **20**, 187-217.

Chapman, L. F., & Wolff, H. G. The cerebral hemispheres and the highest integrative functions of man. *Archives of Neurology*, 1959, **1**, 357-424.

Clausen, J. *Ability structure and subgroups in mental retardation*. Washington, D.C.: Spartan Books, 1966.

Clawson, A. A relationship of psychological tests to cerebral disorders in children: A pilot study. *Psychological Reports*, 1962, **10**, 187-190.

Cobb, W. A. The normal adult EEG. In D. Hill & G. Parr (Eds.), *Electro-encephalography*. New York: MacMillan, 1963.

Cohen, J. Factors underlying Wechsler-Bellevue performance of three neuropsychiatric groups. *Journal of Abnormal and Social Psychology*, 1952, **47**, 359-365.

Cohen, L. Perception of reversible figures after brain injury. *Archives of Neurology and Psychiatry*, 1959, **81**, 765-775.

Cohn, R. Delayed acquisition of reading and writing abilities in children. *Archives of Neurology and Psychiatry*, 1961, **4**, 153-164.

Collins, A. L., & Lennox, W. G. The intelligence of 300 private epileptic patients. *Association for Research in Nervous and Mental Disease*, 1947, **26**, 586-603.

Corfariu, O., Szabo, L., Varilsy, A., & Rado, M. Electroclinical aspects of behavioral disorders in children. *Electroencephalography and Clinical Neurophysiology*, 1967, **22**, 571.

Corkin, S. Tactually-guided maze learning in man: Effects of unilateral cortical excisions and bilateral hippocampal lesions. *Neuropsychologia*, 1965, **3**, 339-351.

Corsi, P. M. Verbal memory impairment after unilateral hippocampal excisions. Paper presented at the meeting of the Eastern Psychological Association, Philadelphia, 1969.

Costa, L. D., Vaughn, H. G., Jr., Horwitz, M., & Ritter, W. Patterns of behavioral deficit associated with visual neglect. *Cortex*, 1969, **5**, 242-263.

Costa, L. D., Vaughn, H. G., Jr., Levita, E., & Farber, N. Purdue pegboard as a predictor of the presence of the laterality of cerebral lesions. *Journal of Consulting Psychology*, 1963, **27**, 133-137.

Crawley, J., & Kellaway, P. The electroencephalogram in pediatrics. *Pediatric Clinics of North America*, 1963, **17**, 17-51.

Critchley, M. *The parietal lobes*. London: Arnold, 1953.

Crockett, D., Klonoff, H., & Bjerring, J. Factor analysis of neuropsychological tests. *Perceptual and Motor Skills*, 1969, **29**, 791-801.

Cronbach, L. J. *Essentials of psychological testing*. New York: Harper & Row, 1969.

Crosby, E. C., Humphrey, T., & Lauer, E. W. *Correlative anatomy of the nervous system*. New York: MacMillan, 1962.

Dailey, C. A. Psychologic findings five years after head injury. *Journal of Clinical Psychology*, 1956, **12**, 349-353.

Darley, F. L. Language rehabilitation. In A. L. Benton (Ed.), *Behavior change in cerebrovascular disease*. New York: Harper & Row, 1970.

Davis, L. J., & Reitan, R. M. Dysphasia and constructional dyspraxia items, and Wechsler verbal and performance IQs in retardates. *American Journal of Mental Deficiency*, 1967, **71**, 604-608.

Davis, W. E., DeWolfe, A. S., & Gustafson, R. C. Intellectual deficit in process and reactive schizophrenia and brain injury. *Journal of Consulting and Clinical Psychology*, 1972, **38**, 146.

Dejerine, J. *Semiologie des affections du système nerveux*. Paris: Masson, 1914.

Dencker, S. J. Closed head injury in twins. *Archives of General Psychiatry*, 1960, **2**, 569-575.

Denny-Brown, D. The nature of apraxia. *Journal of Nervous and Mental Disease*, 1958, **126**, 9-32.

DeRenzi, E., & Faglioni, P. The comparative efficiency of intelligence and vigilance tests in detecting hemispheric damage. *Cortex*, 1965, **1**, 410-433.

DeRenzi, E., & Faglioni, P. The relationship between visuo-spatial impairment and constructional apraxia. *Cortex*, 1967, **3**, 327-342.

DeRenzi E., Pieczuro, A., & Vignolo, L. A. Oral apraxia and aphasia. *Cortex*, 1966, **3**, 327-342.

DeRenzi, E., Pieczuro, A., & Vignolo, L. A. Ideational apraxia; A quantitative study. *Neuropsychologia*, 1968, **6**, 41-52.

De Wolfe, A. S. Differentiation of schizophrenia and brain damage with the WAIS. *Journal of Clinical Psychology*, 1971, **27**, 209-211.

Diller, L. Psychomotor and vocational rehabilitation. In A. L. Benton (Ed.), *Behavior change in cerebrovascular disease*. New York: Harper & Row, 1970.

Dillon, H., & Leopold, R. L. Children and the post-concussion syndrome. *Journal of the American Medical Association*, 1961, **175**, 86-92.

Doehring, D. G., & Reitan, R. M. Concept attainment of human adults with lateralized cerebral lesions. *Perceptual and Motor Skills*, 1962, **14**, 27-33.

Doehring, D. G., Reitan, R. M., & Kløve, H. Changes in patterns of intelligence test performance associated with homonymous visual field defects. *Journal of Nervous and Mental Disease*, 1961, **132**, 227-233.

Dow, R. S., Ulett, G., & Raaf, J. Electroencephalographic studies immediately following head injury. *American Journal of Psychiatry*, 1944, **101**, 174-183.

Dunn, L. M. *Manual for the Peabody Picture Vocabulary Test*. Nashville, Tenn.: American Guidance Service, 1959.

Eaton, M. T., Jr., & Peterson, M. H. *Psychiatry*. Flushing, N. Y.: Medical Examination Publishing Company, 1969.

Eldrige, R., Harlan, A., Cooper, I. S., & Riklan, M. Superior intelligence in recessively inherited torsion dystonia. *Lancet*, 1970, **1**, 65-67.

Enge, S. EEG recording in the acute stage of closed cranio-cerebral injuries. *Electroencephalography and Clinical Neurophysiology*, 1966, **20**, 534.

Ernhart, C. B., Graham, F. K., Eichman, P. L., Marshall, J. M., & Thurston, D. Brain injury in the preschool child: Some developmental considerations: II. Comparison of brain injured and normal children. *Psychological Monographs*, 1963, **77**, 17-33 (Whole No. 573).

Ervin, F. R., Mark, V. H., & Stevens, J. Behavioral and affective responses to brain stimulation in man. In J. Zubin & C. Shagass (Eds.), *Neurobiological aspects of psychopathology*. New York: Grune & Stratton, 1969.

Eysenck, H. J. Cortical inhibition, figural aftereffects, and theory of personality. *Journal of Abnormal and Social Psychology*, 1955, **51**, 94-106.

Fabian, A. A., & Bender, L. Head injuries in children: Predisposing factors. *American Journal of Psychiatry*, 1947, **17**, 68-79.

Faglioni, P., Spinnler, H., & Vignolo, L. A. Contrasting behavior of right and left hemisphere-damaged patients on a discriminative and a semantic task of auditory recognition. *Cortex*, 1969, **5**, 366–389.

Fahy, T. J., Irving, M. H., & Millac, P. Severe head injuries. *Lancet*, 1967, **2**, 475–479.

Fedio, P., & Mirsky, A. F. Selective intellectual deficits in children with temporal lobe or centrencephalic epilepsy. *Neuropsychologia*, 1969, **7**, 287–300.

Fields, F. R. J., & Whitmyre, J. W. Verbal and performance relationships with respect to laterality of cerebral involvement. *Diseases of the Nervous System*, 1969, **30**, 177–179.

Fisher, G. M. Differences in WAIS verbal and performance IQs in various diagnostic groups of mental retardates. *American Journal of Mental Deficiency*, 1960, **65**, 256–260.

Fitzhugh, K. B., Fitzhugh, L. C., & Reitan, R. M. Psychological deficits in relation to acuteness of brain dysfunction. *Journal of Consulting Psychology*, 1961, **25**, 61–66.

Fitzhugh, K. B., Fitzhugh, L. C., & Reitan, R. M. Wechsler-Bellevue comparisons in groups of "chronic" and "current" lateralized and diffuse brain lesions. *Journal of Consulting Psychology*, 1962, **26**, 306–310.

Fogel, M. L. The intelligence quotient as an index of brain damage. *American Journal of Orthopsychiatry*, 1964, **34**, 555–562.

Frantzen, E., Harvald, B., & Haugsted, H. Fresh head injuries. *Acta Psychiatrica Scandinavica*, 1958, **33**, 417–428.

Friedman, S. H. Psychometric effects of frontal and parietal lobe brain damage. Unpublished Ph.D. dissertation, University of Minnesota, 1950.

Gallagher, J. J. A comparison of brain-injured and non-brain-injured mentally retarded children on several psychological variables. *Monographs of the Society for Research in Child Development*, 1957, **22**(2).

Garfield, J. C. Motor impersistence in normal and brain-damaged children. *Neurology*, 1964, **14**, 623–630.

Garfield, J. C., Benton, A. L., & MacQueen, J. C. Motor impersistence in brain-damaged and cultural-familial defectives. *Journal of Nervous and Mental Disease*, 1966, **142**, 434–440.

Gazzaniga, M. S. Psychological properties of the disconnected hemispheres in man. *Science*, 1965, **150**, 372.

Gazzaniga, M. S. *The bisected brain*. New York: Appleton-Century-Crofts, 1970.

Geschwind, N. Disconnexion syndromes in animals and man. *Brain*, 1965, **88**, 237–294; 585–644.

Geschwind, N. Problems in the anatomical understanding of the aphasias. In A. L. Benton (Ed.), *Contributions to clinical neuropsychology*, Chicago: Aldine Publishing Company, 1969.

Geschwind, N. Language disturbances in cerebrovascular disease. In A. L. Benton (Ed.), *Behavioral change in cerebrovascular disease*. New York: Harper & Row, 1970.

Geschwind, N., & Kaplan, E. A human cerebral deconnection syndrome. *Neurology*, 1962, **12**, 675–685.

Geschwind, N., & Levitsky, W. Human brain left-right asymmetries in the temporal speech region. *Science*, 1968, **161**, 186–187.

Ghent, L. Developmental changes in tactual thresholds on dominant and nondominant sides. *Journal of Comparative and Physiological Psychology*, 1961, **54**, 670–673.

Gibbs, F. A., & Gibbs, E. L. *Atlas of electroencephalography*. Vol. 3. Reading, Mass.: Addison-Wesley, 1964.

Goldstein, G., & Neuringer, C. Schizophrenic and organic signs on the Trail Making Test. *Perceptual and Motor Skills*, 1966, **22**, 347–350.

Goldstein, K. *Der Aufbau des Organismus*. Nijhoff, Haag, [Austria] : 1934.

Goldstein, K. *Human nature*. Cambridge, Mass.: Harvard University Press, 1940.

Goldstein, K. The two ways of adjustment of the organism to cerebral deficits. *Journal of the Mount Sinai Hospital*, 1942, **9**, 504–513.

Goldstein, K. The effects of brain damage on the personality. *Psychiatry*, 1952, **15**, 245–260.

Goldstein, K., & Scheerer, M. Abstract and concrete behavior. *Psychological Monographs*, 1941, **53**, (Whole No. 239).

Gomez, M. R. Minimal cerebral dysfunction (maximal neurologic confusion). *Clinical Pediatrics*, 1967, **6**, 589–591.

Goodglass, H., & Kaplan, E. *The assessment of aphasia and related disorders*. Philadelphia: Lea and Febiger, 1972.

Graham, F. K., Ernhart, C. B., Craft, M., & Berman, P. W. Brain injury in the preschool child: Some developmental considerations. I. Performance of normal children. *Psychological Monographs*, 1963, **77**, (Whole No. 573).

Graham, F. K., Ernhart, C. B., Thurston, C., & Craft, M. Development three years after perinatal anoxia and other potentially damaging newborn experiences. *Psychological Monographs*, 1962, **76** (Whole No. 522).

Grant, D. A., & Berg, E. A. A behavioral analysis of degree of reinforcement and ease of shifting to new responses in a Weigl-type card sorting problem. *Journal of Experimental Psychology*, 1948, **38**, 404–411.

Gross, C. G., Bender, D. B., & Rocha-Miranda, C. E. Visual receptive fields of neurons in the inferotemporal cortex of the monkey. *Science*, 1969, **166**, 1303–1306.

Guion, R. M. *Personnel testing*. New York: McGraw-Hill, 1965.

Gunzburg, H. C. Psychological assessment in mental deficiency. In A. M. Clarke & A. D. B. Clarke (Eds.), *Mental deficiency: The changing outlook*. New York: Free Press, 1965.

Gurdjian, E. S., & Thomas, L. M. Organization of services for the treatment of acute head injury in community and industrial practice. *Excerpta Medica International Congress*. (Series No. 93) Amsterdam: Excerpta Medica Foundation, 1965.

Hall, M. M., Hall, G. C., & Lavoie, P. Ideation in patients with unilateral or bilateral midline brain lesions. *Journal of Abnormal Psychology*, 1968, 73, 526–531.

Halstead, W. C. *Brain and intelligence: A quantitative study of the frontal lobes.* Chicago: University of Chicago Press, 1947.

Halstead, W. C. Biological intelligence. *Journal of Personality*, 1951, 20, 118–130.

Halstead, W. C., & Rennick, P. M. Perceptual cognitive disorders in children. In A. H. Kidd & J. L. Rivoire (Eds.), *Perceptual development in children*. New York: International University Press, 1966.

Halstead, W. C., & Shure, G. Further evidence for a frontal lobe component in human biological intelligence. *Transactions of the American Neurological Association*, 1954, 79, 9–11.

Halstead, W. C., & Wepman, J. M. The Halstead-Wepman aphasia screening test. *Journal of Speech and Hearing Disorders*, 1949, 14, 9–13.

Harlow, H. F., Akert, K., & Shiltz, K. A. The effects of bilateral prefrontal lesions on learning behavior of neonatal, infant and preadolescent monkeys. In J. M. Warren & K. Akert (Eds.), *The frontal granular cortex and behavior*. New York: McGraw-Hill, 1964.

Harlow, H. F., & Harlow, M. K. The effect of rearing conditions on behavior. In J. Money (Ed.), *Sex research: New developments*. New York: Holt, 1965.

Harrington, J. A., & Letemendia, F. J. J. Persistent psychiatric disorders after head injuries in children. *Journal of Mental Science*, 1958, 104, 1205–1218.

Hathaway, S. R., & McKinley, J. C. *Minnesota Multiphasic Personality Inventory manual*. New York: The Psychological Corporation, 1967.

Hay, R. H. Neurosurgical aspects of traffic accidents. *Canadian Medical Association Journal*, 1967, 97, 1364–1368.

Hayes, K. J. Genes, drive and intellect. *Psychological Reports*, 1962, 10, 299–342.

Hebb, D. O. *The organization of behavior*. New York: Wiley, 1949.

Heber, R. A manual on terminology and classification in mental retardation. *American Journal of Mental Deficiency*, 1961, Monograph supplement, (2nd ed.).

Hécaen, H. Clinical symptomatology in right and left hemisphere lesions. In V. B. Mountcastle (Ed.), *Interhemispheric relations and cerebral dominance*. Baltimore: Johns Hopkins University Press, 1962.

Hécaen, H., & Ajuriaguerra, J. *Left handedness, manual superiority, and cerebral dominance*. (E. Ponder, Trans.) New York: Grune & Stratton, 1964.

Heilbrun, A. B., Jr. Psychological test performance as a function of lateral localization of cerebral lesion. *Journal of Comparative and Physiological Psychology*, 1956, 49, 10–14.

Heilbrun, A. B., Jr. Issues in the assessment of organic brain damage. *Psychological Reports*, 1962, 10, 511–515.

Heimburger, R. F., & Reitan, R. M. Easily administered written test for lateralizing brain lesions. *Journal of Neurosurgery*, 1961, 18, 301–312.

Hendrick, E. B., Harwood-Hash, D. C. F., & Hudson, A. R. Head injuries in children: A survey of 4465 consecutive cases at the Hospital for Sick Children, Toronto. *Journal of Clinical Neurosurgery*, 1964, 11(6), 46–65.

Hillbom, E. After-effects of brain injuries. *Acta Psychiatrica Scandinavica*, 1959, 34 (Suppl. 137), 7–29.

Hjern, B., & Nylander, I. Acute head injuries in children. *Acta Paediatrica*, (Stockholm), 1964 (Suppl. 152), 1–37.

Horenstein, S., & Casey, T. R. Perceptual defects in both visual fields in attention hemianopia. *Transactions of the American Neurological Association*, 1963, 88, 60–64.

Hughes, J. R., & Parkes, G. E. Electro-clinical correlations in dyslexic children. *Electroencephalography and Clinical Neurophysiology*, 1969, 26, 119.

Hughes, R. M. Rorschach signs in the diagnosis of organic pathology. *Rorschach Research Exchange*, 1948, 12, 165–167.

Jackson, J. H. *Selected Writings of John Hughlings Jackson.* London: Hodder 1931–1932. 2 vols.

Jasper, H., Kershmann, J., & Elvidge, A. Electroencephalography in head injury. *Association for Research in Nervous and Mental Disease, Research Publications*, 1945, 24, 388–420.

Jasper, H., Solomon, P. & Bradley, C. Electroencephalographic analyses of behavior problem children. *American Journal of Psychiatry*, 1938, 95, 641–658.

Jastak, J. F., & Jastak, S. R. *The Wide Range Achievement Test. Manual of instructions.* Wilmington, Del.: Guidance Associates, 1965.

Jensen, A. R. *Environment, heredity and intelligence.* (Reprint Series No. 2) Cambridge, Mass.: Harvard Educational Review, 1969.

Johnson, F. H. Neuro-anatomical tracts considered as correlates of the ascending reticular activating system in the cat. *Anatomical Record*, 1953, 155, 327–328.

Jones, L. V., & Wepman, J. M. Dimensions of language performance in aphasia. *Journal of Speech and Hearing Research*, 1961, 4, 222–232.

Joynt, R. J., & Benton, A. L. The memoir of Marc Dax on aphasia. *Neurology*, 1964, 14, 851–854.

Julesz, B. Binocular depth perception without familiarity cues. *Science*, 1964, 145, 356–363.

Kahn, E., & Cohen, L. H. Organic drivenness: A brain-stem syndrome and an experience. *New England Journal of Medicine*, 1934, 210, 748–756.

Kellaway, P., Crawley, J., & Maulsby, R. The electroencephalogram in psychiatric disorders in childhood. In W. P. Wilson (Ed.), *Applications of electroencephalography in psychiatry.* Durham, N. C.: Duke University Press, 1965.

Kendrick, J. F., & Gibbs, F. A. Interrelations of mesial temporal and orbital frontal areas revealed by strychnine spikes. *Archives of Neurology and Psychiatry*, 1958, 79, 518–524.

Kennard, M. A. Reorganization of motor function in the cerebral cortex of monkeys deprived of motor and premotor areas in infancy. *Journal of Neurophysiology*, 1938, 1, 477–496.

Kennard, M. A. Cortical reorganization of motor function: Studies on series of monkeys of various ages from infancy to maturity. *Archives of Neurology and Psychiatry*, 1942, **48**, 227-240.

Killian, L. R. WISC, Illinois Test of Psycholinguistic Abilities, and Bender Visual-Motor Gestalt Test performance of Spanish-American kindergarten and first grade school children. *Journal of Consulting and Clinical Psychology*, 1971, **37**, 38-43.

Kimura, D. Cerebral dominance and the perception of verbal stimuli. *Canadian Journal of Psychology*, 1961, **15**, 166-171.

Kimura, D. Right temporal-lobe damage. *Archives of Neurology*, 1963, **3**, 264-271.

Kimura, D. Functional asymmetry of the human brain in dichotic listening. *Cortex*, 1967, **3**, 163-178.

Kinsbourne, M. The cerebral basis of lateral asymmetries in attention. Paper presented at the symposium on Human Neuropsychology, American Psychological Association, Washington, D. C., 1969.

Klein, D. F., & Davis, J. M. *Diagnosis and drug treatment of psychiatric disorders*. Baltimore: Williams & Wilkins, 1969.

Klonoff, H. Head injuries in children: Predisposing factors, accident conditions, accident proneness and sequelae. *American Journal of Public Health*, 1971, **61**, 2405-2417. (a)

Klonoff, H. Factor analysis of a Neuropsychological Battery for Children aged 9 to 15. *Perceptual and Motor Skills*, 1971, **32**, 603-616. (b)

Klonoff, H., Fibiger, C. H., & Hutton, G. H. Neuropsychological patterns in chronic schizophrenia. *Journal of Nervous and Mental Disease*, 1970, **150**(4), 291-300.

Klonoff, H., & Robinson, G. C. Epidemiology of head injuries in children. *Canadian Medical Association Journal*, 1967, **96**, 1308-1311.

Klonoff, H., Robinson, G. C., & Thompson, G. Acute and chronic brain syndromes in children. *Developmental Medicine and Child Neurology*, 1969, **11**, 198-213.

Klonoff, H., & Thompson, G. B. Epidemiology of head injuries in adults. *Canadian Medical Association Journal*, 1969, **100**, 235-241.

Kløve, H. Relationship of differential electroencephalographic patterns to distribution of Wechsler-Bellevue scores. *Neurology*, 1959, **9**, 871-876. (a)

Kløve, H. The relationship of sensory imperception to the distribution of Wechsler-Bellevue scores. Paper presented at the meeting of the Midwestern Psychological Association, Chicago, 1959. (b)

Kløve, H. The relationship between neuropsychologic test performance and neurologic status. Paper presented at the meeting of the American Academy of Neurology, Minneapolis, 1963.

Kløve, H. Differential WAIS patterns in lateralized and diffuse encephalopathy. Paper presented at the meeting of the Midwestern Psychological Association, Chicago, 1965.

Kløve, H., & Cleeland, C. S. The relationship of neuropsychological impairment to other indices of severity of head injury. Paper presented at the meeting of the International Neuropsychology Society, Washington, D. C., September 1967.

Kløve, H., & Fitzhugh, K. B. The relationship of differential EEG patterns to the distribution of Wechsler-Bellevue scores in a chronic epileptic population. *Journal of Clinical Psychology*, 1962, **18**, 334–337.

Kløve, H., & Matthews, C. G. Psychometric and adaptive abilities in epilepsy with differential etiology. *Epilepsia*, 1966, **7**, 330–338.

Kløve, H., & Matthews, C. G. Neuropsychological evaluation of the epileptic patient. *Wisconsin Medical Journal*, 1969, **68**, 296–301.

Kløve, H., & Reitan, R. M. The effect of dysphasia and spatial distortion on Wechsler-Bellevue results. *Archives of Neurology and Psychiatry*. 1958, **80**, 708–713.

Kløve, H., & White, P. T. The relationship of degree of electroencephalographic abnormality to the distribution of Wechsler-Bellevue scores. *Neurology*, 1963, **13**, 423–430.

Klüver, H., & Bucy, P. C. An analysis of certain effects of bilateral temporal lobectomy in the rhesus monkey, with special reference to "psychic blindness". *Journal of Psychology*, 1938, **5**, 33–54.

Knights, R. M. *Normative data on tests for evaluating brain damage in children from 5 to 14 years of age.* (Res. Bull. No. 20) London, Ont.: University of Western Ontario, 1966.

Knights, R. M., & Ogilvie, R. M. *A comparison of test results from normal and brain-damaged children.* (Res. Bull. No. 53) London, Ont.: University of Western Ontario, 1967.

Knights, R. M., & Tymchuk, A. J. An evaluation of the Halstead-Reitan Category Tests for Children. *Cortex*, 1968, **4**, 403–413.

Knott, J. R., Muehl, S., & Benton, A. L. Electroencephalograms in children with reading disabilities. *Electroencephalography and Clinical Neurophysiology*, 1965, **18**, 513.

Knott, J. R., Platt, E. B., Ashby, M. C., & Gottleib, J. S. A familial evaluation of the electroencephalogram of patients with primary behavior disorder and psychopathic personality. *Electroencephalography and Clinical Neurophysiology*, 1953, **5**, 363–370.

Kubala, M. J., & Kellaway, P. Cerebral concussion in children: A longitudinal EEG profile. *Electroencephalography and Clinical Neurophysiology*, 1967, **23**, 82.

Lacks, P. B., Harrow, M., Colbert, J., & Levine, J. Further evidence concerning the diagnostic accuracy of the Halstead Organic Test Battery. *Journal of Clinical Psychology*, 1970, **26**, 480–481.

Lancaster, J. B. Primate communication systems and the emergence of human language. In C. Jay (Ed.) *Primates: Studies in adaption and variability*. New York: Holt, 1968.

Lansdell, H. C. Effect of brain damage on intelligence in rats. *Journal of Comparative and Physiological Psychology*, 1953, **46**, 461–464.

Lansdell, H. A sex difference in effect of temporal-lobe neurosurgery on design preference. *Nature*, 1962, **194**, 852–854.

Lansdell, H. Sex differences in hemispheric asymmetries of the human brain. *Nature*, 1964, **203**, 550.

Lansdell, H. A general intellectual factor affected by temporal lobe dysfunction. *Journal of Clinical Psychology*, 1971, **27**, 182–184.

Lashley, K. S. *Brain mechanisms and intelligence*. Chicago: University of Chicago Press, 1929.

Lennox, W. G. *Epilepsy and related disorders*. Vol. 2. Boston: Little, Brown, 1960.

Levine, J., & Feirstein, A. Differences in test performance between brain-damaged, schizophrenic, and medical patients. *Journal of Consulting and Clinical Psychology*, 1972, **39**, 508–511.

Lilliston, L. Tests of cerebral damage and the process-reactive dimension. *Journal of Clinical Psychology*, 1970, **26**, 180–181.

Lindsley, D. B., & Cutts, K. K. Electroencephalograms of "constitutionally inferior" and behavior problem children: Comparison with those of normal children and adults. *Archives of Neurology and Psychiatry*, 1940, **44**, 1199–1212.

Lishman, W. A. Psychiatric disability after head injury: The significance of brain damage. *Proceedings of the Royal Society of Medicine*, 1966, **59**, 261–266.

Lockard, R. B. Reflections on the fall of comparative psychology: Is there a message for us all. *American Psychologist*, 1971, 168–179.

Loewenson, R. B., Comparative morbidity and mortality; case material. Stroke: U.S. and Japan. Part I. *Geriatrics*, 1969, **24**, 85–94. (Monograph)

Lorente de Nó, R. Studies on the structure of the cerebral cortex: Continuation of the study of the ammonic system. *Journal für Psychologie und Neurologie*, 1934, **46**, 113–177.

Lubin, B., Wallis, R. R., & Paine, C. Patterns of psychological test usage in the United States: 1935–1969. *Professional Psychology*, 1971, **2**, 70–74.

Luria, A. R. *Restoration of function after brain injury*. (B. Haigh, Trans.) New York: MacMillan, 1963.

Luria, A. R. Neuropsychological analysis of focal brain lesions. (D. Bowden, Trans.) In B. J. Wolman (Ed.), *Handbook of clinical psychology*. New York: McGraw-Hill, 1965.

Luria, A. R. *Higher cortical functions in man*. (B. Haigh, Trans.) New York: Basic Books, 1966.

MacLean, P. D., & Delgado, J. M. R. Electrical and chemical stimulation of frontotemporal portion of limbic system in the waking animal. *Electroencephalography and Clinical Neurophysiology*, 1953, **5**, 91–100.

Major, I. Electroencephalographic findings in children with behavior disorders. *Electroencephalography and Clinical Neurophysiology*, 1967, **22**, 287.

Marks, P. A., & Seeman, W. *The actuarial description of abnormal personality: An atlas for use with the MMPI*. Baltimore: Williams & Wilkins, 1963.

Marshall, C., & Walker, A. E. The value of electroencephalography in the prognostication and prognosis of post-traumatic epilepsy. *Epilepsia*, 1961, **2**, 138–143.

Matthews, C. G. Problem-solving and experiential background determinants of test performances in mentally retarded subjects. *Psychological Reports*, 1963, **13**, 391–401.

Matthews, C. G., & Booker, H. E. Pneumoencephalographic measurements and neuropsychological test performance in human adults. *Cortex*, 1972, **8**, 69–92.

Matthews, C. G., Folk, E. D., & Zerfas, P. G. Lateralized finger localization deficits and differential Wechsler-Bellevue results in retardates. *American Journal of Mental Deficiency*, 1966, **70**, 695–702.

Matthews, C. G., & Kløve, H. Differential psychological performances in major motor, psychomotor and mixed seizure classifications of known and unknown etiology. *Epilepsia*, 1967, **8**, 117–128.

Matthews, C. G., & Kløve, H. MMPI performances in major motor, psychomotor and mixed seizure classifications of known and unknown etiology. *Epilepsia*, 1968, **9**, 43–53.

Matthews, C. G., & Reitan, R. M. Comparisons of abstraction ability in retardates and in patients with cerebral lesions. *Perceptual and Motor Skills*, 1961, **13**, 327–333.

Matthews, C. G., & Reitan, R. M. Psychomotor abilities of retardates and patients with cerebral lesions. *American Journal of Mental Deficiency*, 1962, **66**, 607–612.

Matthews, C. G., & Reitan, R. M. Relationship of differential abstraction ability levels to psychological test performances in mentally retarded subjects. *American Journal of Mental Deficiency*, 1963, **68**, 235–244.

Matthews, C. G., Shaw, D. J., & Kløve, H. Psychological test performances in neurologic and "pseudoneurologic" subjects. *Cortex*, 1966, **2**, 244–253.

Meier, M. The regional localization hypothesis and personality changes associated with focal cerebral lesions and ablations. In J. N. Butcher (Ed.), *MMPI research developments and clinical applications*. New York: McGraw-Hill, 1969.

Meier, M. J. Effects of focal cerebral lesions on contralateral visuomotor adaptation to reversal and inversion of visual feedback. *Neuropsychologia*, 1970, 8, 269–279. (a)

Meier, M. J. Objective behavioral assessment in diagnosis and prediction. In A. L. Benton (Ed.), *Behavior changes in cerebrovascular disease*. New York: Harper & Row, 1970. (b)

Meier, M. J., & French, L. A. Caudality changes following unilateral temporal lobectomy. *Journal of Clinical Psychology*, 1964, **20**, 464–467.

Meier, M. J., & French, L. A. Lateralized deficits in complex visual discrimination and bilateral transfer of reminiscence following unilateral temporal lobectomy. *Neuropsychologia*, 1965, **3**, 261–273. (a)

Meier, M. J., & French, L. A. Some personality correlates of unilateral and bilateral EEG abnormalities in psychomotor epileptics. *Journal of Clinical Psychology*, 1965, **21**, 3–9. (b)

Meier, M. J., & French, L. A. Longitudinal assessment of intellectual functioning following unilateral temporal lobectomy. *Journal of Clinical Psychology*, 1966, **22**, 22–27. (a)

Meier, M. J., & French, L. A. Readaptation to prismatic rotations of visual space as a function of lesion laterality and extratemporal EEG spike activity after temporal lobectomy. *Neuropsychologia*, 1966, **4**, 151–157. (b)

Meier, M. J., & Okayama, M. Behavior assessment. *Stroke* (Monograph): U.S. and Japan. Part II. *Geriatrics*, 1969, **24**, 95–110.

Meier, M. J., & Resch, J. A. Behavioral prediction of short-term neurologic change following acute onset of cerebrovascular symptoms. *Mayo Clinic Proceedings*, 1967, **42**, 641–647.

Meier, M. J., & Story, J. L. Selective impairment of Porteus Maze Test performance after right subthalamotomy. *Neuropsychologia*, 1967, **5**, 181–189.

Meier, M. J., Story, J. L., French, L. A., & Chou, S. N. Quantitative assessment of behavioral changes following subthalamotomy in the treatment of Parkinson's Disease. *Confinia Neurologica*, 1966, **27**, 154–161.

Mettler, F. A. *Selective partial ablation of the frontal cortex.* New York: Hoeber, 1949.

Meyer, V. Psychological effects of brain damage. In H. J. Eysenck (Ed.), *Handbook of abnormal psychology*. New York: Basic Books, 1960.

Meyer, V., & Jones, H. G. Patterns of cognitive test performances as functions of lateral localization of cerebral abnormalities in the temporal lobe. *Journal of Mental Science*, 1957, **103**, 758–772.

Meyer, V., & Yates, A. J. Intellectual changes following temporal lobectomy for psychomotor epilepsy; preliminary communication. *Journal of Neurology, Neurosurgery and Psychiatry*, 1955, **18**, 44–52.

Miller, H. Accident neurosis. *British Medical Journal*, 1961, **1**, 919–925.

Milner, B. Psychological defects produced by temporal lobe excision. *Association for Research in Nervous and Mental Disease, Research Publications*, 1958, **36**, 244–257.

Milner, B. Laterality effects of audition. In V. B. Mountcastle (Ed.), *Interhemispheric relations and cerebral dominance*. Baltimore: Johns Hopkins, 1962.

Milner, B. Some effects of frontal lobectomy in man. In J. M. Warren & K. Akert (Eds.), *The frontal granular cortex and behavior*. New York: McGraw-Hill, 1964.

Milner, B. Visually-guided maze learning in man: Effects of bilateral hippo-campal, bilateral frontal, and unilateral cerebral lesions. *Neuropsychologia*, 1965, **3**, 317–338.

Milner, B. Brain mechanisms suggested by studies of the temporal lobes. In C. H. Millikan & F. L. Darley (Eds.), *Brain mechanisms underlying speech and language*. New York: Grune & Stratton, 1967.

Milner, B. Visual recognition and recall after right temporal lobe excisions in man. *Neuropsychologia*, 1968, **6**, 191–210.

Milner, B. Memory and the medial temporal regions of the brain. In K. H. Pribram & D. E. Broadbent (Eds.), *Biology of memory*. New York: Academic Press, 1970.

Milner, B., & Kimura, D. Dissociable verbal learning deficits after unilateral temporal lobectomy in man. Paper presented at the meeting of the Eastern Psychological Association, Philadelphia, 1964.

Milner, B., & Teuber, H.-L. Alteration of perception and memory in man: Reflections on methods. In L. Weiskrantz (Ed.), *Analysis of behavior change*. New York: Harper & Row, 1968.

Mishkin, M., & Pribram K. H. Visual discrimination performance following partial ablations of the temporal lobe. I. Ventral vs. lateral. *Journal of Comparative and Physiological Psychology*, 1954, **47**, 14–20.

Misurec, J., & Vzral, J. EEG in children with minimal brain damage. *Electroencephalography and Clinical Neurophysiology*, 1969, **26**, 232.

Money, J. Cytogenetic and psychosexual incongruities with a note on space-form blindness. *American Journal of Psychiatry*, 1963, **119**, 820–827. (a)

Money, J. Two cytogenetic syndromes: Psychologic comparisons. I. Intelligence and specific-factor quotients. *Journal of Psychiatric Research*, 1963, **2**, 223–231. (b)

Morison, R. S., & Dempsey, E. W. A study of thalamo-cortical relations. *American Journal of Physiology*, 1942, **135**, 281–292.

Morrison, D., & Pothier, P. Two different remedial motor training programs and the development of mentally retarded preschoolers. *American Journal of Mental Deficiency*, 1972, **77**, 251–258.

Moruzzi, G., & Magoun, H. W. Brain stem reticular formation and activation of the EEG. *Electroencephalography and Clinical Neurophysiology*, 1949, **1**, 455–473.

Muehl, S., Knott, J. R., & Benton, A. L. EEG abnormality and psychological test performance in reading disability. *Cortex*, 1965, **1**, 434–440.

Nauta, W. J. H. Some projections of the medial wall of the hemisphere in the rat's brain (cortical areas 32 and 25, 24 and 29). *Anatomical Record*, 1953, **115**, 352.

Nauta, W. J. H. An experimental study of the fornix system in the rat. *Journal of Comparative Neurology*, 1956, **104**, 247–271.

Nielsen, H. H., & Ringe, K. Visuo-perceptive and visuo-motor performance of children with reading disabilities. *Scandinavian Journal of Psychology*, 1969, **10**, 225-231.

Norrman, B., & Svahn, K. A follow-up study of severe brain injuries. *Acta Psychiatrica Scandinavica*, 1961, **37**, 236-264.

O'Connor, N., & Hermelin, B. Visual and stereognostic shape recognition in normal children and mongol and non-mongol imbeciles. *Journal of Mental Deficiency Research*, 1962, **6**, 63-66.

Olds, J. Adaptive functions of paleocortical and related structures. In H. F. Harlow & C. N. Woolsey (Eds.), *Biological and biochemical bases of behavior*. Madison: University of Wisconsin Press, 1958.

Osgood, C. E., & Miron, M. S. (Eds.) *Approaches to the study of aphasia: A report of an interdisciplinary conference on aphasia*. Urbana: University of Illinois Press, 1963.

Overall, J. E., & Gorham, D. R. Organicity versus old age in objective and projective test performance. *Journal of Consulting and Clinical Psychology*, 1972, **39**, 98-105.

Parsons, O. A. Clinical neuropsychology. In C. D. Spielberger (Ed.), *Current topics in clinical and community psychology*. Vol. 2. New York: Academic Press, 1970.

Parsons, O. A., & Klein, H. P. Concept identification and practice in brain-damaged and schizophrenic groups. *Journal of Consulting and Clinical Psychology*, 1970, **35**, 317-323.

Parsons, O. A., Vega, A., & Burn, J. Different psychological effects of lateralized brain-damage. *Journal of Clinical and Consulting Psychology*, 1969, **33**, 551-557.

Partington, M. W. The importance of accident-proneness in the aetiology of head injuries in childhood. *Archives of Disease in Childhood*, 1960, **35**, 215-223.

Penfield, W., & Milner, B. The memory deficit produced by bilateral lesions of the hippocampal zone. *Archives of Neurology and Psychiatry*, 1958, **79**, 475-497.

Penfield, W., & Roberts, L. *Speech and brain mechanisms*. Princeton, N. J.: Princeton University Press, 1959.

Pennington, H., Galliani, C., & Voegele, G. Unilateral electroencephalographic dysrhythmia and children's intelligence. *Child Development*, 1965, **36**, 539-546.

Peterson, L. R., & Peterson, M. S. Short-term retention of individual verbal items. *Journal of Experimental Psychology*, 1959, **58**, 193-198.

Petrie, A. *Personality and the frontal lobes: An investigation of the psychological effects of different types of leucotomy*. New York: Blakiston, 1952.

Piercy, M. The effects of cerebral lesions on intellectual function: A review of current research trends. *British Journal of Psychiatry*, 1964, **110**, 310-352.

Piotrowski, Z. A. The Rorschach inkblot method in organic disturbances of the central nervous system. *Journal of Nervous and Mental Disease*, 1937, **86**, 525-537.

Polacek, L., & Tresohlavova, Z. Hyperkinetic syndrome in children. *Electro-encephalography and Clinical Neurophysiology*, 1969, **26**, 231–232.

Poppelreuter, W. *Die psychischen Schadigungen durch Kopfschuss im Kriege 1914. Band I. Die Storungen der niederen und hoheren Schleistungen durch Verletzungen des Occipitalhirns.* Leipzig: Voss, 1917.

Popper, K. R. *The logic of scientific discovery*. London: Hutchinson, 1959.

Porch, B. E. *Porch Index of Communicative Ability*. Palo Alto, Calif.: Consulting Psychologists Press, 1967.

Porteus, S. D. *The Maze Test and clinical psychology*. Palo Alto, Calif.: Pacific Books, 1959.

Prechtl, H. F. R., Boeke, P. E., & Schut, T. The electroencephalogram and performance in epileptic patients. *Neurology*, 1961, **11**, 296–302.

Predescu, V., Roman, I., Costiner, E., Cristian, K., & Oancea, C. Electroclinical correlations in behavioral disturbances in children. *Electroencephalography and Clinical Neurophysiology*, 1968, **25**, 292–293.

Pribram, K. H. *Languages of the brain: Experimental paradoxes and principles in neuropsychology*. Englewood Cliffs, N. J.: Prentice-Hall, 1971.

Pronovost, W., & Dumbleton, C. A picture-type speech sound discrimination test. *Journal of Speech and Hearing Disorders*, 1953, **18**, 258–266.

Ramón y Cajal. S. *Histologie du système nerveux de l'homme et des vertébrés*. Paris: Maloine, 1909.

Ranck, J. B., & Windle, W. F. Brain damage in the monkey, *Macaca Mulatta*, by asphyxia neonatorum. *Experimental Neurology,* 1959, **1**, 130–154.

Rapaport, D., Gill, M., & Schafer, R. *Diagnostic psychological testing*. Vol. I. Chicago: Year Book Publishers, 1945.

Rapaport, D., Gill, M., & Schafer, R. *Diagnostic psychological testing*. Vol. II. Chicago: Year Book Publishers, 1946.

Rapaport, D., Gill, M., & Schafer, R. *Diagnostic psychological testing*. (Rev. ed., R. Holt, Ed.) New York: International Universities Press, 1968.

Read, J. H., Bradley, E. J., Morison, J. D., Lewall, D., & Clarke, D. A. The epidemiology and prevention of traffic accidents involving child pedestrians. *Canadian Medical Association Journal*, 1963, **89**, 687–701.

Reed, H. B. C., Jr. Differentiated impairment on the Wechsler-Bellevue Scale as a function of type and laterality of cerebral pathology. Paper presented at the meeting of the Midwestern Psychological Association, Chicago, 1962.

Reed, H. B. C., Jr. Some relationships between neurological dysfunction and behavioral deficits in children. In *Conference on Children with Minimal Brain Impairment*. Urbana: University of Illinois, 1963.

Reed, H. B. C., Jr., & Fitzhugh, K. B. Patterns of deficits in relation to severity of cerebral dysfunction in children and adults. *Journal of Consulting and Clinical Psychology*, 1966, **30**, 98–102.

Reed, H. B. C., Jr., Reitan, R. M., & Kløve, H. The influence of cerebral lesions on psychological test performances of older children. *Journal of Consulting Psychology*, 1965, **29**, 247–251.

Reed, J. C. Lateralized finger agnosia and reading achievement at ages 6 and 10. *Child Development*, 1967, **38**, 213-220.

Reed, J. C., & Reitan, R. M. Verbal and performance differences among brain-injured children with lateralized motor deficits. *Perceptual and Motor Skills*, 1969, **29**, 747-752.

Reitan, R. M. An investigation of the validity of Halstead's measures of biological intelligence. *Archives of Neurology and Psychiatry*, 1955, **73**, 28-35. (a)

Reitan, R. M. Certain differential effects of left and right cerebral lesions in human adults. *Journal of Comparative and Physiological Psychology*, 1955, **48**, 474-477. (b)

Reitan, R. M. Discussion: Symposium on the temporal lobe. *Archives of Neurology and Psychiatry*, 1955, **74**, 569-570. (c)

Reitan, R. M. The distribution according to age of a psychologic measure dependent upon organic brain functions. *Journal of Gerontology*, 1955, **10**, 338-340. (d)

Reitan, R. M. Investigation of relationships between "psychometric" and "biological" intelligence. *Journal of Nervous and Mental Disease*, 1956, **123**, 536-541.

Reitan, R. M. Contributions of physiological psychology to clinical inferences. Symposium presented at the meeting of the Midwestern Psychological Association, Detroit, May 1-3, 1958. (a)

Reitan, R. M. Validity of the Trail Making Test as an indicator of organic brain damage. *Perceptual and Motor Skills*, 1958, **8**, 271-276. (b)

Reitan, R. M. Qualitative versus quantitative mental changes following brain damage. *Journal of Psychology*, 1958, **46**, 339-346. (c)

Reitan, R. M. The comparative effects of brain damage on the Halstead Impairment Index and the Wechsler-Bellevue Scale. *Journal of Clinical Psychology*, 1959, **15**, 281-285. (a)

Reitan, R. M. Impairment of abstraction ability in brain damage: Quantitative versus qualitative changes. *Journal of Psychology*, 1959, **48**, 97-102. (b)

Reitan, R. M. *The effects of brain lesion on adaptive abilities in human beings.* Privately published by the author, Indianapolis, 1959. (c)

Reitan, R. M. The significance of dysphasia for intelligence and adaptive abilities. *Journal of Psychology*, 1960, **50**, 355-376.

Reitan, R. M. Psychological deficit. *Annual Review of Psychology*, 1962, **13**, 415-444.

Reitan, R. M. *Manual for administering and scoring the Reitan-Indiana Neuropsychological Battery for Children (aged 5 through 8).* Indianapolis: University of Indiana Medical Center, 1964. (a)

Reitan, R. M. Psychological deficits resulting from cerebral lesions in man. In J. M. Warren & K. A. Akert (Eds.), *The frontal granular cortex and behavior.* New York: McGraw-Hill, 1964. (b)

Reitan, R. M. Problems and prospects in studying the psychological correlates of brain lesions. *Cortex*, 1966, **2**, 127-154. (a)

Reitan, R. M. A research program on the psychological effects of brain lesions in human beings. In N. R. Ellis (Ed.), *International review of research in mental retardation*. Vol. I. New York: Academic Press, 1966. (b)

Reitan, R. M. Psychological assessment of deficits associated with brain lesions in subjects with normal and subnormal intelligence. In J. L. Khanna (Ed.), *Brain damage and mental retardation: A psychological evaluation*. Springfield, Ill.: Charles C. Thomas, 1967. (a)

Reitan, R. M. Psychological changes associated with aging and with cerebral damage. *Mayo Clinic Proceedings*, 1967, **42**, 653-673. (b)

Reitan, R. M. *Psychological effects of brain lesions in children*. Privately published mimeographed manuscript, 1967. (c)

Reitan, R. M. *Manual for administration of neuropsychological test batteries for adults and children*. Privately published by the author, Indianapolis, 1969.

Reitan, R. M. Sensorimotor functions, intelligence and cognition, and emotional status in subjects with cerebral lesions. *Perceptual and Motor Skills*, 1970, **31**, 275-284.

Reitan, R. M. Sensorimotor functions in brain-damaged and normal children of early school age. *Perceptual and Motor Skills*, 1971, **33**, 655-664. (a)

Reitan, R. M. Complex motor functions of the preferred and non-preferred hands in brain-damaged and normal children. *Perceptual and Motor Skills*, 1971, **33**, 671-675. (b)

Reitan, R. M. Trail Making Test results for normal and brain-damaged children. *Perceptual and Motor Skills*, 1971, **33**, 575-581. (c)

Reitan, R. M. Neuropsychological correlates of minimal brain dysfunction. Paper presented at the Conference on Minimal Brain Dysfunction, New York Academy of Sciences, New York, March 20-22, 1972.

Reitan, R. M. Psychological testing after craniocerebral injury. In J. R. Youmans (Ed.), *Neurosurgery: A comprehensive reference guide to the diagnosis and management of neurosurgical problems*. Vol. II. Philadelphia: Saunders, 1973.

Reitan, R. M. Psychological testing of epileptic patients. In P. J. Vinken & G. W. Bruyn (Eds.), *Handbook of clinical neurology*. Vols. IX and X. *The epilepsies*. North Holland, in press.

Reitan, R. M., & Fitzhugh, K. B. Behavioral deficits in groups with cerebral vascular lesions. *Journal of Consulting and Clinical Psychology*, 1971, **37**, 215-223.

Reitan, R. M., & Heineman, C. E. Interactions of neurological deficits and emotional disturbances in children with learning disorders: Methods for their differential assessment. In J. Hellmuth (Ed.), *Learning disorders*. Vol. 3. Seattle: Special Child Publications, 1968.

Reitan, R. M., & Shipley, R. E. The relationship of serum cholesterol changes on psychological abilities. *Journal of Gerontology*, 1963, **18**, 350-356.

Reitan, R. M., & Tarshes, E. L. Differential effects of lateralized brain lesions on the Trail Making Test. *Journal of Nervous and Mental Disease*, 1959, **129**, 257–262.

Richardson, F. Some effects of severe head injury. *Developmental Medicine and Child Neurology*, 1963, **5**, 471–482.

Rodin, E. A. Contribution of the EEG to prognosis after head injury. *Diseases of the Nervous System*, 1967, **28**, 595–601.

Rodin, E. A. *The prognosis of patients with epilepsy*. Springfield, Ill.: Charles C Thomas, 1968.

Rorschach, H. *Psychodiagnostics: A psychodiagnostic test based on perception*. (P. Lemkau & B. Kronenberg, Trans.) Bern: Hans Huber Verlag (American Distributor: Grune & Stratton), 1942.

Rosenzweig, M. R., Krech, D., & Bennett, E. L. A search for relations between brain chemistry and behavior. *Psychological Bulletin*, 1960, **57**, 476–492.

Rosner, B. S. Brain functions. In P. H. Mussen & M. R. Rosenzweig (Eds.), *Annual review of psychology*. Vol. 21. Palo Alto: Annual Reviews, 1970.

Ross, A. O. The case of the innocent model. *The Clinical Psychologist*, 1971, **24**, 2–3.

Rosvold, H. E. Some neuropsychological studies relevant to mental retardation. In G. A. Jarvis (Ed.), *Mental retardation*. Springfield, Ill.: Charles C Thomas, 1967.

Rowbotham, G. F., Maciver, I. N., Dickson, J., & Bousfield, M. E. Analysis of 1400 cases of acute injury to the head. *British Medical Journal*, 1954, **1**, 726–730.

Rowley, V., & Baer, P. Visual Retention Test performance in emotionally disturbed and brain-damaged children. *American Journal of Orthopsychiatry*, 1961, **31**, 579–583.

Rubinstein, B. B. Psychoanalytic theory and the mind-body problem. In N. S. Greenfield & W. C. Lewis (Eds.), *Psychoanalysis and current biological thought*. Madison: University of Wisconsin Press, 1965.

Ruch, T. C. Neurophysiology of emotion and motivation. In T. C. Ruch, H. D. Patton, J. W. Woodbury, & A. L. Towe, (Eds.), *Neurophysiology*. Philadelphia: Saunders, 1961.

Ruesch, J. Intellectual impairment in head injuries. *American Journal of Psychiatry*, 1944, **100**, 480–496.

Ruesch, J., Harris, R. E., & Bowman, K. Pre- and post-traumatic personality in head injuries. In *Trauma of the central nervous system*. Vol. 24. Proceedings of the Association for Research in Nervous and Mental Disease, 1945. Baltimore: Williams & Wilkins.

Russell, E. W., Neuringer, C., & Goldstein, G. *Assessment of brain damage*: *A neuropsychological key approach*. New York: Wiley-Interscience, 1970.

Saetveit, J. G., Lewis, D., & Seashore, C. E. *Revision of the Seashore Measure of Musical Talents*. (University of Iowa Studies No. 65) Iowa City: University of Iowa Press, 1940.

Sanders, C. Terminology and classification. In J. Wortis (Ed.), *Mental retardation. An annual review*. New York: Grune & Stratton, 1970.

Sarason, S. B. *Psychological problems in mental deficiency*. (3rd ed.) New York: Harper & Row, 1959.

Satz, P. Specific and non-specific effects of brain lesions in man. *Journal of Abnormal Psychology*, 1966, **71**, 65–70.

Satz, P. Laterality effects in dichotic listening. *Nature*, 1968, **218**, 277–278.

Satz, P. Cerebral mechanisms in motor asymmetry. Paper presented at the meeting of the Academy of Aphasia, New Orleans, October 1970.

Schafer, R. *The clinical application of psychological tests: Diagnostic summaries and case studies*. New York: International Universities Press, 1948.

Schuell, H. Paraphasia and paralexia. *Journal of Speech and Hearing Disorders*, 1950, **15**, 290–306.

Schuell, H. A short examination for aphasia. *Neurology*, 1957, **7**, 625–634.

Schuell, H., & Jenkins, J. J. The nature of language deficit in aphasia. *Psychological Review*, 1959, **66**, 45–67.

Schuell, H., Jenkins, J. J., & Jimenez-Pabon, E. *Aphasia in adults*. New York: Hoeber, 1964.

Scriven, M. Psychology without a paradigm. In L. Breger (Ed.), *Clinical-cognitive psychology*. Englewood Cliffs, N. J.: Prentice-Hall, 1969.

Selecki, B. R., Hay, R. J., & Ness, P. A retrospective survey of neurotraumatic admissions to a teaching hospital. Part I. General Aspects. *Medical Journal of Australia*, 1967, **2**, 113–117.

Semmes, J. Hemispheric specialization: A possible clue to mechanism. *Neuropsychologia*, 1968, **6**, 11–26.

Semmes, J., Weinstein, S., Ghent, L., & Teuber, H. -L. *Somatosensory changes after penetrating brain wounds in man*. Cambridge, Mass.: Harvard University Press, 1960.

Shaffer, J. W. A specific cognitive deficit observed in gonadal aplasia (Turner's syndrome). *Journal of Clinical Psychology*, 1962, **18**, 403–406.

Shure, G. H., & Halstead, W. C. Cerebral localization of intellectual processes. *Psychological Monographs*, 1958, **72**, (12, Whole No. 465).

Sidman, M., & Stoddard, L. T. Programming perception and learning for retarded children. In N. R. Ellis (Ed.), *International review of research in mental retardation*. Vol. II. New York: Academic Press, 1966.

Siegel, S. *Nonparametric statistics for the behavioral sciences*. New York: McGraw-Hill, 1956.

Silverman, D. Electroencephalographic study of acute head injury in children. *Neurology*, 1962, **12**, 273–281.

Small, I. F., Small, J. G., Millstein, V., & Moore, J. E. Neuropsychological observations with psychosis and somatic treatment. *Journal of Nervous and Mental Disease*, 1972, **155**, 6–13.

Smith, A. Changes in Porteus Maze scores of brain-operated schizophrenics after an eight-year interval. *Journal of Mental Science*, 1960, **106**, 967–978.

Smith, A. Duration of impaired consciousness as an index of severity in closed head injuries. *Diseases of the Nervous System*, 1961, 22, 69–74.

Smith, A. Verbal and nonverbal test performances of patients with "acute" lateralized brain lesions (tumors). *Journal of Nervous and Mental Disease*, 1966, 141, 517–523.

Smith, K. U., & Smith, W. M. *Perception and motion: An analysis of space-structured behavior*. Philadelphia: Saunders, 1962.

Sperry, R. W. Cerebral organization and behavior. *Science*, 1961, 133, 1749.

Spreen, O. Language functions in mental retardation: A review. *American Journal of Mental Deficiency*, 1965, 69, 482–494; 70, 351–362.

Spreen, O., & Benton, A. L. Comparative studies of some psychological tests for cerebral damage. *Journal of Nervous and Mental Disease*, 1967, 140, 323–333.

Spreen, O., & Benton, A. L. *Neurosensory center comprehensive examination for aphasia*. Victoria, B. C.: University of Victoria, 1968.

Spreen, O., & Gaddes, W. H. Developmental norms for 15 neuropsychological tests age 6 to 15. *Cortex*, 1969, 5, 171–191.

Stack, J. T. & Phillips, A. R. Performance of medical, brain-damaged, and schizophrenic patients on the Halstead-Reitan Neuropsychological Battery. *Newsletter for Research in Psychology*, 1970, 12(4), 16–18.

Stein, K. B. Manual for the Symbol-Gestalt Test: *A three-minute perceptual-motor test for brain damage*. (Rev. ed.) Mimeographed. Privately published by the author, Berkeley, 1970.

Stevens, J. R., Sachdev, K. K., & Milstein, V. Behavior disorders of childhood and electroencephalogram. *Electroencephalography and Clinical Neurophysiology*, 1968, 24, 188.

Stone, C. P., & Obias, M. D. Effects of hypophysectomy on behavior in rats. II. Maze and discrimination learning. *Journal of Comparative and Physiological Psychology*, 1955, 48, 404–411.

Strauss, A. A., & Werner, H. Deficiency in the finger schema in relation to arithmetic disability (finger agnosia and acalculia). *American Journal of Orthopsychiatry*, 1938, 8, 719-725.

Strauss, A. A., & Werner, H. Finger agnosia in children: With a brief discussion on defect and retardation in mentally handicapped children. *American Journal of Psychiatry*, 1939, 95, 1215–1225.

Strauss, A. A., & Werner, H. The mental organization of the brain-injured mentally defective child. *American Journal of Psychiatry*, 1941, 97, 1194–1203.

Sylvester, P. E. Parietal lobe deficit in the mentally retarded. *Journal of Neurology, Neurosurgery and Psychiatry*, 1966, 29, 176–180.

Sylvester, P. E., & Blundell, E. Parietal lobe inadequacy in mental deficiency. *British Medical Journal*, 1967, 1, 282.

Talland, G. A. *Deranged memory*. New York: Academic Press, 1965.

Talland, G. A. Interaction between clinical and laboratory research on memory. In G. A. Talland & N. Waugh (Eds.), *The pathology of memory*. New York: Academic Press, 1969.

Taylor, M. L. A measurement of functional communication in aphasia. *Archives of Physical Medicine*, 1965, **46**, 101–107.

Tellegen, A., & Briggs, P. F. Old wine in new skins: Grouping Wechsler subtests into new scales. *Journal of Consulting Psychology*, 1967, **31**, 499–506.

Terman, L. M., & Merrill, M. A. *Stanford-Binet Intelligence Scale manual for the third revision. Form L-M*. Boston: Houghton Mifflin, 1960.

Teuber, H.-L. The riddle of frontal lobe function in man. In J. M. Warren & K. Akert (Eds.), *The frontal granular cortex and behavior*. New York: McGraw-Hill, 1964.

Teuber, H.-L., Battersby, W. S., & Bender, M. B. Changes in visual searching performance following cerebral lesions. *American Journal of Physiology*, 1949, **159**, 592–603.

Teuber, H.-L., & Mishkin, M. Judgment of visual and postural vertical after brain injury. *Journal of Psychology*, 1954, **38**, 161–175.

Teuber, H.-L., & Rudel, R. G. Behavior after cerebral lesions in children and adults. *Developmental Medicine and Child Neurology*, 1962, **4**, 3–20.

Turkewitz, G., & Birch, H. G. Comparative Psychology. In J. Wortis (Ed.), *Mental retardation. An annual review*. New York: Grune & Stratton, 1970.

Vega, A., & Parsons, O. A. Cross-validation of the Halstead-Reitan tests for brain damage. *Journal of Consulting Psychology*, 1967, **31**, 619–625.

Walker, A. E., & Erculei, F. *Head-injured men fifteen years later*. Springfield, Ill.: Charles C Thomas, 1969.

Walker, A. E., & Jablon, S. A follow-up of head-injured men of World War II. *Journal of Neurosurgery*, 1959, **16**, 600–610.

Walters, R. H., & Kosowski, I. Symbolic learning and reading retardation. *Journal of Consulting Psychology*, 1963, **27**, 75–82.

Walton, J. N., Ellis, E. & Court, S. D. M. Clumsy children: Developmental apraxia and agnosia. *Brain*, 1962, **85**, 603–612.

Warrington, E. K., James, M., & Kinsbourne, M. Drawing disability in relation to laterality of lesions. *Brain*, 1966, **89**, 53–82.

Watson, C. G. An MMPI Scale to separate brain-damaged from schizophrenic men. *Journal of Consulting and Clinical Psychology*, 1971, **36**, 121–125.

Watson, C. G., Thomas, R. W., Anderson, D., & Felling, J. Differentiation of organics from schizophrenics at two chronicity levels by use of the Reitan-Halstead Organic Test Battery. *Journal of Consulting and Clinical Psychology*, 1968, **32**, 679–684.

Wechsler, D. *The measurement of adult intelligence*. (3rd ed.) Baltimore: Williams & Wilkins, 1944.

Wechsler, D. *Manual: Wechsler Intelligence Scale for Children*. New York: The Psychological Corporation, 1949.

Wechsler, D. *Manual for the Wechsler Adult Intelligence Scale*. New York: The Psychological Corporation, 1955.

Weigl, E. Zur Psychologie sogennanter Abstraktionsprozesse: Untersuchungen über da "Ordnen". *Zeitschrift für Psychologie mit Zeitschrift für Angewandte Psychologie*, 1927, **103**, 1–45.

Weinberg, A. M. The axiology of science. *American Scientist*, 1970, **58**, 612–617.

Weiner, I. B. *Psychodiagnosis in schizophrenia*. New York: Wiley, 1966.

Weinmann, H. M. Post-traumatic electroencephalographic findings in children. *Electroencephalography and Clinical Neurophysiology*, 1966, **20**, 534.

Werner, H. Perceptual behavior of brain-injured, mentally defective children: An experimental study of the Rorschach technique. *Genetic Psychological Monographs*, 1945, **31**, 51–110.

Werner, H., & Thuma, B. B. A deficiency in the perception of apparent motion in children with brain injury. *American Journal of Psychology*, 1942, **55**, 58–67. (a)

Werner, H., & Thuma, B. B. Critical flicker-frequency in children with brain injury. *American Journal of Psychology*, 1942, **55**, 394–399. (b)

Werry, J. Organic factors in childhood psychopathology. In H. C. Quay & J. S. Werry (Eds.), *Psychopathological disorders of childhood*. New York: Wiley, 1972, in press.

Wheeler, L., Burke, C. J., & Reitan, R. M. An application of discriminant functions to the problem of predicting brain damage using behavioral variables. *Perceptual and Motor Skills*, 1963, **16**, 417–440.

Wheeler, L., & Reitan, R. M. The presence and laterality of brain damage predicted from responses to a short aphasia screening test. *Perceptual and Motor Skills*, 1962, **15**, 783–799.

Wheeler, L., & Reitan, R. M. Discriminant functions applied to the problem of predicting cerebral damage from behavior tests: A cross validation study. *Perceptual and Motor Skills*, 1963, **16**, 681–701.

Wigner, E. Events, laws of nature, and invariance principles. *Science*, 1964, **145**, 995–999.

Willett, R. A. The effects of psychosurgical procedures on behavior. In H. J. Eysenck (Ed.), *Handbook of abnormal psychology*. New York: Basic Books, 1960.

Williams, H. L. The development of a caudality scale for the MMPI. *Journal of Clinical Psychology*, 1952, **8**, 293–297.

Winfield, D. L. Intellectual performance of cryptogenic epileptics, symptomatic epileptics and posttraumatic encephalopaths. *Journal of Abnormal and Social Psychology*, 1951, **46**, 336–343.

Windle, C. Prognosis of mental subnormals. *American Journal of Mental Deficiency*, 1962. (Monograph Supplement)

Windle, W. F., & Becker, R. F. Asphyxia neonatorum. *American Journal of Obstetrics and Gynecology*, 1943, **45**, 183–200.

Yates, A. J. Psychological deficit. *Annual Review of Psychology*, 1966, **17**, 111-144.

Zigler, E. Familial mental retardation: A continuing dilemma. *Science*, 1967, **155**, 292-298.

Zurif, E. B., & Carson, G. Dyslexia in relation to cerebral dominance and temporal analysis. *Neuropsychologia*, 1970, **8**, 351-362.

SUBJECT INDEX